THE ROUTLEDGE COMPANION TO NATIVE AMERICAN LITERATURE

The Routledge Companion to Native American Literature explores the historical, political, cultural, and aesthetic tensions that create a problematic legacy in the study of Native American literature. This important and timely addition to the field provides context for issues of community identity, ethnicity, gender and sexuality, language, and sovereignty as they enter into Native American literary texts through allusions, references, and language use.

The volume presents more than forty chapters by leading and emerging international scholars and analyzes:

- regional, cultural, racial, and sexual identities in Native American literature;
- key historical moments from the earliest period of colonial contact to the present;
- worldviews in relation to issues such as health, spirituality, animals, and physical environments;
- traditions of cultural creation that are key to understanding the styles, allusions, and language of Native American literature;
- the impact of differing literary forms of Native American literature.

This collection provides a map of the critical issues central to the discipline and uncovers new perspectives and directions for the development of the field. It is essential reading for anyone interested in the past, present, and future of this literary culture.

Contributors: Joseph Bauerkemper, Susan Bernardin, Susan Berry Brill de Ramírez, Kirby Brown, David J. Carlson, Cari M. Carpenter, Eric Cheyfitz, Tova Cooper, Alicia Cox, Birgit Däwes, Janet Fiskio, Earl E. Fitz, John Gamber, Kathryn N. Gray, Sarah Henzi, Susannah Hopson, Hsinya Huang, Brian K. Hudson, Bruce E. Johansen, Judit Ágnes Kádár, Amelia V. Katanski, Susan Kollin, Chris LaLonde, A. Robert Lee, Iping Liang, Drew Lopenzina, Brandy Nālani McDougall, Deborah L. Madsen, Diveena S. Marcus, Sabine N. Meyer, Carol Miller, David L. Moore, Birgit Brander Rasmussen, Mark Rifkin, Kenneth M. Roemer, Oliver Scheiding, Lee Schweninger, Stephanie A. Sellers, Kathryn W. Shanley, Leah Sneider, David Stirrup, Theodore C. Van Alst Jr., Tammy Wahpeconiah.

Deborah L. Madsen is Professor of American Literature and Culture at the University of Geneva, Switzerland.

ALSO AVAILABLE IN THIS SERIES

The Routledge Companion to Anglophone Caribbean Literature
Also available in paperback

The Routledge Companion to Asian American and Pacific Islander Literature

The Routledge Companion to Experimental Literature
Also available in paperback

The Routledge Companion to Latino/a Literature
Also available in paperback

The Routledge Companion to Literature and Human Rights

The Routledge Companion to Literature and Science
Also available in paperback

The Routledge Companion to Native American Literature

The Routledge Companion to Science Fiction
Also available in paperback

The Routledge Companion to Travel Writing

The Routledge Companion to World Literature
Also available in paperback

THE ROUTLEDGE COMPANION TO NATIVE AMERICAN LITERATURE

Edited by
Deborah L. Madsen

LONDON AND NEW YORK

First published 2016
by Routledge
4 Park Square, Milton Park, Abingdon, Oxon OX14 4RN
605 Third Avenue, New York, NY 10017

First issued in paperback 2023

Routledge is an imprint of the Taylor & Francis Group, an informa business

© 2016 Deborah L. Madsen for selection and editorial matter; individual contributors their contributions.

The right of Deborah L. Madsen to be identified as the author of the editorial material, and of the authors for their individual chapters, has been asserted in accordance with sections 77 and 78 of the Copyright, Designs and Patents Act 1988.

All rights reserved. No part of this book may be reprinted or reproduced or utilized in any form or by any electronic, mechanical, or other means, now known or hereafter invented, including photocopying and recording, or in any information storage or retrieval system, without permission in writing from the publishers.

Trademark notice: Product or corporate names may be trademarks or registered trademarks, and are used only for identification and explanation without intent to infringe.

British Library Cataloguing-in-Publication Data
A catalogue record for this book is available from the British Library

Library of Congress Cataloging-in-Publication Data
The Routledge companion to Native American literature/[edited by] Deborah L. Madsen.
pages cm
Includes bibliographical references and index.
1. American literature—Indian authors—History and criticism 2. American literature—Indian authors—Themes, motives. 3. Indians in literature. 4. Group identity—United States. 5. Indians of North America—Ethnic identity. 6. Indians of North America—Intellectual life. 7. Indians of North America—Social conditions. 8. Indians of North America—Social life and customs. 9. United States—Civilization. I. Madsen, Deborah L., editor. II. Title: Companion to Native American literature. III. Title: Native American literature.
PS153.I52R68 2015
810.9'897—dc23
2015009262

ISBN: 978-1-13-802060-3 (hbk)
ISBN: 978-1-315-77734-4 (ebk)
ISBN: 978-0-367-36562-2 (pbk)

DOI: 10.4324/9781315777344

Typeset in Goudy
by Book Now Ltd, London

Publisher's Note
The publisher has gone to great lengths to ensure the quality of this reprint but points out that some imperfections in the original copies may be apparent.

CONTENTS

List of figures	ix
Notes on contributors	xi
Acknowledgements	xxiii

Introduction: The Indigenous Contexts of "Native." "American." "Literature."
DEBORAH L. MADSEN — 1

PART I
Identities — 13

1 Indigenous American Literature: The Inter-American Hemispheric Perspective
EARL E. FITZ — 15

2 Alaska Native Literature
SUSAN KOLLIN — 28

3 American Imperialism and Pacific Literatures
BRANDY NĀLANI MCDOUGALL — 39

4 Clear-Cut: The Importance of Mixedblood Identities and the Promise of Native American Cosmopolitanism to Native American Literatures
CHRIS LALONDE — 52

5 The Problem of Authenticity in Contemporary American "Gone Indian" Stories
JUDIT ÁGNES KÁDÁR — 64

6 Indigenous Writers and the Urban Indian Experience
CAROL MILLER — 74

CONTENTS

7 Recovering a Sovereign Erotic: Two-Spirit Writers "Reclaim a Name for Ourselves" 84
ALICIA COX

8 Indigenous Feminisms 95
LEAH SNEIDER

PART II
Key Moments 109

9 U.S.–Indian Treaty-Relations and Native American Treaty Literature 111
DAVID J. CARLSON

10 The Marshall Trilogy and Its Legacies 123
SABINE N. MEYER

11 Native Letters and North-American Indian Wars 135
OLIVER SCHEIDING

12 Finding Voice in Changing Times: The Politics of Native Self-Representation during the Periods of Removal and Allotment 146
MARK RIFKIN

13 Assimilative Schooling and Native American Literature 157
TOVA COOPER

14 Federalism Reconfigured: Native Narrations and the Indian New Deal 167
JOSEPH BAUERKEMPER

15 Embodied Jurisgenesis: NAGPRA, Dialogue, and Repatriation in American Indian Literature 181
AMELIA V. KATANSKI

16 Native American Literature and the UN Declaration on the Rights of Indigenous Peoples 192
ERIC CHEYFITZ

PART III
Sovereignties 203

17 "That We May Stand Up and Walk Ourselves": Indian Sovereignty and Diplomacy after the Revolutionary War 205
TAMMY WAHPECONIAH

18 "What Can I Tell Them That They Will Hear?": Environmental Sovereignty and American Indian Literature 217
LEE SCHWENINGER

CONTENTS

19 A Seat at the Table: Political Representation for Animals 229
BRIAN K. HUDSON

20 Where Food Grows on Water: Food Sovereignty and Indigenous
North American Literatures 238
JANET FISKIO

21 (Alter)Native Medicine and Health Sovereignty: Disease
and Healing in Contemporary Native American Writings 249
HSINYA HUANG

22 Religious Sovereignty and the Ghost Dance in Native American Fiction 260
SUSANNAH HOPSON

23 Native American Activism and Survival: Political, Legal, Cultural 273
BRUCE E. JOHANSEN

24 Identity, Culture, Community, and Nation: Literary Theory as Politics
and Praxis 284
KIRBY BROWN

PART IV
Traditions 297

25 Indigenous Literacy and Language 299
BIRGIT BRANDER RASMUSSEN

26 Native American Voices in Colonial North America 307
KATHRYN N. GRAY

27 Early Native American Writing 317
DREW LOPENZINA

28 The Historical and Literary Role of Folklore, Storytelling,
and the Oral Tradition in Native American Literatures 328
SUSAN BERRY BRILL DE RAMÍREZ

29 Spinning the Binary: Visual Cultures and Literary Aesthetics 340
DAVID STIRRUP

30 Indigenous Hermeneutics through Ceremony: Song, Language,
and Dance 353
DIVEENA S. MARCUS

31 Native American Intellectuals: Moundbuilders of Yesterday, Today,
and Tomorrow 364
CARI M. CARPENTER

vii

CONTENTS

PART V
Literary Forms 377

32 Crossing the Bering Strait: Transpacific Turns and Native Literatures 379
IPING LIANG

33 Reverse Assimilation: Native Appropriations of Euro-American
Conventions 390
KENNETH M. ROEMER

34 From As-Told-To Stories to Indigenous Communal Narratives 402
STEPHANIE A. SELLERS

35 Native Short Story: Authorships, Styles 412
A. ROBERT LEE

36 "A New Legacy for Future Generations": Native North American
Performance and Drama 423
BIRGIT DÄWES

37 Native American Poetry: Loosening the Bonds of Representation 435
DAVID L. MOORE AND KATHRYN W. SHANLEY

38 Native American Novels: The Renaissance, the Homing Plot,
and Beyond 448
JOHN GAMBER

39 Film in the Blood, Something in the Eye: Voice and Vision in
Native American Cinema 458
THEODORE C. VAN ALST JR.

40 Indigenous Uncanniness: Windigo Revisited and Popular Culture 469
SARAH HENZI

41 Future Pasts: Comics, Graphic Novels, and Digital Media 480
SUSAN BERNARDIN

Further Reading 494
Index 508

viii

FIGURES

31.1	Three-dimensional reconstruction of a moonrise over the Newark Earthworks	365
39.1	The Mercury Monterey. *Winter in the Blood*	463
39.2	The Boot. *Winter in the Blood*	463
39.3	Hi-Line Sunset. *Winter in the Blood*	463
39.4	The Airplane Man. *Winter in the Blood*	464
40.1	Steven Keewatin Sanderson, *Darkness Calls* (2005), 24–25	474
40.2	Steven Keewatin Sanderson, *Darkness Calls* (2005), 40–41	475
40.3	Steven Keewatin Sanderson, *Darkness Calls* (2005), 44–45	476
41.1	"Shamanic Warrior," from "Super Indian Volume 1."	483
41.2	Cover of "Here Comes the Anthro," "Super Indian Issue #2"	486
41.3	Cover of "The Curse of Blud Kwan'Tum, Part II," "Super Indian Issue #6"	487
41.4	Cover of "INC's Universe #0"	490

CONTRIBUTORS

Joseph Bauerkemper is an Assistant Professor in the Department of American Indian Studies at the University of Minnesota Duluth where his scholarship, outreach, and teaching emphasize politics, literature, governance, and law. He has published in *Studies in American Indian Literatures, American Studies, Journal of Transnational American Studies, Settler Colonial Studies, Visualities: Perspectives on Contemporary American Indian Film and Art, Seeing Red: Hollywood's Pixeled Skins,* and *The Oxford Handbook of Indigenous American Literature,* and he is currently at work on a book project titled "Trans/National Narrations: Networks and Nodes in Native Writing and Governance." Before joining the UMD faculty, Joseph earned his PhD in American Studies from the University of Minnesota Twin Cities, enjoyed one year at the University of Illinois as a Chancellor's Postdoctoral Fellow in American Indian Studies, and enjoyed two years at UCLA as an Andrew W. Mellon Visiting Assistant Professor in the Department of English and in the program for the study of Cultures in Transnational Perspective.

Susan Bernardin is Professor of English and Chair of Women's and Gender Studies at SUNY Oneonta. A co-author of *Trading Gazes: Euro-American Photographers and Native North Americans, 1880–1940* (Rutgers University Press 2003), she also facilitated a new edition of *In the Land of the Grasshopper Song* (Bison Books 2011) in collaboration with Terry Supahan and André Cramblit. She has published articles on foundational and contemporary Native writers, including Gertrude Bonnin, Mourning Dove, Sherman Alexie, Eric Gansworth, Gerald Vizenor, and Louis Owens. She served as guest editor of the 2014 special issue of *Western American Literature* entitled, *Indigenous Wests: Literary and Visual Aesthetics.* She is a two-time recipient of Western Literature Association's Don D. Walker Award for best published essay in Western American Literary Studies.

Susan Berry Brill de Ramírez, Caterpillar Inc. Professor of English, is also the Executive Director for Title IX Compliance at Bradley University. Brill de Ramírez's humanities studies began at St. John's College in Maryland, continued at the University of Wisconsin and the University of Chicago, culminating with nonwestern indigenous studies at the University of New Mexico. As a literature scholar, she is a specialist in the fields of Native American literatures, ecocriticism, folklore, and literary criticism and theory. She is a national Councillor for the Arts & Humanities with the Council for Undergraduate Research, a member of the PMLA Advisory Committee for the Modern Language Association, and the Book Review Editor for the *CUR Quarterly.* A

CONTRIBUTORS

widely published scholar, she is the author of *Wittgenstein and Critical Theory* (1995), *Contemporary American Indian Literatures and the Oral Tradition* (1999), *Native American Life-History Narratives* (2007), and with Evelina Zuni Lucero, co-editor of *Simon J. Ortiz: A Poetic Legacy of Indigenous Continuance* (2009). In her scholarly work, Professor Brill de Ramírez is currently exploring the ecocritical concepts of placefulness and "geographies of belonging" as transformative elements in literary poetics and narrative, and also completing a volume on the ethnographic work of women in the twentieth century.

Kirby Brown (Cherokee Nation) is an Assistant Professor of Native American and Ethnic American literatures in the Department of English at the University of Oregon and an enrolled citizen of the Cherokee Nation. His current research project, *Stoking the Fire: Nationhood in Early Twentieth Century Cherokee Writing*, examines how four Cherokee writers variously remembered, imagined and enacted Cherokee nationhood in the period between Oklahoma statehood in 1907 and tribal reorganization in the early 1970s. Essays in contemporary Indigenous critical theory, constitutional criticism in Native literatures, and Native interventions in the Western have appeared in *Sovereignty, Separatism, and Survivance: Ideological Encounters in Native North America* (2009), *Nakum Journal* (2010) and *Studies in American Indian Literatures* (2011). In addition to serving as an American Council of Learned Societies dissertation fellow, Brown is also the recipient of the Don D. Walker prize for the best essay published in western literary studies in 2012 by the Western Literature Association.

David J. Carlson is Professor of English at California State University, San Bernardino, where he teaches Native American Literature and Early American Literature. He is the author of *Sovereign Selves: American Indian Autobiography and the Law* (University of Illinois Press 2006) and the co-editor of *John Neal and Nineteenth-Century American Literature and Culture* (Bucknell University Press 2011). Professor Carlson's current book project is titled *Sovereign Reading: The Discourse of Self-Determination in American Indian Law and Literature* (forthcoming, University of Oklahoma Press 2016). He is also one of the founding editors of the on-line journal, *Transmotion*, which focuses on the work of Gerald Vizenor and on theoretical, post-modern and avant-garde writing by Native American and First Nation authors.

Cari M. Carpenter is Associate Professor of English at West Virginia University, where she is also a core member of the Native American Studies program and a faculty associate of the Center for Women's and Gender Studies. She is the author of *Seeing Red: Anger, Sentimentality, and Nineteenth-Century American Indians* (2008), editor of *Selected Writings of Victoria Woodhull: Suffrage, Free Love, and Eugenics* (2010), and co-editor with Carolyn Sorisio of *The Newspaper Warrior: Sarah Winnemucca Hopkins's Campaign for American Indian Rights, 1864–1891* (forthcoming 2015 from the University of Nebraska Press).

Eric Cheyfitz is the Ernest I. White Professor of American Studies and Humane Letters at Cornell University, where he teaches American literatures, American Indian literatures, and federal Indian law. He is the author of three books: *The Transparent: Sexual Politics in the Language of Emerson* (1981); *The Poetics of Imperialism: Translation and Colonization from* The Tempest *to* Tarzan (1991, 1997), which was named by *Choice* as one of the outstanding academic books of 1991; and *The (Post)Colonial Construction of Indian Country: U.S. American Indian Literatures and Federal Indian Law*, which appears

CONTRIBUTORS

as Part I of his edited volume, *The Columbia Guide to American Indian Literatures of the United States since 1945* (2006). In addition to these books he has published numerous essays in the fields of law, literature, cultural and postcolonial studies. His most recent publication is an essay, "What Is a Just Society? Native American Philosophies and the Limits of Capitalism's Imagination," which appeared in *Sovereignty, Indigeneity, and the Law*, a special issue of *South Atlantic Quarterly* (110:2, Spring 2011), which he also co-edited and which won the award for the best special issue of an academic journal in 2011 given by the Council of Editors of Learned Journals and was acknowledged for "Outstanding Indigenous Scholarship" in the same year by the American Indian and Alaska Native Professors Association. In addition to his scholarly publications, Cheyfitz has been the director of Cornell's American Indian Program and the faculty coordinator for the Mellon Mays Undergraduate Fellowship Program at Cornell. He has been an op-ed columnist for the newspaper, *Indian Country Today, The Jewish Daily Forward, The Chronicle of Higher Education,* and the London *Times Higher Education* supplement. He has appeared in the award-winning documentary film on Western Shoshone land rights, *Our Land, Our Life* (2007), as well as on public radio, where he has discussed issues of academic freedom, federal Indian law, and Native American literatures. He has served as an expert witness in the academic freedom case of Ward Churchill, and in cases involving Indian rights. Throughout his career, his focus has been to connect his scholarship and teaching to progressive social action.

Tova Cooper's research interests intersect at the disciplinary boundaries of literature, history, education, and visual studies. She is particularly interested in history gleaned from the pages of memoirs and autobiographies, as well as from the archives. Dr. Cooper's book *The Autobiography of Citizenship: Assimilation and Resistance in U.S. Education* appeared in 2014, as part of Rutgers University Press's American Literatures Initiative. Cooper also has an essay forthcoming in *Studies in Law, Politics, and Society* titled "Commercial Leases and Family Realities in Charles Reznikoff's *Family Chronicle*." Currently, Cooper is working on an essay about representations of Asperger's in literature and memoir, titled "The Aspergian Literary Hero and Alternative Ways of Knowing." She is also writing a novel titled *Underwater Subdivision*.

Alicia Cox is currently a University of California President's Postdoctoral Fellow at UC Davis. She is a queer feminist of Cherokee and European heritage. Alicia earned her BA at the University of Kansas, and she completed her PhD in English with a concentration in Native American Studies at the University of California, Riverside. Her dissertation, "Autobiographical Indiscipline: Queering American Indian Life Narratives," seeks to develop a decolonizing practice of reading as-told-to Indian autobiographies, and it focuses on narratives of gender disciplining in Indian boarding schools. Alicia's work has been published in the journal *Studies in American Indian Literatures*. She has served as Events Coordinator and Secretary for the Cherokee Community of the Inland Empire, a Cherokee Nation At-Large citizen organization.

Birgit Däwes is Professor and Chair of American Studies at the University of Vienna. Having taught previously at the Universities of Mainz and Würzburg as well as at National Sun Yat-sen University in Kaohsiung, Taiwan, she has specialized in Native North American literatures and cultures. Next to a monograph study on *Native North*

xiii

CONTRIBUTORS

American Theater in a Global Age (Winter 2007) and the recent collection, *Indigenous North American Drama: A Multivocal History* (SUNY Press 2013), she has also published an award-winning study on fiction as a mode of cultural memory: *Ground Zero Fiction: History, Memory, and Representation in the American 9/11 Novel* (Winter 2011). She is also one of the co-editors (with Karsten Fitz and Sabine N. Meyer) of the international book series *Routledge Research in Transnational Indigenous Perspectives*.

Janet Fiskio is Assistant Professor of Environmental Studies and Comparative American Studies at Oberlin College, where she teaches and researches in the environmental humanities, food justice, and climate change, with a particular focus on the rust belt. She has published in *American Literature* and *The Cambridge Companion to Literature and the Environment*. She is currently at work on a monograph, *Counter Friction*, which examines climate change through literature, art, performance, and protest.

Earl E. Fitz is Professor of Portuguese, Spanish and Comparative Literature at Vanderbilt University, where he teaches courses on Brazilian and Spanish American literature, Comparative Literature, inter-American literature and translation. He is also an Affiliate Faculty for Vanderbilt's Latin American Studies Program. He is the author of such studies as *Rediscovering the New World: Inter-American Literature in a Comparative Context, Brazilian Narrative Traditions in a Comparative Context,* and (with Elizabeth Lowe) *Translation and the Rise of Inter-American Literature*. Professor Fitz is currently working on a new book entitled *Inter-American Literature: Five Case Studies*.

John Gamber is an Assistant Professor at Columbia University in the Department of English and Comparative Literature and the Center for the Study of Ethnicity and Race. His book, *Positive Pollutions and Cultural Toxins* (2012) examines the role of toxicity and contamination in contemporary novels by authors of color. His current project, *International Indians* examines alternative constructions of nationhood in contemporary Native American literature. He has published several articles on Native American literature in edited collections and journals including PMLA, MELUS, and *Western American Literatures*.

Kathryn N. Gray is Associate Professor (Reader) in Early American Literature at Plymouth University and her research focuses on the literatures of the Anglo-American Atlantic world. She has published on the Native American experience of Christianity in particular, and is currently working on a project involving natural history narratives and the production of natural knowledge in the colonial Atlantic world. Her publications include, *John Eliot and the Praying Indians of Massachusetts Bay* (Bucknell University Press 2013), and articles in, for example, *Symbiosis, Journal of Eighteenth-Century Studies* and *The Seventeenth Century*.

Sarah Henzi is an FQRSC-funded Postdoctoral Fellow in the First Nations Studies Program at the University of British Columbia and a Sessional Instructor in the Department of First Nations Studies at Simon Fraser University. She is also Co-organizer of and Lecturer for the International Graduate Summer School on Indigenous Literature and Film, held annually in July at the Centre d'études et de recherche internationales, Université de Montréal. Her current research project, entitled "Indigenous New Media: Alternative Forms of Storytelling," seeks to analyze how more contemporary modes of storytelling,

CONTRIBUTORS

such as the graphic novel, science fiction, speculative fantasy, erotica, slam and spoken word performance, as well as the short film and animation, both complement and inform the already-existing critical theory developed by literary scholars. She has articles published in *Studies for Canadian Literature*, the *London Journal of Canadian Studies*, and *Australasian Canadian Studies*, and is a contributor to the *Oxford Handbook of Indigenous American Literature* (2014). She also has a book project under contract with University of Manitoba Press, entitled *Inventing Interventions: Strategies of Reappropriation in North American Indigenous Literatures*.

Susannah Hopson is currently a PhD student in the Department of History at the University of Hull. Her thesis is entitled "The Process of Memory: A Comparative Study of Native American Massacre Sites, 1863–1890." Her research focuses on the Bear River Massacre (1863), the Sand Creek Massacre (1864) and the Wounded Knee Massacre (1890) in order to consider the complexities of collective memory and memorialization within Euro-American and Native American contexts. She received a First Class Honours degree from the University of Wales, Swansea in 2010, spending one year of this degree at California State University, Fullerton. She gained her MA in English Literature from the University of Lincoln in 2011 and currently works as a PhD tutor for undergraduate students at the University of Hull and as an English literature tutor to GCSE and A-Level students.

Hsinya Huang is Professor of American and Comparative Literature and Dean of the College of Arts and Humanities, National Sun Yat-Sen University, Taiwan. She is the author or editor of books and articles on Native American and Indigenous literatures, eco-criticism, post-colonial and ethnic studies, published in Taiwan and abroad, including *(De)Colonizing the Body: Disease, Empire, and (Alter)Native Medicine in Contemporary Native American Women's Writings* (2004) and *Huikan beimei yuanzhumin wenxue: duoyuan wenhua de shengsi* (*Native North American Literatures: Reflections on Multiculturalism*) (2009), the first Chinese essay collection on Native North American literatures, and *Aspects of Transnational and Indigenous Cultures* (2014). She edited the English translation of *The History of Taiwanese Indigenous Literatures* and is currently editing *Aspects of Transnational* and *Ocean and Ecology in the Trans-Pacific Context*. She is Editor-in-Chief of *Sun Yat-sen Journal of Humanities*. She serves on the Council of the American Studies Association and on the Advisory Board of *The Journal of Transnational American Studies* (*JTAS*) and the Routledge series on "Transnational Indigenous Perspectives" and on the Editorial Board of *Transmotion: A Journal of Vizenorian Indigenous Studies* (University of Kent). Her current research projects funded respectively by the Ministry of Science and Technology (Taiwan) and Chiang Ching-Kuo Foundation investigate Native American and Pacific Islanders' literatures, radiation ecologies in the Pacific, and Chinese railroad workers in North America (in collaboration with Stanford University).

Brian K. Hudson, a citizen of the Cherokee Nation of Oklahoma, recently completed his PhD in English with a concentration in Literary and Cultural Studies at the University of Oklahoma. He recently published a special issue of *Studies in American Indian Literatures* on animal studies and edited Carter Revard's latest collection of poetry, *From the Extinct Volcano, A Bird of Paradise*. He is currently working on the relationships between human and nonhuman animals in Native American literatures.

xv

CONTRIBUTORS

Bruce E. Johansen is a Professor of Communication and Native American Studies, University of Nebraska at Omaha. He has been teaching and writing in the School of Communication at UNO since 1982. He had authored 39 published books as of 2014. Johansen writes frequently about environmental subjects, including *The Encyclopedia of Global Warming Science and Technology* (2 vols., 2009), *Global Warming in the 21st century* (3 vols., 2006), *The Global Warming Desk Reference* (2001), *The Dirty Dozen: Toxic Chemicals and the Earth's Future* (2003), and *Indigenous Peoples and Environmental Issues* (2004), a 200,000-word encyclopedia of indigenous peoples' struggles with corporations with a world-wide scope. He was co-editor of the *Encyclopedia of American Indian History*, a 4-volume set (ABC-CLIO 2007), as well as the *Encyclopedia of the American Indian Movement* (Greenwood 2013). Johansen's first academic specialty was the influence of Native American political systems on United States political and legal institutions; his best-known books in this area are *Forgotten Founders* (1982) and *Exemplar of Liberty* (with Donald A. Grinde Jr.), published in 1991. Johansen has described the present-day debate over this issue in *Debating Democracy* (1998), and *Native American Political Systems and the Evolution of Democracy: An Annotated Bibliography* (Greenwood 1996; volume 2, 1999). He also writes as a journalist in several national forums, including the *Washington Post* and *The Progressive*, with letters to the editor in *The Atlantic, New York Times, National Geographic, Wall Street Journal*, et al.

Judit Ágnes Kádár has taught American and Canadian cultural studies at the Department of American Studies of Eszterházy College in Eger, Hungary for twenty years, more recently with a focus on ethnic and multicultural studies. She published the textbook *Critical Perspectives on English-Canadian Literature* (1996). She has received numerous research grants (FEFA, FEP, FRP/CEACS, JFK, Fulbright), and held temporary positions at Georgia College and State University (2009) and University of New Mexico (2012). As for her field of research, she has studied alternative histories and epistemological relativism in recent western Canadian fiction; she has explored the epistemological, psychological, and sociological implications of indigenous passage rites (Othering/indigenization) in Canadian and American literature and culture, and published *Going Indian: Cultural Appropriation in Recent North American Literature* (2012, University of Valencia Press). In 2013, she completed her habilitation at ELTE University of Budapest. Currently she is exploring mixed blood narratives and the problem of identity negotiation in the context of Southwestern literature and recent *Nuevomexicano* writing. She is the director of the International Relations Center at Eszterházy College.

Amelia V. Katanski is Associate Professor of English at Kalamazoo College in Kalamazoo, Michigan. Dr. Katanski received her PhD in English from Tufts University and earned an MA in English at Tufts and an MA in American Indian Studies from UCLA. Her research and teaching focuses on American Indian literature. She is the author of *Learning to Write "Indian": The Boarding School in American Indian Literature* (University of Oklahoma Press 2005) as well as a number of scholarly articles on American Indian literature and pedagogy. Her research has explored the relationship among educational institutions, US federal law, indigenous customary law, and Native literary traditions. She teaches courses in American Indian Literature, Comparative Indigenous Literatures and "American Indian Literature and the Law," alongside a range of courses in American literature and a first-year writing seminar on food systems called "Cultivating

Community," a service-learning course that examines food justice from a variety of perspectives. Her current research, supported by a faculty fellowship with the Arcus Center for Social Justice Leadership at Kalamazoo College, focuses on the intersection of storytelling, tribal sovereignty, and food sovereignty in Anishinaabeg communities and she is a recipient of an American Midwest Foodways Scholar's Grant to complete a project on the impact of Indian boarding school education on Great Lakes Indigenous foodways.

Susan Kollin is Professor of English and a College of Letters and Science Distinguished Professor at Montana State University for 2011–2014. Her essays on the fiction and film of the American West have appeared in *American Literary History, Modern Fiction Studies, Contemporary Literature, Genre: Forms of Discourse and Culture, Studies in American Fiction*, and other journals. Her books include the edited volume, *Postwestern Cultures: Literature, Theory, Space, and Nature's State: Imagining Alaska as the Last Frontier*. She is presently editing the *Cambridge History of Western American Literature*.

Chris LaLonde is Professor of English and a member of the program faculty in Native American Studies at SUNY Oswego. He has published books on William Faulkner and on the Choctaw-Cherokee-Irish author Louis Owens. He is also the author of numerous articles on Native American literatures and, in particular, the works of Gerald Vizenor and Kimberly Blaeser.

A. Robert Lee, formerly of the University of Kent at Canterbury, UK, retired as Professor of American Literature at Nihon University, Tokyo in 2011. He has held visiting appointments at Princeton, the University of Virginia, Bryn Mawr College, Northwestern University, the University of Colorado, Berkeley and the University of New Mexico. His publications include *Designs of Blackness: Mappings in the Literature and Culture of Afro-America* (1998); *Multicultural American Literature: Comparative Black, Native, Latino/a and Asian American Fictions* (2003), which won the 2004 American Book Award; *United States: Re-Viewing American Multicultural Literature* (2009); *Gothic to Multicultural: Idioms of Imagining in American Literary Fiction* (2009) and *Modern American Counter Writing: Beats, Outriders, Ethnics* (2010). His interests in Native American texts and culture are reflected in *Shadow Distance: A Gerald Vizenor Reader* (1994); *Postindian Conversations*, with Gerald Vizenor (1999); ed. with Deborah Madsen, *Gerald Vizenor: Texts and Contexts* (2010); ed. *The Salt Companion to Jim Barnes* (2010); ed. the four-volume set, *Native American Writing* (2011); ed. with Alan Velie, *The Native American Renaissance: Literary Imagination and Achievement* (2013); and essays on Louis Owens, Simon Ortiz, Carter Revard, Diane Glancy, Kim Blaeser and Stephen Graham Jones.

Iping Liang is Professor of English and American Studies at National Taiwan Normal University. Her research interests include Herman Melville, Global Indigeneity Studies, Native American Literature, and Asian American Studies. She is the author/editor of *The Pacific in Sail: Herman Melville and the South Pacific Indigenous Islanders* (forthcoming); *Asia/Americas: Asian American Literatures in Taiwan* (2013); and *Ghost Dances: Towards a Native American Gothic* (2006). Her recent publications include "The Foreigner at Home: The Politics of Home in Francie Lin's *The Foreigner*" (*Changing Boundaries and Reshaping Itineraries in Asian American Literary Studies*, eds. Liu Kuilan and Elaine Kim, 2014; "'The Sharpest Sight': The Canonical and the Popular in *The Sharpest Sight*" in *Chung-wai Literary Quarterly* 2013; "The Mixedblood Landscape: Life Writing

CONTRIBUTORS

in Louis Owens and Gerald Vizenor" in *Life Writing*, eds. Yuan-wen Chi and Yu-cheng Lee. 2011. Her current research involves the Stanford Project on North American Chinese Railroad Workers and a three-year project on Taiwanese American fiction. She was Editor-in-Chief for *Concentric: Literary and Cultural Studies*, International Representative for the Women's Committee, American Studies Association, as well as Coordinator of the Native American Literature Study Group in Taiwan. She currently serves on the advisory/editorial boards of *Multiethnic Studies in Europe and the Americas* (MELUS); Association for the Studies of Literature and Environment in Taiwan; and *Journal of Overseas Chinese Studies: Connections and Comparisons in East Asia*. She is also the Director of International Cooperation at NTNU, where she is responsible for global partnerships, student mobility, and study abroad programs.

Drew Lopenzina is Professor of Early American and Native American literature at Old Dominion University in Norfolk, VA. His book, *Red Ink: Native Americans Picking up the Pen in the Colonial Period* (SUNY Press 2012) offers a rethinking of indigenous engagements with literacy in America's colonial milieu, detailing how Native communities drew from their own narrative and literary traditions as they forged interactions with western forms of literacy. He has published in the journals *American Literature*, *American Quarterly*, *American Indian Quarterly* and others. Currently he is working on a biography of the nineteenth-century Pequot activist and minister William Apess.

Brandy Nālani McDougall (Kanaka ʻŌiwi/Hawaiian), born and raised on the island of Maui, is of Kanaka Maoli (Hawaiʻi, Maui, Oʻahu and Kauaʻi lineages), Chinese and Scottish descent. She is the author of a poetry collection, *The Salt-Wind, Ka Makani Paʻakai* (Kuleana ʻŌiwi Press 2008), the co-founder of Ala Press and Kahuaomānoa Press, and the co-star of an amplified poetry album, *Undercurrent* (Hawaiʻi Dub Machine 2011). A recipient of both Ford and Mellon-Hawaii postdoctoral awards in 2013–2014, her research focuses on the Hawaiian practice of kaona (veiling and layering meaning) in contemporary Hawaiian Literature. Her monograph will be published by the University of Arizona Press in Spring 2016. She is an Assistant Professor of Indigenous Studies in the American Studies Department at the University of Hawaiʻi at Mānoa.

Deborah L. Madsen is Professor of American Studies at the University of Geneva. Her research focuses on issues of settler-nationalism, indigeneity, and migration, exemplified by her work on American Exceptionalism and the white supremacist ideology of Manifest Destiny. Her most recent books include the edited collections, *Native Authenticity: Transatlantic Approaches to Native American Literature* (SUNY Press 2010) and *Louise Erdrich* (Continuum 2012). She is an Associate Editor of *Contemporary Women's Writing* (Oxford University Press), and has served on the Editorial Board of the *Encyclopedia of American Studies* (published by Johns Hopkins University Press for the American Studies Association) and on the Editorial Advisory Committee of PMLA.

Diveena S. Marcus (Tamalko-California Coast Miwok), is an enrolled member of the Federated Indians of Graton Rancheria. She received her Philosophy degree at the University of Hawaiʻi and holds a Master of Arts degree in Native American Studies from Montana State University. She is a PhD Indigenous Studies candidate at Trent University in Ontario Canada completing a dissertation entitled, "*Hiyaa ʻaa Maa Pichas̲ʻope: Maa Hammaako He Ma Papʼoyyis̲ko (Let Us Understand Again Our Grandmothers and Our*

xviii

CONTRIBUTORS

Grandfathers) Map of the Elders: Cultivating Northern California Indigenous Consciousness." Her interdisciplinary research deals with issues that lie at the intersections of Indigenous studies, Religious Studies, Environmental Studies and Performance.

Sabine N. Meyer is an Assistant Professor of American Studies at the Institute of English and American Studies at the University of Osnabrück and the Coordinator of the Osnabrück Summer Institute on the Cultural Study of the Law. Her research explores the history of American reform movements, concepts of gender, ethnicity, and civic identity in the United States in the nineteenth century, representations of Native Americans in American popular culture, as well as the intersections of law and Native American literature. Her publications include articles on the teaching of U.S. history in German universities (*Journal of American History* 2010), on Native American literature and the transnational turn (*Transnational American Studies*, ed. Udo Hebel 2012), and on representations of Native Americans in television and film (*Ethnoscripts, zkmb* 2013). Her book, *We Are What We Drink: The Temperance Battle in Minnesota*, is under contract with the University of Illinois Press for publication in 2015. She is currently working on her second book project, "The Indian Removal in Law and Native American Literature," which explores the interfaces between removal legislation and literary representations of removal in Native American texts from the nineteenth to the twenty-first centuries.

Carol Miller is a Morse Alumni Distinguished Teaching Professor (Emerita) of the Department of American Indian Studies and the Program in American Studies, University of Minnesota-TC. She is an enrolled member of the Cherokee Nation of Oklahoma.

David L. Moore is Professor of English at the University of Montana. His fields of research and teaching at graduate and undergraduate levels include cross-cultural American Studies, Native American literatures, Western American literatures, Peace Studies, Baha'i Studies, literature and the environment, and ecocritical and dialogical critical theory. He has taught previously at the University of South Dakota, Salish Kootenai College, University of Washington, and Cornell University. He was the recipient of a Post-Doctoral Fellowship at the Society for the Humanities at Cornell University and of the Faculty Research Fellowship in Western Studies at the O'Connor Center for the Rocky Mountain West, among other awards. His book, entitled *"That Dream Shall Have a Name": Native Americans Rewriting America*, is published by the University of Nebraska Press. He currently is editing a collection of essays on prominent author Leslie Marmon Silko, contracted with Bloomsbury Academic Publishers in the UK. Other publications include an edited volume of *American Indian Quarterly* as well as numerous articles and chapters. He co-hosts Reflections West, a short weekly literary program on Montana Public Radio; and he participates in theater productions by the Bearhead Swaney Intertribal Playwrights Project on the Flathead Reservation.

Birgit Brander Rasmussen is Assistant Professor of American Studies and Ethnicity, Race and Migration at Yale University and Global Center for Advanced Studies. She received her PhD from UC-Berkeley's Ethnic Studies Department. Her scholarship focuses on race, writing, colonialism, and American Literature. She is the author of a prize-winning book entitled *Queequeg's Coffin: Indigenous Literacies and the Making of Early American Literature* (Duke University Press 2012). Her work has appeared in anthologies and in *American Literature, PMLA, Early American Literature, Journal*

xix

CONTRIBUTORS

of Transnational American Studies, Interventions: International Journal of Postcolonial Studies, Mississippi Quarterly, and *Modern Language Quarterly*. Her article, "Negotiating Treaties, Negotiating Literacies: A French-Iroquois Encounter and the Making of Early American Literature," won the 2007 Norman Foerster Prize for best essay published in *American Literature*. She is co-editor of *The Making and Unmaking of Whiteness* (Duke University Press 2001). Her next book is tentatively titled *The Fort Marion Sketchbooks: Plains Pictography and the Carceral State*.

Mark Rifkin is Professor of English and Women's and Gender Studies at the University of North Carolina at Greensboro. He is the author of four books, including *Settler Common Sense: Queerness and Everyday Colonialism in the American Renaissance* and *When Did Indians Become Straight?: Kinship, the History of Sexuality, and Native Sovereignty*. He also has served as president of the Native American and Indigenous Studies Association.

Kenneth M. Roemer, a Piper Professor of 2011, Distinguished Teaching Professor, and Distinguished Scholar Professor at the University of Texas at Arlington, has received four NEH grants to direct Summer Seminars and has been a Japan Society for the Promotion of Science Fellow and a Visiting Professor in Japan. He has been a guest lecturer at Harvard and has been an invited lecturer at twelve universities in Japan and in ten other countries. He is past President of the Society for Utopian Studies, past Vice President and founding member of ASAIL, and past Chair of the American Indian Literatures Divisions of MLA. He was Assistant Editor of *American Quarterly* and has served on the Advisory Board of *PMLA* and the Editorial Board of *American Literature*. His articles have appeared in journals such as *American Literature, American Literary History, Modern Fiction Studies, Technology and Culture*, and *SAIL*. His books on Native American literature include *Approaches to Teaching Momaday's The Way to Rainy Mountain* (ed.); *Native American Writers of the United States* (ed.); and *The Cambridge Companion to Native American Literature* (co-ed.). The latter two won Writer of Year Awards from the Wordcraft Circle of Native Writers and Storytellers. He has written four books on utopian literature, including *The Obsolete Necessity*, which was nominated for a Pulitzer in American History, and one personal narrative, *Michibata de Deatta Nippon (A Sidewalker's Japan)*. For twenty years he has been a Faculty Advisor for the Native American Students Association at UT Arlington. In 2011 he was named a Piper Professor (state-wide award) and received a UT System's Regents' Outstanding Teaching Award. In 2014 he was one of five inducted into the UT System Academy of Distinguished Teachers.

Oliver Scheiding is Professor of American Literature and Early American Studies at the University of Mainz, Germany. He is author of *Worlding America: A Transnational Anthology of Short Narratives before 1800* (Stanford University Press 2015), which documents indigenous narrative traditions in the early Americas. He is editor of *Native American Studies Across Time and Space: Essays on the Indigenous Americas* (Winter 2010). He edits the journal *Amerikastudien/American Studies* on behalf of the German Association of American Studies. Currently, he is working on a manuscript tentatively titled "New World Objects: Materiality, Networks, and Agency in the Early Americas."

Lee Schweninger is Professor of English at the University of North Carolina Wilmington where he teaches early American and American Indian literatures and serves as coordinator of the Native American Studies minor. His recent publications include *Listening to the Land: American Indian Literary Responses to the Landscape* (University of Georgia Press 2008); *The First We Can Remember: Colorado Pioneer Women Tell Their Stories* (University of Nebraska Press 2011), and *Imagic Moments: North American Indigenous Film* (University of Georgia Press 2013). He has also recently published essays or book chapters on American Indian literature and/or film in *The Memory of Nature in Aboriginal, Canadian and American Contexts* (ed. Francoise Besson, Cambridge Scholars Publishing 2014); *Elohi* (journal, University of Bordeaux 2013); *Critical Insights: The American Dream* (ed. Keith Newlin, Salem Press 2013); and *Indigenous Rights in the Age of the UN Declaration* (ed. Elvira Pulitano, Cambridge University Press 2012).

Stephanie A. Sellers (Cherokee/Shawnee/Sephardic Jew/European) holds a doctoral degree in Native American Studies with an emphasis on Women of the Eastern Woodlands and is on the faculty at Gettysburg College. Her first book, *Native American Autobiography Redefined: A Handbook*, was published by Peter Lang USA in 2007. Sellers's poetry, essays, and coyote stories have appeared in peer-reviewed journals such as *American Indian Quarterly*, *American Indian Culture and Research Journal*, *Native Literatures: Generations*, and *Calyx: The Journal of Women's Literature and Art*. She has presented her scholarship on Native American Traditions panels at national conferences of the American Academy of Religion, the Modern Language Association, the Association of Eighteenth-Century Studies, and the International Society of American Women Writers, among others.

Kathryn W. Shanley (Nakoda/Fort Peck Assiniboine) is a Professor of Native American Studies at the University of Montana-Missoula, and also works as the Special Assistant to the Provost for Native American and Indigenous Education. Widely published in the field of Native American literature, Dr. Shanley most recently co-edited a volume (with Bjorg Evjen) titled *Mapping Indigenous Presence: North Scandinavian and North American Perspectives* (University of Arizona Press 2015). She also has recent essays in *These Living Songs: Reading Montana Poetry* (2014), *Native American Renaissance: Literary Imagination and Achievement* (2013), and *Re-imagining Nature* (2013). An enrolled Nakoda from the Ft. Peck Reservation, Dr. Shanley co-edits (with Ned Blackhawk) the Yale University Press Henry Roe Cloud American Indians and Modernity series. She served as president-elect, president, and past-president of the Native American and Indigenous Studies Association from 2011–2013, and she has for the past ten years served as regional liaison for the Ford Foundation Fellowship Program.

Leah Sneider earned her PhD in American Literature (Native American emphasis) from the University of New Mexico and is an Assistant Professor of English at Montgomery College in Maryland. Her research focuses on the intersections of race/ethnicity, gender, and nation as depicted in ethnic American literature. She most recently published "Gender, Literacy, and Sovereignty in Winnemucca's *Life Among the Piutes*" in *American Indian Quarterly*. Her developing manuscript, *Decolonizing Gender: Indigenous Feminism and Native American Literature*, explores literary performances of gender through a blended Two Spirit/queer analytics and Indigenous feminist lens.

David Stirrup is Senior Lecturer in American Literature at the University of Kent. His publications include *Louise Erdrich* (Manchester University Press 2010), *Tribal Fantasies:*

xxi

CONTRIBUTORS

Native Americans in the European Imaginary, 1900–2010 (co-ed. with James Mackay. Palgrave 2012), *Parallel Encounters: Culture at the Canada–US Border* (co-ed. with Gillian Roberts, Wilfrid Laurier University Press 2014), and *Enduring Critical Poses: Beyond Nation and History* (co-ed. with Gordon Henry Jr., forthcoming with SUNY Press). His monograph on Visuality and the Visual Arts in contemporary Anishinaabe writing is forthcoming with Michigan State University Press. He is Principal Investigator of the Leverhulme Trust-funded "Culture and the Canada–US Border" International Network, and one of the founding editors of the online journal, *Transmotion*.

Theodore C. Van Alst Jr. is an Assistant Professor of Native American Studies at the University of Montana, and former Assistant Dean and Director of the Native American Cultural Center at Yale University. His most recent work includes the chapters "Navajo Joe," and "The Savage Innocents," in *Seeing Red – Hollywood's Pixeled Skins: American Indians and Film* (2013). His current book-length project is *Spaghetti and Sauerkraut with a Side of Frybread*, and his selected volume *The Faster, Redder, Road: The Best UnAmerican Stories of Stephen Graham Jones* will be published in Spring 2015 by the University of New Mexico Press. He has worked as a consultant for the Disney Channel as well as NPR's *All Things Considered*, and has recently appeared in multiple segments of the History Channel series "Mankind the Story of All of Us," and been interviewed by the *Washington Post*, Canadian Broadcast Corporation, Native America Calling, *Smithsonian Magazine*, and Al-Jazeera America Television.

Tammy Wahpeconiah (Sac and Fox) is an enrolled member of the Sac and Fox Nation of Missouri and teaches American Indian, Ethnic American, and American literatures in the English department at Appalachian State University. Her research interests include early American Indian writers, contemporary American Indian literature, and television. She has published a book entitled *This Once Savage Heart of Mine: Rhetorical Strategies of Survival in Early Native American Writing* focusing on the writings of Joseph Johnson and William Apess, as well as articles on Sherman Alexie and William S. Penn. She is currently writing about the poetry of Gordon Henry and the television series *Sons of Anarchy*.

ACKNOWLEDGEMENTS

For permission to reproduce the illustrations in this volume, we gratefully acknowledge the assistance of John E. Hancock, Alex and Andrew Smith, Steven Keewatin Sanderson, and Arigon Starr. For permission to use her beautiful and evocative painting "Grey Wolves" on the cover of our book, we thank the artist Clarissa Rizal (Tlingit).

Joseph Bauerkemper owes a debt of gratitude to Jill Doerfler for guidance and feedback on his chapter. Kirby Brown sends a big wado to James Cox, Angie Morrill, Brian Klopotek, April Anson, and Taylor McHolm. Alicia Cox would like to thank Susy Zepeda and Sarah Biscarra-Dilley for reviewing a draft of the chapter and offering generous and insightful feedback; and the Intertribal Friendship House in Oakland, California, for hosting the Two-Spirit Honoring Ceremony in December 2014, which acknowledged the place of Two-Spirit peoples in Native American communities and offered a space for healing from centuries of violence. The ceremony was guided by Rodney Littlebird and sponsored by the Intertribal Friendship House, the Native American Health Center, and Wicahpi Koyaka Tiospaye. Janet Fiskio would like to thank Sarah Wald and Ted Toadvine for thoughtful comments on an earlier draft of the chapter, and Kyle Powys Whyte for generously sharing his time and insights. Hsinya Huang is indebted to the Ministry of Science and Technology, Taiwan for funding support. Bruce Johansen would like to acknowledge Vine Deloria Jr., friend and mentor. Iping Liang wishes to thank Gerald Vizenor and A. Robert Lee for support; Keijiro Suga, Ikue Kina, and Huei-chu Chu for advice; and Zhi-chen Lin and Chia-wei Yang for their help with the research. Birgit Brander Rasmussen thanks Benedicte Årestrup; Oliver Scheiding acknowledges the valuable research assistance provided by Patricia Godsave. Ted Van Alst thanks Alex and Andrew Smith, Ken White, Chaske Spencer, Lily Gladstone, Robert Hall, Sterling Holywhitemountain, and Jeff Barnaby.

Deborah Madsen extends the warmest of thanks to Liz Levine, the Commissioning Editor at Routledge, for initially suggesting this volume and for her valuable advice in the early stages, and Ruth Hilsdon for being a constant source of editorial assistance especially during the latter stages of bringing this book into being. Kenneth Roemer displayed his characteristic collegiality by making available to me the results of his bibliographic researches (for his 1997 Dictionary of Literary Biography volume on Native American Writers) while I was compiling the "Further Reading" section of the current volume: a gesture of generosity that went well beyond what he had signed on for. But generosity has marked this project from its very inception, when scholars of Indigenous Studies from all parts of the world – pretty much from the Artic to Australia – offered me help and support of all kinds, for

ACKNOWLEDGEMENTS

which I remain deeply appreciative: Joni Adamson, Ellen Arnold, Kevin Bruyneel, Richard Dauenhauer, Philip Deloria, Joanna Hearne, Shari Huhndorf, Ron Illingworth, Scott Lyons, Sam McKegney, Keavy Martin, David Martínez, Scott Morgensen, Robert Dale Parker, Jessica Bissett Perea, Craig Santos Perez, Joy Porter, LaVonne Brown Ruoff, James Ruppert, Johan Henrik Schimanski, Lisa Tatonetti, Maggie Walters, Robert Warrior, Chong Zhang, and also the seven anonymous reviewers who provided Routledge with a series of probing and insightful reports that helped to make this a better book. The creation of a resource such as this book is a genuine community effort and so the deepest debt of gratitude is owed to the contributors, whose work I am honored to have facilitated.

Permissions

Chapter 2

From *Blonde Indian* by Ernestine Hayes. © 2006 Ernestine Hayes. Reprinted by permission of the University of Arizona Press.

"Saginaw Bay: I Keep Going Back" by Robert Davis in *SoulCatcher*, Raven's Bones Press, 1986; *Alaska Quarterly Review*, Vol. 26 No. 1 & 2, Spring & Summer 2009; *Village Boy: Poems of Cultural Identity*, Robert Davis Hoffmann, 2014.

Chapter 3

From *Coconut Milk* by Dan Taulapapa McMullin (2013) reprinted with permission of the author.

"Sā Nāfanua" by Caroline Sinavaiana (2002) in *Alchemies of Distance* by Caroline Sinavaiana reprinted with permission of the author.

"SPAM's Carbon Footprint [a malologue]" by Craig Santos Perez (2014) in *from unincorporated territory [guma]* by Craig Santos Perez reprinted with permission of the author.

"April 2013" by Lehua Taitano (2014) in *A Bell Made of Stones* by Lehua Taitano reprinted with permission of the author.

"Into Our Light I Will Go Forever" by Haunani-Kay Trask in *Night is a Sharkskin Drum* © 2002. Reprinted by permission of the University of Hawaii Press.

Chapter 4

"Driving in Oklahoma" by Carter Revard (2005) in *How the Songs Come Down* by Carter Revard reprinted with permission of the author.

"The Truth is" by Linda Hogan (1985) in *Seeing Through the Sun* by Linda Hogan reprinted with permission of the author.

"Certificate of Live Birth" and "Downwinders" by Kimberly Blaeser (1996) in *Trailing You* by Kimberly Blaeser reprinted with permission of the author.

xxiv

ACKNOWLEDGEMENTS

Chapter 11

From *Fight Back, For the Sake of the People, For the Sake of the Land* by Simon Ortiz (1980) reprinted with permission of the author.

Chapter 21

From "I Would Steal Horses" by Sherman Alexie reprinted from *First Indian on the Moon* © 1993 by Sherman Alexie, by permission of Hanging Loose Press.

Chapter 28

From "Deer Dance Exhibition" by Ofelia Zepeta (1995) in *Ocean Power* by Ofelia Zepeda reprinted with permission of the author.

From "That's the Place Indians Talk About" by Simon Ortiz (1992) in *Woven Stone* by Simon Ortiz reprinted with permission of the author.

Chapter 29

From "Lone Dog's Winter Count" by Diane Glancy (1991) in *Lone Dog's Winter Count* by Diane Glancy reprinted with permission of the author.

From "Blue Horses" by Gerald Vizenor (2006) in *Almost Ashore* reprinted with permission of the author.

Chapter 31

From *Blood Run* by Allison Adelle Hedge Coke (2006) reprinted with permission of the author.

Chapter 32

From Gerald Vizenor, *Summer in the Spring: Anishinaabe Lyric Poems and Stories*, New Edition (1993) and *The Trickster of Liberty: Native Heirs to a Wild Baronage* (2005) reprinted with permission of the author.

Chapter 33

From *The Sound the Stars Make Rushing Through the Sky: The Writings of Jane Johnston Schoolcraft*, edited by Robert Dale Parker (2007), pp. 49, 99–100, 141–42. Reprinted with permission of the University of Pennsylvania Press.

ACKNOWLEDGEMENTS

Chapter 37

From "The American Artificial Limb Company" by Sherman Alexie. Reprinted from *One Stick Song* © 2000 by Sherman Alexie, by permission of Hanging Loose Press.

"Call Me Brother: Two-Spiritedness, the Erotic, and Mixedblood Memory as Sites of Sovereignty and Resistance in Gregory Scofield's Poetry" by Qwo-Li Driskill, from *Speak to Me Words: Essays on Contemporary American Indian Poetry* edited by Dean Rader and Janice Gould © 2003 The Arizona Board of Regents. Reprinted by permission of the University of Arizona Press.

"Snow" by Janice Gould, from *Earthquake Weather: Poems* by Janice Gould © 1996 Janice Gould. Reprinted by permission of the University of Arizona Press.

"Medicine Song" by Dan Hanna, from *Home Places: Contemporary Native American Writing from Sun Tracks*, edited by Larry Evers and Ofelia Zepeda © 1995 The Arizona Board of Regents. Reprinted by permission of the University of Arizona Press.

"She Had Some Horses," "Two Horses" and "The Woman Hanging from the Thirteenth Floor Window" by Joy Harjo, from *How We Became Human: New and Selected Poems: 1975–2002* by Joy Harjo © 2002 W.W. Norton. Reprinted by permission of W.W. Norton.

From "Manifest Destinations" by Adrian C. Louis (1999) in *Fire* No. 9 reprinted with permission of the author.

"What Indians?" and "Culture and the Universe" by Simon Ortiz, from *Out There Somewhere* by Simon Ortiz © 2002 Simon Ortiz. Reprinted by permission of the University of Arizona Press.

"In Oklahoma" by Carter Revard, from *An Eagle Nation* by Carter Revard © 1993 Carter Revard. Reprinted by permission of the University of Arizona Press.

Gerald Vizenor, "An Envoy to Haiku" from *Shadow Distance: A Gerald Vizenor Reader* © 1994 published by Wesleyan University Press. Used by permission.

Disclaimer

The publishers have made every effort to contact authors/copyright holders of works reprinted in *The Routledge Companion to Native American Literature* to obtain permission to publish extracts. This has not been possible in every case, however, and we would welcome correspondence from those individuals/companies whom we have been unable to trace. Any omissions brought to our attention will be remedied in future editions.

Introduction
The Indigenous Contexts of "Native." "American." "Literature."

Deborah L. Madsen

"When asked by an anthropologist what the Indians called America before the white man came, an Indian said simply, 'Ours'" (346). In this reversal of the dominant colonialist view of New World colonial history, Vine Deloria Jr. highlights an indigenous-centered perspective that is characteristic of Native American Literature and the approaches to it used in this *Companion*. If asked what Indians might call Native American Literature, we could answer simply, "ours." That is to say, the work of indigenous expressive artists in the Americas, since long before contact with Europeans, has constituted the literature of Native peoples in America. In *Red on Red*, Craig Womack uses the metaphor of a tree to challenge the genealogical assumption that indigenous literatures are only one of the ethnic or multicultural "branches" of the canonical U.S. literary tree: "tribal literatures are not some branch waiting to be grafted onto the main trunk," he asserts. "Tribal literatures are the *tree*" (6–7 original emphasis). The inappropriate juxtaposition of Native American texts with other "hyphenated" American literatures (such as African- or Asian-American) obscures fundamental differences between indigenous literatures and the literatures of migrant (all non-indigenous) communities. The most fundamental aim of this *Companion* is to promote the reading of Native American Literature as indigenous literature by providing the contextual information that is needed in order to recognize and appreciate the complex relations among modes of Native identification, historical events, sovereign tribal world-views or cosmologies, indigenous expressive and aesthetic traditions, and the specific traditions of Native American Literature.

One of the most damaging consequences of settler colonialism in the Americas, possibly even beyond the disruption of intimate tribal relations with homelands, has been the attempted erasure of Native artistic presence – through the destruction of written artifacts or ancient mounds and earthworks, for example – in order to validate the claim that New World "savages" possessed no "civilization." The limited visibility of Native peoples (as Brandy Nālani McDougall calls it in her chapter) is a consequence of these efforts at erasure coupled with the prominence given to stereotypes of "the Indian." The chapters that follow elucidate the diverse contexts of indigenous experience that are needed to bring the Native quality of Native American Literature into central focus and heightened visibility. These chapters also survey the rich historical, generic, stylistic, and tribal range of Native literary texts that counter, subvert, and ultimately render irrelevant static Indian stereotypes in favor of the dynamic representation of Native American experience.

While every national literature is distinctive, requiring that readers bring to it a basic competence in terms of historical, social, cultural, intellectual, and aesthetic contexts,

Native American Literature presents a particularly complex case. There are currently more than 560 federally recognized Native American tribes in the United States and Alaska, with many more tribal groups that have not been granted official recognition. Regionally, these tribes have experienced distinct histories of colonial contact – with European powers such as the British, French, Spanish, Dutch – and further radical displacement and reorganization in the period since U.S. independence. Thus, historically, the Native tribes of the United States experienced very different legacies of colonization in the period before the U.S. Supreme Court took control of Native issues and, since then, in terms of distinct state-level interventions. The tribes of Native North America continue to constitute distinct social and cultural communities, each of which has been shaped in particular ways by the impact of European colonization. The interplay between the indigenous cultures that endure and these colonial impacts form a framework of allusions and references that characterize Native American literary texts. These allusions may not be familiar to non-Native readers, or indeed to Native readers whose heritage differs from that represented in a specific literary text. This is what the present *Companion* seeks to provide: a comprehensive yet manageable introduction to the contexts essential to reading Native American Literature. I have been consistently referring to "Native American Literature" (as befits the volume's title) and, while the term has coherence and a powerful conventional meaning, it is essential to remember that the very category "Native American" is itself an invention or product of this history of colonization. So it is worth reminding ourselves about the complex nature of each of the terms used in the title of this volume: "Native. American. Literature."

"Native"

All of the terms "Native American," "American Indian," and "indigenous American" are used to describe people who inherit, by descent from the first inhabitants, claims on the territory now known as the United States of America. These general terms apply to all "first people" regardless of any specific tribal affiliation. However, Native peoples often self-identify according to tribe (Cherokee or Anishinaabe or Tlingit, say) rather than with a generalized or "pan-Indian" term like "Native" or "indigenous" American. The advantage offered by the term "Native American" is its inclusivity, encompassing all tribal groups within the United States and Alaska, as well as the significant number of writers who trace their ancestry to several tribes and those who identify as being of mixed race. The term "Indian" carries strong colonial associations as the preferred term used by the U.S. federal government (to name the Bureau of Indian Affairs, for example) but for this reason is an important reminder of the fact that "Indian" is a legal definition as well as a racial, cultural, social, and personal identity marker. The term "indigenous" is possibly more problematic, especially in literary terms, because of its anthropological connotations; however, in the period since the ratification of the UN Declaration on the Rights of Indigenous People this term has entered more general use to name the important commonalities shared by indigenous communities globally. Throughout this volume all three terms are used by contributors who choose the terminology that is most appropriate to the issues they discuss.

"*Native* American" designates a range of kinds of identities: in settler-colonial terms, "Native" is a racial identity; in tribal terms "Native" is a mode of self-identification that names relationships with family, clan, tribe, and other Native peoples in addition to the

INTRODUCTION

U.S. nation-state. U.S. federal government recognition confers legal identity but is far from the sole determinant of Native identity. It was sadly ironic that in 2007, on the 400th anniversary of the founding of Jamestown and amidst celebratory reminders of that era's most famous story – that of Pocahontas – contemporary tribal communities descended from seventeenth-century Powhatans were still struggling to gain federal recognition. In the document "Procedure for Establishing that an American Indian Group Exists as an Indian Tribe" (1978), the Bureau of Indian Affairs (BIA) sets out the terms under which an indigenous tribe can petition for recognition from the U.S. federal government and makes clear that the burden of proving their indigenous status lies with the tribe. In the latest list of recognized "Indian entities" not one of the Virginia tribal groups – the Mattaponi, Pamunkey, Chickahominy and Eastern Chickahominy, Rappahannock, Upper Mattaponi, Nansemond, Cheroenhaka (Nottoway), and Patawomeck tribes, the Nottoway Indian Tribe, and the Monacan Indian Nation – appears as a legally constituted U.S. indigenous community and in fact Virginia – like many of the originally colonized states – is home to no recognized tribes at all (see Department of the Interior "Indian Entities"; National Parks Service).[1]

The questions surrounding "authenticity" – who is Indian; what is the nature of indigeneity; what counts as "Native" American Literature; who qualifies as a "Native American" writer and how that identity is determined – run through much Native American Literature and scholarly engagements with it, as Judit Kádár explains in her chapter. External criteria include membership of a federally recognized tribe; acceptance as a member of a tribal community; and "blood quantum" (or proportion of Native ancestry). The latter became an influential definition of Indianness only in the latter nineteenth century, following the requirement of the Dawes Act that tribal members formally enroll in order to determine who was entitled to an allotment of land. This "objective" measure of descent becomes especially complicated for individuals who are of mixed blood either due to inter-tribal marriage or inter-racial marriage; this is discussed by Carol Miller in her chapter on literary engagements with urban Native experience. Again in urban contexts, the validation of identity through tribal community recognition can be problematic and, as Miller points out, underlies Native insistence that "urban" refers to a complex and evolving "experience" rather than a category of identity for indigenous people. This distinction also opposes the damaging stereotypes that claim "real" Native people cannot survive in the modern urban environment by focusing instead on the experiential continuance of Native individuals and nations through adaptation and the development of an "indigenous urbanity," as Miller calls it. The mythical figure of the "Vanishing American" is captured in Gerald Vizenor's concept of the "*indian*" – italicized and lower-case – to express the fictional nature of this constructed stereotypical character that is placed in a mythical historical and territorial environment far removed from the contemporary lived world (*Fugitive Poses* 15). The "*indian*" fills the representational gap left by the colonial erasure of real, complex, living Native people.

The mixed-race identity claimed by many canonical Native American writers and represented by the literary protagonists of many canonical texts destabilizes these Native stereotypes. Mixed-blood characters navigating between cultural worlds disturb the normative racial and also gender and sexual values of settler-colonial society. The role of gender and sexuality in the structure of settler colonialism is interrogated and deconstructed by scholars who approach these identities from the perspective offered by indigenous

3

Feminisms and through gender roles such as Two Spirit/Queer Indian identities. The analysis of how patriarchy and heteronormativity operate as strategies of settler colonialism to subvert and erase pre-contact tribal practices of gender and sexuality (by scholars like Mark Rifkin, Andrea Smith, and Deborah Miranda) expose direct links between the violent occupation of colonized lands and colonial violence against women and those of non-normative sexual orientation. Alicia Cox and Leah Sneider explain how violent attempts to dismantle traditional tribal gender and sex roles constitute an attack on tribal sovereignty and self-determination at the most intimate level of self-identification; and remind us of the power of Native challenges to settler normativity. As Chris LaLonde's quotation from Linda Hogan's poem "The Truth is" reminds us: "it is dangerous to be a woman of two countries" (5). The mixed-blood in Native American Literature disturbs U.S. epistemologies by presenting these colonialist ways of knowing as highly contingent when viewed from the perspective of tribal realities. LaLonde refers to this in terms of epistemological disobedience, represented at its most fundamental by the refusal to be defined by or as the "*indian*." A long-running controversy focuses on the degree of emphasis that should be placed on the components of mixed-race identity. Scholars sometimes labelled as "cosmopolitans" like Elvira Pulitano place great emphasis on European rather than indigenous heritage when discussing "hybrid" or mixed-blood identities. But the long history of Native–settler contact repeatedly shows the incorporation of European (and Asian) elements into cultural practices that remain resolutely Native. As contributors to this *Companion* – such as Earl Fitz, Birgit Brander Rasmussen, Drew Lopenzina, Kenneth Roemer, John Gamber, and others – conclusively demonstrate, indigenous writers have consistently included styles of expression borrowed from colonists to produce forms of expressivity that are no less indigenous for making use of foreign materials that could enhance communicative power – often in the interests of cross-cultural explanations or to advance the rights of indigenous communities.

Cross-cultural relations, of course, can be inter-tribal as well as "colonial-cosmopolitan." As I have already mentioned, Native America includes more than 560 tribal nations, though the category "Native American" has been constructed historically as a monolithic identity. Many of the following chapters comment on the difficulty of generalizing across such tribal diversity: from Earl Fitz's overview of the many different indigenous languages and cultures of the American hemisphere that incorporates Anglo-French Canada, the United States, Spanish America, and Brazil; to Birgit Brander Rasmussen's account of indigenous literacies from the Andes to Panama, throughout Meso-America, across the North American Plains to Alaska, in the woodlands, along the eastern seaboard, and throughout the Northeast; to Janet Fiskio's survey of indigenous foodways of North America, which include thousands of practices from the arid farmers of the Sonoran Desert, to the Salmon peoples of the Pacific Northwest. A few specific instances that put into question the concept of "Native America" are singled out for particular attention: Brandy Nālani McDougall offers an overview of the cultural, historical, and political contexts that shape colonial relations between the U.S and the incorporated territory of Hawai'i, the unincorporated territories of Guåhan (Guam) and American Samoa, the Commonwealth of the Northern Mariana Islands (CNMI), and the freely associated states of the Federated States of Micronesia, Palau, and the Marshall Islands; Susan Kollin examines how Aleut, Athabaskan, Eyak, Haida, Iñupuit, Tlingit, Tsimshian, and Yupik literatures have all addressed issues of colonialism through questions of community and identity, land struggles, statehood, tourism, and resource extraction; and

INTRODUCTION

Iping Liang considers the transpacific relations between Native American and indigenous Asian literatures (what Chadwick Allen might call "trans-indigenous" relations).

"American"

The term "American" in "Native American" represents another complex terminological issue. "American" implicitly identifies the geography of North America with the political culture of the United States. Yet Native Americans were largely ineligible for U.S. citizenship until the passage of the Nationality Act of 1940, though the process of granting full citizenship began with the Indian Citizenship Act of 1924. Before 1924, the granting of U.S. citizenship depended upon assimilation and the surrender of tribal citizenship, a sacrifice that many Native people were unwilling to make. The conjunction of the terms "Native" and "American" then exposes a number of key contexts: the ongoing colonized conditions that influence the identities and lifeways of indigenous Americans; the conflictual dynamic that underlies the history of relations between Native American peoples and, initially, the colonies that became the United States, then the United States as an independent nation-state and imperial power; and the importance of U.S. law in attempting to shape Native North America into the desired image of the U.S. federal government – from the period of treaty-making and the Marshall Decisions of the 1830s, through the establishment of reservations and the attempt to dismantle them through the Allotment Act of the late nineteenth century, to the various strategies of forced assimilation and the recent acknowledgements of Native rights in U.S. laws like NAGPRA and the UN Declaration on the Rights of Indigenous Peoples.

The colonial era until around 1830, as David J. Carlson explains, is marked by an uneven history of treaty-making, up to the unilateral suspension of treaty-making by the United States under the Indian Appropriations Act of 1871. Native nations and colonizing states held different views of what a treaty is and what it does; consequently, treaties reveal details of indigenous political thought and cultural practice as well as functioning as a mechanism of colonization. As Bruce Johansen also observes in his chapter, much of the political activism beginning in the 1960s turned to treaty rights as a strategy for reclaiming tribal traditions and preserving access to resources. Carlson highlights the preservation of indigenous traditions in the form of the treaty which functions as a type of performative, dramatic text encoding specific tribal understandings of diplomatic and human relationships. Literary texts may use the history, or individual acts, of treaty-making as part of the story or diegesis while engaging on the rhetorical level with the issues of textual interpretation that are central to the function of treaties. That is, by asking how meanings are constructed that create inter-personal, inter-national, and even inter-species (a topic taken up by Brian Hudson) relations, literary engagement with treaties and treaty history can work as a tool for de-colonization.

The 1830s is often characterized as the start to the Removals era because of the passage of the Indian Removal Act of 1830 and the series of legal decisions by Chief Justice John Marshall that enabled the forced relocation of eastern tribes to "unsettled" and "reserved" territories west of the Mississippi under the Act. In her discussion of the so-called "Marshall Trilogy" Sabine N. Meyer outlines the legal conceptualization of Native sovereignty that emerged in each case and analyzes the legal and cultural fictions that John Marshall employed to validate his arguments. An enduring complication that originates in Marshall's decision in *Cherokee Nation v. Georgia* (1831) is the definition of indigenous tribes as "domestic dependent nations." That is, autonomous nations that are territorially bounded by the United States and ideologically placed as "wards" of the U.S. federal government. This changed the terms by which treaties could be made between nations of equal status, asserting the plenary power of the U.S. Congress over Native tribal nations. In 1851 Congress passed the Indian Appropriations Act, which allocated funds to create reservations ostensibly for the protection of western tribes against the increasing and violent encroachment of settlers on their territory, though the threat may equally have been posed by Native occupation of land and control of resources that threatened to limit the westward expansion of the United States. The latter part of the nineteenth century saw an intensification of the "Indian Wars" that had been continuing since first contact with colonists, with the Seminole, Navajo, Sioux, Apache, Ute, Modoc, Arapaho, Comanche, Cheyenne, Kiowa, and Nez Percé among the tribal nations that engaged the United States militarily. In the stereotypical narrative of the vanishing "*indian,*" indigenous peoples emerge as the tragic victims of these military encounters – perhaps nowhere more so than in accounts of massacres and other atrocities – but Oliver Scheiding reminds us that Native literary responses to warfare are more than defensive strategies of resistance and containment; rather, literature has been a location for the re-evaluation of complex intersections among Native peoples and Euro-American settlers.

The Indian Appropriations Act of 1871 brought to an end treaty-making and all government-to-government negotiations between the United States and Native American tribes, while the decades of the 1870s and 1880s saw moves by Congress to redefine Native people as individuals rather than as members of distinct tribal nations. The General Allotment Act (or Dawes Act) of 1887 empowered the Department of the Interior to divide tribally held lands, to distribute an allotment to each enrolled tribal member, and to sell "excess" lands to U.S. settlers. In the half-century following allotment, approximately two-thirds of formerly tribal land moved into non-Native ownership. Allotment required that all Native people formally enroll as members of their tribal nation; that degrees of Native descent (blood quantum) be recorded and used to determine whether individuals were "competent" to manage their own financial affairs; that allottees adopt U.S. citizenship (which became possible more generally only in 1924); and, at its most basic, the process of allotment transferred legally recognized Native landbases to the trusteeship of Congress, thus giving the United States legal title to the land. As Mark Rifkin makes clear, the aim of this project was to eliminate the tribe as a political entity and to force Native people to assimilate to the individualistic property-owning model of the "proper" U.S. citizen, with corresponding pressure on Native forms of self-representation. The sale of reservation lands raised funds to support new and existing programs to train indigenous people to become citizens. Between 1879 (when the Carlisle Indian Industrial School opened) and 1924 (when full citizenship rights were granted to all Native Americans), the U.S. government sponsored efforts to assimilate Native Americans by educating them in boarding schools located both on and off reservations. As Tova Cooper explains, these effects produced an ongoing and often highly traumatic legacy for Native American identity and culture.

By the early twentieth century, Native–settler relations had seen an end to treaty-making, the imposition of U.S. citizenship, and the abandonment of aggressive allotment and assimilation programs. The ending of organized assimilation efforts was largely the consequence of the critiques of federal Indian policy set out in Lewis Meriam's influential 1928 report, submitted to the Secretary of the Interior as *The Problem of Indian Administration*, which determined many of the provisions of the 1934 Indian Reorganization Act, which is also known as the "Indian New Deal." Under the Commissioner of the Bureau of Indian Affairs, John Collier Sr., the Act reversed the privatization of communally held lands under the Dawes Act; facilitated a return to tribal self-governance, in part by restoring tribal management of resources such as land; and assisted in the creation of tribally controlled educational resources. As Joseph Bauerkemper points out, these policy changes promoted corresponding and long-lasting shifts in tribal discourses regarding kinship and citizenship. However, in 1953 Congress adopted the policy of "Termination" and a return to aggressive assimilation in the effort to make all Native Americans within the territorial limits of the United States subject to the same laws, rights and responsibilities as all U.S. citizens. This meant ending federal recognition of and responsibility for some 109 tribes before the policy was abandoned in 1968. Bureau of Indian Affairs services were discontinued, legal jurisdiction was transferred to state governments, tribal sovereignty was abolished and, under the BIA Relocation Program, Native people were actively encouraged to move from tribal lands to urban centers where they were promised assistance with housing, training, and employment. Carol Miller offers an account of the impacts of termination and relocation on the experience of indigeneity in this period and in literary reflections on the urban Indian experience. Certainly, the power of Congress unilaterally to abolish the existence of tribal nations served to underline the extent of the plenary power that the U.S. federal government could exercise over Native American nations.

The impact of termination on American Indian communities was devastating. In 1968, the Indian Civil Rights Act began the process of restoring Native self-determination by requiring tribal consent for states to assume jurisdiction over Indian land and, by extending some but not all Constitutional protections of individual rights, offered tribal courts the opportunity to interpret the law in terms of specific tribal traditions and so extend the exercise of tribal sovereignty. This period saw renewed the political activism of the Red Power and American Indian Movements, though, as Bruce Johansen points out, indigenous activism and protest had been a necessary response to settler colonialism from first contact. Other legislative acts that continued to promote Native self-determination include the Indian Self-Determination and Education Assistance Act of 1975, the Indian Child Welfare Act of 1978, and the Native American Languages Act of 1990. Two legislative instruments – the American Indian Religious Freedom Act of 1978 and the Archaeological Resources Protection Act of 1979 – were significant forerunners to the 1990 Native American Graves Protection and Repatriation Act (NAGPRA), which answered to a long history of Native outrage concerning the misappropriation of indigenous sacred artifacts and human remains. Amelia Katanski addresses the Act's imperative for communication among groups such as tribal governments, museums, government agencies, scientific organizations, and indigenous advocacy organizations, as a context for her argument that literary texts about repatriation themselves constitute legal co-texts in that they produce and embody dialogue about NAGPRA, its potential and its limitations. In the same way that treaties function in David J. Carlson's account, so texts about NAGPRA work performatively to do that which they are about, communicating both on the level of content and also of rhetorical form. These positive twentieth-century legislative moves towards indigenous self-determination and the reversal of centuries of colonial violence (physical and cultural) must, however, be evaluated in the context of a fundamental and enduring paradox in U.S.–Native relations. This basic contradiction is summed up by Eric Cheyfitz in his account of the UN Declaration on the Rights of Indigenous Peoples. In the Declaration, land is clearly identified as the crucial issue confronting indigenous peoples, but the issue of the rightful possession of this land is rendered ambiguous. The Declaration makes reference to the "dispossession" of indigenous lands by colonial powers and also to indigenous peoples' "rights to their lands" – lands that have already been taken away from them by the invading colonial power. Consequently, Cheyfitz concludes, while the Declaration may intend to endorse the liberation of indigenous peoples it remains a colonial document because it explicitly recognizes the legitimacy of "the territorial integrity" and "political unity" of the dominating settler-colonial states. In the same way, acts by the U.S. Congress may endorse increasing self-determination for American Indian tribes but these legislative moves are always located within the context of congressional plenary power over tribes that in U.S. terms remain largely, as in Chief Justice Marshall's formulation, "domestic dependent nations."

The history of Native American Civil Rights and documents like the UN Declaration conceptualize the possibilities for indigenous sovereignty from the colonial "outsider" perspective of the Westphalian nation-state; but Native writers adopt an indigenous-centered view of this dynamic to assert the continuous existence of tribal world-views, traditions, values, and practices to promote tribal sovereignty in relation to such things as inter-nation diplomacy (discussed here by Tammy Wahpeconiah), management of environments and environmental resources (Lee Schweninger), non-human animals (Brian Hudson), food (Janet Fiskio), health (Hsinya Huang), religion (Susannah Hopson), community (Kirby Brown), and the forms of activism required to ensure the survivance of these forms of tribal sovereignty (Bruce Johansen). These Native-centered ways of knowing and relating to reality are profoundly disturbing to settler-colonial epistemologies and the social, cultural, political, and legal systems they support. The grounds of indigenous epistemology is, literally, the ground – the land that gives meaning to indigeneity. As Jace Weaver describes:

> When Natives are removed from their traditional lands, they are robbed of more than territory; they are deprived of numinous landscapes that are central to their faith and their identity, lands populated by their relations, ancestors, animals, and beings both physical and mythological. A kind of psychic homicide is committed.
>
> (38)

Thus, sovereignty is a claim to land that makes possible the claim to identity – an identity that is defined by a network of relationships that are known in the context of a reality based on these "numinous landscapes." It is this claim to tribal sovereignties that are grounded in Native ontologies that can make Native American literary texts seem obscure. Texts assume some familiarity with the distinctive nature of tribal understandings of what it means to be human in relation to health and spirituality, animals and plants, and to physical environments, as well as the impact on Native communities of environmental devastation and the extinction of animal species in the wake of colonization – and also the interconnectedness of the various expressions of Native sovereignty. As the chapters in this volume make clear, the continuity of Native America, as a distinct group of tribal communities sharing common fundamental values, despite more than 500 years of colonial

INTRODUCTION

onslaught – and the preservation of these values as fundamental to a vital and living Native sovereignty – is an assertion of sovereignty the performance of which takes a variety of expressive or literary forms.

"Literature"

The term "Native American Literature" is complicated not only by the identification of "American" with the United States, as a governmental, social, and cultural entity that continues to claim plenary powers over indigenous nations, but also by the identification of "American" as signifying an anglophone culture. Changes in language usage were an essential impact of colonization: the tribes of the south and southwest encountered Spanish-speaking colonists; those of the northeast experienced first contact with francophone fur-trappers and traders; the tribes of the Atlantic seaboard encountered the English. A fundamental principle of assimilation efforts was the eradication of tribal languages; an effort the reversal of which required the Native American Languages Act of 1990 to guarantee the right of Native people to use their indigenous languages. While English is the language used most commonly by Native American writers – and in all canonical texts in the field – many Native American literary texts use code-switching between English and a tribal language sometimes with the inclusion of elements of a European colonial language, such as French or Spanish, as well. This is only one of the ways in which Native American expressive culture puts into question the issues of language and literacy – questioning the definition of "literature" itself.

Beyond the well-known opposition between oral expression and writing, material cultural forms such as wampum or petroglyphs, pictographs or geoglyphs or earthworks complicate the ways in which literacy is understood in Native American Literatures of all periods. Thus, the ancient mound-builders of what is now Newark, Ohio allow Cari M. Carpenter to orient her discussion of Native American intellectualism through the lunar earthwork that challenges the western equation of literacy with intellect, while Birgit Brander Rasmussen discusses the historic use of hieroglyphic scripts inscribed on the trunks of trees and on birchbark, wampum in the Northeast and quipus in the Andes and then, in the aftermath of colonization, pen and paper. The violent erasure of indigenous expressive cultures in the early contact period marked the beginning of the state of invisibility that has characterized colonial approaches to the systems of indigenous literacy. And yet, as Rasmussen reminds us, the historical record includes examples of intercultural exchange, such as the Franciscan friar Bernardino de Sahagún who worked with Aztec scribes to produce texts that brought into dialogue Spanish and Aztec writing systems and languages, producing culturally hybrid documents uniquely rooted in the colonial context: including work like the *Florentine Codex* and the books of *Chilam Balam*. Or in seventeenth-century New France, the Franciscan missionary Christian Le Clerq attempted to learn the Mi'kmaq writing system and, according to Rasmussen, adding some signs that he invented himself, produced a hybrid writing system. Drew Lopenzina also reminds us that when Native people were introduced to western forms of literacy, these forms were brought into conformity with their own traditions, creating new syncretic forms of expression that had their roots in indigenous customs. He quotes Lisa Brooks' point that "transformations occurred when the European system entered Native space. Birchbark messages became letters and petitions,

9

wampum records became treaties" (13). These forms, which are better described as "syncretic" than "hybrid," enact an interplay of speech acts and visuality that, as David Stirrup explains, expresses particular intellectual, ethical, and aesthetic histories through the performance of relationships between narrative and visual art-forms.

The importance of visuality in Native traditions of expressivity is sadly ironic given the invisibility of Native literacies that has been wrought by colonial violence. Yet traces of indigenous expressivity can be found in representations of Native American identities in key, canonical settler texts of the seventeenth and eighteenth centuries, as Kathryn Gray demonstrates, by attending to how Native American identities are mediated and the ways in which Native American voices are translated and transcribed for English-speaking readers. Drew Lopenzina also finds evidence for Native religion, laws, and writing in the colonial reports of, for example, ceremonies to which settlers were witnesses and sometimes participants. While wanting to deny the "civilization" of Native peoples by denying the existence of expressive tribal cultures, still colonists could not avoid the traces of indigenous cultural presence in their writing, just as Native writers like Caleb Cheeshateaumauk, Samson Occom, Joseph Johnson, William Apess, and George Copway could not but write with both Native and white audiences in mind. While oral tribal traditions could not be denied, oral language was frequently misread and misinterpreted as a simplistic, even primitive, form of expression in contrast to the supposedly more sophisticated form of writing. But as Susan Berry Brill de Ramirez shows, orality is potentially a more complex form than writing (though contemporary Native American writers skillfully incorporate oral techniques into their printed texts). Oral communication is, to use her term, "conversive": supportive of the interpersonal and intersubjective relations that directly affect personal, interpersonal, and community wellbeing. The centrality of community, tribe, nation, place, and interpersonal connection to the hermeneutics of indigenous expressive traditions links these traditions to tribal ceremony, as Diveena Marcus explores in her discussion of the indigenous theory of knowledge that underlies Native practices of song, language, and dance.

These expressive traditions and indigenous literacies lend Native American Literature a range of unique textual and aesthetic forms, forms that facilitate substantive engagement with specific moments in Native history and sovereign tribal world-views. Stephanie Sellers introduces the relatively new literary genre of the Indigenous Communal Narrative which, in contrast to the much older ethnographic genre of the "as-told-to story," works to incorporate an entire community – the earth, animals, plants, and the cosmos as well as the human tribe – into the voice of the narrative. The creation of the text does not involve a monolithic, authoritative, singular voice speaking for the whole nation in the form of an "as-told-to" autobiography but requires consultation and collaboration with the tribal Council, clan historians, and living descendants. As-told-to narratives have been criticized for reproducing a non-indigenous vision of Native lives and, at worst, perpetuating the stereotype of the "*indian*": Birgit Däwes highlights the work being done in drama that parallels the developments in Native-centered life-writing discussed by Stephanie Sellers. Däwes focuses on the innovative strategies used by contemporary playwrights to dismantle and redefine the cultural imaginary of the *indian*, and to replace hegemonic representations with original voices, using the stage in myriad ways to create sites for the negotiation of identity and cultural difference, memory and tradition, as well as issues of sovereignty, agency, and futurity.

INTRODUCTION

The development of the Native American literary tradition is marked by that openness to innovation that I described above as a syncretic trait. Mediations with the Anglo-European tradition are mapped by Kenneth Roemer: Jane Schoolcraft's use of the language and vocabulary of nineteenth-century poetry, Alexander Posey's use of late nineteenth-century satiric dialect sketches, John Joseph Mathews' use of the *Walden* model, the transformations of Anglo-American Modernist conventions in the writings of Scott Momaday, Leslie Silko, and Louise Erdrich, and LeAnne Howe's blendings of historical realism and mythical interventions. John Gamber notes John Rollin Ridge's use of the Western dime novel in *The Life and Adventures of Joaquín Murrieta* (1854) and Alice Callahan's affective use of sentimental interiority in *Wynema* (1891). As Lopenzina shows for the earlier period, in later forms of Native literary expression, indigenous writers exercise their freedom to incorporate dominant literary traditions and conventions in ways that may be variously subversive (in the sense of deconstructing settler-colonial epistemologies) or "indigenizing" (by give these forms new meanings that express Native world-views). This process of borrowing is not restricted to European expressive forms, as Iping Liang shows in her discussion of transpacific literary relations: Native American writers have adopted elements of Asian literary forms and philosophical traditions – most notably haiku poetics – but indigenous Asian writers have also been free to borrow from models made available by Native American Literature. The development of the Native American literary tradition has involved not only influences from outside but also the internal pressures of periodization and canonicity. The novelistic tradition is mapped by John Gamber, the poetic tradition by Kathryn Shanley and David Moore, the tradition of storying through short fiction by A. Robert Lee. Some of the most recent additions to these traditions have been in the area of intermedial or text-and-image expression. In contemporary popular genres, film, and digital media, Native literary expression continues the long traditions set out in this *Companion*: refusing boundaries between the literary and the visual, mediating between Native and non-Native aesthetics, referencing a range of indigenous signifying forms such as birchbark scrolls, codices, petroglyphs, and wampum. In film, the comic, the graphic novel, digital shorts or what Susan Bernardin calls "poemfilms," visual storytelling operates within a network of complex relationships that mediate tradition and innovation.

This *Companion* engages with the long and dynamic traditions of Native American Literature in the broadest sense, relating the distinctive histories, world-views, traditions, aesthetic forms, and cultural contexts – while acknowledging the multiple scenes of tension (historical, political, cultural, and aesthetic) that inform Native literary engagements with issues of community identity, ethnicity, gender and sexuality, language, and sovereignty – all of which are needed to prepare readers to approach the work of writers from diverse Native American tribal backgrounds with an appropriate readiness to appreciate these literatures specifically as forms of indigenous American expressivity.

Note

1 In July 2015, as this volume was going to press, the U.S. Bureau of Indian Affairs announced the federal recognition of Virginia's Pamunkey Indian Tribe. The Pamunkey tribe began the process of applying for U.S. Federal recognition in 1982.

Works cited

Allen, Chadwick. *Trans-Indigenous: Methodologies for Global Native Literary Studies*. Minneapolis: University of Minnesota Press, 2012.

Brooks, Lisa. *The Common Pot: The Recovery of Native Space in the Northeast*. Minneapolis: University of Minnesota Press, 2008.

Deloria, Vine, Jr. *Red Earth, White Lies: Native Americans and the Myth of Scientific Fact*. New York: Scribner, 1995.

Department of the Interior, Bureau of Indian Affairs. [145A2100DD/A0T500000.000000/AAK3000000] "Indian Entities Recognized and Eligible to Receive Services from the United States Bureau of Indian Affairs." The Federal Register 80. 9 (14 Jan. 2015): 1942–1948. Web. Accessed 30 Jan. 2015. http://www.bia.gov/cs/groups/webteam/documents/document/idc1-029026.pdf

——. "Procedure for Establishing that an American Indian Group Exists as an Indian Tribe." *Federal Register*, 43. 106 (1 June 1978).

Hogan, Linda. "The Truth is." *Seeing Through the Sun*. Amherst: University of Massachusetts Press, 1985. 4–5.

National Parks Service, Historic Jamestown, "Meet the State-Recognized Virginia Indian Tribes." Web. Accessed 30 Jan. 2015. http://home.nps.gov/jame/historyculture/virginia-indian-tribes.htm

Pulitano, Elvira. *Toward a Native American Critical Theory*. Lincoln: University of Nebraska Press, 2003.

Vizenor, Gerald. *Fugitive Poses: Native American Scenes of Absence and Presence*. Lincoln: University of Nebraska Press, 1998.

Weaver, Jace. *That the People Might Live: Native American Literatures and Native American Community*. Oxford: Oxford University Press, 1997.

Womack, Craig S. *Red on Red: Native American Literary Separatism*. Minneapolis: University of Minnesota Press, 1999.

Part I
IDENTITIES

1
Indigenous American Literature
The Inter-American Hemispheric Perspective

Earl E. Fitz

In the early decades of the twenty-first century, indigenous American literature can be read in a number of ways. Virtually all the nations of the Americas can claim a Native American literary and cultural heritage, and in many, if not all, of these modern nation-states this heritage lives on, becoming, finally, the common denominator of our multiple American identities. One can, for example, study the Native American cultural experience in Canada (and in both its French and English language traditions), the United States, Spanish America (in all its diversity), the Caribbean, and Brazil. Today, however, one of the most fruitful ways of reading indigenous American literature is comparatively, as separate, distinct components of a larger cultural phenomenon, and from the hemispheric, or inter-American, perspective. Indigenous American literature can, in fact, be said to constitute the very foundation of inter-American literary and cultural study (see Fitz).

Most anthropologists believe that the first Americans were Asians who, pursuing the animals that sustained their lives, crossed the Bering land bridge between 20,000 and 40,000 years ago. Another, less widely accepted, theory posits that the first Americans were Pacific islanders who discovered the American land mass by sailing eastward. And a still newer idea holds that a vast ice sheet once connected southwestern Europe to the Americas and so allowed people to make the trip on foot. Clearly, the origin of the First Americans remains shrouded in mystery. Nevertheless, we do know that the Americas, from the northern reaches of Canada to the southernmost tip of South America, and from the eastern shores of the long American coastline to its rugged western coast, were completely peopled by the momentous (and, for some, catastrophic) year, 1492, and the arrival of the first European conquerors. When Christopher Columbus, a Genoese sailing under the flag of Spain, dropped anchor off a Caribbean island he mistakenly believed lay just off the coast of India, he had no way of knowing that he had stumbled onto a vast and geographically varied land mass.[1] Nor could he have known that the world he had just entered was culturally diverse and that it contained some twenty million people who spoke some 2,000 different languages, many of which are still spoken today.[2] The people he first encountered there, the peaceful Tainos, would, for example, tell him of another people, the fierce, cannibalistic Caribs, who lived to the south.[3] Because, as a man of his time, he was trained to regard the Tainos and the Caribs as "savages," Columbus concluded that "they were fit to be made slaves," according to the Aristotelian doctrine so popular then. "In a single letter," as Emir Rodríguez Monegal points out, "Columbus" laid out "the future of the New World: discovery, conversion, and conquest were all one for him" (4). The profound and too often bloody clash of cultures that resulted from this first encounter, which was based on the deliberate and systematic subjugation of one group by another, set in motion waves of conflict, violence, and tension that continue to challenge our hemispheric sense of identity and justice to this very day.[4]

There was, in 1492, an astonishing diversity among the thousands of different Native American peoples who lived in the Americas, some of whom knew each other and some of whom did not. As Alistair Cooke puts it:

> There were Indian societies that dwelt in permanent settlements, and others that wandered; some were wholly democratic, others had very rigid class systems based on property. Some were ruled by gods carried around on litters, some had judicial systems, to some the only known punishment was torture. Some lived in caves, others in tepees of bison skins, others in cabins. There were tribes ruled by warriors or by women, by sacred elders or by councils, or by fraternities whose rituals and membership were as unknown to the rest of the tribe as those of any college secret society. There were tribes who worshiped the bison or a matriarch or the maize they lived on. There were tribes that had never heard of war, and there were tribes debauched by centuries of fighting.
>
> (24–25)

In short, what Columbus and his men stumbled into in 1492 was a cultural complexity more fantastic than anything they could have ever imagined. Moreover, what they regarded as the "New World" was already an ancient world to the millions of people who lived here.

While we cannot say with any degree of certainty what the literature of these "First Peoples" was like, we can conjecture that it was both oral in nature and deeply integrated into the larger culture that spawned it (see Ong). To a degree, we can think of it as an example of indigenous American performance art, one that, encompassing what we know today as North, Central, and South America, must have included such forms as music and song, dance, and a multitude of different language uses, from the religious to the historical and from the inventive, or "literary," to the very pragmatic. Working in the 1880s, American ethnographer, Daniel Brinton was "among the first" to consider "indigenous American cultural expression as literature" (Adorno 35). Though the historical, cultural, and anthropological value of Native American cultural production was well established, the notion that it would have also possessed a deliberately creative and philosophic dimension, "the literary conceptualization" of indigenous America, has been a more recent development (Adorno 36). The more one delves into it, the more this early, pre-Columbian American literature reveals itself to have been rich, complex, and socially vital, the kind of art, or cultural production, that held a people together, that created its identity by recounting its history, and that showed it the way forward and how its future might be determined.

Arguably the first piece of indigenous American literature that we know to be authentically indigenous in nature (as opposed to being the hybrid product of the imposition[5] of a European culture on an autochthonous one),[6] the *Rabinal Achi* offers us a glimpse into a distant and largely lost American past. It is, therefore, of particular importance to those who wish to know more about the nature of literature and culture in the Americas before the arrival of the Spanish, the Portuguese, the Dutch, the French, and the English. Like the ancient Egyptians, the Mayans had books with hieroglyphic figures, but nearly all of these were destroyed by the zealously religious Spanish or by the ravages of time and weather (Imbert & Florit 2). Involving long, cadenced, and often parallel speeches (Tedlock 16–17), masks, dance, and elaborately ritualized action, the *Rabinal Achi* (or "Man of Rabinal") offers us a Native American, and specifically Maya K'iche' (the most widely spoken of the several Mayan languages) or, possibly, Maya Achi (Tedlock 5), take on a timeless and tragic theme: How two great warriors, once allies, are cast, by fate, into a situation where one of them, the defender of an established but fading order, must execute the other, now judged to be a renegade. Unique for having been originally composed long before the Spaniards first arrived, for dealing with Mayan historical issues still more remote, and for still being performed, even today, in a Mayan language, this play stands as a fascinating example of how sophisticated, in thought and expression, indigenous American literature could be (Tedlock 1–2, 5). To study *Rabinal Achi* is to understand how Native American literature has never left us, how it serves as our oldest common denominator, and how it is both ancient and modern, as alive and vital as its most recent presentation in the highlands of today's Guatemala.

Closely related, linguistically and culturally, to the *Rabinal Achi* is another immensely important pre-Columbian text, the *Popol Vuh*, a creation story that gives us the Mayan version of how men and women came to exist and live on the earth. The original manuscript has been lost. What we have to work with today is the translation to Spanish done by Father Francisco Ximémez. This means that what, in the process of translation, was modified, altered, or simply deleted from or added to the original text cannot be determined. Thus it is that, when we read the Spanish translation called the *Popol Vuh*, we must remember that we are not reading the original but only an approximation, the nature of which is determined not by the original authors or singers but by a translator whose linguistic skills, intentionality, and fidelity to the intent and style of the original are (for religious and cultural reasons) open to question. This situation is true of all translation work, but it is especially acute here, where a serious religious clash is involved. Although it touches on many things, at bottom the *Popol Vuh* relates the stories of how the gods decided to create human beings (who would honor them) and how the sacred twins, Hunahpú and Ixbalanqué, would be conceived in the womb of the virgin mother, Ixquic (Imbert & Florit 3). Although a few other texts of this same nature (translations of lost oral originals or Spanish or Latin copies of copies), the *Popol Vuh* even in translation deserves its ranking as one of the most revealing and complete texts we have of our fascinating pre-Columbian world.[7]

Of the several European powers that came to the New World in the late fifteenth and early sixteenth century, it was the Spanish who encountered indigenous civilizations so sophisticated, complex, and advanced that they rivaled and in many ways surpassed the European civilizations to which they were compared. Chronicler, historian, and eyewitness to the events he recorded, Bernal Díaz recounts, for example, how dazzled he and his compatriots were at discovering the splendor of the Aztec city, Tenochtitlán, which, in 1519, probably enjoyed a population of somewhere around a half-million persons, and this at a time when "London had no more than forty thousand" inhabitants and Paris could boast only "sixty-five thousand" (von Hagen 134). The Aztec citadel was, as anthropologist Victor von Hagen writes, "one of the world's largest cities" (133), as well as one of its cleanest, best planned, and most beautiful. As the Spanish soldiers, seeking an audience with the Aztec emperor, Moctezuma, entered Tenochtitlán on 8 November 1519, they could hardly believe what they were seeing, such was the grandeur of the Aztec capital, which had been erected in the middle of a great lake. Even in translation, the modern reader can still feel the awe of the Spanish soldiers as they gazed upon the wonder that was Tenochtitlán. As Bernal Díaz writes (via his translator, John Cohen):

> We were astounded. These great towns and cues and buildings rising from the water, all made of stone, seemed like an enchanted vision from the tale of Amadis. Indeed, some of our soldiers asked whether it was not all a dream. ... It was all so wonderful that I do not know how to describe this first glimpse of things never heard of, seen or dreamed of before. ... With such wonderful sights to gaze on we did not know what to say, or if this was real that we saw before our eyes.
>
> (214, 216)

While the Portuguese, the French, the Dutch, and the English all made contact with Native American people whose cultures had served them well for countless generations but who were nevertheless warred against, only the Spanish would experience the extraordinary societies of the Aztecs (in central and southern Mexico), the Maya (in southeastern Mexico and Guatemala), and the Inca (in Peru and along the Andean mountain chain). These three indigenous civilizations were brilliant, and, as their records show, the Spanish *conquistadores* marveled at what they were seeing. And, sadly, at what they felt compelled to destroy.[8]

Of the many narratives, poems, and dramas that resulted from the tremendous clash of worlds that was the Spanish invasion of the New World, none is more dramatic than Bernal Díaz's riveting account of the Spanish conquest of the great Aztec empire in Mexico, *The Conquest of New Spain*.[9] The power of this text derives from its being a first-hand account of the struggle for control of Mexico by an actual participant in the fierce hand-to-hand combat that characterized this conflict (1519–1521), the first of a series in which a European power would find and crush an indigenous New World people. While the Aztecs held a significant numerical advantage and were fighting for their homeland and way of life, the Spanish, led by their commander, Hernán Cortés, had access to horses, armor, and superior military technology, and, in the end, these factors would turn the tide of battle in their favor.[10] As would their ability to turn people enslaved by the Aztecs against them in an ever-growing revolt rising up to challenge this powerful, vast, and closely controlled pre-Columbian empire, which, in 1519, reigned over "several million human beings," speaking a variety of languages and stretching from the "Pacific Ocean to the Gulf coast and from central Mexico to the present-day Republic of Guatemala" (León-Portilla xxiii). In the end, though, *The Conquest of New Spain* is the narrative of the winners, the Spanish, and Bernal Díaz, who often recognizes the valor and the courage of the Aztec warriors, never doubts what he feels is the rightness of the Spanish cause.

This is why the most profitable, and moving, way to appreciate the truly gripping Bernal Díaz account is to read it in conjunction with *The Broken Spears*, which tells the same story but from the perspective of the defeated Aztecs, whose language (Nahautl), history, and culture continue to live on, even today, in Mexico and forming, finally, a fundamental part of modern Mexican identity. It is an excellent example of how ancient Aztec culture, symbolized here by means of the great Aztec calendar stone, is understood by modern Mexicans as an icon of their brilliant heritage and one that integrates their past, their present, and their future. Paz, an astute and discerning commentator on the differences between Mexican and U.S. culture, has also observed that the "possibility of belonging to a living order, even if it was at the bottom of the social pyramid, was cruelly denied to the Indians by Protestants of New England," whereas in Spanish America, as ugly as this truth is, the Indians were recognized immediately as heathens to be converted and as a valuable labor force "that should not be wasted," and so had their place in the Spanish social, political, and economic structure (*The Labyrinth of Solitude* 101–02). "It is often forgotten," Paz continues, "that to belong to the Catholic faith meant that one found a place in the cosmos" (102), even if one were a decimated New World people.

Taken together, these two works, the one, *The Conquest of New Spain*, written from the perspective of the victor, the other, *The Broken Spears*, from that of the vanquished, epitomize this terrible event, the violent and bloody collision of hitherto unknown worlds, as it played itself out again and again in other parts of North, Central, and South America. Although the places and adversaries were different, the story, tragically, would always be the same. At the same time, a work like *Sun Stone* reminds us that, for all the violence directed at Native American peoples, indigenous American cultures continue to live on, exhorting us, as Leslie Marmon Silko puts it in her powerful novels, *Ceremony* and *Almanac of the Dead*, to reject the "Destroyers," the sorcerers, and the haters among us and to be better people.

Appearing in 1962, *The Broken Spears* is a translation (by Lysander Kemp) of an earlier work, *Visión de los vencidos* (by Ángel Maria Garibay K. 1959), which was itself a translation of a still earlier text originally written in Nahautl. *The Broken Spears* is thus a translation of a translation. As the eminent Mexican scholar, Miguel León-Portilla writes, in his introduction to *The Broken Spears*:

> This book is the first to offer a selection from those indigenous accounts, some of them written as early as 1528,[11] only seven years after the fall of the city. These writings make up a brief history of the Conquest as told by the victims.
>
> (vii–viii)

Rivaling the epic grandeur achieved by Homer in the *Iliad*, when he sings of the fall of Troy, *The Broken Spears* comes to life even now in "the most vivid" and "tragic realism" (León-Portilla viii). If there is great drama to the Bernal Díaz narrative, the collective Aztec voice in *The Broken Spears* exudes a tremendous pathos, the anguish and pain of a great empire in the throes of defeat but without knowing why.

In the United States of the nineteenth century, the genocidal Indian wars, sanctioned and supported by white, Christian America, effectively exterminated certain tribes while dislocating many others and rendering them impoverished, disinherited, and impotent. The widely accepted premise of the time, that "the only good Indian was a dead Indian," amounts to one of the most shameful periods in the history of the United States of America.[12] The military and civilian campaigns waged against the American Indians were cruelly effective, even as, in the eyes of some observers, they elevated the Indian to iconic status, as a powerful image of something once free, independent, and self-sustaining now desecrated. If, as many commentators have noted, the fate of the African Americans in the

United States was slavery, that of the Native Americans was all but total extermination. As writers like Leslie Marmon Silko, N. Scott Momaday, and Sherman Alexie vividly demonstrate, the pernicious effects of this ugly experience are still being felt today, by both the conquered and the conquerors.

In the Americas, this process of deliberate indigenous recuperation and celebration first began in Brazil, where, in the poetry of Gonçalves de Magalhães and, especially, Gonçalves Dias, and in the prose fiction of José de Alencar, the Brazilians would turn to their native past in order to create their new status as an independent American nation. The superb Indianist verse of Dias (a trained ethnographer and a talented poet) stands out in early nineteenth-century Brazilian literature. Dias's short composition, "I-Juca-Pirama" (1851) stands as one of the best Indianist poems of the entire American nineteenth century (see Merquior 366). In both Spanish America and Brazil, the Indian became, during the nineteenth century, a mechanism for myth-making about the supposed authenticity of American identity. Ironically, the American Indian thus became a force in the creation of American nationality throughout the hemisphere – the same hemisphere in which these "First Peoples" had been so persecuted.

Canada, too, has a long history of indigenous American literature. As elsewhere in the Americas, indigenous Canadian literature was originally oral in nature and tended to feature historical accounts, storytelling, rhythmic language use, song, and ceremony. Oratory was highly prized. As early as 1633, the French Jesuit priest, Paul Le Jeune, commends, in one of his *Relations*, a Montagnais chief "for a 'keenness and delicacy of rhetoric that might have come out of the schools of Aristotle or Cicero'" (Petrone 383). Another Jesuit Father, Jérôme Lalemant, similarly lauds, in a *Relation* of 1645, the rhetorical skills of an "Iroquois spokesman to Governor Montmagny at Quebec" (Petrone 383). Beginning with the arrival of the French and, later, with the arrival of the English, Canadian literature offers a plethora of poems, songs, narratives, and dramas that deal with Indian-related themes.

In the 1860s and 1870s, for example, the Confederation Poets, celebrating Canada's steady progress toward independence, are conspicuous for their sensitivity to the Canadian wilderness and for their championing of Canada's Native American heritage. But these authors, as talented and as sympathetic as they were, were still non-Indian men writing about Indian culture and what they took to be its unique world view or *Weltanschauung*. Appearing earlier in the nineteenth century, the first truly indigenous voices to be regarded as forming part of English Canadian literature, however, are the "Christianized Indians, who themselves became missionaries …" and who "were encouraged to write for an international audience in order to raise money for the Indian people," who were being assimilated into Canadian civilization (Petrone 384). "Their books," as Petrone notes, "comprise the first body of Canadian Indian literature in English" (384). "The first Canadian Indian to publish a book in English was George Copway (1818–1869), Kah-ge-ga-gah-bowh (He who stands forever)" (Petrone 384). His best-known work, *The Traditional History and Characteristic Sketches of the Ojibwa Nation* (1850), was a call for better, more just relations between Canada's indigenous peoples and both the provincial and national governments. In twenty-first-century Canadian letters, however, the question of racial and cultural mixing that so defines Brazil and much of Spanish America has become more complicated.

If, in the nineteenth century, the American Indian was used, ironically enough, to legitimize various forms of New World nationalisms, many of which were based on the exploitation if not the outright extermination of the Indian, in the twentieth and twenty-first centuries we have seen Indian literature not only endure but come to flourish throughout the Americas. One of the earliest and best examples of this kind of artistically and intellectually engaged indigenous literature is *Iracema* (1865), a novel, or prose poem (and subtitled a "legend of Ceará," in Brazil's northeast), that, as Doris Sommer argues, must be regarded as foundational to all of Brazilian literature (138–71). Its author, José de Alencar, sought, with his several Indianist novels, "to create allegories of the genesis of the Brazilian people" (Lindstrom xii). In the United States, James Fenimore Cooper toyed with the idea of doing something similar, though for him the prospect of a sexual union between a white woman and an Indian man was, finally, untenable, as the conclusion of *The Last of the Mohicans* shows. The same question appears in a number of canonical Spanish American texts, though rarely does it get the same degree of positive treatment that it gets in *Iracema*. While it was not written by an Indian author, *Iracema* is, arguably, the most important and influential Native American-related novel of the nineteenth century. Powerfully mythopoetic in nature, and both lyrical and tragic by design, *Iracema* (the title is an anagram for "America") tells the story not only of Brazil's emergence as a modern nation-state but, metaphorically, of the Americas generally.

Although *Iracema* does rest on the historical animosity between two indigenous tribes – the coastal Pitiguaras who have made peace with the Portuguese and with Martim, the novel's main white, male character, and the inland Tabajaras, the people of the Indian woman, Iracema, who is the narrative's true protagonist – at its heart it deals, with one of inter-American literature's most defining themes: racial and cultural mixing. Martim and Iracema (whom we can envision as indigenous and natural "America") will produce a child, Moacir ("child of pain"), who will symbolize the future of not only the Brazilian people but the future people of greater America. Inextricably bound up in the larger issue of identity (both individual and social), this same venerable American theme connects the Americas as few other themes can. In Brazil, and, in different, sometimes more conflicted ways, in Canada and Spanish America as well, miscegenation, both biological and cultural (see Kaup & Rosenthal), has from the very beginning been an accepted and quite natural fact of life.[13] Thematically, however, the enduring importance of *Iracema* is that it makes this more flexible and humane attitude more normative. It is presented to the reader as comprising something close to a national creation myth – one based, however, in historical reality and one with indigenous America at its heart.

The Indian is also a powerful a presence in modern Spanish American literature, so much so that its study sub-divides into two categories: "Indianismo," which, now out-moded, offered a rather romanticized sense of the Indian experience; and the more militant and socially conscious, "Indigenismo," which, like its counterparts in Brazil, Canada, the Caribbean, and the United States, has generated some of our most haunting, beautifully written, and thought-provoking texts. A prime example of "Indigenismo" writing is José María Arguedas' wrenching novel, *Deep Rivers*. First published in Spanish in 1958, *Deep Rivers* tells the story of Ernesto, a boy who, though the product of white parents, is reared by Peruvian Indians who were the servants in the house of a woman, Ernesto's stepmother, who despised them all. At age fourteen, Ernesto is torn from his loving Indian home and sent to a Catholic boarding school. Ridiculed there by the privileged, white boys who surround him, Ernesto, who begins to feel the same hatred of white society that the Indians in his stepmother's house had felt, finds himself to be stuck between two bitterly divided cultures, this being a theme that resonates in indigenous literature throughout the Americas. The terrible tension felt by the young protagonist in this essentially autobiographical novel reflects the tensions that fraught the author's own life, which ended, tragically, in suicide in 1969.

Though this core theme, of being what in English is known, derisively, as a "half-breed," and of therefore being a person whose personal sense of identity is always in question, is endemic to indigenous American literature, the truly extraordinary aspect of *Deep Rivers* is its linguistic complexity, a quality that shines through even in its English-language translation, which is extraordinarily well done by Frances Horning Barraclough. Originally published as *Los ríos profundos* and written in a Spanish that sought to overlay Quechua syntax with a mostly Spanish but also Quechua vocabulary, the novel was intended to give the Spanish-speaking reader of the late 1950s a sense of how the Quechua-speaking Indians of Peru saw and understood the world. *Los ríos profundos* was, in other words, designed to be indigenous not only in theme and content but in its very language. And Barraclough, in her prize-winning translation,[14] captures these same qualities to an exceptional degree, thus allowing the reader of *Deep Rivers* to gain some semblance of the Quechua-driven consciousness that permeates the original text.

A professional anthropologist, Arguedas also wrote poetry, though only in Quechua, a language he felt was rich in poetic potential. And, as John Murra points out, Arguedas always "saw himself as talking not only about the Andean peoples, but for and *to* them" (xi). Striking an inter-American stance, Murra also notes that "Speakers and students of creole and pidgin languages in the Caribbean and elsewhere and readers of George Lamming and Errol Hill will have less difficulty" than Spanish-speakers in "imagining the magnitude of Arguedas's undertaking – how to transmit to the reader of Spanish," or to the reader of the translation, *Deep Rivers*, "not only compassion for the oppressed, but a sense that the latter also had a perception, a world view of their own," one "in which people, mountains, animals, the rain, truth, all had dimensions of their own, powerful, revealing, and utterly unlike the Iberian ones" (xi). As the great Peruvian novelist and social commentator, Mario Vargas Llosa, puts it, Ernesto, the boy whose language and culture-tangled consciousness stand at the center of *Deep Rivers*, "is a child tortured by a double origin, a child with roots in two hostile worlds, ... two mutually unfamiliar worlds that reject one another" and that "are unable to coexist painlessly even within his own person" (235).

The year 1958 also saw the publication of another extraordinary indigenous novel, this time from French Canada. *Agaguk*, a novel by Yves Thériault, offers the reader three separate but interlocking conflicts: the conflict between the Inuit and Montagnais cultures, the conflict between Inuit and white culture, and the conflict between the kinds of people the two main characters (Agaguk and Iriook) want to be and the repressive demands of their Inuit society. In this latter respect, gender expectations loom large for both the man, Agaguk, and the woman, Iriook, who form a couple. With respect to the tension between Inuit and the white society that surrounds it and that encroaches ever more on it, Thériault shows that beyond the several pernicious white men who seek to exploit the Inuit, it is the more anonymous and omnipresent entity known as the "Company" that controls things. While the individual white men can be dealt with, the "Company" is much more insidious and untouchable, even in the Canadian Arctic. While it is the ancient conflict between the Inuit and the Montagnais that ignites the novel, it is the characterization of both Agaguk and Iriook that captures the reader's attention. And though both undergo a transformation, psychologically and in terms of the rigid expectations set by their male-dominated Inuit culture, it is Iriook who takes command of the novel. Iniook grows, as a character, from passivity to agency, an agency that Agaguk comes to accept, though not without some difficulty. She is the one who deals most successfully with their struggle to be individuals and yet remain true to Inuit culture, she saves her mate's life on two occasions, and, most notable of all, she becomes a powerfully sexual being, a young woman who initiates sex, who cultivates it as a vital life force, and who liberates both herself and her partner through its passionate, joyful practice. As Jeannette Urbas writes, "Such attitudes towards sex," and particularly female sexuality, "were not common in the writings of French Canada, nor did they exist in the population at large at the time of the first appearance of *Agaguk* in 1958" (79).

Modern English Canadian literature has also cultivated indigenous life, which it regards, as writers and artists in the rest of the Americas do as well, as being fundamental to Canadian identity. In the early seventeenth century, as Canadian author, Brian Moore, writes, the "Hurons, Iroquois, and Algonkin ... were in no way dependent on the white man and, in fact, judged him to be their physical and mental inferior. ... They despised the 'Blackrobes,'" or Jesuit Fathers,

> for their habit of hoarding possessions. They also held the white man in contempt for his stupidity in not realizing that the land, the rivers, the animals, were all possessed of a living spirit and subject to laws that must be respected.
>
> (Moore ix)

Reminiscent of the basic cultural conflict in *Deep Rivers*, and in a host of other indigenous texts, *Black Robe* is, in the words of its author, "an attempt to show" that the conflicting belief systems of the white French colonists and the Native American peoples they encountered "inspired in the other fear, hostility, and despair," and that eventually this perhaps still irreconcilable conflict "would result in the destruction and abandonment of the Jesuit missions, and the conquest of the Huron people by the Iroquois, their deadly enemy" (Moore ix). In 1991, the novel *Black Robe* was, under the direction of Bruce Beresford, transformed into an excellent film, also titled *Black Robe*.

Since the 1960s, the United States, too, has seen Native American literature establish itself as a mainstream subject. One of the first indigenous novels to gain national celebrity was Silko's *Ceremony*, a painful if poetic narrative that depicts the struggle of its protagonist, Tayo, a mixed-blood Laguna Indian and World War II combat veteran, to reconcile the two largely antithetical worlds he inhabits, his Native American culture and the white culture that surrounds him, that discriminates against him and his people, and that he fought for in the war. For readers interested in the larger, inter-American perspective, however, *Ceremony* stands out because it integrates Tayo's Native American heritage with both the older Spanish heritage of the American southwest and the more modern English-speaking heritage. In the novel's conclusion, the reader realizes that Tayo's struggle is the struggle of all people in the Americas who wish to live in harmony with themselves, each other, and the natural world. The never-ending battle against the "Destroyers," those people of any group who are motivated by hatred, selfishness, and prejudice and who practice violence, against other human beings and against the earth itself, must be fought by all of us working together. And in a democracy, this means we, "the people," must use our votes to resist the defilement of the earth and its people by the "Destroyers."

Silko cultivates the inter-American and Native American connection even more profoundly in her celebrated 1991 novel, *Almanac of the Dead*. Often considered her masterpiece, *Almanac of the Dead* daringly "illustrates this concern for inter-Amerindian culture and geography" (Barrenechea & Moertl 113). Linking together other basic themes germane to Native American literature in the New World, such as race and racial (and cultural) mixing, identity, the environment, and prophecies from such sources as the *Popol Vuh*, Silko "defies imposed divisions between the indigenous peoples of the Americas" to create the "Great American Indian Novel" (Barrenechea & Moertl 115). For Silko, the Americas are a matter, first and foremost, of the land, the natural world, and indigenous America is our most vital link to it. From the perspective of 2015, when issues of the environment and global climate change are more urgent than ever, *Almanac of the Dead* reminds us that the human race must stand united in its opposition to those who would divide us and those who would destroy, pollute, or defile our lives and our world. As Silko's novel makes plain, making reference to humanity's future:

> Nothing could be black only or brown only or white only anymore. The ancient prophecies had foretold a time when the destruction by man had left the earth desolate, and the human race was itself endangered. This was the last chance the people had against the Destroyers, and they would never prevail if they did not work together as a common force.
>
> (*Almanac of the Dead* 747)

In the Americas, "No writer has advocated more fervently for a hemispheric realignment" of indigenous issues "than Laguna Pueblo Indian author Leslie Marmon Silko" (Barrenechea & Moertl 113), and few writers have a message that is as urgent and as important.

Like its hemispheric neighbors, modern Brazil has also seen a surge of indigenous writing. One of the most salient of these efforts is Darcy Ribeiro's hauntingly beautiful novel, *Maíra*. Published in Portuguese in 1978, and in English translation in 1984, *Maíra* "dramatizes ... an explosive, perhaps hopeless situation: the irreconcilable conflict between the rich, complex culture of the Indians of the Amazon and Western modes of living, informed as these are by technology and capitalism," a conflict endemic to the Americas in terms of our Amerindian past and present and one that, more specific to Brazil, casts new light on the so-called "economic miracle" of the U.S.-supported Brazilian dictatorship (1964–1968), a brutal regime that was "realized through the systematic extermination of whole tribes of the indigenous population of the Amazon region."[15] As anthropologist Joyce F. Riegelhaupt writes, "the chapters of the novel are focused ... on events involving the Indians, on Indian myths and on the frontier Brazilian society that is intruding upon tribal culture," and they "include a magnificent portrayal of Brazilian Indian culture and an arresting story of the violent contact between frontier expansionism and the Indian's striking but vulnerable society" (20).

Much more than a protest against the wholesale destruction of our indigenous peoples, *Maíra* also explores the ruinous pathology of the social, political, and economic activity that enables this kind of shameful behavior on the parts of our American nation-states. Read from this perspective, Ribeiro's landmark novel, a classic of modern Brazilian literature, amounts to a searing indictment of who and what we *Homo sapiens* have become. In the parlance of Silko, we, "the people," have abandoned our obligations to justice and

THE INTER-AMERICAN HEMISPHERIC PERSPECTIVE

the preservation of the natural world and allowed the "Destroyers" to desecrate not only the earth but violate its most vulnerable and innocent inhabitants. Importantly, though, even the novel's somber conclusion, where the power of the "Destroyers" to deceive "the people" and to inflict pain and suffering (always in the name of "progress" and profit) seems insurmountable, the engaged reader will also read it as a call to action, as a need to fight for stronger anti-pollution laws, anti-deforestation laws, and for laws that protect the environment and that serve the interests of "the people" (*Almanac of the Dead*, 755), and not the corporations that want to own and exploit our planet for their own, private gain. In *Maíra* (the Tupi word for the god of all life), the fate of the Mairun Indians is made to stand for the fate not just of a lone indigenous people struggling to survive or even for the people of modern Brazil; brilliantly, the fate of the Mairun people comes to stand for the fate of all "the people" of planet earth.

From the northernmost reaches of the Canadian Arctic to the southern tip of Argentina and Chile, and from the sun-splashed beaches of Ipanema and Copacabana in eastern Brazil to the mountainous coast of western North, Central, and South America, Native American culture is the foundation of our collective American identity. At least twenty thousand years old, and permeating our entire hemisphere, the Native American experience binds us together here in the Americas as nothing else can. It is our common American heritage and, as its greatest writers show, we would be wise to heed the many lessons it can teach us.

Notes

1 That Columbus mistakenly believed that he had made landfall close to India led to the people he encountered being referred to as "Indians."

2 In the Valley of Oaxaca, for example, Zapotec, an indigenous language, is still widely spoken. Maya-Quiché remains a living language for people in modern day Guatemala, while in Bolivia both Spanish and some thirty Native American languages are spoken. And in the Andean nations along South America's Pacific Coast, the home of the great Incan empire, millions of people still speak Quechua. In Paraguay, both Spanish and Guaraní are official state languages.

3 It was from this word, "through 'cannibals,'" that Shakespeare "would coin the name 'Caliban' in *The Tempest*" (Monegal 4).

4 Throughout the length and breadth of the Americas, this subjugation would be not only religious but also social, political, and economic in nature. And it would be established by force of arms.

5 Throughout the Americas, the conquest was not only military and religious but also social, political, and economic in nature.

6 Two well-known colonial dramas from Spanish America, the *Apu Ollantay* and the *Tragedia del fin del Atahualpa* (*The Tragedy of Atahualpa's Final Days*) are good examples of these possibly hybrid cultural productions. Both works, however, are "in the tradition of the *wanka*, dramatic compositions enacting historical deeds in which solemnity and sorrow are tempered by humor" (Adorno, citing Lara, 55).

7 For more on the nature of the ancient oral tradition in what we know today as Spanish America, see Adorno, 40-1.

8 The modern capital city of Mexico was built, deliberately, over the top of the ruins of the Aztec capital, which the Spanish razed as their final act of domination.

9 The Bernal Díaz account would inform Archibald MacLeish's later poem, *Conquistador* (1932).

10 As is well known, the Aztecs at first believed, as per their cosmology, that Cortés could have been the reincarnation of their great god, Quetzalcoatl, who, long in exile, was prophesied to return about the time the Spanish landed at Vera Cruz. By the time they realized the error of their ways,

it was too late. Holding back initially because they feared angering one of their primary deities, the Aztec forces held back and did not attack. Had they done so, the Spanish would likely have been annihilated on the beach. For more information on this, see León-Portilla vii, xv, 3–12.

11 As León-Portilla notes, the Aztec writing system, in 1519, is best understood as

> a combination of pictographic, ideographic and partially phonetic characters or glyphs, representing numerals, calendar signs, names of persons, place names, etc. The Aztecs came closest to true phonetic writing in their glyphs for place names, some of which contained phonetic analyses of syllables or even of letters.
>
> (xxvii)

We can conclude, therefore, that while the Aztecs did not, at the time of the conquest, as yet possess fully phonetic writing, they were definitely close to doing so.

12 For purposes of comparison, it is worth noting that the official credo of the Brazilian Indian Protection Service (formed in 1910 by the extraordinary General Mariano Rondon) was built around this position (and formulated by Rondon himself):

> If a stranger entered our homes without permission, he would risk being shot. The interior is the home of the Indian. Now we are going to enter that home. If he attacks us, he will only be defending what is his. If we attack him, we shall be committing a crime. If we kill him, we shall be murderers. We must avoid that. … When he appears, we will place our weapons on the ground. We can die! … But kill, never!
>
> (Kelsey 54–55)

13 The Brazilian flexibility with respect to racial and cultural mixing is often thought to be a function of its similarly flexible Portuguese heritage.

14 For her effort, Barraclough won Columbia University's 1978 Translation Center Award.

15 From the back cover of the Vintage Library/Ventura paperback edition of *Maíra* (1984).

Works cited

Adorno, Rolena. "Cultures in Contact: Mesoamerica, the Andes, and the European Written Tradition." *The Cambridge History of Latin American Literature*, Vol. I. Ed. Roberto González Echevarría & Enrique Pupo-Walker. Cambridge: Cambridge University Press, 1996. 33–57.

Alencar, José de. *Iracema*. 1865. Trans. Clifford Landers. New York: Oxford University Press, 2000.

Apu Ollantay: A Drama of the Time of the Incas. Ed. and trans. Clements R. Markham. Project Gutenberg. Web. Accessed 30 Dec. 2014. http://www.gutenberg.org/files/9068/9068-h/9068-h.htm

Arguedas, José María. *Deep Rivers*. 1958. Trans. Frances Horning Barraclough. Austin: University of Texas Press, 1978.

Barrenechea, Antonio & Heidrun Moertl. "Hemispheric Indigenous Studies: Introduction." *Comparative American Studies*. 11. 2 (June 2013): 109–23.

Cooke, Alistair. *Alistair Cooke's America*. New York: Alfred A. Knopf, 1974.

Cooper, James Fenimore. *The Last of the Mohicans*. 1826. Rpt. New York: Oxford University Press, 1980.

Copway, George. *The Traditional History and Characteristic Sketches of the Ojibwa Nation*. 1850. Rpt. Honolulu: University Press of the Pacific, 2002.

Diaz, Bernal. *The Conquest of New Spain*. Trans. John M. Cohen. London: Penguin, 1963.

Fitz, Earl E. "Native American Literature and Its Place in the Inter-American Project." *Comparative American Studies*. 11. 2 (June 2013): 124–47.

Garibay K., Ángel Maria. *Visión de los vencidos*. México: UNAM, 1959.

THE INTER-AMERICAN HEMISPHERIC PERSPECTIVE

Imbert, Enrique Anderson & Eugenio Florit, eds. *Literatura Hispanoamericana: Antología e Introducción Histórica*. New York: Holt, Rinehart & Winston, 1960.

"The Jesuit Relations and Allied Documents 1610 to 1791." Web. Accessed 30 Dec. 2014. http://puffin.creighton.edu/jesuit/relations/

Kaup, Monika & Debra J. Rosenthal, eds. *Inter-American Dialogues: Mixing Race, Mixing Culture*. Austin: University of Texas Press, 2009.

Kelsey, Vera. *Six Great Men of Brazil*. Boston: D.C. Heath and Company, 1942.

Lara, Jesús, trans. and ed. *La tragedia del fin de Atawallpa*. Cochabamba, Bolivia: Imprenta Universitaria, 1957.

León-Portilla, Miguel, ed. *The Broken Spears: The Aztec Account of the Conquest of Mexico*. Trans. Lysander Kemp. Boston: Beacon Press, 1962.

Lindstrom, Naomi. "Foreword." *Iracema* by José de Alencar. Trans. Clifford E. Landers. Oxford: Oxford University Press, 2000. xi–xxiv.

MacLeish, Archibald. "Conquistador." 1932. *Collected Poems, 1917–1982*. Boston: Houghton, Mifflin, 1985. 169–251.

Merquior, J. G. "The Brazilian and the Spanish American Literary Traditions: A Contrastive View." *The Cambridge History of Latin American Literature*. Vol. 3. Ed. Roberto González Echevarría & Enrique Pupo Walker. Cambridge: Cambridge University Press, 1996. 363–82.

Monegal, Emir Rodríguez with Thomas Colchie. *The Borzoi Anthology of Latin American Literature: From the Time of Columbus to the Twentieth Century*. Vol. I. New York: Alfred A. Knopf, 1984.

Moore, Brian. "Author's Note." *Black Robe*. New York: Plume/Penguin, 1997. vii–x.

Murra, John. "Introduction." *Deep Rivers by José María Arguedas*. Trans. Frances Horning Barraclough. Austin: University of Texas Press, 1978. ix–xv.

Ong, Walter J. *Orality and Literacy: The Technologizing of the Word*. London: Methuen, 1982.

Paz, Octavio. *The Labyrinth of Solitude: Life and Thought in Mexico*. Trans. Lysander Kemp. New York: Grove Press, 1961.

——. *Sun Stone/Piedra de sol* (1957). Trans. Muriel Rukeyser. New York: New Directions, 1963.

Petrone, Penny. "Indian Literature." *The Oxford Companion to Canadian Literature*. Ed. William Toye. Oxford: Oxford University Press, 1983. 383–88.

Rabinal Achi: A Mayan Drama of War and Sacrifice. Trans. Dennis Tedlock. Oxford: Oxford University Press, 2003.

Ribeiro, Darcy. *Maíra*. São Paulo: Editora Brasiliense, 1976.

Riegelhaupt, Joyce F. "Among the Mairun." *New York Times Book Review* (June 1984): 20.

Silko, Leslie Marmon. *Almanac of the Dead*. New York: Penguin, 1991.

——. *Ceremony*. New York: Viking, 1977.

Sommer, Doris. *Foundational Fictions: The National Romances of Latin America*. Berkeley: University of California Press, 1991.

Tedlock, Dennis. "Introduction." *Rabinal Achi: A Mayan Drama of War and Sacrifice*. Oxford: Oxford University Press, 2003. 1–19.

Thériault, Yves. *Agaguk*. Montreal: Quinze, 1980.

Urbas, Jeannette. *From Thirty Acres to Modern Times: The Story of French-Canadian Literature*. Toronto: McGraw-Hill Ryerson, 1976.

Vargas Llosa, Mario. "Afterword." *Deep Rivers*. Trans. Austin: University of Texas Press, 1978. 235–42.

Von Hagen, Victor Wolfgang. *The Aztec: Man and Tribe*. Rev. ed. New York: New American Library, 1961.

2
Alaska Native Literature

Susan Kollin

In her American Book Award-winning memoir, Tlingit author Ernestine Hayes notes that while lawmakers and other experts continue to debate land rights and resource claims across Alaska, issues of ownership and belonging have long been understood quite differently by indigenous populations throughout the state. "Who our land now belongs to, or if land can even be owned, is a question for politicians and philosophers. But we belong to the land ... This is our land ... We can't help but place our love there," she writes (ix). Alaska received its name from the Unangan or Aleut people, who called it "Alyeska," meaning "the Great Land" (Williams 1). The largest state in the United States, Alaska comprises more than 586,000 square miles and spans many ecosystems, from tundra to sea ice, and from boreal forests and coastal rainforests to wetlands, rivers, and lakes ("Alaska's 32 Ecoregions"). Of the 562 federally recognized tribes in the United States, 225 of them are located in Alaska. The state is home to more than 127,000 Alaska Natives who live in over 200 villages and speak twenty indigenous languages (Williams 2–4). Alaska Natives comprise a diverse population that includes Iñupiat and Yuit Eskimos, Aleuts, and Athabascans, as well as Tlingit, Haida and Tsimshian Indians (Haycox xii).

According to oral traditions, Native peoples occupied Alaska for thousands of years before European contact, which began in the mid-eighteenth century with the Russian explorers. The United States later "purchased" the region in 1867, and in 1959 Alaska was granted statehood. Following the 1968 discovery of oil across the North Slope, the federal and state government entered a land grab in the hope of exploring and developing Arctic oil (Williams xv). Because indigenous Alaskans had not relinquished their land rights after statehood, the federal government had to negotiate a settlement. The Alaska Native Claims Settlement Act (ANCSA), the largest land settlement at that time in U.S. history, was signed into law in 1971. ANCSA extinguished indigenous land claims in exchange for forty-four million acres and nearly one billion dollars to be managed through twelve regional Alaska Native corporations (Williams xv). In clearing the way for the construction of the Trans-Alaska pipeline, the settlement act resulted in tremendous political and cultural upheaval that continues to have repercussions for Alaska Natives today.

Indigenous Alaskan writers have responded to these changes as well as other transformations brought about by histories of contact and conflict. In addition to addressing concerns about identity and community, Alaska Native literature has centered on sovereignty and cultural recovery, the meanings of place as well as resistance to assimilation and Americanization. While the name "Alaska Native" carries traces of the negative attitudes about indigenous peoples often found in settler-colonial thinking, it is an accepted designation used by indigenous people throughout the state (Williams 4). The term has been employed strategically as a way of speaking about different cultural groups who frequently face common experiences within the colonial system. Tlingit scholar Maria Shaa Tláa Williams notes, however, that this language is undergoing a process of change, as words established by outsiders including "Eskimo," "Aleut," and "Indian" are being replaced with "self-designative terms such as 'Yup'ik,' 'Yupiaq,' 'Iñupiaq,' 'Unangan,' and 'Alutiiq/Sugpiaq'" (xiv).

Alaska Native literature is a diverse tradition that includes oral narratives, poetry, fiction, and memoir. Although histories of conquest and occupation have meant that some of this literature has been lost or destroyed, there have been efforts to recover the work, with several collections of Alaska Native oral narratives and other literature appearing in recent years. James Ruppert and John W. Bernet note that the act of collecting these text tended to fall into the domain of specific professional groups over the years. From 1870 to 1920, it was primarily missionaries who were involved in this effort. During the next four decades, anthropologists tended to conduct the work, while from the 1960s and on, linguists took up the project (Ruppert & Bernet 15). More recently, however, Alaska Native scholars have begun leading these literary recovery efforts and have taken over the production of knowledge and the role of expert.

With the state located far from major publishing houses, Alaska Native literature has tended to be produced by local or university presses. In 1986, for instance, the *Alaska Quarterly Review*, sponsored by the University of Alaska at Anchorage, put together a special issue on "Alaska Native Writers, Storytellers, and Orators" with a preface by Tlingit poet and scholar Nora Marks Dauenhauer and her husband, the late Richard Dauenhauer. Both of them served as Alaska State poet laureates and eventually edited three collections of Tlingit oral narratives and life stories. These volumes include *Haa Shuká, Our Ancestors: Tlingit Oral Narratives* (1987); *Haa Tuwunáagu Yís, for Healing our Spirit: Tlingit Oratory* (1990); and *Haa Kusteeyí, Our Culture: Tlingit Life Stories* (1994). Recent years have also seen an outpouring of Alaska Native poetry by writers such as Dauenhauer (Tlingit), Mary TallMountain (Koyukon/Athabaskan), Robert Davis Hoffman (Tlingit), and Joan Naviyuk Kane (Iñupiaq).

Autobiographical writings by indigenous Alaskans include one of the earliest known efforts, Paul Green's *I am Eskimo: Aknik My Name* (Iñupiaq) from 1959. Other memoirs include Velma Wallis's *Raising Ourselves: A Gwich'in Coming of Age Story from the Yukon River* (Athabascan) from 2002, Elizabeth Pinson's *Alaska's Daughter: An Eskimo Memoir of the 20th Century* (Iñupiaq) from 2005, Ernestine Hayes' *Blonde Indian: An Alaska Native Memoir* (Tlingit) from 2006, and William L. Iġġiaġruk Hensley's *Fifty Miles from Tomorrow: A Memoir of Alaska and the Real People* (Iñupiaq) from 2009. The biggest selling narrative by an indigenous Alaskan author, Velma Wallis's retelling of an Athabascan narrative in *Two Old Women: An Alaskan Legend of Betrayal, Courage, and Survival*, came out in 2002. It garnered a number of literary awards and saw a third edition appear in 2013. Wallis also adapted another Athabascan story in her second book, *Bird Girl and the Man Who Followed the Sun* (1997). Finally, literary scholarship has produced a number of important critical essays and volumes, with work by Jeane C. Breinig, Shari M. Huhdorf, James Ruppert, and other figures setting the foundations for Alaska Native cultural and literary studies.

Indigenous Alaskan literature has gained increased national and international attention, partly as a result of the larger Native American Renaissance that developed across the Lower 48 in the late 1960s. Various exchanges allowing for the circulation of ideas between Alaska Native and American Indian authors helped generate excitement about literary production in the 1970s and 80s. As Ruppert notes, writers such as Joy Harjo, Geary Hobson, Wendy Rose, Joseph Bruchac, and others visited Alaska and gave public lectures across the state, which had lasting effects on audiences and authors alike ("Alaska Native Literature" 334). Leslie Marmon Silko, for instance, lived in Ketchikan for a few years in the mid-1970s where she wrote most of her novel *Ceremony,* while her short time in Bethel also shaped some of the writings in *Storyteller* (Nelson 248).

Today many new Alaska Native voices are coming into print, and various major publishers are becoming interested in signing on indigenous authors from the state. Memoirs such as Ernestine Hayes's *Blonde Indian* and William Iġġiaġruk Hensley's *Fifty Miles from Tomorrow* are gaining increased attention, due in part to the growing national interest in life writing and autobiographies in general. While a new awareness about Alaska Native literature has created important opportunities for indigenous writers and their communities, problems can also arise with this enhanced interest. The demands of the literary market place, for instance, may place burdens and restrictions on the types of stories indigenous Alaskan writers are able to produce as well as which voices get to be heard. Genre conventions shaping memoirs and autobiographies can also prove troubling in that they may value individuals over communities, placing inordinate worth and meaning on the life of single, isolated self.

Elected to the Alaska House of Representatives and the Alaska Senate and an influential figure who helped pass the indigenous land claims act, Hensley addresses these problems, noting that in his culture there is a "sense of propriety" that cautions against elevating oneself above others. Throughout his memoir Hensley stresses the ways it always "takes many people to create success" and credits other indigenous Alaskans who worked hard to ensure a better future for their communities (8). In a similar way, Ernestine Hayes uses autobiography not only to chronicle her childhood in Southeast Alaska, her travels throughout the West, and her return to the state as an adult, but also as a way of remembering stories her Tlingit grandmother told her about their kinship with bears, spiders, and other life forms, as well as oral narratives about how glaciers shaped their homeland, Lingít Aaní, and how Raven brought light to the people. Ultimately, both Hensley and Hayes place their life experiences in the context of these larger struggles for indigenous rights and survivance, whether it is through their work with legislation and other efforts at creating meaningful political change or through a focus on Alaska Native education, cultural revival, and storytelling.

In *Blonde Indian: An Alaska Native Memoir,* Hayes describes her coming of age in Juneau and the American West as an only child raised by a single mother and devoted grandparents.[1] Born in 1945, the author never met her father and heard only partial stories about him while growing up. The title of her narrative comes from the light-colored hair she had as a child and from a song her grandmother used to share with her. "*Blonde Indian, Blonde Indian,*" her grandmother used to sing, while the author danced and sang along (5). Her grandfather, whose "white man name" she carried, was frequently away from the family for months at a time while fishing (5). Hayes remembers that when he returned home, he enjoyed baking for them, making biscuits in the oven of their wood-burning stove, and sometimes bringing the rare treat of butter for the family to melt on top.

The process of providing, making, and sharing food appears as a central focus of her memoir, an activity that is linked to the challenges of living under a colonial system and a capitalist economic order, which disrupted their relationship to the land and how they traditionally provided food for themselves. Hayes recounts the family's subsistence hunting and fishing in Juneau. "In my grandmother's house back across the channel," she writes, "we ate deer meat and porcupine my uncles poached from land that once belonged to our powerful ancestors, the Kaagwaantaan" (10). Hayes remembers helping her family stay fed, walking along the edge of town "to the cold storage docks past men in yellow rubber suits cutting fish and throwing unwanted fish parts onto the wooden docks where I was often sent to collect the heads for that night's boiled soup" (11). At her Aunt Erm's house where she is sent to stay for a time, Hayes remembers that she "hauled wet seaweed from the beach to feed the garden, weeded the eager potatoes and carrots" while she fed the chickens and looked forward to all the "enchanted dishes" her aunt prepared (25).

When family members succumb to alcoholism, the author's life starts to decline. The crisis becomes visible in the diminished diet that replaces beloved meals she once enjoyed after caregivers lose interest in cooking and other domestic labors. A diet based on subsistence hunting and fishing is thus replaced with processed foods purchased at the store, including canned milk, boxed cereals, "fried potatoes cut up with wiener nickels," as well as canned corned beef "stirred into a frying pan and mixed with hot sticky rice ... canned Spam with canned sweet potatoes ... and hamburger served with dark brown canned gravy poured over rice" (33). At school, Hayes watches the white mothers prepare items for the bake sale – desserts "made of magic" (17) – while she dreams one day that she too will "cast sprinkles on enchanted cakes" (26).

The family's transformed diet ultimately reflects a larger crisis of delegitimization facing many Alaska Natives and is representative of the larger colonial system that disrupts indigenous cultures across the nation as a whole. In *Global Appetites: American Power and the Literature of Food*, Allison Carruth examines the politics of the modern food system along with its failings, linking transformations in the development, preparation, and consumption of food to larger accounts of globalization and post-World War II American power (4–5). For Carruth, literature about food and diets offers connections between "social and interpersonal registers" as well as between "symbolic and embodied expressions of power" (5). From the development of agribusiness to issues of free trade, food justice, global branding, and the transnational networks that rely on "geographic and psychic distance between people and that profit on our enchantment" with "exotic" tastes and products (7–8), the modern food system becomes an important force to examine in making sense of post-war indigenous struggles across Alaska.

Throughout *Blonde Indian*, changes in the author's childhood diet also foreground disruptions in the family's relationships with each other and their community. She remembers the reciprocal food practices she learned from her grandmother. As they sit at the table enjoying a meal together, Hayes' grandmother describes their cousin, the brown bear. She explains that if her granddaughter wanders too far from home and finds herself near the forest while picking berries, she should speak to her "unseen cousin" and say, *"Don't bother me, cousin! I'm only here for my share! I'm not trying to bother you!"* (5). The stories provide the author with a sense of extended family. "I had no sisters or brothers and I had few friends," she writes, but bears were my cousins and the wind was my grandfather. … wild plants grew on the hill beside our old house, and a creek led up the mountain behind me, and seaweed and crabs danced in the ocean channel at my feet. I never questioned that I belonged.

(7)

Hayes remembers lessons too about harvesting food from the abundant life of the sea and the land in Southeast Alaska:

She taught me to dig fast for clams on the rich beach, watch for their squirting spit, run fast, dig fast, place my treasured clams carefully into a pail, fill the pail and carry it home, wet hungry beach sand sucking my untied shoes. Scrub the uncomplaining shells in fresh cold water. Watch her cook the sea-flavored clams. Drink the juice. If there is some butter left over from grandfather's last visit, melt a little butter into the broth. Otherwise, maybe some seal oil. Eat the claims with seaweed and salmon eggs. Chew on some dryfish. … Then fresh berries I may have picked that very day, berries that my cousin the brown bear has so kindly allowed me to take from the edge of the forest, from where he quietly watched.

(5–6)

The passage calls to mind a poem that Tlingit author Nora Marks Dauenhauer wrote a few decades earlier about adapting to dietary changes that were gradually finding their way into her life. In "How to Make a Good Baked Salmon from the River," Dauenhauer offers a recipe for adapting traditional ways of preparing meals to the realities now facing readers. The poet describes how salmon is best prepared when it is cooked at camp near the beach using a fire and a wooden stick. Knowing that many in her community no longer live in rural places or have access to these supplies, she concedes that the food may be prepared in the city in a kitchen with electricity and a black frying pan. Thinking how tasty fresh berries would be alongside the salmon, she again acknowledges limitations and welcomes other cooks to open instead fruit cocktail from a can (*Droning Shaman* 11–13). Growing up in an earlier generation, Dauenhauer struggled to negotiate changes in Tlingit diets, and thus for her a few compromises do not hurt the dish. By the time Hayes returns to Tlingit culture, however, the colonial system has made such dramatic transformations in the modern food system and in Alaska Native communities that it becomes difficult for her to make similar accommodations in recreating traditional meals.

Just as the colonial system diminishes the food traditions of her community, so it brings an educational system that is also damaging. Hayes' memoir addresses her experiences attending what she calls "white people's schools" where teachers did not value her culture (10). She remembers the basement schoolroom that houses "stiffly folded chairs … where dainty little girls and clean little boys stared at me when I entered, always dirty, always hungry, always late" (8). For a student who went on to become an award-winning writer, stories already made a strong impression on her. Hayes remembers the reading groups into which they are divided; Seagulls are the lowest and Bluebirds are the highest. She describes the books they read:

Dick, Jane, and Spot live in an oversized, brightly shuttered house with Mother, a yellow-haired woman with white skin and smiling red lips who waves a morning goodbye across the manicured lawn to Father, dressed in a business suit and stepping into a shiny new car. ... Dick and Jane and Spot frolic with a bright red ball in the sunny yard. Spot is a small, mostly white, frisky dog with a black spot around his eye. It is a clever, playful name. Dick neatly tucks his striped, colorful shirt into belted trousers. I sense that Jane is a Bluebird.

(10)

As a child, Hayes already notes the differences dividing the classroom. While "Bluebirds" move "comfortably and confidently" in the world, she remembers entering it "timid and alone," even though she is one of the strongest readers in the class (13). Yet if Hayes senses that she doesn't belong at the white people's school, she knows she belongs to the land. "I would never be a Bluebird. Nor a Wren, Nor a Seagull," the author writes, but takes comfort in her grandmother's stories. "'Never forget,' she told me daily, 'you are an Eagle. Not Raven. Not Seagull. You will always be an Eagle and a Wolf. You will never be a Bluebird'" (15). These stories provide a different value system, what Ruppert describes as an alternative epistemology that the colonial system has "repressed and supplanted" ("Survivance" 286). Thus, for Hayes, some of the stories her teacher reads to the class do not make sense. She especially remembers a perplexing tale about a princess and a pea. "What makes a woman so precious, so unusual, that she can confidently complain of a trifle, demand and receive such extraordinary favor," she wonders (11).

When her mother enters a hospital in Seward to be treated for tuberculosis, Hayes is often left alone and unsupervised. She ends up being sent to juvenile and reform centers, spending time at Haines House and a missionary boarding school in Valdez. When her mother returns, they leave for California. For many years, Hayes wanders the Lower 48, "like a person in a strange dark forest. ... It was a long time before I finally came back" (26). *Blonde Indian* chronicles her travels through California, Nevada, and Washington, tracing her experiments with the "back-to-nature movement" and the "back-to-jesus movement" (79). She is called Sister Ernestine and teaches Sunday school; she doesn't wear slacks or makeup or any jewelry and doesn't cut her hair, play cards, watch TV, or "say gosh or darn" (80). The author writes about a white man who told her he was Indian, which she believed. "I had no dealings in Alaska with people who claimed to be Native unless they actually were, and I had no reason not to believe him" (78). She has two children and later finds herself in an abusive relationship, facing physical ailments, depression, an attempted suicide, and eventually homelessness.

At age forty, Hayes realizes she needs to "go home now, or ... die with my thoughts facing north" (111). The author enrolls in college, earns an MFA, and works at the Naakaahidi Theater in Juneau performing Tlingit stories. She is eventually hired as a professor in the English Department at the University of Alaska, Southeast in Juneau. In the early years when she first returned to Alaska, Hayes is able to reconnect with her community through her work as a tour guide on ships that travel through the Inside Passage. Her position involves teaching visitors about the region and its indigenous people. As she explains to the tourists, some people believe that the rich and abundant land enabled the Tlingit to develop its complex art, "the yellow cedar carvings, red cedar bentwood boxes and house screens, stylized woven blankets, formline painting and design" (52). They believe the plentiful nature of Lingít Aaní enabled the community to develop an elaborate social order with its matrilineal society and its subgroups, the Eagle and the Raven, who adhere to a reciprocity and balance so that an Eagle traditionally marries a Raven, and when a Raven gets pierced ears, it is traditionally an Eagle who performs the task (53).

The author teaches visitors about the abundant nature of Lingít Aaní – the five kinds of salmon and the different shellfish inhabiting the waters. She tells of the many types of seaweed, which are collected in the spring to be used the rest of the year, often cooked with salmon eggs or enjoyed "dry like popcorn" (52). She describes the berries: "salmonberry, huckleberry, blueberry, raspberry, soapberry, cranberry, nagoonberry, Jacob berry, strawberry, thimbleberry" (52). As the author explains, "When the land was as it should be, there was enough for all the people, and all the bears, and all the eagles and gulls and ravens" (65). For thousands of years, there was enough for all the people; the problem is that new people came who wanted too much. A poem by another Tlingit writer addresses this greed. In his well-known poem, "Saginaw Bay: I Keep Going Back," Robert Davis writes about resource extraction and developers who bulldoze forests across Alaska, leaving the land scarred and bare in their wake. "Some men can't help it," he explains, "they take up too much space, /and always need more" (*SoulCatcher* 19; Kollin 144–46).

Hayes comments on the problems of those who want and have too much. One figure in her memoir describes the Exxon Valdez oil spill. "Why were they still in charge?" he asks. "They elbowed their way in to shit all over everything and then they elbowed their way in to tell everyone how to clean up all the shit" (122). People in the state soon become rich from

> all the workers who went north to Valdez to get paid big money to clean up all the oil all over everything from one of those tankers that spilled millions of gallons and destroyed in a few hours what everyone thought would take at least a few more years to ruin.
>
> (121)

While she chronicles various crises and negative effects brought about by the colonial system, Hayes does not end her memoir on a note of despair. Instead, she concludes with the words of her grandmother. *"Remember that the land is enspirited. It is quickened,"* her grandmother tells her.

> When as you conduct your life you chance to see an eagle, or a wolf, or a bear, remember that it too is conducting its life, and it sees you as well. ... When you remember this, and feel this, and know this, you will want to hug the land. You will want to embrace it.
>
> (173)

In his narrative, *Fifty Miles from Tomorrow: A Memoir of Alaska and the Real People*, William L. Iġġiaġruk Hensley likewise chronicles a history of conflict and survival under the colonial system in the North. The author was born in 1941 near the shores of Kotzebue Sound, less than thirty miles from the Arctic Circle, ninety miles from Russia, and fifty miles from the International Date Line (11). As a child, Hensley faced hardships that led him to be adopted by his mother's uncle, and like Hayes, he spent part of his life outside Alaska, in his case attending boarding school in Tennessee and then university in Washington D.C. While he struggled with issues of identity and belonging, Hensley eventually became an influential figure in state politics and in securing land claims for Alaska Natives in the early 1970s.

While official maps call his hometown Kotzebue, the people who have lived there for thousands of years know it as "Qikiqtaġruk," meaning "small island" (11). As Hensley explains, the land presents many challenges; the winters are nine months long, and when it becomes really cold – around 50 or 60 below zero – the people describe it as "*itraliq*," meaning "bitter cold, so cold it hurts" (16). In this weather, any exposed skin quickly turns white, a sign that frostbite has set in. If someone manages to work up a sweat in that temperature, the person is likely to freeze the moment his or her body starts to cool. Hensley grows up knowing there was "very little room for error" under such conditions and thus maintains a respect for the land (16). "There are few people in America who can say that their forebears were here ten thousand years ago. That is a powerful feeling," he writes (18). The knowledge "that your ancestors played with the same rocks, looked at the same mountains, paddled the same rivers, smelled the same campfire smoke, chased the same game, and camped at the same fork in the river gives you a sense of belonging," he explains. At any moment, one "might unearth an ivory harpoon head or a flint scraper" and suddenly realize that these items are objects that one's "forebears used millennia ago" (18–19).

Because they occupy a relatively isolated region, the indigenous people of Arctic and subarctic Alaska have often experienced a different colonial history from other indigenous groups in the United States. As Yup'ik scholar Shari Huhndorf points out, across regions in the Far North indigenous groups engaged in various forms of political resistance, but did not partake in straightforward warfare with colonizers. This was partly because Europeans arrived in the region in smaller numbers and over a more gradual time period compared to other parts of the United States. Also, because the region was regarded as nearly uninhabitable by the colonizers, interest in the Far North was mostly consigned to resource extraction in the form of fur, minerals, and oil (Huhndorf 101).

In his memoir, Hensley recalls this history of colonial contact and remembers growing up at a time when some white establishments displayed signs that read "NO DOGS OR NATIVES ALLOWED" (213). He also remembers contact with populations from Outside – the name that is given to anyone not from Alaska. As a boy, Hensley looked forward each year in late summer to the arrival of the *North Star* (a ship out of Seattle) that would appear off the shore of Kotzebue, bringing people as well as goods that traders would sell across the region (65–67). The author recalls the circulation of cultural products, including motion pictures, which played at Archie Ferguson's Midnight Sun Theater. Hensley and his friends either paid the twenty-five cents to see the new movie or slipped in underneath someone's parka if they didn't have enough money (62). "Westerns were our favorites," he recalls. "Hopalong Cassidy, Tex Ritter. ... we would really get into the wild western – the fancy horse tricks, the quick draws with the six-shooters, the brawling and the falling off balconies. And the fierce Indians" (62). It was many years before he realized how he and his friends managed to internalize the racial politics of the colonial system. "We took the bait Hollywood gave us," he explains, "and sided with the 'good guys.' We were unaware – entirely – of the fact that our own people had considerably more in common with the Indians than with their onscreen enemies" (62).

Later while writing his memoir, Hensley begins to make connections between his life and "the story of a hundred thousand Alaska Natives of every tribe, spanning several generations ... families and cultures in danger of being obliterated by change, disease, and cultural upheaval" (9). Partly due to his community's isolation and because there were no transnational political organizations linking the Iñupiat with indigenous groups elsewhere,

Hensley didn't make these connections until much later. "I often wonder what might have happened in our world had we been more aware of the catastrophes faced by our fellow indigenous peoples, beginning in Jamestown four hundred years ago," he writes. "Could we have forestalled the negative effects of disease, alcohol, starvation, and people with superiority complexes?" (230).

As a boy, Hensley attends the BIA (Bureau of Indian Affairs) school in Kotzebue which, like other such schools, aimed to assimilate indigenous Alaskans into American life. Because the school only operated through the eighth grade, if students wanted to continue their education, they had to attend boarding schools elsewhere. At his Baptist boarding school in Tennessee, Hensley befriends another athlete who is Cherokee and who invites him home to North Carolina; there he learns for the first time about the struggles of the Cherokee and the Trail of Tears. He goes on to study at George Washington University where he and his new friend Hank Adams, an Assiniboine-Sioux, attend the 1963 March on Washington (105).

Upon his return home in 1956, Hensley enrolls at the University of Alaska at Fairbanks, but finds he needs a job in order to pay his living expenses. He ends up working one summer on the controversial "Project Chariot." In the 1950s and 60s, the nuclear scientist Edward Teller supported "peacetime uses of atomic energy" and developed a project with the Atomic Energy Commission to create a deep-water harbor along the Arctic coast near Kotzebue by detonating up to six thermonuclear bombs. The project would have been situated in the middle of Iñupiat lands. Had the Atomic Energy Commission gone forward, the explosions were estimated to be 160 times more powerful than the atomic bomb dropped on Hiroshima and were guaranteed to have catastrophic effects on the environment as well as the Iñupiaq community for generations to come. Iñupiats along with various environmentalists eventually leaked information that helped stop Project Chariot. Because major state newspapers were generally in support of these developments, Alaska Natives also started their own paper. In 1961, *Tundra Times*, led by Iñupiaq Harold Rock, helped to foster closer ties between Alaska Native groups and later played a role in passing the indigenous land claims act (Hensley 102; Andrews & Creed xxii–xxiii). In his memoir, Hensley confesses that he likes to believe his crew may have contributed to the demise of Project Chariot. That summer, his team managed to complete only half of the holes they were supposed to drill because their equipment could not cut through the dense shale (102).

A key moment in Hensley's political awakening comes in the wake of his family's dispossession. After statehood, the BLM (Bureau of Land Management) decided to send surveyors to Kotzebue to establish lots for individual sale at public auctions. "We did not think of straight lines and pieces of paper as describing our relationship to the land. We had lived on it, gloried in it," he writes. "Thousands of years of our heritage lay just under the surface, and the bones of our ancestors were there among them" (108). When officials discover oil under the surface of the land, more changes arrive in the region. Hensley notes the ways that oil has actually long served at the center of Iñupiaq culture. "For millennia, the Inuit had been aware of oil seeps in the North Slope of Alaska, and had used them for their own fuel" (151). He explains that a "thousand generations of our forefathers powered their bodies and fed their dogs and kept *iglus* warm with seal oil, whale oil, and walrus oil. Seal oil practically runs in our veins" (150). Throughout history, indigenous Alaskans have had a complex relationship with populations who desired oil. The demand for fuel, for instance, originally brought Europeans to Greenland, where in "just a few hundred years, the whales were virtually wiped out in that part of the world" (150). Likewise, whalers from New England hunted with such intensity that by the late 1800s, both whale and walrus populations were almost killed off, causing widespread starvation among the indigenous peoples in the region. In 1865, the discovery of crude oil in Pennsylvania led to the deep decline in whaling along with the economic stability of many Alaska Native communities (150–51).

Struggles for land rights and resource development thus become important issues for Hensley. When he enrolls in a constitutional law class at the University in Fairbanks, he has the opportunity to research the legal issues surrounding Alaska's lands (111). During his studies, he learns that the 1959 Act of Congress admitting Alaska as the 49th state indicated that the United States never won any land from Alaska Natives in battle or through treaty. Because Alaska Natives had not relinquished their land rights, they retained aboriginal title to the land, a discovery that becomes the legal basis for the Alaska Native Claims Settlement Act (112–13). Hensley plays an influential role in passing ANCSA and runs for public office. Later in his career, he becomes involved in setting up the Inuit Circumpolar Council, a transregional and transnational organization that helps unite the Inuit of the polar world, an important development for the political and cultural futures of indigenous peoples across the Arctic (210).

The anthropologist Ann Fienup-Riordan has noted that Alaska Natives have often faced what she describes as a particularly American form of Orientalism that depicts Eskimos in particular – and one could argue indigenous Alaskans in general – as an unchanging and premodern people frozen in time, the embodiment of the prelapsarian origins of western culture, the epitome of nature, and the purest form of "essential man" encountered by modern society (*Freeze Frame* xi). In their memoirs, Hayes and Hensley provide different understandings of indigenous Alaskan identity. Their texts offer an important corrective to settler-colonial understandings of Alaska's Native peoples, while countering misconceptions about its indigenous inhabitants as a premodern people occupying a past and dying world. In the process, their memoirs note affinities and connections that Alaska Native communities have with indigenous peoples across the nation and the world. Indeed, this continued recognition and study of shared histories is likely to inform the literary production and political labors of Alaska's indigenous populations for years to come.

Note

1 Although *Blonde Indian* is marketed as a non-fiction memoir, Hayes includes a parallel fictional narrative alongside her life story. As the author explained to me in email correspondence, current systems of genre classification do not fully describe the diverse narrative practices many Native American writers currently employ.

Works cited

"Alaska's 32 Ecoregions," Alaska Department of Fish and Game. State of Alaska. Web. Accessed 28 Nov. 2014. http://www.adfg.alaska.gov/index.cfm?adfg=ecosystems.ecoregions

Andrews, Susan B. & John Creed. "Introduction." *Authentic Alaska: Voices of Its Native Writers.* Ed. Susan B. Andrews & John Creed. Lincoln: University of Nebraska Press, 1998. xv–xxvii.

Breinig, Jeane. "In Honor of Nastao: Kasaan Haida Elders Look to the Future." *Studies in American Indian Literature* 25 (Spring 2013): 53–67.

Carruth, Allison. *Global Appetites: American Power and the Literature of Food*. Cambridge: Cambridge University Press, 2013.

Dauenhauer, Nora. *The Droning Shaman: Poems*. Haines, AK: Black Current Press, 1988.

Dauenhauer, Nora & Richard Dauenhauer, eds. *Haa Kusteeyí, Our Culture: Tlingit Life Stories*. Seattle: University of Washington Press, 1994.

——, eds. *Haa Shuká: Our Ancestors: Tlingit Oral Narratives*. Seattle: University of Washington Press, 1987.

——, eds. *Haa Tuwanáagu Yís, for Healing Our Spirit: Tlingit Oratory*. Seattle: University of Washington Press, 1990.

Dauenhauer, Nora Marks, Richard Dauenhauer & Gary Holthaus, eds. "Alaska Native Writers, Storytellers, and Orators." Special issue of *Alaska Quarterly Review* 4. 3–4 (1986).

Davis [Hoffmann], Robert. *SoulCatcher*. Sitka, AK: Raven's Bones Press, 1986.

Fienup-Riordan, Ann. *Freeze Frame: Alaska Eskimos in the Movies*. Seattle: University of Washington Press, 1995.

Green, Paul. *I am Eskimo: Aknik My Name*. Juneau: Alaska Northwest Publishing Company, 1959.

Haycox, Stephen. *Alaska: An American Colony*. Seattle: University of Washington Press, 2002.

Hayes, Ernestine. *Blonde Indian: An Alaska Native Memoir*. Tucson: University of Arizona Press, 2006.

——. email correspondence with the author. 13 January 2015.

Hensley, William L. Iġġiaġruk. *Fifty Miles from Tomorrow: A Memoir of Alaska and the Real People*. New York: Farrar, Strauss and Giroux, 2009.

Huhndorf, Shari M. *Going Native: Indians in the American Cultural Imagination*. Ithaca, NY: Cornell University Press, 2001.

Kollin, Susan. *Nature's State: Imagining Alaska as the Last Frontier*. Chapel Hill: University of North Carolina Press, 2001.

Nelson, Robert. "Leslie Marmon Silko: Storyteller." *The Cambridge Companion to Native American Literature*. Ed. Joy Porter & Kenneth Roemer. Cambridge: Cambridge University Press, 2005. 245–56.

Pinson, Elizabeth. *Alaska's Daughter: An Eskimo Memoir of the 20th Century*. Logan: Utah State University Press, 2005.

Ruppert, James. "Alaska Native Literature: An Updated Introduction." *The Alaska Native Reader*. Ed. Maria Shaa Tláa Williams. Durham, NC: Duke University Press, 2009. 333–36.

——. "Survivance in the Works of Velma Wallis." *Survivance: Narratives of Native Presence*. Ed. Gerald R. Vizenor. Lincoln: University of Nebraska Press, 2008. 285–95.

Ruppert, James & John W. Bernet. "Introduction." *Our Voices: Native Stories of Alaska and the Yukon*. Ed. James Ruppert & John W. Bernet. Lincoln: University of Nebraska Press, 2001. 1–37.

Wallis, Velma. *Bird Girl and the Man Who Followed the Sun*. New York: Harper Perennial, 1997.

——. *Raising Ourselves: A Gwich'in Coming of Age Story from the Yukon River*. Kenmore, WA: Epicenter Press, 2002.

——. *Two Old Women: An Alaskan Legend of Betrayal, Courage and Survival*. 1992. 20th Anniversary Reprint. New York: Harper Perennial, 2013.

Williams, Maria Shaa Tláa. "Alaska and Its People: An Introduction." *The Alaska Native Reader*. Ed. Maria Shaa Tláa Williams. Durham, NC: Duke University Press, 2009. 1–11.

3

American Imperialism and Pacific Literatures

Brandy Nālani McDougall

The Pacific Ocean covers one-third of the earth's surface, comprising roughly 64 million square miles. The United States, considered the largest overseas territorial power in the world, currently claims and controls nearly one-third of the Pacific through its territories, freely associated states, and ocean monuments. A product of manifest destiny, American imperialism in the Pacific was and continues to be focused primarily on militarization, nuclearization, and trade in the Asia-Pacific region. Historically, the Pacific has been a "strategic" site of American empire; however, the Pacific has also been strategically invisible to the popular and scholarly American imaginary. At most, Americans view the Pacific as a paradise with hospitable, happy natives. This strategic invisibility and narrow visibility hides the colonial and territorial realities that Pacific Islanders have endured for more than a century of American hegemony. Despite this narrow visibility, according to the 2010 U.S. census, the "Native Hawaiian and Other Pacific Islander alone-or-in-combination population" increased by 40 percent from 2000 to 2010, and constituted the second fastest growing racial group in the United States during the last decade. American imperialism in the region, however, has largely meant Indigenous displacement and a growing Pacific Islander diaspora in the past few decades – to the point that some off-island populations outnumber their on-island kin.

This chapter provides an overview of the literatures and major authors of Pacific Island nations that are now considered part of the United States and its territories, namely Hawai'i, Guåhan (Guam), and Amerika Samoa. The United States formally annexed Hawai'i and Guåhan (Guam) in 1898 and Amerika Samoa in 1900. These countries have different political histories and colonial relationships with the United States, and these political histories and statuses have invariably affected the literatures of the region in their content, language, distribution, and visibility. While there continue to be Pacific writers who write in Indigenous languages, this chapter primarily focuses on writing in English since the 1960s. This new literature is marked by its use of what Albert Wendt, the prolific Samoan writer and artist, describes as indigenized Englishes, which are used alongside Indigenous languages "to declare our independence and uniqueness; to analyze colonialism itself and its effects upon us; to free ourselves of the mythologies created about us in colonial literature" (3). Thus, rather than a sign of colonial assimilation and apathy, the wide use of Indigenous Englishes in contemporary Indigenous Pacific Literatures should be seen as a sign of cultural revitalization and continuity, as well as reflective of strong decolonization and cultural sovereignty movements. Consequently, literary themes include countering colonial hegemony, examining the legacy and impact of colonialism, including the effects of tourism and living in the diaspora, emphasizing a return to ancestral knowledge and culture, reaffirming nationalism and sovereignty, and underscoring the intimate, familial bond with our lands and ocean. Moreover, because these new literatures grow out of long vibrant traditions of orature, distinctive Indigenous cultural symbols, histories, aesthetics, and literary practices are an integral part of contemporary works.

Hawai'i

Hawai'i, now claimed as a state of the United States since 1959, was once an internationally recognized sovereign nation with a constitutional monarchy. The Hawaiian Kingdom was illegally overthrown in 1893 by an oligarchy of wealthy American businessmen with U.S. military backing. Annexation to the United States was solidified five years later in 1898 through a joint resolution, the Newlands Resolution, after a treaty of annexation failed. Incorporated as a territory of the United States for nearly 70 years, Hawai'i became a state through an electoral ballot that listed just two options: statehood or continued territorial status. The U.S. military now controls 231,000 acres or 5.6 percent of Hawai'i for bases and training – part of the lands to which Kānaka Maoli may still lay claim as they were illegally seized from the Hawaiian Monarchy and then "ceded" to the United States.[1]

Because of the illegality of the overthrow and all subsequent U.S. claims to Hawai'i, current discussions question whether Hawai'i is in a state of occupation or colonialism, in turn calling into question if Kānaka should be classified as Indigenous. For the purposes of this discussion of literature, I will continue to refer to Kanaka 'Ōiwi Literature as an Indigenous Literature, as within literary criticism, the term "Indigenous" indicates more than a political status, but a unique culture and deep history within a particular land and the harsh experiences of colonialism following the claims and settlement of a dominating power. In any case, the occupation of Hawai'i and colonial treatment of Hawaiians has prevented written Kanaka literature from flourishing to the extent that was enjoyed under the Hawaiian Kingdom. Hawai'i once boasted the highest literacy rate of any country by the 1850s and created the largest archive of writing in an Indigenous language (over one million manuscript pages) within a 100-year period. However, the intense Americanization campaigns of the twentieth century, coupled with the Republic's English-only law, forced a cultural and language disconnection to assimilate Hawaiians into the American populace. To overturn this, there have been several examples of native-controlled presses and journals, including *Hūlili*, *'Ōiwi: A Native Hawaiian Journal*, Kuleana 'Ōiwi Press, Topgallant Press, Ku Pa'a Press, Ala Press, Kahuaomānoa Press, Kamehameha Schools Press, and 'Ai Pōhaku Press.

John Dominis Holt

John Dominis Holt was among the first major writers in English to publish in the 1960s in Hawai'i. Born in 1919, Holt was descended from ali'i (chiefly) lineage and was the grand-nephew of Queen Lili'uokalani, Hawai'i's last reigning monarch. His publications include *On Being Hawaiian* (1965); a historiography, *The Hawaiian Monarchy* (1971); his novel, *Waimea Summer* (1976), which is recognized as the first contemporary Hawaiian novel; short story collections, *Today Ees Sad-dy Night* (1965) and *Princess of the Night Rides* (1977); a collection of poems, *Hanai, A Poem for Queen Lili'uokalani* (1986) and his memoir, *Recollections: Memoirs of John Dominis Holt 1919–1933* (1993).

Much of Holt's work can be characterized through his emphasis on mo'okū'auhau (genealogy) and ancestral inheritance. In the short story "The Pool" an old caretaker who must feed and care for a great shark who frequents a brackish pool, wants to pass on this knowledge to a young boy. Initially fascinated, the young boy, however, becomes fearful, turns away, and later regrets his choice. This theme may also be seen in Princess Ka'iulani, the protagonist in the short story "Princess of the Night Rides," who after living in exile in England returns to a newly annexed Hawai'i and the impoverishment of her people. Holt's Ka'iulani shares:

> They have taken everything away from us and it seems there is left but little, and that little our very life itself. We live now in such a semi-retired way that people wonder if we even exist anymore. I, too, wonder, and to what purpose?
>
> (40)

Raised since birth to lead and care for her people, Holt's Ka'iulani's grief is lessened when she reconnects with her ancestors during a night horse ride through Nu'uanu, when they assure her of their continuity in the land.

Similarly, in *Waimea Summer*, the young protagonist Mark Hull is urbanized, light-skinned and hapa (half-Hawaiian, half-haole), but the keeper of family mo'olelo (stories), who is, therefore, more sensitive to the ancestral. In visiting relatives in Waimea, and coming from Honolulu, he is, however, fearful of being given ancestral knowledge and ultimately turns away. In *Recollections*, Holt's memoir and final publication, he shares much of his own mo'okū'auhau and his family's personal mo'olelo, sharing his descent from ali'i lineages. Many of his Hawaiian family members are portrayed as being forced to adapt to western ways, caught between supporting the Hawaiian Kingdom and losing hope of seeing their country's sovereignty restored.

Noting how there were no publishing opportunities for Kanaka and other Hawai'i residents, Holt started Topgallant Press in 1974 and published over 20 books focused on Hawai'i, including his own novel and short story collections. He later started Ku Pa'a Press in 1985 and went on to publish at least eight more books before his death in 1993. His dedication to publishing illustrates his belief in the power of the Hawaiian literary continuum to enable ancestral reconnections to transform and strengthen our contemporary relationships with the 'āina and culture.

Victoria Nālani Kneubuhl

Representing both Hawai'i (through her mother's lineage) and Amerika Samoa (through her father's lineage), Victoria Nālani Kneubuhl was awarded the 1994 Hawai'i Award for Literature and the 2006 Elliot Cades Award for Literature. She also served as Distinguished Writer in Residence in the English Department at the University of Hawai'i at Mānoa in Fall 2007. A playwright and a novelist, Kneubuhl's Hawaiian and Samoan genealogies inform her work, which often portrays and examines carefully researched Indigenous histories, cultural practices, and colonial issues in Hawai'i and Samoa. Her novels, *Murder Casts a Shadow* (2008) and its sequel *Murder Leaves its Mark* (2011), are both mystery novels set in the 1930s in Honolulu and feature the Hawaiian heroine, Mina Beckwith, a journalist, alongside the Samoan hero, Ned Manusia, a playwright. Together the intelligent duo solve murder mysteries while also challenging white privilege and plantation-based classism in Hawai'i. In particular, Kneubuhl aims to educate her audiences about the overthrow of the Hawaiian Kingdom, as seen in her play *January 1993*, which is a five-act, nineteen-scene, fifteen-hour dramatization of historical crimes and contemporary loss. Along these lines, Kneubuhl co-founded the Hawai'i Pono'ī Coalition, which has produced her play *Mai Poina* at 'Iolani Palace every September since 2007 (coinciding with Queen Lili'uokalani's birthday).

Her collection *Hawai'i Nei: Island Plays* (2002) assembles three of Kneubuhl's plays: "The Conversion of Ka'ahumanu," "Emmalehua," and "Ola Nā Iwi." The first play, "The Conversion of Ka'ahumanu" has been Kneubuhl's most produced play and has toured Hawai'i, Samoa, Edinburgh, Washington, D.C., and Los Angeles (xv). In 1819, Ka'ahumanu, the favorite wife of Kamehameha I, became kuhina nui (regent) after his death and brought an end to the kapu system. Kneubuhl's Ka'ahumanu is an ali'i in conflict with many of her decisions, but eventually comes to see Christianity as a measure of protection for her country and people:

> There are too many ships, too many guns, too many diseases. If I take up this god perhaps there will be some good, some peace. Other nations will see that we believe in the same god and not think us ignorant savages. ... [S]ome will want to protect a Christian people from wrong.
>
> (68)

Thus, the play ends with Ka'ahumanu's decision to convert. "Emmalehua" and "Ola nā Iwi" depict situations in which Hawaiian women must protect and preserve cultural beliefs and their own power amidst a seemingly uncompromising colonial rigidity. "Emmalehua," Kneubuhl's first full-length play, is set in 1951 during the pressures of Americanization campaigns, and features Emmalehua, a young woman struggling to preserve hula against commercialization. Similarly, "Ola nā Iwi," portrays Kawehi, a Hawaiian woman fighting to repatriate iwi kupuna, or human remains.

Haunani-Kay Trask

Haunani-Kay Trask is an activist, scholar, professor and poet. A chief aspect of Trask's political activism includes her impressive body of literary and academic works. She has published two books of scholarship, *Eros and Power: The Promise of Feminist Theory* (1986) and *From a Native Daughter: Colonialism and Sovereignty in Hawai'i* (1993); as well as two books of poetry, *Light in the Crevice Never Seen* (1994) and *Night is a Sharkskin Drum* (2002). Trask is also the co-producer and scriptwriter of the 1993 documentary, *Act of War: The Overthrow of the Hawaiian Nation*. During her nearly forty-year tenure as professor of Hawaiian Studies, she played a pivotal role in securing and building the Kamakakūokalani

Center for Hawaiian Studies, a five-acre complex, as well as the creation of Hawaiian Studies itself.

Trask frames her work as stemming from her "rage and an insistent desire to tell the cruel truths about Hawai'i" ("Writing" 3). Trask's first collection, *Light in the Crevice Never Seen*, is comprised of several intimate portraits of the poet and her family and close friends alongside horrific and violent images of colonial devastation. The longest poem in the collection, the lyric "Hawai'i," can be characterized through its grieving tone and its articulation of loss of culture, land, and people through various kaona (veiled meaning) references; however, "Hawai'i" also presents smaller snapshot images of Hawai'i as a colonized space.

Images of colonial violence and devastation, but also themes of cultural return and renewal follow in Trask's second collection, *Night Is a Sharkskin Drum*. Several poems, like "The Broken Gourd," frame the "foreigner" as the devourer of Hawaiian culture and land and describe the resulting loss of Hawaiian culture and history. Yet, the collection begins and ends with akua (gods) as in "Night is a Sharkskin Drum," "Hi'iaka Chanting," and "Nāmakaokaha'i" to emphasize the strength in a return to the 'āina (land) and culture. The final poems in the collection depict a return to the lushness and mana (power) of the 'āina as a refuge for healing and decolonization. In the poem "Into Our Light I Will Go Forever," Trask praises several coastal 'āina on O'ahu for the gifts they offer and recognizes the continued presence of Hawaiian gods. Trask takes the reader into "the hum of/reef-ringed Ka'a'awa, /pungent with limu" (61), and later, into "our corals of/far Kahana, sea-cave/ of Hina" (61). She concludes with the lines: "Into our sovereign suns, /drunk on the mana/of Hawai'i" (62). These lines emphasize how Kānaka, who are of the land ourselves, must look toward "our sovereign suns" to strengthen our own sovereignty. Overall, Trask asserts a return to ancestral culture and 'āina, and other forms of resistance as means toward decolonization.

Indeed, Trask's poetry like the work of several other contemporary Kanaka writers, offers the weaponry of fierce hope for justice and sustenance of our sovereignty as native people. This dedication to Hawai'i's decolonization is particularly evident in the rich and growing body of contemporary Hawaiian Literature by writers and Spoken Word artists such as Imaikalani Kalahele, Māhealani Perez-Wendt, Joe Puna Balaz, Leialoha Perkins, Wayne Westlake, Lisa Kanae, ku'ualoha ho'omanawanui, Michael Puleloa, No'ukahau'oli Revilla, Donovan Kūhiō Colleps, Jamaica Osorio, David Keali'i, Sage U'ilani Takehiro, Christy Passion, Kealoha, Matthew Kaopio, Kristiana Kahakauwila, and myself, who employ kaona, along with other Hawaiian literary practices and aesthetic systems.

Amerika Samoa

The Samoan archipelago in the South Pacific is politically divided between the eastern group of islands, now known as Amerika Samoa, an unincorporated U.S. territory, and the western group, once occupied by Germany, then New Zealand, and is now the independent state of Samoa. In the late nineteenth century, the Samoan archipelago was partitioned by the competing imperialist powers of Germany and the United States. Amerika Samoa was governed under the U.S. navy for over 50 years until the insular territory was officially transferred under the Department of the Interior, who appointed governors until 1978, when the first election was held. Due to this militarized history and to severely limited employment opportunities, Samoans serve in the U.S. military at disproportionately high rates.

Since its inception, the partition of Samoa has divided families and altered cultural practices. Caroline Sinavaiana Gabbard notes that while Samoa has turned to Aotearoa/ New Zealand for its literary development, criticism, and publications, Amerika Samoa has, of course, relied largely on the United States, where very little attention has been given to "Pacific Islander" literature ("Amerika" 589). Also among the issues facing writers (and potential writers) of Amerika Samoa is limited access to education (and funding for education) and publishing. With limited federal funding given to Amerika Samoa and limited employment, Samoans have been forced into the diaspora to work and pursue higher education. This experience is clear when examining their contemporary literature and the diasporic experiences of their authors.

Despite these obstacles, Samoans have created a substantial and growing body of contemporary literature in English, employing both introduced and Samoan literary practices and aesthetics, such as fale aitu (literally, house of spirits), satirical sketches that Caroline Sinavaiana Gabbard describes as "represent[ing] a particular type of communication that functions, among other things, to help bridge a historical gap between a cultural past and present, a cultural self and other" ("Comic" 201–02). Though fale aitu is typically thought of as an orally rendered, often comedic, improvised performance, the practice has been adapted to Samoan written literature, as Sinavaiana Gabbard's scholarship has made clear.

John Kneubuhl

The son of a Samoan mother and a white American father, John Kneubuhl was a Samoan playwright and screenwriter who began writing in the 1940s, but who is most famous for his plays of the 1960s. Born in the village of Leone in Tutuila in Amerika Samoa, he used theatre to examine Indigenous identity, especially hapa or bicultural identity, reflective of his own upbringing. After a successful screenwriting career in Hollywood, Kneubuhl returned to Samoa and Hawai'i to write and produce plays that explored both Samoan and Hawaiian heritages, cultures, and histories, with characters forced to face their conflicted identities.

His collection of plays *Think of a Garden and Other Plays* (1997) features three plays, including "Mele Kanikau: A Pageant," his first published play since returning to the islands, and the complex comedy "A Play: A Play." "Think of a Garden," the last play Kneubuhl wrote before his death in 1992, but the first featured in the collection, is set in his home village of Leone in American Samoa in the late 1920s. "Flirt[ing] with autobiography" by Kneubuhl's own admission, "Think of a Garden" examines the aftermath of the partition of Samoa and the Mau Independence Movement of Western Samoa and features the character of the Writer, who speaks in retrospect as an older David Kreber. The Writer opens the play with a brief history:

> Those were the days when Samoa was undivided among foreign powers, its many islands a unified country ... The family had homes and vast lands in Western Samoa and on this island, which, in 1900, was ceded by its chiefs to the United

States of America. Still, my mother always thought of herself as a Western Samoan, and acted like one. In fact, she was supposed to marry into a noble family there. Instead, she met and married my father, an American ...

(3)

As such, the play reflects on the divisions created between families following the partition of Samoa, but it also examines how colonialism becomes internalized in various ways. Lu'isa Kreber, David's mother, is obsessed with light skin and the status it holds, yet she is also grief-stricken following the assassination of her relative, Tupua Tamasese, the resistance leader of the Mau movement for independence. In this way, the story of Samoa's fight for independence mirrors David's fight to survive his childhood amidst colonial trauma.

Caroline Sinavaiana Gabbard

A poet and scholar, Caroline Sinavaiana Gabbard was born in Utulei Village in Tutuila and is an Associate Professor of English, specializing in Pacific Literatures. Her poetry, which uses narrative, lyric, and avant garde aesthetic forms, has been published in journals nationally and internationally. Her first book of poetry, *Alchemies of Distance* (2002), is written in both prose and verse and divulges her personal search for Samoan identity within the diaspora, as a child with a father in the military. She writes in the collection's Introduction:

For me, all journeys are about pilgrimage, and poetry the vessel that carries me back (and forward) to the country of home. But it's more than just the boat. It's the lifeline, too. It's the line that can harness anger. It's the alchemy that can transform loss.

(27)

Consequently, many of the poems in the collection explore how distance and travel, which Sinavaiana Gabbard recognizes "is in [her] blood, in the genes" from her Polynesian ancestors, can be transformative, diasporic living, a regenerative space. In the poem "Sā Nāfanua," dedicated to her sisters, Sinavaiana Gabbard expresses that as descendants of Nāfanua, they "move down to the sea" and "follow [Nāfanua's]/ocean path to the world above" (43). She addresses Nāfanua in the poem directly, asking that she continue to guide the journey:

steady us mother
your eye lights the way
your heart moves our blood
your hand steers our boat
and plants us like seeds in the new land
sing for us Tinā.

(44)

Returning to Tutuila, Samoa, her home(is)land, represents one such journey and her poems "afiafi" and "ianeta's dance" reflect on this return, while other poems, like "married to the moment," "lineage," and "pilgrimage" are rooted in Honolulu, Hawai'i, the part of the Pacific where Sinavaiana Gabbard lives. Each poem brings the reflection and retrospection that can only come with an "alchemy of distance" (in the poem "soiree") that "[gives] voice to the silence/inside."

Sinavaiana Gabbard is also the co-author of *Mohawk/Samoa: Transmigrations* with James Thomas Stevens (Mohawk), a collection of call-and-response poems examining the similarities and differences between Samoan and Mohawk experiences and histories. Her next collection of poems, *Side Effects* will be published in 2015 by Ala Press.

Dan Taulapapa McMullin

Dan Taulapapa McMullin is an award-winning poet, painter, and filmmaker. He has published a chapbook, *A Drag Queen Named Pipi* (2004), and has edited an anthology of contemporary Pacific writing, *Nafanua* (2010). His artwork has exhibited at the De Young Museum, the Gorman Museum, the Bishop Museum, and the Peabody Essex Museum. His film *Sinalela* won the 2002 Honolulu Rainbow Film Festival Best Short Film Award.

Comprised of both narrative and avant-garde poems, *Coconut Milk* (2013), McMullin's first collection of poems, examines Samoan, fa'afafine (literally, in the manner of woman), queer and diasporic identities using a particularly Samoan brand of storytelling and sharp colonial and homophobic critique. McMullin employs language and form to encompass multivocality and multiperspectivism. Written in an unglossed/untranslated Samoan and English, many of his poems are part of a series, demonstrating McMullin's ability to deeply explore the experience of place, diaspora, and fa'afafine culture, as well as his ability to write from multiple perspectives, which is perhaps at the heart of fa'afafine identity – the ability to walk between and embody both the masculine and feminine as part of being third-gender.

His Sa Moana poem series (six poems in all) is comprised of poems centered primarily on his mother and express his love and admiration for her. She becomes his ideal of beauty, affecting not only how he sees other women, but also how he sees himself: "[M]y favorite activity in the world was to listen to her dress for work or something special ... //When she was ready/she would ask me to zip up the back of her dress/the journey of my life began there" (5). The formative bond with his mother provides a foundation for his Fa'a Fafine poem series (numbering 24 in all) to reflect more explicitly on fa'afafine identity and explore gender and sexuality as it is imbricated with Samoan culture. He writes:

Despite the failed attempt among fundamentalists in Samoa
influenced by American televangelism
to force fa'afafine to dress as men in church
Fa'afafine do always dress as ladies in the choir
as businesswomen at work
as Miss at the chalkboard
as Mom at the shop
as Aunty at home.

(50)

AMERICAN IMPERIALISM AND PACIFIC LITERATURES

Whether examining fa'afafine or diasporic Samoan culture, McMullin's poetry is dedicated to showing the strength and resilience of Pacific indigeneity despite colonialism.

Aside from Kneubuhl, Sinavaiana-Gabbard, and McMullin, Amerika Samoa is also home to the novelist Lemanatele Mark Kneubuhl, the nephew of John Kneubuhl and cousin of Victoria Nālani Kneubuhl, and author of the comical novel *The Smell of the Moon* (2007). Finally, novelist, poet, and playwright Sia Figiel, who is of lineages from both Samoa and Amerika Samoa, merits special recognition. Though much of her work, including her novels, *Where We Once Belonged* (1999) and *They Who Do Not Grieve* (2003), are set in Samoa, she now has several works in progress inspired by her time living in Amerika Samoa. She currently lives in Utah, and is actively involved as a health activist raising awareness about diabetes and obesity.

Guåhan

Guåhan (Guam) is the largest of the Mariana Islands of Micronesia and has endured a long and continuous history of colonization since the seventeenth century under Spain, the United States, Japan, and then the United States again. Under competing colonialisms, Guåhan has been separated politically, and in some senses, culturally, from the Northern Mariana Islands, which are now organized as an American commonwealth. Like Amerika Samoa, Guåhan is on the United Nations list of non-self-governing territories awaiting decolonization, but is presently an unincorporated territory of the United States. Guåhan is heavily militarized; the U.S. military currently holds 30 percent of the island for bases and training sites, but has plans to expand. The control of lands by U.S. military parallels the large numbers of Chamorus enlisted in the U.S. armed forces to fight for and defend a nation that currently holds their own native homeland as a colonial possession.

Descended from a rich literary history, contemporary Chamoru writers incorporate Chamoru aesthetics into their written and oral literatures, as Craig Santos Perez's scholarship on the continuity of the Chamoru tsamorita tradition, a call-and-response poetic form, elucidates ("Singing" 156). Tanya Chargualaf Taimanglo's *Attitude 13*, for example, features a short story entitled "Resurfacing" that veers between the ancestral and the contemporary by re-inscribing legendary Chamoru ancestors into the present. Taimanglo and other writers and Spoken Word artists such as Craig Santos Perez and Lehua Taitano, Cecilia "Lee" Perez, Michael Lujan Bevacqua, Bernadita Camacho-Dungca, Evelyn Flores, Clarissa Mendiola, Jay Baza Pascua, Anne Perez-Hattori, Kisha Borja-Kicho'cho', Anghet Hoppe-Cruz, Melvin Won Pat-Borja, and Dåko'ta Alcantara-Camacho contribute to the inafa'maolek (the restoration of harmony and order) of Chamoru literature, culture, and language to subvert and resist American imperialism in Guåhan.

Craig Santos Perez

An activist involved in the demilitarization movement on Guåhan, Craig Santos Perez is a Chamoru from the village of Mongmong. In 1995, his family migrated to California, where he lived for fifteen years before moving to Hawai'i, where he lives now and works as an Associate Professor of English at the University of Hawai'i at Mānoa. Perez is the author of three books of poetry: *from unincorporated territory [hacha]* (2008), *from unincorporated territory [saina]* (2010) – winner of the PEN Center USA 2011 Literary Prize for Poetry – and *from unincorporated territory [gumá]* (2014). He has also recorded an "amplified poetry" album *Undercurrent* (Hawai'i Dub Machine 2011), and co-founded Ala Press, a publisher of Indigenous Pacific literature.

Consisting entirely of excerpts, Perez's first book *[hacha]* ("one" in Chamoru) focused on mapping where he is from – the island of Guåhan – and his home(is)land's omission from imperialist maps. Throughout much of his first collection, Perez traces the complex colonial history of Guåhan, demonstrating the ambiguity of "unincorporated" territorial status, while also re-inscribing a Chamoru history of resistance, recalling the powerful chiefs Gadao and Matapang in poems such as "Achiote." His second collection *[saina]* (meaning "ancestor" in Chamoru) references the sakman, or large outrigger canoe, of the same name, a symbol of Chamoru navigational revitalization. His poetic excerpts continue to uncover what it means to be from (as all of his poems begin with from or ginen, the Chamoru equivalent), but more deeply examine Perez's diasporic experience as a Chamoru, both his roots and his routes. Certain serial excerpts, such as "from Aerial Roots" and "from ta(la)ya" continue in this second collection, though he also introduces new serial poems such as "from all with ocean views," which examines tourism.

His third collection *[gumá]* maps and navigates conceptions of home (the translation of guma) and his home(is)land. In "from Ta(la)ya," a series started in Perez's first book, he explores Chamoru net weaving and fishing, but also recounts the violence of Japanese and American militarization of the island which, as is clear through generations of men in Perez's family, is also a kind of net, trapping Chamorus into military service. However, beyond his own family, Perez lists the names of fallen Indigenous Pacific soldiers, striking through other details of their lives to demonstrate colonial erasure. Similarly, a new poem series "fatal impact statements" gathers several public comments responding to the U.S. military's Draft Environmental Impact Statement (DEIS), prepared in 2009 in order to assess the effects of a proposed U.S. military buildup on Guam.

Also featured in *[gumá]* is Perez's humorous poem "SPAM's Carbon Footprint [a malologue]," which features the legendary Juan Malo, who was said to consistently outsmart and cleverly rebel against Spanish colonial rule without reprisals. Perez's Juan Malo subverts American colonial rule in Guåhan, speaking with heteroglossic agency, constantly shifting registers, thoughts, and voices, sarcastically presenting himself as successfully colonized at times, and revolutionary at others through a series of "malologues." Perez ends his malologue on SPAM with the promise "I will never eat it," at once declaring he will neither eat the unhealthy canned meat, nor buy into the violent, yet numbing imperialism it represents.

Lehua Taitano

Chamoru poet Lehua Taitano is originally from Yigo, Guåhan but currently resides in Sonoma County, California. She is the author of the Merriam-Frontier Award-winning chapbook *appalachiapacific* and the poetry collection *A Bell Made of Stones* (2013), but also writes essays and fiction. Born to a Chamoru mother and a white father in the military, Taitano's family migrated when she was four years old to the Appalachia Mountains of North Carolina. Since that time, she has lived in many different places in the continental United States.

Reflective of this diasporic experience, the poetry in Taitano's collection structurally and metaphorically builds an idea of home through stories and fragments. The title refers to the latte stone megaliths (resembling bells) that form the foundation of ancestral Chamoru houses. The collection contains twenty-one individual poems and five serial poems arranged uniquely. Even though the collection spans nearly 90 pages, the text of the poems only appears on the "recto" pages (the right or front page), while the "verso" pages (left or back page) contains no poetic text. Like the structure and arrangement of the collection, Taitano's poems also experiment with typography and juxtaposition.

The collection begins with a letter addressed to an unnamed reader. The top of the letter is dated "April 2013" and the location is listed as "a little room/in California/with wind and eucalyptus" (9), introducing and situating the theme of disconnection and diaspora. A desire for ancestral connection is encapsulated in a dream in which Taitano's ancestors speak to her, but she doesn't understand their language. Besides not speaking the language of her ancestors, the speaker also worries her ancestors won't recognize her because of her light skin color: "In my bare feet I am Chamoru. And white, yes" (9). This anxiety is extended to Taitano's failure to be brown or white "enough" to fit into recognizable racial categories. Taitano ultimately conceives of this uncomfortable space as a hyphenated space: "This is the hyphen inside of me talking. Fused, spliced, separated, compounded ... These are my intersections of half-ness. Of -lessness" (11). Reflective of her attention to the visual structure of her poems, Taitano examines what it means to live at these visual, racial, diasporic intersections longing for a sense of home.

Compact of Free Association (COFA) Countries and the United States

Once part of the UN Trust Territories, the Federated States of Micronesia (FSM), the Marshall Islands, and Belau are now protectorates with a compact of "free association" with the United States. As part of its "free association," the United States allows for visa-free movement between these countries and the United States (including territories), and provides access to U.S. social services. In return, these countries grant the United States certain exclusive operating rights, primarily related to security and defense. COFA countries have faced the militarization and nuclearization of their islands and people, who have joined the armed forces in disproportionately high numbers per capita and have also endured high rates of exposure-related health issues.

Like their Pacific counterparts, the histories of FSM, the Marshall Islands, and Belau are rich with orature, which has informed and shaped their contemporary literatures. Yet, also like others in the Pacific affected by American imperialism, their writers face education, employment, publishing, and dissemination obstacles. Emelihter Kihleng of Pohnpei (FSM) and Kathy Jetnil-Kijiner of the Marshall Islands are among relatively few published writers in the region. Emelihter Kihleng is the author of the poetry collection *My Urohs* (2006), which examines Pohnpeian diasporic women's identity. Her work has critiqued the ascription of "Micronesian" racialization and scapegoating in Hawai'i and Guåhan, where she has lived for much of her life. Similarly, much of Kathy Jetnil-Kijiner's written poetry and spoken-word performances have focused on facing discrimination as a "Micronesian," but her poems also examine climate change and the rising ocean, militarization, and the history of nuclearization in her home(is)lands. Recently, she was a featured speaker who performed "Dear Matafele Peinam," a poem addressed to her baby daughter, at the UN Climate Summit in New York City in 2014. Her collection *Iep Jeltok* will be published in 2015.

"America's Pacific Century"

Former Secretary of State Hillary Clinton recently described (and rhetorically territorialized) the twenty-first century as "America's Pacific Century." The cornerstone of this "Pacific Pivot" is the Trans-Pacific Partnership (TPP), which aims to remove labor laws and environmental protections, expand corporate investment, and increase U.S. militarization throughout the region, having far-reaching ramifications on global and local territorialities, human rights, and climate change. While the "Pacific Pivot" and the TPP reinforce American imperialism in the Pacific, they are not insurmountable. Indigenous Pacific Literature stands as an important bastion of decolonization and resistance, making Pacific issues visible and reminding us that our islands are regenerative and revitalizing, our ocean, vast and powerful. As Tongan writer Epeli Hau'ofa writes:

> Oceania is humanity rising from the depths of brine and regions of fire deeper still, Oceania is us. We are the sea, we are the ocean, we must wake up to this ancient truth and together use it to overturn all hegemonic views that aim ultimately to confine us …
>
> (39)

Note

1 I use Kanaka Maoli, Kanaka 'Ōiwi, Kanaka, and Hawaiian to refer to the Indigenous people of Hawai'i. With the addition of the macron in Kānaka Maoli, Kānaka 'Ōiwi, and Kānaka, the term becomes plural.

Works cited

Clinton, Hillary. "America's Pacific Century." *Foreign Policy* 11 Oct. 2011. Web. Accessed 1 Apr. 2012.
Colleps, Donovan Kūhiō. *Proposed Additions*. Kāne'ohe, HI: TinFish Press, 2014.
Figiel, Sia. *They Who Do Not Grieve*. Los Angeles: Kaya Press, 2003.
———. *Where We Once Belonged*. Los Angeles: Kaya Press, 1999.
Hau'ofa, Epeli. *We Are Ocean: Selected Works*. Honolulu: University of Hawai'i Press, 2008.
Holt, John Dominis. *Princess of the Night Rides*. Honolulu: Topgallant Press, 1977.
———. *Recollections: Memoirs of John Dominis Holt 1919–1933*. Honolulu: Ku Pa'a Press, 1993.
———. *Waimea Summer*. Honolulu: Topgallant Press, 1976.

Jetnil-Kijiner, Kathy. *Iep Jeltok*. Manuscript in Progress.

Kihleng, Emelihter. *My Urohs*. Honolulu: Kahuaomānoa Press, 2006.

Kneubuhl, John. *Think of a Garden and Other Plays*. Honolulu: University of Hawai'i Press, 1997.

Kneubuhl, Lemanatele Mark. *The Smell of the Moon*. Wellington: Huia Press, 2007.

Kneubuhl, Victoria Nālani. *Hawai'i Nei: Island Plays*. Honolulu: University of Hawai'i Press, 2002.

——. *Murder Casts a Shadow*. Honolulu: University of Hawai'i Press, 2008.

——. *Murder Leaves its Mark*. Honolulu: University of Hawai'i Press, 2011.

McMullin, Dan Taulapapa. *Coconut Milk*. Tucson: University of Arizona Press, 2013.

——. *A Drag Queen Named Pipi*. Kāne'ohe, HI: TinFish Press, 2004.

——, ed. *Nafanua*. Honolulu: Ala Press, 2010.

Perez, Craig Santos. *from unincorporated territory [hacha]*. Kāne'ohe, HI: TinFish Press, 2002.

——. *from unincorporated territory [saina]*. Richmond, CA: Omnidawn Press, 2010.

——. *from unincorporated territory [gumá]*. Richmond, CA: Omnidawn Press, 2014.

——. "Singing Forwards and Backwards: Ancestral and Contemporary Chamorro Poetics." *Oxford Handbook of Indigenous American Literatures*. Ed. James Cox & Daniel Heath Justice. London: Oxford University Press, 2014. 152–65.

Revilla, No'ukahau'oli. *Say Throne*. Kāne'ohe, HI: TinFish Press, 2011.

Sinavaiana Gabbard, Caroline. *Alchemies of Distance*. Kāne'ohe, HI: TinFish Press, 2002.

——. "Amerika Samoa: Writing Home." *Oxford Handbook of Indigenous American Literatures*. Ed. James Cox & Daniel Heath Justice. London: Oxford University Press, 2014. 589–607.

——. "Comic Theater in Samoa as Indigenous Media." *Pacific Studies* 15.4 (December 1992): 199–209.

——. *Side Effects*. Honolulu: Ala Press, 2015.

Sinavaiana Gabbard, Caroline & James Thomas Stevens. *Mohawk/Samoa: Transmigrations*. Oakland, CA: Subpress, 2005.

Taimanglo, Tanya Chargualaf. *Attitude 13: A Daughter of Guam's Collection of Short Stories*. Bloomington, IN: AuthorHouse, 2010.

Taitano, Lehua. *A Bell Made of Stones*. Kāne'ohe, HI: TinFish Press, 2014.

Trask, Haunani-Kay. *Eros and Power: The Promise of Feminist Theory*. Philadelphia: University of Pennsylvania Press, 1986.

——. *From a Native Daughter: Colonialism and Sovereignty in Hawai'i*. Honolulu: University of Hawai'i Press, 1993.

——. *Light in the Crevice Never Seen*. Corvallis, OR: Calyx Books, 1994.

——. *Night is a Sharkskin Drum*. Honolulu: University of Hawai'i Press, 2002.

——. "Writing in Captivity: Poetry in a Time of Decolonization." *Inside Out: Literature, Cultural Politics, and Identity in the New Pacific*. Ed. Vilsoni Hereniko & Rob Wilson. New York: Rowman & Littlefield, 1999. 17–26.

Wendt, Albert, ed. *Nuanua: Pacific Writing in English since 1980*. Honolulu: University of Hawai'i Press, 1995.

4

Clear-Cut

The Importance of Mixedblood Identities and the Promise of Native American Cosmopolitanism to Native American Literatures

Chris LaLonde

Strange though it may seem for a chapter on mixedblood identities and Native cosmopolitanism in a section of a *Companion to Native American Literature* devoted to "Identities," let us begin with a film. *Clearcut* (1991), a little-seen and, I think, under-appreciated film starring First Nations/Native American actors Graham Greene (Oneida), Tom Jackson (Metis), and Floyd Red Crow Westerman (Sisseton-Wahpeton Sioux), focuses on the conflict between logging company interests and the destruction of the natural world resulting from clear-cutting in the name of industry and progress. On one side stands the mill manager Bud Rickets, played by Michael Hogan and, on the other, Natives protesting the proposed road that is necessary in order to get more stems to the mill, the tribe's white lawyer Peter Maguire, played by Ron Lea, who argues their case in court, and the character of Arthur, played by Greene, who after the defeat in court takes Maguire's joke seriously and compels the lawyer to kidnap Rickets. Bound but nevertheless self-assured, even cocky, Rickets tries to engage Arthur on both what his mill has destroyed and native tradition. He rattles off all that mill has brought to the reserve and when Arthur says reserve plumbing doesn't work Rickets replies, "Well get it fixed chief, it's free. Put your bottle on the table and pick up the phone." Pretending to voice Arthur – and, it seems, all Natives – he adds with a tone derisive and sarcastic "look at me, I have an identity." Setting Rickets' derision aside, if only briefly, the proclamation of identity weds nicely with concerns over and articulations of Native identity, both historical and contemporary, that one finds throughout Native American Literature and its criticism. Native literary voices rise from the heart of the Haudenosaunee Confederacy to the Pueblos, from the low lands and hill country of Mississippi and Alabama to the deep woods and urban environs of the upper Midwest, from the Pacific shore and coastal range to the Backbone of the World, from the Nation(s) of Oklahoma, to declare singly and together "we are still here."[1]

Rickets mocks Arthur because with word and deed Arthur lays claim to agency. While Rickets will say that he understands Arthur because he, like Rickets, is a man of action, the truth is that Rickets would have the *indian* remain an object, a construction captured in the word "chief" with which the mill manager hails the *indian*. The italicized lower-case *indian* is White Earth Anishinaabe writer and theorist Gerald Vizenor's, of course, the sign signaling the construction created and perpetuated by the dominant society that renders the Native, in all her/his complexity and richness, absent. In work stretching from *The Everlasting Sky: New Voices of the People Named the Chippewa* (1972) through the aptly titled *The People Named the Chippewa* (1983), *Fugitive Poses* (1998), and on, Vizenor drives home the point that the *indian* has "no native ancestors ... it is a simulation, the absence of natives" (*Fugitive Poses* 15). Writing specifically about the Anishinaabe in 1972, Vizenor says

> the cultural and political histories of the *anishinabe* were written in the language of those who invented the *indian*, renamed the tribe, allotted the land, divided ancestry by geometric degrees – the federal government identifies the *anishinabe* by degrees of *indian* blood – and categorized identity by the geography of colonial reservations.
>
> (*Everlasting Sky* 13)[2]

The *indian*, that is, speaks to and embodies the dominant society's wishes and fears. In Deborah Madsen's fine phrasing, the dominant society "posits insistently Native people as 'Vanished,' or as tragic victims, or as ig/noble savages frozen in a mythical past, or even as ecowarriors in an idealized New Age future" (66). Rickets sees Arthur as savage, locked in the past, unwilling or unable to pick up the phone and call to get reserve plumbing fixed. His admonition for Arthur to "pick up the phone, chief" drives home how information and communication technologies (ICT) are used to perpetuate the othering images captured in the stereotypical "chief."[3]

Whatever clarity of tone and rhythm, of song and thus of vision, the natural world and its other-than-human inhabitants offer is drowned out by the chainsaws felling and limbing trees and the de-barking machinery and saws of Rickets' mill. Native American literatures would have us hear "bell and beat" as well as individual articulations of personhood and subjectivity, the phrasing and celebration of community, and proclamations of sovereignty.[4] There are any number of Native literary texts in which the natural world has something to offer us, to teach us, if only we would listen differently. Chickasaw writer Linda Hogan's work comes to mind, including her novels *Power* and *Solar Storms*, as does Silko's work of course, fitting given that she has written of how landscape is a character in her fiction. So too should "Driving in Oklahoma" by Osage poet Carter Revard. The narrator "grooving down the highway" at 70 mph hears five piercing notes from a meadowlark and is left

> wanting
> to move again through country that a bird
> has defined wholly with song
> and maybe next time see how
> he flies so easy, when he sings.
>
> (11)

With its depiction of the threat clear-cutting poses for the earth and its inhabitants, *Clearcut* sounds a note that resonates with cosmopolitanism, one of the three major critical perspectives on Native literatures, the others being nationalism and indigenism, that Arnold Krupat identified in *Red Matters* (2002). Although eleven years later he re-labels indigenism trans-indigenism and adds a fourth perspective when he again surveys the field,

Krupat continues to hold that the perspectives are not mutually exclusive, writing in 2002 that they are "overlapping and interlinking (1) and in 2013 that there is a "necessary and complementary relationship" between them ("Four Perspectives" 12). One instance of shared concern, germane for our purposes because it resonates with our opening move, has to do with the natural world. While indigenist criticism of Native literature in the United States has, Krupat argues, developed to include a trans-indigenist and comparativist element, particularly in the work of Chadwick Allen, it continues both to "unsettle the epistemological assumptions that underline Western socio-political hegemonies" ("Four Perspectives" 34) and to hold that it is "the *earth* – nature, the ecosphere, or biosphere – that is the source of the knowledge and values a critic must bring to bear on literary analysis" ("Four Perspectives" 11). The same holds, Krupat notes in 2002, for the cosmopolitan perspective (*Red Matters* 23), and in 2013 he extends the connection between the indigenist and the cosmopolitanist approaches to explicitly include, if you will, the ecological: cosmopolitanism being "based upon what I've several times noted, that different as we may be one from another we are all equivalently subject to the risks to the planet and its environment" ("Four Perspectives" 36).[5]

There are multiple cosmopolitanisms or neo-cosmopolitanisms of course, each tending to have a different point of emphasis. In his Introduction to *Indigenous Cosmopolitans: Transnational and Transcultural Indigeneity in the Twenty-first Century* (2010), Maximilian Forte writes:

> There is the spatial definition where the cosmopolitan is someone who moves across global space; the social definition of the stranger who never really belongs to any community; the political definition of a "citizen of the world" whose rights are liberal democratic and individualist ones supported by international institutions; the structural definition of the class position of the cosmopolitan; the moral definition, featuring someone who shows solidarity with strangers; and the essential definition [holding that we are all cosmopolitan because we all have certain natural rights].
>
> (5)

Forte and the contributors to the volume hold for an indigenous cosmopolitanism, one that "can be both rooted and routed, nonelite yet nonparochial, provincial without being isolated, internationalized without being de-localized" (Forte 6).

It bears pointing out that Creek scholar and novelist Craig Womack, in his chapter of *American Indian Literary Nationalism* that he co-authored with Cherokee scholar Jace Weaver and Osage scholar Robert Warrior, noted as a first principle for allies committed to literary nationalism a link between the local and the international:

> Just as tribes are related to the outside world of local municipalities, state governments, federal Indian law, and international relations (American Indian presence on U.N. task forces on indigenous peoples being a key example), literary nationalism can do local work with global implications, thus demonstrating a more profound cosmopolitanism than has been argued for to date [2006], one with strong roots at its base.
>
> (168–69)

MIXEDBLOOD IDENTITIES

Here is the same language of roots and routes that one finds in efforts to articulate an indigenous cosmopolitanism from a social science perspective. What is clear, then, is that place matters, still, and I would say the same holds for sovereignty. With both the local and the global, with the trans-indigenous/transnational and the cosmopolitan, what also matters, critically, are the earth and all its inhabitants.[6]

When Rickets says Arthur's name the pronunciation slides to author and in doing so reminds us that before the filmic, be it moving or still, the written word was, and is, used to position the Native as *indian*. Weaver reminds us that "Three primary stereotypes of Indians dominate literary representations of them: the noble savage (the 'good' Indian), the bloodthirsty savage (the 'bad' Indian), and the half-breed" (*Red Atlantic* 243). In his fiction, Choctaw-Cherokee-Cajun-Irish writer and scholar Louis Owens makes clear the role canonical American literature plays in shaping the American imaginary when it comes to the *indian*. For instance, *The Sharpest Sight*, Owens' second novel, establishes its concern with and over canonical American literature by taking for its epigraph a quotation from Jonathan Edwards' "Sinners in the Hands of an Angry God": "the arrows of death fly unseen at noonday; the sharpest sight cannot discern them." Peppered throughout the novel are references to and discussions of *Moby-Dick*, *Adventures of Huckleberry Finn*, William Faulkner's "The Bear," and other literary texts. Those texts are part of what Luther Cole calls the "romance" whites have "going with death, they love it, and they want Indians to die for them" (216). The dominant society, Luther tells Onatima and Owens tells his reader, tries "to write us to death" (216).

As Weaver points out, miscegenation makes the "half-breed" an especially odious figure in literary representations produced by the dominant culture and that the stereotypes often picture the "half-breed" as trapped between worlds, "distrusted by both whites and Natives" (*Red Atlantic* 243–44). It is, then, perhaps little wonder that when Native artists turn to writing one often finds characters of mixed ancestry populating their texts. In the groundbreaking *Other Destinies: Understanding the American Indian Novel* (1992), Owens rightly observes that again and again the novels produced by Native writers from the 1930s to the early 1990s feature mixedblood characters. While the difficulty of negotiating the terrain of two worlds and cultures, Euroamerican and the particular Native culture of the protagonist(s), is depicted to be sure, as is the case for Archilde Leon in D'Arcy McNickle's *The Surrounded* (1936) and the title character in James Welch's *The Death of Jim Loney* (1979). One sees in texts such as Leslie Marmon Silko's *Ceremony* (1977) ways forward for the mixedblood and her/his people. Beginning with Owens' second novel, one also sees in his work mixedblood characters able to avoid the stereotypical trap of being lost between worlds and doomed as a result. Both Cole McCurtain in *The Sharpest Sight* and *Bone Game* and Will Striker in *Nightland* are able, finally, to embrace community and worldview as they are articulated in and through Choctaw and Cherokee culture respectively.

This is not to say that Native writers and their texts suggest either that negotiating or managing mixed ancestry is necessarily easy and without difficulty or danger. As the poem "The Truth is" by mixedblood Chickasaw writer Linda Hogan reminds the reader, "The truth is/we are crowded together/and knock against each other at night. /We want amnesty' (4). The poem's persona addresses "Linda," reminding her, and us, "Girl, I say/it is dangerous to be a woman of two countries" (5). Left hand red, right white, both driven deep into empty pockets, the poem is well aware that an enemy is in a pocket, that it kills, that it is critical to keep moving.

55

In "Poet Woman's mitosis: Dividing all the cells apart," Miwok-Hopi poet Wendy Rose phrases for the reader the difficulty faced by urban mixedbloods trying to maintain connections with a culture from which they are some distance removed in space and, in generational terms at least, in time. With the poem's first line, following an epigraph quoting a 1950 Tucson Indian School document describing how one cannot expect *indians* to embrace quickly contemporary Euroamerican society and ways, the poem's narrator declares she is a mixedblood from the city trying to learn the songs that singers of an earlier generation know in their being and in the world. The narrator can only mimic the sound of the singers early on, even though she knows she is Hopi in her very being. Still, although she recognizes that the particulars of the song are elsewhere, she declares that she too will sing.

Rose takes the trope to which the dominant society would lay claim in order to create and master the *indian*, skin, and makes it her own. It is the skin that bears the sores born of distance and displacement, to be sure, but it is also the skin, because she is Hopi, upon which the sores will eventually burst so that she might burst forth in traditional song. That song is measured to and with the natural world. Pain then yes, certainly, but not without end, nor without the promise of finding one's voice and community.

In his articulation of cosmopolitanism as the area of inquiry has developed, including the paucity of attention paid in key texts by Ulrich Beck and Paul Gilroy to Native Americans, Krupat draws attention to Walter Mignolo's 2000 essay "The Many Faces of Cosmo-Polis: Border Thinking and Critical Cosmopolitanism." Attention and commitment to border thinking runs through Mignolo's work, from *Local Histories/Global Designs: Coloniality, Subaltern Knowledges, and Border Thinking* (2000) to *The Darker Side of Western Modernity: Global Futures, Decolonial Options* (2011). Border thinking is "epistemically disobedient" ("Geopolitics" 276), as those engaged in it, termed by Mignolo "the anthropos" who "dwell and think in the borders" ("Geopolitics" 276) to which they have been consigned by the "humanitas" that has created them as other, call into question both the construct and the categories of thought that shape people and the world. As Mignolo puts it, succinctly, "the 'other' doesn't exist ontologically. It is a discursive invention" ("Geopolitics" 275). Forcefully in play, the invention can only be countered by border thinking and border epistemology that, having delinked from the thought and constructions of the West and its definition of modernity, would have us think and see differently. In Mignolo's words, "border thinking is by definition thinking in exteriority, in the spaces and time that the self-narrative of modernity invented as its outside to legitimize its own logic of coloniality" ("Geopolitics" 282).

Dwelling and thinking in the borders, being epistemically disobedient, and both recognizing and refusing to be defined and delimited by the construction *indian* created by the dominant society is a cogent, if unintentional, description of the critical projects of two mixedblood Native writers with sustained explorations of mixedblood identity and the natural world: Owens and Vizenor. Owens would have us reclaim the frontier and apprehend its connection to the figure of the mixedblood. Vizenor, for whom "some upsetting is necessary" (Bowers & Silet 46), has devoted his career to pointing out and undoing the sign *indian* in ways that are nothing if not epistemically disobedient.[7]

Some twenty years ago Owens recast territory and frontier in order that we might imagine the latter as "a multidirectional zone of resistance" (*Mixedblood Messages* 41). Revised and retitled for *Mixedblood Messages*, the new title squarely placing the key terms before the reader, "Mapping the Mixedblood: Frontier and Territory in Native America" asks us to see the frontier not in terms of the mastering narrative of the Nation and Manifest Destiny but as a contact zone of possibility and play. As a borderland, the frontier, for Owens, is "a shimmering, always changing zone of multifaceted contact within which every utterance is challenged and interrogated, all referents put into question" (*Mixedblood Messages* 26). Chief among those referents to be questioned are *indian* and mixedblood. With their work, Owens argues in the essay and indeed throughout his critical work on Native literatures and mixedblood identity, Native literary artists and their characters resist the "ideology of containment" that strives to fix the Native as *indian* and "insist upon the freedom to reimagine themselves within a fluid, always shifting frontier space" (*Mixedblood Messages* 27).

Weaver, Creek Craig Womack, and Osage Robert Warrior are careful in *American Indian Literary Nationalism* (2006) not to overtly critique Owens' work, stating in their Preface that a "footloose, rootless, mixed-blood hybridity [is what] people too casually take away from Owens's work" and decrying the fact that the work

> has begun to be taken up methodologically by those opposed to literary nationalism and by others who pay lip service to Native sovereignty, but seem to have little or no attachment to the centrality of Native nationhood to contemporary Native people.
>
> (xx)

Weaver reiterates the point in *Notes from a Miner's Canary: Essays on the State of Native America* (2010), writing that people "too casually take away from Owens's work ... particularly the unfortunate *Mixedblood Messages* ... a vision in which hybridity is all" (9).

I like to imagine that what is unfortunate is that, in seeing Owens' emphasis on mixedblood identity in Native texts – the "core subject" of *Mixedblood Messages* (142) – and what the "problematic word 'mixedblood' means" (142), casual readers may well miss, for instance, that with very nearly the first word of the autobiographical "Blood Trails: Missing Grandmothers and Making Worlds" Owens invokes both Choctaw language and the Cherokee Nation:

> The word "Oklahoma" resonates deeply through my childhood. This state with a Choctaw name meaning the land of the red people was the "Nation" in stories told by my mother, aunt, uncle, and grandmother, a place of great pain and beauty often remembered in the same utterance.
>
> (*Mixedblood Messages* 135)

It is only after hearing for years as a child these stories and their articulation of both family and the Nation that the young Owens came to realize that the Nation "meant Cherokee Nation" (150). An attention to mixedblood identity and an attention to nationalism and sovereignty need not be exclusive. I like to imagine, too, that in essays offering the images of "people surviving together – Indian and white," while it behooves us to see them "as human beings who loved one another while crossing borders and erasing boundaries and, despite immeasurable odds, *surviving* that they deserve our recognition and utmost respect" (148), it is equally the case that we see, no matter the routes either taken or forced upon them – by the promise of a better life, by poverty, by the federal government – being rooted in traditional stories and "generational storytelling" (*Mixedblood Messages* 150) is what helps to make survival – individual, community, Nation – possible for Natives, mixedblood and full.

Owens considers the frontier trickster space and trickster that which "defies appropriation and resists colonization" (*Mixedblood Messages* 26). Like trickster and trickster discourse, mixedbloods, according to Vizenor, "Loosen the seams in the shrouds of identity" ("Crows" 101). "Shrouds" is telling, for it invokes the garment that conceals that which is to be buried. The shroud, then, is the *indian*, that construction that would conceal Natives and lay them to rest once and for all. Specifically for the purposes of this chapter, then, the concealing garment is the construction of the half-breed, or "breed."

Returning a final time to *Clearcut*, the film resonates with a moment in Vizenor's work, for, tellingly, he links clear-cutting and mixedbloods. The passage is rich enough to warrant quoting in full:

> The United States is not the first government in the world to demand so much from racial categories and measurements of blood and tribal descent, but the practice of determining tribal identities by geometric degrees of blood, or blood quantums, as if blood could be measured in degrees, has elevated a racist unscientific method to the level of a federal statute. On the other hand, the federal government pursued policies of both elimination and assimilation of tribal cultures, while on the backhand, mixedbloods were stranded like dandelions between the stumps on new meadows. Some mixedbloods were cast in literature and official reports as the griseous reminders of the romantic past, or the loose coins from the economic rape of the land, but whatever the images, mixedbloods were clearcut, with few exceptions, from the political present.
>
> (Vizenor *People* 106)

Here, Vizenor suggests that the violent removal of mixedbloods from the political landscape, then and now, is, as is the case with clear-cutting, short-sighted and unwise. One also finds in the passage an invocation of the stereotypical *indian* relegated to the past, of an early sounding of the possibility and promise of the trans-indigenist approach, of a transnational turn, of the connections to be made between Native studies and ecocriticism, and of the political emphasis critical to the nationalist approach. The year was 1984.

"American *indians*," Vizenor writes in *Fugitive Poses*,

> are never the same as natives. The *indians* are that uncertain thing of discoveries, and the absence of natives. … the *indigene*, that real sense of presence, memories, and coincidence is born in native stories. The trick is to create a new theater of native names.
>
> (69)

To counter the stereotype, to undo both it and the violent eradication of mixedblood natives from the political present *circa* the early 1980s and I would argue up to the present moment, eradication crystallized with the term "clearcut" (*People* 106), Vizenor invokes the new name "crossblood." At once an invocation and re-appropriation of Natty Bumppo's

MIXEDBLOOD IDENTITIES

continued assertion that he is a man without a cross in his blood, Vizenor's crossblood is a recognition and celebration of mixedblood identity. That identity is a "torsion in the blood." Vizenor's phrase speaks volumes, for the twist of torsion invokes the double helix of identity. What is more, and this is critical, whether one is referring to a single strand or two, or more, strands together, the twist is only possible because the base remains solid, fixed. That base is Native. As Krupat astutely points out in *Red Matters*, more than merely a proclamation of

> "emergent hybridity" … the identity Vizenor has elaborately been defining and redefining has at its base the deep and unmistakable roots of "tribal" values – which can and indeed must be taken along wherever one may go – to the cities, to Europe, to China, anywhere. These values wish to substitute for Western ideologies of "progress" and "dominance," ideologies of what Vizenor has called "continuance" and "survivance."
>
> (112)

What holds for Vizenor holds for other mixedblood writers. Early in her memoir *The Woman Who Watches over the World*, for instance, Linda Hogan writes of sitting and talking before the ocean with her Chumash-Papago friend Georgianna Sanchez; the women eventually grow silent as they fall

> quietly into the rhythms of the shining ocean. It is not insignificant that we are *Native women* [emphasis added], because history lives cell-deep within us. And as we talked we added history to the list of causes of illness. The split of cultures has come to dwell in our skin.
>
> (20)

The split here is not mixedblood identity but that cleaving born of the violent and violating positioning by the dominant, Euroamerican culture of the Native as *indian*.

In the memoir Hogan writes of a trip taken with her father to Oklahoma, of something of the history of her family and of the Chickasaw. She says that following Removal the people seemed lost (117); crucially, she adds a little later that for some mixedbloods this feeling of loss, born due to the dominant society's prohibition against traditional cultural practices and native languages, is especially troubling, for memories and connections to their Native identity are especially important. Although her grandmother's house in the Territory has burned down and there are shards of the material goods of her family left discarded and weathering on the ground, Hogan says the connection to her Chickasaw ancestry and culture remains and is rooted in the traumatic route her people were forced to take West: "I am one of the children who lived inside my grandmother, and was carried, cell, gene, and spirit, within mourners along the Trail of Tears" (123).

Hogan will muse that the betwixt and between the worlds she found herself in as a young girl traveling to Europe with her parents – between not simply cultures but between "girlhood and womanhood" (34) – and that her time as an adult spent traveling between places, might mean that "Perhaps 'between' was, is, at the root of my existence" (34). Nevertheless, she says early on that it is her Chickasaw roots that ground her:

All I know is that my life has never fully existed in the other, mainstream, America. There is a larger sphere of our context to be taken into consideration. It is in the America that reveres the land, that is attached, like the clay woman, to where we dwell. Georgianna and I are from the America of other, first people. Like the broken woman who watches over the injured world, we are connected to the land.
(21)

Although she is well aware that, as a mixedblood, "I contain blood of both victim and victimizer" (119–20), she holds that "there are forces deeper than blood. It is to these that I look, to the roots of tradition and their growth from ages-old integrity and knowledge of the world" (120). The tradition, the integrity, and the knowledge that she invokes, that shape her, is Chickasaw.

Hogan lights upon writing when she acknowledges the blood of the victimizer, telling the reader that "my mother's grandfather wrote in his journal about killing buffalo and how he saw Indians and they seem peaceful" (120). The invocation is fitting, for it is in and with writing that Native literary artists can lay claim to a nuanced and grounded mixedblood identity. This is the, necessary, note sounded at the end of Kimberly Blaeser's "Certificate of Live Birth: Escape from the Third Dimension." There the narrative voice of the poem considers what may have led her mother to misidentify herself as Caucasian on her child's birth certificate and whether now, years later, the daughter, now grown, should correct it. She opts not to, recognizing that the mark "is more accurate/just as it stands" (85), not just as a mark of the mother's life but as "the history of Indian people in this country" (85), a mark that tells a story of capture and of the struggle to survive for both her and all Natives. Let the final word be Blaeser's:

> And, Mother, this poem is the certificate of our live birth
> For together we have escaped their capture
> Our time together outdistances their prison
> It "stands in the ruins" within the circle of our lives:
>> Father, caucasian.
>> Mother, American Indian.
>> Daughter, mixedblood.
>
> (86)[8]

Notes

1 Both non-Native and Native scholars have pointed out the importance of identity to an understanding of Native literature, and indeed of its criticism, from early works such as Charles Larson's *American Indian Fiction* (1978) and Arnold Krupat's *The Voice in the Margin: Native American Literature and the Canon* (1989) and "Identity and Difference in the Criticism of Native American Literature" (1983) to works by White Earth Anishinaabe Gerald Vizenor, his fellow band member Kimberly Blaeser, and Choctaw-Cherokee-Cajun-Irish Louis Owens.

2 Anishinaabe and Anishinabe are both accepted spellings of this particular Native nation.

3 That the line is delivered in a movie is both fitting and telling, for film from its earliest days in the United States has been used to disseminate images of the *indian*. Vizenor voices his awareness of this in the explanatory note for a 1989 essay when he writes, concerning his use of Umberto Eco's term "hyperreality," that "Tribal people, in this sense, have been invented as 'absolute fakes'

in social science models, cinema, and popular media" (*Crossbloods* 55). The late Louis Owens was also acutely aware of cinema's role in disseminating *indian* images, devoting a section of his first collection of essays, memoir, and creative non-fiction, *Mixedblood Messages: Literature, Film, Family, Place* (1998), to films ranging from the Westerns of John Ford and John Wayne to Kevin Costner's *Dances with Wolves*. Of the latter, Costner wrote "It will forever be my love letter to the past" (qtd. in *Mixedblood Messages* 114); a love letter, Owens argues, that is "a cinemagraphically painful, lyrically moving, heart-string pulling love letter to an absolutely fake American past that Euroamericans invented as a sanitized, romantic version of the ugly realities of colonization and genocide. Costner's film buys it all, repackages it, and makes more palatable the age-old clichés and unwavering metanarrative" (*Mixedblood Messages* 115–16). Costner's phrasing is apt, whether he knows it or not, for *Dances with Wolves* is about writing (recall the journal Dunbar goes back to the frontier post in an effort to retrieve); about inscription; about representation. My turn to Vizenor and Owens is calculated, of course, given each's concern with questions of writing, representation, and mixedblood identities.

4 "Bell and beat" are from Miwok-Hopi Wendy Rose's "Poet woman's mitosis: Dividing all the cells apart."

5 In a note a little later in the essay, Krupat makes clear both that he recognizes Beck's "World-Risk Society" at best glosses over the inconvenient truth that we are all in fact not equally at risk, at least in the short-term, and that his commitment to cosmopolitanism does not shy from the fact that people of color and the poor are often first at risk. The poem "Downwinders," by Blaeser, powerfully makes the same point. There, in response to someone saying "'We all live downwind and downstream'" the narrator thinks "about how in this land of equal rights and equal justice/'Some of us are more equal than others'" (*Trailing You* 54).

6 I type this note in the afterglow of an Argentine court having granted basic legal rights to an orangutan named Sandra, her lawyers having successfully argued that she is a person in the philosophical sense and, as such, she was being deprived her basic right to liberty by being held in a Buenos Aires zoo.

7 Given that Mignolo offers an alternative narrative of the West, one that begins not in ancient Greece but in the northwest Mediterranean and on the North Atlantic and the beginnings of "the emergence of the Atlantic commercial circuit in the sixteenth century that linked the Spanish crown with capitalist entrepreneurs from Genoa, with Christian missionaries, with Amerindian elites, and with African slaves" ("Many Faces" 725), given too that Weaver published in 2014 *The Red Atlantic*, a project that Krupat writes of approvingly in its initial essay form, it is worth noting that in his Preface Weaver states in no uncertain terms that, in addition to re-writing the history of the Atlantic to include Natives, he

> intend[s] to explode broadly held (and tenacious) misconceptions about indigeneity that I have been refuting my entire career. Too many want to see mixed bloods, mestizos, metis, or (to use Gerald Vizenor's descriptive term) crossbloods as somehow diminished in Indianness.

This is problematic, at best, wrong at worst. Rather, Weaver continues, "One must interrogate each case individually and examine the figure's self-identification and commitments" (xi).

8 An unfortunate limitation of a chapter such as this is that there is not the space needed to discuss precisely where and how the literary works mentioned are rooted in specific tribal cultures, histories, contemporary circumstances, and worldviews. I have long held, as have others, how critical it is that we attend to and read in light of those roots.

Works cited

Allen, Chadwick. *Blood Narrative: Indigenous Identity in American Indian and Maori Literary and Activist Texts*. Durham, NC: Duke University Press, 2002.

——. "A Transnational Native American Studies? Why Not Studies that Are Trans-*Indigenous*?" *Journal of Transnational American Studies* 4 (2012): 1–22.

Blaeser, Kimberly. *Trailing You*. Greenfield Center, NY: Greenfield Review Press, 1996.

Bowers, Neal & Charles Silet. "An Interview with Gerald Vizenor." *MELUS* 8.1 (1981): 41–49.

Clearcut. Dir. Ryszard Bugajski. Perf. Graham Greene, Ron Lea, and Floyd Red Crow Westerman. Northern Arts Entertainment, 1991. Film.

Forte, Maximilian, ed. *Indigenous Cosmopolitans: Transnational and Transcultural Indigeneity in the Twenty-first Century*. New York: Peter Lang, 2010.

Hogan, Linda. *Power*. New York: W.W. Norton, 1999.

——. *Solar Storms*. New York: Scribner's, 1997.

——. "The Truth is." *Seeing Through the Sun*. Amherst: University of Massachusetts Press, 1985. 4–5.

——. *The Woman Who Watches over the World*. New York: W.W. Norton, 2001.

Krupat, Arnold. "Identity and Difference in the Criticism of Native American Literature." *Diacritics* 13. 2 (Summer 1983): 2–13.

——. "Nationalism, Transnationalism, Trans-Indigenism, Cosmopolitanism: Four Perspectives on Native American Literatures." *Journal of Ethnic American Literature* 3 (January 2013): 5–63.

——. *Red Matters: Native American Studies*. Philadelphia: University of Pennsylvania Press, 2002.

——. *The Voice in the Margin: Native American Literature and the Canon*. Berkeley: University of California Press, 1989.

Larson, Charles. *American Indian Fiction*. Albuquerque: University of New Mexico Press, 1978.

Madsen, Deborah. "On Subjectivity and Survivance: Rereading Trauma through *The Heirs of Columbus* and *The Crown of Columbus*." *Survivance: Narratives of Native Presence*. Ed. Gerald Vizenor. Lincoln: University of Nebraska Press, 2008. 61–87.

McNickle, D'Arcy. *The Surrounded*. 1936. Rpt. Albuquerque: University of New Mexico Press, 1993.

Mignolo, Walter. *The Darker Side of Western Modernity: Global Futures, Decolonial Options*. Durham, NC: Duke University Press, 2011.

——. "Geopolitics of Sensing and Knowing: On (De)coloniality, Border Thinking, and Epistemic Disobedience." *Postcolonial Studies* 14.3 (2011): 273–83.

——. *Local Histories/Global Designs: Coloniality, Subaltern Knowledges, and Border Thinking*. Princeton, NJ: Princeton University Press, 2000.

——. "The Many Faces of Cosmo-Polis: Border Thinking and Critical Cosmopolitanism." *Public Culture* 12. 3 (Fall 2000): 721–48.

Owens, Louis. *Bone Game*. Norman: University of Oklahoma Press, 1994.

——. *Mixedblood Messages: Literature, Film, Family, Place*. Norman: University of Oklahoma Press, 1998.

——. *Nightland*. Norman: University of Oklahoma Press, 1996.

——. *Other Destinies: Understanding the American Indian Novel*. Norman: University of Oklahoma Press, 1992.

——. *The Sharpest Sight*. Norman: University of Oklahoma Press, 1992.

Revard, Carter. *How the Songs Come Down*. London: Salt Publishing, 2005.

Rose, Wendy. *Lost Copper*. Banning, CA: Malki Museum Press, 1980.

Silko, Leslie Marmon. *Ceremony*. 1977. Rpt. New York: Penguin, 1986.

Vizenor, Gerald. *Crossbloods: Bone Courts, Bingo and Other Reports*. Minneapolis: University of Minnesota Press, 1990.

——. "Crows Written on the Poplars: Autocritical Autobiographies." *I Tell You Now: Autobiographical Essays by Native American Writers*. Ed. Brian Swann & Arnold Krupat. Lincoln: University of Nebraska Press, 1987. 99–110.

——. *Fugitive Poses*. Lincoln: University of Nebraska Press, 1998.

——. *The Everlasting Sky: New Voices of the People Named the Chippewa*. New York: Cromwell-Collier, 1972. [Reprinted 2000 with new Introduction and Index.]

——. *The People Named the Chippewa*. Minneapolis: University of Minnesota Press, 1984.

——, ed. *Survivance: Narratives of Native Presence*. Lincoln: University of Nebraska Press, 2008.

Weaver, Jace. *Notes from a Miner's Canary: Essays on the State of Native America.* Albuquerque: University of New Mexico Press, 2010.

——. *The Red Atlantic: American Indigenes and the Making of the Modern World, 1000–1927.* Chapel Hill: University of North Carolina Press, 2014.

Weaver, Jace, Craig Womack & Robert Warrior. *American Indian Literary Nationalism.* Albuquerque: University of New Mexico Press, 2006.

Welch, James. *The Death of Jim Loney.* 1979. Rpt. New York: Penguin, 2008.

5

The Problem of Authenticity in Contemporary American "Gone Indian" Stories

Judit Ágnes Kádár

What is Native American writing and who classifies as a Native writer? Who is Indian and what is the nature of indigeneity? In a colonial sense "Native" is a racial identity, while in a tribal sense it is a mode of self-identification. Interestingly, we can observe a move from the notion of identity towards that of self-identification – and more generally from a mono-lithic sense of American identity to mixed identity/race – in American literature of the last few decades. The question of authenticity is still central in contemporary American ethnic writing in two regards: first, in relation to the ethno-cultural affiliation ("blood quantum" versus self-identification) of the writer, and second in terms of the cultural heritage of the central character of the literary text. There remains great confusion about how to tackle the problem of ethno-cultural affiliation or who is authorized to define identity – whether some sort of law, Indigenous agency, or the individual him/herself – but literature offers answers that clearly acknowledge the individual's right to self-definition.

This chapter engages with the problem of defining "Indian," "Native American," and "Indigenous" identities through the perspectives offered by literary texts authored by non-Native writers about characters who undergo indigenization by "going Indian." The critical understanding of indigenization in American literature has been formulated by scholars like the groundbreaking Robert Berkhofer (specifically on the "white man's Indian" in various areas of culture, and on the invention of the Noble Savage and Vanishing Indian images that serve the agenda of colonization throughout U.S. history); Philip Deloria (on ideological fantasy and the national iconography of "playing Indian" and fixing racial boundaries); Marianna Torgovnick (on Primitivism); Terry Goldie (on the image of indigene); Shari Huhndorf (on the Native as an idealized alter ego); Gerald Vizenor (on "Manifest Manners" and the simulation of the "Indian"); Samira Kawash (on the episte-mology of the color line and its literary subversions in fiction about "passing"); and Dagmar Wernitznig (on European appropriations of Native American culture). However, con-temporary understandings of issues of indigenization, Native authentication, validation, legitimation and critical Otherness can be enhanced through the interdisciplinary insights offered by postcolonial studies and research on the racial implications of non-Indigenous Othering or "passing" narratives. "Passing" refers to the practice of presenting oneself as a member of a different and usually more prestigious racial group, in order to gain acceptance and power or to avoid anxiety and frustration. In the context of Indigenous literature, passing refers to texts that present a central character of Euro-American origins who becomes "indigenized" through various styles of "going Indian." Such texts vary in their representation of passing, from the "Grey Owl Syndrome" and the "white man's Indian" to New Age spiritualism, from wilderness fantasy to some forms of the postcolonial novel. Furthermore, passing can also refer to the identity transformation of persons of mixed heritage, where their Indigenous identity comes to dominate and becomes emphatic. Beyond the wilderness fantasies of what Margaret Atwood has termed the "Grey Owl Syndrome" (35–61), I concentrate on what could be called variations of the "postcolonial novel" by Thomas Berger, Charles Frazier, Jim Fergus, Deborah Larsen and Fintan O'Toole. I suggest that interdisciplinary critical approaches, especially those focused on cross-cultural issues and narrative psychology, are helpful in our investigations of the authentication processes and, in a broader sense, all indigenization- and acculturation-related identity changes that the central characters of these "passing" novels go through.

Narrative psychology investigates the specific processes by which fictional characters struggle for identity, meaningful existence and proper communal attachments: how they redefine their "identity states," the kind of personal and social positioning that characterizes them in their "storied lives" (Rosenwald's title), how "selfing" may serve as psychotherapy (de St. Aubin, et al.), how they cope with the problem of authenticity regarding their ties to Native culture, and the ways in which any claim for authenticity influences them. In this chapter, I can only indicate the means by which narratives restructure the narrator's personal life experiences and the manner in which specific discourses work to produce a narrative self. Within literary studies, Werner Sollors among others calls attention to kinship and/or conscious affiliation, ethnic choice and identity as the result of inter-personal interactions (xix). In her introduction to *Native Authenticity* (2010), Deborah Madsen explores the competing cultural discourses in various definitions of Indianness, from blood quantum to the refusal to identify with the term "Indian" as indicative of victimization based on stereotype, and the effort to regain control over discourse. Susan Bernardin discusses "The Authenticity Game" and authenticity as a cultural value, raising questions about the issue of purity in a neo-primitivistic context and beyond.

Recent U.S. writing addresses authenticity in more than one sense, depending on the agency that may validate it. The word actually refers to the quality of being "real," "genuine," or "accurate, credible and very similar." As can be seen in every work of indigenization literature – from captivity narratives to New Age stories – authentication and Native validation (that is, verification as a group member and acceptance by a particular tribal agency) is an important factor for those who pass, who undergo transcultural experiences and who seek new ethnic identity definitions. In addition to this claim for legitimation by Native peers, the protagonist's non-Native environment may also validate the ethnic identity of the character. Both forms of validation belong to the alter-ascribed definitions (definitions offered by characters other than the "passing" protagonist) that the character in question may or may not acknowledge as relevant forces that shape life and consciousness. However, recent literature calls attention to another kind of authentication, and that is the self-esteem of the protagonist in relation to which the reader is also authorized to judge and validate.

Interdisciplinary critical attention devoted to the problem of transculturation, its background, processes and impacts has been limited mainly to the phenomenon of "playing (the white man's) Indian": for instance, in work by Robert Berkhofer, James Clifton, Terry Goldie, and Daniel Francis. Cultural critics, like Philip Deloria and Ward Churchill, approach this problematic from a more ideological perspective, acknowledging that authenticity is a central problem in all "passing" experiences. Whether a character recognizes the commercial power of Indianness, the spiritual force of Native culture, or a deeper level of genetic, spiritual and mythological identification, the reader is invited to explore the difference between superficial identification based on masking and profound experiences of acculturation and integration. Deloria shows the literary Indian to be an essential part of the U.S. national mythology (73) and the epic national quest for legitimation. However, more recent movements like primitivism and New Age spiritualism have attempted to validate the aspirations of those longing for identification with Native culture. Nevertheless, since the late 1960s, the Red Power and American Indian Movements, which organized social protests and called for the expression of pan-Indianism through activism as well as through the Indian Renaissance in the arts, claimed rights over this kind of legitimation. Native critics like David Treuer argue that their peers have less opportunity to publish their literary work, "unless they lard their prose with perceived Indianisms and authenticating marks" (190). In addition, while the difference between actual Indigenous people and the image of the Noble Savage or Vanishing Indian has encouraged some non-Natives to believe that original tribal cultures have vanished, Natives have been accused of being inauthentic upholders of their traditions (Deloria 69–70, 91). Consequently, the discursive way has been opened for non-Natives to claim equal access to and rights to practice Native lifestyles.

One of the best known examples of "going more Indian than any Native-born person" is the Canadian Armand Ruffo's impressive long poem entitled *Grey Owl: the Mystery of Archibald Belaney*: a postmodern retelling of Archie Belaney's successful shape-shifting life, based on his autobiographical fiction. Ruffo's text scrutinizes the problems of authentication, Native validation, and self-legitimation and it greatly helps us understand American indigenization stories, regardless of their period. The long poem follows Archie's life and transformations in a linear chronological order, depicting how the young orphaned child in Hastings, England becomes obsessed with Indianism, what motivations push him towards making a new home in North America and turning into a "fake Indian" – and then what schizophrenic personality changes make him both the most successful Indian but also the loneliest person on earth. Ruffo presents the protagonist from multiple narrative perspectives, showing how the people in Archie/Grey Owl's environment try to understand him, while they also have constant doubts about his credibility and authenticity as Grey Owl. Manipulation strategies, self-deception, sheer materialism and deep identification with Native American values, these are all part of Belaney's turbulent world. Psychoanalytical investigation is central to the story and to Ruffo's wonderful narrative presentation of it, making this long poem an essential guide for the better understanding of other indigenization stories.

In her essay, "Simulation of Authenticity," Drucilla Mims Wall lists some of the reasons that underlie going or playing Indian, such as an intense longing for meaning, a respect for Mother Earth, eco-tourism, the seeking of connection to sacred places, the search for wisdom and truth, and the "longing for recovery" (97–99). Motives such as these are used to justify the appropriation of Native cultural practices evidenced in the widespread European fascination and even obsession with playing Indian. Especially the German-speaking countries, but also the Czech Republic, Poland, Hungary and even Denmark, have a hundred-year-old tradition of Indian hobbyism that takes various forms in leisure activities and powwow Indianism – like dressing and singing for example – that Dagmar Wernitznig explains in her study, *Europe's Indians, Indians in Europe*. The complex psychological and sociological processes of acculturation, including indigenization and going Indian, as well as some of the motivations for passing and attitudes to Native authenticity are presented in the chart, "The Dynamics of Ethnic Identity Change," in *Going Indian: Cultural Appropriation in Recent North American Literature* (108). From a Native perspective based on Scott Momaday's notion of "blood memory," Chadwick Allen engages with the invisibility, non-articulation, and misrepresentation of Native identity that underpins claims for non-Indigenous "recovery of self, place, voice, and community" and the "rearticulation" (160–61) or "reimagination" (163) of the European as indigenous. In *Fugitive Poses*, Gerald Vizenor argues that the appropriation of Native identity through the simulation of Indianness derives from attempts to control cultural representations that are transmitted though movies and in the media: the "longing for authenticity resides in the sacredness of place, not in imagined Indians, not in any purchased piece of imagined authenticity" (112–13). Authenticity becomes problematic in practical life, too, such as the definition of Indian blood quantum, doubts about the identity of urban versus reservation Natives, distortions in many walks of life (such as literary hoaxes, unauthorized healers, wannabes, white shamans and non-Native "Indian expert" academics), as well as the non-Native claim to share Indigenous spirituality as a common human possession (Churchill 193). Wendy Rose discusses what she calls "whiteshamanism" and Kim Tallbear researches New Age appropriations of indigeneity. These Native critics scrutinize the issue of authenticity from different angles but can be read together with Ward Churchill who describes those who make such spurious claims to Indigeneity as the "Culture vultures" who practice "genocide with good intentions" (185).

These concerns all make authenticity a burning issue for many. One of the problems adding to these, however, is the process of selective legitimation that is both physical and intellectual: "chipped off fragments of Indianness, put them into new contexts, and turned them to new users" (Deloria 179). Selective legitimation here may refer to the display of visible markers of ethnicity, such as clothes or rituals, combined with icons of Native spirituality such as the life circle or medicine wheel, but where this display takes place without any engagement in Native lifestyles, especially not those of the kind we can observe in contemporary reservation or urban Indian environments. Figures like Ruffo's Grey Owl, Sylvester Long Lance, Sir William Johnson, Dances with Wolves, and Hollywood's celluloid Indians all provide ample examples of selective identification and authentication. Obviously, the latter can be a conscious or less-conscious process; an integral attribute of one's intercultural moment or an artificial attempt to transform one's self-image. Non-Indigenous passing narratives present a variety of "experiments" in the process of ethnic authentication, which can sensitize the reader both on a communal level to the complexities of cultural genocide and also on an individual level to the implications of passing or masking, and promote the alternative of developing one's own personal sense of authenticity.

In the domain of these literary texts, various forms of the process that we can call "white man going Indian" are presented in passing or Othering or indigenization stories. Thomas Berger's *Little Big Man* (1964) is probably the first novel that ironically challenges the widespread aptitude to judge by racial preconceptions through the creation of a protagonist who occasionally becomes a "fake Indian." Jim Fergus's *One Thousand White Women* (1998), Deborah Larsen's *The White* (2002), Fintan O'Toole's *White Savage: William Johnson and the Invention of America* (2005), and Charles Frazier's *Thirteen Moons* (2007) are indigenization stories that are more or less based on authentic, direct contact experiences of various kinds. However, the question remains: what happens to that primary experience of inter-ethnic contact in the course of the novel? Furthermore, is authenticity relevant, or to the contrary, is fake or makeshift Indianness central? The latter "makeshift Indianness" would be similar to contemporary Canadian texts like Ruffo's *Grey Owl* – in the sense of being prototypical stories of a white man going Indian – or like Philip Kreiner's 1988 novel *Contact Prints*, where the heroine recognizes the commercial power of Indianness. In contrast, in the indigenization narratives presented by Berger, O'Toole, Frazier, Fergus, and Larsen, the protagonist develops a genuine interest in Indigenous culture and acculturates to tribal community life and rituals, though with motivations and impacts that are totally different to those of the Native characters. Daniel Francis claims that due to a broadly shared inability to adjust to the North American continent, many immigrants consequently search for ways of home-making or engage in a quest for identity or suffer from problems of alienation. Thus, they are led to admire Native ways and attempt to "go Indian" by appropriating elements of Native culture into their own lifeways – all to validate their presence on a land that originally and firstly belonged to Indigenous people (189–90). In a broader sense, and in addition to various other motivations, this immigrant experience provides some of the ideological underpinnings of these literary texts.

Berger's *Little Big Man* and the Canadian Robert Kroetsch's *Gone Indian* (1973) are the forerunners of a trend in contemporary North American literature that is thematically focused on ethic and cross-cultural passing experiences and "going" or "playing" Indian in particular. At the crossroads of the emerging postmodernist and postcolonial movements in North American letters, Berger scrutinizes the problem of how power is constructed through narrative, how colonial discourse can re-establish a white man's authority, and more specifically, how someone with great intercultural skills and experience can present in an ironic way the strategies through which authority and control are obtained in language. Berger's protagonist Jack Crabb fits the tradition of earlier American (auto) biographies where an initial shocking childhood experience motivates the individual to move out of the confines of Anglo-American culture towards the unknown land and people of the frontier which, beyond its physical nature, is conceptualized as providing an expanded sense of identity. The preconceived opposition of civilization versus wilderness, or white versus primitivistic imagination, characterizes Crabb's surroundings until his attachment to the Cheyenne grows substantially and he becomes culturally hybrid: his identification as a Cheyenne through his appearance and self-definition are superficial indicators of his fluctuating ethnic affiliation. Jack remains a visitor and whenever he shifts towards Native culture it is towards a more generic Indianness, while he overtly acknowledges the pragmatic value of pretending Indianness and shifting his loyalties as the moment demands. Jack is legitimized by the Cheyenne and his ironic, honest style of narration sustains the narrative credibility, rendering authenticity an interesting issue in the novel.

Jack Crabb challenges the white stereotypes and myths attached to the intercultural experience of being adopted by the Cheyenne through his enactment of ethnic shape-shifting between the two worlds. He rejects the division between these worlds and highlights the individual differences that diminish the importance of race, especially after its constructed nature has been exposed. Crabb/Little Big Man travels far and wide, but his mental shifting and character development finally place him in an unknown territory where the uncertainties surrounding his narrative credibility and the details of his life story do not challenge his predominantly white cultural affiliation. Nevertheless, these points of uncertainty raise questions concerning his private frontier: a mindscape that facilitates the narrative account of clashing frontier fantasies.

Jim Fergus's *One Thousand White Women* presents the late nineteenth-century figure of May Dodd as a less ironic shape-shifter on the frontier. In the novel she takes the opportunity to escape a Chicago lunatic asylum and become an Indian bride in the totally unknown worlds, first of Camp Robinson, Nebraska and then of Tongue River Indian Reservation in Montana. Seeking only a temporary rescue, she does not plan any major ethnic transformation for herself at all. However, after an initial period of adjustment, she recognizes the potential value of taking fuller control of her life by becoming a culture broker. Her perceived and objective life conditions in her white society of origin make her both disillusioned and at the same time interested in what the western frontier can offer her. From the beginning, the central question forming the axis of the novel is: are whites really civilized and the savages truly barbarous? Obviously her presuppositions are shaken by her experiences in both cultures but her capacity for cultural integration and the resolution of difficulties provides her with new perspectives and opportunities as well. She basically sustains her Anglo-American ethnic affiliation, while becoming highly critical of injustice and inhumanity regardless of the color line: "You realize that you were happy among the Indjuns after leaving" (Fergus 163). The pull and push factors of acculturation and value judgment provide the dynamics of her character development. She learns the gap between white stereotypes that are based on ignorance and racial ideology, and a learning-based understanding of Native people. She evaluates her mixed experiences rationally and dislikes moral hypocrisy such as that expressed by Rev. Hare's prejudiced attitude (168), and the racism expressed by the "Niggah"-hater Daisy Lovelace and by Captain Bourke who believes in "God's natural separation of races" (51). In fact both May and her friend Phemie, a black Indian living among the "savages" (70), transgress racial lines. Though she finds supportive peers, May cannot identify entirely with either culture, her sense of belonging to any community is not strong enough for her to identify fully, and her profound disillusionment with white civilization and the difficulties of identifying with the Native world leave her in a vacuum between the two worlds. May is left without clear direction regarding the orientations of her acculturation, though occasionally she seems strong enough, like Larsen's Mary Jemison figure, to create her own personal universe between cultures.

Larsen's *The White* provides us with a contemporary interpretation of the eighteenth-century story of Mary Jemison/Two Falling Voices. The daughter of Irish immigrants on the Pennsylvania frontier during the French and Indian Wars, at the age of sixteen Jemison witnessed the murder of her entire family by Shawnees and then found herself adopted into a Seneca family. She lived as a tribal member for five decades, marrying twice, raising seven children, and then removing herself to a cultural frontier without fully belonging to either culture:

And so, in 1797, Mary, known to her French captors as l'autre, known to the Seneca as Two-Falling-Voices, known to her first husband as Two, known to her second husband as Two-Falling; known to her white neighbors as Mary; known to her white solicitor as Mrs. Jemison; known to her children as Mother; came to own land: more than ten thousand acres.

(178)

Larsen's psychological approach to Jemison's historical life depicts the process of Jemison's ethnic transformation, her decision to refuse repatriation, the costs and benefits of ethno-cultural affiliation and in-betweenness, all from a gendered perspective. Symbolically, the three valleys in which the heroine lives each signify a stage of Mary's life and character development: separation, transformation, and return or refusal to repatriate. Although her initial extremely negative attitude to tribal culture is mostly due to the trauma she experiences, she gradually adopts a comprehensive intercultural repertoire from language to manners and attitudes and, in something of a contrast with Fergus's May Dodd figure, Mary Jemison's hybrid personality emphatically builds on elements from both cultures. The Noble Savage image of Cooperian and Karl Mayean sentimentalism clashes with the reality of daily life and warfare. In the increasingly complex reality in which she lives, Mary develops her own inner world through language: the act of telling and un-telling (173–74). She becomes sensitive to cultural coding and racism. During her semi-intentional process of acculturation her former ethno-cultural identification is overwritten by Native culture but, in the long run and in order to "de-victimize" herself, she is forced to elaborate alternative modes of being; that is, to construct for herself a transcultural hybrid or even "post-ethnic" identity.

Another example of hybridity and self-empowerment by indigenization is provided in Fintan O'Toole's biography, *White Savage: William Johnson and the Invention of America*. The novel explores the slippage between cultures characteristic of what Homi Bhabha calls the "mimic man" (121) through the highly influential historic person, Sir William Johnson/ Warraghiyagey (1715–1774). "The man between" was a dispossessed Irish Catholic turned Protestant who, in the New World, became an Iroquois while his "white self" continued to serve Britain; he owned huge land possessions in America while he was also accepted as an honorary Indian with a Mohawk family. A frontier chameleon, Johnson's character certainly underlines the constructed nature of ethnic identity. His voluntary and deliberate passing as Native is based on the primary motivations of authority, power, and wealth, as opposed to other racial "shifters" who sought escape, adventure, different values, and new attachments in alternative ethnic identifications. Johnson developed extraordinary intercultural and adaptation skills from childhood. Beyond physically "going Indian" and elaborating extensive family and political ties in both cultures, he also located himself in the imagination of the Mohawk as a sachem and cultural mediator of relevance and impact. His dynamic "swinger shifter" role entailed a frequent shift from one social role to another and moral ambivalence which, in terms of authenticity, might place him in contrast to value-oriented shifters, like those described by the Grey Owl Syndrome, who follow their understanding of the positive features of a Native culture and lifestyle. There is a major difference between the primary motivation of those whose indigenization is based on real or perceived advantages of Native American culture that attract the given person to "pass," and those who are not convinced of any real value or personal benefit from going Native other than the benefits that derive from the opinion and interest of outsiders: that is, a socially and economically acknowledged role. In fact authenticity and legitimation emerge as the central questions in any indigenization story for this reason: as readers, we want to know why someone goes Indian/Native, how they do it, and how s/he is perceived and validated by the original and by the host societies.

The figure of Johnson provides an excellent example of the constant evaluation of the costs and benefits of indigenization by the protagonist himself, the narrator and the reader. His semi-integration and multiply faceted personality not only made him a successful agent in the ever-changing social climate of his age, but also presents an example of the "part-time Indian" whose transcultural and inter-ethnic transformation is authentic, despite his multiple loyalties. What seems problematic is the powerful implication of Johnson's figure: his combination of white racial purity and raw Indian toughness (343), and his image as the charismatic Anglo-American with the "ability to marry whiteness with the best aspect of Indian culture" (345). As such, he is represented as an idealized agent of manifest destiny:

> The racially pure embodiment of American values who is yet at home in the wilderness because he had adopted the best of Indian culture. An American with white skin but Indian dress, Christian decency but Indian simplicity, European accomplishments but Indian skills, would have the right to take the West.
>
> (339)

The story of survival on the frontier with the help of Native Americans is merged with the Jack Crabbian figure of the wanderer in Charles Frazier's historical novel *Thirteen Moons*. In fact there are three mediators or cultural in-betweeners in the story: Colonel Will Cooper, "Duke of the Waste Land" (283), his partner May, and a part-time Indian mediator, Featherstone, who is a father-like figure to Will. Will is an orphan who learns basic survival skills and is helped by the Cherokee, especially a man called Bear. He buys a store and tries his business skills. He is elected an honorary tribal leader, but also becomes a self-made "wilderness lawyer" (349), a senator, and an occasional helper of the Natives. He is tricky, smart and skillful, and an interculturally sensitive communicator, which helps him to diminish any acculturation stress. His adopted Native family and direct contact with the Cherokee in a sense make him Native, but in some situations he presents an ambivalent attitude: he is a "party boy" like Long Lance in New York (197), he praises Cherokee trade over Yankee trade, yet he also expresses a typical Eurocentric attitude in business. Through this character ethnic authenticity is presented as a matter of what the moment demands, not an independent ideal or value to follow.

Similar to Berger's Crabb, Will's notion of ethnic identity is based on the strategy of using ethnic identity as a performative role. He claims, for example, "Since I was there to represent the Cherokee, I dressed the part" (184). He is conscious about his appearance, just like Sir William Johnson and the impostors, and he goes Indian when the situation demands:

> My surrender was a show … . I had changed from my normal dress clothes into breechcloth, greasy buckskin leggings, and moccasins laced with woven strands of horsetail dyed red and blue and strung through eyelets cut from the quill ends of bird feathers. … Me – an attorney, a colonel, chief, and a senator. An acquaintance of presidents. … I became quite rational despite my wild attire … . I was their chief and colonel.
>
> (358)

The self-conscious distance between himself and his appearance here establishes him fundamentally as a white man going Native, while there is an important recognition about ethnic identification offered by the narrator: "We agreed to acknowledge that identity is both who you say you are and who the world says you are" (325); that is, ethnic identity both internally recognized and externally ascribed. Will is adopted by the Cherokee and is considered to be one of them, but he remains a "white Indian" with some significant distance from them; as the narrator comments, "He seems rather among them than one of them .... a sense of belonging to no place, neither this, nor to any other" (298). Will's acculturation lacks the component of total immersion and integration, and he makes no real choice in that regard. The novel dramatizes the way in which ethnicity is applied as a mask; Will is acculturated into a tribal community and he goes Native, but nevertheless, he "plays" Indian.

These novels highlight the correlation between social position, prestige, de-victimization, and ethnic choice or transformation, while they also explore the protagonists' learning of culture. This learning process includes cognitive development and socio-cultural adaptation as well as the costs and benefits of intercultural change. Indigenization or "going white man's Indian" is engaged here with an emphasis on the factor of personal choice. The novels discussed in this chapter are only loosely related to Native American writing, since they are written by Anglo-Americans and they scrutinize the "going Indian" phenomenon thematically. All of these texts address the problem of defining who is Indian, who is Indigenous, who is authorized to legitimize the indigeneity of anyone else, how personal and social positioning can influence one's life in "storied lives," and how as a construct and process certain kinds of ethnic identity can bring benefits to the individual. Epistemological uncertainty about racial identity and narrative credibility is the common marker of all the texts, where the narrative is a site that explores indigenization, re-connection with tribal heritage, the acknowledgement of the potential for hybridity, the re-statement of identity, healing, survival, escape, and the combination of all these. Contemporary writers invite the reader to enter the game of authentication and validation, to challenge our perceptions of race, ethnicity and the right to define who we are.

Works cited

Allen, Chadwick. *Blood Narrative: Indigenous Identity in American Indian and Maori Literary and Activist Texts*. Durham, NC: Duke University Press, 2002.

Atwood, Margaret. "The Grey Owl Syndrome." *Strange Things: The Malevolent North in Canadian Literature*. Oxford: Clarendon, 1995. 35–61.

Berger, Thomas. *Little Big Man*. New York: Dial, 1964.

Berkhofer, Robert F., Jr. *The White Man's Indian: Images of the American Indian from Columbus to the Present*. New York: Vintage, 1979.

Bernardin, Susan. "The Authenticity Game: 'Getting Real' in Contemporary American Indian Literature." *True West: Authenticity in the American West*. Ed. William Handley & N. Lewis. Lincoln: Nebraska University Press, 2004. 155–75.

Bhabha, Homi. *The Location of Culture*. London: Routledge, 1994.

Churchill, Ward. *Fantasies of the Master Race: Literature, Cinema and the Colonization of American Indians*. Monroe, ME: Common Courage, 1992.

Clifton, James A. *Being and Becoming Indian: Biographical Studies of North American Frontiers*. Chicago: Dorsey, 1989.

De St. Aubin, Ed, Mary Wandrei, Kim Skerven & Catherine M. Coppolillo. "A Narrative Exploration of Personal Ideology and Identity." *Identity and Story: Creating Self in Narrative.* Ed. Dan P. McAdams, Ruthellen Josselson & Amia Lieblich. Washington, D.C.: American Psychological Association, 2006. 235–44.

Deloria, Philip J. *Playing Indian.* New Haven, CT: Yale University Press, 1998.

Fergus, Jim. *One Thousand White Women: The Journal of May Dodd.* New York: St. Martin's Griffin, 1998.

Francis, Daniel. *The Imaginary Indian: The Image of the Indian in Canadian Culture.* Vancouver: Arsenal Pulp, 1993.

Frazier, Charles. *Thirteen Moons.* Toronto: Vintage, 2007.

Goldie, Terry. *Fear and Temptation: The Image of the Indigene in Canadian, Australian and New Zealand Literatures.* Montreal: McGill-Queen's University Press, 1989.

Huhndorf, Shari M. *Gone Native: Indians in the American Cultural Imagination.* Ithaca, NY: Cornell University Press, 2001.

Kádár, Judit Ágnes. *Going Indian: Cultural Appropriation in Recent North American Literature.* Valencia: Valencia University Press, 2012.

Kawash, Samira. "The Epistemology of Race: Knowledge, Visibility, and Passing." *Dislocating the Color Line: Identity, Hybridity, and Singularity in African-American Narratives.* Stanford, CA: Stanford University Press, 1997. 124–66.

Kreiner, Philip. *Contact Prints.* Toronto, Doubleday, 1987.

Kroetsch, Robert. *Gone Indian.* 1973. Rpt. Nanaimo, BC: Theytus Books, 1981.

Larsen, Deborah. *The White.* New York: Knopf, 2002.

Madsen, Deborah. "Contemporary Discourses on 'Indianness'." *Native Authenticity: Transnational Perspectives on Native American Literary Studies.* Ed. Deborah Madsen. Albany: State University of New York Press, 2010. 1–18.

O'Toole, Fintan. *White Savage: William Johnson and the Invention of America.* London: Faber & Faber, 2005.

Rose, Wendy. "Whiteshamanism: Just What's All This Fuss About Whiteshamanism Anyway?" Web. Accessed 30 Nov. 2014. http://www.english.illinois.edu/maps/poets/m_r/rose/whiteshamanism.htm

Rosenwald, George C. & Richard L. Ochberg, eds. *Storied Lives: The Cultural Politics of Self-Understanding.* New Haven, CT: Yale University Press, 1992.

Ruffo, Armand Garnet. *Grey Owl: the Mystery of Archibald Belaney.* 1996. Rpt. Regina, SK: Coteau, 2000.

Sollors, Werner, ed. *The Invention of Ethnicity.* New York: Oxford University Press, 1989. ix–xx.

Tallbear, Kim. "Indigeneity and Technoscience." Web. Accessed 30 January 2015. http://www.kimtallbear.com/research.html

Torgovnick, Marianna. "Introduction." *Primitive Passions: Men, Women, and the Quest for Ecstasy.* New York: Alfred Knopf, 1996. 3–19.

Treuer, David. *Native American Fiction: A User's Manual.* Saint Paul, MN: Graywolf, 2006.

Vizenor, Gerald. *Fugitive Poses: Native American Scenes of Absence and Presence.* Lincoln: University of Nebraska Press, 1998.

———. *Manifest Manners: Narratives on Postindian Survivance.* Lincoln: University of Nebraska Press, 1994.

Wall, Drucilla Mims. "Simulations of Authenticity: Imagined Indians and Sacred Landscape from New Age to Nature Writing." *True West: Authenticity in the American West.* Ed. William Handley & N. Lewis. Lincoln: Nebraska University Press, 2004. 97–116.

Wernitznig, Dagmar. *Europe's Indians, Indians in Europe: European Perceptions and Appropriations of Native American Cultures from Pocahontas to the Present.* Lanham, MD: University Press of America, 2007.

6

Indigenous Writers and the Urban Indian Experience

Carol Miller

The most recent U.S. census presents a profile of American Indian/Alaska Native demographics that mostly extends established trends: AI/AN populations continue to grow, now numbering as many as 5.2 million people. Thirty percent of this population is younger than eighteen. Unsurprisingly, poverty and unemployment remain significantly higher among indigenous people than for the general U.S. citizenry. Perhaps more surprising, the percentage of the AI/AN population living in urban areas has reached 71 percent, up from only 8 percent in 1940.

What this data signifies is of particular significance to the now five generations and more of indigenous people whose experience is being described. Insider analysis might provide a more nuanced interpretation of the causes and consequences of a notable diaspora driven by socio-political factors such as two World Wars and federal policies such as allotment, termination, and relocation.

Insider attention is being, and has been, paid – in particular by a cohesive Native insistence that "urban" refers to a complex and evolving "experience" rather than a category of identity for indigenous people. This distinction between experience and identity is crucially relevant as a counter to the stereotypes that, over centuries of contact history, have driven white society's triumphalist assumptions about the doom and vanishing of Native individuals and nations. Experience rather than identity was certainly emphasized even in the title of a 2001 edited collection, *American Indians and the Urban Experience* (Lobo & Peters), whose chapters deliberately avoided the "identity" trap, focusing instead on such topics as cultural adaptations and continuance, indigenous health and wellness, and representations of the urban in various artistic genres.

Examination of representations of urban experience in contemporary American Indian literature is the subject of this chapter. Although present constraints insure that such an examination can in no way be exhaustive, in particular I want to explore: 1) how some Native writers have presented urban experience in contexts reflecting the circumstances of particular tribal cultures in specific historical times and places; 2) how distinctive features and values of an indigenous "urbanity" have been frequently shown in contrast with non-Native philosophies related to urbanity; and 3) how writers' presentations of indigenous urban experience have, especially in recent work, evolved in directions that serve the interests of both Native and non-Native audiences. My focus here is on contemporary fiction because, over now more than a century of print-language narrative, Native storytellers have returned insistently to the topic, doing so in a variety of iterations that have frequently exhibited what writer and critic Gerald Vizenor (Ojibwe) has called "survivance," his useful amalgam of survival and resistance – both necessary to Native cultural continuance.

This is a rich field of examination indeed, since Native communities have had long engagement with threats to their survival, resulting in part from the disparities between the metaphorical rhetoric of the colonizers' idealized "city on a hill" and the ambivalence they felt about their errand into a primitive wilderness that had to be tamed and civilized before that city could be constructed. Urban centers such as Boston, Washington, and New York very early became not only beachheads of exploration and conquest but the very epitomes of distinctions between Euro-American "civilization" and indigenous "primitivism." Over many centuries, Native leaders made endless arguments addressing the ruinous misconceptions that rationalized the theft of tribal homelands and the dispossession of those who lived on them. The world-traveling Oglala holy man Black Elk even crossed the "big water" with Buffalo Bill's Wild West Show, visiting the cities of Europe to, as he said, bring back to his people what he could learn from such contact with white urbanity. Black Elk was little impressed.

> Then we went roaring on again, and afterwhile we came to a still bigger town – a very big town … . I did not see anything to help my people. I could see that the Washichus did not care for each other the way my own people did before the nation's hoop was broken … . They had forgotten that the earth was their mother. This could not be better than the old ways of my people.
> ("Across the Big Water" Neihardt 166–67)

Black Elk's assessment of the urban spaces he visited is essentially a reversal of categories of civilized and primitive. The "Washichus" he observed fit the latter category, based on their failure to value either one another or the natural world. This is a telling judgment because it is Black Elk's early, independent expression of some of the features of an indigenous notion of what constitutes civilized behavior that literary critic William Bevis has linked to a culturally determined "urbanity."

In his seminal essay, "Native American Novels: Homing In" (1987), Bevis presents a matrix of converging ideas that distinguish American Indian narrative from its western counterparts, based in part upon a working understanding of what a Native urbanity signifies. "Native American nature is urban …" Bevis asserts. "The woods, birds, animals, and humans are all 'downtown,' meaning at the center of action and power, in complex and unpredictable relationships" (601). In tribal cosmology, the human and natural worlds have always been joined, never divided as in much western thought, and thus, "… when Native Americans imagined man and nature joined, they assumed the combination would be 'human,' 'civilized,'" with Nature being a "part of the tribe" (602).

In this sense, the traditional Indian "urban" describes a complexly inclusive symbiosis of human and natural worlds in which the social glue depends upon maintaining (or recovering), a transpersonal, rather than an individualist, sense of self comprised of a society, a past, and a place. Bevis links these components to an assertive theme within indigenous narrative that distinguishes it from western fiction: "American whites keep leaving home" (581), he writes. Instead, Native American narrative draws upon a centripetal energy in which "homing in" – staying home, returning home, and, in recent manifestations, deploying storytelling to re-constitute home or protect it – is a pervasive manifestation of the transpersonal. Just as important, the transpersonal is not just the protagonist's recovery of his relation to society. It is society's recovering of its relation to him or her as well.

This is the indigenous urbanity that Ella Cara Deloria (Yankton Dakota) describes so effectively in her novel *Waterlily*, unpublished until 1988, and also in its ethnological companion piece, *Speaking of Indians* (1944). Both books were originally written during World War II when Native people had left their reservation communities in large numbers to serve in the military or take part in war-effort employment. In both *Waterlily* and *Speaking of Indians*, Deloria describes the highly civilized and complexly organized "corporate" life of the traditional Dakota "tiyospaye" or camp community, as a "scheme of life that worked" (*Speaking of Indians* 24). Deloria wrote about an exemplary useable past whose values might be adapted to meet the needs of an accelerated post-war future in which many Native people would return "home" to both tribal and urban communities. Apprehensive about how Native people might achieve the adaptation that would be necessary to effect successful re-entry into a hopefully more equitable American society, Deloria offered the highly civilized values of traditional Dakota life as a means to that end – and hoped that non-Native American society would do its part in making re-entry possible.

In fact, many factors, deriving in largest measure from conditions put in place by two World Wars and by federal policies that sought to break up Native communities, would indeed radically accelerate and complicate indigenous urban experience. During World War I, ten thousand American Indians left their home communities to participate in the war. In World War II, twenty-five thousand, a preponderance of them volunteers, served in every branch of the military (Bernstein). Many others left reservations for war work in cities often very distant from their reservations. Thousands remained in cities after the war.

Increases in numbers of indigenous people living in urban settings were also fueled by generations of federal policies that sought to deal in one way or another with the "Indian problem." One of the earliest of these policies was allotment, formalized by the Dawes Act of 1887, which undid traditional communal property ownership and authorized the division of tribal land holdings into parcels to be assigned to individuals and families, with surpluses to be sold to non-Indian purchasers. The consequences of this policy were ruinous to Native families and communities: over its course, 90,000,000 acres of land were removed from native ownership and control; 27,000,000 of these were lost when Native "owners" were deemed incompetent or could not pay taxes. In addition to loss of tribal land holdings, allotment's goal of assimilation was to be met by private property ownership that would undermine tribal cohesiveness and force Native people to "adopt the habits, practices, and interests of the American settler population" ("History of Allotment" n. pag.). Although some tribal groups welcomed this policy, many did not, and one of its outcomes was that Native people were indeed over time dispersed from tribal communities. Many, including my own Oklahoma Indian Territory forebears, became migrants forced to re-establish themselves in neighboring towns or farther-away cities. The weakening of group bonds of kinship and proximity certainly meant an undermining of traditional cultural values and support systems and a resulting vulnerability to new risks.

This is at least a sub-text in one of the earliest novels by an American Indian woman. In Mourning Dove's (Okanogan) western melodrama *Cogewea, the Half-Blood* (1927), Cogewea's 80-acre allotment, mentioned almost as an afterthought at the end of the narrative as evidence of Cogewea's lack of wealth, is essentially economically useless to her. Cogewea lives with her sister Julia and Julia's white husband on the Horseshoe Bend cattle ranch in a ranch house constructed on Julia's allotted land (31). The ranch itself represents the new post-allotment economy for Mourning Dove's "go-between" mixed-bloods, an economy in which financial security depends upon cattle rather than the vanished buffalo.

But as a writer and as a woman of the twentieth century, Mourning Dove is eager to show that neither she nor her capable heroine is vanishing. Cogewea and the "true Americans" of the H-B ranch are adapting to the changing conditions of modernity, and the ranch is the mediated ground upon which this is occurring. Polson, on the other hand, the nearby town to which Cogewea goes on the Fourth of July holiday to compete in the Ladies' and Squaws' horse races, is presented as a physical space emblematic of cultural alienation and physical risk for the ranch's mixed-bloods. At the other polarity is the undisrupted traditional power of nearby Buffalo Butte, Cogewea's "beautiful Eden" (109), an unspoiled sacred site in which spirit voices still have the power to speak.

Even the names of the "Ladies'" and "Squaws'" competitions show the bigotry Mourning Dove presents on the part of the prejudiced town. After Cogewea wins both races, she is humiliated by white judges who deny both of her victories since in their estimation, she is neither "lady" nor "squaw" (68–69). No recourse to justice is possible in the threatening town space where her mixed-blood defender, the ranch foreman Jim LaGrinder, who loves Cogewea, is threatened with jail and physical assault.

Mourning Dove's melodramatic climax occurs when Cogewea, rejecting the warnings of her traditional grandmother, plans to elope to the city with the villainous fortune-hunter Densmore. Again, in another instance of the urban as a false and dangerous destination for indigenous people, it is to the city that Densmore flees, knowing that there he will be safe from any consequence after abusing and abandoning Cogewea. Having made the wrong choice, Cogewea over time will make the right one when she ultimately chooses Jim – and chooses as well the "splendid world" (284) that can be apprehended from her rightful place looking out from the spirit-infused space of Buffalo Butte.

Even in this early example, an indigenous writer presents the non-Native urban as a site of alienation for Mourning Dove's "true Americans," shown as targets of bigotry and exploitation at the hands of their white peers at the same time federal policies and more general social pressures attempted to coerce their assimilation to the values of those peers. In 1934, the Wheeler–Howard Act, also known as the Indian Reorganization Act, put an end to the official allotment of Indian lands. But new federal programs to facilitate assimilation would soon be legislated into place.

These new mid-century programs approached the "Indian problem" with macro and micro strategies. The ominously titled legislative initiative called "Termination" embodied the macro by systematizing the federal government's intention to close rolls and liquidate tribal assets with a single per capita payment to each tribal member. The desired outcome was to put an end to the protected status Indian nations might be owed in any future interactions with the federal government. Although Congress began sixty termination proceedings against individual tribes, most Native groups resisted, understanding that such a policy would not in the long term work to the good of the nations. Until the termination program was itself terminated by President Richard Nixon in 1970, another three million acres of tribally held land were forfeited, and numerous "terminated" tribes lost their status as sovereign nations.

But it was the government's Relocation Program, put in place during the post-war period and lasting through the 1950s, that ultimately did the most damage to individuals and tribal communities. Relocation was a systematized effort to entice Native people to voluntarily migrate to urban centers such as Chicago and Los Angeles by offering financial incentives to those who could be convinced to leave their reservations. Although some individuals and families prospered as a result of this urban migration (the family of the notable Cherokee Principal Chief Wilma Mankiller was one), many found only economic hardship, discrimination, and dead-end futures in their relocated new lives.

The damage done by the false allure of such futures is central to the story told in *House Made of Dawn* (1968), one of the most celebrated novels of the twentieth century. N. Scott Momaday (Kiowa) follows his war-traumatized protagonist Abel in his anguished attempts to reconnect with the traditional values of his home community. Even before he left home to join the military and certainly after his return, Abel has suffered from a lifetime of detachments from disrupted family and cultural traditions. His initial attempts to re-integrate himself are blasted by the presence of the "albino," a malevolent destructive force associated with such timeless and powerful evil that any easy equating of the figure with white identity seems simplistic. Abel comes to recognize the need to kill such a being if one can – and eventually he does so. Released from prison and "relocated" with his friend Benally to Los Angeles, Abel hits a rock bottom that promises only annihilation rather than any possibility of re-integration with ancient Pueblo beliefs that preserve the joined human and natural worlds as home, an aptly metaphorical "house made of dawn" holding all of creation.

Abel's friend Benally, however, is the character whose deluded hopes for his new urban life illustrate how completely Momaday imagines the city as a site of ultimate exile and disillusion. Benally's experience of the urban is of an alien space where "it's dark ... all the time, even at noon" (140), where you don't understand what people are saying, and where "You know, you have to change. That's the only way you can live in a place like this. You have to forget about the way it was, how you grew up and all" (148). Benally has internalized the materialist pipe dreams – "money and clothes and having plans and going someplace fast" (158) – that life in Los Angeles is supposed to promise. He rationalizes that in the tribal world he has left behind, "there's nothing there ... just the land, and the land is empty and dead. Everything is here. Everything you could ever want. You never have to be alone" (181). In his new urban place, Benally seems to deny every component of Bevis' indigenous "homing" as a matrix of society, place, and past.

But Benally is stuck in a dead-end job that will never bring his pipe dreams to fruition, and his only escapes are alcohol and self-deception. Momaday allows Benally another means of escape, however, when he can occasionally call up childhood remembrances of his grandfather telling stories in the firelight of the family's sheep camp. At least in those memories, Benally is able to home in, re-creating the transpersonal place and time when he had been "right there in the center of everything, the sacred mountains, the snow-covered mountains and the hills, the gullies and the flats, the sundown and the night, everything – where you were little, where you were and had to be" (157) – securely inside the house made of dawn.

Momaday's novel, however, finally is not a portrait of doomed Native victimization because Abel, the narrative's true center, resists the city and its soul-killing brutality. Beaten to near death by a sadistic cop, lying in a liminal space where he can hear the sounds of both the sea and the city, Abel is aware of something else as well: a vision of the runners after evil, the timeless beings who, within the traditional belief system that he has previously found impenetrable, engender balance and design within the universe. This vision will eventually be part of a process leading Abel homeward, away from the city. But its timing and location also suggest a transcendent agency linking landscapes that are simultaneously tribal and urban, ancient and contemporary. In the novel's variously interpreted concluding scene, Abel, back at home, will himself begin to run, taking a place in a traditional order and recovering the ability to sing in his own language.

House Made of Dawn, appearing in the activist 60s, is a Pulitzer-prize winning performance, one that, like American Indian writing that comes before and after it, presents non-Native urbanity as potentially toxic. Leslie Marmon Silko's (Pueblo) 1977 novel *Ceremony* essentially re-tells a similar story, focusing on another young Native man struggling to re-enter his community. Although much of Silko's telling takes place in and around the Laguna pueblo to which her mixed-blood protagonist Tayo returns after a disastrous experience as a prisoner-of-war in World War II, some of the story unfolds in nearby city spaces – Gallup and Albuquerque – presented as dehumanizing outlands that pervert and destroy those who are attracted to them. Tayo's mother is one of those who has been destroyed, and Tayo's memories of his time living with her in a tin shelter thrown together in a camp for vagrants in Gallup are nightmarishly sordid: a toddler's bewildered endurance of neglect, alcoholism, promiscuity, and violence.

The meanness of Gallup is far removed indeed from Ella Deloria's civilized, complex scheme of life that worked. Tayo's mother has internalized what whites have communicated about "the deplorable ways of the Indian people" (68). But the shame that seals her fate is not hers alone. It is a collective guilt that infects her family and her entire community: "For the people, it was that simple, and when they failed, the humiliation fell on all of them; what happened to the girl did not happen to her alone; it happened to all of them" (69).

Ceremony's narrative movement is about how the personal and collective consequences of internalized guilt create an out-of-balance world that jeopardizes the interdependent fates of individuals and the entirety of creation. This balance must be restored by a process of curative ceremonies – laid out in both Tayo's contemporary story and in a parallel story from ancient oral traditions. In Silko's cosmology, the past, present, and future are simultaneous and interconnected, as are the fates of individuals and human kind collectively. "Destroyers," those both white and Native who take malevolent pleasure in destruction, are a threat to Tayo's future as well as to humanity's. At the novel's end, the Destroyers are foiled, at least temporarily, by ceremonies which have led Tayo to a liberation from self-blame, delivering him from violence, bringing him to an epiphany in which he understands "the convergence of patterns" (254) signified by the timeless stars and an eternally benevolent earth – and sending him home to tell his story to the elders in the kiva.

But Tayo's "homing" in *Ceremony's* resolution is only possible when one has a home – and in Silko's radically polemic novel *Almanac of the Dead* (1991), the original conquest and theft of the American continents have been compounded by rapacious materialism that threatens the earth itself. Silko's almost parodic urban metaphor for exponential postcolonial devastation is Venice, Arizona, real-estate developer Leah Blue's dream city. Blue and the capitalist establishment she represents don't care that the canals and waterways of their faux-Venice-in-the-desert will require deep-water drilling: the ultimate penetration and despoiling of the Mother for profit. In *Almanac*, this perversion of urban possibility is only one component of a debased global inhumanity so destructive that the very preservation of the sacred earth depends upon no less than a wish-fulfillment reversal of history and the restoration of tribal possession of the land.

Almanac of the Dead recasts earlier iterations of the tribal/urban dichotomy as an issue of global consequence, but this may not be enough of an evolution to satisfy the prolific author Sherman Alexie (Coeur d'Alene/Spokane), who has objected to the homing plot and the celebration of a sacred landscape as among several features of contemporary Native literature accounting for a "lack of innovation" (Gamber 189). Alexie – who grew up on a reservation, now lives in Seattle, and has set his own work both in reservation and urban settings – is quoted as saying, "I think a lot of Native writers are pretending, writing about the kind of Indians they wish they were, not the kind of Indians they are" (203). It is true that many Native writers live or have lived in cities, have ties to academia, and may or may not have lived on tribal land or in reservation communities. But, though the character and depth of their connections to community may be very different, by telling (and re-telling) the effecting particularities of many versions of people's lived experience at "home," wherever that may be, Native writers are indeed creating new understandings of how "indigenous" and "urban" come together.

Although they are certainly not the only examples, recent works by Linda LeGarde Grover (Bois Forte Ojibwe) and Thomas King (Cherokee) present meaningful new versions of Native lives in relation to urban landscapes. Grover is the author of a short story collection, *The Dance Boots* (2010), and a novel, *The Road Back to Sweetgrass* (2014), which may be productively read as companion pieces. Each builds upon the related histories of the extended families of the fictional "... Mozhay Point and allotment lands ... in the heart of the six reservations of the Minnesota Chippewa Tribe, a few hours' drive north of Duluth, Minnesota" (*The Dance Boots* Preface). An overview might conclude that the main focus of *The Dance Boots* is the importance of recounting and remembering the suffering boarding schools caused generations of Indian individuals and families. And the dominant narrative emphasis of *The Road Back to Sweetgrass* might be read as a charting of the equally destructive impacts of many iterations of Native people's "relocations." In both books, however, Grover refuses to end on the old assumptions of victimhood. Not all of Grover's damaged characters thrive or even survive, but many do, drawing upon personal and transpersonal sources of strength and resilience that Gerald Vizenor would surely recognize as survivance.

The several protagonists of both of Grover's books re-connect their families and create new ones, allowing Grover to illustrate how "home" can be sustained, by effort and need, not only on the long-held if contested space of the Sweetgrass allotment but, less predictably, in Native households in the west end of urban Duluth. Taken together, the human actions and geographies of both books involve generations of movement back and forth between the rural reservation Mozhay Point and the city landscapes of Duluth, Minneapolis, and, in *Sweetgrass*, Chicago, where young Dale Ann is transplanted in a disastrous female instance of the federal relocation policy.

At the beginning of *The Dance Boots*, the culturally functional powwow boots are a gift from one generation of LaForce family women to the next as a material marker of each generation's storykeeper's responsibility to pass on the family's history, especially concerning the horrendous abuses of enforced attendance at boarding schools. Their new owner breaks in her inherited boots at a Duluth powwow – and begins a story that allows Grover very early to establish an important narrative thread: how Duluth becomes sanctuary and home for several generations of extended Mozhay Point kin.

THE URBAN INDIAN EXPERIENCE

It is to Duluth that one of the collection's central characters, Maggie LaForce, flees from her abusive first husband Andre with her younger children (the others are already in boarding school). There, using her first paycheck from a job at a mattress factory, she rents a house for her own family and for her school-abused sister Helen. Over time, Duluth becomes another home for Maggie's extended family members as surely as Mozhay Point is. It is to Duluth that Sonny and Waboos head when they run away from Harrod Boarding School. It is to Duluth that the children come home in the summers. For Maggie's generation, male or female, and for the ones that follow, town may not mean upward mobility or even complete security, but it does become another site of "Indian country."

A late story, "Refugees Living and Dying in the West End of Duluth," flashes forward to 1970 and the occasion of the funeral of Maggie's beloved second husband Louis. On this day, Cousin Babe's west-end Duluth house is perfumed by Mozhay Point comforts: fry bread, bologna, Manishcewitz wine, cigarettes, olive sandwiches toasted on hamburger bun – and generations of kinship. In an even later story, Sis, another LaForce relation, sums up Grover's reconstituting view of what "homing" means:

> What I have learned is that we have a place where we belong, no matter where we are, that is as invisible as the air and more real than the ground we walk on. It's where we live, here or aandakii: those of us who returned to the old LaForce allotment, those of us in Duluth, or those of us far away. It doesn't matter if we leave, or if we think we will never come back. It's where our grandparents, and their grandparents, lived and died; it's where we and our grandchildren will too ... . We are just part of it; we are in the picture. It's home.
>
> (99–100)

As its title indicates, *The Road Back to Sweetgrass*, introducing several new characters and story threads, shifts the narrative focus back to the reservation, and in particular to the Sweet Grass homestead, once possessed by generations of the "renegade" Muskrat/Washington family but more recently re-assigned by allotment to the ownership of the LaForces. Life in cities in this book is more temporary than permanent, as when one character's flight to Minneapolis is compared by Grover to the migration of wild geese. Indians from the reservation fly south to the cities, Grover writes,

> ... looking for work, for opportunity, for relatives who were homesick. To escape for a while. When their hearts' seasons changed, they flew back home, in a migratory pattern that had come to seem as natural and inevitable as the patterns of birds.
>
> (107)

In the heartbreaking section, "Niizh: Termination Days," a much more injurious migration has happened to smart, studious Dale Ann who is persuaded by the low expectations of government-sponsored relocation recruiters that life on the reservation is a dead end. But the real dead end is Dale Ann's move to Chicago to be trained as a long-distance operator. There she is raped by her white roommates' college friend, becomes pregnant, and endures the baby's coerced adoption and a forced sterilization. The real meaning of relocation for Dale Ann is a horrific termination of the life aspirations she began with. What remains is an emotionally constrained if still productive future back in her Mozhay Point community.

By dexterous storytelling, Grover weaves the disparate fates of several generations of LaForces and Muskrat/Washingtons – and even Dale Ann and her reclaimed adult son – together in a promising resolution that unites the blended families at Sweetgrass. Showing her characters culturally adaptive in tribal communities *and* in urban ones and eloquently articulating the migratory patterns that bind those communities, Grover creates something positive from even a vexed urban experience in a new conclusion that complicates Mourning Dove's or Momaday's.

Finally, we come to Thomas King's recent award-winning *The Back of the Turtle* (2014), a novel that in some ways appears to extend themes, including homing in, that have been present in much of King's earlier work, such as *Medicine River* (1990), *Green Grass, Running Water* (1993), and *Truth and Bright Water* (1999). Like King's masterful *Green Grass, The Back of the Turtle* is a wonderfully complex, multi-layered, highly allusive text. In this case, King interweaves a real-world contemporary story with two others drawn from distinctively different cultural sources: the Iroquois origin story "The Woman Who Fell from the Sky" and Milton's *Paradise Lost*. The novel touches on complicated ideas – like the nature of existence, the presence or absence of God, the moral implications of one origin story privileged against another – and certainly repays more detailed critical attention than it can receive here.

But its primary relevance to this analysis is its damning presentation of a contemporary urban landscape as soulless backdrop for a run-amok global capitalism that threatens the existence of all living things on the planet. In King's imagining, Toronto is the corporate home of Domidion, the agribusiness conglomerate responsible for an accumulating series of untrammeled environmental depredations. The city is a shell, a materialist urban center of no art, no culture, populated by a mostly invisible citizenry whose interests are entirely irrelevant to Domidion. As CEO Dorian Asher is ferried around Toronto in his limo, he appears to have only two passions. One is manipulating the short-memory outrage on the occasions when Domidion's environmental rapaciousness come to public attention. The other is shopping for items of conspicuous consumption – designer watches, ties, suits, multi-million dollar condos – that satisfy Dorian's obsessive materialist pursuit of success and security. Perhaps terminally ill with a cancer that mirrors a corporate soul-sickness, Dorian is entirely without moral compass, and King's city is just the place to accommodate an uber-Destroyer who has no need for one.

Posed against urban-headquartered global Monsanto-madness is the aptly named Samaritan Bay community, located a continent away on the coast of British Columbia. Samaritan Bay is neighbor to a First Nations reserve that has been previously decimated by an environmental spill caused by Domidion and Gabriel, its guilt-ridden, now suicidal indigenous chief chemist. "GreenSweep," the defoliant that has destroyed the life of the reserve and the river that flows through it to the sea, has the potential to do the same for the whole earth.

In *Ceremony*, Leslie Silko declared almost four decades ago that stories are "all we have to fight off illness and death" (2). King tells a complicated story indeed, one that will involve a character who may be the devil; another who may be the "poorly lit" son of God; a talking dog who has apparently survived death in a previous King novel; a romance between two Native people who, having left home, are now attempting to return to it; and a contingent of ship-wrecked Taiwanese boat people also seeking a home. If the poisoned natural world and its damaged human beings have any chance, it will indeed take a village, another kind of "downtown" very different than Toronto, one that resists the mis-directions of materialism, oligarchies, science, or divisive religiosity – and chooses another ethos acknowledging that the back of the turtle is our indispensable collective home.

In King's new work, indigenous value systems are offered as a means of co-operative survivance not just for Native people but for everyone. Linda LeGarde Grover's perspective is more local but no less innovative, claiming "home" for Native people in tribal *and* urban communities. Both strategies defend cultural continuance in ways that engage the changing circumstances of contemporary living, and both are empowering additions to the long tradition of Native authors telling the urban experience of indigenous people.

Works cited

Bernstein, Alison. *American Indians and World War II: Toward a New Era in Indian Affairs*. Norman: University of Oklahoma Press, 1991.

Bevis, William. "Native American Novels: Homing In." *Recovering the Word*. Ed. Brian Swann & Arnold Krupat. Berkeley: University of California Press, 1987. 580–620.

Deloria, Ella Cara. *Speaking of Indians*. Lincoln: University of Nebraska Press, 1998.

——. *Waterlily*. Lincoln: University of Nebraska Press, 1988.

Gamber, John. "We've Been Stuck in Place since *House Made of Dawn*." *The Native American Renaissance: Literary Achievement and Imagination*. Ed. Alan R. Velie & A. Robert Lee. Norman: University of Oklahoma Press, 2013. 189–206.

Grover, Linda LeGarde. *The Dance Boots*. Athens: University of Georgia Press, 2010.

——. *The Road Back to Sweetgrass*. Minneapolis: University of Minnesota Press, 2014.

"History of Allotment," *Indian Land Tenure Foundation*, 2014. Web. Accessed Dec. 2014. https://www.iltf.org/resources/land-tenure-history/allotment

King, Thomas. *The Back of the Turtle*. Toronto: Harper Collins Publisher, 2014.

——. *Green Grass, Running Water*. New York: Bantam Books, 1994.

——. *Medicine River*. Toronto: Viking Canada, 1989.

——. *Truth and Bright Water*. Toronto: Harper Flamingo Canada, 1999.

Lobo, Susan & Kurt Peters, eds. *American Indians and the Urban Experience*. New York: Alta Mira Press, 2001.

Momaday, N. Scott. *House Made of Dawn*. New York: Harper & Row, 1968.

Mourning Dove. *Cogewea the Half-Blood: A Depiction of the Great Montana Cattle Range*. Lincoln: University of Nebraska Press, 1981.

Neihardt, John G. *Black Elk Speaks*. Lincoln: University of Nebraska Press, 2000.

Silko, Leslie Marmon. *Almanac of the Dead*. New York: Simon & Schuster, 1991.

——. *Ceremony*. New York: Penguin, 1977.

7

Recovering a Sovereign Erotic

Two-Spirit Writers "Reclaim a Name for Ourselves"

Alicia Cox

What's in a name: then and now

"Some Like Indians Endure" is the leading work in both the first and the latest collections of literature by Two-Spirit writers.[1] In this poem, Paula Gunn Allen (Laguna Pueblo) compares "dykes" to Indians and claims that both lesbians and Native Americans – and lesbian Native Americans – have struggled to survive by crafting identities that inform the ways we belong and relate to one another (Allen 12). Allen's poem address the significance of a shared self-conception that helps Indians and lesbians find a home in each other and endure together despite centuries of patriarchal, settler colonial violence. Identities are formed in part through acts of naming whereby we assign words to the ideas we have about ourselves. Qwo-Li Driskill (Cherokee) claims that "an intense power to shape reality" inheres in "words" (Driskill, "Call," 222). Many Two-Spirit writers insist that "directly naming things constitutes a valuable form of power," and this is a belief that, according to Craig Womack (Creek), Indians "have long maintained" ("Suspicioning" 146).[2] Deborah Miranda (Ohlone/Costanoan-Esselen) asserts that Native people have always acknowledged the "right to produce self-names as utterances of empowerment," and she claims that the first task of contemporary Two-Spirit people is to "reclaim a name for ourselves" in order to take back the right to define our genders and sexualities ("Extermination" 277, 260). This chapter will address the history of academic study of so-called berdache people by primarily non-Native anthropologists and give an account of Native peoples' interventions into berdache studies. It will then define and contextualize the term *Two-Spirit*, which queer Native people developed to replace the term *berdache*. Since many Two-Spirit writers author both literary and critical works, this essay interweaves reviews of Two-Spirit critique with representative readings of poetry and prose by Two-Spirit authors.

The issues of gender and sexuality are central to the history of settler colonization in the Americas. As Andrea Smith explains, "It has been through sexual violence and through the imposition of European gender relationships on Native communities that Europeans were able to colonize Native peoples in the first place" (139). Prior to colonial contact, many – if not most – Native American societies recognized the existence of multiple genders, and indigenous languages included words that named men, women, and people

84

of a third gender.[3] European explorers were ignorant of the fact that Native Americans' construction of gender was based on occupational preferences and spiritual gifts rather than on biological sex, so when they met Native males who wore Native women's clothing, specialized in Native women's arts and occupations, or engaged in sexual partnerships or marriages with Native men, they mistook these third-gender people to be homosexual men. Thus, in colonial documentation of these encounters, third-gender people are labeled with the name *berdache*, a Persian word that has been translated as "'kept boy,' 'male prostitute,' and 'catamite'" ("Call" 224). Since Christian dogma forbids homosexual behavior, colonizers routinely punished and/or summarily executed third-gender people.[4]

Due to the violence inflicted on third-gender people, Native Americans were terrorized into discontinuing multiple-gender systems and conforming to the western sex/gender binary. The disappearance of third-gender roles was linguistic as well as social. Miranda explains that the "Erasure of tribal terms" for third-gender people "was a strategy used by European colonizers throughout the Americas" to eradicate the presence of viable roles for people whose gender did not align with their biological sex ("Extermination" 260). However, third-gender people did not cease to be born merely because of the loss of names for them and the roles they once filled in their communities. Rather, Miranda reasons, a "spiritual-sexual splitting of the [third-gender] role" resulted from the colonial imposition of the binary system of gender; consequently, the only way queer Natives could identify was as homosexual, using the terminology of the dominant culture ("Extermination" 274). Beth Brant (Bay of Quinte Mohawk) also sees the rending of spirituality from sexuality as a result of colonization; she writes, "Our sexuality has been colonized, sterilized, whitewashed. Our sense of spirit has been sterilized, colonized" (*Writing* 60). With no third-gender roles to fill or models to follow, queer Natives became outcasts among their own people who had internalized the homophobic views of the dominant culture.[5] This especially became the case during the federal Indian policy era of assimilation. As M. Owlfeather (Shoshone-Metis/Cree) writes,

> in the period of 1880 to 1910, if you were found or caught practicing Indian beliefs or dress, you could be jailed … . So it was with little wonder that the vision of the berdache was forgotten or suppressed to the point that it was no longer mentioned and barely remembered. When it was mentioned, it was with shame and scorn, due to the influence of Christianity on Indian people.
>
> (100–01)

Queer Native Americans who endured hatred and exclusion in their home communities often moved to urban areas where they sought understanding and solidarity.

In San Francisco in 1975, Randy Burns (Northern Paiute) and Barbara Cameron (Lakota) founded Gay American Indians, "the first gay Indian organization in the United States" (Burns in Roscoe *Living* 3). The formation of GAI was necessary to address the particular needs of queer Indians who endured homophobia among Indian communities and racism among mainstream gay communities. Burns explains that "gay American Indians face *double oppression* – both racism and homophobia" because "discrimination against nonwhite people [exists] within the lesbian/gay community" (2). The white-biased objectives of the gay movement did not serve the interests of most Indian people whose primary goal was to unify their sexual, gender, and ethnic identities and gain acceptance in their Native communities. One strategy toward that end was to research and record the identities and roles of their "gay Indian ancestors" (Burns 2). Through collaboration with anthropologist Will

Roscoe, GAI formed the Gay American Indian History Project to compile a bibliography of sources on the subject of the berdache and catalogue the existence of multiple-gender systems in over 130 North American tribes.

Another outcome of Roscoe's alliance with GAI was the publication of *Living the Spirit: A Gay American Indian Anthology* (1988), a collection of essays, prose, poetry, and visual art by LGBT Native people. This text marks the intervention of Native writers into berdache studies which had previously been dominated by non-Native anthropologists. *Living the Spirit* includes the seminal essay written by Maurice Kenny (Mohawk), titled "Tinselled Bucks: A Historical Study in Indian Homosexuality," that was originally published in the 1975 issue of *Gay Sunshine*. In "Tinselled Bucks," Kenny characterizes the berdache as an Indian sort of homosexual, and he gives an overview of berdache roles among various tribes, names celebrated berdache individuals, and quotes and interprets historical and anthropological sources written by non-Indians. The essay by Midnight Sun (Anishnawbe) in this anthology, titled "Sex/Gender Systems in Native North America," is similar to Kenny's as it provides the perspective of a queer Native American on non-Native ethnographic material; however, its focus on Native gender complicates Kenny's use of the term *homosexuality*. Midnight Sun explains:

> If a culture's sex/gender system makes it possible for a biological female to become a social man, then "he" is not ... engaging in lesbian behavior by having sexual relations with women. Because he is a socially recognized man, such relations would be defined as "normal."
>
> (35)

For most Native peoples, homosexual activity in itself did not determine a person's social identity; "the homosexual" as a social type – a person of one sex/gender whose sexual desire is solely oriented toward people of the same sex/gender – is a western construction that does not make sense in a cultural context in which gender is not determined by biological sex.

Living the Spirit was likely inspired by Beth Brant's edited collection, *A Gathering of Spirit: A Collection by North American Indian Women* (1984), which includes the work of twelve lesbian-identified writers. Speaking of the collection's contributors, Brant declares, "We are here. Ages twenty-one to sixty-five. Lesbian and heterosexual. Representing forty Nations ... . we believe together, in our ability to break ground. To turn over the earth. To plant seeds. To feed" (*Gathering* 12). The groundbreaking work that *A Gathering of Spirit* performs through literary practices of naming fulfills the need of queer Native women to express themselves and know each other. Quoting a letter she received from one contributor, Brant shares her words: "'I feel new ... . Our struggle is so much easier, knowing we have each other'" (13). Brant's politically potent gathering has influenced the creative work of queer Native writers ever since.

Whereas many Native authors featured in *A Gathering of Spirit* and *Living the Spirit* identify as LGBT and use the term *berdache* to refer to traditional Native third-gender roles, subsequent queer Natives desired a word that would distinguish them from non-Native LGBTQ people. They wanted a name that would signal their contention that their right to sexual and gender self-determination is a matter of Native sovereignty, not U.S. civil rights, and that would restore the spiritual component of third-gender roles to sexual identity. "This, in fact, is a crucial point," according to Miranda: "the words *gay* and *lesbian*" are inadequate for defining queer Native people "because those labels are based on an almost exclusively sexual paradigm inherited from a nonindigenous colonizing culture" ("Extermination" 277). Native queers became increasingly dissatisfied with *berdache* due to its European origin, elision of female third-gender people, and derogatory connotation of child abuse.

As a replacement of *berdache*, the term *Two-Spirit* was coined by Albert McLeod during the Third Annual Inter-tribal Native American, First Nations, Gay and Lesbian American Conference held in Winnipeg in 1990. According to Driskill, "Using *Two-Spirit*, or *Two-Spirited*, rather than, or in addition to" the labels abbreviated as LGBTQ,

> creates a sovereign label for Native people to discuss our traditional and contemporary gender and sexual identities. It helps us decolonize our bodies and minds from the homophobic, sexist, transphobic, and racist ideologies that are entrenched in European occupation of Turtle Island.
>
> ("Call" 224–25)

The creation of the term *Two-Spirit* answers Owlfeather's call that "somehow, there should be a blending of the old with the new" (104). That blending is precisely the promise of Two-Spirit identities and the work of Two-Spirit writers who blend old traditions with new transformations for the purpose of healing queer Native erotics and decolonizing sexuality.

A critical intersection: Native American studies and queer theory

Scholarly projects to recover the names and histories of traditional Two-Spirit roles are aligned with the politics of American Indian literary nationalism. Proponents of literary nationalism assert that any meaningful analysis of American Indian literature must be grounded in knowledge of the Native national context from which a text arises.[6] In the hands of non-Native scholars, the study of American Indian literatures has tended to perpetuate stereotypes and generalizations about Indian people as a racial type rather than as members of distinct and diverse sovereign nations. As a critical methodology, American Indian literary nationalism holds scholars accountable for producing work that is useful to Native peoples. Womack argues that tribally specific examination of the "histories, cultures, and commitments to community that literatures reflect" is a "key method for decolonizing the study of Indigenous literatures" (Womack in Driskill et al. *Queer* 4–5). *Decolonization* and *sovereignty* are key words for understanding the work of Two-Spirit authors who work to "reclaim our histories from the colonizer's records even as we continue to know and adapt our lives to contemporary circumstances and needs" (Miranda "Extermination" 277). Driskill defines *sovereignty* as

> an issue of vital importance to Native people, not only as a right we have as independent nations within the borders of colonial governments, but also as a struggle to define ourselves outside of Eurocentric and racist notions of our lives as First Nations people.
>
> ("Call" 222)

Two-Spirit writers point out that settler colonial politics are inherently heteronormative, and colonial institutions and policies resulted in the oppression of queer Native traditions. Two-Spirit writers desire the restoration of viable social roles that existed within their Native communities prior to colonization.

Indeed, the goal of decolonization is at the heart of Two-Spirit organizing and writing. Brant, Miranda, Driskill, and others propose that "decolonizing sexuality is one of the many tasks of contemporary Two-Spirits" (Driskill "Call" 229). In 2004, Driskill published a landmark article titled "Stolen from Our Bodies: First Nations Two-Spirits/Queers and the Journey to a Sovereign Erotic" in the journal *Studies in American Indian Literatures*. Lisa Tatonetti notes that this essay marked "queer American Indian literatures' transition into a new era of politics and promise, a period in which conversations about sovereignty and sexuality entwine" (154). "Stolen from Our Bodies" takes up the issue of historical trauma, such as the sexual abuse and heteronormative gender disciplining that Native children endured in Indian boarding schools, and relates it to the current presence of homophobia in Indian communities. Sexual abuse of Native children was rampant within Indian boarding schools (known as residential schools in Canada) where children were vulnerable to the sadistic natures and pedophilic desires of white teachers, priests, nuns, and other staff members. These abuses resulted in terror, shame, and silence around Native erotics, and they have contributed to ongoing intergenerational abuse among Native communities. As Chris Finley (Colville) explains,

> shame around sex started in the boarding schools, and sexual shame has been passed down for generations. Throughout the imposition of colonialism in the United States, one of the methods Native communities have used to survive is adapting silence around sexuality. The silencing of sexuality in Native studies and Native communities especially applies to queer sexuality.
>
> (32)

Consequently, contemporary Two-Spirit people have been at a loss for role models who might show them how to live their identities in culturally relevant ways. In her 1993 essay titled "Giveaway: Native Lesbian Writers," Brant writes, "I had no models for being an Indian lesbian, much less one who wrote. I fumbled and wrote in aloneness ("Giveaway" 945). For these reasons, Two-Spirit writers insist on the importance of writing our erotic experiences as a way of both healing our own historical trauma as well as helping other Two-Spirit people to heal in turn. In "Stolen From Our Bodies," Driskill calls for Indians to embark on a journey to recover a sovereign erotic, a relation to our bodies and sexualities that refuses the U.S. nation-state's compulsory heteronormativity and the silencing and shaming of sexual identities and practices. As Driskill explains elsewhere, the U.S. "dominant culture's notions of the erotic ... are often accompanied by the sexism and racism infused into its fiber" ("Call" 229). Conversely, a "Sovereign Erotic relates [Native peoples'] bodies to our nations, traditions, and histories" (Driskill "Stolen" 52). The projects of decolonizing our nations and decolonizing our sexualities are not mutually exclusive; in the words of Daniel Heath Justice (Cherokee), "To ignore sex and embodied pleasure in the cause of Indigenous liberation is to ignore one of our greatest resources ... . Every orgasm can be an act of decolonization" ("Fear" 106). Indians must take back our bodies and break the silence surrounding our erotic lives in order to shirk colonial legacies of shame and internalized hatred.

Since 2004, scholarly conversations on the mutual significance of sexuality and Native sovereignty have proliferated. The critical alliance of queer theory and Native American studies methodologies was cemented in 2010 by the publication of a special issue of *GLQ: A Journal of Lesbian and Gay Studies* titled *Nationality, Sexuality, Indigeneity: Rethinking the State at the Intersection of Native American and Queer Studies.* This project was vital because queer of color theory had previously tended to ignore indigenous peoples and issues of settler colonialism while Native American studies had tended to ignore issues particular to queer people and women. The conversations featured in this issue are rooted "in indigenous feminisms … and larger decolonial movements" that seek to understand "the entwined nature of colonization and heteropatriarchy" (Driskill et al. *Sovereign* 6). The introduction to this issue asks how a dialogue between the fields of queer and Native American studies might help us understand the U.S. nation-state, which has sought to delimit queer people's access to legally recognized kinship, particularly through marriage and adoption, and restrict Native people's ability to exercise sovereignty, especially regarding taxation and land claims. Native scholars like Andrea Smith and Craig Womack theorize the utility of queer studies methodologies for shrugging off the burden of ethnographic representation that has long plagued Native writers. Non-Native contributors to the issue, like Scott Morgensen, Mark Rifkin, and Bethany Schneider, draw on insights and methods from Native American studies to critique the settler colonial foundations of queer politics.

Daniel Heath Justice's essay, "Notes toward a Theory of Anomaly," attends to an urgent political issue in the Cherokee Nation: the 2004 ban of same-sex marriage. Justice points out that the new legislation, rather than protecting or upholding Cherokee tradition, actually violates traditional philosophies within Cherokee culture, particularly the worldview that honors anomaly as a necessary feature of social life. Whereas the European worldview pathologizes difference and demands conformity to the normal, Justice asserts that the Mississippian worldview from which Cherokee culture arises has a precedent of honoring anomalous beings for their unique gifts. Justice cites oral traditions that champion anomalies in nature, such as the bat (a four-legged with wings that can fly like a bird) and the bear (a four-legged that can walk on two legs like a human). Justice suggests that we may think of queer Cherokees as anomalies, and he urges the Cherokee Nation to remember the traditions that value difference as sacred and honor diversity as necessary for the balance of the planet. By reminding us of the stories that teach the value of all life and that narrate how each person, no matter how odd, has a place in the circle of the community, Justice calls on tradition to restore a place for contemporary queer Cherokees.

Miranda's essay titled "Extermination of the *Joyas*: Gendercide in Spanish California" considers the particular case of the *joyas*, the Spanish colonizers' name for third-gender people among Native Californians. Miranda outlines the social role of *joyas* who had a unique spiritual function as undertakers to mediate the space between this life and the afterlife. Since specialized communal responsibilities were inherent in the third-gender role, Miranda explains, the extermination of *joya* people was detrimental to Native societies as a whole and necessitated a redistribution of social responsibilities. In part by recovering these histories and remembering the traditional role of the *joya*, Miranda claims that "third-gender people are reemerging … as contemporary Two-Spirit people" (260, 274).

Miranda's recent publication of *Bad Indians: A Tribal Memoir* (2013) in many ways constitutes an extension of her *GLQ* article. This mixed-genre work features Miranda's interpretation of ethnographic and historical research on her Native Californian ancestors as well as poetry, short stories, and other creative offerings to the mosaic of her tribe's presence. The short story "Coyote Takes a Trip," which was previously anthologized in *Sovereign Erotics: A Collection of Two-Spirit Literature* (Driskill et al. 2011), narrates a day in the life of a cruising, trickster Coyote who decides to leave his Venice Beach camp and take a trip to visit his brother in New Mexico. However, on his bus ride to the airport, Coyote becomes fascinated by an elderly Indian woman passenger. Coyote nearly misses his stop while daydreaming about past lovers, and during his scramble to pull the stop request cord, his baggy pants fall down around his ankles: "Not only was his butt hanging out for all the world to see, but so was his pride and joy, and wouldn't you know it, right at eye level with the old *Indita*" (*Bad Indians* 183). Coyote wonders that the "old Indian lady" seemed to be "giving him the *eye*," and contemplating this after exiting the bus, Coyote realizes that "that was no little old lady. The qualities that had so intrigued Coyote, that mix of strength and serene femininity … that old lady was a glammed-up – *and impressed* – old man" (183). This epiphany sends Coyote on a mental journey to remember the appropriate name for the old *Indita*'s gender identity:

> Not exactly a man. What was that old word? Joto? No, older than that, and sweeter. *Joya? Jewel of the People?* Nope, still Spanish, and just thinking it conjured up vile images of humiliation before loved ones, being stripped naked, mastiffs set loose, flesh and souls mutilated. "No, we had our own words before the padres and *soldados de cuero*," Coyote thought; it was coming back to him now, how many beautiful words, each tribe creating a title as unique as the being it described.
>
> (183–84)

Coyote's mental trip through his memory is just as embodied as was his physical trip down the aisle of the bus. While searching for that old "word that meant honor, medicine, truth," Coyote "rolled his slippery pink tongue around in his mouth as if he could rattle the lost names out from between his teeth somewhere … . then his mouth remembered, and Coyote cried the Chumash word aloud: '*aqi!*" (184). In the end, Coyote abandons his plan to travel to New Mexico and decides to meet the '*aqi* when s/he returns from the grocery store. The margins of this story's pages are adorned with quotations from Miranda's ethnographic research on the *joya*, and Miranda's blend of critical and creative storytelling opens a space for Coyote's sovereign erotic to emerge.

Two-Spirit writers and organizers argue that in order to nurture the lives and work of today's queer Natives, recovering third-gender histories is not enough. Brant claims that

> stories of Two-Spirits being revered *because* of their blurred gender and uncompromising ways of living within their clan or tribal unit … are important ones to treasure and repeat to our young, but … they cannot take the place of living and breathing lesbians and gay men who can be role models if we are able to jump over the chasm that homophobia has blasted into our Nations.
>
> (*Writing* 58)

As Miranda notes, we cannot recreate the traditional roles of our ancestors, but the knowledge of their previous existence may help us imagine and build a future:

> As long as you are attempting to *recreate*, you are doomed to fail! ... when something is that broken, more useful and beautiful results can come from using the pieces to construct a mosaic. You use the same pieces, but you create a new design from it ... . if we pick up the pieces and use them in new ways that honor their integrity, their colors, textures, stories – then we do those pieces justice.
>
> (*Bad Indians* 135)

Miranda's metaphor of contemporary Native life as a mosaic made from the shards of old traditions is a perfect conceptualization of Two-Spirit identity.

For Two-Spirit people, the work of writing erotica complements the decolonial task of recovering third-gender traditions. Miranda argues that erotica portrays Indians as humans rather than as static racial types, and she declares that "if we want [decolonial] justice, we must work for the erotic" ("Dildos" 147). She explains that the suppression of Native erotica has been systematized through "five hundred years of erotic murder in this country" to dehumanize and disappear Indians; indeed, the American "Indian as *human* is still unthinkable for most Americans" whose primary cultural references for Indians are mascots, margarine labels, and prefabricated Halloween costumes ("Dildos" 145). Brant advocates writing workshops for Indian women to practice the "use of erotic imaging" as "a tool by which we heal ourselves" and recuperate our bodies and sexualities, exorcising internalized hatred (*Writing* 17). Menominee poet Chrystos is a paragon of the use of erotic imaging as a tool of healing, decolonization, and community building. Most of the poems in her first collection, *Not Vanishing* (1988), are dedicated to a particular person, indicating that the work of crafting words is a labor of nurturing relationships, creating community, and being responsible to our relations. Chrystos' poetry deals with a plethora of issues, including racism, poverty, rape, and cultural appropriation. Yet her love poetry and explicit depictions of Native lesbian erotics have proven to be incomparable sources of inspiration for Two-Spirit writers.

Chrystos' poem "O Honeysuckle Woman" depicts the speaker's desire for lesbian intimacy. The apostrophe hails, or conjures, an abstract woman lover. Written in the second-person narrative voice, the poem is a sexual invitation; the speaker proposes, "won't you lay with me ... /O honey woman/won't you suckle me" (Not Vanishing 6). The speaker tries to persuade her intended that with their "tongues flowering/open-throated" in oral sex, they "could drink one another," tasting the "golden pollen" that resides "sticky sweet & deep" within "our bodies" (36).

The action verbs "suckle" and "suckling" play on the name of the honeysuckle flower and also call to mind the nurturing and nourishing action of a mother breastfeeding a baby – an image that suggests that the two women lovers' oral stimulation of each other's breasts and genitals is an act not only of giving and receiving pleasure but also of caretaking and feeding one another's spirits; it is an act of sexual decolonization.

The decolonial potential of erotic pleasure is also a theme in "Double Phoenix." The mythical reference in the title alone suggests that through sex the lovers are realized; they rise together from the proverbial ashes and are reborn. "Double Phoenix" is a poem of re-emergence. Anticipating Driskill's call for Indians to take back our bodies and recover a sovereign erotic, the poem calls out the speaker's and the lover's body parts using scientific terms rather than flowery metaphors so that there is no ambiguity: "hands," "thighs," "ear," "vulva," "mouth," "tongue," "fingers," "bones," "blood," "breasts," and "hips" are named into being on the page (Chrystos *Not Vanishing* 43). The poem narrates the lovers' body parts' relation with one another in acts that engender a new reality:

hands skimming my thighs she whispers into my ear
I want you my vulva shivers clenches
her mouth takes me her
tongue tells long dancing stories of flight stars darkness burst
fingers flicker in my bones
she enters me in the moment when my blood begs her.

(43)

At the moment of orgasm, the speaker's face is buried in her lover's chest, but she is also flying: "my toes skim stars/I'm wings in the night sky crying out in her breasts" (43). Through the lovers' encounter with one another, they are returned to their cosmic home. They ascend from the dust of colonial destruction and restore one another's bodies to their sovereign erotic.

Chrystos' erotic poetry has been and continues to be instrumental for Two-Spirit people who had been lacking representations of queer Native sexuality. The character of Rabbit in Craig Womack's *Red on Red* expresses how crucial it is for queer Native people to have access to literature with which we can identify. Rabbit states that we need to consider:

what happens to the Indian gay guy or gal writing today? Will they speak the truth about their lives and places in their tribes? ... What's the future for Indian gay and lesbian readers wanting to read something honest about theyselves? ... if writers don't write about things, they is partly responsible for turning kids into ghosts.

(309)

Rabbit's provocative line about "turning kids into ghosts" alludes to the alarming rate of suicide by Native youth as well as the death of Two-Spirit people due to hate-fuelled homicides. Womack argues that "Native two-spirits, gays, lesbians, and transgendered folks desperately need ... community. They need to see images of themselves reflected in books and in many other aspects of their lives" ("Suspicioning" 146). Womack suggests that it is imperative that Two-Spirit people write honestly about their experiences so that future generations of queer Natives will be able to identify with the stories of their people, have models to follow, and know that they are not alone and that their lives matter.

Breaking silence, releasing shame, and telling stories are necessary actions for Indians to heal our spirits and bodies and take back power over our lives and ultimately, one may hope, our lands. Two-Spirit authors assert that erotic life is a source of sovereignty. Explicitly defining and narrating our sexual lives and genders as integral parts of our Native identities are crucial aspects of the process of healing from colonial violence and the intergenerational abuses that have perpetuated in its wake. Through recovering names for ourselves and voicing our stories in the face of colonial erasures, we reclaim our bodies as part of the land to which we belong and are responsible, and we resituate our lives among the circle of our communities.

Notes

1 See Roscoe, and Driskill et al., *Sovereign Erotics*. In this essay, I use *queer* as an umbrella term for lesbian, gay, bisexual, transgender, and queer identities, and I use *Two-Spirit* as an umbrella term that encompasses the LGBTQ identities of Native American people in particular as well as the myriad traditional, tribally specific third-gender identities. Not all Two-Spirit people identify as lesbian, gay, bisexual, transgender, or queer; some prefer to use Native language terms to name their identities. Additionally, not all LGBTQ Native people identify with the term *Two-Spirit*; some feel that *Two-Spirit* lacks the political visibility of terms like *queer* while others contend that not all tribes are known to have harbored such a role traditionally. *Two-spirit* is a translation of the Anishinaabemowin term *niizh manidoowag*. Since the origin of this term is specific to the Anishinaabe people and language, many take issue with the use of *two-spirit* to name all queer Native people. I agree with Driskill et al., the editors of *Queer Indigenous Studies*, who argue that "When linked, *queer* and *Two-Spirit* invite critiquing heteronormativity as a colonial project, and decolonizing Indigenous knowledges of gender and sexuality as one result of that critique" (3). Like any umbrella term, I consider *Two-Spirit* to be a moveable shelter under which those who choose to may stand as a strategy for staying dry; rather than a confining box or a restrictive label, the umbrella term is a tool that allows us to move freely through the rain while we wield it.

2 I use the term *Indian* here in accordance with its use by Womack. Generally, I use the terms *Indian*, *American Indian*, *Native*, *Native American*, and *First Nations* interchangeably depending on the context.

3 Some tribes recognized as many as five genders. In this essay, I use the term *third-gender* to refer to any traditional Native non-cisgender identity. Although scholars have used *third-gender* to represent Native gender possibilities beyond the man/woman binary, the term, like all language, has its limits. While I use the term *third-gender* here for ease of communication, I do not mean to disregard the multitude of gender expressions represented in Native communities historically and in the present.

4 The extermination of the *berdache* can also be seen as part of the campaign to establish male dominance, or patriarchy, in the so-called New World. As a hierarchical organizing logic, patriarchy requires that gender be constituted by one's biological sex in order to clearly distinguish between men and women. Christian dogma has long been used to justify patriarchy as a righteous logic for ordering societies.

5 Miranda theorizes the term *gendercide* to name the systematic murder of Native third-gender people by Europeans ("Extermination" 259). She argues that what many consider to be the existence of homophobia among Native communities is actually internalized gendercide, a legacy of colonial violence. For novels that deal with the issue of homophobia among Native American communities, see Sarris, and Womack, *Drowning in Fire*.

6 See Warrior, *Tribal Secrets: Recovering American Indian Intellectual Traditions* (1994); Womack, *Red on Red*; and Weaver, Womack, and Warrior, *American Indian Literary Nationalism*.

Works cited

Allen, Paula Gunn. "Some Like Indians Endure." Roscoe, *Living the Spirit*. 9–13.

Brant, Beth, ed. *A Gathering of Spirit: A Collection by North American Indian Women*. 1984. New York: Firebrand Books, 1988.

——. "Giveaway: Native Lesbian Writers." *Signs: Journal of Women in Culture and Society* 18. 4 (1993): 944–47.

——. *Writing as Witness: Essay and Talk*. Toronto: Three O'Clock Press, 1994.

Burns, Randy. "Preface." Roscoe, *Living the Spirit*. 1–8.

Chrystos. *Not Vanishing*. Vancouver: Press Gang Publishers, 1988.

Driskill, Qwo-Li. "Call Me Brother: Two-Spiritness, the Erotic, and Mixedblood Identity as Sites of Sovereignty and Resistance in Gregory Scofield's Poetry." *Speak to Me Words: Essays on*

Contemporary American Indian Poetry. Ed. Dean Rader & Janice Gould. Tucson: University of Arizona Press, 2003. 222–34.

——. "Stolen From Our Bodies: First Nations Two-Spirits/Queers and the Journey to a Sovereign Erotic." *Studies in American Indian Literatures* 16. 2 (2004): 50–64.

Driskill, Qwo-Li, Chris Finley, Brian Joseph Gilley & Scott Lauria Morgensen, eds. *Queer Indigenous Studies: Critical Interventions in Theory, Politics, and Literature*. Tucson: University of Arizona Press, 2011.

Driskill, Qwo-Li, Daniel Heath Justice, Deborah Miranda & Lisa Tatonetti, eds. *Sovereign Erotics: A Collection of Two-Spirit Literature*. Tucson: University of Arizona Press, 2011.

Finley, Chris. "Decolonizing the Queer Native Body (and Recovering the Native Bull-Dyke): Bringing 'Sexy Back' and Out of Native Studies' Closet." *Queer Indigenous Studies*. Ed. Driskill et al. Tucson: University of Arizona Press, 2011. 31–42.

GLQ: A Journal of Lesbian and Gay Studies, special issue "Nationality, Sexuality, Indigeneity: Rethinking the State at the Intersection of Native American and Queer Studies." 16. 1–2 (2010).

Justice, Daniel Heath. "Fear of a Changeling Moon: A Rather Queer Tale of a Cherokee Hillbilly." *Me Sexy: An Exploration of Native Sex and Sexuality*. Ed. Drew Hayden Taylor. Vancouver: Douglas & McIntyre, 2008.

——. "Notes Toward a Theory of Anomaly." *GLQ: A Journal of Lesbian and Gay Studies* 16. 1–2 (2010): 207–42.

Midnight Sun. "Sex/Gender Systems in Native North America." *Living the Spirit*. Ed. W. Roscoe. New York: St. Martin's Press, 1988. 32–47.

Miranda, Deborah. *Bad Indians: A Tribal Memoir*. Berkeley, CA: Heyday, 2013.

——. "Dildos, Hummingbirds, and Driving Her Crazy: Searching for American Indian Women's Love Poetry and Erotics." *Frontiers* 23. 2 (2002): 135–49.

——. "Extermination of the *Joyas*: Gendercide in Spanish California." *GLQ: A Journal of Lesbian and Gay Studies* 16. 1–2 (2010): 253–84.

Owlfeather, M. "Children of Grandmother Moon." Roscoe, *Living the Spirit*. 97–105.

Roscoe, Will, ed. *Living the Spirit: A Gay American Indian Anthology*. New York: St. Martin's Press, 1988.

Sarris, Greg. *Watermelon Nights*. New York: Penguin, 1999.

Smith, Andrea. *Conquest: Sexual Violence and American Indian Genocide*. New York: South End Press, 2005.

Tatonetti, Lisa. "The Emergence and Importance of Queer American Indian Literatures; or, 'Help and Stories' in Thirty Years of *SAIL*." *Studies in American Indian Literatures* 19. 4 (2007): 143–70.

Warrior, Robert. *Tribal Secrets: Recovering American Indian Intellectual Traditions*. Minneapolis, MN: University of Minnesota Press, 1994.

Weaver, Jace, Craig S. Womack & Robert Warrior, eds. *American Indian Literary Nationalism*. Albuquerque: University of New Mexico Press, 2006.

Womack, Craig S. *Drowning in Fire*. Tucson: University of Arizona Press, 2001.

——. *Red on Red: Native American Literary Separatism*. Minneapolis, MN: University of Minnesota Press, 1999.

——. "Suspicioning: Imagining a Debate between Those Who Get Confused, and Those Who Don't, When They Read Critical Responses to the Poems of Joy Harjo, or What's an Old-Timey Gay Boy Like Me to Do?" *GLQ: A Journal of Lesbian and Gay Studies* 16. 1–2 (2010): 133–55.

8

Indigenous Feminisms

Leah Sneider

According to the National Congress of American Indians' "Fact Sheet on Violence Against Women in Indian Country," based on a U.S.-based study from 2000:

> American Indians, in general, experience per capita rates of violence that are much higher than those of the general population. In particular, the rate of aggravated assault among American Indians and Alaska Natives is roughly twice that of the country as a whole.

The fact sheet further states that non-Natives perpetrate 70 percent of these crimes and that "one out of three American Indian and Alaskan Native women are raped in their lifetime, compared with about one out of five women in the overall national statistic" (n. pag.). To help address these issues, in 2010 President Obama signed the Tribal Law and Order Act, which allows for more tribal law enforcement and prosecution of sexual assault and other forms of violence against Native women. Yet, the U.S. federal government alone is responsible for prosecuting crimes committed by non-Native people on Native land and continuously fails to do so (see Mark Rifkin's blog on the subject at: http://www.firstpeoplesnewdirections.org/blog/?p=5446 [accessed 9 Dec. 2014]). Tribal courts, therefore, cannot prosecute the majority of crimes against Native women, severely limiting tribal autonomy and the tribe's ability to protect their women.

Our neighbors to the north have done much to address similar problems for Canadian Aboriginal/First Nations people. The Ontario Native Women's Association and the Ontario Federation of Indian Friendship Centres created "A Strategic Framework to End Violence Against Aboriginal Women," which addresses eight interconnected areas for change including: research, legislation, policy, programs, education, community development, leadership, and accountability. However, of particular importance is area number 5 involving education and including the two following goals:

> 5.1: To develop an ongoing, integrated public education campaign that teaches communities and stakeholders about the root causes of violence against Aboriginal women, violence prevention, and how to develop and maintain *healthy relationships* while opening up an ongoing dialogue about *respectful relationships*.

> 5.3: Strengthen public knowledge and understanding of the historical context of violence against Aboriginal women.
>
> ("A Strategic Framework," n. pag. emphasis added)

Of note is the emphasis here on healthy and respectful relationships while engaging in dialogue and public education that reveal a fundamental ethic or ideology necessary for individual, communal, and social balance. These goals rely on academics and theorists across disciplines to develop an understanding of the root causes, historical context, and contemporary consequences of violence against Native/Aboriginal women. Academics are then charged with following the lead of activists and non-profit organizations in developing the means by which college students can study and instructors can teach methods for prevention and healing necessary for decolonization, while maintaining this fundamental ethic of social balance. Doing so requires the transformative power of healthy and respectful relationship between theory and practice. Extending this ethic to the study of literature, students and scholars of Native/Aboriginal literature must engage texts responsibly and respectfully through an Indigenous feminist methodology.

What IS Indigenous feminism?

Indigenous feminism is more than a theory, political position, or way of thinking. Indigenous feminist scholars claim that "a monolithic approach to a Native feminism is not possible ... rather, there are multiple definitions and layers of what it means to do Native feminist analysis [as a means of addressing] 'sexism and promote indigenous sovereignty'" (Goeman & Denetdale 10). Although we discuss it in the singular form, there are many Indigenous feminisms, not just one. Thus, Indigenous feminism most broadly defined means the shared responsibility for the nurturance and growth of Native communities through communal practices and actions that reflect and promote personal and tribal autonomy. The basic tenets of Indigenous feminism include respect, relationship, reciprocity, and responsibility as a means to decolonization while maintaining self-determination and sovereignty. As Indigenous feminist scholar Sandy Grande explains, "for indigenous women, the central dominating force is colonization, not patriarchy; and the definitive political project is decolonization, not feminism," which drastically separates Indigenous feminism from mainstream feminism (152). Decolonization first requires stripping away colonial ideologies that have become imbedded in tribal identities and, as Maori scholar Linda Tuhiwai Smith elucidates, have "left a permanent wound on the societies and communities who occupied the lands named and claimed under imperialism" (21). Indigenous feminist theory helps to contextualize the history of colonization and opens "a space to plan, to strategize, to take greater control" in establishing self-determination (Smith 38). More to the point, Indigenous feminism advances the process of decolonization primarily through the recovery and commemoration of Native experiences and histories. However, Indigenous feminism is not limited to the literary realm but also includes those many courageous activists fighting for decolonization for their tribal nations, cultures, and the land.

Recent Indigenous feminist scholars have given voice to Native histories and women's experiences in particular. For instance, in her text *Conquest: Sexual Violence and American Indian Genocide*, Andrea Smith reveals the patriarchal and colonial roots of sexual violence against Native women and posits that sexual violence against women was and still is a primary tool of genocide and colonization in America. Smith cites several forms of sexual and gender violence against women, including forced sterilization, rape, environmental racism, and boarding school policies. She asserts that sexual and gender violence includes any strategy that seeks to "not only destroy peoples, but to destroy their sense of being a people" (3). Betty Bell explains that

> "the story" of Native women and their relation to power and authority is often told, or lived, between conflicting "traditions": on the one hand, the precolonial or "traditional" status of women; on the other, the postcolonial advance of patriarchy into tribal nations.
>
> (307)

Patriarchy as an ideology is another form of colonization impacting tribes. Restoring Native women's identities and traditional roles as caregivers thus requires them to combat racist and sexist ideologies. In *Mapping the Americas: The Transnational Politics of Contemporary Native Culture* (2009) Shari M. Huhndorf asserts that the "ways in which colonization has positioned indigenous women demand a feminist rethinking of Native politics and culture, a task to which nationalism is inadequate" (4). Huhndorf's work on Native women's dramatic and literary productions attends to "the role of patriarchy in colonization, figures of Native women in colonial national origin stories, and the emerging transnational politics of indigenous feminism" (4).

Indigenous feminism leads us to an understanding of the ways in which race and gender ideologies are intimately and equally connected to national identity and self-determination. In her article "Race, Tribal Nation, and Gender: A Native Feminist Approach to Belonging" (2007) Renya Ramirez emphasizes that

> race, tribal nation, and gender should be non-hierarchically linked as categories of analysis in order to understand the breadth of our oppression as well as the full potential of our liberation in the hope that one day we can belong as full members of our homes, communities, and tribal nations.
>
> (22)

Race and gender ideologies and corresponding hierarchical dominance helped fuel and perpetuate the stripping of Native tribal sovereignty in paternalistic U.S policies that conceived of Native nations as inferior and in need of protection. Mishuana Goeman's *Mark My Words: Native Women Mapping Our Nations* extends our application of Indigenous feminism to the ways in which colonization informs the physical demarcations of land, space, and time as connected to national sovereignty. By focusing on the ways Native women writers "map" their lives, she explains, "Alternative conceptions of borders, nations, and place are subversive to the masculine project of empire building. American Indian women are seeking to (re)map first encounters and mediate ongoing spatial relations by writing in the form of these alternative maps" (29). She hopes that these alternative ways of mapping help inform social and political movements and an understanding of nationhood. In her chapter in *Making Space for Indigenous Feminism* (2007), Emma LaRocque explains that

> self-determination must mean that all individuals have a basic right to a certain quality of life, free from the violence of colonialism, racism/sexism and poverty, as well as from the violence of other humans, even if these other

humans are one's people, or even one's relations, or are themselves suffering from colonial conditions.

(61–62)

Furthermore, LaRocque notes that "it is in moments of nationalisms that we are most vulnerable not only to essentialisms/fundamentalisms, but to the disempowerment of women" (68). LaRocque classifies a move towards nationalism as exclusive, static, and therefore masculine in character. However, understanding nationalism from this colonial ideological standpoint limits its potential. An Indigenous feminist understanding of a national character is more inclusive, fluid, and gender-balanced as a process of continual negotiation and decolonization focused on the people as a whole. Furthermore, such decolonization first requires sovereignty.

For example, I have written elsewhere that Sarah Winnemucca Hopkins's *Life Among the Piutes: Their Wrongs and Claims* (1883) reveals the ways in which gender is tied to national sovereignty. I explain that,

> sovereignty, particularly in rhetorical form, has been long debated and continually transforming in meaning across different tribal nations and as needs shift. Self-determination defines the ability and will of a people to establish themselves as a nation in culturally appropriate ways. Relationship recognizes and negotiates differences for the sake of communal self-determination and sovereignty. How those relationships are built and maintained reveals information regarding a group's perceived and enacted sovereignty.

(Sneider 260)

Winnemucca attempts to build and maintain balanced relationships with her readers by sharing her culture and acknowledging differences and similarities across cultures.[1] Her rhetorical sovereignty, however, originates from her personal self-determination to overcome restrictive colonial gender roles and voice her concerns while maintaining a constant focus on her people's welfare as a distinct nation. Such a focus attempts to reveal, critically assess, and decolonize the effects of colonial ideologies and violence on herself and her people. I conclude that:

> *Using* Indigenous feminism as a theoretical approach concurrently *enacts* Indigenous feminism by attempting to broaden the understanding and practice of sovereignty and more effectively listening to the various complementary parts of the much larger story. An unbalanced theoretical approach to Native literature and culture reproduces rather than transcends colonial oppression.

(260)

As demonstrated above, Indigenous feminism offers a method for analyzing literary practices that attempt to deconstruct ideological oppression with a focus on concepts of gender and race identity. As Lisa Kahaleole Hall writes, "Indigenous feminism grapples with the ways patriarchal colonialism has been internalized within Indigenous communities as well as with analyzing the sexual and gendered nature of the process of colonization" (278). In "Land Claims, Identity Claims: Mapping Indigenous Feminism in Literary Criticism and in Winona LaDuke's *Last Standing Woman*," Cheryl Suzack helps to explain the dual demands to which Indigenous feminism must tend:

> on the one hand, how to take issue with the call by contemporary American Indian critics for an unproblematized historical representation and reconstruction in American Indian writing, and, on the other, how to participate in a process of cultural reinvention and renewal that illuminates how the revival and preservation of tribal identity must of necessity engage with the inheritances of a colonial past.
>
> (*Reasoning Together* 172)

Native women can preserve Indigenous social balance by helping to renew *both* male *and* female leadership roles in the community as a method of decolonization. Therefore, an Indigenous feminist approach is not limited to constructions of gender but more specifically addresses the colonial ideologies that inform constructions of gender, race, class, nationality, geopolitical space, physical ability, etc. Indigenous feminist practices seek to expose these colonial ideologies and decolonize while asserting sovereignty.

A very brief history of Indigenous feminism

Indigenous feminism is as old as Native women; as long as there have been Native women, there has been some form of Indigenous feminism. Native women historically held leadership roles within many tribal nations. One example is the Cherokee Beloved Woman position last held by Nancy Ward. As the Beloved Woman, Ward acted as advisor and spokesperson for her tribe and often gave speeches in which she

> used the rhetoric of motherhood to convey her desires and hopes for peaceful relations between the US government and Cherokee people. Underpinning her language was the esteem, prestige, and authority enjoyed by Cherokee women; rather than being a sentimental appeal to motherhood – which in white culture would have been an appeal to "influence" – her speeches attempt to establish a relationship of kinship, centered on women, fundamental in traditional Cherokee culture.
>
> (in Kilcup 26)

Ward's speeches appeal to establishing relationship or kinship between the orator and the listeners, between Native American and Western American peoples. The rhetoric of kinship, "brother" and "father" especially, was common in oratory at this time. Rarely do we see mention of mothers or sisters other than in Ward's speeches. The topics of such oratory are typically of creating peaceful relationships. The Cherokee men in power extinguished the role of Beloved Woman shortly after Ward's death in 1822 indicating a major shift in gender roles due to colonization. M. Annette Jaimes explains: "the reduction of the status held by women within indigenous nations was a first priority for European colonizers eager to weaken and destabilize target societies" (319). One strategy included simply refusing to deal politically with women based on Eurocentric gender roles. Tribes had to send replacement representatives when their leaders were, in fact, women.

However, as a gender/sex-focused academic analytic Indigenous feminism is fairly new, having only emerged since the early 1980s and most prominently with Laguna Pueblo/ Lebanese literary author and scholar Paula Gunn Allen and, more specifically, her feminist critiques of Leslie Marmon Silko's novel *Ceremony* (to be discussed momentarily). Kate Shanley's "Thoughts on Indian Feminism," in Beth Brant's edited collection *A Gathering of Spirit: A Collection by North American Indian Women*, was one of the earliest texts focusing on the development of the concept as an analytical and activist tool. Shanley frames her exploration of American Indian feminism's differences from white feminism around the 1983 Ohoyo Indian Women's Conference on Leadership that resulted in the publication of *Words of Today's American Indian Women, Ohoyo Makachi: A First Collection of Oratory by American Indian/Alaska Native Women*. Shanley's construction of "Indian feminism" is directly tied to tribal sovereignty. She writes:

> The importance Indian people place on tribal sovereignty [is] the single most pressing political issue in Indian country today. For Indian people to survive culturally as well as materially, many battles must be fought and won in the courts of law, precisely because it is the legal recognition that enables Indian people to govern ourselves according to our own world view ... equality for Indian women within tribal communities, therefore, holds more significance than equality in terms of the general rubric "American."
>
> (215)

Shanley's short declaration spurred a flurry of academic discussion that has strengthened into a theoretical approach as well as an established social movement in contemporary times. Indigenous feminist scholars from across the globe have since developed the discourse through various disciplines and applications but all maintain the focus on tribal sovereignty and decolonization. Some of the other most prominent Indigenous feminist scholars include Jennifer Denetdale, Linda Smith, Mishuana Goeman, Lisa Kahaleole Hall, Renya Ramirez, Sandy Grande, Reyna Green, Kim Anderson, Emma LaRocque, and Cheryl Suzack.

Indigenous feminist literary texts and practices

Paula Gunn Allen's *The Sacred Hoop: Recovering the Feminine in American Indian Traditions* was the first scholarly publication focused on Native American women. Allen explains that Native genocide originated out of the fear of gynocracy, or female rule/women-centered society, and the study of Native literatures by non-Natives are "erroneous at base because they view tribalism from the cultural bias of patriarchy and thus either discount, degrade, or conceal gynocratic features or recontextualize those features so that they will appear patriarchal" (4). Allen distinguishes Native literature from Western literatures based on cultural differences, particularly in terms of relatedness. Native American societies, she states, "relate events and experiences to one another [and not] in terms of dualities or priorities" (59). The literature, therefore,

> does not rely on conflict, crisis, and resolution for organization, nor does its merits depend on the parentage, education, or connections of the author. Rather, its

significance is determined by its relation to creative empowerment, its reflection of tribal understandings, and its relation to the unitary nature of reality.

(59)

She identifies the two basic and interrelated forms of Native literature as ceremony and myth: "The ceremony is the ritual enactment of a specialized perception of a cosmic relationship, while the myth is the prose record of that relationship" (61). In applying this understanding to Leslie Marmon Silko's *Ceremony*, Allen argues that the novel is

about two forces: the feminine life force of the universe and the mechanistic death force of the witchery. And Ts'eh [aka Yellow Woman] is the central character of the drama of this ancient battle as it is played in contemporary times [because she is] the matrix, the creative and life-restoring power.

(119)

Allen claims that it is the loss of this worldview and associated traditions that encompass the main form of ongoing genocide and which, thus, must be captured in Native literatures through the power of the feminine.

One of the earliest and most important Indigenous feminist literary collections is Paula Gunn Allen's *Spider Woman's Granddaughters: Traditional Tales and Contemporary Writing by Native American Women* (1989). As the title indicates, the collection brings together women's stories from across time and, by juxtaposing them, puts them in conversation with each other. In her introduction, Allen explains that "The aesthetic imperative requires that new experiences be woven into existing traditions in order for personal experience to be transmuted into communal experience; that is, so we can understand how today's events harmonize with communal consciousness" (8). In essence, Allen's collection creates these important, affirming relationships across time and space as a means to sustain tribal cultures while assisting in the transformations necessary for decolonization. The best example involves the various Yellow Woman stories included as part of the ongoing cycle and as a means to understanding changing needs across time. She explains, "Silko's use of the Yellow Woman stories, for example, leans more toward isolation of the protagonist from her people than toward connectedness – though even here her connection to herself is of necessity through the stories by way of her family" (23). Silko's story, then, is one part of the "collective unconscious [that] is the ever-renewing source" for all Native stories (23). However, more importantly, Allen claims that Native American women differ drastically from dominant American women because "[they] are women at war [which] is as much a matter of metaphysics as of politics" (24). Their war stories, thus, depict

the turmoil that ensues when one meets the enemy ... combat ... survival, death, mutilation, indignity, and community destruction. Above all, they are about transformation, which is another term for ritual. Sometimes transformation occurs as a consequence of victory, but as often occurs as a consequence of defeat. These stories of women at war are about the metaphysics of defeat. They are about being conquered, about losing the right and authority to control personal and community life.

(24)

With this understanding in place, Allen's collection is broken into three parts – The Warriors, The Casualties, and The Resistance – that focus on feminine power and blend traditional with modern stories. There have been quite a few other collections of Native women's creative writing including *American Indian Women: Telling Their Lives* (1984), *A Gathering of Spirit: A Collection of North American Indian Women* (1989), *Reinventing the Enemy's Language: Contemporary Native Women's Writing of North America* (1997), *Spider Woman's Web: Traditional Native American Tales About Women's Power* (1999), and *Native American Women's Writing 1800-1924* (2000). However, Native authors tend to blend genres making it difficult to separate creative writing from all other types of writing (historical, political, sociological, cultural, analytical, etc.). Of course, there are also several novels, short story collections, and poetry collections that have been analyzed through an Indigenous feminist lens. Following is a brief overview of just *some* of these works and their corresponding Indigenous feminist analysis.

Considered the first written by a Native American woman, S. Alice Callahan's novel *Wynema: A Child of the Forest* (1891) presents a biting criticism of sexism and U.S. Indian policies (such as allotment) through the story of a young Muscogee Indian girl's experiences navigating the white world. In this way, it very much falls in line with Allen's assertions of Native women writing war stories. In A. Lavonne Brown Ruoff's introduction to the novel, she calls Callahan a "'woman word warrior' creating 'strong-hearted,' intelligent heroines and sensitive heroes who educate her audience about Muscogee culture, Indians' and women's rights, and the mutual respect between the sexes essential to happy marriages" (xliii). Of particular note is Callahan's use of Muscogee dialect within the novel as a means to demonstrate the protagonist's negotiation of white culture. The mixture of Indigenous languages with English is one way in which Native female authors strategically engage tribal knowledge as a means to decolonize.

As mentioned earlier, Laguna Pueblo/Mexican/European author Leslie Marmon Silko's novel *Ceremony* is one of those most widely recognized as "feminist" because of the role of the main female character, Yellow Woman/Ts'eh, in healing the male protagonist, Tayo, from Post-Traumatic Stress Disorder after serving in World War II and returning to the Laguna pueblo in New Mexico. Feminist critics focus on literary elements that emphasize feminine powers such as connections to land and sexuality and also the blending of masculinity and femininity. Kristin Herzog's article "Thinking Woman and Feeling Man: Gender in Silko's *Ceremony*" explores the healing powers of such literary gender blending as cultural epistemology. She writes that "For American Indians, spirit ties all human beings to each other and to the whole cosmos; therefore it also unifies the genders. Spirit does not dissolve gender distinctions, but it renders certain gender traits as interchangeable" (33). However, what makes *Ceremony* more an *Indigenous feminist* novel is the ways in which it uses this gender blending to respond to the damaging effects of colonial hyper-masculinity. An Indigenous feminist reading focuses on the ways in which the novel grapples with ideological conflicts and how traditional practices must adapt to these conflicts in contemporary times. Therefore, Tayo's healing process adapts traditional practices to contemporary needs while making political commentary on the importance of traditional Native religious practices that were not considered legal at the time (the American Indian Religious Freedom Act of 1978 was passed a year after the novel's publication). Furthermore, the story itself adapts cultural traditions by placing Tayo in the role of Yellow Woman based on traditional stories and because of his contemporary differences as a mixed-blood war veteran.

Silko's other immense novel, *Almanac of the Dead*, presents a modern apocalyptic world developed over centuries and crossing various colonially inscribed borders. Depicting mixed-breed struggles, the borderlands drug trade, witchcraft/shamanism, and revolution against ongoing colonial oppression, the novel predicts many of our twenty-first-century conflicts with unnerving precision. Mishuana Goeman dedicates a chapter of her book *Mark My Words* to exploring how the novel can be read as an Indigenous feminist decolonial map, "an active apparatus that restructures spatial domination, social relations, and epistemological violence [and] moves away from romanticized notions of resistance" (166). Her final assessment shows how the novel's depiction of historical and contemporary Native struggles maps the "destruction of the patriarchal nation-state [necessary for] decolonization and globality" (202). In other words, the novel's recovery of and emphasis on Native story, history, and perceptions of land and space leads towards decolonization across the globe.

Ojibwe author Lois Beardslee's *The Women's Warrior Society* (2008) playfully depicts modern-day versions of the original woman warrior, Ogitchidaakwe. These educated women meet in the library to plan their response to the "Abusers [who are] born of tradition, tradition of history, tradition of eminent domain, manifest destiny, slave-holding" (8). Like fellow Ojibwe author Louise Erdrich, Beardslee's narrative voice shifts constantly and includes the perspectives of the women warriors and the "abusers" in order for readers to truly understand Native women's experiences with and responses to institutionalized racism and colonization. For example, when one of the women sees a book that inaccurately depicts Native people, she uses a permanent marker to boldly write that the book is "bad for Indians [because] it promotes damaging stereotypes" about Native women (89). The chapter "Initiation" responds to colonial oppression through educating and empowering Native children within a supportive community setting. Nine-year-old Cinqala attends the library sweatlodge with the women warriors and shares her damaging story about a Thanksgiving-time class project. She comes to recognize her teacher's arrogance and ignorance and the women warriors symbolically arm her with cultural support to overcome such offenses. Ultimately, the collection emphasizes that women warriors are not born but trained by the women elders who encourage sharing stories and continually resisting oppression in new and meaningful ways. In sharing their stories within the circle of women warriors and within this collection, these Indigenous feminist women shape-shift and elude containment of any kind.

Originating from the Turtle Mountain Band of the Chippewa/Ojibwe Nation and also part German and Métis, Louise Erdrich is perhaps the most prolific Native female author, having published fourteen novels, three poetry collections, six children's books, and two non-fiction books. She is best known for the novels *Love Medicine* (first published in 1984) and *Tracks* (1988), which are part of a series of novels that focus on interconnected family relationships and struggles that take place in or near the North Dakota reservation, and start in the late nineteenth century. The families include hereditary tribal leaders and mixed-blood Métis all of whom challenge social, cultural, and religious taboos in their interactions and as they experience ongoing colonization with loss of land and cultural traditions. Most of the novels depict violence against women in various forms but also very strong women who overcome these struggles and work to lead the people. Another distinguishing feature is the ways in which these novels constantly shift narrative voice in order to present stories from multiple perspectives, making them uniquely communal in form. Erdrich's most Indigenous feminist and most recent novel is *The Round House* (2012), which is told from the perspective of a 13-year-old boy who tries to find the perpetrator of his mother's severe beating and rape. Because his mother is a tribal enrollment specialist and his father a tribal judge on the Ojibwe reservation, the novel explores the politics involved with gender and leadership roles, as well as cultural conflicts. Most importantly, however, the novel reveals the complications regarding land ownership, legal jurisdiction for prosecuting certain crimes, and tribal sovereignty. Although this novel won the National Book Award for fiction, it has not yet garnered critical attention merely because it is so very new. However, an Indigenous feminist reading of the novel would focus on the ways in which it grapples with real contemporary issues connecting gender and tribal sovereignty based on an ongoing colonization of Native lands and bodies.

Muscogee Creek poet Joy Harjo is perhaps the best-known Native female poet, whose poems are diverse and unique in both topic and form. She has written six poetry collections, two children's books, and a memoir and is also an accomplished musician and playwright. Harjo is also highly regarded for her co-editorial role in the collection *Reinventing the Enemy's Language: Contemporary Native Women's Writings of North America*. In the editors' introduction, she writes:

> To understand the direction of a society one must look toward the women who are birthing and intimately raising the next generation … to speak at whatever cost, is to become empowered rather than victimized by destruction. In our tribal cultures the power of language to heal, to regenerate, and to create is understood.
>
> (21–22)

She explains that the collection of Native women's work represents a promise to bring the people together and be strengthened by their unified voices. Goeman's Indigenous feminist analysis of Harjo's body of work, in *Mark My Words*, focuses on the ways in which she creates global relationships while honoring Creek history and culture through what Goeman calls "spatial poetics," which rely on language and metaphor. More specifically, Goeman analyzes the ways in which Harjo uses Creek philosophies concerning spirals, stomping grounds, music, dance, and the sun as a means to "counter forms of knowledge that would erase and deny Native presences" and imagine global relationships across time and space (135). Goeman further explains that "maneuvering between local epistemologies and global frameworks strengthens the notion that Indigenous people, though they experience the material realities of globalization, do not necessarily have to be determined by a global world of faceless systems and institutions" (153). Instead, spatial poetics, story more generally, and the relationships stories create reflect a cultural mapping of decolonized possibilities on a global scale.

Recent changes in tribal jurisdiction with the Tribal Law and Order Act and the Violence Against Women Act reveal that Indigenous feminism is working well in conjunction with other Indigenous movements. Several tribal nations now recognize gay marriage and are rethinking if not yet allowing women to take leading positions in tribal government. Most importantly, tribal nations are working towards and, in some cases, fighting for the recognition of tribal sovereignty and, ultimately, decolonization. The most recent example is the Sioux nation's determination that the U.S. federal government's passing of any legislation that allows companies to drill oil pipelines through their land will be considered an act of war against a sovereign nation and will be met with resistance. Indigenous feminism is also exemplified in the now internationally known and supported First Nations' Idle No More movement, which "calls on all people to join in a peaceful revolution to honour [sic] Indigenous sovereignty, and to protect the land and water" ("The Vision" n. pag.). Attawapiskat First Nations Chief Theresa Spence helped shape this movement through her six-week hunger strike demanding that the Canadian government honor treaties and First Nations' sovereignty ("The Vision" n. pag.). However, as I have argued throughout this chapter, all of this work towards decolonization relies on the sharing of tribal stories and the recovery and honoring of tribal history. Experiencing the greatest oppression due to Western/colonial gender roles, Native women and their stories work to amplify and employ the power of the feminine for the sake of cultural survival, tribal sovereignty, and global decolonization.

Note

1 In LeAnne Howe's essay "A Story of America: A Tribalography," she writes that tribalography theoretically captures an epistemology that "comes from the native propensity for bringing things together, for making consensus, and for symbiotically connecting one thing to another."

Works cited

"A Strategic Framework to End Violence Against Aboriginal Women." Ontario Native Women's Association & the Ontario Federation of Indian Friendship Centres. Sept. 2007. Web. Accessed 10 Sept. 2007. http://www.oaith.ca/assets/files/Publications/Strategic_Framework_Aboriginal_Women.pdf
Allen, Paula Gunn. "The Feminine Landscape of Leslie Marmon Silko's *Ceremony*." *Studies in American Indian Literatures: Critical Essays and Course Designs*. New York: MLA, 1983. 127–33.
——.*The Sacred Hoop: Recovering the Feminine in American Indian Traditions*. Boston: Beacon, 1992.
——, ed. *Spider Woman's Granddaughters: Traditional Tales and Contemporary Writing by Native American Women*. New York: Fawcett Columbine, 1989.
Anderson, Kim. *A Recognition of Being: Reconstructing Native Womanhood*. Toronto, Ontario: Sumach Press, 2000.
Bataille, Gretchen M. & Kathleen Mullin Sands. *American Indian Women: Telling Their Lives*. Lincoln: University of Nebraska Press, 1987.
Beardslee, Lois. *The Women's Warrior Society*. Tucson: University of Arizona Press, 2008.
Bell, Betty. "Gender in Native America." *A Companion to American Indian History*. Ed. Phillip J. Deloria & Neal Salisbury. Malden, MA: Blackwell, 2002. 307–20.
Brant, Beth, ed. *A Gathering of Spirit: A Collection by North American Indian Women*. Ithaca, NY: Firebrand Books, 1989.
Callahan, S. Alice. *Wynema: A Child of the Forest*. Ed. A. Lavonne Brown Ruoff. Lincoln: University of Nebraska Press, 1997.
Denetdale, Jennifer Nez. "Chairmen, Presidents, and Princesses: The Navajo Nation, Gender, and the Politics of Tradition." *Wicazo Sa Review* 21. 1 (Spring 2006): 9–28.
Erdrich, Louise. *Love Medicine*. New York: Holt, 1993.
——. *The Round House*. New York: HarperCollins, 2012.
——. *Tracks*. New York: Harper, 1988.
Goeman, Mishuana R. *Mark My Words: Native Women Mapping Our Nations*. Minneapolis: University of Minnesota Press, 2013.

——. "Notes Toward a Native Feminism's Spatial Practice." *Wicazo Sa Review* (Fall 2009): 169–87.

Goeman, Mishuana R. & Jennifer Denetdale, "Native Feminisms: Legacies, Interventions, and Indigenous Sovereignties." *Wicazo Sa Review*, 24. 2 (2009): 9–13.

Grande, Sandy. "Whitestream Feminism and the Colonialist Project: Toward a Theory of Indigenísta." *Red Pedagogy: Native American Social and Political Thought.* Lanham, MD: Rowman & Littlefield, 2004. 123–57.

Hall, Lisa Kahaleole. "Strategies of Erasure: U.S. Colonialism and Native Hawaiian Feminism." *American Quarterly* 60. 2 (June 2008): 273–79.

Harjo, Joy & Gloria Bird, eds. *Reinventing the Enemy's Language.* New York: W.W. Norton & Co., 1997.

Hazen-Hammond, Susan. *Spider Woman's Web: Traditional Native American Tales About Women's Power.* New York: Perigee Press, 1999.

Herzog, Kristin. "Thinking Woman and Feeling Man: Gender in Silko's *Ceremony*." *MELUS* 12. 1 (1985): 25–36.

Hopkins, Sarah Winnemucca. *Life Among the Piutes: Their Wrongs and Claims.* Reno: University of Nevada Press, 1994.

Howe, LeAnn. "The Story of America: A Tribalography." *Clearing a Path: Theorizing the Past in Native American Studies.* Ed. Nancy Shoemaker. New York: Routledge, 2002. 29–50.

Huhndorf, Shari M. *Mapping the Americas: The Transnational Politics of Contemporary Native Culture.* Ithaca, NY: Cornell University Press, 2009.

Jaimes, Annette M. & Theresa Halsey. "American Indian Women at the Center of Indigenous Resistance in Contemporary North America." *The State of Native America: Genocide, Colonization, and Resistance.* Ed. M. Annette Jaimes. Boston: South End Press, 1992. 311–44.

Kilcup, Karen, ed. *Native American Women's Writing* c. *1800–1924: An Anthology.* Cambridge, MA: Blackwell, 2000.

LaRocque, Emma. "Métis and Feminist: Ethical Reflections on Feminism, Human Rights and Decolonization." *Making Space for Indigenous Feminism.* Ed. Joyce Green. New York: Zed Books, 2007. 53–71.

National Congress of American Indians, "Fact Sheet: Violence Against Women in Indian Country." n.d., n. pag. Web. Accessed 10 Feb. 2010. www.ncai.org

Ramirez, Renya. *Native Hubs: Culture, Community, and Belonging in Silicon Valley and Beyond.* Durham, NC: Duke University Press, 2007.

——. "Race, Tribal Nation, and Gender: A Native Feminist Approach to Belonging." *Meridians* 7. 2 (2007): 22–40.

Shanley, Kate. "Thoughts on Indian Feminism." *A Gathering of Spirit: A Collection by North American Indian Women.* Ed. Beth Brant. Ithaca, NY: Firebrand Books, 1988. 213–15.

Silko, Leslie Marmon. *Almanac of the Dead.* New York: Penguin Books, 1991.

——. *Ceremony.* New York: Penguin Books, 1977.

——. *Yellow Woman and a Beauty of the Spirit: Essays on Native American Life Today.* New York: Simon & Schuster, 1996.

Smith, Andrea. "American Studies Without America: Native Feminisms and the Nation-State." *American Quarterly* 60. 2 (June 2008): 309–15.

——. *Conquest: Sexual Violence and American Indian Genocide.* Cambridge, MA: South End Press, 2005.

——. "Native American Feminism, Sovereignty, and Social Change." *Feminist Studies* 31. 1 (Spring 2005): 116–32.

Smith, Linda Tuhiwai. *Decolonizing Methodologies: Research and Indigenous Peoples.* London: Zed Books, 1999.

Sneider, Leah. "Gender, Literacy, and Sovereignty in Winnemucca's *Life Among the Piutes*." *American Indian Quarterly* 36. 3 (Summer 2012): 257–87.

Suzack, Cheryl. "Land Claims, Identity Claims: Mapping Indigenous Feminism in Literary Criticism and in Winona LaDuke's *Last Standing Woman*." *Reasoning Together.* Ed. Craig S. Womack, Daniel Heath Justice & Christopher B. Teuton. Norman: University of Oklahoma Press, 2008. 169–92.

"Tribal Law and Order Act." *Tribal Law and Order Act*. The United States Department of Justice. Web. Accessed 14 Dec. 2014. http://www.justice.gov/tribal/tribal-law-and-order-act

"Violence Against Women Act." *Violence Against Women Act*. The United States Department of Justice, 7 March 2013. Web. Accessed 14 Dec. 2014. http://www.justice.gov/tribal/violence-against-women-act-vawa-reauthorization-2013-0

"The Vision." Idle No More Movement. Web. Accessed 26 Nov. 2014. www.idlenomore.ca

Words of Today's American Indian Women, Ohoyo Makachi: A First Collection of Oratory by American Indian/Alaska Native Women. Washington, D.C.: U.S. Dept. of Education; Wichita Falls, TX: Prepared and distributed by Ohoyo, Inc., 1981.

Part II
KEY MOMENTS

9
U.S.–Indian Treaty-Relations and Native American Treaty Literature

David J. Carlson

In 1871, through a rider attached to an appropriations bill, the U.S. government ostensibly called an end to the era of treaty-relations with American Indian tribes, an era that began in 1778 with the Treaty of Fort Pitt. To paraphrase a well-known American writer of that time, however, the report of the death of the treaty was greatly exaggerated. Before and after 1871, treaties have enjoyed a particular status as fundamentally important texts within the framework of U.S. Indian law. Other than during a brief period at the start of the twentieth century, treaties have consistently served as crucial rallying points in American Indian political discourse and resistance movements. Furthermore, from the beginning of contact with Euro-Americans in the territory that would become the United States, treaties and treaty-making have provided central themes and tropes in American Indian cultural history and literary production. What Chadwick Allen refers to as a "treaty discourse" informs a broad and rich tradition of what we might call "treaty literature."

Scholarly overviews of the history of treaty-making have taken a number of different forms. Francis Paul Prucha, for example, approaches the Indian treaty as a type of legal and political "anomaly." Working primarily from a U.S. legal perspective, Prucha tends to frame the history of treaty-making as the story of the gradual erosion of tribal sovereignty in the face of waxing American power. For him, the historical significance of treaties is to be found in their revelation of the process whereby Indian tribes gradually became what Chief Justice John Marshall designated them in *Cherokee Nation v. Georgia* (1831) – "domestic dependent nations."[1] While rooted in immense erudition, then, Prucha's approach to Indian treaties is in many ways what Gerald Vizenor would characterize as a "tragic" one, enclosing American Indian political potentiality within a type of "terminal creed." Evidence of this appears in Prucha's summary dismissal of the treaty-centered activism of the American Indian Movement (AIM) in the late 1960s and 1970s. In Prucha's view:

> Ignoring or consciously rejecting the anomalous situation in regard to treaties that a detailed historical analysis depicts, advocates of renewed treaty status proposed an idealistic return to the past or some new construct that fitted a particular theory. For some Indians, it was merely an exercise in nostalgia; for others, a handle with which to pressure the government for attention to the Indians' troubles; for a few, a hoped-for theoretical status looking back to some idea of absolute sovereignty.
>
> (411)

In marked contrast to these Indian activists, Prucha accepts the logic that ostensibly ended treaty-relations in 1871 as a given, albeit an unfortunate one.

In contrast with Prucha, Lumbee legal scholar Robert A. Williams Jr. has argued that an appreciation of the history of treaty-making that more fully takes into account tribal perspectives opens up a different set of possibilities. Williams urges us to recover an understanding of the "shared legal world" dominant during the colonial era, when the balance of power between Indian nations and European settlers was more equal (Williams 9). This alternate history, he suggests, supports the idea advanced by other scholars, such as Charles Wilkinson, that a firm legal foundation still exists for a form of measured separatism for tribal nations. Crucially, Williams argues, framing treaty history in a way that highlights the reciprocal diplomatic processes that dominated in the middle ground of early America (and that continued to manifest themselves during the nineteenth century) yields a "countermythology" that challenges the frontier thesis advanced by Frederick Jackson Turner (24). The core of this latter, imperial myth was written into American Constitutional law in key opinions of the Marshall Court – *Johnson v. McIntosh* (1823), *Cherokee Nation*. Those opinions, with their particular incorporation of the law of discovery and narratives of conquest into American jurisprudence, provided the logical foundation for subsequent diminishments of tribal sovereignty through the abandonment of treaty-relations. Williams opposes this with a rather different ethos. He reminds us that in the "shared legal world" of the colonial period it was widely understood that a "treaty," in its fullest sense, was not just a written text, but also the act of negotiating and *relating* peacefully with others. As he puts it, "Treaty making fulfilled what tribal Indians regarded as a sacred obligation to extend their relationships of connection to all of the different people of the world" (50). When one conceives of treaties and treaty-making in this broader fashion, it is possible to rewrite the tragic story that Prucha tells and transform it into one with more progressive possibilities. American Indian literary engagements with treaties and treaty-making, I would argue, have often essayed precisely that kind of re-scripting.

It is useful to imagine the relationship between treaty literature and treaty history as a series of intersections with a continuum bounded by the two theoretical models I have identified with Prucha and Williams. Native American literature often witnesses, and critiques, the ways that Indian treaties have been used as instruments of colonization by an increasingly domineering U.S. government. Numerous texts and artists draw attention to the misuse, manipulation, or abrogation of the treaty documents and to the effects on tribal communities of policies put into effect through often coercive negotiations. Some obvious examples would include Diane Glancy's *Pushing the Bear* (1996) and James Welch's *Fool's Crow* (1986), novels focused on Cherokee Removal and the confinement of Plains Indian nations to reservations during the nineteenth century. Louise Erdrich's 1988 novel *Tracks*, to take another example, depicts the allotment policy as a vehicle for assimilation and dispossession built on the foundations of the (treaty-based) creation of reservations. Supplementing works that document and reimagine historical injustices surrounding treaty history, though, we can also find numerous texts that lean toward Williams's end of the spectrum. Such works focus attention on the enduring potential of treaties (as historical documents and cultural forms) to advance the cause of sovereignty and to redefine the relationships between Indian communities and the United States. Examples of works that gesture in this direction would include William Apess's *A Son of the Forest* (1829) and Elizabeth Cook-Lynn's *Aurelia: A Crow Creek Trilogy* (1999). It is worth noting, of course, that many texts include a mixture of these modes of engagement with treaty history. This point, along with the fact that there are significant historical shifts in the nature of treaty-making that go beyond what brief summaries of Prucha's and Williams' work can show, suggests the value of looking in more detail at a set of examples of treaty literature with an eye toward their particular historical entanglements.

Following Williams' lead, we should begin by recognizing the foundations of U.S.–Indian treaty-making in colonial-era diplomacy. Doing so also allows us to initiate a broad and deep literary history that simultaneously supports Robert Warrior's call for the cultivation of tribal "intellectual sovereignty" (through a recognition of the rich cultural heritage to be found in the oral tradition and early non-fiction writing) while also highlighting the "multicultural" nature of treaty-writing that interests Williams.[2] As historians James Merrell and Colin Calloway have pointed out, treaties have been part of "American" writing and literature since the very beginnings of colonial contact. William Bradford, for example, recorded the terms of the 1621 treaty with the Wampanoag people led by Massasoit as part of *Of Plymouth Plantation*, and Lisa Brooks and Betty Booth Donohue have both suggested that we can reread that kind of colonial text as evidence of the emergence of an early form of transcultural treaty literature. Without question, treaties had become highly visible transatlantic literary productions by the eighteenth century, with Benjamin Franklin regularly printing the proceedings of negotiations with tribal nations and publishing these for sale in England (see Kalter). Franklin would put out thirteen of these volumes, and treaties have been available in print ever since (Calloway 6). Canon formation, then, might start there.

One prominent example of eighteenth-century treaty literature (the 1844 Treaty of Lancaster between the Iroquois Confederacy and the colonies of Pennsylvania, Virginia, and Maryland) offers an excellent example of Williams's "shared legal world." While there are problematic limitations in the text printed by Franklin (based on minutes taken by Penn family agent Richard Peters), James Merrell rightly characterizes the Lancaster text as a "hybrid Iroquois-European creation" (18). To be sure, the published work leaves out key parts of what mattered, from an Indian perspective, in the negotiations. The full scope of what constitutes a "treaty" for the Iroquois participants, we should recall, would include the informal conversations taking place outside of the formal speech making. These are missing from Franklin's text. We can also be sure that elements of the translated speeches were not conveyed entirely accurately or in their full complexity, and we know for a fact that some of the more difficult moments in the negotiation were left out of the final text, while some statements not actually made by the Commissioners of Virginia were put in the textual record. Franklin gives us a somewhat sanitized, idealized version of a treaty, in other words.

Despite these limitations, though, this piece of treaty literature does manage to capture much of the cultural breadth and complexity that Williams describes. The text conveys a clear sense of tribal sovereignty and agency, elements that Williams is keen to highlight in his argument that early treaties are clear precedents for contemporary assertions of measured separatism. As Merrell notes, reflecting their power as mediators between European colonial rivals and various tribal groups, "at Lancaster the Iroquois leaders, were, to a remarkable degree, running the show, conducting negotiations on their terms and not the colonists'" (viii). Not surprisingly, then, the book that emerged from the Lancaster proceedings draws considerable attention to indigenous diplomatic protocols, cultural practices, and linguistic forms. This attention to custom was vitally important for the Iroquois, for the essence of friendship, as they understood it, was in the process, and not just the final product of diplomatic relations (Merrell 16). The final written agreement (the "treaty" as the British understood it) was seen by the Iroquois as a somewhat superfluous reflection of the Europeans' needs. When the Onondaga orator Cannassatego comments on the nature of the proceedings, however, he instead draws attention to a broader sense of the "performative" elements of treaty-making. In just one small phrase printed by Franklin – "By these treaties we became Brethren," – the Lancaster text gestures toward a different kind of tradition of Native American treaty literature.

Merrell rightly observes that Franklin's book reads as a form of "compelling theater, a lively stage on which the peoples of early America acted out their contest for the continent" (10). It is no doubt true that many elements of the text (its listing of participants as if they were *dramatis personae* and presentation of diplomatic speeches as oratorical set pieces) create a sense of resemblance between the negotiation and a formal stage play. But even if European readers of the time were inclined to view the "book" of the Lancaster treaty as a theatrical performance, from a modern perspective we can discern a much more complex form of cultural performativity on display. Read from a viewpoint closer to the Iroquois one, as Williams suggests, we find in the document examples of the use of language to create what legal scholar Robert Cover calls stories of "jurisgenesis." Understood in a tribal context, the Lancaster treaty involved "the creation of new legal meanings" and the redefinition of a shared normative universe (or "nomos") between different polities, achieved through an act of collaborative and recursive storytelling (Williams 28). In this piece of treaty literature, then, we find many examples of the creation of relationships (kinship being the central concept underlying Iroquois diplomacy) on display. We see that no speech made by either side was answered immediately (allowing for time for communal reflection, and leading to subsequent effort to engage interlocutors in narrative compromises). We see that wampum belts were exchanged regularly as symbols of faithfulness (and as evidence of the approbation of Indian women – who were the primary makers of wampum – toward the speeches of their orators). We see the fact that the Indians and Europeans adopted a common metaphorical language of diplomacy. And through all of these elements, we find seeds of future expressions of the spirit and forms of the treaty in Native American literature.

A suggestive example of some of the ways that this early treaty history (and literature) informs subsequent indigenous expression can be found in the work of William Apess (1798?–1839). As I have argued elsewhere, Apess's 1829 autobiography *A Son of the Forest* subtly employs the rhetorical structures of colonial-era treaty-making (specifically Iroquoian) in his broader effort to engage with the language of antebellum American law. While Apess's primary focus in his autobiography (and in later works like *Indian Nullification*) was to manipulate the discourse of liberal property theory and subjectivity to defend Indian sovereignty in the northeast, he does so, in part, by employing "statements of mourning" to initiate a process of engagement (Carlson 95). This approach precisely mirrors the ways in which the Iroquoian Condolence ritual was adapted to undergird the system of Indian treaty-making (Williams 54). By opening his act of autobiographical self-definition with a traditional "lament" from the woods' edge, Apess signals that his text be read as a kind of treaty itself, as "an act of diplomatic engagement" focused on "the creation of cross-cultural connections and bonds of kinship" (Carlson 96).

Apess's invocation of King Philip (the Wampanoag sachem Metacomet), with whom he identifies as kin, highlights other ways that his broader literary oeuvre engages with the history and forms of colonial treaty-making. The most well-known of Apess's texts in his lifetime was his "Eulogy on King Philip," first delivered publicly at the Odeon theatre in Boston in 1836. There, Apess frames Philip as a heroic patriot who represents an earlier era of "international" relations between European and Indian sovereigns, mediated primarily by treaty-relations. Implicitly invoking the way that the Marshall Court had eroded treaty-based sovereignty through its application of the law of discovery to U.S. law, Apess notes that one of his goals in eulogizing Philip is to "melt the hearts of those who are in possession of his soil, and only by the right of conquest" (Apess 277). Beyond this, the "Eulogy" contains numerous references to the treaty-relations that existed between the Wampanoag people and the early English settlers; the fidelity of tribal leaders to those agreements and relationships contrasts directly with the perfidy of the English that led to the outbreak of war in 1675. Philip's resistance to the English abrogation of treaty-relations emerges, in Apess's prose, as a clear assertion of sovereignty, one that Apess apparently felt still had the potential to gain some traction even in the Jacksonian era. "I shall treat of peace only with a king, my brother," Apess reports Philip to have replied to messengers from the colonial leadership in Boston and, in doing so, he (Philip) conveyed clearly that "he felt his independence more than they thought he did" (294). The subsequent epic narrative of Philip's doomed war of resistance locates Apess's work of treaty literature as a rallying cry for Indian people in the early nineteenth century. Apess notes that "A foundation was laid in the first [colonial] Legislature to enslave our people," before imploring his audience to "Look at the treaties made by Congress, all broken" (306). In offering this type of testimonial, and by invoking the present-day controversies surrounding Indian removal through new, coerced treaties, Apess looks backward toward an alternate model where treaty-relations had the potential to establish and preserve tribal autonomy and reciprocal relationships between the inhabitants of New England.

To be sure, much of the essence of colonial-era diplomacy and history that we find recorded in the Treaty of Lancaster and reinterpreted by Apess dissipated during the nineteenth century. As Calloway has pointed out, early (colonial) treaties often revolved around trade and military alliances and, as such, they both required Indian cooperation and manifested an ethos of reciprocal recognition that would quite understandably be invoked by later writers, such as Apess and Williams. With some notable exceptions, though, the treaties signed after American Independence more typically focused on land cessions and Indian dispossession in a very different political climate and balance of power. Immediately after the 1783 Peace of Paris ending the Revolutionary War, American negotiators attempted to designate all Indian tribal nations as conquered peoples and aggressively imposed treaty terms upon them. One can find evidence of this in the 1784 Treaty of Fort Stanwix, which took a far different form from its 1768 colonial predecessor. American power was not *always* sufficient to dictate treaty provisions throughout the period from 1783 to 1871, of course. The American military suffered a series of defeats in its conflict with Ohio Valley nations during the late 1780s and early 1790s, for example, which led to a strategic rejection of Indian policy based purely on assertions of conquest. And the content of the 1868 Treaty of Fort Laramie, to take a later example, was largely shaped by the victorious Sioux at the end of Red Cloud's War.

Despite the aforementioned examples, it is nevertheless clear, as Stuart Banner has pointed out, that the general tendency of nineteenth-century Indian treaty-making was towards relatively involuntary and coercive contracts that employed U.S. legal frameworks as a structure through which to legitimize claims of title to Indian lands. Reciprocal relations were not a nineteenth-century American goal. Native American literary invocations of treaty-making from 1783–1871, however, often involve carefully crafted, pragmatic attempts to impel the American government and society to live up to the legal obligations encoded in even those ambiguous documents. Despite the fact that nineteenth-century U.S.–Indian treaty-making does not embody the same kind of relative balance of sovereignty we find during the colonial period, indigenous people nevertheless recognize, as Calloway puts it, that "[U.S.] Indian treaties have life and power. They are foundational documents in the nation's history. Alongside 'sacred texts' like the Declaration of Independence and the Constitution, and, like them, they are open to interpretation by subsequent generations" (10).

One interesting example of Native American literary engagement with the problematic history of nineteenth-century treaty-making can be found in Agua Caliente (Cahuilla) leader Francisco Patencio's *Stories and Legends of the Palm Springs Indians*. Patencio's book reveals how adaptations of the oral tradition into print can comprise another significant part of the modern body of treaty literature. *Stories and Legends* is divided into two parts: "The Creation," which contains a series of traditional Pass Cahuilla narratives about the origin of the world and the migrations and deeds of the early people; and "Patencio's Life," which incorporates more conventionally autobiographical and historical materials, while also offering a range of highly specific references to Cahuilla place-names in the Palm Springs area. In this respect, this act of storytelling functions as a kind of map, one with particular relevance to Agua Caliente concerns with treaty history. Patencio's version of the Cahuilla creation cycle contains a considerable amount of material not appearing in other printed versions. His extensive use of Cahuilla language-markers, for example, offers a rigorously localized form of his people's creation story, much of which would be shared universally by Cahuilla people throughout Southern California, but parts of which are par-ticular to the Agua Caliente band and their experience of place. The development of those connections extend across both Parts One and Two.

Patencio's storytelling generates the textual equivalent of a boundary map, one that functions both as a claim to the recognition of Cahuilla lands that should have been acknowledged by treaty and also as a way of reimagining the nature of treaty-relations to emphasize the importance of sharing space – of recognizing the presence of others, over time, in a mutually occupied landscape. "I know about all the Treaties from the time of the Missions and Spanish Grants," Patencio tells us. "All the agreements since Spain, Mexico, and United States have taken the land." (63). Knowing this history (and its ongoing effects in the 1930s), of course, Patencio also knew that none of the eighteen treaties negotiated with California Tribes in the early 1850s, which would have formally recognized some of their lands, were ever ratified by the U.S. Senate. As Van Garner has documented, however, the failure of the Senate to ratify these agreements was not communicated to the California tribes resulting in even further dispossession and land loss. To challenge this lack of recognition of Cahuilla territory and disrespect of treaty-relations, Patencio employs a densely *placed* narrative to mark out the boundaries that need to be recognized. Significantly, Patencio also recounts a number of stories that focus on the movements of others through Agua Caliente territory, not with the intent of undermining his own peo-ple's land claims, but rather as an acknowledgment of the fact that indigenous models of land ownership allow for multiple groups to share use of some of the same spaces. When, in Part Two of his text, Patencio recalls the presence of several American 'pioneers' in the

Coachella Valley (and even includes place names of stagecoach stations in the territory), then, he is not conceding title to colonial conquerors. Rather, he is reasserting an ethos that demands the recognition of the presence of others in the landscape, not their erasure. This is a powerful model of how treaty literature can emerge in response to the complexities of the history of colonization.

A more indirect, but perhaps more conventionally literary response to this history would be Thomas King's 1993 comic novel *Green Grass, Running Water*, the title of which playfully invokes the regularly broken promises of written treaty-agreements.[3] The problem of "time" as it relates to treaty-making (and particularly to shifting American interpretations of the meaning of treaties) is the serious theme underneath the surface of King's playful postmodernism. In his book, *American Indians, Time, and the Law*, Charles Wilkinson draws attention to the ways that the American legal system has historically attempted to undermine the sovereignty of tribal communities and alter the terms of its own relationship with those communities by designating them as "belated" and outside of the framework of modernity. (Political scientist Kevin Bruyneel traces this phenomenon as well in his book *The Third Space of Sovereignty*.) Tribes have been particularly vulnerable, Wilkinson reminds us, to arguments based on "waiver, laches, forfeiture, statutes of limitation, adverse possession, and other doctrines premised on dilatory conduct" (37). The historical fact that tribal governments have often "gone dormant" (at least in the eyes of courts) has also been regularly used against them. The best example of this, perhaps, is the concept of "termination," which was employed in the mid-twentieth century as a way of severing federal relations with tribal nations that were deemed no longer historically viable as political entities. And as Wilkinson notes, "The notion that tribal existence could be terminated because of the passage of time, [even] without congressional action, continued to be reflected in numerous federal and state cases during the twentieth century" (35).

The most significant counterweight to the tendency to erase tribes from the modern world, is the huge corpus of extant treaties (even those problematic and coercive nineteenth-century versions). As Wilkerson points out, "Indian law ... is a time-warped field," in no small measure because courts regularly are drawing meaning from statutes of another age (13). These "old laws" are most often "the treaties and treaty substitutes that established Indian reservations" (14). And the central thrust of those old laws, Wilkinson argues, was to create a form of measured separatism that preserved significant elements of tribal sovereignty. *Green Grass, Running Water* is, in many respects, a literary exploration of the idea that a conscious embrace of this "time warp" is empowering to tribal communities. King's book is structured around four tellings of tribal creation stories, narrated by four unaccountably old Indians who also share the names of famous "colonial" Euro-American figures well-known for their Indian sidekicks (Cooper's Hawkeye, Melville's Ishmael, Defoe's Robinson Crusoe, and the Lone Ranger). The creation tales told by these figures intertwine throughout the book with the present-day experiences of contemporary Indian characters wrestling with questions of identity, relationship to kin, and land rights. While a major thrust of the novel is obviously satirical, one should also note that its postmodern play with time and inter-textuality has the effect of making a wide range of characters and types of stories *co-present* throughout the novel. Distinctions between the "mythic" past, literary history, and current events dissolve in the novel, as do firm lines between the Indian world and the Euro-American one. In this respect, *Green Grass, Running Water* is a language game whose stakes mirror those of the legal struggles being waged in the "real" world surrounding treaty rights. In the context of modern litigation, as Wilkerson points out, tribes have "continually sought to prevent the use of time against them" (30). By working through a narrative form to prevent the Indian world from being relegated to a "savage" past (one that can be dismissed by the American legal system or placed in a state of "domestic dependency"), King's form of treaty literature complements tribes' contemporary efforts to "make time work in their favor" by reasserting the sovereignty embedded in treaty relations.

This type of reassertion, of course, has been the hallmark of much of the activism of the national (and indeed, international) Indian movement that began in the late 1960s and continues to have an impact in the present. Vine Deloria's *Behind the Trail of Broken Treaties* is both a compelling historical account of why treaty-making continues to matter in Indian Country today and an example of treaty literature in its own right. Deloria's immediate purpose in writing the book was to clarify for American readers the historical context and motivations behind the American Indian Movement-led "Trail of Broken Treaties" march on Washington, D.C. in 1972, as well as the subsequent occupation and standoff at Wounded Knee in 1973. In laying out the colonial and legal history behind these events, though, his larger purpose was to suggest the viability of a return to treaty-relations between the United States and tribes, relations that might take the form of "quasi-protectorate" status for what would be largely independent tribal nations. Deloria embraces demands 1, 2, 4, 5, 6, 7, and 8 of the famous "Twenty Points" document submitted to the Nixon Administration by the Trail of Broken Treaties leadership. Those demands involved calls for the

> restoration of the authority to make treaties with Indian communities, with the need to enforce treaty provisions for the protection of Indian individuals and with the need to place all Indian people under a new general category of status to be known as "treaty relations."
>
> (Deloria xii)

In this respect, Deloria not only documents the political events of his own time, he also calls for a broad refocusing on treaty discourse throughout Indian Country. Even if he is sometimes critical of their poor strategizing, Deloria embraces much of what the activist leadership of groups like AIM (led by figures such as Russell Means and Dennis Banks) achieved – reawakening a sense of Indian pride and assertiveness and reminding Indian people that an alternative, and potentially decolonizing history of treaty-making might be told. "On a deeper, more intellectual level, and of world significance," Deloria writes,

> Wounded Knee marked a historic watershed in the relations of American Indians and Western European peoples. The theory of treaties as articulated by the Oglalas called for a reexamination of the four centuries of contact between Indians and whites on the continent. In demanding independence for the Oglala nation, the people at Wounded Knee sought a return to the days of pre-discovery, when the tribes of this land had political independence and sovereignty ... Wounded Knee marked the first sustained modern protest against the Western European interpretation of history.
>
> (80)

A significant strain of contemporary treaty literature has taken up this spirit of resistance.

Means's autobiography, *Where White Men Fear to Tread*, is an interesting example of how the activist spirit of the 1960s and 1970s, particularly in its emphasis on treaty-based sovereignty, has been translated into literary forms. Means's account of his life is structured, explicitly and implicitly, around the concept of treaty-making and the history of specific agreements. He opens the text, significantly, with a discussion of place, locating himself and the reader in the South Dakota landscape of the Yankton Reservation (his mother's ancestral homeland). Means reminds us of the Yankton's fully sovereign possession of this land, before the era of reservations and the federal hydroelectric projects changed the Missouri river and flooded tribal lands. Significantly, he then connects his sense of "national' consciousness and memory of place to a treaty – the agreement signed between representatives of the Yankton and the U.S. Government in Washington, D.C. in 1858. Means presents the history of the 1858 Treaty in a decidedly negative light. He notes that while it is commemorated by a stone monument (made by whites) on the reservation, the treaty was signed under dubious circumstances, with the Yankton delegation essentially confined and misled in the nation's capital until they signed an agreement. The 1858 treaty, then, represents for Means the colonizing power of the United States, a power that corrupts by destroying tribal unity.

The struggle against that power becomes the central metaphor for Means's own life struggle, described in the rest of the autobiography. This is the battle of an urban Indian, cut off from his heritage and shamed by the history of dispossession, to recover a sense of tradition and take his place in "a long line of patriots" (8). Significantly, Means positions another treaty, the 1868 Treaty of Fort Laramie that inspired and mobilized much of the AIM activism of which he was a part, against what was represented in the 1858 document. The first treaty reveals a divided, outmaneuvered, and dispossessed people. The second represents a united, potently resurgent, and sovereign people. The central theme of *Where White Men Fear to Tread*, then, is that it is possible to live one's life in a kind of treaty-spirit, and that doing so provides not only a path forward for tribal nations but also a source of personal, individual redemption. This idea informs the sub-theme of the autobiography – gender imbalance and problems with Indian masculinity as a result of the disruption of traditional lifeways and the diminishment of the roles women play in them. It is no coincidence that Means began his book *on his mother's land* and stressing the matrilineal traditions of his people. In the end, the narrative suggests that Means's reconnection with tradition through his treaty-centered activism allowed him to master the personal addictions and anger that created damaging effects on himself and those around him. Treaty literature links diplomacy and family for Means in a way that might recall the earlier history of treaty-making celebrated by Williams, with its emphasis on kinship relations.

Elizabeth Cook-Lynn provides a final example of how complex the interplay between law and literature can be in modern Native American writing. Throughout her career, Cook-Lynn has focused not only on creating tribal-centered works of fiction and poetry but also on consistently advocating for a new treaty-based defense against dispossession of resources and lands. As she has also argued with some frequency, then, a full understanding of the significance of her fiction (even such short, enigmatic pieces as the story "Mahpiyato" that opens her collection *The Power of Horses*) requires an awareness of the centrality of treaty-relations to her own thinking and to the history of the Dakotah people. Cook-Lynn's reasons for placing written treaties with the United States, specifically, at the heart of her thinking and writing are simultaneously philosophical, historical, and personal.

Skepticism regarding the utility of other legal strategies (such as suits within the United States court system or constitutional reform) as effective vehicles for pursuing sovereignty has been a key element. Additionally, her understanding of sovereignty as an expression both of tribal autonomy in governance and of indigenous knowledge rooted in a specific land base intersects very explicitly with the Dakotah experience of nineteenth-century treaty-making. In particular, the traumatic theft of the sacred site of the Black Hills, in violation of the 1868 Fort Laramie agreement, provides a central rallying cry in her work. Finally, the common misreading of the history of the American West as the "conquest" of the Plains Indians has caused Cook-Lynn to invoke treaty history as a means of countering that narrative; this move is central to her efforts to challenge the controlling legal doctrine of "discovery." One might say with some justification, then, that for Cook-Lynn the 1868 Treaty of Fort Laramie is both the discursive cause of, and the essential context for all of her critical work as well as for the writing of her own fiction and poetry.

Cook-Lynn's vision also demands the creation of a new critical paradigm for Native American Studies, one that we might call "treaty-criticism," or "treaty-reading." In her *Notebooks*, she provides a "reading guide" for her novel trilogy *Aurelia*, foregrounding a series of treaties and land claim cases and suggesting that the work is "mostly, a story about crime, both the institutional crime of theft of tribal lands and individual crimes like murder and rape" (Cook-Lynn *Notebooks* 51). One facet of the "treaty-reading" she advocates, then, is the need to view documents like the 1868 Treaty of Fort Laramie as the implied context for many other pieces of writing, even pieces that do not directly or obviously reference them; this considerably broadens the scope of what might be considered treaty literature. The aforementioned short story "Mahpiyato" implicitly offers both a complement to the 1868 agreement (fleshing out the tribal understanding of their relationship to some of the territory in question) and a corrective to its subsequent interpretation in the courts (the land claims cases surrounding the Black Hills controversy). Similarly, in much of Cook-Lynn's other poetry and short fiction, the legal context of treaty history provides a necessary element for the reader who is responding to what might otherwise seem fragmentary or ambiguous musings. Taken in toto, then, Cook-Lynn's oeuvre offers a strikingly synthetic approach to integrating treaties into both critical and literary work.

As Vine Deloria has argued:

> The treaty process is a shorthand way of viewing the history of America's expansion. The evolution of the treaty – from a mutual agreement between sovereigns, each ostensibly giving and receiving, to the rubber-stamp land conveyances that opened the West – reflects a concept of sovereignty that is not static or absolute ... It varies according to time and place.
>
> (108)

What Deloria says here of treaty history is equally true of Native American treaty literature. As I have tried to suggest, there already exists a highly varied and politically engaged "canon" of treaty-centered texts within the field of Native American Studies. And treaties are only increasing in importance, both as objects of historical study and as loci for literary production. We find today a significant upswing of treaty-centered writing. Going forward, we might anticipate even greater emphasis on treaty history and treaty discourse, reflecting the increasing internationalization of the field and the ratification of the United Nations

Declaration on the Rights of Indigenous Peoples. The type of grounded knowledge base one can develop from the close study of treaty-making and treaty literature in a U.S. context, then, will also serve as a vital point of contact with new forms of transnational indigenous studies that are emerging today.

Notes

1 Key excerpts from the Marshall decisions can be found in Francis Prucha, ed. *Documents of United States Indian Policy*. 3rd ed. Lincoln: University of Nebraska Press, 2000 or in the online (accessed 16 Oct. 2014) database https://supreme.justia.com/
2 We might note, in passing, that this type of integrative project was anticipated in some ways decades ago by Lawrence Wroth in a 1928 *Yale Review* essay titled "The Indian Treaty as Literature."
3 Interestingly, as Vine Deloria points out, the phrase "as long as the rivers flow and the grass grows" appears frequently in treaty proceedings, but it is only actually found in one of the treaties between the Confederacy and the Five Civilized Tribes at the start of the American Civil War (*Behind the Trail* 132).

Works cited

Allen, Chadwick. *Blood Narrative: Indigenous Identity in American Indian and Maori Literary and Activist Texts*. Durham, NC: Duke University Press, 2002.

Apess, William. *A Son of the Forest, and Other Writings*. Ed. Barry O'Connell. Amherst: University of Massachusetts Press, 1997.

Banner, Stuart. *How the Indians Lost Their Land: Law and Power on the Frontier*. Cambridge, MA: Harvard University Press, 2005.

Bradford, William. *Of Plymouth Plantation, 1620–1647*. New York: McGraw-Hill, 1981.

Brooks, Lisa. *The Common Pot: The Recovery of Native Space in the Northeast*. Minneapolis: University of Minnesota Press, 2008.

Bruyneel, Kevin. *The Third Space of Sovereignty: The Post-Colonial Politics of U.S.–Indigenous Relations*. Minneapolis: University of Minnesota Press, 2007.

Calloway, Colin G. *Pen and Ink Witchcraft: Treaties and Treaty Making in American Indian History*. Oxford: Oxford University Press, 2013.

Carlson, David J. *Sovereign Selves: American Indian Autobiography and the Law*. Urbana: University of Illinois Press, 2006.

Cook-Lynn, Elizabeth. *Aurelia: A Crow Creek Trilogy*. Niwot: University of Colorado Press, 1999.

——. *Notebooks of Elizabeth Cook-Lynn*. Tucson: University of Arizona Press, 2007.

——. *The Power of Horses and Other Stories*. Tucson: University of Arizona Press, 2006.

Cover, Robert. M. "The Supreme Court, 1982 Term – Foreword: Nomos and Narrative" (1983). *Faculty Scholarship Series*. Paper 2705. Web. Accessed 16 Oct. 2014. http://digitalcommons.law.yale.edu/fss.papers/2705

Deloria, Vine, Jr. *Behind the Trail of Broken Treaties: An Indian Declaration of Independence*. New York: Dell Publishing, 1974.

Donohue, Betty Booth. *Bradford's Indian Book: Being the True Root and Rise of American Letters as Revealed by the Native Text Embedded in of Plimoth Plantation*. Gainesville: University Press of Florida, 2011.

Erdrich, Louise. *Tracks*. New York: Harper Perennial, 2004.

Garner, Van H. *The Broken Ring: The Destruction of the California Indians*. Tucson, AZ: Westernlore Press, 1983.

Glancy, Diane. *Pushing the Bear: A Novel of the Trail of Tears*. New York: Harcourt Brace, 1996.

Kalter, Susan. *Benjamin Franklin, Pennsylvania, and the First Nations: The Treaties of 1736–1762*. Urbana: University of Illinois Press, 2006.

King, Thomas. *Green Grass, Running Water*. New York: Bantam Books, 1993.

Means, Russell. *Where White Men Fear to Tread*. New York: St. Martin's Press, 1995.

Merrell, James H., ed. *The Lancaster Treaty of 1744, with Related Documents*. New York: Bedford St. Martins, 2008.

O'Connell, Barry, ed. *On Our Own Ground: The Complete Writings of William Apess, a Pequot*. Amherst: University of Massachusetts Press, 1992.

Patencio, Chief Francisco. *Stories and Legends of the Palm Springs Indians*. Los Angeles: Times-Mirror, 1943.

Prucha, Francis Paul. *American Indian Treaties: The History of a Political Anomaly*. Berkeley: University of California Press, 1997.

———, ed. *Documents of United State Indian Policy*. 3rd ed. Lincoln: University of Nebraska Press, 2000.

Turner, Fredrick Jackson. *The Significance of the Frontier in American History*. New York: Penguin, 2008.

Vizenor, Gerald. *Manifest Manners: Narratives on Postindian Survivance*. Lincoln: University of Nebraska Press, 1999.

Warrior, Robert. *The People and the Word: Reading Native Nonfiction*. Minneapolis: University of Minnesota Press, 2005.

Welch, James. *Fool's Crow*. New York: Penguin, 2011.

Wilkinson, Charles F. *American Indians, Time, and the Law: Native Societies in a Modern Constitutional Democracy*. New Haven, CT: Yale University Press, 1988.

Williams, Robert A., Jr. *Linking Arms Together: American Indian Treaty Visions of Law and Peace, 1600–1800*. London: Routledge, 1999.

Wroth, Lawrence. "The Indian Treaty as Literature." *Yale Review* (July, 1928): 749–66.

10

The Marshall Trilogy
and Its Legacies

Sabine N. Meyer

The Marshall trilogy

The three famous opinions by the U.S. Supreme Court's Chief Justice John Marshall between 1823 and 1832 have shaped the contours of federal Indian law up to the present day (Fletcher, "Iron Cold" 626). *Johnson v. McIntosh* (1823), *Cherokee Nation v. Georgia* (1831), and *Worcester v. Georgia* (1832) – first described as a "trilogy" by Charles Wilkinson (24) – need to be read as attempts: 1) to define and codify the legal relationship between the United States and Native American tribes by defining the extent of their sovereignty and the nature of their property rights; and 2) to construct a coherent imperial geography by defining Native legal subjectivities which could be absorbed into this geography and incorporated into U.S. hegemonic jurisdictional structures (see Banner; Rifkin).

Johnson v. McIntosh (1823)

Johnson v. McIntosh marked a shift in property relations between Native Americans and the colonizer. By the mid-eighteenth century, official British colonial policy was firmly based on the assumption that Native Americans owned all their land, which could be obtained from them through purchase only. While individual settlers often violated this colonial policy by trespassing on Native lands, it remained firmly in place, even after the American Revolution (Banner 157). The early nineteenth century, however, witnessed a transformation in legal thought. Because of an ever-expanding market in pre-emption rights, Native Americans came to be considered occupants rather than owners of the land, with the fee simple resting with the state and federal governments (Banner 150, 174).

By legally codifying the relatively new concept of Native occupancy, *Johnson* "put a final nail in the coffin of the older view of Indian property rights" and conquered Native America through law (Banner 179; Robertson xiii). Chief Justice Marshall legitimized "the Indian right of occupancy" (Johnson n. pag.) by recurring to both a legal and a cultural fiction. The legal fiction he employed was the so-called discovery doctrine. "[D]iscovery," Marshall argued,

> gave title to the government by whose subjects, or by whose authority, it was made, against all other European governments, which title might be consummated

by possession. The exclusion of all other Europeans, necessarily gave to the nation making the discovery the sole right of acquiring the soil from the natives, and establishing settlements upon it.

(Johnson n. pag.)

After formally adopting the discovery doctrine into federal common law (Fletcher "Iron Cold" 631), Marshall elaborated how the doctrine limited Native rights to their land. While they "were admitted to be the rightful occupants of the soil, with a legal as well as just claim to retain possession of it, and to use it according to their own discretion," "their power to dispose of the soil at their own will, to whomsoever they pleased, was denied." The European powers exercised "ultimate dominion": "a power to grant the soil, while yet in possession of the natives" (Johnson n. pag.).

By sleight of hand, Marshall turned Natives from owners into occupants of the soil. The pre-emption right as well as the title to the land he assigned to "either the United States or the several states" (Johnson n. pag.). The alienation of Native lands and thus the extinguishment of Native title, the Chief Justice further argued, could take place "either by purchase or by conquest" (Johnson n. pag.).[1] While hinting at the fact that the Court did not necessarily approve of the "extravagant … pretension of converting the discovery of an inhabited country into conquest," Marshall emphasized that "[c]onquest gives a title which the Courts of the conqueror cannot deny …" (Johnson n. pag.). He conceded that the law clearly regulated the relations between the conqueror and the conquered but then proceeded to apply the long-held cultural fiction of Native savagism in order to justify that "under such circumstances" an application of the law of nations was not possible:

But the tribes of Indians inhabiting this country were fierce savages, whose occupation was war, and whose subsistence was drawn chiefly from the forest. To leave them in possession of their country was to leave the country a wilderness; to govern them as a distinct people was impossible, because they were as brave and as high spirited as they were fierce, and were ready to repel by arms every attempt on their independence.

(Johnson n. pag.)

The savage character of Native Americans, elaborated by Marshall at length, thwarted adherence to principles of humanity. His writing into law of the legal and cultural fictions of the discovery doctrine and Indian savagism became instrumental in removing the southeastern tribes (see Krupat 133; Robertson 118–25).

Cherokee Nation v. Georgia (1831)

Cherokee Nation v. Georgia immediately resulted from the Cherokee tribe's quarrels with the state of Georgia over the latter's unlawful extension of its jurisdiction over their tribal lands and centered upon the question of states' rights. Early in 1831, on behalf of the Cherokee Nation as a foreign nation, the attorneys John Sergeant and William Wirt petitioned the Supreme Court, asking the judges to grant an injunction interdicting enforcement of Georgia's jurisdiction laws within the territory of the Cherokee Nation. Notwithstanding the fragmentation of the Court's eventual decision, the majority of judges decided against conceptualizing the Cherokee Nation as a foreign nation capable of suing under the Court's doctrine of original jurisdiction (Norgren 99–100; Burke 503; Fletcher "Iron Cold" 639).

In his lead opinion, Marshall never addressed the question of whether Georgia's extension laws violated treaty agreements or the American Constitution. Instead, he inquired into whether the Cherokee Nation could be considered "a foreign state in the sense of the Constitution." The Chief Justice concluded that

> it may well be doubted whether those tribes which reside within the acknowledged boundaries of the United States can, with strict accuracy, be denominated foreign nations. They may, more correctly, perhaps, be denominated domestic dependent nations. They occupy a territory to which we assert a title independent of their will, which must take effect in point of possession when their right of possession ceases. Meanwhile they are in a state of pupilage. Their relation to the United States resembles that of a ward to his guardian.
>
> (Cherokee n. pag.)

"Marshall," as Jill Norgren has pointed out,

> represented Indian nations as being *domestic* in the sense that their territories were located within the exterior boundaries of the United States, *dependent* because of the limitations placed on them with respect to war and foreign negotiations, and *national* because they were distinctly separate peoples outside the American polity.
>
> (103)

Through this oxymoronic classification, Marshall reaffirmed the idea of Native rights of occupancy developed in *Johnson*, while at the same time strengthening Native rights to self-governance. He also extricated the Court from the struggles for power between the federal government and the states over Native affairs and from the debates about Native rights. While conceding that "[t]he mere question of right might perhaps be decided by this court in a proper case with proper parties," he concluded his ruling with the following disheartening words:

> If it be true that the Cherokee Nation have rights, this is not the tribunal in which those rights are to be asserted. If it be true that wrongs have been inflicted, and that still greater are to be apprehended, this is not the tribunal which can redress the past or prevent the future.
>
> (Cherokee n. pag.)

Despite the Court's unwillingness to grant the desired injunction, *Cherokee Nation* became one of its most famous decisions due to Marshall's extensive discussion of the nature of Native tribal sovereignty (Banner 219).

Worcester v. Georgia (1832)

The question of Cherokee rights continued to haunt the Supreme Court. In late 1830, Georgia's legislature implemented a bill prohibiting the passage of "any white person" onto the territory of the Cherokee Nation without the permission of the state. A group of missionaries, headed by Samuel A. Worcester, defied the law, declaring it to be violating Cherokee sovereignty. As a consequence, they were arrested by Georgia state police and sentenced to four years hard labor in the state penitentiary. These events enabled Wirt and Sergeant to challenge Georgia's extension laws in the U.S. Supreme Court once again, using the white missionaries as plaintiffs. The question at hand in *Worcester v. Georgia* was whether the missionaries had been arrested, tried, and sentenced under a state law violating the Constitution's Commerce Clause. The appeal also asked the Marshall Court to decide whether the Cherokee Republic was a sovereign nation recognized by treaties and outside the jurisdiction of the single states (Norgren 112–15).

On 3 March 1832, Chief Justice Marshall – writing for himself and three other justices – ruled against the state of Georgia, declaring the condemnation of the missionaries and the act on which this condemnation was based as "repugnant to the Constitution, treaties or laws of the United States." He also modified the Court's previous rulings, in particular *Johnson*. While in *Johnson* Marshall had claimed that "discovery gave title," in *Worcester* he announced that discovery gave the discoverers "exclusive right to purchase," that is, it merely conferred a right of pre-emption (Worcester n. pag.). Contrary to *Johnson*, he also dismissed the idea of the extinguishment of title through conquest and considered the charters "blank paper so far as the rights of the natives were concerned." The Revolutionary War, he claimed, was not a war of conquest and consequently "did not assert any right of dominion" over Natives. While treaties were absent from *Johnson*, *Worcester* included the history of treaty-making from 1778 to 1832, emphasizing the treaties' "language of equality." Marshall paid particular attention to the Treaty of Hopewell, from which he quoted extensively in order to demonstrate that it "explicitly recogniz[ed] the national character of the Cherokees and their right to self-government, thus guarantying (sic) their lands, assuming the duty of protection, and of course pledging the faith of the United States for that protection ..." (Worcester n. pag.). While in *Johnson* he had spoken out against Native ownership and unlimited disposition after discovery, in *Worcester* the Chief Justice asserted that the tribes had lost their unlimited disposition rights but retained ownership and possession of their lands after discovery (Watson 999).

In contrast to the cultural fiction of Native savagism he had propagated in *Johnson*, in *Worcester* Marshall explicitly referred to the civilizational progress the Cherokees had made and to the encouragement they had received from the U.S. government. The Chief Justice also elaborated on, and attenuated, the concept of "domestic dependent nation" he had developed in *Cherokee Nation*, this time emphasizing the tribes' political independence:

> The Indian nations had always been considered as distinct, independent political communities, retaining their original natural rights as the undisputed possessors of the soil from time immemorial, with the single exception of that imposed by irresistible power, which excluded them from intercourse with any other European potentate than the first discoverer of the coast of the particular region claimed .... The very term "nation," so generally applied to them, means "a people distinct

from others." The Constitution, by declaring treaties ... to be the supreme law of the land, has adopted and sanctioned the previous treaties with the Indian nations, and consequently admits their rank among the powers who are capable of making treaties. The words "treaty" and "nation" are words of our own language, selected in our diplomatic and legislative proceedings by ourselves, having each a definite and well understood meaning. We have applied them to Indians as we have applied them to the other nations of the earth. They are applied to all in the same sense.

(Worcester n. pag.)

In his argumentative conclusion, Marshall again emphasized that state law did not apply on tribal lands and that the intercourse between Natives and the United States was the legal prerogative of the federal government:

The Cherokee nation, then, is a distinct community, occupying its own territory, with boundaries accurately described, in which the laws of Georgia can have no force, and which the citizens of Georgia have no right to enter but with the assent of the Cherokees themselves, or in conformity with treaties and with the acts of Congress. The whole intercourse between the United States and this nation is, by our Constitution and laws, vested in the Government of the United States.

(Worcester n. pag.)

"*Worcester* was intended to prove *Johnson*'s undoing," to use Lindsay Robertson's words (133). However, although Georgia's governor eventually pardoned and released the missionaries (Norgren 128), *Worcester* did not help the Cherokees to avert removal. "The Court," as Stuart Banner has argued, "lacked the power to invalidate acts of the government of Georgia that did not contribute to Worcester's conviction, and it certainly could not order the federal government, which was not a party to the case, to intervene" (Banner 222).

The significance of the Marshall trilogy for Native American literature

The trilogy's legal repercussions can still be felt today. Legal scholars have expounded the import of Marshall's conception of Native sovereignty and Native rights in modern federal Indian law (Tsosie & Coffey 192–94; Fletcher "Iron Cold" 648–67). As the foundation of federal Indian law, the trilogy and its legal implications have dominated all facets of Native American life, including Native literary production. Native American literature and the trilogy, I argue, are interrelated in three different ways.

First, federal Indian law, including the Marshall trilogy, constitutes the socio-legal context in which Native literary texts are produced. Pleading for the "intimacy of law and literatures" in the field of Native American Studies, Eric Cheyfitz has argued that "federal Indian law has been the indispensable but obscured text and context to an understanding of U.S. Native American oral and written expression" (8). "Due to the fact that non-indigenous institutions legally define and regulate the 'political rights and sovereignty' of native peoples," Mark Rifkin argues by borrowing from Dale Turner, "negotiation with the 'intellectual landscapes' of imperial authority is necessary" (74). Native American texts – both non-fictional and fictional – have inevitably had to engage, thematically as well as aesthetically, with the legal discourses and legal landscapes put in place by the colonizer. As such, they can only be understood by placing them within the historical and legal framework of federal Indian law.

Second, Native American fictional and non-fictional texts "actively participate in the process of lawmaking, legal interpretation, and policymaking" (Katanski 53). By engaging with federal Indian law, Native American literature adds its own legal vision to that law, so that we can conceive of the relationship between Native American literature and federal Indian law as a dialogical one. Beth Piatote, for instance, has described the added value of a contrapuntal reading of law and literature as follows:

> The law names particular subjects, but unnamed subjects remain within its grasp. By viewing law and literature together, it is possible to see the effects upon the unnamed as well as the named subjects in the ordering of social hierarchies and the distribution of political rights.
>
> (10)

Christine Metteer Lorillard even claims that literature "make[s] the law free" by "[illuminating] [its] shadowy dictates" (252–53). And Kristen A. Carpenter points out that the need to contextualize legal rules through Native American literature is "particularly acute" with respect to federal Indian law; due to its rootedness in the colonizers' legal traditions, it alienates, and oppresses, its "Indian constituents" (605; see also Duthu 143; Rifkin 25–31; Carlson 7).

Native American literary texts critically reflect upon how federal Indian law, in general, and the Marshall trilogy, in particular, have affected Native identities, forms of governance, and notions of property, as well as the Natives' relationship to the land. They address the trilogy's impairment, even abrogation, of Native sovereignty and explore the legal subjectivities it has created and superimposed upon the tribes. They intervene in the legal discourses imposed by the colonizer, sometimes appropriating and at other times subverting and decentering the language of the law. Many Native American writers emphasize the effectiveness of their storytelling to achieve justice and to break through the hegemonic structures of the Anglo-American legal system. The most famous example might be Leslie Marmon Silko, who decided to quit law school to become a writer because she felt that law was unable to administer justice:

> When I was a sophomore in high school I decided that law school was the place to seek justice. I majored in English ... only because I loved to read and write about what I'd read. ... but my destination was law school where I planned to learn how to obtain justice.
>
> ...
>
> I completed three semesters in the American Indian Law School Fellowship Program before I realized that injustice is built into the Anglo-American legal system. ...
>
> I decided the only way to seek justice was through the power of stories.
>
> (19–20)

Third, Native American literature plays a pivotal role in the creation of an alternative to the tribal sovereignty crafted on the basis of the Marshall trilogy and subsequent legislation (see Fletcher "Looking"; Singel; Tsosie & Coffey). Tribal sovereignty has, in past years, come under increasing attack. Thus, Tsosie and Coffey appeal to Native Americans to turn their backs on a sovereignty defined and circumscribed by the American legal system:

> Too often, we as Indian people are forced to litigate our rights within the dominant society's appraisal of tribal sovereignty. We cite the Marshall Trilogy as if the concept of "domestic dependent nation" really means something in terms of our legal rights. ... We enter the court citing *Cherokee Nation* and *Worcester* as our charter of sovereignty ... . To the extent that we litigate our right to sovereignty within this legal framework, we have lost the true essence of our sovereignty.
>
> (196; see also Fletcher "Looking" 3)

Instead of seeking to achieve tribal sovereignty through the American legal system, Native Americans should – according to Tsosie and Coffey – strive for "cultural sovereignty," that is, "the internal construction of sovereignty through Native peoples themselves" (Tsosie 1). Native storytelling and literature are at the center of such a construction of cultural sovereignty from within. "Tribal law and culture," Fletcher claims, "are collections of stories. The same stories that scholars study as snapshots of tribal culture are also stories about a tribe's law" ("Looking" 3).

While John Borrows writes about how the old stories, such as trickster tales, can form the basis of tribal law, Fletcher highlights the significance of new stories, "the stories that interpret the old stories for the new era" (Borrows 13–23, 46–54; also Fletcher "Looking" 4). Fundamental questions such as the shape and form of legal identity under tribal law need to be answered by taking into account the modern experiences of Native Americans (and not by studying U.S. American laws). Only by restoring the old stories of historic sovereignty and by integrating them with contemporary Native stories can Native Americans define, assert, insist upon, and protect cultural sovereignty (Fletcher "Looking" 19; Tsosie & Coffey 196).

Native American writers have become aware of the central role they and their stories play in the development of modern tribal law. Gerald Vizenor drafted the recently adopted Constitution of the White Earth Nation, emphasizing the inextricable link between Native storytelling and cultural sovereignty in its preamble: "The Anishinaabeg create stories of natural reason, of courage, loyalty, humor, spiritual inspiration, survivance, reciprocal altruism, and native cultural sovereignty" ("Constitution of the White Earth Nation").

The Marshall trilogy in selected Native writings

Initial indigenous responses to the Marshall trilogy included that of John Ross, Chief of the Cherokee Nation, who first responded to *Johnson* in 1828. That year, the state of Georgia had begun to annex parcels of Cherokee land with the intent to distribute them among settler-citizens. Georgia state authorities legitimized their actions by recurring to *Johnson* (Robertson 118–25). Therefore, in his annual message to the Cherokee tribe on 13 October 1828, Ross challenged the ruling by questioning the doctrine of discovery:

> In the first place, the Europeans ... discovered this vast Continent, and found it inhabited exclusively by Indians of various Tribes, and by a pacific courtesy and designing stratagems, the aboriginal proprietors were induced to permit a people from a foreign clime to plant colonies, and without consent or knowledge of the native Lords, a potentate of England whose eyes never saw, whose purse never purchased, and whose sword never conquered the soil we inhabit, presumed to issue a parchment called a "Charter," to the Colony of Georgia, in which its boundary was set forth, including a great extent of country inhabited by the Cherokees and other Indian Nations. ... Thus stands the naked claim of Georgia, to a portion of our lands. The claim advanced under the plea of discovery, is preposterous. Our ancestors from time immemorial possessed the country, not by a "Charter" from the hand of a mortal King, who had no right to grant it, but by the Will of the King of Kings, who created all things and liveth for ever & ever.
>
> (qtd. in Moulton 142–43)

In this indigenous version of the European discovery of the New World, Ross expanded Marshall's Eurocentric tale by Native agency. It had been the Natives – the owners of the soil – who had granted the discoverers the right to plant settlements. He also considered the charters, described by Marshall as "purport[ing] to convey the soil as well as the right of dominion" (Johnson n. pag.), incapable of transferring Native property rights to Europeans, as their issuance involved neither purchase nor conquest. Ross deemed the idea of Indian occupancy as such preposterous. The Cherokees had received the land from God rather than from a mortal king a time long before Europeans had set foot on the North American continent. In several other writings, the Chief countered the Chief Justice's cultural fiction of Native Americans as "fierce savages" by developing – what Timothy Sweet has called – a "counternarrative of improvement" (122), outlining the Cherokees' agricultural pursuits, Christianization, education, and their adoption of governmental structures akin to American ones (see, for instance, Moulton 157).

Despite his severe critique of *Johnson*, Ross later argued that the Cherokees' only chance to halt Georgia's increasing encroachment on Cherokee territory and her onslaught on tribal culture was another intervention through the U.S. Supreme Court. On 1 June 1830, by the force of Georgia law, the Cherokee Nation, its constitution, its courts, and its laws were abolished, and all Cherokees remaining in the state became subject to the state's laws and jurisdiction (Garrison 104). In July 1830, the Cherokee Chief asked the members of the tribal council

> to consult and employ counsel to defend our cause before the Supreme Court of the United States, in which tribunal, as the conservatory of the Constitution, Treaties, and laws of the Union, we can yet hope for justice, and to which we should fearlessly and firmly appeal.
>
> (qtd. in Moulton 191)

Especially after the *Worcester* decision, the Cherokee leader saw the Marshall Court as a protective shield against the infringement of indigenous rights (see Moulton 243).

When it became evident that the *Worcester* ruling could not avert removal, Ross felt deprived of all means of "legal self-defense" (qtd. in Moulton 459). In a memorial to the

Senate and House of Representatives from May 1834, he and several tribe members complained that the Cherokee Nation had been

> stripped of its territory, and individuals of their property, without the least color of right, and in open violation of the guarantee of treaties. At the same time, the Cherokees, deprived of the protection of their own government and laws, are left without the protection of any other laws, outlawed as it were, and exposed to indignities, imprisonment, persecution, and even to death ...
>
> (qtd. in Moulton 291)

The application of the Cherokee concept of outlawry to the tribe's current status – characterized by the abrogation of all Cherokee laws by Georgia and the non-enforcement of federal Indian laws and *Worcester* – reveals that Ross and his co-complainants interpreted the law, both Cherokee and Anglo-American, as an integral part of their self-conception. Their exclusion from all legal protection amounted to life as social outcasts whose physical and spiritual being was in acute danger.

Ross's diverse writings exemplify the complex Cherokee perception of and relation to the U.S. Supreme Court. Rather than positioning the tribe outside American law, he and many other Cherokee leaders, aimed to fight for indigenous rights from within the American legal system, sometimes criticizing, at other times working within and strategically appropriating the language of Anglo-American law (see Meyer). Through their intense engagement with the Marshall trilogy, they added a Native perspective to an imperial legal tale and strove hard to correct its fictions and historical falsifications. Their writings emphasize the significance of Native self-government, defined by Vine Deloria and Clifford M. Lytle as "those forms of government that the federal government deems acceptable and legitimate exercises of political power and that are recognizable by the executive and legislative branches" (18).

While almost two hundred years later Native writers continue to engage with the Marshall trilogy and its effects on Indian Country, they have increasingly focused on the limits and shortcomings, rather than on the positive effects, of Native self-government on the reservations. Instead of advocating Native self-government, they have positioned themselves in favor of indigenous self-determination. Deloria and Lytle have asserted that, in contrast to self-government, self-determination exists independently from the U.S. federal government and "requires the perpetuation of customs, beliefs, and practices whose origin can be traced to precontact times" (19). Self-determination is thus inextricably linked to the concept of cultural sovereignty.

Gerald Vizenor's 2012 campus novel *Chair of Tears* is one of the texts that views Native self-government critically, arguing in favor of indigenous self-determination. It is a literary reflection on the limits of tribal sovereignty as constructed by the Marshall trilogy and the need of Native Americans to construct a cultural sovereignty from within their tribes; it also sheds light on the role of literature in this construction of cultural sovereignty. Before acquainting the reader with the protagonist Captain Shammer and his efforts to decolonize the University of Minnesota's Native American Indian Studies Department, *Chair of Tears* maps and engages with the legal geographies of Indian Country – largely a result of the Marshall trilogy. Like the Chief Justice, the novel envisions the sovereignty exercised by Native American tribes as operating in the shadow of U.S. plenary power. The reservation is consequently represented as a product of imperial domination and as an outpost of colonial surveillance and control. It is a locus of "domestic dependence" in the sense of *Cherokee Nation* rather than one of "political independence" in the sense of *Worcester*.

Chair of Tears also suggests why the reservation constitutes the absence of sovereignty:

> Federal agents were the most notorious abusers of natural reason and the ordinary rights of animals and birds. The agents scorned the stories and visions of hereditary flight, maligned the sovereignty of treaty citizens and the continental liberty of our native ancestors by declarations of civil war, and by the cruel calculations of birth counts, blood rights, and cultural termination.
>
> (2)

Federal agents maligned Native self-government and curtailed Native customs and traditions through their adherence to the formal mechanisms of federal Indian law. "Continental liberty" – a phrase also used by Vizenor in the Constitution of the White Earth Nation – roots Native sovereignty in the pre-contact era and is associated both with Native mobility across the continent and their "sophisticated sense of rights" ("Constitution of the White Earth Nation: Definition of Selected Words"). The novel here advocates Native cultural sovereignty and self-determination (and not self-government) as ways to escape the overriding federal authority of the United States.

The novel then presents the houseboat "Red Lust" as a trope of continental liberty and the epitome of Native self-determination. By roaming "just outside the treaty boundary to escape the capricious authority of federal agents and sleazy reservation politicians" (2), it provokes federal agents and questions their authority. By re-enacting the unrestricted movements of Native Americans in the pre-contact era, boat and crew defy the physical and legal colonial geographies of Indian Country, rendering the containment and control of reservation spaces incomplete, and undoing the propertization of indigenous lands. Long before casinos emerged on reservation lands, the houseboat members engaged in playing games, which is deeply rooted in the traditions of many tribes. Thus they thwart the federal agents' attempts at "cultural termination" through acts of cultural sovereignty.

Captain Shammer's efforts to decolonize the Native Studies department need to be read as a continuation of the houseboat crew's defiance of and resistance to the overriding sovereignty of the United States. *Chair of Tears* narratively links the establishment of the White Earth Reservation and the Department of Native American Indian Studies at the University of Minnesota (37), and constructs Dean Colin Defender as the equivalent of the federal agents on the reservation (26). The Native faculty are presented as quietly enjoying "the privileges of tenure" offered to them by the state government (36). The term "tenure" clearly evokes Marshall's conception of Native Americans as tenants-at-will rather than owners of the land in *Johnson*.[2] The Native faculty's acceptance of tenure implies their acquiescence to practices of colonial dominance. This acquiescence is fostered, as the narrator states, "by some obscure sense of entitlement and right of discovery" (36), once again echoing Marshall.

Shammer's multiple measures to reform the department can be interpreted as attempts to shatter the Native faculty's state of dependency and to create – from within – a self-determined Native academic community with a "sophisticated sense of rights ... and native liberty." At the end of the novel, the department is sold to the Earthdivers, "an association of Native storiers," who want to overturn "[t]he notion that history is a more significant

THE MARSHALL TRILOGY AND ITS LEGACIES

narrative than native stories and literature" (132). Storytelling, as the novel argues, is an act of agency. Exerting such control over tribal culture and tradition is at the heart of cultural sovereignty, which the novel advocates as a viable alternative to tribal sovereignty. The latter is presented as tainted, as it is rooted in a legal system that continues to view Native nations as domestic and dependent. Indigenous rights, *Chair of Tears* argues, have to be traced back to their pre-contact roots, and indigenous rights discourses need to be disentangled from the language and structures of colonialism.

Notes

1   The United States ... hold and assert in themselves the title by which it was acquired. They maintain, as all others have maintained, that discovery gave an exclusive right to extinguish the Indian title of occupancy either by purchase or by conquest, and gave also a right to such a degree of sovereignty as the circumstances of the people would allow them to exercise.

(Johnson n. pag.)

2 Both the novel's title, as well as Shammer's policy of removal, evoke, of course, the larger legal-historical context of the Marshall trilogy – the struggle about removal during the Jackson administration.

Works cited

Banner, Stuart. *How the Indians Lost their Land: Law and Power on the American Frontier*. Cambridge, MA: Belknap Press, 2005.

Borrows, John J. *Recovering Canada: The Resurgence of Indigenous Law*. Toronto: University of Toronto Press, 2002.

Burke, Joseph C. "The Cherokee Cases: A Study in Law, Politics, and Morality." *Stanford Law Review* 21 (1969): 500–31.

Carlson, David J. *Sovereign Selves: American Indian Autobiography and the Law*. Urbana: University of Illinois Press, 2006.

Carpenter, Kristen A. "Contextualizing the Losses of Allotment through Literature." *North Dakota Law Review* 82 (2006): 605–26.

Cherokee Nation v. Georgia. 30 U.S. 1. Supreme Court of the United States. 1831. *Supreme Court Collection*. Legal Information Inst., Cornell University Law School, n.d., n. pag. Web. Accessed 10 Feb. 2012.

Cheyfitz, Eric. "The (Post)Colonial Construction of Indian Country: U.S. American Indian Literatures and Federal Indian Law." *The Columbia Guide to American Indian Literatures of the United States since 1945*. Ed. Eric Cheyfitz. New York: Columbia University Press, 2006. 3–124.

"Constitution of the White Earth Nation." *White Earth Reservation Tribal Council*. 2009. Web. Accessed 5 May 2014.

"Constitution of the White Earth Nation: Definition of Selected Words." *Anishinaabeg Today* [White Earth] 2 Sept. 2009: 19. Web. Accessed 5 June 2014.

Deloria, Vine, Jr., & Clifford M. Lytle. *The Nations Within: The Past and Future of American Indian Sovereignty*. Austin: University of Texas Press, 1998.

Duthu, N. Bruce. "Incorporative Discourse in Federal Indian Law: Negotiating Tribal Sovereignty through the Lens of Native American Literature." *Harvard Human Rights Journal* 13 (2000): 141–89. HeinOnline. Web. Accessed 24 Nov. 2014.

133

Fletcher, Matthew L. M. "The Iron Cold of the Marshall Trilogy." *North Dakota Law Review* 82 (2006): 627–96. Michigan State University Legal Studies Research Paper No. 04-07. Web. Accessed 5 Nov. 2014.

———. "Looking to the East: The Stories of Modern Indian People and the Development of Tribal Law." *Seattle Journal for Social Justice* 5.1 (2006): 1–26. Seattle University School of Law Digital Commons. Web. Accessed 3 Sept. 2014.

Garrison, Tim Alan. *The Legal Ideology of Removal: The Southern Judiciary and the Sovereignty of Native Americans*. Athens: University of Georgia Press, 2002.

Johnson & Graham's Lessee v. McIntosh. 21 U.S. 543. Supreme Court of the United States. 1823. *Supreme Court Collection*. Legal Information Inst., Cornell University Law School, n.d., n. pag. Web. Accessed 10 Feb. 2012.

Katanski, Amelia V. "Writing the Living Law: American Indian Literature as Legal Narrative." *American Indian Law Review* 33. 1 (2008–2009): 53–76. HeinOnline. Web. Accessed 15 Nov. 2014.

Krupat, Arnold. *Ethnocriticism: Ethnography, History, Literature*. Berkeley: University of California Press, 1992.

Metteer Lorillard, Christine. "Stories that Make the Law Free: Literature as a Bridge between the Law and the Culture in Which It Must Exist." *Texas Wesleyan Law Review* 12 (2005–2006): 251–70. HeinOnline. Web. Accessed 26 Nov. 2014.

Meyer, Sabine N. "In the Shadow of the Marshall Court: Nineteenth-Century Cherokee Conceptualizations of the Law." *Twenty-First Century Perspectives on Indigenous Studies: Native North America in (Trans)Motion*. Ed. Sabine N. Meyer, Birgit Däwes & Karsten Fitz. New York: Routledge, 2015.

Moulton, Gary E., ed. *The Papers of Chief John Ross*. Vol. 1. Norman: University of Oklahoma Press, 1985.

Norgren, Jill. *The Cherokee Cases: The Confrontation of Law and Politics*. San Francisco: McGraw-Hill, 1996.

Piatote, Beth H. *Domestic Subjects: Gender, Citizenship, and Law in Native American Literature*. New Haven, CT: Yale University Press, 2013.

Rifkin, Mark. *Manifesting America: The Imperial Construction of U.S. National Space*. Oxford: Oxford University Press, 2009.

Robertson, Lindsay G. *Conquest by Law: How the Discovery of America Dispossessed Indigenous Peoples of Their Lands*. Oxford: Oxford University Press, 2005.

Silko, Leslie Marmon. "Introduction." *Yellow Woman and a Beauty of the Spirit: Essays on Native American Life Today*. New York: Simon & Schuster, 1996. 13–24.

Singel, Wenona T. "Cultural Sovereignty and Transplanted Law: Tensions in Indigenous Self-rule." *Kansas Journal of Law & Public Policy* 15 (2005–2006): 357–69. Digital Commons at Michigan State University College of Law. Web. Accessed 3 Sept. 2014.

Sweet, Timothy. *American Georgics: Economy and Environment in Early American Literature*. Philadelphia: University of Pennsylvania Press, 2002.

Tsosie, Rebecca. "Introduction: Symposium on Cultural Sovereignty." *Arizona State Law Journal* 34 (2002): 1–14. Social Sciences Research Network. Web. Accessed 1 Sept. 2014.

Tsosie, Rebecca & Wallace Coffey. "Rethinking the Tribal Sovereignty Doctrine: Cultural Sovereignty the Collective Future of Indian Nations." *Stanford Law & Policy Review* 12. 2 (2001): 191–221.

Vizenor, Gerald. *Chair of Tears: A Novel*. Lincoln: University of Nebraska Press, 2012.

Watson, Blake A. "The Doctrine of Discovery and the Elusive Definition of Indian Title." *Lewis and Clark Law Review* 15. 4 (2011). Social Science Research Network. Web. Accessed 3 Nov. 2014.

Wilkinson, Charles F. *American Indians, Time, and the Law: Native Societies in a Modern Constitutional Democracy*. New Haven, CT: Yale University Press, 1987.

Worcester v. Georgia. 31 U.S. 515. Supreme Court of the United States. 1832. *Supreme Court Collection*. Legal Information Inst., Cornell University Law School, n.d., n. pag. Web. Accessed 10 Feb. 2012.

11
Native Letters and North-American Indian Wars

Oliver Scheiding

In light of current scholarship that refocuses Native agency in the context of "The Red Atlantic" (Weaver), this chapter surveys selected key moments in the history and literature of Indian upheavals to discuss representations of North American Indian struggles on historical levels as well as on the level of the personal depicted in social conflict or in conflict with the self. In doing so, the chapter looks at Native responses to warfare as more than defensive strategies of resistance and containment. Instead, I will consider different genres used by Native American writers to re-evaluate the complex intersections among Native peoples, Euro-American powers, borderlands, and homelands.

The opening pages of Leslie Marmon Silko's epic text, *Almanac of the Dead* (1991), reprints what she calls the "Five Hundred Year Map" of European and Native American encounters with the claim that "The Indian Wars have never ended in the Americas" (n. pag.). Such statements show that both "non-Indians and Indians have different stakes in the history of the Indian Wars" (Elliott 15). What also becomes obvious is the fact that besides the fascination of war and violence, the Indian Wars had a formative impact on print, writing, and literature. From the earliest local clashes in the sixteenth and seventeenth centuries, to the French and Indian Wars (1754–1763) that was part of a worldwide imperial conflict, and to the more than forty battles against Native Americans in the nineteenth century, the many Indian wars produced countless pamphlets, sermons, petitions, letters, newspaper reports, poems, and plays that shaped public history and popular forms of memorialization, as discussed by Michael Elliott in his seminal study on the enduring legacy of the Indian Wars and General Custer's defeat at the Battle of the Little Bighorn. While most accounts created what has been called "the anti-Indian sublime" (Silver xx) – a rhetoric built upon horrific accounts of violence and victimization – Native Americans actively participated in responding to the growing industry of war accounts by applying different forms of literacies or "mediascapes" (Cohen & Glover); that is, modes of written and nonwritten communication inscribed on pieces of bark, animal skins, paper, and other kinds of material artifacts that intersect themes evolving from the Euro-American wars and other intertribal conflicts.

The enduring emphasis on static definitions and cultural essentialisms in depicting the Indian Wars has contributed to what Vine Deloria Jr. calls the "the 'cameo' theory of history" (39): Indigenous peoples make dramatic entrances, stay briefly on the stage, and then fade out as the main history of European expansion and progress resumes. However, these one-sided official war accounts were already being reassessed in journalism, autobiography, and historiography by early Native American writers such as Samson Occom and William Apess, and by nineteenth- and early twentieth-century Native non-fiction writers such as Charles Eastman, Sarah Winnemucca, and E. Pauline Johnson, who all served as cultural critics and produced entangled histories of complex intergroup relations as they documented the loss of tribal lands and Indian imprisonment on reservations.

Non-fictional Native accounts form an important archive in Native American letters and should be read in conjunction with Native American fiction, and especially alongside the novel, which had its breakthrough only in the 1960s with writers such as N. Scott Momaday, James Welch, and Leslie Marmon Silko. More recently Louise Erdrich, Linda Hogan, and Gerald Vizenor have contributed to the bourgeoning list of indigenous novels portraying warfare and armed conflict as central to Native American life in both the past and present (see Warrior). While the novel has certainly become the dominant genre in Native American literary history over past decades, this chapter surveys the archive of Native letters by first discussing an early case of colonial Native non-fiction writing circulated in the context of Metacom's War (1675–1676), one of the most ruinous battles in colonial North America. The second part of this chapter draws attention to poetry as central to Native expression. Volumes of indigenous verse frequently mix traditional forms of storytelling, lyrical elements, and prose to leave a "legacy of resistance" (Dunbar-Ortiz ix) and to create sites of memory as seen in Simon J. Ortiz's *Fight Back: For the Sake of the People, For the Sake of the Land* (1980), Joy Harjo's *The Woman Who Fell From the Sky* (1994), and Gerald Vizenor's *Bear Island: The War at Sugarpoint* (2006), in which he recounts the so-called last battle between Native Americans and the U.S. Army in a conflict fought in 1898. This chapter will draw attention to the regions of instability in the Southwestern United States and discuss Ortiz's volume of poems in which he commemorates the Pueblo Revolt (1680–1692) that started the opposition to Spanish authority and the rebellion against the exploitation of the indigenous peoples in the Americas. The final example highlights Hanay Geiogamah's pan-Indian playwriting and his use of a communal form of theater to "stop the erosion of our Indian way of life" (Geiogamah n. pag.). In his path-breaking early play *Foghorn* (1980), Geiogamah portrays the corruption of Native American ways of living in the Americas ranging from Columbus's accidental discovery in 1492 to the Wounded Knee massacre in 1890 to the uprising on the Pine Ridge Reservation in 1973. The examples chosen here – non-fiction, poetry, and drama – attempt to communicate the Native peoples' presence and "survivance" (see Vizenor *Survivance*) in the overlapping temporalities and warring spaces of the Americas.

Writing is fighting: James Printer and Metacom's War

Metacom's War, sometimes better known as King Philip's War, captivated contemporaries and posterity as perhaps no other Indian war in the colonial history of America (see Lepore). One reason for the continuing fascination with this war lies in the dazzling figure of the Wampanoag leader Metacom, who was called by New Englanders for propaganda purposes (somewhat hyperbolically) "King Philip." Chief Metacom came to serve as an eponym for a war that, historically speaking, he did not cause, nor was he the main

NATIVE LETTERS AND NORTH-AMERICAN INDIAN WARS

driving force behind all the incidents and atrocities that were later ascribed to him. His iconic potential to figure both as a "doleful, great, naked, dirty beast" (Church 45) and as a romanticized "noble savage" brought about an image of Metacom/Philip as a model Indian that could be adjusted to the changing political and cultural needs of post-revolutionary America (see Scheiding "Indian Chief").

The Puritans demonized the Indians as "Monsters shapt and fac'd like men" (Tompson 19), and in numerous sermons ministers "prayed the bullet into Philips heart" (I. Mather 10). Metacom's War resulted in creating a racialized iconography that portrayed Native Americans as "Devils in this Wilderness" (C. Mather 198), demonizing and dehumanizing the Indian. This representation lasted throughout the colonial period, only to be revived during the American Revolution (see McWilliams 106–33). The romanticizing of the Wampanoags' struggle in the first half of the nineteenth century resulted from the idea, as expressed by Edward Everett, that "Although the continent of America, when discovered by the Europeans, was in the possession of the native tribes, it was obviously the purpose of Providence, that it should become the abode of civilization, the arts, and Christianity" (589). Nineteenth-century American art and belle-letters appropriated the "Indians" in terms of the nation's progress, making their disappearance from history appear inevitable. Images of the "vanishing Indian" were widely circulated and served as "mimetic capital" (Greenblatt 6) for America's ongoing westward expansion.

Mary Rowlandson's captivity narrative, which chronicles the events of Metacom's War, certainly plays a central role in fabricating such an imaginative archive. Since its first publication in 1683, Rowlandson's account was not only a steady transatlantic seller, but it has been rewritten and parodied by Native American authors, such as Louise Erdrich's poem and Sherman Alexie's short story, both titled "Captivity." Recent editions of Rowlandson's narrative also reveal the problematic nature of the text's authorship, unearthing the involvement of Native Americans in composing the account. Present scholarship draws attention to the so-called Praying Indians – Native Americans who converted to Christianity – in early American printing and manuscript publications. Language, literacy, and religion make up the cultural in-betweenness of converts and play a significant role in the biography of James Printer, the compositor of Rowlandson's New England edition (see Brooks).

James Printer, a second-generation Praying Indian, was born the son of Noas, a leading member of the Christian Church in Hassanamessit. From an early age Printer had been exposed to Christian knowledge, and being born into a praying family made him realize what living in two worlds requires. While Native American converts formed a "proto-elite" (Peyer 52) in Christian Indian communities, they were frequently considered dubious figures both within and outside those communities – neither fully Christian nor fully Indian. Printer became an apprentice to Samuel Green's Cambridge print shop in 1659. Serving as typesetter and translator, Printer was exposed to New England's growing book business; he even helped facilitate John Eliot's Indian Library, a collection of instructional texts that initiated American publishing history.

In light of Printer's role as a translator and scribe, Metacom's War marks a moment of transition in his life. At the outbreak of the war, he had decided to ally with Metacom to fight the English. After the Indian raid on Medfield in February of 1675, the colonial militia found an "Indian letter" that the attackers had left on their retreat. The authorship of the so-called Medfield note has provoked heated debates among scholars; while there is no clear evidence that James Printer himself drafted the note, it has been attributed to him. The letter reads:

> Know by this paper, that the Indians that thou hast provoked to wrath and anger, will war this twenty one years if you will; there are many Indians yet, we come three hundred at this time. You must consider the Indians lost nothing but their life; you must lose your fair houses and cattle.
>
> (Salisbury "Indians' Letter" 132)

The short text illustrates that writing enabled Native Americans not only to wield power but also to gain access to agency. To claim the written word is to claim authority and threaten settler hegemony. Exposing their lust for land and property – obviously in conflict with Puritan theology – challenges the ideological premises of this very hegemony. It is undeniable that the composer of this note was familiar with the use of the English language; the writer is also sensitive to religious matters and quite conscious of the white settlers' expectations. This cultural literacy is characteristic of early Native American writing as it was practiced, for instance, by Native scribes: "[L]and ownership, social order, and literacy were inextricably intertwined in this early period of Native writing" (Round 69). The Indian letter is thus performative in nature and reveals the transliteral practices Native Americans used during the war. "Writing," as Laura Donaldson argues, "worked alongside … more overt weapons" (47). Writing practices, such as the "Indians' Letter," were thus integral to "doing" war.

Numerous letters of negotiation were circulated among the different parties involved in Metacom's War. Both sides discussed terms of captivity and release. Despite the concessions made by Native Americans in a series of letters, the one thought to have been written by James Printer provoked harsh reactions from the English. In a letter dated 28 April 1676, colonial officials angrily retorted: "We received your letter by Tom and Peter, which doth not answer ours to you: neither is subscribed by the sachems nor hath it any date, which we know your scribe James Printer doth well understand should be" (Salisbury, "Letter from" 136; see also Printer). The English complaint about their opponents' inappropriateness in handling the rules of warfare demonstrates that writing is integral to the self-perception of the English. They are the ones who are familiar with the practices of war, which often involves writing, signing, and delivering dated letters. The response letter seeks to claim authority over writing as a social tool in negotiating war, and as such it has to follow specific conventions. That the Native side fails to adhere to these conventions is a major point of critique as voiced by the English. Since the writer acknowledges Printer's familiarity with the established standards of communication, the alleged failure can also be read as challenging the discursive superiority that the English believe they possess. Although Rowlandson's account depicts the Praying Indians as uncivilized heathens, it is their writing upon which her own release ultimately depends. As one usually tends to consider war and captivity in terms of battles, conquest, and open violence, the so-called Medfield note, the letters of negotiation, and Rowlandson's captivity narrative demonstrate that Native letters were an important strategic and creative tool in presenting contrasting spiritual and epistemological systems that demarcate different cultures' worldviews; these early sources also signal the erasure of Native subjectivity in the telling of this war's history (Tinker 144–49).

The shatter zone of the West: the Pueblo Revolt of 1680 and Simon J. Ortiz's *Fight Back* (1980)

In her study *Imperial Eyes: Studies in Travel Writing and Transculturation* (1993), Mary Louise Pratt popularized the term "contact zones" to refer to a space of colonial encounters, the place where people who are geographically and historically separated come into contact with each other and establish ongoing relations. As the encounter takes place in a colonial context, the contact is not an exchange of equal partners because it frequently involves coercion, inequality, and conflict. In recent years, the notion of contact zones has developed into a productive concept for reassessing colonial encounters in larger geopolitical contexts. This concept helps to explore the complex mix of transformations that affected the spiritual, cultural, and material worlds of all who were involved in it, especially those of Native peoples.

Simon J. Ortiz's third collection of poems *Fight Back: For the Sake of the People, For the Sake of the Land* (1980), written "In Commemoration of the Pueblo Revolt of 1680 and our warrior Grandmothers and Grandfathers" (n. pag.), provides a geopolitical reassessment of the Southwest as a "shatter zone" (Ethridge & Shuck-Hall) devastated by the consequent exploitation of the land and the people over centuries. In her preface, Roxanne Dunbar-Ortiz notes:

> For centuries the indigenous people of the western hemisphere have worked for various masters – for the Spanish church and state officials; for English planters, traders, and industries; for French fur merchants; for Portuguese colonialists; and for the wealthy of the United States, Canada, Colombia, Peru, Guatemala, Bolivia.
>
> (vii)

Ortiz's volume unfolds a panoramic history of the region that blurs time and space and thus connects the past to modern-day America, the communal to the personal, and the land to a people of mixed ethnic heritage. In his 1992 introduction to *Woven Stone*, Ortiz refers to *Fight Back*, concluding: "The American political–economic system was mainly interested in control and exploitation, and it didn't matter how it was achieved – just like the Spanish crown had been ignorant of people's concerns and welfare" (31). Ortiz wrote *Fight Back* for the tri-centennial celebration of the "1680 All Indian Pueblo Revolt" (Dunbar-Ortiz viii): a unified revolt of the poor from the entire region of what is now New Mexico – mestizos, mulattoes, captive Indians from other tribes, Mexican Indians, Navajos, and Apaches – who fought together under Pueblo leadership against the oppressive labor conditions forced upon them by the Spanish settlers. Combining autobiography, history, storytelling, poetry, and prose, Ortiz creates a continuous history ranging from political to economic oppression in colonial America that shapes the present-day fight against the poisoning of land by uranium mines in the Southwest. Since the unified rebellion was successful in asserting sovereignty over indigenous homelands, Ortiz seeks to inspire the continuation of this struggle, particularly with regard to the land which transcends race and culture. The poet includes every reader in the "we" in his "Mid-American Prayer": the poem that begins the volume by proposing solidarity among all marginalized people in modern America.

The opening prayer connects the historic past, the land, and the people. Similar to Zuni mythology, it recalls a ceremonial cycle that brings the community together.

> Standing again
> with all things
> that have been in the past,
> that are in the present,
> and that will be in the future,
> we acknowledge ourselves
> to be in a relationship that is responsible
> and proper, that is loving and compassionate,
> for the sake of the land and all people.
>
> (1)

The first part of the book is comprised of poems that deal with the exploitation of the land and the people through the uranium mines in New Mexico. It conveys an economic history of the area around Grants, New Mexico, which is located about eighty miles west of Albuquerque and is nicknamed the "Uranium Capital of the World." This part interweaves biographical and anecdotal material exploring the people's connection to the land. In a personal note, Ortiz tells the reader: "I never worked for the railroad, but for a while I worked in the uranium mills and mines … Many Acoma, Laguna, and Navajo people whose homeland is mid-northwest New Mexico work in the underground and open pit mines" (2). The longest poem of the section, "To Change in a Good Way," relates the story of two families who become close friends while working in the mines: Pete and Mary, a Laguna couple, and Bill and Ida, a white couple from Oklahoma. Their enduring friendship and connection to the land help overcome racial and cultural barriers, symbolized in Pete's gift of a traditional medicine bundle and some corn to which Bill turns after his brother's death in Viet Nam. In the gift-giving ceremony Pete notes:

> You and Ida are not Indian,
> but it doesn't make any difference.
> It's for all of us, this kind of way,
> with corn and this, Bill.
>
> (23)

The second part of this book, titled "No More Sacrifices," offers both history and personal narrative. Ortiz chronicles the history of encounters in New Mexico from before the arrival of the Spanish in 1540 to the 1980s. Utilizing Acqumeh language to capture ante-colonial Pueblo life and its changes, the poet records Pueblo interaction with the Spanish and later with Anglo-Americans, but he also includes other groups, such as Navajos and Chicanos. Ortiz blurs temporal distinctions in a vision of the land and the people that unifies the history of the Southwest, the oral tradition, memory, and his own experiences. Making a connection between past and present, Ortiz weaves a genealogy of the shared fates of indigenous peoples and the Euro-American population. In doing so, he links the Pueblo Revolt to the history of the Indian Wars and the men who battled a "ruthless, monopolistic U.S. empire" (58; see also Sayre):

The action swept on. Tecumseh, the Shawnee freedom fighter, had been courageous in the early nineteenth century and Osceola led his people desperately in the 1820s and 30s, both trying to save lands and people, and they both were killed. Crazy Horse organized a freedom movement on the Plains, but he was assassinated. Sitting Bull submitted and was paraded like a clown. (60)

Despite five hundred years of domination by foreign powers and a devastating history that transformed this region into "the national sacrifice area in the Southwest" (72), the Pueblo people – who are noted for their resiliency – continue to survive. In light of writing and storytelling as a communal performance of fighting back, Ortiz's poetic re-enactment of the Pueblo revolt ends with a plea for cooperative action: "Only when the people of this nation, not just Indian people, fight for what is just and good for all life, will we know life and its continuance" (73). *Fight Back* provides a reciprocal reassessment of the rebellion's long history using language as a force for positive change. Ortiz's volume ultimately illuminates within the context of Indian resistance the dialogic rather than oppositional nature of Indigenous nationhood.

The heirs of Columbus and staging Indian wars: Hanay Geiogamah's *Foghorn*

At the time of *Foghorn*'s first production in 1973 Hanay Geiogamah, a young Kiowa-Delaware activist and journalist who was publicly speaking out for the emancipation of Native Americans in social, political, and artistic terms, was well aware of a long history of persistent misrepresentation of the "Indi'n" not only on the American stage, but also in films and on television (see Darby). His collection of plays, *New Native American Drama: Three Plays*, first published in 1980, made him a key figure in ethnic theater. In *Foghorn*, the play that opens the collection and was first performed in Germany, Geiogamah retraces the violent history of the Indian–white relationship in eleven scenes that shift from major events of colonization to the Native population of the Americas. In doing so, Geiogamah re-enacts Native resistance to the numerous colonizing endeavors in the long history of discovery and civilization. The series of events is interspersed with three scenes dedicated to Native rebellions: the occupation of Alcatraz Island in 1969 (scene 2), the history of treaty-signing between the U.S. government and Native tribes (scene 9), and the outbreak of violence in 1973 at Wounded Knee (scene 11). The history of white hegemony reproduces well-known stereotypes of Native Americans, depicting them as either noble savages or as immoral heathens whose fate is simply to vanish from the annals of history.

The play reveals the history of Indian–white relationships as a complex fabric of interrelated developments, beginning with an episode that re-enacts the very first encounter between Europeans and the indigenous population of the Americas. Columbus and his crew land on the shores of the New World and see themselves suddenly confronted with Native people. This first encounter is symbolized by a huge "Indian" face projected onto the back of the stage. Immediately – without knowing anything about them – the sailors call the "Indians" "Vermin! Varmints! Vermin! Varmints! Vermin! Varmints!" (52). The fear of cohabitation in the New World makes Columbus and his men ultimately decide to dispossess the Native Americans and to set their land free for the progress of civilization. Subsequently, a group of Native Americans is symbolically pushed from the stage, only to make room for the appearance of a U.S. senator who steps to the front of the stage and declares to the audience that the "Indian" case is now a legal issue to be dealt with in the courtroom.

The Indian face at the back of the stage serves as the key symbol of the colonizer's mind, serving as a Western icon picturing the cruel and cunning other. It hangs there before even one "Indian" actor enters the stage. The red face is not the outcome of first contact, but an image that has a long history of othering in European thought that led to repeated military and legal transactions. Expressing the suppressed cultural anxieties of their white neighbors, the stereotype of the "red villain" discloses the hegemonic social reality that Native Americans face. By twisting stereotypes into new configurations, *Foghorn* reassesses predominant prejudices and seeks to exorcise them with knowledgeable laughter, illustrating how the world is perceived normatively and not objectively.

Scene 2 enacts the symbolic repossession of Alcatraz Island in 1969 by several hundred Native Americans from various tribes; the Indian actors perform a song in front of a picture of the island. One of the actors suddenly steps to the front of the stage and recounts the whole event from a Native American point of view. Finding a voice, the self-conscious speech of the play's narrator problematizes the way American officials silence tribal history. Telling the story on his own terms, the narrator states: "We, the Native Americans, reclaim this land, known as America, in the name of all American Indians, by right of discovery" (55). This statement, made in the first person plural, can be read as a phatic speech act that gives a specific historical meaning to this event. Furthermore, the Native American actor takes over a position that is usually reserved for white officials: that is, determining via language what constitutes history and which role Native Americans should play in it. This is the first time in the play that a Native American uses the English language, speaks for himself, and directly addresses the audience. In the light of a long history of military conflicts and dispossessions, tribal self-representation is linked to a move from non-verbal to verbal action.

The play's dynamic of self-empowerment is intensified in scene 9, in which important Indian treaties that were signed between the U.S. government and Native tribes are named. While the actors read aloud the legal titles of each Indian treaty since the 1850s, the rest of the group sings Gene Kelly and Fred Astaire's 1943 musical blockbuster hit "Pass That Peace Pipe and Bury That Hatchet." The scene's introduction is as follows:

> The performing group lines up in a choreographed pattern as the piano begins "Pass that Peace Pipe." Between each of the stanzas of the song, delivered as a wild production number, an actor wearing a bull's head is spotlighted with a pretty girl in pigtails, who reads from a giant roll of toilet tissue. The bull also holds a roll, and unwinds enough tissue to wipe his behind each time a treaty is called out.
>
> (75)

In between the historical treaties – such as the "THE TREATY OF FORT LARAMIE" (76, capitalization in original) that declared the independence of the Oglala Sioux Nation from the United States in 1868 – there are mock treaties that have been completely made up by the playwright, such as "THE TREATY OF POINT NO POINT" (76, capitalization in original). These announcements run parallel with the almost scatological performance of the bull-actor who repetitively wipes his behind with toilet paper each time a treaty's name is read aloud. The scene is an example of how the play uses Native humor to unearth "everything from the past that we've brought forward with us, our memories, ancestors, ... singing, dancing, stories, suffering, all of that" (Lincoln 336). Thus, the symbolic props, the direct address to the audience, the employment of music, and the play's loose scenic structure blur the space between actor and audience in a humorous way. The audience is slowly immersed in a performance context to reassess the past. The play's sometimes chaotic agglomeration of images, remembrances, and audience interplay also replaces a Western dramatic sense of progressive act-building and climax by using instead repetitive and cyclical patterns of Native American modes of world-making. The play destroys an all-too-comfortable form of romanticizing illusions, traditionally used in nineteenth-century "Indian" plays such as *The Indian Princess* (1808) or *Metamora; or, The Last of the Wampanoags* (1829), in favor of foregrounding the theatricality and fictitiousness of official history.

In the final scene (80–82), the "Indians" fully establish themselves within the realm of action. Scene 11 reconstructs the violent events of the 1973 occupation of Wounded Knee – the site of the 1890 massacre of Big Foot's Oglala Sioux – when two Indians were shot and a federal marshal was paralyzed by gunfire. Toward the end of the scene, when the actors have finished chanting the "American Indian Movement Song," the "Indians" are surrounded by the marshal's crew and advised to cooperate because they have been "unlawfully trespassing on private property" (80). At the end of the marshal's speech, the play's narrator steps to the front of the group and calls out: "We move on" (81). Performers respond by naming and identifying with various tribes: "I am Creek," "I am a Winnebago," "I am a Sioux" (81). The narrator ultimately ends this call and response performance of Native American tribal memory by "compassionately" claiming, "I am ... NOT GUILTY" (82, capitalization in original). Performers' acts of naming tribes symbolize emancipation from past "Indian" stereotypes and imposed representational forms. The "Indians" position themselves in their stories and remember themselves by means of their own dramatic and innovative enactments of history.

Conclusion

Over the past several decades, scholars have conceived entirely new ways of thinking about Native Americans, Euro-Americans, and their shared histories. Moving beyond conventional top-down narratives that depict Indians as bit players in imperial struggles or as tragic victims of colonial expansion, today's scholarship portrays them as full-fledged historical actors who played a formative role in the making of the modern world. Rather than a seamless, preordained sequence, the colonization of the Americas should be seen as a dialectic process that created new worlds for all involved. Indigenous societies did not simply vanish in the face of Euro-American wars. Many adjusted and endured, rebuilding new economies and identities from the fragments of the old ones. Others fought and resisted, but eventually cooperated and coexisted with the newcomers to create new hybrid worlds that were neither wholly Indian nor wholly European.

This chapter endeavors to go beyond a reductionist view of the history of Indian wars that tends to interpret Native responses in terms of mere strategies for survival. Especially in Indian–Euro-American studies, this practice has led to a focus on Native Americans as "fringe peoples" that ignores broader historical and cultural struggles, or relegates them to the "background of the central story of cross-cultural cooperation and assimilation"

(Hämäläinen 12). Native letters, both non-fiction and fiction, are not ethnographic curiosities but must be seen as part of a continuing debate about colonialism, frontiers, and borderlands in the Americas that includes consideration of the diverse historical actors involved in creating new worlds for all – Native Americans and Euro-Americans alike.

Works cited

Alexie, Sherman. "Captivity." *First Indian on the Moon*. Brooklyn, NY: Hanging Loose Press, 1993. 98–101.

Brooks, Lisa. "Turning the Looking Glass on King Philip's War: Locating American Literature in Native Space." *American Literary History* 25. 4 (2013): 718–50.

Church, Benjamin. *Entertaining Passages Relating to Philip's War which Began in the Month of June, 1675. As also of Expeditions more Lately Made Against the Common Enemy, and Indian Rebels, in the Eastern Parts of New-England: With some Account of the Divine Providence towards Benj. Church Esqr*. Boston: Bartholomew Green, 1716.

Cohen, Matt & Jeffrey Glover, eds. *Colonial Mediascapes: Sensory Worlds of the Early Americas*. Lincoln: University of Nebraska Press, 2014.

Darby, Jaye T. "Introduction: A Talking Circle on Native Theater." *American Indian Theater in Performance: A Reader*. Ed. Hanay Geiogamah & Jaye T. Darby. Los Angeles: UCLA American Indian Studies Center, 2000. iii–xv.

Deloria, Vine, Jr. *We Talk, You Listen: New Tribes, New Turf*. New York: Macmillan, 1970.

Donaldson, Laura. "Writing the Talking Stick: Alphabetic Literacy as Colonial Technology and Postcolonial Appropriation." *American Indian Quarterly* 22 (1998): 46–63.

Dunbar-Ortiz, Roxanne. "Preface." *Fight Back: For the Sake of the People, For the Sake of the Land*. Las Lomas: University of New Mexico Press, 1980. vii–ix.

Elliott, Michael A. *Custerology: The Enduring Legacy of the Indian Wars and George Armstrong Custer*. Chicago: University of Chicago Press, 2007.

Erdrich, Louise. "Captivity." *Jacklight*. New York: Holt, 1984.

Ethridge, Robbie Franklyn & Sheri M. Shuck-Hall, eds. *Mapping the Mississippian Shattering Zone: The Colonial Indian Slave Trade and Regional Instability in the American South*. Lincoln: University of Nebraska Press, 2009.

Everett, Edward. "Address Delivered at Bloody Brook, in South Deerfield, September 30, 1835, in Commemoration of the Fall of 'The Flower of Essex,' at that Spot, in King Philip's War, September 18, 1675." *Orations and Speeches, on Various Occasions*. 1836. New York: Arno, 1972. 587–637.

Geiogamah, Hanay. *Foghorn. New Native American Drama: Three Plays*. Norman: University of Oklahoma Press, 1980. 46–82.

Greenblatt, Stephen. *Marvelous Possessions: The Wonder of the New World*. Oxford: Clarendon, 1991.

Hämäläinen, Pekka. *The Comanche Empire*. New Haven, CT: Yale University Press, 2008.

Harjo, Joy. *The Woman Who Fell from the Sky: Poems*. New York: Norton, 1994.

Lepore, Jill. *The Name of War: King Philip's War and the Origins of American Identity*. New York: Vintage, 1999.

Lincoln, Kenneth. "Interview with Hanay Geiogamah." *Indi'n Humor: Bicultural Play in Native America*. Oxford: Oxford University Press, 1993. 326–38.

Mather, Cotton. *Magnalia Christi Americana: or, The Ecclesiastical History of New-England, from its First Planting in the year 1620, unto the Year of our Lord, 1698*. London: Thomas Parkhurst, 1702.

Mather, Increase. *An Historical Discourse Concerning the Prevalency of Prayer Wherein is Shewed that New-Englands late Deliverance from the Rage of the Heathens, is an Eminent Answer of Prayer*. Boston: John Foster, 1677.

McWilliams, John. *New England's Crises and Cultural Memory: Literature, Politics, History, Religion, 1620–1860*. Cambridge: Cambridge University Press, 2004.

Ortiz, Simon J. *Fight Back: For the Sake of the People, For the Sake of the Land*. Las Lomas: University of New Mexico Press, 1980.

———. *Fight Back: For the Sake of the People, For the Sake of the Land. Woven Stone*. Tucson: University of Arizona Press, 1992. 286–365.

———. "Introduction." *Fight Back: For the Sake of the People, For the Sake of the Land. Woven Stone*. Tucson: University of Arizona Press, 1992. 3–33.

Peyer, Bernd C. *The Tutor'd Mind: Indian Missionary-Writers in Antebellum America*. Amherst: University of Massachusetts Press, 1997.

Pratt, Mary Louise. *Imperial Eyes: Studies in Travel Writing and Transculturation*. London: Routledge, 1993.

Printer, James et al. "Letter to John Leverett et al., *ca.* April 1676." *The Sovereignty and Goodness of God with Related Documents*. Ed. Neal Salisbury. Boston: Bedford, 1997. 135–36.

Round, Philip H. "Early Native Literature as Social Practice." *The Oxford Handbook of Indigenous American Literature*. Ed. James H. Cox & Daniel Heath Justice. Oxford: Oxford University Press, 2014. 65–80.

Salisbury, Neal, ed. "Indians' Letter to English Troops at Medfield, 1675." *The Sovereignty and Goodness of God with Related Documents*. Boston: Bedford, 1997. 131–32.

———, ed. "Letter from the Massachusetts Governor's Council to 'Indian Sachems,' April 28, 1676." *The Sovereignty and Goodness of God with Related Documents*. Boston: Bedford, 1997. 136–37.

Sayre, Gordon M. *The Indian Chief as Tragic Hero: Native Resistance and the Literatures of America, from Moctezuma to Tecumseh*. Chapel Hill: University of North Carolina Press, 2005.

Scheiding, Oliver. "The Indian Chief as Federalist Icon: Washington Irving's Refigurations of Philip of Pokanoket." *American Cultural Icons: The Production of Representatives Lives*. Ed. Günther Leypoldt & Bernd Engler. Würzburg, Germany: Königshausen, 2010. 365–81.

Silko, Leslie Marmon. *The Almanac of the Dead*. New York: Simon & Schuster, 1991.

Silver, Peter. *Our Savage Neighbors: How Indian War Transformed Early America*. New York: Norton, 2008.

Tinker, George E. "'To the Victor Belong the Spoils': An Afterword on Colonialist History." *Buried in Shades of Night: Contested Voices, Indian Captivity, and the Legacy of King Philip's War*. Billy J. Stratton. Tucson: University of Arizona Press, 2013. 144–49.

Tompson, Benjamin. *New Englands Crisis. Or A Brief Narrative, of New-Englands Lamentable Estate at Present, Compar'd with the Former (but few) Years of Prosperity. Occasioned by Many Unheard of Crueltyes Practised upon the Persons and Estates of its United Colonyes, without Respect of Sex, Age or Quality of Persons, by the Barbarous Heathen Thereof. Poetically Described. By a Well Wisher to His Countrey*. Boston: John Foster, 1676.

Vizenor, Gerald. *Bear Island: The War at Sugarpoint*. Foreword by Jace Weaver. Minneapolis: University of Minnesota Press, 2006.

———, ed. *Survivance: Narratives of Native Presence*. Lincoln: University of Nebraska Press, 2008.

Warrior, Robert. *The People and the Word: Reading Native Nonfiction*. Minneapolis: University of Minnesota Press, 2006.

Weaver, Jace. *The Red Atlantic: American Indigenes and the Making of the Modern World, 1000–1927*. Chapel Hill: University of North Carolina Press, 2014.

12

Finding Voice in Changing Times

The Politics of Native Self-Representation during the Periods of Removal and Allotment

Mark Rifkin

Over the course of a century from the 1820s to the 1930s, Native peoples were subjected to a series of invasive displacements. While conducted under various policy rubrics, which were configured differently and articulated disparate aims, the effect of these disposses-sions was to limit the lands held by Indigenous nations and to incorporate them (both the territory and the people) into overarching U.S. legal categories and norms.[1] As policy formulations, removal – the dominant agenda for Indian affairs in the 1820s and 1830s – and allotment – operative from the 1880s through the 1930s – both sought to insert Native peoples into U.S. legal mappings. In doing so, they imposed particular kinds of legal subjectivities, whether the centralized state-like polity of the treaty-system (through which removal was conducted) or the property-owning individualism of the allotment program. Having to speak within and through these roles meant that Native peoples altered their forms of self-representation in order to engage with the policy language and frameworks of non-natives. Native writing in this period registers and responds to these impositions, ten-sions, and struggles over how to portray Indigenous personhood and peoplehood. Through discussion of two paired sets of texts – Elias Boudinot's *Letters and Other Papers Relating to Cherokee Affairs* (1837) and Black Hawk's *The Life of Ma-Ka-Tai-Me-She-Kia-Kiak or Black Hawk* (1833); and Sarah Winnemucca Hopkins's *Life Among the Piutes: Their Wrongs and Claims* (1883) and Alice Callahan's *Wynema* (1891) – this chapter will survey some of the difficulties of articulating forms of public voice for Native peoples in light of shifting legal paradigms, addressing the complex ways Native authors engaged, appropriated, acquiesced to, and deferred the imperative to speak in ways that fit into the dominant structures of U.S. Indian policy.[2]

The push for Indian removal did not begin in 1830 with the passage by Congress of the Indian Removal Act, nor did it arise as a completely separate policy goal from the recognition of Native nations as such through the treaty-system.[3] If removal indicates the effort to displace an entire nation wholesale at once, dislocating them from one landbase to an entirely different one further west, it also can be understood as intensifying previous efforts to displace Indigenous people(s) from areas sought by non-natives (see Jones; Rockwell; Wallace). After a good deal of armed struggle in the southeast and the Great

Lakes region in the 1780s and 1790s, the federal government adopted a process of formal negotiation with Native nations, drawing on the provisions for treaty-making within the new Constitution that had been written in 1787. Characterized in the Constitution as "the supreme law of the land," treaties held a different status than ordinary legislation, requiring a vote of two-thirds by the Senate alone in order to be ratified and marking a formal diplomatic relation that exceeded the ordinary parameters of "domestic" law. However, such agreements had been used prior to the war as a means of officially securing Native consent to the transfer of land to English colonies and colonists, much of which was already occupied by non-natives. The scene of treaty-making could recast an overall coercive context as a moment of free assent by independent sovereigns in ways that effaced how Indian policy actually produced forms of duress and incited unofficial forms of settler invasion that would be made good through later treaties. Thus, even while the signing of treaties with Native nations indicated recognition that they and their territories lay outside of the ordinary jurisdiction of the U.S. government, that very act of political acknowledgment could function as a means of legitimizing the annexation of Indigenous lands. Beginning in the early 1800s under the administration of President Thomas Jefferson, the federal government began to push toward more large-scale displacements of entire nations, rather than the piece-meal acquisition of various parts of a people's territory.

Elias Boudinot's *Letters and Other Papers* reflects the tensions generated by the U.S. insistence that Native peoples speak in centralized ways through the treaty-system and the emergence of disagreements within the Cherokee Nation over how to conceptualize Indigenous territoriality and peoplehood (on the pre-removal Cherokee Nation, see Justice; McLoughlin; Perdue; Rifkin *Manifesting* 37–74). Over the course of the 1810s and the 1820s, the Cherokees developed a formal national government, one that contrasted with previous forms of decentralized governance in which each town acted autonomously and in which decision-making largely worked through consensus. This consolidation of Cherokee political authority largely was a response to U.S. efforts over the previous few decades to pick and choose chiefs with whom the federal government would engage in treaty negotiations that affected all Cherokees. In order to further coalesce and establish the legitimacy of their sovereignty and self-rule, the Cherokees in 1827 adopted a constitution, modeled on that of the United States, and this action was taken by Georgia as a challenge to its claims to Cherokee lands, setting in motion a series of political and legal maneuvers (at the state and federal levels) that would eventuate in the passage of the Indian Removal Act. Despite having repeatedly failed to gain the consent of the Cherokee national government to a removal treaty, federal agents kept trying, and in 1835, they were able to secure consent from a group of Cherokees, including Boudinot, who were not officials of the Cherokee Nation. That document, known as the Treaty of New Echota, was ratified by the U.S. Senate in May 1836, and on the basis of that supposed agreement, the Cherokees were rounded up in 1838 and removed to what would come to be known as Indian Territory in a journey known as the Trail of Tears. Boudinot had served as the editor of the *Cherokee Phoenix*, the national newspaper, from its creation in 1828 to his forced resignation in 1832 due to his burgeoning support for removal. *Letters and Other Papers* originally was printed as a pamphlet in Georgia and then was circulated to members of the U.S. Senate.

More than simply providing a retrospective justification for what could be, and largely was, construed as treason against the Cherokee Nation, Boudinot's text develops an argument about the nature of Cherokee collective identity and forms of political representation that registers the profound effects of U.S. policy on Cherokee governance. One of the principal conceptual moves the text makes is to separate the nation as a group of persons from the nation as a bounded territory. Boudinot observes:

> I may say that my patriotism consists in the *love of the country*, and *the love of the People*. These are intimately connected, yet they are not altogether inseparable ... But if the country is lost, or is likely to be lost to all human appearance, and the people still exist, may I not, with a patriotism true and commendable, make a *question* for the safety of the remaining object of my affection?
>
> (172)

Saying that "the country" could be "lost" while "the People" remain suggests not merely that a collection of individual Cherokees could survive the expropriation of their homeland but that the Cherokee Nation as such could continue to exist in the absence of its traditional territory – including as an object of "patriotism." The potential for imagining such a wholesale disjunction between the polity and the land it occupies can be seen as a function both of the previous centralization of Cherokee legal and administrative authority (all Cherokees belong to a single, unified entity rather than a collection of autonomous towns cross-cut by clan affiliations) and the kinds of subjectivity envisioned in treaty-discourse. In calling on representative leaders to sign agreements that would divorce a people entirely from their prior lands, U.S. Indian policy creates the potential for envisioning a kind of Native national identity that bears no inherent relationship to a particular place and that, theoretically, could come to occupy anywhere. Even as Boudinot seeks to imagine possibilities for Cherokee nationality that avoid "com[ing] under the dominion of the oppressor" by removing beyond the reach of Georgia's grasp (173), his text rhetorically severs the relationship between the people and the land that had driven Cherokee resistance to removal up to that point. In addition, he suggests that national leaders' support for "the contemptible prejudice founded upon the *love of the land*" functions as a form of deception (198), "humor"-ing a "delusion" by playing to the people's ignorance about the actual conditions they face (213). He asserts, "They have been taught to feel and expect what *could not* be realized – and what Mr. [John] Ross [the Principal Chief of the Cherokee Nation] himself must have known *would not* be realized" (161), and he suggests that "our most intelligent citizens ... would, no doubt, sustain me, from a proper view of things" (166), insisting that those who supported the treaty did "what the majority *would do* if they understood their condition" (162). Boudinot presents the elected leaders as a misguided (if not outright corrupt) elite whose pandering to public sentiments endangers the people's welfare, and he casts himself and the other treaty-signers as a different kind of elite – the "intelligence of the country" (189) – acting as true patriots in the population's interest. While the adoption of the Treaty of New Echota operated outside the parameters of the Cherokee Constitution and the official forms of Cherokee national governance, Boudinot implicitly invokes the kind of national representativity (in contrast to localized modes of direct consensus) that characterize treaty relations with the United States and that shaped the construction of a centralized Cherokee national administration in response. Thus, even as Boudinot challenges the actions of the Cherokee government, he draws on the kinds of unified political subjectivity that emerged in negotiating the demands of the treaty-system, in the struggle over who legitimately could speak for/as the Cherokee people.

FINDING VOICE IN CHANGING TIMES

In contrast to Boudinot, Black Hawk's text refuses the centralization of Native governance, even while drawing on the ways he had been cast by the U.S. government as the exclusive source of Sauk resistance to removal. He became famous as the putative leader of what was treated as a military campaign in the spring and summer of 1832; he and dozens of others (including Foxes, Kickapoos, and Potawatomies) crossed the Mississippi at what is now the border between Illinois and Iowa from the area to which the Sauks officially had been removed a few years prior in order to return to reclaim their traditional lands (on the Black Hawk War and the history leading up to it, see Nichols; Thorne; Trask). The Sauks' dislocation from their territory east of the Mississippi was based on a treaty signed in 1804 that supposedly ceded those lands. It was part of the Jefferson administration's efforts to expand non-native control westward in the wake of the Louisiana Purchase the previous year, in which the United States acquired from France a territory stretching from the Mississippi to the areas claimed by Spain in the west and south (despite the lack of any meaningful French jurisdiction – or that of Spain before it – in virtually any part of that area). The treaty of 1804 gave the Sauks the right to occupy the ceded territory so long as it remained U.S. public land (had not been purchased by individuals as private property), and for decades, the Sauks periodically contested the validity of the treaty on the basis of both its illegitimacy (the chiefs who signed it were not authorized to enter into such a negotiation) and fraudulence (the terms were quite different than those to which the chiefs believed themselves to be agreeing). Settlers began moving into the main Sauk village in the winter of 1828–1829 while the Sauks were away on their annual hunt, a process that directly led to their official removal. In the wake of the "war" in 1832, which largely involved flight from the U.S. military and the murder of numerous Native noncombatants, the Sauks were forced to sign a treaty that year surrendering extensive lands west of the Mississippi, and Black Hawk was taken into custody and jailed for a little over a year, after which he was taken on a several months' long tour of eastern cities which was meant to show him the folly of opposing white expansionism. Instead, the tour created notoriety for him on which he capitalized in the production and circulation of his text. The *Life* was translated and transcribed by Antoine LeClaire, a Potawatomi who had served as an official interpreter for the U.S. government, and it was published by local editor John B. Patterson.

Like Boudinot, Black Hawk was not an official leader, but rather than arguing for his ability to speak for the Sauk people as a political collective in ways consistent with the treaty-system, Black Hawk insists on the illegitimacy of treaties, and U.S. Indian policy more broadly, in how they envision Native identity and territoriality. As against a notion of the Sauks as owning the land, such that they could decide to sell it to the United States, the text insists on inhabitance rather than possession as the basis for understanding relations to place:

> My reason teaches me that *land cannot be sold*. The Great Spirit gave it to his children to live upon, and cultivate, as far as is necessary for their subsistence; and so long as they occupy and cultivate it, they have the right to the soil – but if they voluntarily leave it, then any people have a right to settle upon it.
>
> (101)

In this vein, he suggests that the Sauk chiefs could not possibly have conceptualized the agreement in 1804 as one of sale, characterizing that fundamental mistranslation of Sauk intent as "the origin of all our difficulties" (54). He further presents the negotiation of treaties, and U.S. administrative conduct generally, as an extended process of deception, observing, "What do we know of the manner of the laws and customs of the white people? They might buy our bodies for dissection, and we would touch the goose quill to confirm it, without knowing what we are doing" (87). More than indicating the problems of translating English words into Sauk, the text emphasizes the mutual unintelligibility of Native and settler understandings of landedness, political authority, and collective accountability. Black Hawk suggests that whites intentionally play on this disjunction in order to secure apparent assent to written agreements that are radically different from what Native interlocutors believe them to mean and that do not conform to extant Native philosophies and practices. He notes, "How smooth must be the language of whites, when they can make right look like wrong, and wrong like right" (102). While Boudinot charges Cherokee officials with misleading the people in the relations between the Cherokee Nation and the United States, Black Hawk suggests that those recognized as Sauk leaders by the United States only have such authority due to the United States. He particularly singles out Keokuk for rebuke, who also was not a traditional chief but who gained increasing prominence through the 1820s and became the federally recognized spokesperson for the Sauks by the end of the decade. The text characterizes Keokuk as possessing a "smooth tongue" like the whites (107), and Black Hawk contrasts federal favoritism toward Keokuk (he "stood high in the estimation of our Great Father [meaning the U.S. government], because he did not join me in the war" [143]) with his own commitment to protecting Sauk connections to place (including the women's corn-fields and the graves of their ancestors [107–8]). Rather than presenting his account as important due to his status as part of an elite (Boudinot's "intelligence of the country" – which includes literacy in English), Black Hawk draws on his fame as a result of the "war" to use print publication to reach a non-native audience, even as the text foregrounds forms of Native popular understanding that do not conform to those of non-natives and that, therefore, challenge the principles at play in Indian policy and the attendant validity of the treaties negotiated within that framework.

Congress brought an end to treaty-making in 1871, as a rider to an appropriations bill.[4] If the treaty-system often worked to cast relations of coercion as acts of consent on the part of Native peoples, it, at least, presented itself as an acknowledgment of Native nations as autonomous political entities with whom the United States was engaging in diplomatic relations. By the mid-nineteenth century, though, the federal government increasingly portrayed the legal recognition of Native territories as if it were a gift of land from the United States, a compassionate gesture of sympathy for a less enlightened population in need of white care. Within that process, Indian agents, those individuals appointed to oversee particular peoples, were granted huge discretion in exerting authority over virtually all aspects of Native life. Reservations came to be far more carceral than they had been previously, and the military was used to police movements off-reservation and to capture/ punish those persons and bands deemed "hostile" due to their refusal of federally sanctioned forms of superintendence. Indian policy had been committed to "civilizing" Native peoples since at least the 1810s, but in the late nineteenth century, that supposed aim served as a justification for vastly increased intervention within Native affairs, eventuating in the passage of the General Allotment Act in 1887 (otherwise known as the Dawes Act, after the Massachusetts senator who proposed it).[5] Far surpassing anything in federal policy that preceded it,[6] that law sought to eliminate the existence of Native nations as such by dividing up

FINDING VOICE IN CHANGING TIMES

Native lands into individual parcels (usually distributed to nuclear family units). Breaking up the landbases of Native nations into private property-holdings was cast as teaching Native people how to be citizens, a status which was extended through allotment. The achievement of citizenship was presented as a sign of Indian competence to participate in modern life but also as an indication of having left behind all things "tribal," such that being seen as deserving autonomy from suffocating federal management (as well as from potential subjection to military assault) was also tantamount to agreeing to abandon Native collective identities and sovereignties.

In her novel *Wynema*, Alice Callahan draws on the representation of Native people as in need of governmental care as a way of arguing against the imposition of allotment. Not all peoples were directly subject to the Dawes Act, at least initially. Among those exempted were those Native nations that had been removed from the southeast to what came to be known as Indian Territory – over top of which the state of Oklahoma would be created in 1907 – including the Creek Nation (on the post-removal history of the Creek Nation, see Debo; Chang; and Saunt). The removal treaty for the Creeks was ratified in 1832, and it allowed for those who desired to do so to take up residence as citizens on lands that they would own as private property, rather than relocate west – a model much like that of allotment. However, the undeclared war by local whites against those who had stayed led to the removal of the remaining Creeks three years later. In Indian Territory, the Creeks re-established their government, eventually siding with the Confederacy during the Civil War (due to both U.S. duplicity and intrusion and the fact that a number of Creeks were slaveholders who wanted to retain their property in human chattel). In 1866, in the wake of the war, Creeks signed a new treaty with the United States emancipating their slaves and enfranchising them, and they established a constitutional government with a bicameral legislature based on representation by town. Callahan's father served in a number of roles within that government, including as a clerk within the legislature, a clerk to the Supreme Court, and a justice of that court, suggesting that she would have been well aware of the dynamics of Creek governance in the late nineteenth century. While initially exempted from allotment, the Creeks, and other peoples in Indian Territory, were subjected to it under the Curtis Act (1898). *Wynema* was written and published in the period between the passage of the Dawes Act and the Curtis Act, when discussion of allotment was prevalent but it had not yet been federally mandated for the Creek Nation.

The novel appears to endorse forms of white paternalism, yet it presents the kinds of humanitarian concern that officials and legislators often claimed as the motivation for Indian policy as a basis for rejecting (or at least significantly deferring) the atomizing and detribalizing force of allotment. Rather than casting itself as a form of Creek self-representation, the text tells the story from the point of view of Genevieve Weir, a white woman from the South who comes to the Creeks as a teacher. While offering a rather skewed portrait of Creek life (including describing them as living in "tepees" and offering virtually no sense that Creeks have a national government), the text illustrates the growing affection between Genevieve and her charges, including Wynema. Her effectiveness as a teacher results from the ways that "the influence of love open[s] doors that giant force could not set the least ajar" (23), and that rhetoric of benevolent care provides the frame through which the novel approaches the question of allotment. In a conversation in which Wynema initially endorses allotment, Genevieve notes that it "sounds like the lands will be allotted whether the Indians like or no ... It will do very well for the civilized tribes, but they should never consent to it until their weaker brothers are willing and able," adding, "Do you think the western tribes sufficiently tutored in the school of civilization to become citizens of the United States[?]" (52). Later, Gerald Keithly, a missionary among the Creeks whom Genevieve eventually marries, remarks, "'The strong should protect the weak' says chivalry; but there seems to be very little if any chivalric spirit shown in the case of these Indians" (57). While not contesting the notion of whites' civilizational superiority, the novel mobilizes such sentiments to argue against subjecting Native peoples to mandatory allotment, on the basis that they are not now (and may never be) ready "to become citizens" and that they need *protection* until that point. Callahan emphasizes that gap between such compassionate instruction and supervision and existing government actions in the text's discussion of the spectacular violence of the Wounded Knee massacre, which is referenced toward the end of the novel. Characters to whom readers have been introduced go to missionize among the Lakota just before the army's murder of Ghost Dancers in their camp in December 1890 as they were in the peaceful process of moving toward the Pine Ridge agency (on the massacre and the history leading up to it, see Ostler). Genevieve's brother, Robin, observes of the vicious assault,

> is all this right, this treatment of the Indians, this non-fulfillment of treaties, this slaughter of a defenseless people, living in the light of wards of the Government? Can it be right for the strong to oppress the weak, the wise to slay the ignorant?
>
> (102)

Here the language of care, of truly treating Native people as "wards," serves as a counterpoint to the brutality of military aggression for which Wounded Knee serves as the iconic instance. The novel, then, counterpoises a policy of loving "influence" and *chivalrous* guardianship, in which the question of allotment is suspended (perhaps indefinitely), to a politics of "giant force," in which the United States seeks to destroy Native peoples as such in ways that are inhumane at best and, at worst, downright bloodthirsty.

While written a few years before the passage of the Dawes Act, Sarah Winnemucca Hopkins's *Life Among the Piutes: Their Wrongs and Claims* argues for allotment as a way of countering the dire effects of Indian agent discretion and the absence of security for Native lands. Unlike the other peoples I've discussed, the northern Paiutes were not a coherent political entity, instead comprising loosely organized bands of shifting size (usually in the dozens) that were organized around kinship relations (see Blackhawk; Smoak; Zanjani). There was not a centralized government (as with the Cherokees and Creeks) or a collective council (as with the Sauks), and the bands did not have permanent village sites, instead moving in seasonal patterns within a regular area in what is now northwest Nevada and southeast Oregon. Although occasionally trappers and explorers came through the territory in the 1830s, consistent contact with Euramericans did not begin until the late 1840s and early 1850s, after the Mexican–American War, and while northern Paiutes were affected to some extent by the patterns of trading, raiding, and captivity occurring to the south, they remained largely distant from the networks of commerce and slaving spurred by Hispanophone presence from the sixteenth century onward. During the 1860s and 1870s, a number of armed conflicts occurred in the northern Paiute region due to forms of settler invasion and assault (often sexual violence against Paiute women), the most explosive of which was the Bannock War in the summer of 1878, about which Winnemucca writes at length. As a result of these conflicts, the federal government both formally created reservations for the northern Paiutes (including Pyramid Lake, Walker Lake, and Malheur) and abolished them as punishment for perceived complicity in violence against settlers. Given that they were not created through treaties, these reservations remained particularly vulnerable to executive action on the part of the President, the Secretary of the Interior, and/or the Office of Indian Affairs. Winnemucca was the daughter of a man she refers to as "Chief Winnemucca" who was often cast by army and Indian bureau officials as the leader of the northern Paiutes, and in addition to serving as a translator both on-reservation and for the military, she lectured extensively, which brought her to the attention of the Peabody sisters (Elizabeth Peabody and Mary Mann) – Boston-based philanthropists and activists who supported her efforts to advocate in the east and Washington, D.C. for the Paiutes and who aided her in the publication of *Life*.

Winnemucca's text highlights the kinds of arbitrary authority exercised by agents on-reservation while positioning the Paiutes as upstanding subjects and herself as a representative speaker due to her status as the daughter of a chief. The body of *Life* (prior to an appendix of letters of support and explanation) closes with a memorial in which Winnemucca

> petition[s] the Honorable Congress of the United States to restore to them said Malheur Reservation [from which they had been removed to the Yakima reservation following the Bannock War] ... where they can enjoy lands in severalty without losing their tribal relations, so essential to their happiness and good character, and where their citizenship, implied in this distribution of land, will defend them from the encroachments of white settlers.
>
> (247)

Allotment – dividing "lands in severalty" – appears as the only recourse from invasive "encroachments," but rather than indicating the loss of Native nationhood, it becomes the vehicle for maintaining "their tribal relations," with "citizenship" as a form of legal recognition/protection through which Paiutes can exert political agency/voice. This seemingly paradoxical vision of allotment as a means of preserving Paiute collectivity emerges out of being subjected to the vicissitudes of the will and policy of different agents, each with their own conception of Native rights or the lack thereof. One agent, Parrish, tells them, "The reservation is all yours. The government has given it to you and your children" (106), whereas a previous agent had insisted that if they did not submit to his demands for what amounts to tribute "you must leave the reservation," claiming that his graft was simply "what the government orders" (95). The agent who replaces Parrish, Reinhard, insists, even more strongly, "This land which you are living on is government land," to which Egan, one of the Paiute leaders, responds, "we don't want the Big Father in Washington to fool with us. He sends one man to say one thing and another to say something else" (124). Yet, even as the text chronicles the many causes of Native discontent and dismay produced by the agents' capricious control of conditions on-reservation, it distinguishes between the Paiutes and those who fail to conform to government dictates. These groups include the Columbia River Indians and the Bannocks. The former are designated as "bad Indians" due to their refusal to stay within reservation boundaries and their continuance of older, regional trade patterns (110), and even though the latter go to war as a result of being punished for seeking to avenge sexual assaults on Bannock women (138–45), Winnemucca distances her people from them, despite ample evidence in the text and elsewhere that many of those who fought with the Bannocks were Paiutes. These differentiations from those who are "bad Indians" work to cast her people as undeserving of the forms of (mis)management and dispossession they face. In addition to rhetorically hardening the distinctions between the Paiutes she associates with her family and other Native people(s), Winnemucca presents herself as a representative figure due to her father's supposed status as "head chief of the Piute nation" (67), a claim often belied in the text by the fact of his long periods away from Paiute people on-reservation (see, for example, 85, 103, 112, 154–62). Such a consolidation of political identity/authority among the Paiutes provides the sense of a more orderly form of government, while also suggesting the kind of "tribal" cohesion that allotment might facilitate and the appropriateness of Winnemucca serving in the public role of advocate for it.

The various texts I've been discussing do not have the same perspective on how to understand Native sovereignty and how to negotiate its relation to U.S. impositions. Boudinot seeks to speak for a unified Cherokee Nation while displacing the authority of the constitutional Cherokee government; Black Hawk aims to challenge the legitimacy of centralized Sauk political authority (as exerted by Keokuk) in favor of a more flexible kind of collectivity emerging out of connection to their historic homeland; Callahan largely effaces the existence of Creek governance as such in order to highlight relations of tutelage with whites; and Winnemucca generates an exaggerated (if not outright fictitious) vision of singular Paiute leadership in ways that help cast them as good subjects, worthy of the protection/recognition offered by "severalty" and "citizenship." Amid the changing conditions and indeterminacies of federal Indian policy over the course of the nineteenth century, Native writers adopted a range of strategies for navigating those ongoing transformations and ambiguities. The absence of unanimity among them indicates the complexities of their varied histories, the situations they faced, and how they sought to inhabit and shift the kinds of public voice available to them while also highlighting the inadequacy of simplistic binaries like "tradition" vs. "assimilation" as a way of understanding the variability of Native modes of textual self-expression in this period (or, really, any other).

Notes

1 In my previous work, I have raised questions about applying the language of nationhood to Indigenous peoples, since historically it has taken part in imposing Euramerican modes of governance (see Rifkin, *Manifesting*).
2 Due to the brevity of this chapter and the number of texts I'll be addressing, I will not engage directly with existing literary criticism on each of the texts. For such scholarship, see the Further Reading section at the end of the volume.
3 The Indian Removal Act allocated $500,000 for the President to purchase Native lands east of the Mississippi and to remove Native peoples to lands to the west (see Prucha, 52–53).
4 While that action did not invalidate existing treaties, it reflected a growing tendency to treat Native peoples as objects of U.S. benevolence/discipline. On the history of this period, see Genetin-Pilawa; Hoxie; Piatote; Rifkin *When* 143–80; Trennert.
5 The allotment period formally was brought to an end by the passage of the Indian Reorganization Act (1934). During the fifty-year period in which it was in effect, Native peoples lost approximately 90 million acres of land.
6 Late-nineteenth-century federal policy, though, can be seen as reflecting earlier developments in New England (see Den Ouden; Mandell; O'Brien).

Works cited

Black Hawk. *Life of Ma-Ka-Tai-Me-She-Kia-Kiak or Black Hawk* (1833), reprinted as *Black Hawk: An Autobiography*. Ed. Donald Jackson. Champaign: University of Illinois Press, 1955.

Blackhawk, Ned. *Violence Over the Land: Indians and Empires in the Early American West*. Cambridge, MA: Harvard University Press, 2006.

Boudinot, Elias. *Letters and Other Papers Relating to Cherokee Affairs: Being a Reply to Sundry Publications Authorized by John Ross* (1837), in *Cherokee Editor: The Writings of Elias Boudinot*. Ed. Theda Perdue. Athens: University of Georgia Press, 1996. 155–234.

Callahan, S. Alice. *Wynema: A Child of the Forest* (1891). Lincoln: University of Nebraska Press, 1997.

Chang, David A. *The Color of the Land: Race, Nation, and the Politics of Landownership in Oklahoma, 1832–1929*. Chapel Hill: University of North Carolina Press, 2010.

Debo, Angie. *The Road to Disappearance: A History of the Creek Indians*. Norman: University of Oklahoma Press, 1941.

Den Ouden, Amy E. *Beyond Conquest: Native Peoples and the Struggle for History in New England*. Lincoln: University of Nebraska Press, 2005.

Genetin-Pilawa, C. Joseph. *Crooked Paths to Allotment: The Fight over Federal Indian Policy after the Civil War*. Chapel Hill: University of North Carolina Press, 2012.

Hopkins, Sarah Winnemucca. *Life Among the Piutes: Their Wrongs and Claims* (1883). Reno: University of Nevada Press, 1994.

Hoxie, Frederick E. *A Final Promise: The Campaign to Assimilate the Indians, 1880–1920*. 1984. Cambridge: Cambridge University Press, 1992.

Jones, Dorothy V. *License for Empire: Colonialism by Treaty in Early America*. Chicago: University of Chicago Press, 1982.

Justice, Daniel Heath. *Our Fire Survives the Storm: A Cherokee Literary History*. Minneapolis: University of Minnesota Press, 2006.

Mandell, Daniel R. *Tribe, Race, History: Native Americans in Southern New England, 1780–1880*. Baltimore, MD: Johns Hopkins University Press, 2008.

McLoughlin, William G. *Cherokee Renascence in the New Republic*. Princeton, NJ: Princeton University Press, 1986.

Nichols, Roger L. *Black Hawk and the Warrior's Path*. Arlington Heights, IL: Harlan Davidson, Inc., 1992.

O'Brien, Jean. *Firsting and Lasting: Writing Indians Out of Existence in New England*. Minneapolis: University of Minnesota Press, 2010.

Ostler, Jeffrey. *The Plains Sioux and U.S. Colonialism from Lewis and Clark to Wounded Knee*. New York: Cambridge University Press, 2004.

Perdue, Theda. *Cherokee Women: Gender and Cultural Change, 1700–1835*. Lincoln: University of Nebraska Press, 1998.

Piatote, Beth. *Domestic Subjects: Gender, Citizenship, and Law in Native American Literature*. New Haven, CT: Yale University Press, 2013.

Prucha, Francis Paul. *Documents of United States Indian Policy*, 3rd ed. Lincoln: University of Nebraska Press, 2000.

Rifkin, Mark. *Manifesting America: The Imperial Construction of U.S. National Space*. New York: Oxford University Press, 2009.

——. *When Did Indians Become Straight? Kinship, the History of Sexuality, and Native Sovereignty*. New York: Oxford University Press, 2011.

Rockwell, Stephen J. *Indian Affairs and the Administrative State in the Nineteenth Century*. New York: Cambridge University Press, 2010.

Saunt, Claudio. *Black, White, and Indian: Race and the Unmaking of an American Family.* New York: Oxford University Press, 2005.

Smoak, Gregory E. *Ghost Dances and Identity: Prophetic Religion and American Indian Ethnogenesis in the Nineteenth Century.* Berkeley: University of California Press, 2006.

Thorne, Tanis C. *The Many Hands of My Relations: French and Indians on the Lower Missouri.* Columbia: University of Missouri Press, 1996.

Trask, Kerry A. *Black Hawk: The Battle for the Heart of America.* New York: Owl Books, 2007.

Trennert, Robert A., Jr. *Alternative to Extinction: Federal Indian Policy and the Beginnings of the Reservation System, 1846–1851.* Philadelphia: Temple University Press, 1975.

Wallace, Anthony F.C. *Jefferson and the Indians: The Tragic Fate of the First Americans.* Cambridge, MA: Harvard University Press, 1999.

Zanjani, Sally. *Sarah Winnemucca.* Lincoln: University of Nebraska Press, 2004.

13
Assimilative Schooling and Native American Literature

Tova Cooper

The involvement of the U.S. government in Native American education dates back to 1819, when the Indian Civilization Fund Act provided funds for Protestant missionaries to establish Indian schools. Assimilative education did not gain significant momentum, however, until 1879, when Carlisle, the first government-funded boarding school for Native Americans, opened its doors. The government's education policy was championed both by government officials who devalued native traditions, and by ostensibly pro-Indian reformers who thought that assimilation was preferable to extinction, which they feared was the inevitable alternative.

Assimilative education was a central component of the Dawes (or General Allotment) Act of 1887. This law promised citizenship to Native Americans who had fulfilled three requirements: abdicated tribal membership, allowed the government to subdivide and privatize their land (allotment in severalty), and agreed to become Americanized. The Dawes Act targeted both communal land ownership and economies based on hunting, fishing, and gathering. It stipulated that reservation land could be sold to white settlers, with the profits earmarked for both assimilative schooling and the purchase of farming equipment for natives living on allotted land.

After passage of the Dawes Act, the U.S. government coerced native children (as young as five and six years old) to attend day or boarding schools both on and off reservations. Early on, children were taken forcibly from their parents; later, parental consent was required, though some schools prohibited contact between parents and children. In 1891 Congress made attendance at assimilative schools compulsory, and in 1893 it authorized the Indian Office to "withhold rations, clothing, and other annuities from Indian parents" who refused to send their children to school (Adams 63). Alongside federally funded institutions, religious groups also operated assimilative schools both on and off of reservations.

Native children who attended government schools (particularly boarding schools) were abruptly deprived of contact with their families and tribes. Native students labored to operate and in some cases help build the schools. Weakened by forced labor and malnutrition – subsisting in some cases on bread, boiled potatoes, black coffee, and syrup – the young children at these schools often became sick and died from outbreaks of infectious disease (Churchill 36). Massive attrition resulted from the housing of children in small, densely packed living quarters with little air circulation, and from the schools' failure to quarantine infected children (Churchill 36–37). Those who did not become ill often ran away; others, who remained at school, underwent systematic tribal disidentification through a curriculum that imposed a generic "Indian" identity on all students, regardless of their tribal affiliation. Motivated by Carlisle founder Richard Henry Pratt's motto, "Kill the Indian … and save the man," government schools imposed a military regime on students. They replaced native clothing with military dress, prohibited the use of native languages (a policy intensified by isolating children from members of their own tribes), and responded to infractions against school policy with corporal punishment.

Various literary genres emerged from assimilative schooling. Many native students and teachers wrote autobiographical texts about their experiences at government and parochial schools. These citizenship autobiographies offer detailed accounts of students' experiences before, during, and after attending such schools. They recount tribal practices and reservation conditions that students left behind; document the methods by which government agents lured children away from their homes; and convey students' attitudes – ranging from acceptance to active resistance – towards their schooling. These autobiographies also illustrate the range of outcomes faced by native students who attended assimilative schools, whether they returned to their reservations, became teachers at assimilative schools, or entered mainstream U.S. society. These narratives reveal that students who returned to their reservations often faced alienation or hostility from their tribes or families, while those who entered mainstream U.S. life encountered racism and difficult working conditions. A handful of former students sought to preserve tribal cultures and cultivate respect for native values by publishing native myths and stories. Some of these same authors wrote essays and speeches calling for self-determination, critiquing the Bureau of Indian Affairs (BIA), and demanding passage of comprehensive citizenship legislation.

From reservation to school and beyond

Three Sioux authors – Zitkala Ša (Gertrude Bonnin), Charles Eastman, and Luther Standing Bear – published the best-known autobiographical accounts of their assimilative education at religious and government schools. All three authors detail the tribal rituals and practices that not only had been weakened by the tribes' confinement to reservations, but were further threatened by their subjection to the terms of the Dawes Act.

Of these three authors, Zitkala Ša (Dakota Sioux) is most critical of assimilative schooling and its effects on Native American children and their families. Though Zitkala Ša attended Quaker schools, her account of White's Manual Labor School evokes conditions shared by government schools. Zitkala Ša's writing also recounts her experience as a teacher at the Carlisle Indian Industrial School. In "Impressions of an Indian Childhood," the first of three autobiographical essays that Zitkala Ša placed in the *Atlantic Monthly* in early 1900, she acknowledges the painful repercussions of contact with whites on Sioux culture. At the same time, she presents an idealized portrait of the tribal education she received from her mother and community, one centered on treating others with dignity and respect. By contrast, in "School Days of an Indian Girl," Zitkala Ša reveals her shock at teachers who patronize and humiliate her. At one point, she recounts the shearing of her hair, horrifying because for the Sioux, only mourners and captured warriors wear their hair short or shingled. At other moments, she shares her objection to religious indoctrination. Throughout, Zitkala Ša dramatizes the confusion and chaos resulting from a prohibition on the use of native languages.

Though Zitkala Ša emphasizes moments of rebelliousness against her schooling, she also thematizes the sad irony of its effect on her family life. Out of respect for her daughter's wishes, Zitkala Ša's mother allowed her to leave home with school recruiters even though her mother distrusted their Edenic promises of a land filled with "big red apples" ("Impressions" 18–21). Though her mother's decision arose from a respect for Zitkala Ša, assimilative education ultimately estranged them from each other. In recounting her experience as a teacher at Carlisle in "An Indian Teacher Among Indians," Zitkala Ša attributes her state of physical and spiritual depletion to assimilative education. Shortly after publishing this third essay, Zitkala Ša left Carlisle. Instead of returning to her reservation, however, she led a peripatetic – but not unproductive – life. She published *Old Indian Legends* (1901); worked with her husband Ray Bonnin on the Ute Reservation; wrote the libretto for *The Sun Dance* opera; and, as Secretary for the Society of American Indians (SAI) and editor of its *American Indian Magazine*, spoke out about a variety of issues, including corruption within the Bureau of Indian Affairs (BIA).

Charles Eastman (Dakota Sioux) was another prolific author who wrote about assimilative education. While Eastman's 1902 memoir *Indian Boyhood* dramatizes his upbringing as a Sioux hunter and warrior, his 1916 book, *From the Deep Woods to Civilization: Chapters in the Autobiography of an Indian*, recounts his schooling in a series of institutions, including the Santee Normal School (which was unusual in that it offered instruction in Sioux), a variety of Midwestern colleges, Dartmouth, and Boston University School of Medicine. In *Deep Woods*, Eastman offers an account of assimilative education that is less openly critical than that of Zitkala Ša. Eastman has been critiqued for being an enthusiastic assimilationist, particularly because he frames his life story in terms of his progress from savagery to civilization. Much of the time, however, Eastman invokes a mainstream concept of savagery ironically, as a means of critiquing U.S. culture from an "Indian" perspective that he defines in terms of communal ownership of goods, respect for nature, and a rejection of materialism.

Unlike Zitkala Ša and Charles Eastman, the educational memoir of Luther Standing Bear (Oglala Sioux) – *My People the Sioux* (1928) – offers a relatively positive account of his transformation from a tribal youth to a government-educated man. Standing Bear explains that when he chose to attend Carlisle, he did not realize he was going away "to learn the ways of the white man"; instead, he thought he was going off to "do some brave deed" before returning to his people (182). Nonetheless, Standing Bear embraces the experience, excels at his schooling, and agrees with his father that education will facilitate his successful adaptation to the dominant white culture. This text also narrates Standing Bear's return from school, work as a reservation teacher, success as a tribal leader, and fight to gain legal citizenship. In the book's most incisive criticism of assimilationist ideology, he shares his knowledge, upon returning home from school, that "there would be no more hunting – we would have to work now for our food and clothing. It was like the Garden of Eden after the fall of man" (254). Standing Bear became increasingly critical of the Dawes Act and the impact of assimilationist ideology on tribal culture and reservation life, a position he expresses in his ethnography of Lakota life, *Land of the Spotted Eagle* (1933).

Some Native American intellectuals who underwent assimilative schooling established the Society of American Indians (SAI) in 1911. This pan-Indian organization connected many Native Americans – including Zitkala Ša and Eastman – who had attended assimilative boarding schools and now worked as doctors, lawyers, teachers, anthropologists, activists, and government employees. Many SAI members shared a commitment to improving the perception of Native Americans by outsiders. They sought to demonstrate that natives could not only assimilate into mainstream U.S. culture but also could reshape it with tribal values. Zitkala Ša's *Old Indian Legends* (1901) exemplifies this trend. Featuring traditional Sioux stories about the tricky but hubristic Iktomi, the book symbolizes the assimilative schools' failure to eradicate tribal cultures. Zitkala Ša's "Preface" to *Old Indian Legends* illustrates the dualistic objective shared by many native authors from this period. Zitkala Ša claims that these stories "belong quite as much to the blue-eyed little patriot as to the black-haired aborigine" but also expresses hope that they will help white readers develop respect for the "American aborigine," who "seems at heart much like other peoples." In a similarly bicultural vein, Zitkala Ša and William Hanson co-authored *The Sun Dance* opera, which "melded Native American ritual with the standard European operatic tradition" in its attempt to translate the power of the Sioux Sun Dance "for predominantly white audiences" (Davidson & Norris xx). In other respects, however, Zitkala Ša clung to native traditions, for instance in her preference for native spirituality over Christianity, which she writes about in her 1902 essay, "Why I am a Pagan."

Like Zitkala Ša, Charles Eastman defended native land claims settlements, supported Native American citizenship, and sought respect for Sioux culture – publishing Sioux myths and stories, for instance, in *Old Indian Days* (1907). Eastman was particularly passionate in his objection to the corruption of reservation life, which likely motivated his unarguable support for assimilation. Nonetheless, Eastman did not embrace assimilation blindly, but rather promoted a dual-directional assimilation through which he sought to infuse mainstream U.S. culture with "Indian" values. Eastman had critiqued the selfish and wasteful habits of white culture as early as 1904, with *Red Hunters and the Animal People* (1904). A decade later, he published a collection of curricular materials that he had created for the scouting movement. In this text, *Indian Scout Talks: A Guide for Boy Scouts and Campfire Girls* (1914), Eastman offers lessons for white scouts in native values and practices.

In his journalistic and political writings, Eastman developed progressive solutions for troubles faced by Native Americans. He advocated the legalization of Native American citizenship on the basis that the best qualities of U.S. culture derived from Native Americans. In his "Opening Address" at the SAI's Annual Conference, Eastman stated: "we Indians started the whole basis of Americanism … [we] laid the foundation of freedom and equality and democracy long before any white people came here and those who took it up, but they do not give us credit ("Opening Address" 145). Likewise, in "The Indian's Plea for Freedom" (1919), Eastman enumerated Indians' many contributions to U.S. cultural, civic, and military life (164). In *The Indian To-day: The Past and Future of the First American* (1915), Eastman promoted the racial "amalgamation" of Indians and whites; as a mixed-race person himself, Eastman felt strongly that racial mixing resulted in American qualities such as "unequalled logic," "wonderful aggressiveness," and "dauntless public service" (124). For Eastman, the problems resulting from assimilative ideology could be assuaged by intermarriage, which would save the Indian's "physique" and "philosophy" even if it was too late to "save his color" (147).

ASSIMILATIVE SCHOOLING

Resisting recruitment and returning home

Helen Sekaquaptewa's *Me and Mine: The Life Story of Helen Sekaquaptewa* and Polingayse Qoyawayma's *No Turning Back: A Hopi Indian Woman's Struggle to Live in Two Worlds* were co-authored by white intermediaries – in other words, "told to" and written by Louise Udall and Vada F. Carlson, respectively. Nonetheless, these texts comment insightfully on the conflict between two Hopi factions, those who accepted government schooling and those who resisted it actively. Both autobiographies are useful for their representations of how these women returned from government schools to their Hopi communities and achieved a balance between their assimilative education and a traditional Hopi lifestyle.

In narrating her experience at the day school situated just outside the Hopi Mesa, Helen Sekaquaptewa dramatizes the tension between and ultimate estrangement of the "friendlies" and the "hostiles" in her tribe: those who embraced white culture and those who clung to Hopi traditions. As hostiles, Helen's parents took extreme measures to evade the school authorities who regularly scouted the Hopi mesa for truant children, accompanied by Navajo policemen (the Hopi's traditional enemies). Though the children's efforts to hide from the authorities were both inventive and persistent, ultimately Helen and many other children like her were sent to the government day school bordering the Hopi Mesa or to Keams Canyon boarding school a few hours away. Sekaquaptewa explains that few students were ever allowed to leave the school grounds, and the children of hostiles – unlike the children of friendlies – were not even allowed to vacation with their parents.

Sekaquaptewa enjoyed school, aside from the relentless teasing she encountered from the children of friendlies. She notes, however, that many students, particularly at the Keams Canyon boarding school, found its military-style discipline problematic. The most far-reaching consequence of schooling for Sekaquaptewa was estrangement from her family after attending school for thirteen years. Though her mother accepted her, Sekaquaptewa "didn't feel at ease" at her parents' house, a feeling that intensified once her mother died and Sekaquaptewa's traditionalist sister took over the family home (144). Nonetheless, Sekaquaptewa explains how she finally learned to balance Hopi culture with American customs, and explains that the lives of her and her husband "were a combination of what we thought was the good of both cultures, the Hopi way and what we had learned at school" (186).

Polingayse Qoyawayma's memoir is particularly unusual in that its co-author, Vada Carlson, narrates Qoyawayma's story in the third person. Nonetheless, the memoir offers an important account of Qoyawayma's struggle to balance her Hopi upbringing with the lessons of assimilative education. After defying her family to attend the reservation day school, Qoyawayma is lured to the Sherman Institute, a California boarding school, with the promise of "orange trees, heavy with fruit" (51). Though boarding school created an intense loneliness in Qoyawayma, she claims it was a diffuse loneliness, which was not for the "pattern life" of the Hopi or for the near destitute living conditions of her family (65). Ultimately, Qoyawayma finds her calling as a teacher at a series of government day schools near the Hopi Mesa. Determined to make school a pleasant experience for her students, Qoyawayma defies the prohibition against bringing Hopi culture into the classroom; knowing that the "white-man stories" meant little to Hopi children, Qoyawayma taught them English and other subjects by drawing on what they already knew in the form of familiar everyday words. As Carlson explains, "Instead of cramming Little Red Riding Hood into the uncomprehending brains of her small students, she substituted familiar Hopi legends, songs, and stories" (125). This technique garnered Qoyawayma fame among progressive educators, and her methods were upheld as a model for other Indian Service teachers (158).

Native-run schools: an alternative to assimilationist ideology

The story of assimilative education would be incomplete without attention to the schools either operated or authorized by the relocated Cherokee, Choctaw, Chickasaw, Seminole, and Creek (now Muskogee) nations to which the U.S. government referred in the nineteenth century as the "Five Civilized Tribes." Mixed-blood elites within these tribes often adopted Euro-American dress, manners, and practices (living in plantation-style homes, owning slaves, and in some cases practicing Christianity). These assimilative practices increased the cultural capital of tribal leaders in dealings with white outsiders, ultimately strengthening their tribal sovereignty. These elites saw no incompatibility between their adoption of Euro-American cultural practices and their primary identification as tribal members, in part because they opposed the native–white binary that aligned natives unequivocally with primitivism. Whereas most schools run by missionaries and the federal government emphasized obedience as the end result of assimilative education (either through the internalization of spiritual values or willingness to do manual work), wealthy native elites who had little interest in becoming laborers saw education as a means of harnessing the social power wielded by their white counterparts.

Not surprisingly, these tribal political leaders opposed the logic and provisions of the Dawes Act. This opposition gained them a period of self-government, which ended in 1898 when the Curtis Act extended the provisions of the Dawes Act to the five nations. In 1906, the Five Civilized Tribes Act terminated all tribal governments in Indian Territory, and gave the federal government (specifically the Bureau of Indian Affairs) control of all native-run educational institutions. Before 1906, the five nations allowed certain religious institutions to operate schools within their territories, with the caveat that the schools would not interfere with tribal sovereignty. The tribes also operated their own schools, ranging from bilingual primary schools to college-preparatory academies, typically called seminaries, which were modeled on the private boarding schools common in white society. Though both the male and female students who attended these seminaries studied academic subjects, the women received additional instruction in the ideas and habits (such as piety, purity, submissiveness, and domesticity) central to the Victorian Cult of True Womanhood. At the English-language Cherokee Female Seminary, for instance, students produced a newspaper, *A Wreath of Cherokee Rose Buds*, in which they articulated a Cherokee identity compatible with the dominant tenets of white femininity, while also asserting equality with whites based on their embrace of civilized ideas and behavior. This seminary was so much like an elite, private school for white women that the federal government objected to its curriculum, complaining that topics like Latin and mathematics were being prioritized over agricultural and domestic work, and the "dignity" of manual labor (Mihesuah 60).

This history is useful for understanding the conditions of production and plot elements of *Wynema: A Child of the Forest*, published by Alice Callahan (Muskogee [Creek]) in 1891.

For a decade following their Removal to Indian Territory, the Creek prohibited the practice of Christianity in their territory, but in 1842 they allowed a handful of missionary schools to open on tribal lands (Debo 117–19). Callahan, who studied at the Wesleyan Female Institute and later taught at the Methodist boarding school, Wealaka, used both as models for the setting of *Wynema* (Ruoff xvi–xvii). While the novel's sentimental style misrepresents some aspects of native culture, it addresses the repercussions of the Dawes Act on Creek culture and offers an insightful portrait of the assimilationist alternative developed by the Creek.

In particular, *Wynema* addresses the rift between full-blooded, monolingual Creeks and English-speaking mixed-bloods, which was worsened by the English-only curriculum at schools like Wealaka (Debo 309). Though in reality full-bloods often failed to thrive at these schools, the novel's title character Wynema learns English effortlessly from her Methodist teachers, Gerard Keithly and Genevieve Weir; likewise, she approves of allotment because it will benefit "industrious and enterprising" Creeks like herself and harm only the "idle and shiftless Indians who do nothing but hunt and fish" (51). By contrast, the novel portrays Wynema's Methodist teachers as champions of Creek culture and critics of the Dawes Act, a law which, as Weir explains to Wynema, would result in the loss of land and community among the Creeks (52). By having her full-blooded protagonist embrace assimilation, Callahan may be pointing to the futility of holding on to a traditional way of life in the face of the inevitable changes hastened by the Dawes Act.

Aside from the native-run bilingual schools discussed above, very few such institutions existed during this period. Therefore, the anomalous existence of Sara Winnemucca Hopkins's (Piute) short-lived Peabody School deserves mention. This school, which operated in Nevada from 1884 to 1887, represents Winnemucca's attempt to create a bilingual, native-controlled school on the Piute reservation. Though Winnemucca's 1883 autobiography, *Life Among the Piutes: Their Wrongs and Claims*, was published before the school opened, her book justifies the need for native-run schools. In her extended diatribe against the BIA – the federal agency that controlled reservation schools and managed Native American funds held in trust by the government – Winnemucca exposed the racist antipathy of BIA agents towards natives and decried their co-optation of government funds earmarked for the improvement of reservation life.

The Peabody School attracted full-blooded Piutes seeking an alternative to the coercive educational policies of the BIA and the dominance of English-only boarding schools. Unfortunately, Winnemucca had trouble raising funds for her school, in part because the BIA retaliated against her attacks on it with a campaign to smear her name. The BIA circulated rumors among government officials and professional reformers that Winnemucca was a "disreputable person" who was "unworthy of trust" (Zanjani 269–70). As a result, Winnemucca failed to raise adequate operating funds, conducted classes in a brush shelter, and was forced to close the Peabody School only three years after it had opened.

What we know about Peabody derives from two pamphlets published by the school's primary financial supporter, Elizabeth Peabody. In the first of these, *Sara Winnemucca's Practical Solution of the Indian Problem* (1886), Peabody emphasizes Winnemucca's commitment to bilingualism. Peabody argues that bilingualism is a necessary prerequisite to making English the vernacular of bilingual students. She attributes this view to Winnemucca, whom she quotes as saying, "the most necessary thing for the success of an Indian school is a good interpreter, a perfect interpreter" (3–4). Echoing the Hopi memoirs discussed above,

Peabody also lauds Winnemucca for defending her people's right "to select the best things in civilization" while remaining "free to retain whatever of the inherited tribal customs [that] are necessary to preserve their social life heart-whole" (qtd. in Zanjani 265).

Post-Assimilation Era literature

In the period immediately following the Assimilation Era, D'Arcy McNickle published *The Surrounded* (1936), a tragic novel about an educated student's return to his reservation. McNickle was the son of an Irish father and Cree mother, and grew up on the Flathead Reservation in Montana after the Salish people adopted him and his family. McNickle attended a day school on the Flathead Reservation, as well as Chemawa Indian School, a government boarding school in Oregon. Though McNickle published many books, fiction and non-fiction, he is most famous for *The Surrounded*. Set at the end of the Assimilationist Era, this novel tells the story of the mixed-blood Indian Archilde, who returns from boarding school to the bleak conditions of the Flathead Reservation. While at first frustrated with his mother's generation for its attachment to traditions that have become unviable, Archilde develops an understanding of that generation's struggle after he becomes entangled in a violent drama that plays out between members of his family and local officials. These figures – including the warden, the sheriff, a Jesuit priest, and an Indian Office agent – symbolize the ongoing repercussions of the U.S. colonialist policy of assimilation, which characterized reservation life in the New Deal era.

Several contemporary Native American authors have represented the history of assimilative education in both fiction and non-fiction. Most notably, Leslie Marmon Silko (Laguna Pueblo) has addressed this topic in *Storyteller* (1981) and *Gardens in the Dunes* (1999). In *Storyteller*, Silko shares the living memory of assimilative schooling in her own family when she recounts a heated argument between her great grandmother, Grandma A'mooh, and her (great) Aunt Susie, both of whom attended Carlisle. As Silko tells it, the argument occurred when Susie objected to Grandma A'mooh's plan to burn her copy of *Stiya: An Indian Girl at Home*. The Carlisle teacher and editor Marianna Burgess published *Stiya* in 1891 in an effort to prevent students who were returning to their reservations from "going back to the blanket" – the government's term for returning to a tribal lifestyle. *Stiya* tells of a fictional Pueblo Indian who, upon returning to her reservation, is disgusted by her tribe's way of life. By distributing the book to former Carlisle students, Burgess sought to continue indoctrinating them with a hatred for tribalism. As an example of how school policies continued to affect Native Americans long after they left government institutions, Silko explains how Grandma A'mooh desired to burn the book as "racist, anti-Indian propaganda," while Susie, "a scholar and a storyteller," wanted to preserve the book "as important evidence of the lies and the racism and bad faith of the US government with the Pueblo people" (164).

In *Gardens in the Dunes*, Silko uses fiction to explore the destructive impact of assimilative policy on Native American families. The novel is about the fates of two sisters from the fictional Sand Lizard tribe – Indigo and Sister Salt – who are taken from their home near the Colorado River in Arizona and sent, unwillingly, away from their mother and grandmother to the Sherman Institute in Riverside, California. Both girls, desperate to escape from the harrowing and unhealthy conditions of the boarding school, run away only to find that they no longer have a home to which they can return. Sister Salt becomes involved with the motley group of laborers, drifters, and displaced natives living near the worksite of the Colorado Dam, while Indigo is taken in by a white woman who develops an emotional attachment to her yet feels compelled to help the girl locate her family. The novel is particularly interesting in its portrayal of the lessons that Hattie and Edward, the white couple who informally adopt Indigo for a time, give her in being a proper lady. By having Indigo leave boarding school only to become a surrogate daughter to Hattie, Silko draws a parallel between assimilative education at government boarding schools and the adoption of Native American children by white families.

Sherman Alexie (Spokane/Coeur d'Alene) similarly aligns these two historical developments in his novel *Indian Killer* (1996). This novel tells the story of John Smith, a Native American child who was born to a teenage mother on an unknown reservation and adopted by a childless white couple. Because John's adoptive mother does not know what tribe he is from, she teaches him about being "Indian in the most generic sense" (28). Abandoning realist literary conventions, the novel collapses historical time to juxtapose discussions of the government's attack on tribal sovereignty during the assimilative period with representations of homelessness and alcoholism in urban Indians. In so doing, Alexie reminds the reader that the detribalized "Indian" identity circulating in contemporary U.S. culture is a direct product of the schools that produced such an identity through ideological reprogramming. He also suggests that the activities of John Smith, a serial killer who scalps his white victims, might be a contemporary manifestation of the Ghost Dance movement of the 1890s. As a symbol of this movement, Smith avenges both historical and contemporary problems of detribalized Native Americans, a move Alexie signals by referring to events that occur "on this reservation or that reservation. Any reservation, a particular reservation" (419). Alexie's ironic figurations of the detribalized "Indian" emphasize the most damaging consequences of assimilationist ideology and associate the effects of assimilative education with the lack of historical consciousness arguably characteristic of mainstream U.S. society.

Works cited

Adams, David Wallace. *Education for Extinction: American Indians and the Boarding School Experience, 1875–1928*. Kansas: University Press of Kansas, 1995.

Alexie, Sherman. *Indian Killer*. New York: Grove Press, 2008.

Callahan, Sophia Alice, *Wynema, a Child of the Forest*. Lincoln: University of Nebraska Press, 1997.

Churchill, Ward. *Kill the Indian, Save the Man*. San Francisco: City Lights, 2004.

Davidson, Cathy & Ada Norris, "Introduction." Zitkala-Ša, *American Indian Stories, Legends, and Other Writings*. New York: Penguin, 2003.

Dawes Act. An Act to Provide for the Allotment of Lands in Severalty to Indians on the Various Reservations (General Allotment Act or Dawes Act), Statute at Large, 24, 388–91.

Debo, Angie. *The Road to Disappearance*. Norman: University of Oklahoma Press, 1941.

Eastman, Charles. *From the Deep Woods to Civilization: Chapters in the Autobiography of an Indian*. 1916. Ed. Raymond Wilson. Lincoln: University of Nebraska Press, 1977.

——. *Indian Boyhood*. 1902. New York: Dover, 1971.

——. *Indian Scout Talks: A Guide for Boy Scouts and Campfire Girls*. Boston: Little, Brown & Company, 1914.

——. *Old Indian Days*. 1907. Rpt. Introduction A. LaVonne Brown Ruoff. Lincoln: University of Nebraska Press, 1991.

——. "Opening Address." *The American Indian Magazine* 7:3 (1919): 145–48.

——. *Red Hunters and the Animal People*. New York: Harper, 1904.

——. *The Indian To-Day: The Past and Future of the First American*. Garden City, NY: Doubleday, Page & Company, 1915.

——. "The Indian's Plea for Freedom." *The American Indian Magazine* 6:4 (1919): 162–64.

Hopkins, Sarah Winnemucca. *Life Among the Piutes: Their Wrongs and Claims*. 1883. Web. Accessed 10 Jan. 2015. http://digital.library.upenn.edu/women/winnemucca/piutes/piutes.html

McNickle, D'Arcy. *The Surrounded*. 1936. Rpt. Albuquerque: University of New Mexico Press, 1978.

Mihesuah, Devon. *Cultivating the Rosebuds*. Chicago: University of Illinois Press, 1993.

Peabody, Elizabeth. *Sara Winnemucca's Practical Solution of the Indian Problem*. 1886. Web. Accessed 10 Jan. 2015. https://archive.org/details/sarahwinnemuccas00peab

Qoyawayma, Polingayse. *No Turning Back: A Hopi Indian Woman's Struggle to Live in Two Worlds*. Albuquerque: University of New Mexico Press, 1977.

Ruoff, A. Lavonne Brown. "Introduction." *Wynema, a Child of the Forest*. Lincoln: University of Nebraska Press, 1997.

Sekaquaptewa, Helen. *Me and Mine: The Life Story of Helen Sekaquaptewa*. Tucson: University of Arizona Press, 1969.

Silko, Leslie Marmon. *Gardens in the Dunes*. New York: Simon & Schuster, 1999.

——. *Storyteller*. New York: Penguin, 2012.

Standing Bear, Luther. *Land of the Spotted Eagle*. 1933. Rpt. Lincoln: University of Nebraska Press, 2006.

——. *My People, the Sioux*. 1928. Rpt. Lincoln: University of Nebraska Press, 1975.

Zanjani, Sally. *Sarah Winnemucca*. Lincoln: Bison Books/University of Nebraska Press, 2001.

Zitkala Ša (Gertrude Bonnin). "An Indian Teacher among Indians." *Atlantic Monthly* 85 (March 1900): 381–87.

——. *Dreams and Thunder: Stories, Poems, and The Sun Dance Opera*. Ed. P. Jane Hafen. Lincoln: University of Nebraska Press, 2001.

——. "Impressions of an Indian Childhood." *Atlantic Monthly* 85 (January 1900): 37–47.

——. *Old Indian Legends*. 1901. *American Indian Stories, Legends, and Other Writings*. Ed. Cathy Davidson & Ada Norris. New York: Penguin, 2003.

——. "Schooldays of an Indian Girl." *Atlantic Monthly* 85 (February 1900): 185–94.

——. "Why I Am a Pagan." *Atlantic Monthly* 90 (1902): 801–03.

14
Federalism Reconfigured
Native Narrations and the Indian New Deal

Joseph Bauerkemper

Domesticating dual citizens

Building slowly from Chief Justice John Marshall's 1831 invention of "domestic dependent nations" (*Cherokee Nation v. Georgia* 30 U.S. 1, 1831) and motivated by the festering irritation that House members felt when compelled to make appropriations for treaties negotiated by the executive branch and ratified by the Senate, in 1871 Congress attached a rider to the annual Indian affairs funding bill proclaiming "That hereafter no Indian nation or tribe within the territory of the United States shall be acknowledged or recognized as an independent nation, tribe, or power with whom the United States may contract by treaty" (25 U.S.C. § 71). When pressed about this incursion into the constitutional powers of the President and Congress, Senator John P. Stockton defended the measure by invoking Indian domestication:

> Hereafter the Indians within our borders, within our limits, shall not be treated as foreigners. We know that these Indians are daily and constantly leaving their nomadic life, that they are becoming merged in many places with our own citizens; we know that they desire, in many instances, themselves that this process shall continue. … The question is, are they foreign nations? I insist that Congress has the perfect right to declare whether these tribes are independent nations in its view, for the purpose of making treaties with them or not.
>
> (Deloria & DeMallie 239)

Despite much ambivalence and some opposition to the rider within the Senate, it was ultimately retained and became law, establishing an ongoing moratorium on Indian treaty-making that marks a prominent moment in federal efforts to neutralize American Indian nations by way of their incorporation into U.S. federalism.

Yet as conspicuous as the treaty moratorium appears, its practical effects would only accrue slowly across the subsequent half-century. Throughout the late nineteenth and early twentieth centuries, the executive branch continued negotiating agreements with tribes and sending them to Congress for approval. The impact of the 1871 rider was that both chambers would assess and vote on the agreements, approving them with simple majorities. Adding to the 370 treaties ratified before 1871, more than four dozen negotiated agreements were approved by Congress over the next several decades (Wilkins & Stark 88, 100;

Special Committee 41). As late as 1922, bicameral acts affirming negotiated tribal land cessions continued (Deloria & DeMallie 1479).

By the mid-1920s, however, negotiated agreement-making had waned. The actual cessation of U.S.–Indian treaty-making thus coincides and perhaps correlates with the blanket conferral of U.S. citizenship upon American Indians. Marking the culmination of federal assimilationist Indian policy, the mid-1920s paired the collective domestication of tribes as entities unworthy of diplomatic relations with the individual domestication of Indians as U.S. citizens. The Indian Citizenship Act of 1924 granted U.S. citizenship to (or imposed it upon) all American Indians who at that time were not citizens. A primary influence on this policy was the Society of American Indians (SAI), a rights organization of prominent Native professionals. Among the objectives included in the SAI Statement of Purposes is a progressivist affirmation of "the natural laws of social evolution" and the ambition "To promote citizenship and to obtain the rights thereof" (Martínez 93). Often assailed as assimilationist, the SAI no doubt found early twentieth-century Indian policy to be fertile ground for their citizenship cause.

While the 1924 Indian Citizenship Act did universally establish citizenship for Indians, that status was by no means unfamiliar in Indian Country. Because of previously instituted policies, the majority of American Indians were already citizens before 1924. As explained by Felix S. Cohen in his *Handbook of Federal Indian Law*:

> Prior to the Citizenship Act of 1924 approximately two-thirds of the Indians of the United States had already acquired citizenship in one or more of the following ways: (a) treaties with Indian tribes, (b) special statutes naturalizing named tribes or individuals, (c) general statutes naturalizing Indians who took allotments, or (d) general statutes naturalizing other special classes [such as Indian women married to U.S. citizens and World War I veterans].
>
> (153–54)

Yet even with U.S. citizenship conferred, many Indians found that the full rights thereof were not forthcoming. Women Indians that became U.S. citizens prior to the 1920 ratification of the nineteenth amendment to the U.S. Constitution encountered inconsistent and often non-existent voting access, and it would not be until 1962 that all states acknowledged the right of Indian citizens to vote (Hafen 215n8).

Prior to the 1924 Citizenship Act, the policy of allotment served as the primary pathway for Indians to access U.S. citizenship. As originally passed, the 1887 General Allotment Act (GAA) – which divided collectively held Indian reservations into 160-, 80-, and 40-acre plots and assigned titles to individual Indians – also conferred U.S. citizenship upon those Indians who accepted land allotments and the attendant lifestyle:

> Every Indian born within the territorial limits of the United States who has voluntarily taken up within said limits his residence, separate and apart from any tribe of Indians therein, and has adopted the habits of civilized life is hereby declared to be a citizen of the United States.
>
> (24 Stat., 388)

In 1906, the Burke Act amended the GAA, establishing that instead of U.S. citizenship being conferred immediately upon the issuance of a land allotment, it would be delayed until the land passed from trust to fee status. The Act also intervened in the standard twenty-five year trust period for allotments by authorizing the Secretary of the Interior to impose fee status on lands held by Indians determined to be "competent" to manage their own affairs (121).

Both in its original and Burke Act-amended form, the GAA not only dealt in U.S. citizenship, but also in tribal citizenship. Because membership in a tribe was a prerequisite for receiving an allotment, the GAA precipitated the need to document tribal citizenship. As Jill Doerfler explains:

> While the act required that those receiving allotments were members of Indian tribes, many tribes did not have official written membership or citizenship policies at this time or complete lists of citizens. Thus, the act signaled the most critical period in the evolution of U.S. involvement in citizenship among tribal nations because this new federal policy required an official census to determine who was a tribal citizen and, therefore, who would receive an allotment. The resulting "census," then, effectively became a primary source in determining who was a citizen of a band or nation.
>
> (310)

The mutually implicating relationship between U.S. citizenship and tribal citizenship cultivated great confusion both within tribes and throughout mainstream society. As both Jill Doerfler and David Beaulieu have explored in detail, the "competency" threshold established by the Burke Act and similarly addressed by the Clapp Rider (also of 1906 and amended in 1907) engendered the use of racialist metaphors of blood quantum to determine tribal membership rolls and therefore to establish eligibility for U.S. citizenship. As mixed-blood (pseudo-scientifically defined and designated) came to serve as a proxy for competence, and as competence came to serve as the trigger for moving an Indian's allotment from trust status to fee status, mixed-blood came to have a transitive relationship with U.S. citizenship.

In order to determine competence, inquiries into the blood lineage of individual Indians would often encounter confusion, both genuine and rhetorical, within tribal communities. When pressed to comment upon the lineage of a fellow community member, tribal members would often rely upon their perspectives regarding culture and kinship (Harmon 194–95; Doerfler 314–18). This tendency would irritate federal agents. According to R. David Edmunds, "During the 1890s when federal officials allotted the reservations, they refused to accept tribally defined membership, demanding that Native Americans enroll with federal allotment agents and state their 'blood quantum,' or degree of Indian ancestry" (733–34; see LaVelle). While many tribal communities resisted blood quantum demands with their own sophisticated approaches to affiliation, federal pressures rarely relented.

Even while federal interests dictated that citizens of tribes be incorporated as citizens of the United States, the dual citizenship status propagated by allotment and other targeted policies and made universal by the 1924 citizenship act caused much consternation within the halls of power in Washington, D.C. Up through the late nineteenth century, U.S. citizenship and Indian status were often configured as mutually exclusive. If one was a U.S. citizen, then by definition one was not an Indian in the political sense (Spruhan 26). Only with the rulings in *United States v. Sandoval* (231 U.S. 28, 1913) and *United States v.*

Nice (241 U.S. 591, 1916) did it become legally established that Indians who became U.S. citizens still remained Indians. Despite such rulings, confusion endured. In 1941 Nathan R. Margold notes in his introduction to Cohen's *Handbook* that dominant misunderstandings of U.S./tribal dual citizenship persist:

> The popular view of the Indian's legal status proceeds from the assumption that the Indian is a ward of the Government, and not a citizen, that therefore he cannot make contracts without Indian Bureau approval, that he holds land in common under "Indian title," that he is entitled to education in federal schools when he is young, to rations when he is hungry, and to the rights of American citizenship when he abandons his tribal relations. This is, on the whole, a thoroughly false picture, although historical exemplification may be found for each feature.
>
> (IX)

The framework of dual tribal/U.S. citizenship was never universally embraced within Indian communities and intellectual circles. After all, the most common pathways to U.S. citizenship were either associated with land dispossession or with a unilateral imposition that did not contemplate Indian consent. Moreover, the retention of tribal citizenship, as underscored within *Sandoval* and *Nice*, was emphasized by federal powers not for the benefit of Indians, but for the purposes of continuing to subject Indians to paternalistic federal oversight and intervention. Finally, the dual citizen framework re-inscribes the federal assertion that tribes as collectives are domestic, dependent, and subject to unrestrained congressional power. Tsianina Lomawaima brings these factors together, noting that "conceptions of citizen-but-ward and sovereign-but-domestic dependent served the agendas of settler colonial entitlement and federal plenary power" (343).

Robert Porter's incisive critique of dual citizenship goes so far as to indict it as genocidal. Noting that the 1924 Act "was notably different from previous efforts to confer American citizenship upon Indians in that consent or any other precondition was not required" (124), Porter goes on to suggest that "forcing American citizenship upon Indigenous peoples was undisputedly part of a concerted and comprehensive effort to destroy the unique Indigenous way of life" (161). The dual citizenship framework was such that dimensions of Indian identity and life, both individual and collective, that the federal government found objectionable were to be set aside, while the dimensions of Indian status that entail unhindered federal control were to be retained. It is little wonder, then, that the assimilationist aspirations of late nineteenth- and early twentieth-century Indian citizenship policy wrought such disruption across Indian Country. Those consequences did not go unnoticed, however, even if the causes continued to be ignored.

The problem of Indian administration

According to Vine Deloria Jr. and Clifford M. Lytle, the post-World War I period brought a shift in the forces that rationalized federal Indian policy. Up until this point, personal beliefs and individual political perspectives drove policy. The emergent reform movement, however, focused on the generation and use of data regarding the conditions of Indian communities (*Nations* 42). This work entailed the creation of numerous reports focused on various areas of Native life. The 1919 report "The Red Man in the United States" brought attention to poverty, the lack of educational opportunities, and poor health. In 1923 "A Study of the Need for Public Health Nursing on Indian Reservations" underscored the latter (Deloria & Lytle *Nations* 42–43). The 1924 report "Oklahoma's Poor Rich Indians: An Orgy of Graft and Exploitation of the Five Civilized Tribes, Legalized Robbery" – which was co-written by Yankton writer, musician, and activist Gertrude Bonnin – called attention to the mistreatment of Indians with a focus on the corruption that ensued when county authorities administered probate (Hafen 204–05). Laurence F. Schmeckebier's 1927 book *The Office of Indian Affairs* offered a detailed historical account and analytical critique of federal administration. The "Preston–Engle Report," issued in 1928, focused on reservation irrigation and revealed endemic mismanagement of land and agricultural projects. The crest of the reformist reporting wave arrived with the 1928 *Problem of Indian Administration*, also known as the "Meriam Report." Produced under the direction of Lewis Meriam for the Brookings Institution, the report – which would soon be joined by a follow-up Brookings report on law and order as well as a reservation economic survey – received much attention upon its release and it has continued to garner scholarly interest (Deloria and Lytle *Nations* 43–46).

In 1923 Calvin Coolidge's Secretary of the Interior Hubert Work convened a massive Indian affairs advisory committee of celebrities, activists, and prominent tribal members (41). This "Committee of One Hundred" included several members of the Society of American Indians such as Henry Roe Cloud, Sherman Coolidge, Charles Eastman, Arthur C. Parker, Thomas Sloan, and J.N.B. Hewitt. Feedback from the committee compelled the Department of the Interior to arrange for the production of the Meriam Report, in which Henry Roe Cloud was directly involved and which Bernd Peyer has described as "painting a grim picture of the contemporary Indian Service, particularly in the field of education, and initiating a marked ideological shift in American Indian policy" (24).

As its formal title not so subtly suggests, the Meriam Report addresses federal management of the "Indian problem." This "problem" was (and from a settler-colonial perspective, still is) the mere fact of Indigenous continuance. The endurance of Native peoples as nations throws a wrench into the cogs of settler federalism. Native presence prevents historical and ongoing injustices from being swept into idle memory, and the differential reserved rights of Indians and tribes confound dominant liberalism's ostensible commitments to equality. The Meriam Report essentially asks, then, how to administer the pesky resilience of Indigenous America and how to neutralize the disruptive questions impelled by the tenacity of Native nations.

Because the Meriam Report focuses primarily on the failed execution of policy rather than its failed orientation, the centrality of citizenship in the recommended educational objectives is of little surprise. Indeed, the report affirms U.S. citizenship for Indians and advocates for policies ensuring that "the Indian is economically on his feet and able to support himself by his own efforts according to a minimum standard of health and decency in the presence of white civilization" (48). Ultimately, the report asserts, "Indians must eventually merge into general citizenship" (552). In support of this end, the report offers a section titled "Specific Training for Future Citizenship Among Whites" (636).

The most compelling feature of the Meriam Report is its sustained critique of allotment policy by which "acts of Congress have resulted in the wholesale exploitation of the Indians" (471). The report observes that allotment "has largely failed in the accomplishment of was expected of it. It has resulted in much loss of land and enormous increase in the details of administration without a compensating advance in the economic ability of the Indians" (41). The report suggests that the problem was not allotment policy itself, but its implementation: without sufficient educational resources "to train him to some extent in business matters and give him a start in the proper care of private property," the assimilationist objectives of allotment remained out of reach (787). In sum, the Meriam Report affirms and defends the assimilationist impulse of late nineteenth- and early twentieth-century policies that had devastating impacts across Indian Country, while also calling for institutional reform and a paradigm shift in the execution, but not the aspirations of, governmental administration. In pursuit of these goals, the report encouraged a significant expansion in budget, personnel, and agency authority and "a substantial immediate increase in appropriations for the Indian Service" (106). Such a posture of administrative growth did not portend mitigation of the paternalism undergirding federal dictation of Indian affairs.

John Collier's nearly new deal

While serving as a social worker for immigrants in New York City, John Collier developed an appreciation for cultural traditions and dismay at their fragmentation in the crucible of U.S. society. These sensibilities would be heightened by visits to Taos and other Pueblos in the 1920s. Collier's romantic yet genuine affinity for Indian peoples and his sense that tribal lifeways offer correctives to the mistaken trajectories of mainstream society led him to establish the reformist American Indian Defense Association and to become a prominent critic of the assimilationist policies of the time (Calloway 485–86). In the aftermath of the Meriam Report and in the thick of the Great Depression, in 1933 Franklin D. Roosevelt appointed Collier to serve as Commissioner of Indian Affairs in order to reform the administration from within. According to Deloria and Lytle, the extent of Collier's ambitions for reform were exceptional and sought not merely reform but transformation (*Nations* 55). Between his fascination with tribal culture, his commitment to Native continuance, his opposition to allotment, and his interest in equipping tribes for the future, Collier's concerns resonated extensively with the disclosures and recommendations of the Meriam Report. Yet while the Meriam Report was essentially about *administrative* reform, Collier's energies were directed toward *political* reconfiguration.

He took up this effort legislatively, collaborating with Felix Cohen and Nathan Margold to draft a hefty (by the standards of the day) forty-eight page bill proposing a complete overhaul of Indian affairs. Known as the "Collier Bill," its title on "Indian Self-Government" would have instituted a draw-down of federal restrictions on the inherent powers of tribes and facilitated tribal government control over reservations lands and tribal members. One of the title's many noteworthy provisions would have established tribal authority to appoint the BIA personnel assigned to their reservation. The least controversial title of the proposed bill emphasized the educational needs of tribes, though it did include bold language on cultural preservation. The Collier Bill's title on "Indian Lands" called for the full termination of allotment, permanent trust status for all tribal lands, and return to tribes of unoccupied lands previously designated as surplus territory and made available for non-Indian settlement. The title also would have invested the Secretary of the Interior with authority to create new reservations and to assist tribes in expanding land holdings. The bill also mandated that the Secretary and tribal governments work together to consolidate reservation lands previously titled to individual Indians. The radical nature of Collier's approach to Indian lands met resistance from Congress and from many tribal members holding title to individual allotments. "Though he could prevent future loss of Indian land," Deloria and Lytle write,

> he could not erase the effects of half a century of allotment and forced land sales without trampling on the rights of individual Indians, many of whom had made their peace with the idea of private property and wanted to keep what little remained to them personally.

> (*Nations* 76)

The bill's final proposed title would have created an entirely new federal court, a "Court of Indian Affairs," that would assume responsibility over Indian-related cases that tend to go before federal district courts. This arrangement would have extended the provisions of the U.S. Constitution to all such cases and, while remaining entrenched in non-Indian jurisprudence, presumably cultivated a judicial system cognizant of Native issues.

In addition to the necessity of defending his bill before congressional committees, Collier arranged a series of ten regional tribal consultation congresses. While the Indian congresses did not provide the enthusiastic grassroots support hoped for by Collier, they did offer some tribes a rare opportunity to impact the proposed legislation. Participants questioned the proposal's mandate to return individual land holdings to the tribal collective and articulated introspective skepticism regarding tribal readiness for self-government. At a mere five pages, the Indian Reorganization Act (IRA) as passed by Congress in 1934 reflects the diverse ambivalence with which tribes greeted the Collier Bill and the dismissive reception many of the proposal's provisions received in Congress. For Deloria and Lytle, "The final version bore little if any resemblance to what [Collier] had originally suggested" (*Nations* 138). Even so, the IRA marked a pronounced paradigm shift in federal Indian policy. And while they are significantly pared in comparison to Collier's original design, the most important provisions of the IRA are indeed drawn from the Collier Bill.

The opening section of the IRA prohibits allotment, bringing to a close a policy whose legacy would nevertheless persist. Subsequent sections extend indefinitely the trust period of already-allotted and unallotted Indian lands and authorize the Secretary of the Interior to restore to tribes available surplus lands. In a departure from the Collier Bill, the act includes significantly softened language on land consolidation, approving land swaps and buy-backs, but also affirming conventional state and federal probate procedures. The IRA creates secretarial authority to acquire land for tribes and to hold it in trust, to expand existing reservations, and to create new reservations. Because property held in trust on behalf of Indian tribes is inalienable and therefore not conducive to collaterally secured financing, the IRA established a ten million dollar revolving line of credit devoted to tribal economic development. The Act also provided a separate credit line for vocational and trade school tuition.

One of the more consequential and continually controversial components of the IRA encourages tribes to establish their own constitutional systems of governance. While the Collier Bill's intricate framework for instituting and cultivating tribal self-government suggested a more nuanced approach, the entire IRA process for ratifying and amending tribal constitutions completely subjects tribal decision-making to federal oversight (Deloria & Lytle *Nations* 67–71; Wilkins & Stark 130). In this regard, Elmer R. Rusco suggests that "Secretarial approval of written constitutions limited tribal self-government, and in practice gave the bureaucracy more control than was healthy" (52). In another noteworthy departure from Collier's original proposal, the IRA is silent regarding any "Court of Indian Affairs," leaving tribes to continue taking claims to district courts. Finally, the IRA includes a stipulation that the Act would not apply to a tribe unless affirmed by tribal referendum. According to Vine Deloria Jr. and Clifford Lytle, 181 tribes accepted the IRA while 77 rejected it (*American* 15). The structuring of this consent provision and its results, however, deserve scrutiny. David E. Wilkins and Heidi Kiiwetinepinesiik Stark point out that according to the Department of the Interior's interpretation of the consent provision "all eligible Indian voters who opted not to vote would be counted as being in favor of adopting the act. For seventeen tribes, this opinion reversed an otherwise negative vote" (64).

With its prohibition of allotment, the extension of the protections and limitations of trust land status, the possibility of expanded tribal land bases, resources for education and economic development, cultivation of severely constrained self-governance, and its tentative gesture toward tribal consent, the IRA is both remarkably ambitious and exceedingly ambiguous. As Stephen Pevar puts it:

> The IRA has been criticized as paternalistic, because tribes were not consulted in its development, ethnocentric, because it promoted a system of government inconsistent with traditional Indian values, and insufficient, because tribes remained subject to substantial federal control. Yet despite its shortcomings, the IRA was a giant step in the right direction.
>
> (11)

Focusing his criticism on the role of Collier, Laurence Hauptman similarly suggests that

> the good intentions of Commissioner John Collier, architect of the policy of self-government for Indians, were undermined by his paternalistic attitude toward Indians, by his naive and often romantic perceptions of modern Indian life, by his abrasive and authoritarian personality, and even by his general lack of understanding of Native American cultures and diversity.
>
> (133)

Yet in defense of Collier, Elmer Rusco asserts that he

> strongly opposed allotment, and the first section of the Indian Reorganization Act (IRA) followed his lead by halting allotment. Although Congress would not go along with Collier's plans to force return of allotted lands to tribal ownership, it did agree to a provision allowing the purchase of lands to augment the Indian land base. Congress never appropriated enough funds to make this very meaningful, but the Indian land base did expand during the Collier era. Moreover, Collier never advocated ... assimilation.
>
> (49)

Along with the documentary record itself, the assessments made by Pevar, Hauptman, Rusco, and many others collectively suggest that the IRA presented a mode of assimilation distinct from the individualistic citizenship-based approach that preceded Collier's tenure as Indian Commissioner. The IRA's approach to Indian incorporation sought not only to continue the integration of individual Indians as U.S. citizens, but more importantly to stabilize, domesticate, and entrench tribal nations within U.S. federalism.

While neither Congress nor the BIA sought to reconfigure the tribal position in U.S. federalism by directly forcing pre-fabricated constitutions upon tribes, detailed guidance and pressures certainly came to bear. A "Model Constitution" was distributed to a number of tribes for their consideration as they drew up instruments of their own (Cohen *On the Drafting* 173–77). Because tribal citizens by definition have access to federal programs and services for Indians, the criteria for tribal citizenship were of great concern to federal interests. As Congress deliberated the IRA's conception of Indian status, Senator Burton Wheeler, the Montana legislator who co-sponsored the IRA and significantly influenced its final form, reflected the expediency of federal interests:

> I do not think the government of the United States should go out there and take a lot of Indians in that are quarter bloods and take them in under this act. If they are Indians in the half blood then the government should perhaps take them in, but not unless they are. If you pass it to where they are quarter blood Indians you are going to have all kinds of people coming in and claiming they are quarter blood Indians and want to be put on the government rolls, and in my judgment it should not be done. What we are trying to do is get rid of the Indian problem rather than to add to it.
>
> (qtd. in Spruhan 46)

Wheeler's statement clearly reflects the racialist and assimilationist logics often underpinning federal Indian policy. Judith Resnik has shown these logics as they consistently manifest in BIA practice. A 1935 Department of the Interior circular uncovered by Resnik and titled "Membership in Indian Tribes" insisted that tribal constitutions limit membership and suggested that this be done by strict residency requirements, dual-parent descent, or the use of minimum blood-quantum standards (Resnik 715). Five decades later, this pursuit would continue. The BIA's 1987 guide titled *Developing and Reviewing Tribal Constitutions and Amendments: A Handbook for BIA Personnel* reveals federal support for restrictive tribal membership criteria and posits heightened scrutiny of tribal proposals to change membership criteria in ways that would increase populations (Resnik 714). An important pattern of fallout from ongoing federal encroachment into and manipulation of tribal "self"-government has been an increasing lack of regard for IRA-oriented tribal governments within tribes themselves (Wilkins & Stark 236). This pattern is evident not only in the political life of American Indian nations, but also in their literatures.

Narration now and then

While this chapter devotes the vast majority of its attention to conveying an understanding of historical and political contexts indispensable for considerations of Native literature written during or about the early twentieth century, a cursory look at a single exemplary novel should serve as a useful case study for viewing this period's Native American literature through a policy-oriented lens. As the previous section of this chapter indicates, many tribal governments formally constituted under the IRA remain precariously situated in relation to the populations they govern. Even while it is never directly mentioned in the book, this governance anxiety is, I argue, central to the conceptual and contextual foundations of Dakota writer and ethnologist Ella Cara Deloria's novel *Waterlily*. The temporal diversity of the novel – set in the nineteenth century, written in the 1940s, and published in the 1980s – lends itself nicely to a multifaceted consideration of the interface between policy and literature.

The novel also serves as one of the most prominent Native literary works written during the immediate post-IRA period, an era not known for robust productivity. Synthesizing insights from Jace Weaver, Daniel Heath Justice, Robert Warrior, Sean Teuton, Craig Womack, and Scott Lyons, James Cox emphasizes the absence of cohesion and the lack of publication that marks the terrain of American Indian literature during the early twentieth century (1–2). Because it was written in the 1940s yet remained unpublished until 1988, *Waterlily* is precisely the exception that proves the rule. Widely read both within and beyond the academy (Gardner viii–ix), *Waterlily* is typically appreciated for the contributions it makes to ethnographic discourses (DeMallie 233). Drawing extensively from Deloria's anthropological research and writing, the novel narrates the childhood, adolescence, and young adulthood of its titular character, a Dakota woman living prior to her people's encounter with European settlers. "The story's real core," Carol Miller explains, "centers on the kinship rules and complex balance of individual and social responsibilities that make one a good relative – and make possible the interdependent communality which undergirds successful Dakota society." In her nonfiction study *Speaking of Indians*, which was published in 1944 as she was at work on *Waterlily* and which was brought back into print following the success of *Waterlily*'s belated publication, Deloria emphasizes this theme:

> Kinship was the all-important matter. Its demands and dictates for all phases of social life were relentless and exact; but on the other hand, its privileges and honorings and rewarding prestige were not only tolerable but downright pleasant and desirable for all who conformed. By kinship all Dakota people were held together in a great relationship that was theoretically all-inclusive and co-extensive with the Dakota domain.
>
> (24)

According to Deloria, the intricate and expansive system of kinship explored throughout the novel's pages served (and serves) the Dakota as "the scheme of life that works" (24).

Encompassing the entire "Dakota domain," this scheme of life serves to govern all aspects of relational and public life, and it therefore clearly entails a comprehensive political dimension. With an emphasis on gender, Maria Cotera underscores both the pedagogical and political facets of *Waterlily*'s invocation of kinship:

> *Waterlily* itself might fruitfully be read as a pedagogical and political project that contributes to tribal revitalization by attempting to "teach" a generation

of Dakota – suffering from the effects of half a century of government policies designed to destroy their traditional modes of social organization – about the importance of the kinship system and its relationship to the codes of conduct governing "proper" Dakota behavior.

(55)

As Cotera notes, the novel's narrative of the nineteenth century is nevertheless in direct conversation with federal policy of the decades up through its composition. Miller concurs:

Although *Waterlily* might appear to some readers to be an idealized or romanticized account, it is more accurately an exemplary one – figuratively re-membering the personal/communal and cultural/spiritual values of an undisrupted functional past in the service of a more functional present.

The novel, then, explores a usable past for twentieth-century Dakota socio-political continuance in the face of disruptions brought on primarily by federal policy.

The novel repeatedly (and in several instances, rather didactically) invites the reader to join Waterlily as she receives instruction in kinship relations and obligations. "The first thing to learn," Deloria writes,

was how to treat other people and how to address them. … You must not call your relatives and friends by name, for that was rude. Use kinship terms instead. And especially, brothers and sisters, and boy cousins and girl cousins must be very kind to each other. That was the core of all kinship training.

(34)

Just as Deloria notes in *Speaking of Indians*, the web of kinship pertains well beyond both the immediate and the extended family. When an enemy war party attack leaves Waterlily's mother, Blue Bird, and great-grandmother without any other surviving immediate relatives, the pair finds their way to an unfamiliar Dakota camp where they are at least fortunate enough to encounter a community that speaks their same dialect. Immediately Dakota kinship obligations and networks emerge to provide for the welfare of the two women:

On learning of their plight and their recent tragedy, the magistrates sent the crier out from the council tipi to announce their arrival and rally the people to their aid. The response was quick. Someone gave the newcomers a tipi to live in, while public-spirited collectors carried around the circle a great bull hide into which contributions were placed. … And thus all in a day Blue Bird and her grandmother were equipped to start life anew. … [T]hey had been taken in as relatives in social kinship.

(11)

The efficiency and unrestrained hospitality with which Blue Bird and her grandmother are integrated into their new tiyospaye (camp circle or village) suggests not only the flexible sophistication of Dakota kinship but also the breadth of its inclusive applicability to address the challenges and opportunities of community life.

Deloria also offers in the novel a broader view of culturally grounded tiyospaye governance in her discussion of the six core Dakota ancient societies:

> The executive Chiefs' Society and the advisory Owl Headdress were composed of elderly, venerable worthies who did much sitting and deliberating. The remaining four, known as Badgers, Scout Hearts, Crow-keepers, and Kit Foxes, were military orders ever alert for action. It was not demanded of them, or of any man, to go to war unless he wanted to go. The military orders functioned rather as messengers, scouts, camp police, in short, as guardians of the camp circle and its people. They patrolled and regulated the communal hunt and in every way carried out the orders of the magistrates and the council.
>
> (97)

The membership of these societies was constituted by the selection of those community members most highly regarded not only for their adroitness with applicable skills, but also for their reputations in minding their kinship relations: "[E]very candidate must have a record of consistent hospitality and generosity, which were the qualities that marked a good citizen of the camp circle" (96). Deloria's novel thus narrates a kinship-oriented "scheme of life that works" not only to cultivate functional families, but also to do the fundamental work of governance: policy deliberation, communication, domestic and external security, and the conservation and allocation of resources (Richland & Deer 61).

As an archive simultaneously attributable to the nineteenth century, the 1940s and the 1980s, *Waterlily* and its detailed tour of Dakota communal kinship reflect and figuratively comment upon the long histories and interactions of Native nationhood and federal Indian policy. In the opening line of the optimistic 1998 preface to the second edition of *The Nations Within*, Vine Deloria Jr. and Clifford Lytle write: "When the first edition of this book was released in 1984, feelings still ran high against tribal governments organized under the Wheeler-Howard, or Indian Reorganization, Act (IRA)" (vii). Reflecting those feelings, in the original text Deloria and Lytle note, "Recent evaluations of the IRA suggest that even limited self-government was a mirage" (215). "It is little wonder, Laurence Hauptman writes, "that by the 1970s these 'IRA councils' became the focus of 'Red Power' militancy that sought to restore traditional government to some reservations" (143). While the belated publication of *Waterlily* amid a resurgence of anti-IRA sentiment and disquiet with IRA-style self-governance is very likely a mere coincidence, there is nevertheless a conceptual correlation. This is a novel, after all, that offers an assertive and committed narration of traditional tribal governance against two backdrops: the IRA's implementation and the IRA's subsequent near-unraveling. While the IRA is duly recognized as a beneficial policy shift away from the aggressive assimilationism and dispossession that preceded it, it ultimately did little for the inherent traditions of tribal governance. As Frank Fools Crow saw it: "The years from 1930 to 1940 rank as the worst ten years I know of, and all the Oglala as old as I am will agree. In that one single period we lost everything we had gained" (qtd. in Mails 148).

According to Maria Cotera,

> *Waterlily* represents an attempt to revive the kinship system by offering a compelling guidebook designed to help Indian people reestablish healthy and rational social

relations in the wake of assimilationist policies that sought to undermine and even erase kinship as a form of social organization.

(56)

By paying attention also to the late twentieth- and early twenty-first-century contexts into which the book was eventually released and continues to be read, we might understand it as an exemplary "guidebook" relevant as well for tribes grappling decades on with the ambiguous legacies of the IRA and for the wave of Native nations currently pursuing political revolution by way of comprehensive and actually self-governed constitutional reform.

Works cited

Beaulieu, David L. "Curly Hair and Big Feet: Physical Anthropology and the Implementation of Land Allotment on the White Earth Chippewa Reservation." *American Indian Quarterly* 8. 4 (1984): 281–314.

Calloway, Colin G. *First Peoples: A Documentary Survey of American Indian History*. 4th ed. Boston: Bedford/St. Martin's, 2012.

Cohen, Felix S. *Handbook of Federal Indian Law*. Washington, D.C.: United States Government Printing Office, 1941.

——. *On the Drafting of Tribal Constitutions*. Ed. David E. Wilkins. Norman: University of Oklahoma Press, 2006.

Cotera, Maria Eugenia. "'All My Relatives Are Noble': Recovering the Feminine in Ella Cara Deloria's *Waterlily*." *American Indian Quarterly* 28. 1–2 (2004): 52–72.

Cox, James H. *The Red Land to the South: American Indian Writers and Indigenous Mexico*. Minneapolis: University of Minnesota Press, 2012.

Deloria, Ella Cara. *Speaking of Indians*. 1944. Lincoln: University of Nebraska Press/Bison Books, 1998.

——. *Waterlily*. 1988. Lincoln: University of Nebraska Press/Bison Books, 2009.

Deloria, Vine, Jr. & Raymond J. DeMallie. *Documents of American Indian Diplomacy: Treaties, Agreements, and Conventions, 1775–1979*. Norman: University of Oklahoma Press, 1999.

Deloria, Vine, Jr. & Clifford M. Lytle. *American Indians, American Justice*. Austin: University of Texas Press, 1983.

——. *The Nations Within: The Past and Future of American Indian Sovereignty*. 2nd ed. Austin: University of Texas Press, 1998.

DeMallie, Raymond J. "Afterword." *Waterlily*. 2nd ed. Lincoln: University of Nebraska Press/Bison Books, 2009.

Doerfler, Jill. "An Anishinaabe Tribalography: Investigating and Interweaving Conceptions of Identity During the 1910s on the White Earth Reservation." *American Indian Quarterly* 33. 3 (2009): 295–324.

Edmunds, R. David. "Native Americans, New Voices: American Indian History, 1895–1995." *The American Historical Review* 100. 3 (June 1995): 717–40.

Gardner, Susan. "Introduction." *Waterlily*. 2nd ed. Lincoln: University of Nebraska Press/Bison Books, 2009.

Hafen, P. Jane. "'Help Indians Help Themselves': Gertrude Bonnin, the SAI, and the NCAI." *Studies in American Indian Literatures* 25. 2 (2013): 199–218.

Harmon, Alexandra. "Tribal Enrollment Councils: Lessons on Law and Indian Identity." *Western Historical Quarterly* 32 (2001): 175–200.

Hauptman, Laurence M. "The Indian Reorganization Act." *The Aggressions of Civilization: Federal Indian Policy since the 1880s*. Ed. Sandra L. Cadwalader and Vine Deloria Jr. Philadelphia: Temple University Press, 1984. 132–48.

LaVelle, John P. "The General Allotment Act 'Eligibility' Hoax: Distortions of Law, Policy, and History in Derogation of Indian Tribes." *Wicazo Sa Review* 14. 1 (1999): 251–302.

Lomawaima, K. Tsianina. "The Mutuality of Citizenship and Sovereignty: The Society of American Indians and the Battle to Inherit America." *Studies in American Indian Literatures* 25. 2 (2013): 331–51.

Mails, Thomas E, assisted by Dallas Chief Eagle. *Fools Crow*. Garden City, NY: Doubleday, 1979.

Martínez, David. *Dakota Philosopher: Charles Eastman and American Indian Thought*. St. Paul: Minnesota Historical Society Press, 2009.

Meriam, Lewis, et al. *The Problem of Indian Administration*. Baltimore, MD: Johns Hopkins Press, 1928.

Miller, Carol. "Ella Cara Deloria." *Voices from the Gaps* 1996 (updated in 2005 by Lauren Curtright). n. pag. Web. Accessed 12 Nov. 2014. http://voices.cla.umn.edu/artistpages/deloriaElla.php

Pevar, Stephen L. *The Rights of Indians and Tribes*. 4th ed. New York: Oxford University Press, 2012.

Peyer, Bernd C., ed. *American Indian Nonfiction: An Anthology of Writings, 1760s–1930s*. Norman: University of Oklahoma Press, 2007.

Porter, Robert B. "The Demise of the Ongwehoweh and the Rise of the Native Americans: Redressing the Genocidal Act of Forcing American Citizenship upon Indigenous Peoples." *Harvard BlackLetter Law Journal* 15 (1999): 107–83.

Resnik, Judith. "Dependent Sovereigns: Indian Tribes, States, and the Federal Courts." *University of Chicago Law Review* 56 (1989): 671–759.

Richland, Justin B. & Sarah Deer. *Introduction to Tribal Legal Studies*. 2nd ed. Lanham, MD: AltaMira Press, 2010.

Rusco, Elmer R. "John Collier: Architect of Sovereignty or Assimilation?" *American Indian Quarterly* 15. 1 (1991): 49–54.

Schmeckebier, Laurence. *The Office of Indian Affairs: Its History, Activities, and Organization*. New York: AMS Press, 1972.

Special Committee on Investigations of the Select Committee on Indian Affairs, United States Senate. *A New Federalism for American Indians*. Washington: U.S. Government Printing Office, 1989.

Spruhan, Paul. "A Legal History of Blood Quantum in Federal Indian Law to 1935." *South Dakota Law Review* 51. 1 (2006): 1–50.

Wilkins, David E. & Heidi Kiiwetinepinesiik Stark. *American Indian Politics and the American Political System*. 3rd ed. Lanham, MD: Rowman & Littlefield, 2011.

15

Embodied Jurisgenesis

NAGPRA, Dialogue, and Repatriation in American Indian Literature

Amelia V. Katanski

The Native American Graves Protection and Repatriation Act (NAGPRA) was passed into law in 1990, the result of decades of activism by indigenous people and communities fighting for a legal path to repatriate human remains and cultural objects held by federal agencies and public and private museums that receive federal funding, and to protect extant gravesites from disturbance. NAGPRA is human rights legislation, working to ensure that the gravesites, bodies, and sacred objects of American Indian and Native Hawaiian people will be treated with the same respect and care as those of non-Indians and redressing centuries of unequal treatment resulting in the desecration, removal, and trafficking of human remains and sacred and cultural items. The need for repatriation of indigenous bodies and cultural items held a prominent place in the discourse of American Indian communities – and, thus, Native American writers – well before the passage of NAGPRA. This discourse played a significant role in shaping the legislation that would become NAGPRA, and it continues to play an important role by articulating and analyzing the law's successes and failures. NAGPRA itself relies upon dialogue in order to function as legislation. Congress believed that the law would "encourage a continuing dialogue between museums and Indian tribes and native Hawaiian organizations, and … promote greater understanding between groups" (qtd. in Trope & Echo-Hawk 140). The law relies upon consultation and discussion among groups including (but not limited to) lineal descendants, tribal governments, museums, government agencies, scientific organizations, and indigenous advocacy organizations; and the structure of the NAGPRA Review Committee, which handles complexities involved in determining affiliation and administering the process of repatriation, is designed to foreground this intergroup dialogue and, particularly, to give voice to indigenous definitions and perspectives. In practice, the dialogue about repatriation built into the structure of NAGPRA encompasses sharing knowledge, finding ways to work together, and narrating profoundly different understandings of the value and meaning of the bodies and objects the law addresses.

The discursive space of NAGPRA is not limited to its direct administration. Literary texts about repatriation are a significant space in which discussion of the law, and the historical and cultural information that contextualize it, take place. These texts produce and embody dialogue about NAGPRA, its potential and its limitations, and insist upon the process of indigenous jurisgenesis, or the development of legal meaning that embodies indigenous values.[1] Texts that open up space for consideration of the core issues at stake in repatriation enact the dialogue the law requires, and thus are significant legal co-texts – not merely commenting on the law or the issues it takes up, but also playing a significant role in its actual practice.

Historicizing NAGPRA

Indigenous burial sites have been excavated and looted since the beginning of European colonization of the Americas. *Mourt's Relation, or a Journal of the Plantation at Plymouth* (1622) recounts more than one occasion when that most iconic group of settlers, the Pilgrims, dug up burial mounds and appropriated some of the items they contained (Winslow & Bradford 32–34). And Thomas Jefferson's *Notes on the State of Virginia* lays out, in some detail, the actions of the then amateur archaeologist and later President Jefferson, as he unearthed and studied a large burial mound near his boyhood home (97–100). The collection of, and traffic in, American Indian human remains and cultural objects increased during the mid-nineteenth century, when Dr. Samuel Morton, a Philadelphia physician, collected a large number of Indian skulls in an attempt to develop "an empirical means to discover human temperament and intelligence and how these were distributed among racial groups" (Bieder 23). Morton and other pseudoscientists (such as phrenologists) hired Indian agents, military personnel, and others with access to indigenous communities to gather Indian crania. As scholar Robert Bieder writes, "Grave robbing kept many people busy on the frontier supplying Morton and other phrenologists" (24). Morton's studies of Indian crania grew out of his beliefs in white superiority, and that other races "were not varieties of humankind but separate inferior species" and Morton claimed that his "data" supported these assumptions (Bieder 25). This "scientific" racism was widely used as justification for Indian removal and the taking of indigenous lands and resources (Trope & Echo-Hawk 126). The study of indigenous human remains became a more explicitly national project when the U.S. Surgeon General issued an order in 1868 directing Army physicians and other military personnel to gather Indian bodies for the Army Medical Museum (Trope & Echo-Hawk 126). By the end of the nineteenth century, "collecting crews from America's newly founded museums [including the Smithsonian, the American Museum of Natural History in New York, Harvard's Museum of Comparative Zoology, and the Field Museum in Chicago] engaged in competitive expeditions to obtain Indian skeletons" (127). The Antiquities Act of 1906, while purporting to protect archaeological sites from looters, redefined native human remains as federal property, "archaeological resources" that could be dug up (with a federal permit) in order for the remains to be placed on permanent display in a federal museum (127). By the mid-1980s, the Smithsonian Institution acknowledged housing over 18,500 American Indian human remains (NARF Legal Review 16.1 (1991): 1), and by September of 2014, the number of Indian human remains museums indexed as eligible for repatriation under NAGPRA numbered 50,518; museums also documented over 1.4 million funerary objects, sacred objects, and objects of cultural patrimony eligible for repatriation (FAQ).

Native resistance to grave-robbing and desecration also dates back hundreds of years. Bieder notes that the efforts of distraught and angry indigenous communities to stop the looting were often thwarted by the realities of epidemics, removal from tribal lands, and military occupation (24). Activists in the 1960s and 70s brought the issue of the collection, study, and display of indigenous remains and cultural objects to national attention. Maria Pearson, an Ihanktonwan (Yankton Sioux) woman, is often credited with starting the repatriation movement in 1971, when she protested the treatment of two indigenous bodies unearthed in a non-Indian cemetery that was being relocated because of a highway project. The non-Indians in the cemetery were immediately reinterred, while the indigenous woman and child were turned over to the state archaeologist to be studied (Zimmerman). Pearson's protests, which drew the attention and support of the American Indian Movement (AIM) and the International Indian Treaty Council, resulted in an Iowa law ensuring that Indian and non-Indian bodies and gravesites would be equally protected (Obituary). By the mid-1980s, several bills addressing repatriation were introduced in Congress and refined through a process of negotiation between the Native American Rights Fund, the National Congress of American Indians, the Society of American Archaeology, and others (Zimmerman). In 1989, the National Museum of the American Indian Act (NMAIA) became law. This act both created a National Museum of the American Indian within the Smithsonian Institution, and addressed the repatriation of human remains and cultural objects at the Smithsonian. With this important legislative precedent paving the way, NAGPRA was signed into law a year later.

NAGPRA has a broader scope than the NMAIA (both in the institutions it addresses, in the kinds of objects it seeks to protect and repatriate, and in the kinds of evidence – including tribal oral tradition – it requires to be considered when determining the cultural affiliation of items). Under NAGPRA, museums and federal agencies must provide an inventory of American Indian human remains and funerary objects (ceremonial items placed with individual human remains at the time of death or later), and written descriptions of other objects, including sacred objects (objects needed by traditional Native religious leaders for current religious practice) and objects of cultural patrimony (objects "having ongoing historical, traditional, or cultural importance central to the Native American group or culture itself, rather than property owned by an individual").[2] Part of the inventory process is the identification of cultural affiliation of the items. The museum may itself identify cultural affiliation, or Indian tribes or Native Hawaiian organizations may attempt to prove their cultural affiliation with items. Items and remains that have been identified and affiliated are subject to repatriation upon request of a lineal descendant, or a tribe or Native Hawaiian organization. The process of determining affiliation has remained one of the most challenging and contentious parts of the administration of the law, and several high profile cases, such as the Kennewick Man/Ancient One case and the Blood Run Historic Site, have highlighted the limits of the law in addressing cases involving ancient human remains and remains associated with non-federally recognized tribes. Penelope Kelsey and Cari Carpenter assert that "NAGPRA's current definition of American Indian identity falls short of tribal sovereign conceptions of identity and tribal responsibility for caretaking human remains" (56). Kelsey and Carpenter look both to how NAGPRA has been applied in practice, and to Allison Hedge Coke's poetry about repatriation struggles at the Blood Run Historic Site, to find "'creative' applications of NAGPRA ... that illustrate the limitations of NAGPRA's legislative rhetoric and enact a more empowering model of American Indian identity and community" (57). Both realms – the practical application of the law, and literary texts that address the law – are engaged in interpreting its meanings and both, as Kelsey and Carpenter demonstrate, seek to establish indigenous jurisgenesis.

Literary embodiments

Many American Indian authors, including Louise Erdrich, Gerald Vizenor, Allison Hedge Coke, Gordon Henry, Sherman Alexie, Winona LaDuke, and Susan Power significantly engage the issue of repatriation, focusing both on human remains and on other cultural objects. Legal scholar Bruce Duthu explains that "both law and literature share a concern with interrogating the imaginative possibilities of relationships between all living beings, not merely between privileged ones." Indigenous narrative traditions, in particular, "challenge the law to move beyond its tendency to speak 'univocally' (that is, in terms that exclude many other voices) to a mode of discourse that is truly multivocal and inclusive of other voices" (Duthu 2). Indeed, reading American Indian literature alongside U.S. Indian law is critically important, says Duthu, because:

> Such an incorporative discourse serves ... to ignite the imaginative possibilities of more inclusive, respectful, and peacefully co-existing communities ... . Inclusion of indigenous narrative traditions in this legal discourse encourages, and indeed often requires, lawmakers and law advocates to cross intercultural boundaries to examine the extent to which emergent legal structures and rules respect cultural differences or reveal jurisprudential myopia.
>
> (Duthu 1)

In other words, literary texts can open up a multivocal space in which indigenous values and meanings can be stated and heard, and indigenous jurisgenesis can prevail. This is particularly important with repatriation, where hearings and debates tend to become polarized, pitting "Indians" against "scientists" (as if that was a stable dichotomy), and where beliefs about the sanctity of burials, connections between past and present, and the validity of different kinds of evidence clash. Literary texts that engage with repatriation frequently present and move beyond these dichotomous positions, radically centering indigenous worldviews. Two such texts are D'Arcy McNickle's *Wind from an Enemy Sky* and Anna Lee Walters' *Ghost Singer*.

Repatriation of a sacred object is central to D'Arcy McNickle's novel *Wind from an Enemy Sky*. McNickle (Salish Kootenai) wrote and rewrote this novel from the late 1930s until his death in 1977. It was posthumously published in 1978, and its focus on repatriation is evidence of the continuing significance of this issue to Native writers and communities throughout the twentieth century. The novel is set in the Northwestern U.S. and tells the story of the fictional Little Elk tribe's struggle to regain their medicine bundle (a sacred object that holds the meaning of their community and recalls the story of Feather Boy, "the great story of our people" (204). This bundle had been given away by Henry Jim, a member of the community who embraced the assimilation programs of the government and missionaries, and it ended up in a museum, where it was not properly cared for and was eventually destroyed by neglect. The loss of the bundle divides the Little Elk people (who do not know of its destruction) and when Henry Jim is about to die, he realizes the error of his actions and seeks to regain the bundle to reunite his people and to renew their belief in their ability to survive. Due to the bungled actions of a well-meaning but selfish and senseless "collector," who not only runs the Museum of Americana where the bundle is held, but also owns a company responsible for building a dam and "killing the water" in the river that ran through Little Elk land, the story ends in tragedy. Bull, a Little Elk traditionalist, shoots and kills both the Indian agent, Rafferty, and the collector, Adam Pell, and is himself shot and killed by a tribal policeman, while the community reels in anger, shock, and fear from the knowledge that their medicine bundle has fallen into irreparable pieces due to the negligence of the museum.

Agent Rafferty, who is honest and committed to his work with the community, recognizes the reticence of the Little Elk people to trust him or partner with him. He says, toward the end of the novel:

> These people find it difficult to believe that a white man, any white man, will give them respect, as it is difficult for me to understand why they push me away and keep me from coming into their confidence. The answer, obviously, is that we do not speak to each other – and language is only a part of it. Perhaps it is intention, or purpose, the map of the mind we follow.

> (125)

Bull, the Little Elk leader who most resists contact with the Agency, similarly reflects, "How to translate from one man's life to another's – that is difficult. It is more difficult than translating a man's name into another man's language" (26). Rafferty and Pell, in particular, fail to understand the role of the medicine bundle in the community, and do not communicate about its condition or location openly or effectively, and the Little Elk people, too, must learn to bridge verbal and ideological rifts between those who adhere to traditional cultural practices and speak the tribal language, and those who do not. The novel itself becomes dialogic and translational as it moves back and forth between the Little Elk people's thoughts about and responses to events and the responses of Rafferty and Pell. These various positions and worldviews are each presented as pieces of a puzzle that the reader can assemble in order to form a fuller understanding of the violence, reconciliations, betrayals and allegiances among the characters.

Despite the fuller understanding that comes from this nascent dialogue, the Little Elk people do not experience justice. After discovering that the Feather Boy bundle has been destroyed, and insulted by Adam Pell's attempt to "make up" for this loss by giving the tribe, in its place, a gold statue he has, in essence, removed from a Peruvian Indian community without permission, an angry Bull shoots and kills both Pell and Rafferty, and is himself shot and killed (256). This tragic ending indicates what happens, according to McNickle, when a tribe loses its spiritual, cultural, core. This loss was caused, and exacerbated, by Pell's arrogance: "Because of his place in the world, his success, he assumed that he could restore a lost world by a simple substitution of symbols. Hell, that's what an Indian superintendent is supposed to do," says Rafferty, "to supply substitute symbols. I know it can't be done, and I'm just a bureaucrat" (249). It is this cultural arrogance – and the legacy of neglect, disrespect, and inattentiveness that allows the medicine bundle to deteriorate in the first place – that crushes Bull and breaks apart the understanding he, the Little Elk people, and Rafferty have tried to construct. In the novel's final words, "the world fell apart" (256).

While intercultural understanding – and the process of repatriation – fail *within* the novel, reading *Wind from an Enemy Sky* as a discursive space, a text that should "send [the reader] off with the will to make use of his best quality, which is his understanding,"[3] as

McNickle claimed all good fiction should do, generates a different, and ultimately more hopeful, interpretation of the text. Showing us the damaging impact of the reckless disregard of tribal culture, McNickle asks us – as his protagonist Bull continually asks his grandson, Antoine – "What did you see? What did you learn? What will you remember?" (116). He explains, in a letter to his editor:

> It may be true, as you suggest, that 999 out of 1000 readers will be familiar with the conduct of Indian affairs, but their knowledge is generalized, and often inaccurate … Most critics of government policy in Indian affairs seem unaware of their own involvement in support of the very morality which informs that policy.
> ("Letter to Douglas Latimer")

Developing that awareness in his readers, McNickle informs the editor, "is part of the argument of the book" ("Letter to Douglas Latimer"). As readers of McNickle's work, we should learn and remember that American Indian communities, grounded in their own values and institutions, can and do determine their own futures. Repatriation is central to these acts of self-determination, and the novel makes a strong case for centering the values and institutions of tribal nations in the process of repatriation. In other words, it embodies jurisgenesis.

While McNickle's novel was written over a 40-year period and published just as the repatriation movement was gaining momentum in the mid-1970s, *Ghost Singer*, a novel by Pawnee/Otoe author Anna Lee Walters, was published in 1988, the year before the National Museum of the American Indian Act became law, as several repatriation bills were working their way through Congress. *Ghost Singer* tells the story of a Navajo man who comes across a Navajo scalp while researching at the Smithsonian. He becomes ill after physical contact with the scalp, as have the white anthropologists who work with the human remains at the Smithsonian. In an attempt to contain and reverse this illness, and to honor the dead who are held at the museum, tribal healers come to the Smithsonian to confront the racism and close-minded ideology of the anthropologists. The novel displays a Euro-American social scientific apparatus built upon a narrative of white domination and manifest destiny, a narrative that must be disrupted to right the wrongs done to Indian people at the hands of museums and historians. *Ghost Singer* is, therefore, about two related issues: Indian remains held in museums, and white control of the narrative of history that insists upon the death of American Indian people – the idea of the disappearing Indian who cannot survive in the face of European-American culture, science, and technology. What is needed, the novel reveals, is a mutually respectful, incorporative discourse to deal with the issue of repatriation. Science and history must consider and value native knowledge, must listen to – and really hear – American Indian counternarrative, embodied or literally incorporated, in Walters' text, as the angry Indian ghosts who force the researchers to confront that which falls outside their understanding of the scientifically explainable, or the "real." In insisting on the meaningful and continuing corporeality of American Indian people, Walters works toward a discourse that takes into account American Indian values, beliefs, and sovereign rights.

The complete lack of respect for the bodies and body parts of Indian people on the part of the Smithsonian staff is evident from the beginning of the novel. While the family of Navajo student Willie Begay preserves and protects the story of how their ancestor White Sheep was scalped by slave traders in 1830, the white anthropologists carelessly handle the human remains they are supposed to be tending at the museum. For instance, anthropologist Geoffrey Newsome sorts through the collection and comes across

> a necklace of twenty human fingers, the nails on the fingers blue-tinged. Geoffrey had seen the necklace many times. On occasion he'd playfully put the necklace on. He was the kind of man who did that, and he did it now. The necklace lay on his plaid shirt, the fingers pressed against him.

> (Walters 42)

"The kind of man" who denies the humanity of others, who views Indian flesh as a trophy to be worn and discarded at will, Geoffrey demonstrates the philosophy articulated by his colleague Donald Evans, who explains to Indian scholar George Daylight:

> "The items in this collection ... are no longer in the possession of any Indian people. ... George, the fact is that these items are *here*. ... These objects and items stored up here are from dead cultures, George, dead! When will you people wake up to this realization? There's no point in trying to revive the dead. Life can't be breathed into these things."

> (125)

Donald's scientific rationalism is quickly proven wrong, as he and Geoffrey come face to face with the revived – and furiously angry – dead, who are able literally to push the researchers around, to squeeze their fingers around the necks of the anthropologists who deny their humanity and the continuing lives of their communities and descendants. Faced with the embodiment of that which they thought impossible, with an utterly unscientific and obstinately corporeal Indian resistance, Geoffrey is pushed off a balcony to his death, another Smithsonian "suicide," and the frightened Donald questions his sanity, eventually forced to turn to George Daylight and his friends for help, since as Anna Snake, a powerful elder notes:

> It don't have to happen the way it's been going. Our folks see spirit peoples all the time, we know them. People don't have to run around like chickens with their heads cut off about it. We cross the paths of spirit peoples all the time. We have to because lotsa peoples have lived and then went on since the world began. That's how come our folks told us how to treat them, so we won't go crazy when we run across them.

> (148)

Through Anna's words, the novel insists that indigenous knowledge and tribal narratives must be heard and understood to redress the deadly situation at the Smithsonian. These stories cannot be denied, just like Donald and Geoffrey find it impossible, in the end, to deny the presence, anger, and strange vitality of the Indian dead they treated like objects. Nevertheless, in a parallel plotline involving a white historian who claims that he wants to write history from a Navajo perspective, Walters shows the pernicious tendency of academia to discredit the native voice. Historian David Drake, a brother of one of the Smithsonian suicides, approaches Willie Begay's grandfather, Jonnie Navajo, and asks him to work with him as a consultant on a history of the Navajo people. Of course, as Jonnie Navajo quickly discovers, Drake retains all control as the teller of the history, deciding when (or whether) to include the information Jonnie shares with him. And when, in return, Jonnie asks Drake to help to locate the granddaughter of his ancestor White Sheep, who was stolen in the slave raid that cost White Sheep his scalp, Drake completes only a minimal search for information about the raid. As he works on his manuscript, Drake reflects:

> at this minute he really did think it would have been much easier to do without the old man's input. He wouldn't have had to listen to the old man's long tale, and he wouldn't have had to rethink his own history of the Navajos. So far, the use of the old man had only caused him a great deal of inconvenience. ... Yes, David had decided he would do what was right – for him. He would only do so much for the old Navajo man, and that was all. He would do only that which was required of him in exchange for what he wanted from the old man – his history, to interpret at his leisure and discretion.
>
> (227–28)

Drake attempts, in short, to deny Jonnie Navajo semiotic sovereignty, while *he* claims the position of interpretive determination for himself – a white academic with the weight of innumerable histories written by men just like him to back him up. His conclusion that "he wasn't a cowboy, or an Indian. He was a historian, and a damn good one, too" demonstrates how David Drake ignores the politics of history-writing, of narrating the past, seeing himself as somehow "innocent," "scientifically objective," and a seeker of "pure" knowledge without "bias" (228).

Jonnie Navajo recognizes Drake's positioning, his apparently inextricable connection to the systems of knowledge that produce the body-clogged museums and the culture-killing narratives, ending their collaboration. An accomplished tribal historian, Jonnie recognizes that as a bearer of Navajo history, he must also be a productive part of the tribe's present, and work to affirm and ensure its future. Part of that work is performing a ceremony for Willie, to cure him of the illness he comes down with after inadvertently touching what may have been the scalp of his ancestor, White Sheep. As Willie explains to his grandfather:

> In Washingdoon, I discovered through the papers and other things there that Navajos and other Indians weren't supposed to have survived this long. ... I think that discovery hurt me very much, more than I dared to admit, but I am recovering from it.
>
> (247)

Jonnie is responsible, in his role as a singer or healer, for reintegrating Willie into the tribe, making him whole once more after his contact with the bodies fragments his living self. History is not, for Jonnie, a recording of past defeats. Instead, it is a lived, continuing reality that teaches him, and his descendants, how to live on their land and tend to their dead while keeping themselves in balance.

The novel's penultimate scene in the Smithsonian mirrors the sense of possibility lost that we have seen in Jonnie's working relationship with David Drake. Donald Evans requests the help of native people to make sense of the encounters he has had with the increasingly angry Indian dead within the museum, but when he brings them up to his attic office, the place where the collection of bodies and sacred objects was stored, he proceeds to give them a mini-lecture on how and why the museum protected and preserved these items benevolently. As he goes on about the museum's drive to "preserve specimens of ancient and extinct Indian cultures," powerful tribal elder Wilbur Snake tunes out Donald's narrative, as does Jonnie Navajo. The older men notice, though, how Willie and his contemporaries, educated in schools that provided them with unrelenting examples of this same narrative of Indian death and white benevolence, hang on Donald's every word. Over the course of the dramatic and emotionally trying ceremony that Wilbur leads to attempt to heal the situation, the spirit people in the museum become visible to everyone present, and the furious warrior attacks Donald physically, punching and slapping him. Wilbur Snake repeatedly tells Donald that to stop the beating, the anthropologist should look at *him*, the living, powerful, contemporary native person instead of the so-called "specimen" retained at the museum for his "study." Donald is still unwilling or unable to focus on the contemporary Indian people, and passes out with terror. While the ceremony fails to change Donald's perceptions of Indian people, and therefore fails to contain the violence in the museum, it does have a significant impact upon the younger Indian people present. Their lives have been filled with conflicting narratives about science, truth, and tribal philosophies, but they can clearly see what Donald has trouble acknowledging – the events in the museum, the presence of the animated bodies, makes sense according to *indigenous* ways of knowing. Science has failed to explain what they have experienced, and therefore semiotic sovereignty rests with Wilbur and the other tribal elders present. Their interpretation of events proves accurate and reliable, and the young native people are able to use this experience to revision themselves as part of the vibrant, continuing contemporary Native community.

Changes in mindset are slow and incremental in *Ghost Singer*, and yet the novel asks its readers – both native and non-native – to interrogate their own positions and beliefs. The novel strongly challenges narratives of the supremacy of science, the absolute accessibility of knowledge, and the "inevitability" of colonization and white ownership of the land of the Americas and all it contains. Since the novel was written before NAGPRA, Walters does not have access to a legal apparatus for repatriation. And yet, her text suggests that legally enforcing repatriation of remains is not enough to heal these rifts and wounds. Social scientists like Donald and David must acknowledge Indian interpretive authority, must value the ability of tribal epistemologies to explain the relationship between body and spirit, between death and life – and American Indian people who have continually encountered European-American historical, legal, and moral narratives that claim the status of "truth" must likewise rethink this received message. The imperative to work toward this indigenous jurisgenesis, to encourage the dialogue that is such an important part of NAGPRA is clear – the novel ends with Willie visiting the grave of the proud, dignified, and extremely knowledgeable Jonnie Navajo, who has passed away after a long and fruitful life. As he tends to his grandfather's grave, Willie wonders if it, too, will one day be in danger of looting, thinking "If only he could be sure his grandfather's grave would be safe there … ." The novel actually ends with ellipses, indicating that, of course, this story is not over, that this narrative itself must work to create the possibility of the additional dialogue that will enable legal channels to function. What *Ghost Singer* tries to teach its readers – even more successfully than it teaches its characters – is to listen to these words, to see the connection native peoples insist on between human remains and living cultures, and to experience an "awakening of understanding" by embracing the incorporative discourse that may begin the process of adjustment of dominant systems of belief that is necessary to successfully enact repatriation.

Twenty-five years after its passage into law, NAGPRA remains a work in progress. Even Native critics of NAGPRA, such as James Riding In, acknowledge the significance of the legislation: "Both NMAIA … and NAGPRA … represent major accomplishments in the Indigenous struggle against contemporary colonialism and oppression" (54). And a 2012 survey of repatriation workers employed by tribal governments to apply NAGPRA concluded that "these tribal repatriation workers see NAGPRA as a temporarily imperfect but fundamentally important law" (Colwell-Chanthaphonh 289). Nevertheless, Native writers and NAGPRA practitioners alike are clear that there are things about the law itself and the way it has been applied that need to change in order for the human rights intention of the law to be realized. Riding In speaks of this as a decolonization of NAGPRA, and the NAGPRA practitioners believe that tribes need more direct involvement in determining cultural affiliations, more information on collections and more meaningful and thorough consultation with museums in order to improve the law (Riding In 61; Colwell-Chanthaphonh 289). As a law that arises from and responds to indigenous perspectives on the sanctity of bodies and the continuity of indigenous cultures, NAGPRA is worth the effort, and the ongoing conversation. American Indian literary texts that address repatriation both reflect and *shape* the broader discourse about repatriation in which the law is applied. This can clearly be seen in the impact that Allison Hedge Coke's "free verse play," *Blood Run* has had. As Hedge Coke's website proclaims,

> After years of lobbying for the protection of Blood Run [burial mounds], some of these very poems composed during the process proved to be the breakthrough testimony that compelled the Game, Fish, & Parks Commission to come to a unanimous vote in favor of acquisitioning and preserving the SD side of the site.
>
> (*Allison Hedge Coke*)

Like McNickle's and Walters' novels, Hedge Coke's poetry functions as a co-text to the law. Engaging with the dialogic process of NAGPRA's construction, these authors' incorporative discourse can be read as supplemental narratives that create the discursive space in which the law can function to assert sovereignty and protect Native bodies and cultural items. By articulating indigenous values and perspectives, her collection and other Native literary discussions of repatriation assert indigenous jurisgenesis that shapes the interpretation and application of law, providing a dynamic example of the decolonizing power of Native American literature.

Notes

1 My use of the term jurisgenesis draws on the work of legal scholar Robert Cover, who explained that "the creation of legal meaning – jurisgenesis – takes place always through an essentially cultural medium. Although the state is not necessarily the creator of legal meaning, the creative process is collective or social" (11). Robert Williams brings this term into indigenous studies in *Linking Arms Together* (e.g. 28–29).

2 These definitions are provided in Section 2 of NAGPRA.
3 These are McNickle's words, from a document entitled "Exhibit C" in McNickle's correspondence, housed at the Newberry Library, which was likely sent with his letter of 25 May 1934, to John Collier as part of his application for the Indian Service.

Works cited

Allison Hedge Coke. Site produced by: Travis Hedge Coke & Ryan DeMoss. 2010. Web. Accessed 15 Jan. 2015.

Bieder, Robert. "The Representations of American Indian Bodies in Nineteenth-century American Anthropology." *Repatriation Reader*. Ed. Devon Mihesuah. Lincoln: University of Nebraska Press, 2000. 19–36.

Colwell-Chanthaphonh, Chip. "The Work of Repatriation in Indian Country." *Human Organization* 71. 3 (2012): 278–91.

Cover, Robert. "Foreword: Nomos and Narrative," *Harvard Law Review* 97. 4 (1983–84): 4–68.

Duthu, N. Bruce. "Incorporative Discourse in Federal Indian Law: Negotiating Tribal Sovereignty through the Lens of Native American Literature." *Harvard Human Rights Journal* 13 (Spring 2000): 141–89.

Frequently Asked Questions (FAQ). *National NAGPRA Project*. National Parks Service, U.S. Department of the Interior. n.d. Web. Accessed 15 Jan. 2015.

Hedge Coke, Allison Adele. *Blood Run*. London: Salt, 2006.

Jefferson, Thomas. *Notes on the State of Virginia*. Ed. William Peden. New York: Norton, 1972.

Kelsey, Penelope & Cari Carpenter. "'In the End, Our Message Weighs': *Blood Run*, NAGPRA, and American Indian Identity." *American Indian Quarterly* 35. 1 (Winter 2011): 56–74.

McNickle, D'Arcy. "Exhibit C." undated (*c.* 1934). McNickle Papers, Newberry Library. Box 18, folder 157.

———. "Letter to Douglas Latimer." 23 March, 1977. McNickle Papers, Newberry Library. Box 20, folder 170.

———. *Wind from an Enemy Sky*. Albuquerque: University of New Mexico Press, 1988.

"Obituary for Maria 'Running Moccasins' Pearson." *NativeWeb.org*. n.d. Web. Accessed 15 Jan. 2015.

Riding In, James. "Decolonizing NAGPRA." *For Indigenous Eyes Only: A Decolonization Handbook*. Ed. Waziyatawin Angela Wilson & Michael Yellow Bird. Santa Fe, NM: School for Advanced Research, 2005. 53–66.

Trope, Jack F. & Walter R. Echo-Hawk. "The Native American Graves Protection and Repatriation Act: Background and Legislative History." *Repatriation Reader*. Ed. Devon Mihesuah. Lincoln: University of Nebraska Press, 2000. 123–68.

Walters, Anna Lee. *Ghost Singer*. Albuquerque: University of New Mexico Press, 1988.

Williams, Robert. *Linking Arms Together: American Indian Treaty Visions of Law and Peace 1600–1800*. New York: Oxford University Press, 1997.

Winslow, Edward & William Bradford. *Mourt's Relation, or a Journal of the Plantation at Plymouth* (1622). Intro. Henry Martyn Dexter. Boston: Rand & Avery, 1865.

Zimmerman, Larry J. "Repatriation." *Encyclopedia of the Great Plains*. Ed. David J. Wishart. Web. Accessed 24 Jan. 2015. http://plainshumanities.unl.edu/encyclopedia/doc/egp.na.095

16
Native American Literature and the UN Declaration on the Rights of Indigenous Peoples

Eric Cheyfitz

The Declaration on the Rights of Indigenous Peoples was ratified by the UN General Assembly in 2007. What it represents in the first instance, as the preamble states, is the recognition by the UN of over 500 years of predominantly European settler colonialism in lands held originally by Indigenous Peoples:

> ... indigenous peoples have suffered from historic injustices as a result of, inter alia, their colonization and dispossession of their lands, territories and resources, thus preventing them from exercising, in particular, their right to development in accordance with their own needs and interests.

Thus, the preamble of the Declaration recognizes

> the urgent need to respect and promote the inherent rights of indigenous peoples which derive from their political, economic and social structures and from their cultures, spiritual traditions, histories and philosophies, especially their rights to their lands, territories and resources.

The Declaration never defines what it means by the term "indigenous." But Steven Newcomb notes:

> According to UN working definitions, peoples said to be "indigenous" were existing freely in a particular place. Then, eventually, another people of a different "race" or "ethnic origin" arrived there, and the new arrivals gradually became dominant through conquest, settlement, and other means. In other words, the UN working definitions tell us that the original peoples were reduced down "to a non-dominant or colonial situation.[1]

In this chapter I use "Indigenous" in approximately the same way to mean "first peoples," that is, the people who were in *place* when Europeans or other outsiders, bent on exploitation, arrived in their territories. Thus, while this chapter focuses on the Indigenous peoples of the United States (American Indians, Alaska Natives, and Native Hawaiians), I also understand that the term *Indigenous* includes, for example, the Palestinian people, currently suffering under the colonial occupation of the state of Israel. In what follows I capitalize the term *Indigenous* to mark it as a proper noun, indicating specific peoples who can claim original habitation on their lands.

As the Declaration makes clear, land is the crucial issue facing Indigenous communities. But in the preamble the Declaration is ambiguous, referring at once to the "dispossession" of Indigenous lands by colonial powers and Indigenous peoples' "rights to their lands," without specifying whether "lands" refers to original lands forcibly taken or lands remaining after such takings. However, Article 26 (1) of the Declaration states: "Indigenous peoples have the right to the lands, territories and resources which they have traditionally owned, occupied or otherwise used or acquired." Nevertheless, Article 28 (1) implicitly recognizes that this right to their original lands has been abrogated by the invading colonial power:

> Indigenous peoples have the right to redress, by means that can include restitution or, when this is not possible, just, fair and equitable compensation, for the lands, territories and resources which they have traditionally owned or otherwise occupied or used, and which have been confiscated, taken, occupied, used or damaged without their free, prior and informed consent.

In this respect, the Declaration is both retrospective, looking back at the colonial history to which it is responding, and prospective, looking forward to the redress of that ongoing history. But it holds the present in suspension, precisely because it recognizes, without ever commenting on the fact, that the Indigenous peoples for whom it speaks are located within the power of the nation-states from which they are seeking redress. Article 38 makes this plain: "States in consultation and cooperation with indigenous peoples, shall take the appropriate measures, including legislative measures, to achieve the ends of this Declaration." But while "the ends of this Declaration" would seem to be the liberation of Indigenous peoples from colonial domination, the Declaration itself is a decidedly colonial document, precisely because it recognizes the legitimacy of "the territorial integrity" and "political unity" of the dominating states:

> Nothing in this Declaration may be interpreted as implying for any State, people, group or person any right to engage in any activity or to perform any act contrary to the Charter of the United Nations or construed as authorizing or encouraging any action which would dismember or impair, totally or in part, the territorial integrity or political unity of sovereign and independent States.
>
> (Article 46 [1])

There is barely an article in the Declaration that does not reference the "States" as the primary agent of restoring the usurpations, principally of land, that constitute the ground of their sovereignty. Taken as a whole, then, the Declaration on the Rights of Indigenous Peoples is a contradictory statement; explicitly anticolonial, it affirms the very colonialism it counters. What other choice did it have within the organization, the United Nations, that legitimizes it?

This contradiction is implicit in Article 4: "Indigenous peoples, in exercising their right to self-determination, have the right to autonomy or self-government in matters relating to *their internal and local affairs*, as well as ways and means for financing their autonomous functions" (my emphasis). What is not addressed here and, indeed, in the entire Declaration is the contradiction inherent in a "self-determination" of "internal and local affairs" that is dependent on the legal framework of the colonial state within which this "self-determination" must operate. The results of such a contradiction can be represented by the definition of Indian communities in U.S. federal Indian law as "domestic dependent nations," an oxymoron (for nations are defined under international law as independent and foreign) formulated by Chief Justice John Marshall in the Supreme Court's 1831 decision in the generative case of *Cherokee Nation v. Georgia*. The Cherokee Nation, rightly considering itself as a *foreign* nation because it had signed treaties with the U.S, came before the Court in order to sue the state of Georgia for violating these treaties. But it left the Court with a diminished status, which disallowed its suit. That definition became doctrine for all the federally recognized tribes in the lower forty-eight states, solving the problem in one stroke of federal recognition of foreign nations within the nation. But Marshall's definition of Indian tribes solved the federal problem by violating the Supremacy Clause (Article VI, ¶2) of the U.S. Constitution, which recognizes treaties as among "the supreme law of the land."

There is, perhaps, something deeply ironic in thinking about what is intended to be an anticolonial document, the UN Declaration, in terms of a decidedly colonial body of law. For that is precisely how U.S. federal Indian law functions and has functioned historically. Nevertheless, there are clearly a significant number of Indigenous peoples or, rather, their representatives,[2] authors of the Declaration, who read the document without any irony or, if they do, are prepared to live with that irony and deal with its contradictions.

However, even if one is prepared to live with the irony, focusing not on context but only on the specifics for which the Declaration seeks redress, the problem of implementation arises, lest the Declaration remain a purely virtual document, a utopian text. In order to address this problem, in September of 2014 the UN convened a "high-level plenary meeting of the General Assembly known as the World Conference on Indigenous peoples" (See "Outcome document"). Preparing for this meeting, representatives of "the 7 global geo-political regions including representatives of the women's caucus and the youth caucus" convened from 10–12 June 2013 a "Global Indigenous Preparatory Conference" in "the traditional territories and lands of the Sami People at Alta, Norway" (see "Global Indigenous Preparatory Conference"). Anticipating the "UN Outcome Document," which would be the document representing the deliberations of the "World Conference," the Alta Conference issued the "Alta Outcome Document." While this document indicted the genocidal "colonial strategies, policies, and actions designed to destroy Indigenous Peoples," it "reaffirm[ed] that the [UN] Declaration [on the Rights of Indigenous Peoples] must be regarded as the normative framework and basis for the Outcome Document [of the 'World Conference'] and its full realization." Having unequivocally affirmed the Declaration as an anticolonial document, it is not surprising, though perhaps disturbing (if one recognizes its colonial framework), that the preamble to the Alta document went on to

UN DECLARATION ON RIGHTS OF INDIGENOUS PEOPLES

affirm that the inherent and inalienable right of self determination is preeminent and is a prerequisite for the realization of all rights. We Indigenous Peoples, have the right of self determination and permanent sovereignty over our lands, territories, resources, air, ice, oceans and waters, mountains and forests.

To "have the right" is of course one thing; to achieve it quite another. In this context of the primacy of the nation-state, the former is rhetorical; the latter, revolutionary, as the U.S. Declaration of Independence might remind us or, more recently, the Bolivian revolution of 2000–2005, which ultimately led to the election of Evo Morales, the first Indigenous president of Bolivia, and an end to neoliberal governance there, certainly in theory and to a significant degree in practice.[3]

Under the heading of "four themes" ("Indigenous Peoples' lands, territories, resources, oceans and waters"; "UN system action for the implementation of the rights of Indigenous Peoples"; "Implementation of the Rights of Indigenous Peoples"; and "Indigenous Peoples' priorities for Development with free, prior and informed consent"), the Alta document makes "specific and concrete recommendations for inclusion in the final Outcome Document of the HLPM/WCIP." If implemented, the forty-three Alta recommendations would constitute an institutional revolution within the nation-states that would in effect reconstitute these states as plurinational polities after, for example, the model of the Bolivian constitution. To this end, Article 10 of Theme 3 recommends

> that States fully honour and in conjunction with Indigenous Peoples create conditions for the right of self determination of Indigenous Peoples including through formal decolonization processes to those Indigenous Peoples who seek it, and that all administering powers of non-self governing territories take all steps necessary to eradicate colonialism in all its forms and manifestations.

What this article would mean if accepted by American Indian nations in the lower forty-eight states of the U.S. and implemented by the federal government would be the total dismantling of federal Indian law, which confers on Congress "plenary power" over Indian affairs, a power administered by the colonial apparatus of the Bureau of Indian Affairs under the Department of the Interior. What would be put in place of the colonial apparatus remains speculative, indeed under the current regime, entirely utopian. It would require, in one format we might imagine, the rewriting of the U.S. Constitution to give plurinational representation to the 564 Native nations (336 American Indian tribes and 228 Alaska Native villages) in the United States, while also representing Native Hawaiians, who currently have no separate legal relationship as a people with the federal government. But it is on the ground of utopian thinking that actual revolutions commence.

In comparison to the utopian, or if you will, revolutionary thinking of the Alta document, the UN "Outcome document," representing "the Heads of State and Government, ministers and representatives of Member States" (Article1), is reactionary. While the UN document "welcome[s]" the Alta statement and "reaffirm[s] ... support for the United Nations Declaration on the Rights of Indigenous Peoples" (Article 2, 3), it implicitly rejects both through dilution or omission of all the recommendations of Alta. Nowhere in the forty articles of the UN Outcome document, which continually refers to the "rights" of Indigenous peoples, do we read the words "colonialism" or "self-determination." And nowhere in the document are there any specific suggestions for the implementation and enforcement of these rights; so that when in its fortieth article, the document "request[s] the Secretary-General ... to report to the General Assembly at its seventieth session on the implementation of the present outcome document," one wonders how exactly a document of such monumental generality can be implemented, precisely when all of its appeals for justice are to the nation-states historically in violation of Indigenous rights. Reading both the Alta and the UN Outcome documents, which ground their statements in interpretations of the UN Declaration, we can understand how the Declaration is in conflict with itself, at once a colonial and an anticolonial document.

Within this context, I want to suggest the outlines of a strain of U.S. Native literatures – fiction and non-fiction, poetry and prose – that have historically engaged the anticolonial position that we find in the Alta reading of the UN Declaration on the Rights of Indigenous Peoples.[4] I am referring, then, to literatures of resistance, of which I take the Alta document to be an example, if we can suspend the problem of its own allegiance to the contradictory Declaration. I am writing here of literatures written in English, which necessarily exclude a vast oral and graphic tradition. Given that the word "resistance" is a vexed term generally and a particularly vexed term in U.S. Native studies, because of the nuances of critical reading coupled with the precarious positions in which Native subjects have found themselves historically, one person's resistor may be another's collaborator. The tension between the Alta and the UN Outcome documents as critical readings of the UN Declaration make this point. Clearly, I find the former resistant and the latter collaborative (decidedly in the negative sense of that term), while, for example, others might find them both *collaborative* (within a range of meanings of the term, positive and negative), given that they have both accepted the framework of the UN Declaration. But it is not my intention to parse the term "resistance" here. Rather, it is to suggest by way of example some texts that one may find useful in thinking critically about the historical issues that the UN Declaration on the Rights of Indigenous Peoples engages and raises. Readers of this chapter will necessarily want to add their own suggestions. I am not creating a canon, then, but proposing a figure for thought.

We could begin a sketch of this resistance literature with the antebellum writings, autobiographical and polemical, of the Pequot Williams Apess, who in his public address *Eulogy on King Philip* (1836) effectively rewrites U.S. history from a "Native point of view" (a rhetorical construction no doubt but a politically strategic one nevertheless constitutive in fact of the UN documents I am reviewing). The text Apess turns on its head in this instance is Increase Mather's Puritan polemic *A Brief History of the War with the Indians in New England* (1676), a justificatory tract for the English genocide committed against the Wampanoag and Naragansett Indians and their allies, 40 percent of whom perished in King Philip's War in 1675–1676 (Strong 85). In celebrating the life of "Philip," the name the English gave to the Wampanoag sachem Metacomet or Metacom, who died resisting the colonizer's murderous land grab, Apess not only indicts early settler colonialism but also the legal regime being put into place by the Andrew Jackson administration with the support of Congress and the Supreme Court, which set the stage for the Indian removals of the 1830s: the ethnic cleansing of the eastern United States. Apess's *Eulogy* gives the U.S. its first declaration of Indigenous rights and the strain of Native literatures I am suggesting a sure focus: resistance to settler colonialism. This resistance takes two interwoven forms: political and cultural, which are the categories of redress in the UN documents. While, as noted, Apess's political resistance is clear enough in his outspoken opposition to federal policy, his cultural resistance, as a converted Christian, is literally to turn Christianity Native in the *Eulogy*, indicting white Christians for their lack of Christian charity, while finding that characteristic precisely in Native practices of hospitality generated through extended kinship.

Apess's mode of attack in the *Eulogy* is irony, a figure the Anishinaabe poet, novelist, and critic Gerald Vizenor uses as well to turn colonialism on its head in his postmodern writing. In his novel *The Heirs of Columbus* (1991), in a way reminiscent of Apess's translation of Christian charity into Native kinship, Vizenor translates Columbus into "a trickster healer in the stories told by his tribal heirs" (3). As with Apess, the force at play in Vizenor is to reset the terms of the historical narrative in order to stress Native "sovereignty," the term driving the UN Declaration yet nowhere written in it except in Article 46 where it refers with unintentional irony solely to "the territorial integrity or political unity of sovereign and independent [nation] States." Thus, in effect, the Declaration bars the use of the key term "sovereignty" in relation to Indigenous peoples, substituting for it "self-determination," in order, one assumes, not to call into question the legal dominance of nation-states over the Indigenous peoples whose polities are situated within them because of the very colonialism the Declaration is intended to redress. But what, the Native texts I am citing and the anticolonial tradition they represent ask, does "self-determination" mean without "sovereignty"? The question is not rhetorical. While, unsurprisingly, the UN Outcome document does not use the term "sovereignty" in relation to the rights of Indigenous Peoples, the Alta document specifies in its preamble that "Indigenous Peoples,[sic] have the right of self determination and permanent sovereignty over our lands, territories, resources, air, ice, oceans and waters, mountains and forests," thus joining "self-determination" and "sovereignty."

Article 13 (1) of the UN Declaration states: "Indigenous peoples have the right to revitalize, use, develop and transmit to future generations their histories, languages, oral traditions, philosophies, writing systems and literatures, and to designate and retain their own names for communities, places and persons." In the texts under consideration, both Apess and Vizenor are exercising this "right," specifically in relation to the key term "sovereignty," which has an ongoing contested history in both law and literature within Native studies. That is, "sovereignty" is in the first place a term of art in Western law and politics used to translate Native polities, which operated through horizontal, non-representational consensual modes of governance, into the hierarchical Western nation-state system. Chief Justice John Marshall makes this clear in his majority opinion in the case of *Worcester v. Georgia* (1832), which confirmed the pre-eminence of federal over state and tribal jurisdiction in federal Indian law:

> The words "treaty" and "nation" are words of our own language, selected in our diplomatic and legislative proceedings, by ourselves, having each a definite and well understood meaning. We have applied them to Indians, as we have applied them to the other nations of the earth. They are applied to all in the same sense.
>
> (31 US at 559–60)

For Native communities to be represented before the law, then, they must speak in the alien language of the nation-state, which recognizes their "sovereignty" but only in order to subordinate them to its sovereignty.

The way the UN documents on Indigeneity engage the term "sovereignty" reflects the double-edged force of its usage. Works like *Eulogy on King Philip* and *Heirs of Columbus* can act as commentary on the UN Declaration precisely because they direct our attention to the problematics of the document, the way it tries to address Indigenous political–cultural issues with a Western vocabulary grounded in the terminology of "sovereignty" and "rights." In *Heirs*, for example, Vizenor has the character of a judge shake the term sovereignty loose from its Western legal moorings and, as he does with Columbus, translate it into an Indigenous form:

> "The notion of tribal sovereignty is not confiscable, or earth bound; sovereignty is neither fence nor feathers. The essence of sovereignty is imaginative, an original tribal trope, communal and spiritual, an idea that is more than metes and bounds in treaties."
>
> (7)

Mohawk political theorist Taiaiake Alfred puts it matter of factly: "The challenge for indigenous peoples in building appropriate postcolonial governing systems is to disconnect the notion of sovereignty from its Western legal roots and transform it" (42). This is the task, then, of the U.S. Native American literary project figured by Apess and Vizenor.

We can find this project articulated in a range of Native texts from Apess to the present. Native Hawaiian scholar and activist Haunani-Kay Trask's *From a Native Daughter: Colonialism and Sovereignty in Hawai'i* (1999) takes as its text what was then the working draft of the UN Declaration and reads it as unequivocally anticolonial: "In the context of international law ... continued American claims to political and cultural superiority are seen as merely the ideology of a colonizing power" (31). While operating with the vocabulary of "sovereignty" and "rights," Trask's definition of Indigenous peoples works against their subordination within a nation-state framework:

> Indigenous peoples are defined in terms of collective aboriginal occupation prior to colonial settlement. They are not to be confused with minorities or ethnic groups within states. Thus "indigenous rights" are strictly distinguished from "minority rights." The *numbers* of indigenous peoples, therefore, does not constitute a criterion in their definition.
>
> (33)

Trask's definition has the force of taking the idea of "Indigenous rights" out of the Western colonial framework, where it becomes only an amelioration or redress of colonial history, and recognizing it as an absolute value, an intrinsic part of a prior, Indigenous history, which requires legal recognition.

Central to this history is what Trask, representing a range of Indigenous philosophies and practices, understands as the "cultural ... bond between people and land," and all that exists in and on the land and waters, a bond expressed *literally* through extended kinship relations, which "is not possible to know ... through Western culture. This means that the history of indigenous people cannot be written from within Western culture" (120–21). In his book *Fight Back: For the Sake of the People, For the Sake of the Land* (1980), which in poetry and prose focuses Indigenous resistance from the Pueblo Revolt of 1680 through union organization of Native workers in the Grants uranium mining belt in the post-World War II era, Acoma writer Simon Ortiz, like Hawaiian Native Trask, articulates the bond between the land and the people. The reciprocal rhythm of the lines of the poem emphasizes the reciprocal relationship between land and people that the poem expresses.

For the Tlingit people of Alaska, the historical bond with the land is expressed through the Tlingit relation to the salmon. Tlingit poet Nora Marks Dauenhauer explains:

> Not only have we used salmon as our main diet, and not only has it been the mainstay of our subsistence and commercial economies, but the different varieties of salmon are a part of our social structure and ethnic identity as well ... . This enduring relationship between the Tlingit people, the fish and animals, and the land, and the connection of all of these to our social structure, took many generations to evolve.

But "[w]ith the arrival of Euro-Americans, many Tlingit and other Alaska Native people were separated from their land and resources base." The Europeans built canneries and turned a "subsistence," or sustainable, way of life, which maintained a balance with the land, into industrial fishing on the capitalist model with the result that

> [e]ntire salmon runs were depleted by fish traps and by logging practices that ruined the habitat ... . The controversy over subsistence fishing continues to rage ... . As with land, subsistence is at the very core of our ethnic identity and tribal existence. The importance of salmon goes beyond the question of calories. It is part of our identity. We need salmon to continue as physically, mentally, and spiritually healthy people.

> (Dauenhauer 3–6)

For the Tlingit people, then, sovereignty means salmon.

Crucially for Indigenous peoples, land is beyond the Lockean paradigm; it is not fungible; it is not "property."[5] It is a relative in Ortiz's sense of family, a non-human person. But it should be emphasized here that Indigenous languages appear not to make absolute distinctions between the human and the non-human.[6] Chickasaw poet and novelist Linda Hogan understands the relation as contractual:

> It is clear that we have strayed from the treaties we once had with the land and with the animals. It is also clear, and heartening, that in our time there are many – Indian and non-Indian alike – who want to restore and honor these broken agreements.

> (11)

What Hogan and the other Indigenous writers I have been citing suggest is that the energy driving the UN Declaration on the Rights of Indigenous Peoples but not, because of its colonial framework, realized in it is fundamentally the energy of a sustainable life, not just for Indigenous peoples, though this life would take an Indigenous form, but for the entire planet. Such a life can be figured in the Quechua phrase *Sumak Kausay*, translated in Spanish as *Buen Vivir*. Paraphrasing Alberto Acosta, the President of the 2007–2008 Constitutional Assembly of Ecuador, Thomas Fatheuer notes:

For him and other Buen Vivir theorists, it is important to distinguish this concept from the Western idea of prosperity. Buen Vivir is not geared toward "having more" and does not see accumulation and growth, but rather a state of equilibrium as its goal. Its reference to the indigenous world view is also central: its starting point is not progress or growth as a linear model of thinking, but the attainment and reproduction of the equilibrium state of *Sumak Kausay* ... . Buen Vivir is a culture of life based on the ancestral knowledge of indigenous peoples that aims to strike a balance, striving for harmony between humans and nature alike, and which foresees a return to a way of life that had been suppressed by colonization. "We must return to being, because colonization has made us into 'wanting to be'. Many of us want to be, but as of yet, we are not. We now want to return to our own path to our being."

(16, 19)

This is what "sovereignty," "rights," and "self-determination" would mean in a world of Indigenous being. Such a world is continually spoken and written in Indigenous literatures around the globe. To understand the limits and the promise of the UN Declaration on the Rights of Indigenous Peoples, one must understand these literatures.

Notes

1 See Newcomb. As I do, Newcomb reads the Declaration as a fundamentally colonial document, though I arrived at my reading before I read the Newcomb essay. For a working definition of the term "indigenous," see Article 1, no.1, of Convention 169 of the International Labor Organization: Indigenous and Tribal Peoples Convention, 1989. This Convention, which forms a basis for the UN Declaration on the Rights of Indigenous Peoples, is a rewriting of the 1957 Convention on Indigenous and Tribal populations with the express purpose of "adopt[ing] new international standards on the subject with a view to removing the assimilationist orientation of the earlier standards" and instituting standards "Recognizing the aspirations of these peoples to exercise control over their own institutions, ways of life and economic development ... ." But the same problem inheres in the 1989 Convention that I am noting in the Declaration: the fact that these aspirations for autonomy are circumscribed by the (post)colonial agendas of the nation-states within which Indigenous communities by reason of conquest find themselves located.

2 The UN Permanent Forum on Indigenous Issues is the representative body of the 370 million Indigenous peoples in the world. Necessarily the question of representation here raises significant questions about voicing this vast population, which exists in "some 70 countries worldwide" ("United Nations Permanent Forum on Indigenous Issues" in Wikipedia).

3 See Hylton & Thomson 3–7. Drafted as the first act of the Morales regime, the new Bolivian constitution announces the "refound[ing] of Bolivia as a 'plurinational state,'" which leaves "the colonial, republican and neoliberal State in the past" and is committed to the "distribution and redistribution of the social product." The constitution is both actual and virtual. The state has nationalized its hydrocarbons and instituted land reforms, both of which have led to a significant redistribution of wealth from which the people have benefited:

The nationalization of the oil and gas industry resulted in a tripling of the state budget in a short time (in the years 2005 to 2008) and let the country implement social programs for families with children and the elderly. Per capita income also rose by more than 50 percent during the same period.

(Fatheuer 12)

At the same time, neoliberal markets in hydrocarbons remain instrumental in driving certain economic sectors and there is concomitantly resistance from Indigenous communities whose environment is negatively impacted by extractive industries.

4 See Cheyfitz *Columbia Guide*. The *Guide* understands American Indian literatures as forms of resistance to an ongoing U.S. colonialism in "Indian Country," which includes all reservation land held in "trust" by the federal government (approximately fifty-four million acres), all of the 336 federally recognized tribes (most of which occupy this land), and all Indian allotments still held under "trust" status in the lower forty-eight states. The "trust" relationship in effect creates Indian nations as "minors" within the confines of U.S. federal Indian law. Because of a different history from Native peoples in the lower forty-eight and while still impacted by U.S. federal Indian law in some respects, Alaska Natives have to deal with U.S. colonialism in various forms, though where land is concerned under a different legal regime: the Alaska Native Claims Settlement Act of 1971 (ANCSA), which ended all land claims in Alaska and transferred the forty-four million acres that remained of Native land into Native held corporations, both regional and local. Of this settlement, Roy M. Huhndorf and Shari M. Huhndorf wrote in 2011:

> Four decades after the act's passage, the effects of ANCSA remain complicated and contradictory. The settlement raises crucial questions about whether traditional Native practices and social structures are compatible with the capitalist system and about the possibilities of corporations to serve the interests of Native communities. Additionally, its failure to adequately address vital sovereignty and subsistence rights engenders conflicts between Native, state, and federal interests that occupy the center of contemporary Alaska Native politics, making these the most actively litigated Native issues.
>
> (385–86)

As for Native Hawaiians, writing at the very end of the twentieth century scholar and activist Haunani-Kay Trask noted:

> Preyed upon by corporate tourism, caught in a political system where we have no separate legal status – unlike other Native peoples in the United States – to control our land base (over a million acres of so-called "trust" lands set aside by Congress for Native beneficiaries but leased by their alleged "trustee," the state of Hawai'i, to non-Natives), we are by every measure the most oppressed of all groups living in Hawai'i, our ancestral land.
>
> (16)

5 See Cheyfitz, *The Poetics of Imperialism*. I argue throughout this book that "property" is a specifically Western term containing within it the Lockean idea of a resource that becomes fungible through the investment of individual labor in it. The Indigenous idea of land and the practice of inhabiting it is decidedly antithetical to the theory and practice of "property" ownership.

6 See, for example, Cajete. "Most Native languages," Cajete tells us,

> do not have a specific word for "animals." Rather, when animals are referred to they are called by their specific names. The fact that there are no specific generic words for animals underlines the extent to which animals were considered to interpenetrate with human life. Animals were partners with humans even when humans were abusive.
>
> (152)

Works cited

Alfred, Taiaiake. "Sovereignty." *Sovereignty Matters: Locations of Contestation and Possibility in Indigenous Struggles for Self-determination.* Ed. Joanne Barker. Lincoln: University of Nebraska Press, 2005. 33–50.

Apess, William. *Eulogy on King Philip*. 1836. Rpt. *On Our Own Grounds: The Complete Writings of William Apess, a Pequot*. Ed. Barry O'Connell. Amherst: University of Massachusetts Press, 1992. 275–310.

Cajete, Gregory. *Native Science*. Santa Fe, NM: Clear Light Publishers, 2000.

Cheyfitz, Eric, ed. *The Columbia Guide to American Indian Literatures of the United States since 1945*. New York: Columbia University Press, 2006.

———. *The Poetics of Imperialism: Translation and Colonization from* The Tempest *to* Tarzan. 1991. Exp. ed. Philadelphia: University of Pennsylvania Press, 1997.

Dauenhauer, Nora Marks. *Life Woven with Song*. Tucson: University of Arizona Press, 2000.

Fatheuer, Thomas. *Buen Vivir: A Brief Introduction to Latin America's New Concepts for the Good Life and the Rights of Nature*. Heinrich Böll Stiftung Publication Series on Ecology. Vol. 17. Berlin: HBS, 2011.

"Global Indigenous Preparatory Conference for the United Nations High Level Plenary Meeting of the General Assembly to be known as the World Conference on Indigenous Peoples 10–12 June 2013, Alta: Alta Outcome Document." Web. Accessed 29 Jan. 2015. http://www.ohchr.org/Documents/Issues/IPeoples/EMRIP/Session6/A.HRC.EMRIP.2013.CRP.2.pdf

Hogan Linda. *Dwellings: A Spiritual History of the Living World*. New York: W.W. Norton & Company, 1995.

Huhndorf, Roy M. & Shari M. Huhndorf. "Alaska Native Politics since the Alaska Native Claims Settlement Act." *South Atlantic Quarterly* 110. 2 (Spring 2011): 385–86.

Hylton, Forrest & Sinclair Thomson. *Revolutionary Horizons: Past and Present in Bolivian Politics*. London: Verso, 2007.

Newcomb, Steven. "The United Nations' High Level Outcome Document." Web. Accessed 16 Jan. 2015. http://indiancountrytodaymedianetwork.com/2014/12/10/united-nations-high-level-outcome-document

Ortiz, Simon J. *Fight Back: For the Sake of the People, For the Sake of the Land*. Albuquerque, NM: INAD Literary Journal. 1. 1 (1980).

"Outcome document of the high-level plenary meeting of the General Assembly known as the World Conference on Indigenous Peoples." 15 September 2014. Web. Accessed 29 Jan. 2015. http://cdn7.iitc.org/wp-content/uploads/2014/10/N1453491-WCIP-FINAL-DOCUMENT-EN_web.pdf

Strong, Pauline Turner. *Captive Selves, Captivating Others: The Politics and Poetics of Colonial American Captivity Narratives*. Boulder, CO: Westview Press, 1999.

Trask, Haunani-Kay. *From a Native Daughter: Colonialism and Sovereignty in Hawai'i*. 1993. Rev. ed. Honolulu: University of Hawai'i Press, 1999.

Vizenor, Gerald. *The Heirs of Columbus*. Hanover, NH: Wesleyan University Press, 1999.

Part III
SOVEREIGNTIES

17

"That We May Stand Up and Walk Ourselves"

Indian Sovereignty and Diplomacy after the Revolutionary War

Tammy Wahpeconiah

Sovereignty is an ideal so inherent in the American psyche that we rarely, if ever, use the term to describe our relational position within and among the nations of the world. To simplify what is not a simple concept, sovereignty is, at its base, the recognition and acknowledgment from other nations. Sovereignty also assumes a freedom from outside control while at the same time understanding that no nation exists in isolation. However, for American Indian peoples, sovereignty is a term fraught with tension, especially as so many Native intellectuals have attempted to specify what sovereignty actually means for tribal nations.[1]

An important aspect of sovereignty for American Indians has always been tied into the ideas of cultural integrity and cultural identity. Tradition and ritual can and do distinguish tribal nations from one another as well as from other nation states, in particular the United States. For tribal peoples, the sense of and commitment to the community is paramount to the continuation of the nation. Therefore, sovereignty is vital to the sustained existence of the group, not just to ensure the rights of the individual.

Although cultural integrity and identity is a significant part of sovereignty for American Indians, we cannot dismiss the real political and legal powers that go along with it. As David Wilkins explains, tribal sovereignty includes "the power to adopt its own form of government; to define the conditions of citizenship/membership in the nations; to regulate the domestic relations of the nations' citizens/members; [and] to administer justice" as well as other political and legal functions (20). These political and legal aspects of tribal sovereignty have been and remain especially important to Native peoples since the coming of Europeans to the North American continent. Around the time of the American Revolution, the notion of tribal sovereignty was highly significant to Native peoples trying to determine their place within this new country and their position relative to the new government. Some Indian nations were being decimated, while others were searching for a new homeland. In the midst of this upheaval, Hendrick Aupaumut, a Mohican sachem, undertook a diplomatic mission that attempted to engender peace between Indian nations living west of the Ohio River and the new American government. His "Narrative of an Embassy to the Western Indians" (1827) portrays tribal leaders who realize what is necessary

205

Historical background

While some historians and literary scholars know of Hendrick Aupaumut, he remains virtually unknown to the larger world, thus his background as well as some Mohican history is beneficial. Captain Hendrick Aupaumut was born in 1757 in Stockbridge, Massachusetts. The Reverend John Sergeant, a Protestant missionary, taught Aupaumut to read, write, and speak English. Aupaumut earned the title of "Captain" during the Revolutionary War, fighting in the Mohican Company under George Washington. Because of his bravery and leadership, Aupaumut earned a commendation from Washington and rose from the rank of private to the rank of captain.

At the end of the Revolutionary War, Aupaumut returned to Stockbridge, Massachusetts where he became sachem, or leader, of the Mohicans. As Alan Taylor explains in his article on Aupaumut, the Mohican tribe should not be confused with the Mohegans of southern New England or James Fenimore Cooper's invented Mohicans. Aupaumut's Mohicans were a combination of Mahicans, Wappingers, and Housatonics who dwelled between the Hudson and Connecticut valleys (Taylor 432). The Mohicans called themselves Muhheakunuk, but both British and Americans referred to them as Mohicans or "Stockbridge Indians."

Aupaumut's grandfather believed that adopting the Protestant religion and English agricultural methods would ensure the tribe's survival. Suffering the derision of neighboring tribes, the Mohicans farmed the land, lived in permanent farmhouses, owned cattle, and sent their children to the Protestant mission school (Taylor 441). Thus, as a third-generation Christian and Stockbridge inhabitant, Aupaumut saw the benefits of adaptation and accommodation.

Although the Mohicans integrated European religious and cultural customs into their everyday lives, the result was not total acculturation. They were able to integrate those European practices and customs that they determined would enrich their lives without turning away from their own customs and traditions. As Taylor states:

> the New Stockbridge Mohicans cherished their distinct identity as a native people. They adopted "white" techniques and beliefs that would help them persist as Mohicans in a changed world – not that they might pass as white men and women. They retained their Algonquian language (while adding English), matrilineal inheritance, clan system, and hereditary chieftainship and much of their folklore. In particular they clung to traditional diplomatic rituals, considering their precise renewal the essence of a native identity.
>
> (441)

One example of Mohican diplomacy is Aupaumut's attempt to convince the Delaware to adopt white farming techniques. In doing so, he was not asking them to forsake their culture, but rather he was working to ensure Indian survival and sovereignty in an increasingly white world.

"THAT WE MAY STAND UP AND WALK OURSELVES"

In June 1791, Timothy Pickering, the United States Indian commissioner, traveled to central New York to meet with potential diplomatic delegates for a mission to the Western tribes. He found the Iroquois wary and unwilling, but received an offer of assistance from the New Stockbridge Mohicans. In a speech to Colonel Pickering, Aupaumut "'offered to effect a western reconciliation as both a sincere friend to the United States' and 'a true friend to the people of my own colour'" (Taylor 435).[2] Aupaumut's knowledge of both Indian and white culture made him a prime candidate for the post of emissary to the Western tribes. However, Aupaumut's offer to Pickering was not based on blind faith in the American government. The Mohicans resented the treatment they had received from New York officials as well as the lack of payment from American officials for Mohican service in the Revolutionary War. In a conversation with Pickering, Aupaumut stated:

> Since the British and Americans lay down their hatchets, then my nation was forgotten. But sometimes I feel sorrow, and shame, that some of my great brothers have forgotten me – that all my services & sufferings have been forgotten – and that I – my nation remain[s] neglected ... Perhaps I am too small to be regarded. My friendship however is strong; my friendship I do not forget.
>
> (qtd. in Taylor 442)[3]

Aupaumut takes the Americans to task for their behavior toward the Mohican nation. Although he questions his people's status with the Americans – "Perhaps I am too small to be regarded" – the sense one gets from his admonishment is one of disappointment in the Americans' behavior. His words are not that of an inferior but of a wise brother who seeks to correct his brother's mistakes. Aupaumut's diplomatic maneuvering is superb. His use of the words *sorrow* and *shame* are more effective than an outright display of anger. Anger may have made Pickering wary, concerned about Aupaumut's reliability in pleading the American cause to Mohican allies. By invoking the emotion of sadness, Aupaumut assures Pickering of his own integrity, while stating his awareness of unfair American treatment toward Indian nations.

In addition, Aupaumut placed the blame for the war between the Western Indians and the American settlers firmly on the shoulders of the settlers. In another speech to Pickering, Aupaumut criticized "the inhuman practices of your people on the frontiers, who ought to have set good examples; but ... these cruel people have kindled the bad fire, and so raised the evil smoke" (qtd. in Taylor 442).[4] Aupaumut clearly states that it is not the Indians who are acting *inhuman*; it is the whites. However, the atrocities begun by the whites, the *bad fire*, could affect more than the nearby tribes. The *evil smoke* can spread even farther, influencing those who are now at peace.

Still, if the situation could not be rectified, if the Americans reneged on their promise, Aupaumut was more than willing to assist the Western tribes in repelling the American settlers. In a speech to the Shawnee, unknown to Pickering and other American officials, Aupaumut concluded, "We now tell you [that] if these people with whom you are at war shall refuse to listen to a just and honourable peace, and remove all obstacles on their part, then we can join with you against them" (qtd. in Taylor 442).[5] These excerpts from Aupaumut's speeches indicate a man with knowledge of political maneuvering. Aupaumut knew where to place the blame for the ongoing troubles along the Ohio frontier and he was not afraid to voice his opinion to Colonel Pickering, or to ensure the Western nations of Mohican support. Furthermore, he let Pickering know that he had not forgotten the payments owed to his tribe for service during the Revolutionary war even if the Americans had forgotten the Mohicans. Of course, Aupaumut wanted to solidify his tribe's position with the Americans, but he also wanted to strengthen the bonds between the Mohicans and their western allies. Therefore, his motives in accepting the mission to the Western tribes were more complicated than just blind loyalty to the Americans.

Aupaumut's report

Aupaumut opens his "Narrative of an Embassy to the Western Indians" explaining why he accepts the mission on behalf of the U.S. government and then explains the connections between his nation and the Western nations. He defines his nation's connections with the Western nations in familial terms, showing Pickering that deep ties connect these nations (Wheeler 203). For example, the Delawares are Grandfathers to the Mohicans; the Monthees are brothers, while the Miamies and the Ottawas are grandchildren. Aupaumut states early on that both the United States and the Western nations were concerned about his ability to negotiate peace; nevertheless, he believes

> that if the Western Nations could be rightly informed of the desires of the United States, they would comply for peace, and that the informer should be an Indian to whom they look upon as a true friend, who has never deceived or injured them.
>
> (76)

Thus, Aupaumut's diplomatic position allows him to understand the position of the United States, while as an Indian he provides the American government a level of access to the Western Nations not necessarily available to a white emissary.

Throughout the report, Aupaumut maintains the sovereignty of both the Western Nations and the United States. When he delivers the United States' message, he does so without prejudice. He condemns the position of neither the United States nor the Western Nations during council meetings. However, he does note his skepticism of the American government and their treatment of Indian nations, his in particular. Aupaumut never encourages the Western Nations to assimilate or acculturate. He does not assume to tell the nations what position they should take. All Aupaumut does is present the words of the U.S. government – he leaves the decision on whether or not to accept these words to the leaders themselves:

> I have delivered you a great Message in your hands, and you must exert yourselves, and consider it seriously – and to remember our children, women, young men, and old people, and take the wisest part; and as I am here with you, I will endeavour to assist you as far as I can.
>
> (95)

Nor does Aupaumut argue that by accepting the terms of the United States, the Indian nations will better themselves. They may better their condition – they will avoid war – but he never assumes to determine their future or undermine their sovereignty.

Aupaumut acknowledges that the United States can help the Indian nations by assisting them, not controlling them, thereby ensuring the sovereignty of the Western nations. As he tells the Delaware, the United States endeavors

> to lift us up the Indians from the ground, that we may stand up and walk ourselves; because we Indians, hitherto have lay flat as it were on the ground, but which we could not see great way; but if we could stand then we could see some distance.
>
> (127)

Aupaumut fully believes in the Indian's ability to control his own destiny, to "stand up and walk ourselves," albeit with some assistance.

Aupaumut's narrative differs from many Indian reports in that he provides us mostly with the Indian voice. The bulk of his narrative is the Western Nations' response to the American offer and to the problems with white settlers. In doing so, Aupaumut challenges the pervasive notion that the only way of survival was through Euroamerican culture. Aupaumut and the Western nations understand and are willing to accept American help "to lift the Indians up," but are determined to "stand up and walk" themselves, to maintain the inherent sovereignty of each nation.

Wampum and the language of diplomacy

In *Indian Giving*, David Murray argues that wampum performs various functions as "currency, ceremonial gift, … and form of writing, or mnemonic system" (120). Because it operates on so many cultural levels, it behooves us to analyze each situation where Aupaumut makes use of wampum. For Aupaumut, and for the Western nations whom he approaches on behalf of the U.S. government, wampum serves as both mnemonic device and ceremonial gift. As mnemonic device, wampum gives Aupaumut "communal authority" to speak as a representative of his people and the U.S. government. Thus, the dialogue between Aupaumut and the Western nations takes on a material reality, a physical presence unfamiliar to American officials. Furthermore, wampum as ceremonial gift becomes a physical manifestation of Aupaumut as leader, in a spiritual, cultural, and economic context. The importance of wampum as a cultural device is evident in Aupaumut's requesting his brother "to fetch [his] bag of peace, in which there is ancient wampom [sic]" before starting out on his journey (78).

We cannot gloss over the significance of this gesture. Aupaumut's presence at the council fires, or his speech alone, is not enough to convince the sachems of the importance of his mission. The idea of diplomacy, the act itself, must be visible to leaders of the Western nations. Aupaumut must present physical proof of the United States' intentions: their desire for peace and their willingness to negotiate the terms of that peace is written in the wampum. In addition, Aupaumut must assert his position as an ally of the Western nations and a worthy advocate for the United States. His bag of peace, then, carries a presence that goes far beyond the symbolic or the imagined. It becomes, in effect, the material presence of peace, the concrete manifestation of the goals Aupaumut attempts to achieve.

As ceremonial gift, the exchange of wampum honors both giver and receiver. However, in this function, wampum can serve as both gift and mnemonic device. For example, when

Aupaumut sends runners to invite the Monthees to the Delaware camp, he sends "three strings of wampum" (84). Thus, the ceremonial gift of wampum illustrates to the Monthees the importance of their attendance to Aupaumut. Furthermore, the wampum serves as mnemonic device informing the Monthees of the importance of Aupaumut's message. This action supports David Murray's argument that wampum "operates as a sort of official seal," and without this seal, Aupaumut's message may not be taken into account (133).

In addition to wampum serving as ceremonial gift and mnemonic device, the giving and receiving of wampum acts as an object of value. It is this value that imbues the wampum with cultural significance. In trade exchanges between Indians and whites, wampum serves as interchangeable currency; however, Aupaumut uses the wampum not only as currency but also as a culturally significant manifestation of the diplomatic act. As Daniel Richter argues, "In both internal politics and external diplomacy, gifts symbolized a close relationship between a leader's roles as a speaker of words, a representative of his kin and followers, and a provider and distributor of economic resources" (qtd. in Murray 135). Wampum, therefore, imbues Aupaumut with the authority to act as representative of the United States and as leader of his nation.

Wampum serves not only as a physical manifestation of diplomacy – as the exchange reveres both speaker and audience – but both parties instill the wampum itself with a belief in its commensurability: the administration of what is morally right must be visible between the United States and the Western tribes. Wampum, then, implies that one good can equal another; and to renege on diplomatic promises demands equal reaction.

One example of the physical manifestation of diplomacy is made evident in one of the first interactions between Aupaumut and the Iroquois. At the very beginning of his journey, Aupaumut meets with members of the Iroquois confederacy, explaining the reasons behind the urgency of his mission as well as the United States' choice of him as intermediary. Before he takes leave of the confederacy, however, Farmers Brother, an Iroquois sachem, asks Aupaumut to deliver a message to the Delaware. Evidently, Iroquois warriors, "led astray by the big knifes," have killed two Delaware.[6] In his message, Farmers Brother apologizes for the actions of these "foolish young men" and reassures the Delaware of their continued alliance. He concludes his speech with the promise to "wipe of [sic] your tears which runs down your cheeks," and he ensures the importance and truth of his statement with five strings of wampum (81). Thus, Aupaumut will deliver to the Delaware material proof of both sorrow and justice as felt by the Iroquois.

For Aupaumut and the Western Tribes, material reality is not only evidenced by the exchange of wampum, speech itself takes on a physical aspect. In a speech by Tautpuhgtheet, a Delaware sachem, to Aupaumut, sorrow and its elimination have a material reality:

> You have come from great way off to see and visit us – you have seen many dismal objects for which your tears droping [sic] down. Our good ancestors did hand down to us a rule or path where we may walk. According to that rule I now wipe off your tears from your eyes and face that you may see clear. And since there has been so much wind on the way that the dust and every evil things did fill your ears, I now put my hand and take away the dust from your ears, that you may hear plain – and also the heavy burden on your mind I now remove, that you may feel easy, and that you may contemplate some objects without burden.
>
> (87)

By invoking a physical act – the wiping of tears and the clearing of ears – Tautpuhgtheet acknowledges Aupaumut's emotional state – his sorrow at seeing so "many dismal objects" – and not so subtly attempts to ensure that Aupaumut will hear and properly respond to Tautpuhgtheet's message. Thus, the acts of seeing, hearing, and thinking become more than just sensate experiences: for all of the nations with whom Aupaumut will come into contact, these sensory acts are manifested physically. Words cannot be misinterpreted because those who are speaking will first "take away the dust" that fills the recipient's ears and remove any "heavy burdens" that may trouble the recipient's mind. In doing so, the speaker ensures that his message will be understood and interpreted correctly.

Although Aupaumut understands Tautpuhgtheet's actions, he also is aware that diplomatic offers from the United States to the Western nations have been either misinterpreted or ignored. Therefore, he couches the words given to him by the U.S. government in physical terms: "It has been feared that our word of peace has not reached your ears, but has fallen and been buried under ground, or gone into the air by means of malignant birds" (93). Words, therefore, have a physical life of their own. They carry a materiality that, if not received correctly, may result in their being entombed in the ground or snatched away in transit by "malignant birds."

Reading Aupaumut's narrative, we can see that, for Aupaumut and the Western nations, the language of diplomacy does have a material reality, a physical presence that does not exist in the Euroamerican language of diplomacy. Furthermore, the exchange of wampum is the transmogrification of words into object, a transmogrification that ensures understanding between the conversants. The language of diplomacy carries with it a weight that cannot be easily dismissed. Acts, such as Aupaumut's, became more than just an exchange of words that could be easily forgotten when considered to be no longer beneficial. Long after the speeches had ended and the council fires had been extinguished, those present had material proof of what had occurred.

Indian politics and the language of diplomacy

Hendrick Aupaumut was not the United States' first choice as emissary to the Western nations. Henry Knox had hoped to convince either Joseph Brant or the Seneca chief, Red Jacket, to deliver the Americans' message to the Western nations as both men were well known to the Americans and the Indian nations. In addition, other nations opposed Aupaumut as it placed the Mohicans in a position of some authority. Aupaumut responds to the Mohawks who disapproved of his election as an emissary to the Western tribes, stating that the "principal chiefs of the Five Nations" opposed his mission, contending "that it would be folly for the United States to send [him] on that business ... the Western Nations will not regard the voice of One Nation – but the business ought to be negotiated by the Five Nations and the British" (76). It is likely that Aupaumut's critic was Joseph Brant, the Mohawk sachem, who repeatedly attempts to undermine Aupaumut's mission. Brant's connection with the British and the powerful Iroquois confederacy placed him in a formidable position, factors of which Aupaumut was well aware.

Although the Five Nations greatly outnumbered the Mohicans, Aupaumut fell back on his tribe's history as diplomats and negotiators. Aupaumut alludes to the honor and integrity of the Mohicans in their dealings with other tribes, implying that the Mohawks could not be trusted implicitly. As he remarks: "... the informer should be an Indian to whom they look upon as a true friend, who has never deceived or injured them" (76). He will remind the Western tribes, later in the narrative, of the Mohawks' past deception:

> But you look back and see heaps of your bones, wherein the Mauquas [Mohawks] have deceived you repeat[ed]ly. I think I could have good reason to tell you not to believe the Message or words of the Mohawks, for they will deceive you greatly as Usual – but I forebear.
>
> (129)

Without directly naming Brant, Aupaumut implies that Brant and the Mohawks are untrustworthy and deceitful, and therefore, because of their connection with Brant, the British cannot be trusted.

That Aupaumut should begin his narrative with a retort to Brant's criticism is very telling. His concerns are not with American apprehension over his ability, but rather with the Western Indians' perception of his people as loyal friends. However, we must remember that Aupaumut writes this narrative in English for American officials and it will likely never be seen by any Indian. Why, then, does he make this statement? When the Americans decided that Brant was unreliable because of his connection with the British, the government still wanted another sachem from the powerful Iroquois confederacy. In putting himself forward as a candidate for the emissary position, Aupaumut was invoking the Mohican past as intercultural brokers. The United States had a skewed conception of Iroquois influence and Aupaumut sought to convince the Americans of the benefits of a Mohican/American alliance.

In his second paragraph, Aupaumut shrewdly refers to Mohican diplomacy and his support of the United States' peace efforts: "... I conclude that I could acquaint them my best knowledge with regard of the dispositions, desires, and might of the United States, without partiality ..." (76). Aupaumut is able to *acquaint* the Western tribes with the intentions of the United States because his knowledge encompasses both white and Native American culture and language. He is telling his readers – Henry Knox, Timothy Pickering – that his familiarity with the United States runs deep enough to enable Aupaumut to articulate the moods and aspirations of the American government. Coming immediately after Brant's criticism, Aupaumut implies that American officials could not expect this depth of knowledge from one whose loyalties lay with the British.

Aware of his American audience, Aupaumut then proceeds to narrate the Mohicans' diplomatic history. He explains that the connections with the Western tribes are old friendships established by his "forefathers" (76). As mentioned earlier, Aupaumut describes all connections in familial terms. Using labels such as *grandfather, nephew, uncle,* and *brother,* Aupaumut allows his readers insight into the hierarchical nature of intertribal relationships. Besides laying bare the structure of these relationships, Aupaumut's specific portrayals of those relationships further enhance his position as emissary. As he states at the end of this description, "It was the business of our fathers to go around the towns of these nations to renew the agreements between them, and tell them many things which they discover among the white people in the east, &c" (78). This statement illustrates that this diplomatic mission was a continuing vocation for the Mohican people.

"THAT WE MAY STAND UP AND WALK OURSELVES"

When Aupaumut meets with the Delaware and the Shawnee, four British delegates are present, including Captain Elliot, who is an associate of Joseph Brant. In one speech, Aupaumut makes a subtle comparison between the Americans and the British, a comparison which shows the British in an unfavorable light. Aupaumut tells the Delaware sachem that the Mohican nation lives in peace with the Americans and "that the great men of the United States wished to live in peace with all Indians ..." (89). He then goes on to state that "there are some wars among the great people over the waters – and that negroes also have cut off many of their masters – which the Indians [are] glad to hear ..." (89). Aupaumut is referring to a slave uprising in a British colony in the Caribbean (Tanner 32). In bringing this information up, he compares the United States' treatment of Indians to the British treatment of those living in British colonies.

The following day, in a council session, Aupaumut uses the Mohican position as cultural emissary to explain his reasons for his intervention on behalf of the Americans. During this speech, he reveals the unfair treatment from the Americans toward his nation:

> In order to have you to understand our business, I will acquaint you some things of our situation, lest you may have wrong apprhensions [sic]. Since the British and Amaricans [sic] lay down their hatchets, then my nation was forgotten. We never have had invitation to set in Council with the white people – not as the Five Nations and you are greatly regarded by the white people – but last winter was the first time I had invitation from the great man of the United States to attend Council in Philladelphia [sic]. According to that invitation I went – and after we arrived at Philadelphia, I find that the business was for the wellfare [sic] of all nations – and then I was asked whether I would carry a message of peace to you here. I then reply that I would – for I know that it would look unfriendly to you, had I refuse[d] to bring good tidings, and for the sake of our good friendship, and for peace, I was willing to take this long journey, &c.
>
> (92)

Clearly, Aupaumut wants the Western tribes to understand that he is not acting as a pawn for the U.S. government. He brings up his grievances with the Americans to illustrate that any misplaced loyalty has not blinded his perceptions regarding them. Furthermore, Aupaumut uses this statement as a deliberate reminder to his American readers that he expects something in return for his efforts. This statement also serves to inform Knox, Pickering and others that he is cognizant of their failure to fulfill their promises.

Furthermore, he lets the Americans know of his disappointment in there not being a voluntary meeting between his people and the U.S. government. He tells the Shawnee and the Delaware, and therefore the Americans, that he approached the whites, not the other way around. Had he not volunteered for this mission, it is likely that the Mohicans never would have sat down with the Americans in council. In addition, he states that he was quick to respond to the Americans' invitation. Aupaumut concludes his opening with yet another reminder of the diplomatic past of the Mohican people.

At this point in the narrative, near the halfway point, Aupaumut delivers the speech of the U.S. government. He refers to them as the *15 sachems* and the *15 United Sachems*, respectively. Within the speech Aupaumut, speaking for the Americans, explains that he was chosen because he is of their "own colar" [sic] and because he will "faithfully" and "impartially" deliver to them the "dispositions of the United States" (93). Again, Aupaumut reassures the Indians, through the voice of the U.S. government, that his loyalty lies with his own people. The United States assures the Indians that they will deal with the "big knives" and will remove the forts standing on their lands if the Western tribes call in their war parties and agree to a treaty regarding settlement along the Ohio River. Hobakon, the Delaware sachem, agrees to deliver the United States' message back to the nations (Wyandots, Ottawas, Chippewas, etc.) and encourages those present to accept the terms.

Aupaumut continues onto the Forks, the meeting of the Maumee and Au Glaize rivers, where he meets with Big Cat, another Delaware sachem. It is here, once again, where Brant and the British confront Aupaumut's mission. However, it is not Aupaumut who answers the charges regarding his expedition. Captain Elliot, the British emissary, makes the mistake of questioning Big Cat about Aupaumut's diplomatic position. Although the Algonquian nations depended heavily on British aid for food and other supplies, Big Cat tells Aupaumut of a severe rebuke he gives to Elliot for overstepping his boundaries:

> Then I replied, how came you to ask us such questions? Did you ever see me at Detroit or Niagara, in your councils, and there to ask you where such and such white man come from? or what is their Business? Can you watch, and look all around the earth to see who come to us? or is what their Business? Do you not know that we are upon our own Business? and that we have longed to see our friends, who now come to us, and for which we rejoice?
>
> (103)

Aupaumut then says that Elliot was silenced and all the other Indians who were present "laughed at him to scorn" (103). His reasons for recounting this incident are varied. Big Cat's defense illustrates Aupaumut's reputation as a diplomat. It also shows the Americans that the British hold on the Western nations was precarious. Furthermore, Aupaumut is able to portray his defeat of Brant and the British who had plagued him throughout his mission.

As the narrative nears the end, Aupaumut lists the Indian arguments against accepting the terms for peace and his refutations of those arguments. He blames the deceit of white people on British law, stating that the laws have changed with the American victory over the British. The Indian confederacy recounts numerous tales of deceit and murder perpetrated by the "big knives." Aupaumut argues that the "big knives" should not be confused with the American officials. To support his argument, he says "if the great men of the United States have the like principal [sic] or disposition as the Big Knifes had, My nation and other Indians in the East would been along ago anihilated [sic]. But they are not so" (127). He asks the confederacy to look at the actions of the United States so that they may see the difference between the American officials and the white settlers.

Aupaumut goes on to say that the British do not want the Indians to be self-sufficient; rather they want to "cover them with blanket and shirt every fall, and the Indians feel themselves warm, and esteem that usage very high – therefore they remain as it were on the ground and could not see great way these many years" (127). In contrast, the Americans want to lift the Indians off the ground so "that we may stand up and walk ourselves" (127). Aupaumut believes that British affiliation would lead to stagnation, but an alliance with the Americans would lead to growth among the Indian nations.

However, in an address to his American audience Aupaumut states that he did not tell the Indians the complete tale of his dealings with white people:

> In all my arguments with these Indians, I have as it were oblige to say nothing with regard of the conduct of Yorkers, how they cheat my fathers, how they taken our lands Unjustly, and how my fathers were groaning as it were to their graves, in loseing [sic] their lands for nothing, although they were faithful friends to the Whites; and how the white people artfully got their Deeds confirm in their Laws, &c. I say had I mention these things to the Indians, it would agravate [sic] their prejudices against all white people, &c.
>
> (128)

With this statement, Aupaumut demonstrates how strong is his desire for peace. He is willing to hold back information from his "family" so that war can be averted. The above excerpt also shows Aupaumut's shrewdness in diplomatic circles. He and the American officials know that such information could destroy any chance of a peaceful settlement. Therefore, it would behoove the Americans to amend any problems that exist between the State of New York and the Mohican tribe.

Conclusion

Aupaumut's mission was thought to be a success and he accompanied a U.S. delegation that was to meet with the Indian confederacy at Lake Erie in the summer of 1793. However, the attempt to reach an agreement failed when the confederacy demanded that the United States remove all settlers and forts from the Ohio country and designated the Ohio River as the boundary (Taylor 449). In the summer of 1794, the American army advanced upon the confederacy and defeated the Indians at Fallen Timbers on August 20, 1794.

Although the United States would increasingly turn to white men for its diplomatic missions, Aupaumut's narrative stands as a singular text within the genre of the Indian report with its detailed look at Indian diplomatic rituals. Aupaumut fought to ensure survival not only for the Mohican people, but also for numerous other Indian nations. His narrative displays the struggle within a man determined to survive as an Indian in an increasingly white world. Through this work, we are able to see a man who strongly believed in Indian sovereignty.

Furthermore, Aupaumut's narrative allows us to understand the ways in which Native Americans viewed the language of diplomacy and justice. For Aupaumut and the sachems of the Western nations, language has an objective reality that is absent in the Euroamerican language of diplomacy and justice. Commensurability is evident in the exchange of wampum and in the physical gestures that accompany diplomatic speech. We can see, therefore, the need to use Native American modes of diplomacy and sovereignty to understand the political moves tribal people made to ensure their survival.

Notes

1 For example, see Forbes 14; Davies & Clow; Cobb; Alfred; Wilkins & Lomawaima; Wilkins; Deloria & Lytle.
2 Aupaumut, Speech, 20 June 1791, in Pickering, Newtown Point Council Journal, Timothy Pickering Papers, Massachusetts Historical Society, vol. 61, item 200. Spelling in this, and all subsequent quotations, has not been corrected.
3 Aupaumut, Speech, 20 June 1791, in Pickering, Newtown Point Council Journal, Timothy Pickering Papers, Massachusetts Historical Society, vol. 60, item 70.
4 Aupaumut, Speech, 20 June 1791, in Pickering, Newtown Point Council Journal, Timothy Pickering Papers, Massachusetts Historical Society, vol. 60, item 70.
5 Aupaumut, Speech to the Shawnees, quoted in Sergeant, Journal, 9 June 1791, Society for Propagating the Gospel among the Indians and Others in North America, Box 1, Massachusetts Historical Society.
6 In the familial terms by which various nations refer to one another, members of the Iroquois confederacy act as "uncles" to both the Delaware and to Aupaumut's Mohican nation.

Works cited

Alfred, Taiaike. "Sovereignty." *A Companion to American Indian History*. Ed. Philip Deloria & Neal Salisbury. New York: Blackwell, 2004. 460–74.

Aupaumut, Hendrick. "Narrative of an Embassy to the Western Indians." *Memoirs of the Historical Society of Pennsylvania* 2 (1827): 76–131.

Cobb, Amanda J. "Understanding Tribal Sovereignty: Definitions, Conceptualizations, and Interpretations." *American Studies* 46. 3/4 (2005): 115–32.

Davies, Wade & Richmond L. Clow, *American Indian Sovereignty and Law: An Annotated Bibliography*. Lanham, MD: Scarecrow Press, 2009.

Deloria, Vine, Jr. & Clifford M. Lytle. *The Nations Within: The Past and Future of American Indian Sovereignty*. New York: Pantheon Books, 1984.

Forbes, Jack. "Intellectual Self-determination and Sovereignty: Implications for Native Studies and for Native Intellectuals." *Wicazo Sa Review* 13. 1 (1998): 11–24.

Murray, David. *Indian Giving: Economies of Power in Indian–White Exchanges*. Amherst: University of Massachusetts Press, 2000.

Tanner, Helen Hornbeck. "The Glaize in 1792." *Ethnohistory* 25 (1978): 15–39.

Taylor, Alan. "Captain Hendrick Aupaumut." *Ethnohistory* 43 (1996): 431–57.

Wheeler, Rachel. "Hendrick Aupaumut: Christian-Mahican Prophet." *Journal of the Early Republic* 25. 2 (2005): 187–220.

Wilkins, David. *American Indian Sovereignty and the U.S. Supreme Court: The Masking of Justice*. Austin: University of Texas Press, 1997.

Wilkins, David & K. Tsianina Lomawaima, *Uneven Ground: American Indian Sovereignty and Federal Law*. Norman: University of Oklahoma Press, 2001.

18

"What Can I Tell Them That They Will Hear?"

Environmental Sovereignty and American Indian Literature

Lee Schweninger

Confronted with a non-Native legal system and the denial of the legitimacy of Indigenous knowledge, the narrator in Linda Hogan's novel *Power* (1998) ranges through her mind looking for a way to share her knowledge with the non-Taiga (a fictional tribe) members of the courtroom that would help them understand the killing of a Florida panther for which her friend and mentor Ama is on trial: "what can I tell them that they will hear?" the young woman asks herself. And by way of response, she suggests (again to herself) that "in the swamps that surround them, their houses, their children, an older world exists, a hungry panther, a woman who doesn't think like them" (131). In the contexts of land rights and Indigenous sovereignty suggested by such a moment in the novel, this chapter investigates the connective lines between literature and environmental issues in parallel with ideas of Indigenous sovereignty and Indigenous knowledge, including Native notions of access to and control of resources, preservation of sacred sites, and of retaining or regaining a homeland more generally. The chapter thus looks at different types of literature by several different American Indian writers, arguing in part that the loss of homelands and the concurrent Indigenous resistance to colonization are often critical underlying features of American Indian works of fiction. This chapter investigates such writers as Linda Hogan (Chickasaw), Gerald Vizenor (Anishinaabe), and Leslie Marmon Silko (Laguna Pueblo), arguing that these writers articulate a sense of self-determination and revitalized notions of intellectual sovereignty, which in turn have to some extent morphed into implied, if not reasserted, land claims and Indigenous environmental activism.

As a number of scholars have argued, the West's general unwillingness to accept the validity of what has come to be called Indigenous knowledge is inseparable from the colonial enterprise in general; that is to say, the dominant, mainstream attitude toward Indigenous knowledge is indicative of a colonial attitude toward Indigenous peoples and their political rights, their sovereignty, and their individual cultures. In representing and insisting on the validity of alternative Indigenous viewpoints, in contrast, American Indian writers can be seen to take part in a form of decolonization, insisting on sovereignty and intellectual property rights. As Anishinaabe scholar Deborah McGregor maintains, the "recognition of Indigenous Knowledge coincides with the increasing assertion by

Indigenous people of their rights and the recognition of these rights by the international community" (389). The rights concern intellectual property, of course, and thus have to do with forms of sovereignty. First Nations writer and activist Leanne Simpson (Mississauga Nishnaagbeg) states the connections between recognition of intellectual property, sovereignty, and environmental degradation bluntly: "Our knowledge comes from the land, and the destruction of the environment is a colonial manifestation and a direct attack on Indigenous Knowledge and Indigenous nationhood" (377). Furthermore, she argues, "Recovering and maintaining Indigenous worldviews, philosophies, and ways of knowing and applying those teachings in a contemporary context represent a web of liberation strategies Indigenous Peoples can employ to disentangle themselves from the oppressive control of colonizing state governments" (373).

In these contexts, then, this chapter attempts to trace the links between Indigenous environmental sovereignty and Western versus non-Western ways (specifically Indigenous North American ways) of imagining the environment and understanding the "resources" of the natural world as those links show up in Native American fiction. I suggest that different Native American writers advocate the importance of challenging and simultaneously harmonizing Western scientific world views and Native ontological and epistemological schemes. In so doing, their literature takes steps in the process of decolonization, steps which are arguably also toward regaining or reasserting forms of sovereignty.

Although this is not an essay on Indigenous knowledge, as such, it is important to offer a definition and to pause a moment on an articulation of its connection with settler culture. Simply put, Indigenous knowledge combines the knowledges that Indigenous peoples hold and practice worldwide, practices these peoples have in some cases held, developed, and practiced for millennia. Oneida writer Pamela Colorado, who is credited with coining the phrase "Indigenous Science," maintains that Indigenous knowledge results from a science that effectively "synthesizes information from the mental, physical, social and cultural/historical realms" (50). In his book *Native Science*, Tewa Pueblo writer Gregory Cajete defines Native science as "a metaphor for a wide range of tribal processes of perceiving, thinking, acting, and 'coming to know' that have evolved through human experience with the natural world" (2). He also asserts that "Coming-to-know is the goal of Indigenous science, a different goal from that of Western science" (81). That Indigenous knowledge is defined in contrast to a Western world view makes manifest its integral connection with the colonial legacy. Dakota writer and activist Waziyatawin Angela Wilson argues that

> recovery of Indigenous knowledge is a conscious and systematic effort to revalue that which has been denigrated and revive that which has been destroyed. It is about regaining the ways of being that allowed our peoples to live a spiritually balanced, sustainable existence within our ancient homelands for thousands of years.
> (359)

Given its insistence on a connection with the colonial enterprise, it is no surprise that Indigenous science has its detractors among academics in the mainstream. According to David Gordon and Shepard Krech in the introduction to their book-length collection of essays, for example, Indigenous knowledge "offers an alternative to the power-knowledge nexus of Western thought, and yet it introduces its own modalities of power" (1). The authors do acknowledge, however, that "Native Americans developed IKs to preserve access to resources and to defend cultural and religious identities when faced with colonial violence" (15).

Where the mainstream has been interested in Indigenous knowledge, it has been primarily to extract specific knowledge that might be immediately helpful for particular Western enterprises. Simpson makes this point in an interview with Naomi Klein:

> Extraction and assimilation go together. Colonialism and capitalism are based on extracting and assimilating. My land is seen as a resource. My relatives in the plant and animal worlds are seen as resources. My culture and knowledge is a resource. ... That's always been a part of colonialism and conquest. Colonialism has always extracted the indigenous – extraction of indigenous knowledge, indigenous women, indigenous peoples.
>
> (Klein n. pag.)

As Deborah McGregor puts it, there is "a lack of respect for traditional knowledge," and thus "For Aboriginal people this issue presents a rather disturbing dilemma: they wish to share knowledge, but the context has changed and knowledge now has to be protected to avoid exploitation" (397). The interchange does not necessarily have to be confrontational, however, argue Clifford Trafzer, Willard Sakiestewa Gilbert, and Anthony Madrigal: "Using cultural science or an integrated scientific approach ... can provide valuable insights, augmenting Western science with cultural knowledge" (1850). Because of the lack of appreciation and cooperation on the part of mainstream Western science and the perceived incompatibility of Indigenous knowledges with that science, a colonial power dynamic lingers and festers. In her essay "Anticolonial Strategies for the Recovery and Maintenance of Indigenous Knowledge," Simpson writes of the inextricable link between colonial power and lack of respect for Indigenous knowledge:

> The depoliticizing of Indigenous Peoples and TEK [Traditional Environmental Knowledge] serves to make the discussion of TEK more palatable to scientists by sanitizing it of the ugliness of colonization and injustice, so scientists can potentially engage with the knowledge but not the people who own and live that knowledge.
>
> (376)

In an effort to bridge the apparent gap between differing world views, Pat Lauderdale suggests that Indigenous knowledge cannot necessarily

> provide all the answers to current environmental problems; however it can provide *us* with ideas about how to improve *our* questions and, therefore, improve *our* potential to provide more equitable, less oppressive structures from which to approach numerous problems.
>
> (1842, my emphasis)

Even though Lauderdale creates a grammatical us–them dichotomy that implicitly reinforces the power dynamic divide between the two systems of thought, he does nevertheless argue importantly that ideas in general might be more important than specific applications.

The stress on idea or principle can be seen as a transformative consideration in the context of intellectual property rights and sovereignty.

As suggested at the outset, a brief discussion of a central issue in Linda Hogan's novel *Power* (1998) provides the groundwork for the larger issue under discussion in this chapter in that the novel deals directly with the links between Indigenous knowledge, tribal sovereignty, and both spiritual and literal survival. The novel's basic plot is easily recounted: the young Tiaga woman, sixteen-year-old Omishto, visits her tribal elder friend Ama, shelters with her during a hurricane, and accompanies her as she hunts down and kills a Florida panther. She then serves as a witness during the subsequent court trial of Ama who is accused of killing the Florida panther, a member of an endangered species. In the course of the trial, Hogan raises the issue of legality (read sovereignty) coupled with a notion of Indigenous knowledge.

On the one hand, Ama's killing of the panther is guaranteed as "a treaty right," as one of the tribal elders argues: "He says it is right, by treaty, all our rights" (132). That is a truth. But, as Omishto realizes, "Inside marble halls there's another kind of truth and it lies down over everything" (135). Ironically, however, the lack of a verdict, ultimately, suggests that the mainstream is simply unable to comprehend a different point of view. Dilek Direnc argues that, according to her reading of the novel, "America can be remade" only so long as "it remains open to the contributions of Native Americans and their diverse cultural traditions" (52). But that openness, of course, does not seem to exist among the mainstream characters in Hogan's novel. As Jesse Peters points out, the "non-Indian participants in their center of European American power become the tourists so fascinated with their own definitions that they exclude Ama from meaningful dialectic interaction" (115). In excluding Ama and failing or refusing to understand her world view, they deny her standing, unable to recognize either her intellectual or her political sovereignty.

Thus, what's important in the context of Indigenous sovereignty as presented in this novel is that Hogan makes manifest and insists on the gap between a sovereignty based on treaty rights and the mainstream's inability or unwillingness to comprehend and respect such rights. This neglect is coupled with or is a result of a concurrent disrespect for Indigenous ways of seeing the world. Hogan's narrator makes overt the connections between colonialism and cultural disrespect when she links the "legal" history of loss of land and a tribal woman standing trial for violating a law that should actually be protected as a treaty right. As Omishto realizes, "it was in this very building of power that our land and lives were signed away not that long ago" (136). With this one sentence Hogan is able to link the loss of land and sovereignty with the inability of the mainstream to appreciate other ways of knowing; that is, with any sort of Indigenous knowledge, a knowledge embodied in the very complex reasons that Ama had for killing the panther in the first place.

A similar understanding of the relationships between Indigenous knowledge, sovereignty, and decolonization is evident in *Ceremony* (1977), the first novel by Laguna Pueblo writer Leslie Marmon Silko. According to Adrienne Akins, for instance, "Through its representation of various ways of knowing and its exposé of the dangers of science divorced from ethical concerns, *Ceremony* challenges the conception that Western science has a monopoly on truth" (8). This separation of science and technology from ethical concerns is evident in Silko's references to assimilation efforts through Indian education, as Akins stresses, but it is also very prominent through Silko's depictions of the uranium mining and the development and detonation of the atomic bomb during the Second World War.

"WHAT CAN I TELL THEM THAT THEY WILL HEAR?"

Shamoon Zamir notes the appropriateness of Silko's setting and of her use of the uranium mine for the novel's climactic scene, pointing out that the Four Corners area (Navajo and Pueblo land, that is) was to be designated a National Sacrifice Area; land, in short, which would be made uninhabitable. Accordingly, the "effect of this global and sacrificial penetration in *Ceremony* is a state in which local cultural codes are either totally erased or radically dislocated and distorted" (Zamir 399). Meanwhile, according to Bruce Johansen, beginning in the 1940s Native American "miners hauled radioactive uranium ore out of the earth as if it [were] coal" (Johansen 393). The ore was mined with total disregard for any and all health hazards associated with the radioactive waste.

When in the nineteenth century many of the reservations were being set up by the federal government, the United States was still primarily an agrarian nation. Logically then, the reservations were established on lands that were essentially unfit for agriculture; that is, on lands for which the members of the mainstream settler culture thought they had no use. Dry, rocky, arid land that without serious irrigation would hardly be missed by the European-American settlers looking for land to farm (or briefly, but repeatedly, land to mine for its gold or other precious metals). Within a few decades, however, those same "desert" lands became extremely valuable for the minerals they contained deep within; gold and silver, of course; but also oil, coal, and – in the context of Silko's novel – uranium. The sad irony is that although the land was given in perpetuity to the tribes forced to settle there, rarely did those tribes retain the mineral rights to that land. (A noteworthy exception, of course, would be the Osage in Oklahoma whose land was discovered to be oil rich.) The Laguna Pueblo, for example, leased their lands to corporations such as the Kerr-McGee Company, and members of the tribe then worked the mines. As Winona LaDuke puts it, major mining companies came to the Southwest and elsewhere and established a plethora of mining agreements: "While the federal government had a trust responsibility to protect the interest of the tribes, those interests were pretty much disregarded. ... [T]he disparities are widely recognized as vast environmental injustices" (36).

In the midst of the environmental and social injustices resulting from mining on Pueblo land, Silko sets the climax of her novel at an abandoned uranium mine, where her Pueblo character Tayo makes the connections between uranium mining, exploitation of natural resources, environmental degradation, and an individual's mental health – and these in turn are coupled with the land itself and with "the fate of all living things" (*Ceremony* 258). As he stands at the site of the mine, Tayo has an epiphany of sorts:

> He had been so close to it, caught up in it for so long that its simplicity struck deep inside his chest: Trinity Site, where they exploded the first atomic bomb, was only three hundred miles to the southeast, at White Sands. And the top-secret laboratories where the bomb had been created were deep in the Jemez Mountains, on land the Government took from Cochiti Pueblo: Los Alamos, only a hundred miles northeast of him now, still surrounded by high electric fences and the ponderosa pine and tawny sandrock of the Jemez mountain canyon where the shrine of the twin mountain lions had always been. There was no end to it; it knew no boundaries. He had arrived at the point of convergence where the fate of all living things, and even the earth, had been laid.
>
> (257–58)

James Tarter argues that this scene in the novel provides Silko "the ground for the articulation of a demand for environmental justice" (98). And indeed, in the context of environmental degradation and lack of tribal sovereignty, the passage is worth quoting at length as a close reading will demonstrate. The idea of a place that is "top-secret" yet on Pueblo land implies both the loss of land and the lack of sovereignty. And indeed the land has been taken from the Cochiti Pueblo people; that is, as Silko insists, the land has been stolen. Like the mine tailings themselves, the government facility is deep within the mountains, and the phrase recalls an image a few paragraphs earlier, in which Tayo notices the bitter taste of the water. He refers to the "sandstone and dirt they had taken from inside the mesa" as earth that is "piled in mounds, in long rows, like fresh graves" (256). These graves, of course, both foreshadow and echo mention of the victims of the atomic bomb: "victims who had never known these mesas, who had never seen the delicate colors of the rocks which boiled up their slaughter" (258). The passage also juxtaposes pine trees with the electric fences at Los Alamos; that is, it opposes life with death. The fences at Los Alamos mirror the barbed wire left behind at the site of the abandoned uranium mine where Tayo stands: "They left behind only the barbed-wire fences, the watchman's shack, and the hole in the earth" (256). Readers will immediately recognize the danger the watchman connotes:

> "Something is wrong," he said
> "Ck'o'yo magic won't work
> if someone is watching us."
>
> (259)

The passage also juxtaposes the mainstream world of science, technology, and destruction with the world of legend, story, and the history of the Pueblo people; that is, the electric fences and the site itself are not only on stolen land, they are at the shrines of the legendary twin mountain lions.

In this sense, then, the land can be seen as both literal and as "an *ideological or epistemological* 'ground' where differing concepts of 'ownership' are capable of writing over Native narratives of identity, belonging, and physical presence" (Holm 263). It is just this sort of loss of identity or search for identity in a disrupted social world that motivates the plot of the novel. Tayo and his cousin Rocky go to war in the first place because they have been stripped of their ideological ground as well as their Native land:

> They had seen what the white people had made from the stolen land. ... Every day they had to look at the land, from horizon to horizon, and every day the loss was with them; it was the dead unburied, and the mourning of the loss going on forever. So they tried to sink the loss in booze, and silence their grief with war stories about their courage, defending the land they had already lost.
>
> (178)

Tayo's awareness of the paradox in this instance highlights the connection with issues of sovereignty, and such a passage implies the socio-economic pressures on the Laguna people to accept the mine (or the war) that is imposed on them. It is in a sense their sovereign status that sets them up as vulnerable to mining companies looking for cheap labor and lax environmental standards. But ironically, of course, benefits are short-lived and are vastly outweighed by subsequent environmental devastation. In "Police Zones: Territory and Identity in Leslie Marmon Silko's *Ceremony*," Karen Piper argues that Native American sovereignty is always and already diminished:

> While reservations have been technically granted "sovereignty," it is sovereignty only under the umbrella of U.S. protectionism. So even where Indians have occupied the same land, the mental mappings of cultural patterns that established the perception of the landscape have been reorganized.
>
> (487)

Silko's novel is thus a veritable testing ground for issues of sovereignty set against capitalism, exploitative enterprise, environmental degradation, international conflict, and the federal government itself.

In Silko's novel, the unconventional medicine man, Betonie, explains the location of his hogan this way: "They keep us on the north side of the railroad tracks, next to the river and their dump. Where none of them want to live" (123). Although the dump to which Betonie refers is not necessarily a toxic or hazardous site, several communities in New Mexico have storied histories concerning uranium mining and the waste the industry produces (see Johanson 396–97). Otherwise, however, the link between Silko's novelistic exploration between the fact of stolen land and the lack of tribal sovereignty may perhaps be more obvious, more overt than what one sees in a writer like Gerald Vizenor (Anishinaabeg), but Vizenor too presents characters who are environmentally aware as well as fully cognizant of their status vis-à-vis the U.S. nation state. In the story "Landfill Meditation" (1991), for example, the character Martin Bear Charme both confronts and capitalizes on the country's propensity for creating trash, garbage, solid waste, and swill: "we are culture bound to be clean, but being clean is a delusion, a separation from our trash and the visual energies of the earth" (105). Bear Charme's philosophy contrasts starkly with the platitudes and clichés (the terminal creeds) mouthed by the character Belladonna. "We are tribal," she claims, "and that means that we are children of dreams and visions. Our bodies are connected to mother earth" (109). Belladonna insists that "tribal people are closer to the earth, to the meaning and energies of the woodlands and mountains and plains" (111). Bear Charme opposes the terminal creeds Belladonna espouses, and his comments seem just paradoxical and elusive enough to be worthy of their trickster creator, Vizenor himself.

Martin Bear Charme "made his fortune hauling trash and filling wetlands with urban swill and solid waste. ... Now his lush refuse reservation ... is worth millions" (100–01). After this introduction Vizenor raises, in a single sentence, the issues of sovereignty and environmentalism, issues which are particularly pertinent in the context of environmental degradation associated with waste disposal: "Charme has petitioned the federal government for recognition as a sovereign meditation nation" (101). The passage is deeply ironic. There is of course the irony of needing permission for sovereignty, but that is the case anyway. Native sovereignty depends on the will of the U.S. federal government, which has a history of granting or refusing recognition and thus the status of "domestic dependent nations." The passage also evokes the issue of certain tribal governments actually inviting waste disposal on reservation lands as a means of making money. The passage thereby also implies the sometimes uninvited use of tribal land for waste disposal.

The pertinence of the passage in the context of environmental issues is immediately apparent, and the idea of the ecocide of American Indians has been in circulation for several decades. In *Changes in the Land* (1983) William Cronon discusses the changes in early New England that had immediate adverse effects on Native Americans environmental practices, and in *Ecocide of Native America* Donald Grinde and Bruce Johansen argue that ecocide has long been partner to the colonial enterprise. One can certainly see this in the context of waste dumps on reservations. As recently as 2011 there were "more than 650 sites where solid waste is stored on Indian lands and proposals to construct hazardous waste facilities on those reservations are underway." Furthermore, "almost all waste sites on reservations are classified as open dumps." In addition to the "legal" dumping or storing of waste on tribal lands, there is also a "proliferation of open, illegal dumping on reservations" (432, 433). Overarching all of these immediate and concrete issues is the lingering question of the role that environmental racism plays in industries' targeting of Indian reservations as sites for waste disposal. As A. Cassidy Sehgal writes in "Indian Tribal Sovereignty and Waste Disposal Regulation," some argue that "building waste facilities on reservations is motivated by industries which desire to exploit the economic situation of tribes and the current loopholes in environmental law regarding regulation of the tribal environment" (434). According to Kevin Kamps, in an effort to find disposal sites for nuclear waste, the U.S. government "sent letters to every federally recognized tribe in the country, offering hundreds of thousands and even millions of dollars to tribal council governments for first considering and then ultimately hosting the dump" (Kamps n. pag.). Such a focused and specific targeting of American Indians as potential "clients" clearly suggests environmental racism. The targeting takes full advantage of the notion of tribal sovereignty and at the same time threatens it. Toxic waste cannot go unregulated, of course, and the regulations impose limitations on sovereignty. According to Sehgal, for instance, the

> extent of tribal sovereignty has … dramatically changed over the course of the last 150 years, with promises of recognition of tribal self-determination today juxtaposed against the broad federal regulatory power of the past. The evolution of the federal/Indian relationship reveals how the motivations and impacts of the law have often been contradictory and inconsistent, usually resulting in harm to the tribes.
>
> (435)

Another irony inherent in the Vizenor passage, quoted above, is evident in that Bear Charme's petition is based on his wealth, accrued from solid waste; he has turned reservation land into landfill land. Again, Vizenor is not writing in a vacuum. Money talks, and the theory is that impoverished people will be the least likely to turn down such lucrative rewards for accepting hazardous waste. A small band of Indians, the Skull Valley Goshutes in Utah, in one particular instance, have been fighting for years against the storage of nuclear waste on their land, whereas the Mescalero Apache in another instance are agreeing to store, "temporarily," approximately "10,000 metric tons of irradiated fuel rods in sealed containers above ground" (Sehgal 457). The arguments justifying the storing of waste vary, but seem always to come down to profit margins.

Whether or not he gets his "sovereign meditation nation" as a result of his petition, Bear Charme maintains that on the old reservations the tribes were the refuse. We were the waste, solid and swill on the run, telling stories from a discarded culture to amuse the colonial refusers. Over here now, on the other end of the wasted world, we meditate in peace on this landfill reservation.

(Vizenor 101)

The idea of amusing the colonial refusers evokes the idea expressed by Leanne Simpson, noted above, when she argues that "Colonialism and capitalism are based on extracting and assimilating. ... My culture and knowledge is a resource" (Klein n. pag.). Vizenor and Simpson thus make very much the same point concerning the connections between trash, the potential for environmental degradation, and tribal sovereignty. Furthermore the pun on refuse and refusers calls attention to an individual's complicity in producing waste. As Jennifer Gillan writes, "By re-establishing a connection between people and their wastes, refuse meditation makes them confront the results of their actions, forcing them to take responsibility for their lives" (249). Refusers are also "nay sayers," those who deny their complicity. It is Bear Charme who refuses to let anyone forget.

An irony inherent in the controversy over how, when, and if Native tribes take waste onto the reservations is that the process has brought attention to the environmental dilemma posed by unregulated waste disposal. For the Environmental Protection Agency and the federal government to have control over the methods by which waste is disposed or stored necessitates the diminishment of tribal sovereignty. Thus when Bear Charme petitions for sovereignty because of his willingness and desire to use his land for waste disposal, he is at the same time implicitly acknowledging that he will lose control over how and precisely where that waste will be located and stored. This implication is evident in that "recent Supreme Court decisions on federal, state and tribal jurisdiction of land-use" have tended to limit or even ignore tribal sovereignty. According to Sehgal, that is, "modern courts have increasingly ignored sovereignty and eroded related principles, despite the intentions of Congress and the executive branch to encourage tribal independence" (434). As one also sees in Silko's novel, for instance, one notes here the irony inherent in the concept of a sovereign but domestic dependent nation. The federal government retains the power to intervene at any point, but also reserves for itself the right to look the other way. Meanwhile, the trash piles up.

In her book *Sightings* (2002), co-authored with Brenda Peterson, Linda Hogan, Chickasaw poet, novelist, and activist, responds not to the burden of trash and hazardous waste disposal as it relates to Native American environmental sovereignty, but to sovereignty as it relates to the hunting of whales. The Makah's hunting and killing of a grey whale in 1999, she suggests, is a result of the tribe blindly pursuing a treaty right rather than listening to and appreciating the knowledge of the elders, specifically the tribal women, who insist on an identity relationship with the whale rather than a hunter–hunted relationship. The women have been silenced, she laments, and their wisdom has been disregarded (see Peterson & Hogan 154). Hogan argues that wisdom, imagination, memory, story, are all needed to keep the balance in a fragile world, and she looks to a pre-colonial philosophy to bolster her argument. In his chapter "Marine Tenure of the Makahs," Joshua Reid, in contrast, argues that the Makah express "ownership of nearby ocean waters and resources through indigenous knowledge of their marine environment and through customary practices such as whaling ... Their current revival of an active whaling practice reflects their efforts at reclaiming the sea" (243, 244). The issues surrounding Makah whaling rights are thus especially interesting and apropos in the context of environmental sovereignty because arguments about this tribe's right to hunt whales include references to land (marine) tenure, sustainability, environmentalism, sovereignty, citizenship, tribal affiliation, and globalization.

Opponents to the legality of the hunting of whales by the Makah argue in part, for example, that allowing the Makahs the treaty right to resume whaling is inappropriate if not illegal because the United States is a non-whaling nation. Allowing Makah whaling runs the risk of setting a precedent that could have adverse international consequences. Supporters of the hunt point out, however, that the Makahs retain treaty rights that include the "right of taking fish and of whaling or sealing at usual and accustomed grounds and stations," and thus, as if they were peoples of a sovereign nation, they should be free from U.S. legal restrictions in this regard. At the same time, however, the treaty reads that the Makahs "acknowledge their dependence on the Government of the United States" (United States). Should the Makah be considered a sovereign nation separate from the United States? One can certainly argue that by allowing Makah whaling, the United States government is shirking its global responsibility as one of the world's strongest opponents of commercial whaling. Yet to do so, not only ignores issues of tribal sovereignty, it also fails to distinguish between "commercial" and other forms of (or reasons for) whaling. Given a certain specific interpretation of the law, the Makah have the legal right to hunt whales. They have tradition and the treaty interpretation on their side. Peterson and Hogan suggest however that whaling is fraught with serious ethical questions beyond the legal rights of an individual tribe and issues of that tribe's sovereignty:

> if the Makah choose not to continue whaling, it could truly make a statement about how strong a culture can be, as it looks to other means for the true and deep wellspring of a culture, of a people, one that holds to a reverence for life.
>
> They will set an example for others by which part of the culture they decide to cultivate. And for the children at Makah, what better example than seeing their own people take the side of life, as part of the sacred. That might very well restore tradition until the whale and the people reestablish a relationship of offering and receiving from one another. The way it used to be. The heart of the hunter has to care.
>
> (Peterson & Hogan 154, Hogan's emphasis)

Perhaps the questions specific to whaling can be extended to several other important environmental sovereignty issues facing Native America regarding Indian lands, such as other hunting practices, controversial dam building, strip coal mining, uranium mining, oil refining, and waste disposal. Environmental issues are at the fringes if not at the center of a multitude of Native American works of fiction: the illegal dumping of toxic waste plays a role in Cherokee writer Thomas King's novel *Truth and Bright Water* (1999), for example. In several novels – *Wind from an Enemy Sky* (1978) by D'Arcy McNickle (Cree/Salish), *Green Grass, Running Water* (1993) by Thomas King, and *Solar Storms* (1995) by Linda Hogan (Chickasaw) – the building of dams is a central issue. Mining and logging are central to Choctaw/Cherokee writer Louis Owens's novel *Wolfsong* (1995). In *Mean Spirit* (1990) Linda Hogan explores the exploitation of the Osage in the context of drilling for oil on their land. Mining is also an important thematic issue in the novel *Powwow Highway*

(1989) by David Seals (Huron). Perhaps most immediate in such contexts is the question of how a turn from literary analysis to discussions of actual American Indian controversies can further our understanding of the larger issues of Indigenous knowledge, environmental sustainability, global citizenship, and tribal sovereignty.

Works cited

Akins, Adrienne. "'Next Time, Just Remember the Story': Unlearning Empire in Silko's *Ceremony*." *Studies in American Indian Literatures* 24. 1 (Spring 2012): 1–14.

Cajete, Gregory. *Native Science: Natural Laws of Interdependence*. Santa Fe, NM: Clear Light Press, 2000.

Colorado, Pamela. "Bridging Native and Western Science." *Convergence* 21. 2&3 (1988): 49–68.

Cronon, William. *Changes in the Land: Indians, Colonists, and the Ecology of New England*. New York: Hill & Wang, 1983.

Direnc, Dilek. "From a New Paradise to a New Earth: European Myths and New World Alternatives Converse in Linda Hogan's *Power*." *Litteraria Pragensia: Studies in Literature and Culture* 15. 30 (2005): 51–57.

Gillan, Jennifer. "Restoring the Flow: Comic Circulation in Gerald Vizenor's Fiction." *North Dakota Quarterly* 67. 3–4 (2000): 242–55.

Gordon, David M. & Shepard Krech III. "Indigenous Knowledge and the Environment." *Indigenous Knowledge and the Environment in Africa and North America*. Ed. David M. Gordon & Shepard Krech III. Athens: Ohio University Press, 2012. 1–24.

Grinde, Donald A. & Bruce E. Johansen. *Ecocide of Native America: Environmental Destruction of Indian Lands and Peoples*. Santa Fe, NM: Clear Light, 1995.

Hogan, Linda. *Mean Spirit*. Cambridge, MA: Atheneum, 1990.

———. *Power*. New York: Norton, 1998.

———. *Solar Storms*. New York: Scribner, 1995.

Holm, Sharon. "The 'Lie' of the Land: Native Sovereignty, Indian Literary Nationalism, and Early Indigenism in Leslie Marmon Silko's *Ceremony*." *American Indian Quarterly* 32. 3 (Summer 2008): 243–74.

Johansen, Bruce. *Indigenous Peoples and Environmental Issues: An Encyclopedia*. Westport, CT: Greenwood, 2003.

Kamps, Kevin. "Environmental Racism, Tribal Sovereignty, and Nuclear Waste." *Nuclear Information and Resources Service*, 2001. n. pag. Web. Accessed 10 Dec. 2014. http://www.nirs.org/factsheets/pfsejfactsheet.htm

King, Thomas. *Green Grass, Running Water*. New York: Houghton Mifflin, 1993.

———. *Truth and Bright Water*. 1999. Rpt. New York: Grove Press, 2000.

Klein, Naomi. "Dancing the World into Being: A Conversation with Idle No More's Leanne Simpson." *Yes Magazine* 5 March 2013. n. pag. Web. Accessed 10 Dec. 2014. http://www.yesmagazine.org/peace-justice/dancing-the-world-into-being-a-conversation-with-idle-no-more-leanne-simpson

LaDuke, Winona. *Recovering the Sacred: The Power of Naming and Claiming*. Cambridge: South End Press, 2005.

Lauderdale, Pat. "Indigenous Peoples in the Face of Globalization." *American Behavioral Scientist* 51. 12 (2008): 1836–43.

McGregor, Deborah. "Coming Full Circle: Indigenous Knowledge, Environment, and Our Future." *American Indian Quarterly* 28. 3&4 (2004): 385–410.

McNickle, D'Arcy. *Wind from an Enemy Sky*. Albuquerque: University of New Mexico Press, 1978.

Owens, Louis. *Wolfsong*. Norman: University of Oklahoma Press, 1994.

Peters, Jesse. "Everything the World Turns On: Inclusion and Exclusion in Linda Hogan's *Power*." *American Indian Quarterly* 37. 1–2 (Winter–Spring 2013): 111–25.

Peterson, Brenda & Linda Hogan. *Sightings: The Gray Whale's Mysterious Journey*. Washington: National Geographic, 2002.

Piper, Karen. "Police Zones: Territory and Identity in Leslie Marmon Silko's *Ceremony*." *American Indian Quarterly* 21. 3 (1997): 483–97.

Reid, Joshua. "Marine Tenure of the Makahs." *Indigenous Knowledge and the Environment in Africa and North America*. Ed. David M. Gordon & Shepard Krech III. Athens: Ohio University Press, 2012. 243–58.

Seals, David. *The Powwow Highway*. 1979. Rpt. New York: Plume, 1990.

Sehgal, A. Cassidy. "Indian Tribal Sovereignty and Waste Disposal Regulation." *Fordam Environmental Law Review* 5. 2 (2011): 431–58.

Silko, Leslie Marmon. *Ceremony*. New York: Viking, 1977. Rpt. New York: Signet, 1977.

Simpson, Leanne R. "Anticolonial Strategies for the Recovery and Maintenance of Indigenous Knowledge." *American Indian Quarterly* 28. 3&4 (2004): 373–84.

Tarter, James. "Locating the Uranium Mine: Place, Multiethnicity, and Environmental Justice in Leslie Marmon Silko's *Ceremony*." *The Greening of Literary Scholarship: Literature, Theory, and the Environment*. Ed. Steven Rosendale & Scott Slovic. Iowa City: University of Iowa Press, 2002. 97–110.

Trafzer, Clifford E., Willard Sakiestewa Gilbert & Anthony Madrigal. "Integrating Native Science into a Tribal Environmental Protections Agency." *American Behavioral Scientist* 51 (2008): 1844–66.

United States. "Treaty of Neah Bay." 1855. *History Link*. n. pag. Web. Accessed 22 Dec. 2014. http://www.historylink.org/index.cfm? DisplayPage=output.cfm&file_id=2632

Vizenor, Gerald. "Landfill Meditation." *Landfill Mediation: Crossblood Stories*. Hanover: Wesleyan University Press, 1991. 98–115.

Wilson, Waziyatawin Angela. "Introduction: Indigenous Knowledge Recovery is Indigenous." *American Indian Quarterly* 28. 3&4 (2004): 359–72.

Zamir, Shamoon. "Literature in a 'National Sacrifice Area.'" *New Voices in Native American Literary Criticism*. Ed. Arnold Krupat. Washington: Smithsonian Institution Press, 2003. 396–415.

19

A Seat at the Table

Political Representation for Animals

Brian K. Hudson

When I mention that I study animals and Native American literature to almost anyone outside the field of Native studies, they almost invariably reference familiar stories of American Indian oral traditions in which animals feature prominently. At some point in the conversation, quite frequently some variation arises of the question, "Did Indians [rarely is the question formed in the present tense] really believe animals could think or were they just telling these stories to teach their children?" My answer to such a question is always, "It's more complicated than that." I try to follow this claim with an explanation that varies in length according to the interest level of the questioner. In the shorter version, I concede that some narratives, such as the Cherokee story "Why Possum Has a Naked Tail," are clearly intended to teach the listener about problems that are caused by moral vices, such as vanity in one's appearance (Caduto & Bruchac 173). This story explains how the possum brags about his tail and his vanity leads others to conspire to shave his bushy tail. The possum, unaware that his tail has been shaved, dances before the other animals while singing about the beauty of his tail. When he realizes it has been shaved, he falls over, frozen from embarrassment. Although this story provides a good lesson about the consequences of vanity, human vices (and virtues for that matter) must in actuality mean little to the mammals of the family *Didelphimorphi*. The aforementioned story deploys a figurative usage of a possum to literally satirize vanity, but has little to say about human interactions with possums beyond an anthropomorphic narrative that humorously explains the behavior of the species when it is threatened. Human qualities, we must infer, would be meaningful to other animals only when they directly influence our interactions with those animals. There are, however, many examples of traditional animal stories in which the wellbeing of animals themselves is the thematic focus, and such tales complicate a simple understanding of traditional animal stories. These more complicated types of stories can be found within creation narratives, the origins of which stretch back to time immemorial, up through contemporary novels and poetry.

Several traditional Native American animal stories reinforce cultural values while also portraying how we should behave toward other species. For example, the collection *Keepers of the Animals: Native American Stories and Wildlife Activities for Children* retells animal stories from several tribal nations in an attempt to help children understand proper behavior toward animals. These stories are followed by exercises that are meant to educate children about particular species through a variety of methods. In the foreword to the collection, the late Sioux theorist Vine Deloria Jr. explains that we owe other animals "the respect that they deserve and the right to live without unnecessary harm" (*Keepers* xii). This respect stems from the realization that other animals can suffer harm and "have thought processes, emotions, personal relationships and many of the experiences that we have in our lives" (*Keepers* xii). An illustrative example from this collection, a story that examines the themes of respect and harm, is the Seneca story "The Dogs Who Saved Their Master." In this story, the narrator explains how a hunter's having treated his dogs with respect and compassion results in those animals defending the human from a monster at the cost of their own lives. The story concludes with the hunter rescuing another dog from a cruel master (Caduto & Bruchac159–60). This Seneca story, rather than being focused on the virtue of kindness as applied toward other humans, instead illustrates the need to avoid harming animals, especially in those instances in which they reciprocate our loyalty. This story is one of many examples that show respect for the thoughts, emotions, relationships, and general wellbeing of animals.

As opposed to the dominant narratives of Western philosophy, which place humanity in a category separate from and above all other living beings, many Native traditional stories teach us that we should realize with humility our place as one of many species. These stories also caution that with this realization, we should be mindful about the repercussions of our actions on other species. This humbler understanding of humanity can also take the form of recognizing the interests of animals in our political narratives, specifically in the ways we conceptualize the sovereign status of our tribal nations. For instance, Chickasaw novelist and poet Linda Hogan has explained that many traditional stories about animals reflect a relationship that has political as well as cultural importance and even directly reference treaties with other species. She writes:

> That we held, and still hold, treaties with the animals and plant species is a known part of tribal culture. The relationship between human people and animals is still alive and resonant in the world, the ancient tellings carried on by a constellation of stories, songs, and ceremonies, all shaped by *lived* knowledge of the world and its many interwoven, unending relationships. These stories and ceremonies keep open the bridge between one kind of intelligence and another, one species and another.

> > (10; italics in original)

Hogan claims here that traditional stories illustrate the existence of treaties with the nonhuman world that recognize the capabilities of animals as well as our obligations to other species. These treaties, furthermore, are not relegated to the past but are instead "alive and resonant in the world." Animals, then, not only hold significance culturally and ethically, but also continue to occupy a place of importance in Native ways of understanding politics.

Along with Linda Hogan, Seneca philosopher John Mohawk understands that traditional animal stories recognize a political relationship with other species. In his article, "Animal Nations and Their Right to Survive," Mohawk makes a clear and emphatic case for the recognition of other species in our political philosophies. Mohawk explains how this lack of representation and respect is the result of what he calls "Economic Man." For Mohawk, "Economic Man" is ideologically driven to monetize nature. This ideology is what leads large companies (and the countries that support them), for example, to ignore tribal interests in pursuit of natural resources. In his critique of Economic Man, Mohawk refers to the political autonomy of animal nations. He mentions only briefly our individual relationships with animals, focusing instead upon our collective obligations to all animals. Mohawk references the many traditional understandings that value protecting the environment we share with animals. Integral to these traditions, as Mohawk explains, is "respect for the power and sacredness of the bird and animal life" (20). Referencing this respect, Mohawk explains how, when speaking in 1977 to the United Nations, Onondaga artist and faithkeeper Oren Lyons questioned the lack of political representation for nonhuman interests by declaring, "We see no seat at the U.N. for the eagle ... No seat for the whales, no representation for the animals" (19). The lack of political representation for animals, as Lyons points out here, is a glaring omission from the point of view of traditional Native understandings. Lyons, Mohawk, and Hogan all claim that Native traditional understandings about animals show they matter in Native political philosophies and should matter in dominant Western political philosophies.

It is with the assertion that animals can be recognized as holding political status that I turn to a tribally specific example of how human-centered definitions of sovereignty can be expanded to include other animals. To do so, I refer to a Cherokee traditional narrative, a story from my own tribe, "Origin of Disease and Medicine." This story illustrates how we as Cherokees have narrated our relationships with other animals and have always recognized them as political entities. Taking this story into account, only one example of how a traditional narrative can help us understand inclusion of animals in political philosophy, means revising our current formulations of sovereignty to include the interests of animals in practical ways.

Native theorists have used sovereignty most often to signify political agency. David E. Wilkins and K. Tsianina Lomawaima give us the clearest definition of a "sovereign nation" as a group that

> defines itself and its citizens, exercises self-government and the right to treat with other nations, applies its jurisdiction over the internal legal affairs of its citizens and sub-parts (such as states), claims political jurisdiction over the lands within its borders, and may define certain rights that inhere in its citizens.
>
> (4)

Moreover, they explain that all sovereignty is limited in that it contains "constraints," not least of which are "the terms of its treaties with other sovereign nations" (5, 4). Here we have a definition of sovereignty as political power that is mediated by certain obligations and constraints in relation to other sovereign entities. This more practical formulation of the way that sovereign nations exercise power leaves little room for the meaningful involvement of animals. Our practical conceptualizations of sovereignty, however, can be expanded to include the recognition of other animals, or animal nations as Mohawk refers to them, who possess a type of sovereignty.

Such explicit, legally codified formulations of sovereignty rest on broader notions of what sovereignty is and how it can be defined. The broader notions inherent in the process of defining sovereignty allow us to theorize how sovereignty can be recognized and acknowledged by examining Indigenous stories about animals. Many Native theorists are reluctant to pin down broader philosophical definitions of the word "sovereignty." Instead, they would rather concentrate on the ways in which it could be defined strategically. In *We Talk, You*

Listen, Vine Deloria Jr. defines sovereignty first and foremost as a process. Deloria writes that "the responsibility which sovereignty creates is oriented primarily toward the existence and continuance of the group" (123). The most pertinent of Deloria's arguments pertaining to the recognition of sovereignty of animals rest on recognition as a process. In explaining his reasoning for conceptualizing sovereignty in this way, Deloria insightfully argues that "implicit in the sufferings of each group is the acknowledgment of the sovereignty of the group" (*We Talk* 117). Deloria's asserts here that suffering predicates sovereignty. If we extend this to animals, our recognition of other animals' ability to suffer signals an ethical obligation to recognize that they possess the sovereignty to avoid such suffering.

This understanding of a political relationship with animals and a recognition of their sovereignty is illustrated in the Cherokee story "Origin of Disease and Medicine." The story explains how human ailments began, along with how humans discovered cures for those ailments. Anthropologist James Mooney collected the story as one of many Cherokee stories for the U.S. Bureau of American Ethnology in 1887–1888. Mooney gathered or transcribed manuscripts from several Cherokee medicine men among the Eastern Band Cherokees and confirmed these narratives with elders in Indian Territory, where the Cherokee Nation of Oklahoma (CNO) resides. He categorized these collected stories as either sacred or secular. The categories of sacred and secular, however, are not always separate.[1] A few of the stories concerning animals, according to Mooney, belong to both categories. Mooney writes that "the shorter animal myths have lost whatever sacred character they once had, and are told now merely as humorous explanations of certain animal peculiarities." He concedes, however, that in "rare instances" these animal stories can also be sacred (231). The sacred stories, as Mooney categorizes them, belong to a class that includes Cherokee stories of the origin of the world. "Origin of Disease and Medicine" is an example of one of these "rare instances" in which a story belongs to the categories of both sacred and secular and in fact is printed in both Mooney's *Myths of the Cherokees* and *Sacred Formulas of the Cherokees*. It is likely that the medicine men whose counsel Mooney sought understood the political implications of recounting such a sacred story to Mooney, who was, after all, a non-Indian anthropologist employed by the U.S. government.

"Origin of Disease and Medicine" can be understood as instituting a recognition that animal suffering leads to human suffering and it establishes that recognizing the sovereignty of other species is integral to healthier relationships with animals. The story begins with a description of a time when humans and animals related to each other on much more equal terms than they do now. It begins:

> In the old days quadrupeds, birds, and insects could all talk, and they and the human race lived together in peace and friendship. But as time went on the people increased so rapidly that their settlements spread over the whole earth and the poor animals found themselves beginning to be cramped for room. This was bad enough, but to add to their misfortunes man invented bows, knives, blowguns, spears, and hooks, and began to slaughter the larger animals, birds and fishes for the sake of their flesh or their skins, while the smaller creatures, such as the frog and worms, were crushed and trodden upon without mercy, out of pure careless-ness or contempt. In this state of affairs the animals resolved to consult upon measures for their common safety.
>
> (319)

A SEAT AT THE TABLE

Some might characterize the use of animals in this story as anthropomorphic, as many Native animal stories are understood; this particular story, however, proves too complex an example for such a dismissive reading. Clearly, we would also be mistaken to read this somber narrative as one of the "humorous explanations" of animal behavior. It does, however, include small elements of such stories, such as when it explains the reason for stripes on the back of ground squirrels and why the grubworm "wiggles off on his back" (321). But these examples are overshadowed by the way the story articulates the valid concern of various species in avoiding suffering caused by humans. Therefore, it is vital to recognize the political importance of this story as it applies to human relationships with other sentient species. Indeed, the political importance of "Origin of Disease and Medicine" is evident, as it is a traditional example of how we as Cherokees have narrated our relationships with other animals. The assertion that animals and humans "lived together in peace and friendship" characterizes an ideal ethics of our relationships with animals – here, an obligation on our part to minimize suffering. Such ethics include, at the very least, an obligation to avoid killing animals to the point of extinction or "out of pure carelessness or contempt." This ideal can and should extend to our treatment of other animals more generally.

The first part of the narrative establishes that Cherokees do have an existing political relationship – or treaty, as Hogan terms it – with animals. The story continues by explaining that this ideal relationship was compromised by the problem of human greed. Humans began to kill other animals not solely for sustenance but to trade their hides, which led the various animal tribes to form a council to "begin war at once against the human race" (320). As part of their tactics in this war, the animal tribes created diseases for humans, including "rheumatism" and infected dreams to make humans "lose appetite, sicken, and die" (321). To avoid these afflictions, the story explains, hunters are required to ask for forgiveness from the animal who has been killed. If the hunter fails to do this, the spirit of the animal will afflict the hunter with a particular disease.[2]

This traditional narrative serves as a warning, by representing hunting in an ethical way, against transgressing treaties with animals. But this story also establishes an ethical baseline for the treatment and killing of animals. While praying for an animal after death does not alleviate its suffering (from a secular standpoint), it may help to create a culture of hunting that is more mindful of the suffering of animals while they are alive. "Origin of Disease and Medicine" enunciates a concern for how other species use the power of disease to avoid suffering due to carelessness and the inevitabilities of human overpopulation, or "settlements spread over the whole earth." At the council meeting with the other animal tribes, the Frog who leads the meeting entreats, "We must do something to check the increase of the race or people will become so numerous that we shall be crowded from the earth" (Mooney 321). The solution for the animals of this story to avoid suffering and extinction is to use their powers to create diseases for man. This traditional Cherokee story, with its figurative use of animals carefully understood, clearly recognizes the suffering of animals being hunted for sport or profit. With several types of species given voice in the story, it is proper to include all sentient animals in the formulation of those who are recognized as having power and exercising it. Those beings who can suffer, according to this Cherokee narrative, should not suffer without apology.

"Origin of Disease and Medicine" has also been referenced recently within a Cherokee political text, suggesting that it has importance both culturally and politically. In 2002, officials of the Cherokee Nation of Oklahoma included a shortened version of this story in a political document titled "Disease and Genocide." The document, authored by former chief Chad Smith and former deputy chief Hastings Shade, was part of a more comprehensive manuscript titled *Declaration of Designed Purpose* meant to elucidate the political philosophy of the Smith administration. Smith and Shade summarize "Origin of Disease and Medicine" by writing that:

> From the beginning, there had been an agreement between the Cherokees and the animals that the animals would sacrifice some of their own to sustain the Cherokee people, provided the people took no more than they needed to live, and provided they showed the proper honor and respect to the animal at the time of the kill. For many generations, the Cherokees had abided by this agreement as they hunted the animals, and the animals had given their lives without remonstrance.
>
> ("Disease and Genocide" n. pag.)

Smith and Shade continue by explaining how the demand for European goods caused the over-hunting of deer in particular. According to the authors, this practice predicated a plague of smallpox in 1738 that killed half of the tribe and another wave of the disease forty years later that killed another third of the Cherokee population. Smith and Shade go on to explain that the plague was followed by failed political alliances with the French and British. All these factors, Smith and Shade claim, led to a weakened and thereby increasingly centralized Cherokee governmental structure. The formation of a unified governing body occurred in response to a tribe that could not battle against the genocidal agenda of the burgeoning United States in the seventeenth century (Smith & Shade "Disease and Genocide" n. pag.).

It is clear here that Smith and Shade are arguing that relationships with animals maintained by Cherokees changed with European contact. They also posit that this change predicated diseases, specifically smallpox, which led to the Cherokees' inability to defend themselves in war with the invading colonists. As Jared Diamond explains in his popular history of colonization and inequality, European germs played a decisive role against the political resistance of Native American tribes. Diamond writes that "diseases introduced with Europeans spread from tribe to tribe far in advance of the Europeans themselves, killing an estimated 95 percent of the pre-Columbian Native American population" (78). The introduction of unknown diseases traveled along trade routes between Europeans and Native American tribes but also spread among tribes faster than the "Europeans themselves" with devastating effect.

"Origin of Disease and Medicine" is a prescient warning against future mistreatment of animals. The origins of many of the most devastating human diseases, including smallpox, are unknown. The Center for Disease Control claims that "smallpox is not known to be transmitted by insects or animals." However, a recent scientific study suggests that smallpox was likely mutated from a pathogen originally present in domesticated animals (Wolfe, Dunavan & Diamond 279). Domesticating animals, something not done on a large scale in the Americas pre-Columbus, likely allowed the disease originally to mutate. And, as the authors of the scientific study readily concede, most human diseases originate in animals particularly in regions where domestication became a common practice very early.

Smith and Shade construct this political document, "Disease and Genocide," to demonstrate how a change in relationships with animals led to several autonomous Cherokee towns consolidating into a nation. Rather than over-hunting, however, a difference in the prevalence of domestication, keeping other animals in greater numbers and increasingly confined spaces, likely led to the mutation of smallpox and other diseases deadly to humans. Smallpox, and other diseases, spread to Cherokees and other tribes with increasing contact from those newly arrived to the Americas. In this political document, Smith and Shade allude to a non-Indian way of conceptualizing human relationships with other animals. An increase in domestication led to the susceptibility of Cherokees to the diseases from settlers and eventually contributed to American campaigns of confinement and genocide. This was because for seventeenth-century Cherokees, as Smith and Shade write, "the balance of their world was gone" ("Disease and Genocide" n. pag.). A lack of balance in relationships with animals, as the authors argue, was partly responsible for the consolidations of autonomous towns into a centralized Cherokee Nation.

Declaration of Designed Purpose, of which "Disease and Genocide" was excerpted for the CNO website, was published the same year the Oklahoma Water Resources Board took steps to study pollution in the scenic rivers of Oklahoma. These studies provided evidence of phosphates from Arkansas poultry farms which polluted water sources, such as the Illinois, within the borders of Oklahoma and the CNO. The lawsuit was filed by the state of Oklahoma against Tyson and eleven other large poultry companies in September of 2009. CNO attempted to join the state of Oklahoma in this lawsuit to protect the Illinois River from pollution produced by the waste created by the large poultry farming operations. Federal courts denied CNO entry into the lawsuit and also denied it upon appeal (Chavez). By attempting to join this lawsuit, the CNO demonstrated a common grievance with the state of Oklahoma. Both the CNO and Oklahoma attempted to seek damages from the poorly regulated poultry companies in Arkansas.

The CNO, in its attempt to join the lawsuit, asserted its sovereign right to "preserve the watershed for cultural, religious and recreational usage" (Chavez). The balance of phosphates in the CNO watershed was compromised by poultry operations. Smith and Shades focus on the imbalance of our relationships with animals. This focus allows "Origin of Disease and Medicine" – which is alluded to in "Disease and Genocide" – to operate politically. Had the CNO not been denied as plaintiff, this allusion would have positioned the CNO strategically against Tyson and the other poultry companies. It would have allowed the CNO grounds to claim the Arkansas poultry companies had transgressed Cherokee sovereignty. This transgression would have been more than the addition of phosphates to a water resource but, more broadly, an offense to Cherokee cultural and traditional values.

In using a version of "Origin of Disease and Medicine" to assert their sovereignty, the CNO also implicitly recognized the disrespect and suffering, and per Deloria, the sovereignty of animals, such as chickens in these large poultry companies. The large-scale poultry operations not only pose a danger to the environment (and sovereign control over water sources) but induce more suffering in the animals themselves than other methods of farming or hunting. As Annie Potts explains in her history of the species *Gallus Gallus*, chickens raised for consumption in large operations such as Tyson suffer acutely and en masse: 8–10 billion chickens each year in American alone (139). Standard breeding practices which privilege weight gain above all else lead to "up to 30 percent suffer[ing] severe lameness and swelling, and at least that many suffer[ing] chronic pain" (155). Even chickens kept for egg-laying live under "constrained conditions" that, in most instances, do not allow them to turn around" (Potts 160). The overcrowded conditions of these chickens are responsible for the sickness and death of many of these nonhuman animals by way of "extreme suffering" of the species "at every stage of processing prior to slaughter" (167). Since, as Potts writes, the Animal Welfare Act and Humane Slaughter Act disregards chickens, it is noteworthy that the CNO implicitly recognizes the suffering of that species, especially since that suffering leads to human disease.

The imbalance in the U.S. poultry industry, which the CNO political document "Disease and Genocide" critiques, is caused by disregard for the suffering of chickens and disregard for the pollution and disease created by such farming practices. In 1998, Tyson was sued for contributing "coliform bacteria, phosphorous and nitrogen" to water sources in Maryland (Potts 170). The pollution of local rivers and the possibility of new diseases suffered by humans and animals are the unfortunate but likely outcome of this disregard for the suffering of other animals and a disregard for ecological balance which "Origin of Disease and Medicine" clearly warns against. These lessons taught by traditional Native stories about animals can help us consider the possibility of more balanced relationships with other species. These more balanced relationships can recognize the ethical, ecological, and political importance of how we treat them.

Native American oral stories about animals are often viewed as merely anthropomorphic depictions of human cultural values. But many examples show us that this is a reductive way to read them. Understanding our traditional stories as depicting treaties with animals that are more than figurative should lead to better treatment of all species, individually and collectively. Some of these stories – "Origins of Disease and Medicine" for example – show that the wellbeing of animals matters to Cherokee culture and politics. This is only one tribally specific example of how our traditional relationships with animals are important to both current Native American cultures and also are significant to contemporary tribal politics.

Notes

1 Robert Conley also recounts this story from Mooney, as an introduction for non-Cherokee readers to Cherokee traditions, in his biography of a Cherokee medicine man who resides within the Cherokee Nation of Oklahoma.
2 Bears, interestingly enough, do not require such prayers because they disengaged from war with the humans in this particular version collected by Mooney. This exception, however, is complicated by stories of Cherokees turning into bears. For more on bears, including their human origins, see Mooney on "Origin of the Bear: The Bear Songs" (*Myths* 231).

Works cited

Caduto, Michael J. & Joseph Bruchac. "The Dogs Who Saved Their Master." *Keepers of the Animals: Native American Stories and Wildlife Activities for Children.* Golden, CO: Fulcrum, 1991. 158–61.
——. "Why Possum Has a Naked Tail." *Keepers of the Animals: Native American Stories and Wildlife Activities for Children.* Golden, CO: Fulcrum, 1991. 173–74.
Chavez, Will. "Appeals Court Again Denies Cherokee Nation from Poultry Case." *Cherokee Phoenix,* 19 November 2010. Web. Accessed 18 Jan. 2012.

Conley, Robert. "A Brief History of the Cherokees and the Origins of Medicine." *Cherokee Medicine Man*. Norman: University of Oklahoma Press, 2005. 8–30.

Deloria, Vine, Jr. "Foreword." Michael J. Caduto & Joseph Bruchac. *Keepers of the Animals: Native American Stories and Wildlife Activities for Children*. Golden, CO: Fulcrum, 1991. xi–xii.

——. *We Talk, You Listen*. Lincoln: Nebraska University Press, 2007.

Diamond, Jared. *Guns, Germs, and Steel: The Fates of Human Societies*. New York: W.W. Norton & Company, 1999.

Hogan, Linda. "First People." *Intimate Nature: The Bond between Women and Animals*. New York: Ballantine, 1998. 6–19.

Mohawk, John. "Animal Nations and Their Right to Survive." *Daybreak*. Summer 1988. 19–22.

Mooney, James. "Origin of Disease and Medicine." *Myths of the Cherokee and Sacred Formulas of the Cherokees*. Nashville: Charles and Randy Elder, 1982. 250–52.

"Oklahoma Scenic Rivers Phosphorus Criteria Review." *Oklahoma Water Resources Board*, 10 Apr. 2012. Web. Accessed 22 Aug. 2014.

Potts, Annie. "Meat Chicks and Egg Machines." *Chicken*. London: Reaktion Books, 2012. 139–73.

"Smallpox Disease Overview." *Emergency Preparedness and Response – CDC*. Centers for Disease Control and Prevention, 30 Oct. 2004. Web. Accessed 29 Jan. 2015.

Smith, Chad & Hastings Shade. *Cherokee Nation Tomorrow: Declaration of Designed Purpose*. Tahlequah, OK: Cherokee Nation, 2002.

——. "Disease and Genocide." *The Official Homepage of the Cherokee Nation*. Cherokee Nation. n.d., n. pag. Web. Accessed 29 Jan. 2015.

Wilkins, David and Tsianina Lomawaima, *Uneven Ground: American Indian Sovereignty and Federal Law*. Norman: Oklahoma University Press, 2002.

Wolfe, Nathan D., Claire Panosian Dunavan & Jared Diamond. "Origins of Human Infectious Diseases." *Nature* 447 (2007): 279–83.

20
Where Food Grows on Water
Food Sovereignty and Indigenous North American Literatures

Janet Fiskio

The windigo, "an ice spirit of awful hunger" emerges from the storytelling traditions of the Anishinaabeg (*Antelope Wife* 190). Stories of this cannibal spirit precede colonization by Europeans, but in the fiction of Louise Erdrich, the windigo figures the cannibalism of European American imperialism as well as the awful hungers – physical and spiritual – produced by colonization (Brozzo 1). In his work *Cannibal Fictions*, Jeff Berglund describes the way that the figure of the cannibal was originally manipulated by European settlers to rationalize colonization, but argues that, more recently, indigenous writers "use the subject of cannibalism to highlight the cannibalistic and self-consuming nature of the colonialist project" (8). *The Antelope Wife* offers a description of Anishinaabe land soon after military conquest: "an earthscape of sloughs and lakes, potholes, woods of delicate yellow-green lace, undulant hills. Into that perfectly made land they wandered, searching out the people now confined to treaty areas, reservations, or as they called them ishkonigan, the leftovers" (239). As the novel details, this land of abundance has been transformed into a landscape of disease and starvation under settler colonialism: it is a perfect land possessed by hunger. Under this regime the people have been devoured; those who have survived this nightmarish feast are "leftovers."

The awful hunger of the windigo is not merely metaphorical, though it has many meanings in indigenous literatures.[1] Recent historical studies of colonization practices in Canada reveal that hunger was used to torture and subjugate First Nations peoples. In *Clearing the Plains*, for example, James Daschuk examines "the politics of famine" in Western Canada during colonization, arguing that the rapid decline of bison herds, a crucial food source, led to starvation (xix–xx). During this period the government failed to meet its treaty commitments for food and medical assistance, instead using food as a political tool (Daschuk xx–xxi). First Nations adults and children in boarding schools were subjected to sadistic experiments on malnutrition (Mosby 2013; see also Daschuk "When Canada Used Hunger"). In addition to these deliberate uses of hunger, colonization produced famine as indigenous peoples in the United States and Canada were removed from their territories and confined to reservations, unable to engage in subsistence practices and forced into dependence on government food aid (Daschuk xxi; Winter 44). Indigenous North

American literature describes the impact of these colonial tactics and the ongoing resistance to settler colonialism through the practice of indigenous subsistence and foodways and efforts to maintain and recover indigenous food sovereignty.

Joshua Nelson notes that speaking of Native American literature risks erasing "the diversity within the diversities of indigeneity" (28). Similarly, it is impossible to generalize about the complex systems of indigenous foodways of North America, which range from arid land farming in the Sonoran Desert, to coastal fishing in the Pacific Northwest, to hunting, fishing, gathering, and farming in the Great Lakes and the eastern woodlands, to the Arctic fishing and hunting of Nunavut. These foodways take place within philosophical and ecological epistemes that engage with questions including but not limited to relationships with nonhuman others (both animals and plants) through hunting, gathering, and agriculture; cuisine, food preparation, recipes, and food preservation; intellectual property rights; tribal hunting and fishing rights; cultural survival and indigenous languages – and, more recently, climate change. As a way of negotiating this complexity and respecting indigenous diversity in literature and foodways, in this chapter I focus in particular on two authors from the Anishinaabeg community (also called Ojibwe and Chippewa), Louise Erdrich and Winona LaDuke.[2] Through multiple genres, both of these writers have articulated the centrality of food to understanding indigenous life and literature and of food sovereignty to indigenous cultural survival. I trace an historical trajectory that focuses on resistance to colonization and struggles to preserve food sovereignty from Erdrich's novel *Tracks* (which takes place in the early twentieth century) through LaDuke's collection of essays, *All Our Relations*, which details indigenous activism for food sovereignty in the present situation of environmental and structural racism. In *Tracks*, we see the result of land dispossession and the reservation system: the destruction of indigenous foodways and famine. LaDuke details the seizure of land that we also witness in *Tracks*; but in LaDuke's essays, we see the resurgence of indigenous food sovereignty even as her essays warn of continuing threats to indigenous lands and communities. Through these works the impact of colonization on the indigenous body comes into view. But unlike the pathologizing discourses of medical and colonialist texts, these writers disclose the indigenous body as a locus of power, knowledge, life, and continuance. This focus on the body emphasizes the importance of indigenous food sovereignty and ongoing resistance to toxic colonization within the context of climate change, particularly as it is revealed in current fossil fuels mining and pipeline projects.

Famine

One of the foremost authors in the United States, Louise Erdrich is an enrolled member of the Turtle Mountain Band, who have lived "since time immemorial in birchbark country" (Lischke 221). Winona LaDuke – writer, activist, vice-presidential candidate – is a member of the Mississippi Band and lives on the White Earth Reservation in Minnesota. Anishinaabe territory includes the Great Lakes region from Michigan to Minnesota and across to Ontario, which Karl Hele describes as a borderland where "some boundaries are mere lines drawn upon the water, often disrupted or even erased altogether by the lived experiences of First Nations people" (Whyte 5, Hele xvi).[3] This ecosystem is shaped by multiple lakes and watersheds, northern hardwood forests, and severe winters. Traditional subsistence practices included hunting, fishing, farming, and gathering, including the wild rice (*manoomin*) that gives the region the name "the place where food grows on water," as well as varieties of corn that can grow so far north, and the spring delight of maple sugaring (Erdrich, *The Birchbark House*; LaDuke, "White Earth" *Relations*). Before European colonization in the 1600s, the Great Lakes region was home to thousands of distinct indigenous nations (Hele xiii).[4]

In the United States, capitalist agriculture and land dispossession acted in concert to threaten indigenous cultural and material survival. Diachronic, sophisticated indigenous scientific knowledge of ecological systems was disregarded as Western agricultural systems and dependence on commodity foods were forced on indigenous nations through legislation and the boarding school system.[5] Frieda Knobloch argues that agriculture was a central technology of colonization, deployed to "recode a 'wild' landscape as quickly as possible by creating vast domesticated fields" while engaging in seizure of indigenous lands through the Homestead Act of 1862 and the Dawes Act of 1887 (55). Knobloch documents the collusion of "federal agencies [that] dispossessed, removed, abducted, and indoctrinated Native Americans, [opening] hundreds of millions of acres of the American West [to be] secured for colonization" (61). The Dawes Act, which divided collectively held tribal lands into individual family plots, was a key instrument used by the federal government to appropriate indigenous lands. The federal government excluded members of the community through the use of blood quantum requirements, deceit, and coercion, and then sold the allegedly unclaimed tribal lands to white settlers and corporations (Knobloch 58; LaDuke, *Relations* 119). In addition, agriculture itself was a form of cultural imperialism, imposed on indigenous peoples as a civilizing practice:

> Native farmers – women – not already overtaken by warfare or disease were encouraged by force to become 'housewives,' separated from their productive art and expertise, and at the same time Native American hunters were expected to harness horses, plow fields, and raise cash crops.
>
> (Knobloch 49)

The practice of Western agriculture not only impacted indigenous foodways but also introduced destructive gender norms and exploitative relationships with nonhuman animals.[6] Further, Joni Adamson links the imposition of wage labor economy to the loss of traditional subsistence practices and subsequent indigenous malnutrition, since workers in agriculture or the logging industry were unable to "plant, tend, and maintain their fields or collect wild foods," leading to diet-related diseases such as diabetes ("Medicine Food" 219).

The construction of hunger and dispossession of land frames Louise Erdrich's novel *Tracks*. In the opening pages, the character Nanapush describes the devastating year of 1912, when consumption killed "Whole families" and "Our tribe unraveled like a coarse rope" (2). The novel traces the intertwined processes of disease, famine, and dispossession: Nanapush recalls "the last buffalo hunt," "the last bear shot," and the treaty, and refuses "to sign the settlement papers that would take away our woods and lake" (2). The woods and lake are strong presences in this novel, sources of power, resistance, and survival for the central characters, and especially for Fleur Pillager. The Pillagers' land is on the lake, and Fleur has an extraordinary relationship with the lake spirit. However, grief, the loss of land, and the threat of famine shadow the events in *Tracks*. After the disease that destroys so many of their loved ones, Fleur and Nanapush are nearly devoured by grief:

WHERE FOOD GROWS ON WATER

We had gone half windigo. I learned later that this was common, that there were many of our people who died in this manner, of the invisible sickness. There were those who could not swallow another bite of food because the names of their dead anchored their tongues.

(6)

Although colonization brings the windigo spirit, food is a medicine that helps to sustain and heal.[7] After Fleur miscarries her second child and is beset by fears, Nanapush realizes that "a cure, an easing, must take place" (187). This healing ceremony, narrated by Nanapush, involves "two plants. One is yarrow and the other I will not name. These are the sources of my medicine" (188). With these herbs Nanapush is able to "plunge my arms into a boiling stew kettle, pull meat from the bottom, or reach into the body itself and remove [...] the name that burned, the sickness" (188). As part of Fleur's healing ceremony, Nanapush feeds Fleur "choice meat" that gives her "strength" (189). Similarly, during a harsh winter Nanapush and Eli are saved from starvation by Nanapush's ecological knowledge, as he guides Eli through song, vision, and prayer. Eli tracks the moose along the lakeshore and down into a slough, staying downwind and under the cover of brush (101–03). Kari Winter notes that in this scene, "Survival is dependent on knowledge, discipline, and respect for animals as well as people" (50). Intergenerational scientific knowledge within an indigenous episteme enables Nanapush and Eli to endure.

But as the "Skeleton Winter" continues, Nanapush's family accepts government commodities and hears, at the same time that the food rations are delivered, about "the annual fee lists and foreclosure notices sent by the Agent" (165, 172). The healing ceremony and subsistence practices cannot forestall the corruption of the settler government. The need for government commodities follows not only a harsh winter but the decimation of the people from disease and confinement to reservation lands; Nanapush earlier observes that "Anishinabe land ... was nibbled at the edges and surrounded by farmers waiting for it to go underneath the gavel of the auctioneer" (99). This conjunction of events – famine, food relief, and land grabs by settlers and lumber companies – reveals the way colonization exploited hunger to subjugate indigenous peoples and undermine resistance. The government map depicts:

> The lands that were gone out of the tribe – to deaths with no heirs, to sales, to the lumber company ... painted a pale and rotten pink. Those in question, a sharper yellow. At the center of a bright square was Matchimanito, a small blue triangle I could cover with my hand ... My concern was the lapping pink, the color of the skin of lumberjacks and bankers, the land we would never walk or hunt, from which our children would be barred.
>
> (173–74)

Matchimanito is the traditional land of the Pillagers on the shore of the lake. In these creeping colors we witness the process of "colonial erasure of Native peoples" through the project of mapping described by Shari Huhndorf in *Mapping the Americas* (2). Working together, Nanapush, Fleur, and their family once again turn to traditional subsistence practices, gathering cranberry bark, hunting fur animals, and making "quill boxes, rabbitskin blankets, dried fish" (190–91). But even with this skilled work and the money the family has saved, with the government late fee, it is only enough to save one allotment, and

Nanapush's wife Margaret chooses her family's land. *Tracks* ends with the lumber company clearcutting Fleur's family land. The centrality of Native foods and foodways to indigenous life and community is clear in *Tracks*, as well as the catastrophic consequences of the erosion of indigenous land claims and subsistence practices for spiritual and mental well-being, and for tribal sovereignty.

Food sovereignty

Indigenous scholars and activists have theorized the meaning and practice of food sovereignty in profound ways, placing indigenous scientific knowledge of plants, nonhuman animals, and the natural world within Native cultures and landscapes, as Enrique Salmón describes:

> I learned the names of plants, their uses, and their place in Rarámuri culture, philosophy, and cosmology. I understood them to be relatives and living beings with emotions and lives of their own. I learned that they were part of my life as well and that I should always care for them. In short, my family led me into the traditional ecological knowledge of the Rarámuri.
>
> (1–2)

While the emergence of food studies as an academic discipline has brought new attention to food in indigenous life and literature, work for food sovereignty in indigenous communities precedes this movement by centuries. The history of colonially produced famine reveals that indigenous struggles to maintain food sovereignty have been constant since the incursion of settlers and settler governments.

Food sovereignty has a complex meaning in indigenous communities. It is not merely about access to food but rather about self-determination within a framework of sovereignty: control of the land, water, and seeds necessary to sustain Native food traditions (Salmón 14849). The international movement of peasants, La Via Campesina, defined food sovereignty at the World Food Summit in 1996 in this way: "Food sovereignty is the right of peoples to healthy and culturally appropriate food produced through sustainable methods and their right to define their own food and agriculture systems" (La Via Campesina).[8] As the food justice movement has gained momentum, communities have offered different visions of what food sovereignty means within their particular contexts. Philosopher Kyle Powys Whyte (an enrolled member of the Citizen Potawatomi Nation in Shawnee, Oklahoma) coins the term *"collective food relations"* to express the ways in which "The concepts of community self-reliance, collective meals, community rights and food sovereignty express claims about the value of food as a contributor to a group's *collective* self-determination" (4). Whyte uses the example of seasonal practices among the Anishinaabeg to emphasize the focus on community and reciprocal relationship:

> Each year, the activities associated with first foods renew the family, community, cultural, economic, social and political relationships that connect Anishinaabe persons with one another and with all the plants, animals and other entities in the environment, such as water, that are associated with these foods.
>
> (5)

In addition, indigenous food traditions are complexly integrated with intergenerational knowledge and Native languages, many of which are threatened (Nabhan *Cultures* 258). Food sovereignty thus requires structural changes that include protection of indigenous land rights, languages, and intellectual property rights (IPRs), as well as respect for indigenous scientific knowledge.[9]

Joni Adamson is one of the first scholars to address the importance of food sovereignty to indigenous literature in *American Indian Literature, Environmental Justice, and Ecocriticism*, where she details the significance of indigenous agriculture as a "middle place" between the Western constructions of wilderness preserves and industrial sacrifice zones. More recently, Adamson has analyzed the intersection of food, IPRs, and colonialism in the novels *Last Standing Woman* by Winona LaDuke and *Gardens in the Dunes* by Leslie Marmon Silko. These novels, Adamson argues, "[enhance] understanding of the reasons real-world indigenous communities are organizing around foods such as wild rice and amaranth and creating international documents that position them to take a stand on global debates surrounding biodiversity, trade liberalization and food sovereignty" ("Medicine Food" 216). Adamson places these novels in the context of decades of organizing in the Americas for food sovereignty, "which called attention to the ideologies and external forces that have been threatening indigenous food systems for hundreds of years" ("Medicine Food" 215). In particular, Adamson articulates the central importance of resistance to biopiracy and the significance of "medicine foods" in the current situation of environmental racism ("Medicine Foods" 219).

As Adamson describes, Winona LaDuke's writing and activism recognize the continuing impact of colonial occupation but center on indigenous resistance and continuance. *All Our Relations: Native Struggles for Land and Life*, a multivocal text shaped by indigenous storytelling traditions, offers a series of portraits of indigenous communities facing the consequences of environmental racism. Each essay in the collection opens with a map of the current territory of the nation, making land central to the dialogue of voices of elders and activists, oral literature and traditions, indigenous ecological knowledge, historical records, and LaDuke's own voice as narrator, archivist, and activist. *All Our Relations* gathers stories and, through direct quotation and dialogue, transcribes these voices in the written text. The collection places food sovereignty within a constellation of indigenous cultural survival issues, including species conservation, activism against extractive energy industries and toxics, and renewable energy. Writing within indigenous worldviews and storytelling practices, the collection recognizes members of the nonhuman world as peoples to whom humans owe responsibility: they are "the relations all around," "the ones who came before and taught us how to live" (2). LaDuke opens the collection with a discussion of the interrelation of indigenous cultures and biodiversity (1). Native environmentalism, for LaDuke, is the labor to protect and restore rivers, forests, deserts, and grasslands for all the peoples who depend on them.

On the lands indigenous people have maintained, a new form of imperialism threatens food sovereignty: toxic colonization. Toxic colonization includes pollution from uranium mining and nuclear waste storage, from mining and extractive industries – coal, tar sands, metals, lumber – and bioaccumulative chemicals from industrial manufacturing that contaminate watersheds, making traditional subsistence practices like fishing and hunting untenable. Toxic colonization thus violates the hunting and fishing rights guaranteed by treaties. LaDuke opens the essay "Akwesasne: Mohawk Mothers' Milk and PCBs" with a photograph and written portrait of Katsi Cook, a member of the Mohawk nation and midwife. Akwesasne bears the toxic burdens from a series of manufacturing industries located on the St. Lawrence River because of access to inexpensive electricity and shipping lanes from the Great Lakes (*Relations* 15). Heavy use of polychlorinated biphenyls (PCBs) by these corporations have contaminated the watershed – and thus fish, wildlife, and human bodies:

> GM has tainted the land, water, and ultimately the bodies of the Mohawk people, their babies included. Katsi's work is precedent-setting environmental justice work that links the intricate culture of the Mohawk people to the water, the turtles, the animal relatives, and ultimately the destruction of the industrialized General Motors Superfund site.
>
> (12)

PCBs are linked to a range of devastating health problems, including cancers, reproductive health problems, breast tumors, and development delays in children exposed while in the womb (*Relations* 15–16).

LaDuke begins her portrait of Akwesasne with a map of the border region, marked by the location of tribal nations and unwanted industries, followed by a detailed history of the stages of dispossession. The essay thus places current disruption to subsistence within a history of appropriation and resistance. Indigenous bodies are impacted by this toxic colonization, by the disruption of traditional fishing and hunting practices, and by the poisonous impact of commodity foods.[10] The essay centers in particular on the impact of PCBs on human breast milk in Akwesasne: a collaborative epidemiological study, initiated by Katsi, revealed "greater concentrations of PCBs in the breastmilk of those mothers who ate fish from the St. Lawrence River" (19). Thus, these women women's bodies have been invaded, forcing them to cease traditional subsistence practices to protect their children. LaDuke documents the rage and pain felt by the women whose bodies have been contaminated: not only land but also bodies are colonized. The impact of this toxic invasion extends to all reservation members:

> Today, 65 percent of the Mohawks on Akwesasne reservation have diabetes ... "Our traditional lifestyle has been completely disrupted, and we have been forced to make choices to protect our future generations," says Lickers. "Many of the families used to eat 20–25 fish meals a month. It's now said that the traditional Mohawk diet is spaghetti."
>
> (18)

As Mary-Ellen Kelm articulates in her study of First Nations in British Columbia in the early twentieth century, *Colonizing Bodies*, "subsistence meant strength and, through access to food, the 'land question' was reified in Aboriginal bodies" (19). By limiting access to traditional hunting and fishing territories, the reserve system made people more vulnerable to starvation (Kelm 27–28). Toxic colonization now limits access to traditional subsistence practices on tribal lands, making people more vulnerable to disease: diabetes and other food-related illnesses are the way the land question is currently imprinted on Native bodies (see Whyte on recent research in Akwesasne).

One of the most powerful aspects of LaDuke's essays, Erdrich's novels, and Native American literature more broadly is that, unlike colonial propaganda, these genres and writers do not conceptualize the indigenous body or Native communities as "inherently unwell" (Daschuk "When Canada Used Hunger"). Kelm describes how early twentieth-century colonial policies and medical discourse naturalized illness among First Nations and the ways in which indigenous peoples have resisted this process, instead locating "social and physical pathologies *outside* themselves" (xvii). In literature of indigenous food sovereignty, the suffering of the indigenous body is clearly depicted as a result of colonization, a situation in which daily acts of cooking and provisioning are forms of resistance. As Enrique Salmón explains:

> It's not just about the food. The food that reaches the table is the final product of a process that is currently threatened. In this case, the food and food choices have become political symbols, revealing struggles for self-determination in places such as New Mexico. Eating a bowl of posole made from locally grown corn, lamb, and chili is equal to going to the state legislature to demand fair water rights.
>
> (148)

In this way, as Devon Mihesuah argues, for Native people restoring ancestral foods is a mode of decolonization.

In the essay "White Earth: A Lifeway in the Forest," LaDuke describes precisely this work of decolonization through land recovery and restoration of indigenous foodways. The essay opens with an epigraph from tribal elder Lucy Thompson that evokes the ravenous cannibal spirit: "'Now the white people claim everything that the Indians used to use in the olden days … . If they could do it, they'd take everything … the only thing they'd leave us is our appetites'"; in the last sentence, LaDuke also employs the imagery of the cannibal, observing that "the rapacious culture eaters, the loggers, the miners" have not quenched the "spirit and lifeway [that] have sustained a community for generations" (*Relations* 112, 134). In this essay, LaDuke brings her experience into the dialogue about indigenous cultural survival, positioning herself not only as narrator and archivist but also as a member of the community, a voice in a continuing storytelling tradition. Like each essay in the collection, the chapter begins with a map. Two smaller maps inset at the top, labeled "Big Woods of Minnesota," show the extent of tribal land loss from 1830 to 1990 (114). The larger map depicts the complex patchwork of land ownership in White Earth, including lands promised in different treaties as well as federal, state, county, corporate, and private lands, the lands claimed by contested settlements, and the lands reclaimed by the White Earth Land Recovery Project (WELRP). While the map in *Tracks*, with its patches of "pale and rotten pink," figures the deployment of the map as an imperial technology, in this text the map documents the work of WELRP and thus supports the efforts toward "retaking land" (Huhndorf 141). In this way, as Shari Huhndorf explains, cartography can be utilized in visual cultural productions and literary texts as a "protest that challenges colonial constructions of land ownership and history" (140–41).

The first part of the essay details the process of dispossession of White Earth land through treaties and allotments as land was transferred to logging and mining companies and, more recently, through the White Earth Land Settlement Act. As land was taken, the people suffered from disease and population declined, spurred on by "the so-called Relocation

Act of the 1950s, under which tribal members (and native people across the country) were offered one-way bus tickets to major urban areas" (121). In response to these historical depredations and contemporary opposition to Native treaty rights, LaDuke and others created WELRP, which utilizes a variety of strategies to reclaim title to tribal lands and to protect "Native cemeteries, forests, and other endangered ecosystems" (126). These lands include "maple sugarbush, the most endangered ecosystem on the reservation ... The project works aggressively to preserve Native languages and culture, restore traditional seed stocks, and reinstate self-determination and self-reliance" (126–27). This description articulates the central elements of food sovereignty embedded within a wider vision of self-determination. WELRP has worked to reduce mercury contamination of local lakes to support indigenous fishing, to restore farming, and to reclaim "local food self-reliance" (130). LaDuke reflects that:

> There is nothing quite like walking through a small field of hominy corn, corn you know your ancestors planted on this same land a thousand years ago. Corn is in the recipes and memories of elders. The inherited memory is the essence of cultural restoration and the force that grows with each step toward the path – the 'lifeway' – as some of the Anishinaabeg call it.
>
> (130)

This restoration project has deep meanings that take place within memory, cosmology, and identity; it shows that food sovereignty is essential to, and cannot be separated out from, the encompassing frame of tribal sovereignty.

LaDuke concludes her essay on her homeland with a portrait of Lennie Butcher, a member of White Earth who has been repeatedly arrested for subsistence practices on what "the state considers its property" (133). Lennie places his actions within a framework of sovereignty, explaining that "Freedom is living how I choose to in my people's way'" (134). In closing with this act of traditional subsistence that transgresses the land claims of the settler government, LaDuke subtly links this practice of civil disobedience to more direct forms of action, such as the armed uprising of 1898, when "The military came to the defense of the lumber companies" that were logging White Earth (118). As LaDuke demonstrates in her work on Akwesasne, toxic colonization is only the most recent threat to indigenous food sovereignty. In recent years, indigenous peoples in the United States and Canada have employed a series of tactics to protest encroachment on Native land, especially by the fossil fuel industry. The fight against the Keystone Pipeline (KXL), for example, has been led by indigenous nations who refuse to allow the pipeline to cross their lands and threaten the Ogallala aquifer (see Owe Aku Bring Back the Way and International Justice Project). In an act of resistance to KXL, activists planted sacred Ponka red corn on the Tanderup family farm (members of the Cowboy and Indian Alliance) in the proposed route of the pipeline (Andrei). As Mekasi Horinek (member of the Ponca Tribe, Oklahoma) explains:

> "Together our families will plant sacred red corn seed in our ancestral soil. As the corn grows it will stand strong for us, to help us protect and keep Mother Earth safe for our children, as we fight this battle against the Keystone XL pipeline."
>
> (Andrei)

This planting both illuminates the importance of Native foods and indigenous agriculture and asks the corn to help the people resist this most recent form of land dispossession. Native American literature reveals the rich and complex food traditions that have sustained indigenous peoples in North America since time immemorial, relations that have survived colonization and will continue to oppose the cannibal spirit that seeks to consume land and bodies.

Notes

1 See Shirley Brozzo, "Food for Thought: A Postcolonial Study of Food Imagery in Louise Erdrich's *Antelope Wife*" for a discussion of the complexity of food and hunger imagery in this novel.
2 Throughout this chapter I have followed the author's uses of terms such as First Nation, Aboriginal, Native, and indigenous. Spelling of indigenous words such as windigo and Anishinaabe vary between authors, so I have chosen to standardize, recognizing that all renditions of Native languages into English are at best approximations. I have used "indigenous" and "Native" interchangeably and have referred to Canadian indigenous communities as "First Nations." My choice to write about Anishinaabe literature and foodways also reflects my current location in northeastern Ohio near Lake Erie, part of the Great Lakes watershed.
3 Akwesasne, the Mohawk reservation that is the focus in LaDuke's essay, is also located in the Great Lakes borderlands. The Mohawk are part of the Haudenosaunee people (13).
4 Kyle Powys Whyte notes that as a result of the reservation system some Anishinaabeg peoples were displaced to Oklahoma and Kansas (5).
5 I use the term "indigenous scientific knowledge" (and sometime "indigenous ecological knowledge") rather than the more well-known "Traditional Ecological Knowledge" (TEK) to recognize the epistemic parity of indigenous knowledge with Western science and to avoid the static connotations of the word "traditional."
6 Kari Winter offers a powerful reading of exactly this dynamic in her analysis of *Tracks*, 49.
7 For links between food, medicine, and sovereignty, see Adamson, "Medicine Foods."
8 For a detailed account of the place of food sovereignty within the United Nations Declaration of the Rights of Indigenous Peoples (UNDRIP), see Adamson, "Medicine Food."
9 Winona LaDuke discusses the importance of IPRs in defending against "biocolonialism" in her essay "Ricekeepers."
10 For a nuanced discussion of the impact of commodity foods on indigenous health in relation to diabetes, see Gary Paul Nabhan, "Discerning the Histories encoded in our Bodies": chapter 1 of *Why Some Like It Hot*.

Works cited

Adamson, Joni. *American Indian Literature, Environmental Justice, and Ecocriticism: The Middle Place.* Tucson: University of Arizona Press, 2000.
——. "Medicine Food: Critical Environmental Justice, Native North American Literature, and the Movement for Food Sovereignty." *Environmental Justice* 4. 4 (2011): 213–19.
Andrei, Mary Anne. "Cowboy and Indian Alliance Plants Sacred Ponka Red Corn in the Path of the KXL." 22 June 2014. Web. Accessed 31 Jan. 2015. http://boldnebraska.org/cowboy-and-indian-alliance-plants-sacred-ponka-red-corn-in-the-path-of-kxl/
Berglund, Jeff. *Cannibal Fictions: American Explorations of Colonialism, Race, Gender, and Sexuality.* Madison: University of Wisconsin Press, 2006.
Brozzo, Shirley. "Food for Thought: A Postcolonial Study of Food Imagery in Louise Erdrich's *Antelope Wife*." *Studies in American Indian Literature* 17. 1 (Spring 2005): 1–15.

Daschuk, James. *Clearing the Plains: Disease, the Politics of Starvation, and the Loss of Aboriginal Life*. Regina, SK: University of Regina Press, 2013.

——. "When Canada Used Hunger to Clear the West." *The Globe and Mail*. 19 July 2013. Web. Accessed 2 Jan. 2015. http://www.theglobeandmail.com/globe-debate/when-canada-used-hunger-to-clear-the-west/article13316877/

Erdrich, Louise. *The Antelope Wife*. New York: HarperFlamingo, 1998.

——. *The Birchbark House*. New York: Hyperion, 1999.

——. *Tracks*. New York: Henry Holt, 1988.

Hele, Karl S., ed. Introduction. *Lines Drawn Upon Water: First Nations and the Great Lakes Borders and Borderlands*. London, ON: Wilfred Laurier Press, 2008. xiii–xxiii.

Huhndorf, Shari M. *Mapping the Americas: The Transnational Politics of Contemporary Native Culture*. Ithaca, NY: Cornell University Press, 2009.

Kelm, Mary-Ellen. *Colonizing Bodies: Aboriginal Health and Healing in British Columbia, 1900–50*. Vancouver, BC: University of British Columbia Press, 1998.

Knobloch, Frieda. *The Culture of Wilderness: Agriculture as Colonization in the American West*. Chapel Hill: University of North Carolina Press, 1996.

La Via Campesina. Web. Accessed 2 Jan. 2015. http://viacampesina.org/en/index.php/organisation-mainmenu-44/what-is-la-via-campesina-mainmenu-45

LaDuke, Winona. *All Our Relations: Native Struggles for Land and Life*. Cambridge, MA: South End Press, 1999.

——. *Last Woman Standing*. St. Paul, MN: Voyageur Press, 1997.

——. "Ricekeepers." *Orion Magazine* (July/August) 2007. Web. Accessed 2 Jan. 2015. https://orionmagazine.org/article/ricekeepers/

Lischke, Ute. "Louise Erdrich and the Lines Drawn Upon the Waters and Lands." *Lines Drawn Upon Water: First Nations and the Great Lakes Borders and Borderlands*. Ed. Karl S. Hele. London, ON: Wilfred Laurier Press, 2008. 219–32.

Mihesuah, Devon A. "Decolonizing Our Diets by Recovering Our Ancestor's Gardens." *American Indian Quarterly* 27. 3/4 (Summer–Autumn 2003): 807–39.

Mosby, Ian. "Administering Colonial Science: Nutrition Research and Human Biomedical Experimentation in Aboriginal Communities and Residential Schools, 1942–1952." *Social History* 46. 91 (May 2013): 145–72.

Nabhan, Gary Paul. *Cultures of Habitat: On Nature, Culture, and Story*. Washington, D.C.: Counterpoint Press, 1997.

——. *Why Some Like it Hot: Food, Genes, and Cultural Diversity*. Washington, D.C.: Island Press, 2004.

Nelson, Joshua B. "The Uses of Indigenous Literatures." *World Literature Today* 88. 5 (Sept.–Oct. 2014): 28–32.

Owe Aku Bring Back the Way and International Justice Project. Web. Accessed 2 Jan. 2015. http://www.oweakuinternational.org

Salmón, Enrique. *Eating the Landscape: American Indian Stories of Food, Identity, and Resilience*. Tucson: University of Arizona Press, 2012.

Silko, Leslie Marmon. *Gardens in the Dunes: A Novel*. New York: Simon & Schuster, 1999.

Whyte, Kyle Powys. "Food Justice and Collective Food Relations." *The Ethics of Food: An Introductory Textbook*. Ed. Anne Barnhill, Mark Budolfson & Tyler Doggett. New York: Oxford University Press, 2015. 1–18.

Winter, Kari J. "The Politics and Erotics of Food in Louise Erdrich." *Studies in American Indian Literatures* 12. 4 (Winter 2000): 44–64.

21

(Alter)Native Medicine and Health Sovereignty

Disease and Healing in Contemporary Native American Writings

Hsinya Huang

In the study of literature, we frequently come across "disease" as an archetypal thematic concern that transcends both time and space: the plague spreads across texts from the Bible, Sophocles' *Oedipus the King*, and Boccaccio's introduction to the *Decameron* (1348), to Daniel Defoe's *Journal of the Plague Year* (1722), Thomas Mann's *Death in Venice* (1930), Albert Camus' *The Plague* (1947) and many more. R. Gordon's selections in his *Literary Companion to Medicine* (1996), for instance, range from the Bible, Boccaccio, William Shakespeare, Rabelais, Daniel Defoe, and Schiller all the way down to nineteenth- and twentieth-century works about disease and medicine, providing an array of historical touchstones that offer windows onto the medical and literary history from yesteryear to now. Whereas diseases do spread across texts from the ancient to the contemporary, Gordon's Eurocentric work omits any mention of the indigenous tribes of the Americas and how they have fought fierce wars of resistance against diseases and plagues since Discovery.

In response to this critical deficit in the mainstream narratives of literature, disease, and medicine, I examine Native American illness and healing in contemporary writings by underscoring Native American alternative medical practices and health sovereignty. I argue that Native American health sovereignty relies on indigenous knowledge of the interconnected web between humans and non-humans, conveyed by their ancestral stories and storytelling (see "Sovereignty" WHO). According to the World Health Organization (WHO), "health sovereignty is the exercise of a state's sovereign power to protect and promote health and provide health services." This definition, which centers on the sovereign power of the modern nation-state, has unfortunately bypassed North American Indian nations, due to the political status of Native Nations within the borders of what is today the United States and Canada. In this chapter, I redefine sovereignty as the right or capacity of American Indian Nations to determine their own affairs, which are not to be influenced by colonial or hegemonic forces of the U.S. or Canadian nation-state. Sovereignty over Native bodies should be recognized as the premise for Native Americans to gain self-governance, determination, and autonomy, because the body is the material base and cultural/historical text upon which "power relations have an immediate hold," to borrow Michel Foucault's famous phrasing in *Discipline and Punish* (25). The notion of health sovereignty denotes the exercise of the tribal sovereign power to protect and promote health and provide health practices and services.

As early as the Discovery, the Western world benefited from Native American medical and herbal practices. The introduction of quinine, extracted from a Native American traditional medicine, Peruvian bark, for instance, marked the beginning of modern Western pharmacology and made possible the extensive European settlement of America because with quinine these colonists acquired cures for the dreadful disease of malaria (Weatherford 177). Old World doctors constantly turned to the pharmacy of the Americas for cures. In addition to quinine, Native American medicine provided cures for numerous diseases, such as amoebic dysentery, scurvy, non-venereal syphilis, and goiter problems. More than two hundred Native American drugs have been appropriated as official entries in the *Pharmacopeia of the United States of America* since the first edition appeared in 1820, and in the *National Formulary* since it began in 1888 (Vogel 6). Native American medical knowledge has been appropriated by the colonial power that usurped not only their lands but their cultural heritage. Through patenting, their medicine has been pirated in the name of protecting knowledge and preventing piracy. Their ancestral knowledge about seeds and herbs has been claimed as an invention of U.S. corporations and U.S. scientists. Lecha and Zeta, the protagonists of Leslie Marmon Silko's *Almanac of the Dead*, find that patent-drug companies have disseminated their ancestral medicine books and given away ancient almanacs as advertisements in medicine shows. For them, not even the parchment pages or fragments of ancient paper could be trusted. For these pirated medicine books all bear "clever forgeries, recopied, drawn, and colored painstakingly," of the colonial script (Silko *Almanac* 570). Thereby, tribal medicine has been inextricably bound to the ongoing colonial enterprise of domination, appropriation, and abuse (see Huang).

In his discussion of medicinal plant use and health sovereignty, Karim-Aly Kassam contends that health sovereignty concerns how individuals and communities exercise their agency, including the ability to choose medicines that are socio-culturally and ecologically appropriate, thereby providing practical, reliable, and culturally and eco-logically relevant health care (817–29). Native Americans have the inherent power and right to govern and protect their health and wellbeing by resorting to their traditional medical knowledge. Their tribal medicine evolves around the ecological possibilities of their homeland, cultural and ritual significance, traditional knowledge capacity, and communal governance structures with respect to meeting their food and health needs. It attends to a state of holistic wellbeing. This indigenous right to their traditional knowl-edge of medical care is constituted and protected in the "United Nations Declaration on the Rights of Indigenous Peoples":

> Indigenous peoples have the right to their traditional medicines and to maintain their health practices, including the conservation of their vital medicinal plants, animals and minerals. Indigenous individuals also have the right to access, with-out any discrimination, to all social and health services.
>
> (2008, Article 24, Section 1)

Native American people before the Conquest lived a healthy life without much inter-ference from outside sources, despite the harsh continental environment. Diseases such as smallpox, trachoma, measles, influenza, cholera, typhoid, and certain venereal diseases did not exist among the aboriginal populations of the Americas prior to the arrival of Europeans (Trennert 3). The greatest and most tragic irony, however, is that this relatively good health of Native Americans and power over their bodies prior to the coming of the European colonists became a key cause of their disastrous undoing. In their thousands of years of isolation from the rest of the world, they were spared from contact with the cataclysms of disease that had wreaked havoc in the "Old World." The outbreak of such epidemics as smallpox took place as a result of Contact and the devastating contagion hardly spared any of the indigenous tribes of the newly "discovered" continent.

Consequently, while colonial invasion invited determined resistance from Native Americans, European colonists survived the warfare because of the microscopic smallpox bacillus. It became catastrophic as it spread among a people with no previous exposure to it. In conceptualizing what he calls the "American holocaust," David Stannard stresses the devastating effects of Old World diseases in the Americas alongside the colonists' subsequent massacres of Native people (57–95). Nonetheless, he fails to specify that New World massacres and Old World diseases are in effect two sides of the same coin, with the latter disguising, rationalizing, and legitimating the former. It is not simply disease but the colonial gaze on the diseased Native body that finally legitimated the colonists' desire to erase the supposedly inferior savages who contracted diseases to which the colonists were largely immune. In fact, as Louis Owens discloses, British agents intentionally gave indigenous tribes blankets that were contaminated with smallpox virus (120, 241). Over 100,000 died among the Mingo, Delaware, Shawnee, and other Ohio River nations. The colonists' army followed suit and used the same method on the Plains tribal populations with similar success (see Welch *Killing Custer* 33; qtd. in Owens 241, n.5). While diseases were deliberately spread among Native people, these purposeful slaughters brought on a demographic drop in the Native American population. Never in history have so many deaths impacted an ethnic group than Native Americans since 1492, due to the combined forces of microbial pestilence and human genocide (see Arnold *Problem of Nature*78).

Sherman Alexie's poems recapitulate brutal historical realities of the smallpox-infected blankets. In the powerful refrains of his poem "I Would Steal Horses," Alexie recalls the killing of native people by the smallpox-infected blankets. Blankets mirror a diseased history of colonial conquests and loss of tribal sovereignty. Demarcated as a space of suffering, Alexie's reservation is a place where indigenous people are tormented by collective memories of a genocidal past prefigured in smallpox-infected blankets.

Likewise, Louise Erdrich's novel *Tracks* (1988) commences with the onslaughts of the epidemics of smallpox and tuberculosis that had swept through Native American communities since 1492. The first chapter, narrated by the old medicine man Nanapush, opens as the tribe recovers from a devastating smallpox epidemic that is followed in turn by "consumption":

> *We* started dying before the snow, and like the snow, we continued to fall … . For those who survived the *spotted sickness* from the south, our long fight west to Nadouissioux land where we signed *the treaty*, and then a wind from the east, bringing exile in a storm of *government papers* … . By then [1912], we thought disaster must surely have spent its force, *that disease* must have claimed all of the Anishinaabeg that the earth could hold and bury. But the earth is limitless and

so is luck and so were our people once … . *A new sickness* swept down … . *The consumption* … . This disease was different from the *pox* and *fever*, for it came on *slow*. The outcome, however, was just as certain.

(1–2; emphasis added)

"Consumption" was used as a synonym for pulmonary tuberculosis as early as 1398 in medieval Europe (Sontag 14). By de-nominating "the consumption" as "a new sickness," Nanapush draws a demarcation line in New World disease history. The lethal disease that Europeans carried to the New World repeatedly "consumed" the indigenous people who were not immunized. As the colonial medical historian Alfred W. Crosby has found, epidemic diseases wiped out up to 50 percent of Native Americans while warfare killed only an estimated 10 percent (196). Nanapush specifically emphasizes the horror of the newly introduced epidemics – he articulates this horror by repeatedly pronouncing "the last":

I guided *the last* buffalo hunt. I saw *the last* bear shot. I trapped *the last* beaver … . I spoke aloud the words of the government treaty, and refused to sign the settlement papers that would take away our woods and lake. I axed *the last* birch that was older than I, and I saved *the last* Pillager.

(2; emphasis added)

In this way, Erdrich discloses the limits of documentary history by supplying the testimony from "the last" surviving tribal witness. The contrast between the pre- and post-Contact eras are indeed striking. The earth, as "it was before," contained "no fences, no poles, no lines, no tracks" (159). Yet, after the whites came, "those who starved, drank, and froze, those who died of the cough" (159–60) covered the lands. The devastating epidemics in effect resulted in the destruction of the total population inhabiting Native lands: human and non-human.

Nanapush bypasses the official markers of disease as he refers to "the spotted sickness" instead of smallpox, and to "a new sickness," "invisible sickness," and "slow" disease rather than tuberculosis or "the consumption" as Father Damien calls it. He uses the traditional tribal names "Anishinaabeg" and "Nadouissioooux" rather than anglicized ones like "Chippewa" and "Sioux"; he refers to "government papers" without ever naming specific documents, ignoring their official designations. Consequently, "consumption" refers also to the colonists' stealing of natural resources in native lands because "diseases" and "treaties" alternate in Nanapush's narrative to constitute a stark picture of the plight of the tribe. In all this, as Nancy J. Peterson insightfully pinpoints, Erdrich insists on the need for tribal people "to tell their stories and their own histories" (985) even as they are endangered by disease. It is an act of empowerment, of reclaiming sovereignty over their bodies as well as their lands as the "earth body" that is central to tribal survival.

Winona LaDuke's *Last Standing Woman* touches on colonial disease in much the same way that Erdrich's novel does. Her story is imbedded within recurring images of "disease": the pox and coughing brought by the French (45); the Church having come to the tribe in the early 1800s, bringing both the Bible and the smallpox (47); fully 60 percent of the Native Americans being afflicted with tuberculosis, 30 percent with trachoma and 20 percent with syphilis (86); and the death of old woman Ishkweniibawiikwe and Situpiwin due to coughing disease (87).

Leslie Marmon Silko's novel *Almanac of the Dead* chronicles epidemic diseases, too. The novel spans 500 years, with the ancient almanac, transmitted from generation to generation, as its pivotal text. The first accurate year of the almanac is 1560, identifying the first impact of colonial disease in the novel:

> The year of the plague – intense cold and fever – bleeding from nose and coughing, twisted necks and large sores erupt. Plague ravages the countryside for more than three years. Smallpox too had followed in the wake of the plague. Deaths number in the thousands.
>
> (577)

The more spectacular examples follow the first outbreak after the Contact: "1590 – In the sixty-seventh year after the alien invasion, on January 3, 1590, the epidemic began: cough, chills, and fever from which people died" (577); "1617–24 – Smallpox" (578); "1621 – Five Ah, the plague began to spread" (578); and "[t]he Great Influenza of 1918" (579). Yoeme, the keeper of the ancient almanac, records in her notebooks:

> At first the officials refuse to believe the reports of so many sick and dead. Influenza travels with the moist, warm winds off the coast. Influenza infects the governor and all the others. The police chief burns to death from fever.
>
> (579–80)

Historical references to colonial diseases in Native American literature abound. Gerald Vizenor's *Hotline Healers: An Almost Browne Novel* uses Peggy Lee's song "Fever" as an ironic reminder of the endemic disease in the history of Euro-American Conquest. James Welch's Native American classic, *Fools Crow*, is still another example. Yellow Kidney finds himself in a lodge filled with bodies of those with "white scabs" (see Vernon). Smallpox destroys Native lives and medical ways. These epidemics decimated the indigenous population with infections to which the conquerors themselves were largely immune. It turns out that disease was a potent factor in the European conceptualization of indigenous society. That the indigenous population contracted fatal diseases is considered to be evidence of their racial and physical inferiority. This was especially so by the close of the nineteenth century when Europeans began to pride themselves on their scientific understanding of disease causation and mocked what they saw "as the fatalism, superstition and barbarity of indigenous responses to disease" (Arnold "Introduction" 7). The association of diseases like smallpox, plague, cholera and malaria with the indigenous population – a development fostered by the growing understanding of disease etiology and transmission in the late nineteenth century – encouraged European pride in their innate racial and physical superiority: their physical constitution made these colonists ideal for inhabiting the New World (Arnold "Introduction" 8; Wisecup 199). This "innate racial and physical superiority" legitimated Euramerican colonial expansion. The destruction of many of the indigenous societies by "germs" contributed to the fulfillment of what the white colonists regard as "Manifest Destiny."

While the destruction of Native bodies by germs coincides with loss and degradation of Native lands and environment, "Manifest Destiny" is the destiny which imprisons common humanity across the Americas. More precisely, in *Sacred Water*, Silko notes that uranium mine waste and contamination from underground nuclear tests ruin the dwindling supplies of fresh water (75). Silko specifically identifies the site of the uranium mine located near Paguate, one of seven villages on the Laguna Pueblo reservation in New Mexico. The disappearance of Beautiful Lake, Kawaik, where, in Navajo cosmology, mortals emerge as living souls from the Fourth World below, becomes a drastic reality as the tribe cannot prevent the mining of their land. All that Yoeme identifies as "a great misfortune for us" in her old notebooks actually occurs (Silko *Almanac* 135).

In Silko's first novel, *Ceremony*, this misfortune strikes Tayo, the protagonist, as a sort of apocalyptic revelation. Soon after the end of the Second World War, as Tayo returned and approached his old home, the sandstone and dirt taken from inside the mesa, piled up in mounds and in long rows, "like fresh graves" (245), stood as evidence of colonial exploitation of tribal lands. This echoes the two photos taken in the 1950s and 1960s as described in *Storyteller*, which Silko sets off in contrast: the mesas and hills that appear in the first photo are gone and swallowed by the mine in the second (80–81). As he progresses in his journey back home along Route 66, Tayo realizes:

> Trinity Site [in Alamogordo of New Mexico], where [the whites] exploded the first atomic bomb, was only three hundred miles to the southeast, at White Sands. And the top-secret laboratories where the bomb had been created were deep in the Jemez Mountains, on land the Government took from Cochiti Pueblo.
>
> (245–46)

Linking "the Cebolleta land grant" where uranium mining took place with "Cochiti Pueblo" where uranium bombs were created and Alamogordo of New Mexico where the bombs were tested, Silko inserts Native American lands into the "space of death," from which Native Americans find no escape. It is this apocalyptic vision that connects Tayo's fragmentary memory of his days on the Asian battlefield with those with his tribal people in his homelands and he arrives at a point of what would be called "convergence," where the fates of "all living things" and "the Earth" have been laid (246). While the two atomic explosions in Hiroshima and Nagasaki resulted in one of the greatest casualties in human history, Laguna people and lands continue to suffer from the drastic consequences of colonists' evil doings:

> [H]uman beings were one clan again, united by the fate the destroyers planned for all of them, for all living things; united by a circle of death that devoured people in cities twelve thousand miles away, victims who had never known these mesas, who had never seen the delicate colors of the rocks which boiled up their slaughter.
>
> (246)

Mining destroys lives across time and distance, fatefully connecting people in Hiroshima and Nagasaki with tribal people in the Americas, or rather virtually enclosing human beings in "a cycle of death" from which no one could possibly escape. Tracing the damage to global health by atomic bombs, Gerald Vizenor's *Hiroshima Bugi: Atomu 57* begins in the ruins of the Atomic Bomb Dome, where the protagonist Ronin Browne creates a new calendar that starts with the first use of atomic weapons, Atomu One. The documentary *Village of Widows*

(Dir. Peter Blow) is another example of how the health of indigenous people (the Sahtu Dene people across the U.S. and Canadian borders) was threatened when they were forced to transport uranium for the bombs that devastated Hiroshima and Nagasaki. The colonialist governments sacrifice not merely Native American benefits but the relationship of humans to the natural world. The result is the disappearance of indigenous peoples and species over the last 500 years since Contact, which Winona LaDuke in her prose writing, *All Our Relations: Native Struggles for Land and Life*, characterizes as "a great holocaust" (1). Native illness emerges out of environmental catastrophe in the global scale.

Reading *Almanac of the Dead*, Joni Adamson insightfully points out that Euramericans continue to stray away from the value of interconnectedness of all lives in a unified eco-system, which "sections of late-seventeenth-century American almanacs" evidence (143). Native health sovereignty thus resides in recovering the ancient medicine ways, which employ "earth mother imagery in profusion" and advise colonial farmers about "how to make healing herbal remedies" (Adamson 143). Silko's novel *Gardens in the Dunes*, for instance, begins by tracing tribal life back to the years before white exploitation and uncovers a garden of vegetation with abundant water: "precious moisture from runoff that nurtured the plants; along the sandstone cliffs above the dunes, dampness seeped out of cracks in the cliff" (14). Amaranth grows profusely at the foot of the dunes. When there is nothing else to eat, there is amaranth; Sister Salt boils up amaranth greens as Grandma Fleet has taught her. *Gardens in the Dunes* epitomizes the deep and intricate connections between the animate and inanimate and among living beings, which is the very basis of Native health sovereignty. In Laguna cosmology, the earth is a living character endowed with the powers of healing and contains all the living spirits existing in the medicines the Pueblo people use. In *Almanac of the Dead* coca leaves serve as a prominent example of Native medicine. The leaves are governed by the deity of Mama Coca, who "had loved and cared for the people for thousands of years" (502). Donald L. Fixico notes that Native Americans "found themselves constantly dependent upon their natural environment … . Plants and herbs provided them with medicine … . Such plants and herbs had spiritual powers to help the people" (34).

In *Gardens in the Dunes*, Indigo receives a package "that held a small silk-bound notebook where Aunt Bronwyn hand-printed the names (in English and Latin) of medicinal plants and the best conditions and methods to grow them" and adds other names: monkshood, wolfsbane, aconite, *Aconitum napellus*, etc. (268). She copies medicinal uses of these herbs – "anodyne, febrifuge, and diuretic" – and writes their definitions: "Anodyne" is Greek for "no pain"; "febrifuge" she remembers as "refuge from fever"; the English word "febrile" comes from the Latin *febris*, for "fever"; "diuretic" is from the Greek for "urine" (282). In this way, Indigo works together with women of different ethnic origins to complete a medicine book. It is a medical text of hybridity, mingling both the pre-modern and the tribal to combat the modern tyranny of science, capitalism, and colonialism. A down-to-earth practicality is privileged as women plant the seeds, nurture and gather the flowers, and share a connected consciousness. In her notes on the novel, Silko points out that she mingled many elements including "orchids, gladiolus, ancient gardens, Victorian gardens, Native American gardens, Old European figures of Snake-bird Goddesses" to write the novel about Indigo's journey (480). The authorial act of naming is redemptive. Those elements nominated in Silko's narrative can be arranged into four basic elements which "have ever danced together": "women, magic, tribes, and Earth," to borrow Paula Gunn Allen's words (*Sacred Hoop* 24). Silko's

Gardens in the Dunes demonstrates how these four elements "have ever danced together" and how these four elements had once been repressed and sundered apart but have now been recovered. Different plants, trees, and herbs permeate *Gardens in the Dunes* and constitute a strong sense of Native sovereignty over lands and bodies. Passages concerning planting, flowers, and herbs become the major threads that tie the characters intimately together. After the first "beans and squash" are harvested, Grandma Fleet leaves her shelter by the "peach seedlings" less and less often. The girls help her walk through the gardens, where she surveys "the sunflowers, some small and pale yellow, others orange-yellow and much taller than they were; then she examined the brilliant red amaranth. ... The gardens were green with corn and bush beans" (50–51). And the night Indigo dreams, she comes back home to the old gardens "where the sunflowers and corn plants and squash" once grew, "the tall gladiolus bloom[s] in all colors" (304). As the twins Maytha and Vedna arrive at the garden, even from a distance "the bright ribbons of purple, red, yellow, and black gladiolus flowers were impossible to miss, woven crisscross over the terrace gardens, through the amaranth, pole beans, and sunflowers" (474). The twins especially like the "speckled corn" effect of the color combinations that Indigo makes with the "gladiolus," which she plants in rows to resemble corn kernels. Maytha as well as Indigo favors "lavender, purple, white, and black planting," but Sister Salt and Vedna prefer the dark red, black, purple, pink, and white planting. In the morning sky "blue morning glories wreathed the edges of the terraces like necklaces" (476). Down the shoulder of the dune to the hollow between the dunes, silver white gladiolus with pale blues and pale lavenders glows among the great dark jade datura leaves. "Just wait until sundown – the fragrance of the big datura blossoms with the gladiolus flowers [will] make them swoon," Indigo promises (476). They are medicine women in Paula Gunn Allen's definition as they develop "refined powers of observation and discernment in the ritualist and extensive knowledge of seasons, weather, astronomy, and healing, conferring on its devotee a degree of mental sophistication that rivals that of physicians, scientists, computer experts, or metaphysicians" (*Grandmothers of the Light* 12).

Fleur in Erdrich's *Tracks* participates in tribal medicine, too, as she knows "the secret ways to cure" (2). Fleur's power specifically resides in what Paula Gunn Allen terms "the way of the mother." The disciplines of the medicine woman's way, as Paula Gunn Allen describes, include the ways of all women as well as those of advanced practitioners or specialists in the medicine path. These ways include the way of the daughter, the way of the householder, the way of the mother, the way of the gatherer, the way of the ritualist, the way of the teacher, and the way of the wise woman (*Grandmothers* 10). In delivering her daughter Lulu, Fleur exemplifies the spirit of tribal healing – the interconnectedness of the cosmic web – in her way of being a mother. During her labor, "it is as if the Manitous all through the woods spoke through Fleur, loose, arguing: Turtle's quavering scratch, the Eagle's high shriek, Loon's crazy bitterness, Otter, the howl of Wolf, Bear's low rasp" (*Tracks* 59). The bear is summoned into the birth house. Fleur is soon filled with such power that she raises herself on the mound of blankets and gives birth. Fleur does not open her eyes until Nanapush's wife Margaret saves her by packing wormwood and moss between her legs, wrapping her in blankets heated with stones, then kneading Fleur's stomach and forcing her to drink cup after cup of boiled raspberry leaf until at last Fleur groans, draws the baby against her breast, and regains life (60). Herbs are used to lend their spirit and power to humans. In all this, Erdrich inscribes the medicine of tribal practitioners, dismissing any association with Western gynecology.

(ALTER)NATIVE MEDICINE AND HEALTH SOVEREIGNTY

Disease carries a potential for salvation. In *Gardens in the Dunes*, the plague "fever" is transformed into pledged "fervor" for the return and rebirth of the Earth while the land is an animate "Mother" (625). This rebirth is embodied in the performance of the Ghost Dance both at the outset and near the end of the novel:

> I]f the Paiutes and all the other Indians danced this dance, then the used-up land would be made whole again and the elk and the herds of buffalo killed off would return. The dance was a peaceful dance, and the Paiutes wished no harm to white people; ... . If they danced the dance, then they would be able to visit their dear ones and beloved ancestors. The ancestor spirits were there to help them. ... [T] hey all were happy and excited because they had seen the Earth reborn.
>
> (23–24)

The spirits and specters come back not to haunt but to "help." The dancers are careful to drag their feet lightly along the ground to keep themselves in touch with the Mother Earth. As they move from right to left, because that is the path followed by the sun, the indigenous bodies correspond to the Earth body to uncover a cosmic harmony that has long been disturbed by the alien invasion. Only by dancing can they hope to bring the Messiah, who would bring back with him all their beloved family members and friends who have moved on to the spirit world after "[t]he invaders made the Earth get old and want to die" (*Gardens* 26). To the end of the novel, the bodily practice of the Ghost Dance, a dance attuned to cosmic rhythms, evidences a form of Native American health sovereignty "to repel diseases and sickness, especially influenza," which killed millions of people at its outbreak at the turn of the century (32). It is in the similar spirit of reclaiming Native American health sovereignty that Sherman Alexie transforms the "smallpox blanket" into a desired blanket of warmth, faith, honor and grace in his poem "Blankets."

While "blankets" carry on the "thematic primacy in the lives and histories of Native people" (de Ramírez 124), contemporary Native American writers rise above the stereotypical Vanishing Indian (of the smallpox-infected blankets) to re-inscribe repressed medical knowledge and to reclaim the sovereignty of Native people. This chapter started with the anger and pain of smallpox and other colonial diseases wreaking havoc along with military slaughter, which deprived Native Americans of sovereignty over their bodies. Whereas their herbal knowledge was appropriated and patented and the medicine way of spirituality demonized as a sign of savagery, Native American bodies perished as the result of massive epidemics introduced by European intruders, bringing social and cultural degeneration, colonial greed and intemperance in their wake. Disease has functioned as a nexus for white–red conflict since the Discovery. In disease narratives where medicine is a critical site of contact and conflict between white (State) authorities and red (tribal) people, the link is made explicit between European colonial hegemony and medicine, between imperialism and disease. Following the medicine ways as delineated in contemporary works about disease and healing, the medical discourse which this chapter has explored provides not only a unique point of entry for examining Native American collective loss at the time of lethal plagues but also an avenue to formulating a model of health sovereignty for contemporary indigenous groups.

Health is not just culture but a way to tribal sovereignty for Native Americans. Tribal knowledge about the causation of illness, the rules of healthy living, and the interconnection

257

between the human and non-human worlds should be retrieved as integral to the global health agenda. Rather than viewing Natives as only bodies that lacked crucial immunities, contemporary scholars have begun to view Native people as valuable sources of medical knowledge (Wisecup 202–03). With specific textual examples from prominent Native American authors, this chapter reverses the optimism of Western medicine based on scientific rationality, not to return to a false notion that "primitive" practices can provide a panacea for the world's health problems but, rather, to recover a medicine that incorporates myriad cultural formulations in tribal contexts, as a powerful and radical challenge to Western medical hegemony. It demonstrates, as Neil Safier puts it, "deep histories of science" (133) in (alter)native medicine, which also embodies a resistance politics, rendering the discourse of medicine a ground for contesting the ethnic identity of the Native as the Other. In Native medicine, the world envisions alternative conditions of wellbeing and wholeness, in the context of the American continent as Native American homelands: lands that resist the binary divisions between man and nature, human and non-human, and Us and Them.

Works cited

Adamson, Joni. *American Indian Literature, Environmental Justice, and Ecocriticism: The Middle Place.* Tucson: University of Arizona Press, 2001.

Alexie, Sherman. *First Indian on the Moon.* Brooklyn, Hanging Loose Press, 1993.

Allen, Paula Gunn, ed. *Grandmothers of the Light: A Medicine Woman's Sourcebook.* Boston: Beacon Press, 1991.

——. *The Sacred Hoop: Recovering the Feminine in American Indian Traditions.* Boston: Beacon Press, 1992.

Arnold, David. "Introduction: Disease, Medicine and Empire." *Imperial Medicine and Indigenous Societies.* Ed. David Arnold. Manchester: Manchester University Press, 1988. 1–26.

——. *The Problem of Nature: Environment, Culture, and European Expansion.* Oxford: Blackwell, 1996.

Crosby, Alfred W. *Ecological Imperialism: The Biological Expansion of Europe, 900–1900.* Cambridge: Cambridge University Press, 1986.

de Ramírez, Susan Berry Brill. "The Distinctive Sonority of Sherman Alexie's Indigenous Poetics." *Sherman Alexie: A Collection of Critical Essays.* Ed. Jeff Berglund & Jan Roush. Salt Lake City: University of Utah Press, 2010. 107–33.

Erdrich, Louise. *Tracks.* New York: Henry Holt, 1988.

Fixico, Donald L. "The Struggle for Our Homes: Indian and White Values and Tribal Lands." *Defending Mother Earth: Native American Perspectives on Environmental Justice.* Ed. Jace Weaver. New York: Maryknoll, 2001. 29–46.

Foucault, Michel. *Discipline and Punish: The Birth of the Prison.* Trans. Alan Sheridan. New York: Vintage Books, 1979.

Gordon, R., ed. *The Literary Companion to Medicine.* New York: St. Martin's Press, 1996.

Huang, Hsinya. *(De)Colonizing the Body: Disease, Empire, and (Alter)Native Medicine in Contemporary Native American Women's Writings.* Taipei: Bookman, 2004.

Kassam, Karim-Aly S. "Medicinal Plant Use and Health Sovereignty: Findings from the Tajik and Afghan Pamirs." *Human Ecology* 38. 6 (Dec. 2010): 817–29.

LaDuke, Winona. *All Our Relations: Native Struggles for Land and Life.* Boston: South End Press, 1999.

——. *Last Standing Woman.* Stillwater, MN: Voyageur Press, 1998.

Owens, Louis. *Mixedblood Messages: Literature, Film, Family, Place.* Norman: Oklahoma University Press, 1998.

Peterson, Nancy J. "History, Postmodernism, and Louise Erdrich's *Tracks*." *PMLA* 109. 5 (1994): 982–94.

Safier, Neil. "Global Knowledge on the Move: Itineraries, Amerindian Narratives, and Deep Histories of Science." *Isis* 101.1 (2010): 133–45.

Silko, Leslie Marmon. *Almanac of the Dead*. New York: Penguin, 1991.

———. *Ceremony*. New York: Penguin, 1977.

———. *Gardens in the Dunes: A Novel*. New York: Simon & Schuster, 1999.

———. *Sacred Water*. Tucson, AZ: Flood Plain Press, 1993.

———. *Storyteller*. New York: Arcade Publishing, 1981.

Sontag, Susan. *Illness as Metaphor*. New York: Penguin, 1987.

"Sovereignty." World Health Organization. Web. Accessed 6 Jan. 2015. http://www.who.int/trade/glossary/story082/en/

Stannard, David E. *The American Holocaust: The Conquest of the New World*. Oxford: Oxford University Press, 1992.

Trennert, Robert A. *White Man's Medicine: Government Doctors and the Navajo, 1863–1955*. Albuquerque: University of New Mexico Press, 1998.

"United Nations Declaration on the Rights of Indigenous Peoples." Web. Accessed 6 Jan. 2015. http://www.un.org/esa/socdev/unpfii/documents/DRIPS_en.pdf

Vernon, Irene S. "'A Happiness that Sleeps with Sadness': An Examination of 'White Scabs' in *Fools Crow*." *American Indian Quarterly* 29. 1–2 (2005): 178–97.

Village of Widows. Dir. Peter Blow. Lindum Films, 1999.

Vizenor, Gerald. *Hiroshima Bugi: Atomu 57*. Lincoln: University of Nebraska Press, 2010.

———. *Hotline Healers: An Almost Browne Novel*. Hanover, NH: Wesleyan University Press, 1997.

Vogel, Virgil J. *American Indian Medicine*. Norman: University of Oklahoma Press, 1990.

Weatherford, Jack. *Indian Givers: How the Indians of the Americas Transformed the World*. New York: Fawcett Columbine, 1990.

Welch, James. *Fools Crow*. New York: Penguin, 1987.

———. *Killing Custer: The Battle of the Little Bighorn and the Fate of the Plains Indians*. New York: Norton, 1994.

Wisecup, Kelly. "Microbes and a 'Magic Box': Medicine and Disease in Early American Studies." *Early American Literature* 47. 1 (2012): 199–216.

22

Religious Sovereignty and the Ghost Dance in Native American Fiction

Susannah Hopson

The history of Native American religious sovereignty is a highly complex one, rooted in intercultural conflict and incomprehension. Indigenous religious practices cannot be equated simply with Western concepts of religion since Native American religion encompasses sacred land use, tribal practices and aspects of daily life. As the Santee Sioux writer, Charles Alexander Eastman professes: "Every act of [an Indian's] life is, in a very real sense, a religious act" (*Soul of the Indian* 47). Thus Native American religious sovereignty cannot be parsed separately from wider Native American sovereignty with its long and profoundly contested history within the United States legal framework.[1]

As the Cherokee scholar Jace Weaver has pointed out, problems surrounding the expression of Native American religious freedom are bound centrally to the United States' founding documents and to the cultural incomprehension and dissonance that has accompanied settler history within colonial and "post-colonial" America. The Establishment and Free Exercise clauses are two of several pronouncements that make up the First Amendment of the United States Constitution. Read together these clauses state: "Congress shall make no law respecting an establishment of religion, or prohibiting the free exercise thereof." Theoretically this implies that Native American tribes have the freedom to practice their varied tribal religions without interference from the state. However, as Weaver states, the First Amendment can never afford full protection to Native religious traditions because, "although it has a particular conception of religion, it lacks a concept of the sacred or the holy" ("Losing My Religion" 180). Fundamentally, the First Amendment fails to account for the sacred interconnectedness in Native religions between land, culture and community. Furthermore, the term "religion" is in itself problematic when applied to Native American spirituality and ceremonial practice because it implies a dogmatic theology that can be isolated from other areas of life. As Osage theologian George Tinker writes: "Indian religions are so thoroughly entwined with and infused in their cultures that we cannot conceive of a theology that deals only with 'religion'" (*American Indian Liberation* 1). Thus, any discussion of Native theology must take seriously the differences between Western and Native worldviews aiming, as Weaver stresses, to "encompass – as much as possible – the entirety of the Native community" (*That the People* 31).

The long history of colonial aggression and interaction between indigenous Americans and settler communities has always involved conflict over land and resources and has been accompanied by simultaneous conflicts over religious or spiritual supremacy. Crucially, resistance to settler encroachment has consistently involved the use of religious or spiritual power between and across Native communities. Christianity expanded across Native lands as settler communities spread through indigenous communities through forced conversion or elective adoption. Despite displacement, encroachment and engulfment by settlers, diverse Native spiritual traditions have persisted and continue to flourish. As Weaver writes: "Because of the intimate connection between Native religion and Native culture and community, Christianity has been unable to displace traditional religious practices and belief, despite more than 500 years of ongoing colonist attempts to do so" (*That the People* viii).

Attacks on tribal religious sovereignty were particularly acute during the 1880s and 1890s as part of the drive to assimilate Native Americans into mainstream American culture, when Christianity, enshrined in U.S. law, was crucial in repressing religious freedom for Native Americans. In his annual report of 1882 the Commissioner of Indian Affairs, Hiram Price, praised Christian missionaries working to "educate" young Natives in government boarding schools:

> In no other manner and by no other means, in my judgment, can our Indian population be so speedily and permanently reclaimed from the barbarism, idolatry, and savage life, as by the educational and missionary efforts of the Christian people of our country.
>
> (Prucha 158)

Dancing and the ritual expression of Native spirituality remained an ongoing point of conflict, in part because of the legacy of conflict with paganism Christian settlers brought with them from Europe.[2] In 1883 Secretary of the Interior, Henry M. Teller, established the Court of Indian Offenses which aimed to punish by law anyone engaging in "savage and barbarous practices" which were "a great hindrance to the civilization of the Indians" (Prucha 158). Such practices included tribal ceremonial dancing, which, as legal scholar Allison Dussias points out, was seen as a direct threat to Christianity because of its religious nature (798). The government's determination to suppress ceremonial dancing culminated in the massacre of Sioux Ghost Dancers at Wounded Knee in 1890. When John Collier was appointed to the Bureau of Indian Affairs in 1932, he stopped overt persecution of Native American religions by ending official prohibitions against Native spiritual and ceremonial practices. However, over the next three decades, Native Americans fought a continuing series of battles to regain and maintain some religious sovereignty.

The 1970s ushered in a new era of federally supported Native American self-determination. The American Indian Movement (AIM) prompted Native Americans to organize politically against such attacks on sovereignty as restrictions against the use of the ceremonial drug peyote, the failure of museums to return remains and sacred objects, and limited access to sacred sites. Native groups across America demanded a congressional bill to protect their religious freedom. On 11 August 1978 the American Indian Religious Freedom Act (AIRFA) was signed into law. Section One of the bill stated:

> Henceforth it shall be the policy of the United States to protect and preserve for American Indians their inherent right to believe, express and exercise the traditional religions of the American Indian, Eskimo, Aleut, and Native

Hawaiians, including but not limited to access to sites, use and possession of sacred objects, and the freedom to worship through ceremonials and traditional rites.

(Public Law 95–341)

Although the AIRFA laid the groundwork for Native religious freedom, there were often difficulties translating the law into practice. Often Euro-American property rights took precedence over freedom to practice Native religion at sacred sites. In the case of *Wilson v. Block* (1983), for example, Navajo and Hopi religious leaders sought to prevent expansion of a ski area in the San Francisco Peaks. Although the proposed area was on federal land, it was regarded as sacred by the tribes. However, the courts stated that the "spiritual inconvenience" (O'Brien 37) caused by a ski bowl did not constitute a violation of the tribes' free exercise of religion. Distinction was made between "offending" and "penalizing" adherence to religious beliefs (37). Similarly in *Lyng v. Northwest Indian Cemetery Protective Association* (1988) the court refused to prevent the construction of a logging road that would impact land considered sacred to Yurok, Karok, and Tolowa tribes. The economic benefits of the road outweighed the tribes' free exercise of rights and the courts ruled that federal construction of the road would not impede free exercise of religion. Another landmark case was *Employment Division v. Smith* (1983) where the state of Oregon was entitled to deny employment benefits to a person fired for using peyote, even though the drug was part of a religious ceremony. In all these cases the AIRFA failed to protect Native American free exercise rights because of what John Petoskey refers to as "religious ethnocentrism" (221). The courts judged Native religions by Judeo-Christian standards. Also, as Weaver has pointed out, Petoskey failed to note the absence of the sacred or the holy in the First Amendment. The courts thus failed to understand the religious resonance of these tribal sites.

Subsequent amendments to the AIRFA include the Native American Free Exercise of Religion Act (NAFERA) of 1993 and the American Indian Religious Freedom Act Amendments of 1994, both of which legalized the use of peyote for religious ceremony. A number of critics have pointed out, however, that these victories by no means preclude the necessity for further defense of Native rights to the sovereign exercise of spiritual freedom. Weaver notes, for example, that there will "continue to arise conflicts between the dominant whitestream culture and Native religious traditions, and these will continue to be decided against Native interests" ("Losing My Religion" 178). The prizewinning advocate for Native rights, Suzan Shown Harjo, also believes that the most glaring failure of the AIRFA and its amendments remains that it has not created a course of action for protecting sacred sites (136).

Other Native scholars have discussed the ongoing need to defend religious sovereignty. A key text in the debate remains Vine Deloria Jr.'s *God is Red* (1973), which details traditional Native American religious views and their relationship to Christianity. Osage scholar Robert Warrior has noted that when Deloria wrote *God is Red* he believed that the "key to an American Indian (and planetary) future was the return to Native ceremonies and traditions within a framework of sovereignty." ("Intellectual Sovereignty" 1). Other scholars such as Tinker argue that for native peoples today religious sovereignty is about liberation, reclamation of religion, and healing. He points to the current poverty and unemployment as a result of conquest:

RELIGIOUS SOVEREIGNTY AND THE GHOST DANCE

This situation reasonably requires that a Native American theology begin with this context as political reality and move quickly to press for a new vision of health and wellbeing ... for the people. Thus, an American Indian theology must be a theology of liberation.

(*Spirit and Resistance* 4)

The push for Native American religious sovereignty today includes reclaiming traditional religious practices from the dominance of the U.S. government and Christian religion, but also the transformation of Native religion within a colonized space. Simon Ortiz, in "Towards a National Indian Literature: Cultural Authenticity and Nationalism," explains that many Christian religious rituals, brought to Southwest tribes by the Spanish in the sixteenth century, are no longer Spanish but have been transformed into a Native American belief system (7–10). Weaver, Warrior and Womack state in *American Indian Literary Nationalism* that Ortiz's process of transformation is "markedly different than that of hybridization" (xix). This adaptation of Christianity is a key part of contemporary Native American religion. Some of its earliest roots can be found in the Native/Christian writing of Mohegan, Samson Occom (1723–1792) and Pequot, William Apess, (1798–1839), two of the earliest known indigenous authors. Both were Christian Native Americans whose work was published for a largely white audience. Both use a Christian platform to denounce the maltreatment of Indians. Using a framework of redemptive Christian sermons, Occom and Apess subverted and transformed Christian theology to fit the plight of Native Americans, their "poor kindred." Often their choice of language appears deeply self-debasing, but it attracted the sympathy of a white audience. Although Occom and Apess worked within a Western literary canon, this does not deny the authority or authenticity of their voices. Literary scholar David Murray argues that by reflecting the views of a largely white audience, Occom and Apess were able to exploit their status as civilized Indians (*Forked Tongues* 57). Robert Warrior notes that Apess's work in particular demonstrates the way Native writers have always used their literary skills to serve the interests of Native people (*People and the Word* 1–48).

Samson Occom was born in 1723 in Connecticut. He began to read Christian scriptures after his village was visited by Christian missionaries in 1739. Following his conversion to Christianity he learnt English and gained a formal education, acquiring a reputation as an impressive preacher. Occom's first ten-page autobiography, *A Short Narrative of My Life*, detailing his conversion and desire to help his "Poor Brethren," remained unpublished until 1882. Perhaps the most well-known of Occom's work is his 1768 Execution Sermon (*A Sermon Preached at the Execution of Moses Paul, an Indian*) which is thought to be the earliest published Native American writing in existence. Invited by whites as a "pious Indian," Occom originally delivered his sermon at the public hanging of the Mohegan, Moses Paul, who had drunkenly killed a white man. Murray writes: "By having the sermon actually preached by a white Indian ... it was possible to stage a sort of moral tableau which encapsulated the moral capacities and disabilities of the Indians" (*Forked Tongues* 47). Murray points to Occom's significant awareness of his multiple audiences (74–75). Occom targeted his "poor unhappy brother Moses," telling the condemned man: "You are an Indian, a despised creature, but you have despised yourself; yea you have despised God" (Occom *A Sermon Preached* 12). He admonishes the drunken behavior of Moses and addresses the Native Americans in the audience: "My poor kindred, do consider what a dreadful abominable sin drunkenness is. God made us men, and we choose to be beasts and devils" (16). While he appealed to his fellow Native Americans to resist the evils of alcohol, he also called upon the white audience to recognize that alcoholism was among the detrimental effects of colonization. Weaver sees the overarching message of the Execution Sermon as "more accusatory of Whites who created the situation by introducing alcohol and by hating the Indians than it is of the condemned and unfortunate Paul" (*That the People* 53). For Weaver, Occom's intent is "clearly subversive," an attempt to "affirm Native personhood" (53).

William Apess also used his status as an educated Christian to emphasize the poor treatment of Native Americans by the colonizers. Weaver writes that for Apess: "conversion to Christianity was not a rejection of Indian ways but a breaking through of personal isolation felt by individual Natives whose traditional lifeways were being eradicated" (*That the People* 58). Born in Massachusetts in 1798, Apess was raised by the white Forman family, where he received his only formal education. He became a prominent Methodist minister who was influenced by radical abolitionism. He was heavily involved in arguing for the sovereign rights of the Mashpee of Cape Cod, which he documents in *Indian Nullification of the Unconstitutional Laws of Massachusetts Relative to the Marshpee Tribe* (1835). Apess often applied the format of a redemption narrative, aimed primarily at a white audience and addressing their misapprehensions about Native Americans, whilst also voicing a "conscious raising call to fellow Indians" (Murray "Translation" 75). This was apparent in his first book, the autobiographical *A Son of the Forest* (1829). Apess counteracted the expected stereotypical language of Indians by referring to King Philip, Native defender of the sovereign rights of the Pequot tribe, and by writing from a Christian perspective. He thereby condemned the Puritans' treatment of the Indians. Brend Peyer notes: "As far as Apess was concerned, American racism actually had its roots in the 'sins' perpetrated by the select Pilgrim Fathers" (113). To publish a work that condemned the heralded Pilgrim Fathers and elevated the inferior Indian by means of the application of Christian scripture was an extraordinary achievement. Occom's and Apess's power lies in their transformation of Christian messages to criticize whites. Their Christian writing remains a powerful expression of Native sovereignty within a colonized landscape. Their work is thus resistance literature, affirming Indian cultural and political identity over the dominant culture. Weaver calls this "communitism," a combination of community and activism, implying resistance. (*That the People* 32, 55). As Weaver notes, any discussion of religion must include Native concepts of community: "The topic of theology is how humanity relates to ultimate reality. Natives define their identities in terms of community and relate to ultimate reality through community" (32). All Native writing is thus an important space in which Native authors can assert religious sovereignty. Community, Weaver explains "has assumed an important role for modern-day Native peoples, especially urban Natives separated from their tribal lands and often from their cultures and religions as well" (xii). Native fictions such as N. Scott Momaday's *House Made of Dawn* (1968) and Leslie Marmon Silko's *Ceremony* (1977) reference the loss of sacred spaces and identity when Native Americans are removed from their lands. Stories and literature remain a vital way to reconnect communities, heal and reclaim traditional practices. The strength of narrative cannot be underestimated in its "tremendous power" to create community. As Weaver explains, Native literature "prepares the ground for recovery, and even the re-creation, of Indian identity and culture" (44).

Weaver's contemporary, Robert Warrior, also places huge value on community in reaffirming a Native sovereignty that is religious, political, and cultural. Warrior's study of two prominent Native American intellectuals, Vine Deloria Jr. and John Joseph Mathews, considered the impact these men have had in the fight for tribal sovereignty. Warrior argued that both Deloria and Mathews portrayed the conflict between Native Americans and whites as a religious one that is founded in land and community ("Intellectual Sovereignty" 1). For Warrior, the struggle for "sovereignty is not a struggle to be free from the influence of anything outside of ourselves, but a process of asserting the power we possess as communities and individuals to make decisions that affect our lives" (19). When Native American fiction and intellectual writers work within the Western canon, they can assert sovereignty whilst also creating literature that is uniquely Native American. In *The People and the Word: Reading Native Nonfiction*, Warrior writes:

> This tradition of writing is the oldest and most robust type of modern writing that Native people in North America have produced as they have sought literate means to engage themselves and others in a discourse on the possibilities of a Native future.
>
> (xx)

It is through writing as emblematic of community that Native Americans are able to resist attacks on their religious sovereignty. "The decision of sovereignty provides the beginning point from which resistance, hope, and most of all, imagination issue" ("Intellectual Sovereignty" 19).

The historical event that has perhaps most frequently been discussed by contemporary writers as they explore Native American religious sovereignty has been the Ghost Dance. It is a spiritual Native expression that emerged during the late 1800s as a desperate response to death, starvation, displacement, and loss of traditional tribal culture. The movement spread rapidly during the 1880s and 1890s amongst the Plains tribes of the United States, chiefly the Cheyenne, Arapaho, Kiowa, Shoshone, Paiute, and the Sioux. The movement was rooted in a vision which came to the Northern Pauite, Jack Wilson (Wovoka). He claimed that the time would come when the Indian race, living and dead, would be reunited upon a regenerated earth, free from death, disease, and misery. Crucially, Wovoka's prophecy was peaceful and did not involve warring with the whites. The white race would not be part of the regeneration but would be left behind. Delegates from different tribes visited Wovoka and returned home with various versions of his prophecy, which they spread amongst their own communities.

News of the Ghost Dance first came to the Sioux in the fall of 1889. Facing starvation, the Ghost Dance prophecy offered the Sioux hope. Led by Sitting Bull, a Hunkpapa Lakota chief, the Sioux believed all white men would be smothered by a giant landslide. White fear of the Sioux dancers spread from the Standing Rock reservation in South Dakota and on 15 December 1890 Indian police surrounded Sitting Bull's cabin, intending to arrest him. When Sitting Bull exited his house, one of his supporters fired a rifle at Indian policeman, Bull Head. Although trying to shoot his attacker, Bull Head fatally shot Sitting Bull. Fearing violence, a number of Hunkpapas made their way to Big Foot's Miniconjou

Sioux encampment in central South Dakota. Big Foot (Spotted Elk) had briefly followed the Ghost Dance and was regarded as a "troublemaker" amongst white authorities. On 17 December 1890 the War Department issued orders for Big Foot's arrest. When he heard of Sitting Bull's death, Big Foot moved with his followers to the Pine Ridge Reservation, hoping to find protection. On 28 December soldiers searched Big Foot and his followers for guns. A shot was fired by Sioux warrior, Black Coyote, after which the soldiers opened fire indiscriminately. Around 300 Sioux were killed, nearly 200 of whom were women and children. The Wounded Knee Massacre was widely regarded as the end of the Ghost Dance, though in fact it continued in diminished form but would never reach the same fever pitch it did during the 1880s and 1890s.

The Ghost Dance ceremony itself has received cross-disciplinary attention. In particular, *The Ghost Dance Religion and the Sioux Outbreak of 1890* (1896), by Irish ethnographer James Mooney, contributed to its wider understanding. Importantly, Mooney compared the movement to other religions that turn to Messianic figures in times of need. Mooney further suggested that the movement created a pan-tribal brotherhood in desperate times. The Ghost Dance has also received attention from contemporary Native American authors whose tribes were not historically part of the movement, such as Sherman Alexie and Leslie Marmon Silko. In their work, the Ghost Dance is seen as a transformative source of pan-tribal resistance and revival, an important assertion of communal strength and cultural sovereignty. Its re-contextualization is important because of the dislocation caused by colonization. Disparate tribal groups were brought together in the Ghost Dance to form a central core of Native resistance against Anglo domination. The ceremony's continued employment in contemporary Native American fiction counters the myth of the "Vanishing Indian," offering the opportunity for a revival of Native practices. By the late nineteenth century the frontier was closed, as signaled in Frederic Jackson Turner's seminal work, *The Significance of the Frontier in American History* (1893). The Ghost Dance then took on an emblematic status, marking the defining moment of frontier closure when Natives were deemed to have vanished. As a result, the Ghost Dance resonated within non-Indian writing as symbolic of desperate Native people clinging onto their last hopes of cultural and religious survival. Because it has so often been put forward as symbolic of Indian decline, it has attracted continued attention from contemporary Native writers at pains to re-inscribe its significance. Nineteenth- and early twentieth-century writers such as S. Alice Callahan and Charles Alexander Eastman in contrast, struggled to reconcile the Ghost Dance with their desire for Indian assimilation.

S. Alice Callahan's (Muscogee Creek) only novel, *Wynema: A Child of the Forest* (1891), is the first novel known to be published by a Native American woman. *Wynema* tells the story of a Muscogee girl, Wynema, and her journey to civilization. Callahan uses the conventional sentimental novelistic framework of nineteenth-century literature to portray Wynema's acculturation into a domesticated and Christian American society. Scholar Kathleen Grace Washburn writes: "By taking the form of the sentimental novel, Callahan rewrites the story of the vanishing Indian through Wynema's education and marriage into a national domestic order" (216). The second part of the novel is a fictional documentation of the Ghost Dance and the Wounded Knee massacre. Callahan's use of Wounded Knee disrupts the dominant romance plot, demonstrating that sentimentalism and romance are inadequate literary forms to portray the depredations committed on the Ghost Dancers. Washburn writes: "Callahan's novel reveals the incompatibility of different modes – tragic vanishing and visionary prophecy" (184). On the one hand *Wynema* supports assimilation and education, but on the other hand simultaneously suggests that a new prophetic future should be imagined for Native Americans. Callahan's introduction of new Sioux characters, as well as a variety of conflicting newspaper accounts in the second section of the novel, demonstrates her own mixed feelings regarding the events of that winter. The fictional warrior Wildfire acknowledges that resistance to the whites will have a disastrous impact on the Sioux, though he would rather die than surrender: "If we cannot be free then let us die. What is life to a caged bird, threatened with death on all sides?" (81). The narrator directly addresses the reader, drawing attention to the indirect nature of the sentimental plot of the first half of the novel: "It is not my province to show how brave it was for a great, strong nation to quell a riot for the dancing of a few 'bucks' – for *civilized* soldiers to slaughter indiscriminately women and children" (92).

Callahan deplored the murder of the Ghost Dancers but it is unclear whether she believed the Sioux were right to disobey the government or if she thought a more submissive attitude would have been preferable to the slaughter of innocents. Washburn argues that *Wynema* stages the tensions between Wounded Knee as "terminal plot and the New Indian as narrative of the future." (229). Callahan closed her novel with a prophetic vision of the future for Native Americans. Fictional missionary Carl Peterson offers a final prayer with an apocalyptic vision of a future where whites will pay for the depredations they have committed on Native Americans: "The subjects of the government will rise up in defiance of the 'authorities that be'" (102). Carl goes on to appeal to Congress to change its conduct towards Native Americans. He invites Congress to avoid the consequences of Native defiance which, as Washburn argues, will "correspond in many respects to the destruction of the whites as foretold by Wovoka" (222). Callahan applied the prophecy of the Ghost Dance in her writing to imagine a new future for Native Americans that counters her earlier romanticized visions of assimilation. Whilst critic Craig Womack has argued that Callahan failed to engage Creek culture, history, or politics in what he refers to as the "silencing of Wynema" (109), I maintain that *Wynema* provides a detailed and important account of the conflicting issues of sovereignty: the pull between assimilation and a new Native future.

Like Callahan, Charles Alexander Eastman (Sioux) was torn between assimilation and his tribal roots. As Hertha D. Sweet Wong wrote: "This theme of trying to reconcile two worlds, Native American and Euro-American, becomes central to twentieth-century Native American fiction" (138). This is evident in the work of Eastman, one of the most prolific Native writers of the early twentieth century. With the help of his wife, Elaine, Eastman wrote his autobiographical account, *From Deep in the Woods to Civilization* (1916). Here Eastman documented his move from a traditional Sioux upbringing to life as an educated Indian and doctor on the Pine Ridge Reservation in 1890. As Eastman told his readers, "a 'white doctor' was something of a novelty" (45), thus emphasizing his status as an assimilated Indian who is clearly distinguished from his tribe. However, Eastman was also acutely aware of the starvation facing the Sioux at Pine Ridge, following the government's reduction of beef rations in 1889. Wong points out Eastman's contradictory stance: "Internalizing the roles of Native informant and editor, Eastman critiques 'civilization' and Christianity as manifested in American society, yet seeks membership in both" (138). Eastman's struggle to square his views of assimilation on the one hand and Native sovereignty on the other is clear in his words: "At times I felt something of the fascination of the new life, and then again there would arise in me a dogged resistance, and a voice seemed to be saying, 'It is cowardly to depart from old things'" (27). Eastman's inner conflict was obvious in his attitude to the Ghost Dance: "... the last hope of race entity had departed, and my people were groping blindly after spiritual relief in their bewilderment and misery" (55). Recognizing the desperation of the movement, Eastman nevertheless asserted his loyalty to the government in the face of an Indian uprising. However, despite this desire for government allegiance, Eastman was horrified after the Wounded Knee massacre: "All this was a severe ordeal for one who has so lately put his faith in the lofty ideals of the white man" (66). An educated Native American like Callahan, Eastman's ties to the Native community had been fractured by assimilation. This left him in the difficult position of struggling to reconcile the peaceful hope of the Ghost Dance with the horrific reality of massacre, provoked by resistance to assimilation.

Written much later than Eastman's work, Leslie Marmon Silko's (Laguna Pueblo) 1999 novel, *Gardens in the Dunes*, makes pivotal use of the Ghost Dance. Set in nineteenth-century America and Europe, Silko's novel both begins and ends with the Ghost Dance, each time using it as a symbol of the unfulfilled hope for the return of both the Messiah and the lost mother of the two Sand Lizard sisters, Indigo and Sister Salt. For Silko, the Ghost Dance indicates the tragic vanishing of Indian community as well as a desperate holding on to ritual-based thinking. Yet her view is only partly negative. Indeed, the adaptive, resilient nature of Native Americans Indigo, Sister Salt, the Chemahuevi twins and trickster Delena offers a way forward via resistance and assimilation. A. M. Regier notes, *Gardens* "functions as a literary compendium of multiple, changing discourse of the Ghost Dance movement, then and now dedicated to social and environmental change" (136). Like the work of Eastman and Callahan, Silko's novel works within the Western literary canon, using the historical novel form, thus addressing a white as well as Native audience. Her reach is broad, covering questions of "botanical and financial entrepreneurship, religious discussions of paganism and early Christianity, and women's positions in the Native and white world" (Nelson 255). The ideals of Christianity and Native culture, both encapsulated by the Ghost Dance, are drawn upon in this fiction with what Regier usefully calls "narrative syncretism" (the attempt to reconcile opposing beliefs, philosophies and practices) (136). Indigenous resistance is thus linked to white concerns about the impact of industrialization. However, it is the Native characters who gladly accept cultural hybridization as a strength: they welcome European botanical knowledge, and see interbreeding with other races as strengthening and identify cultural religious links with Europe's ancient ceremonies. In this way, Silko depicts the ending of tribal lives and practices but also the resurgence of a hybridity that allows tribal continuity in adapted form. Each time the Ghost Dance is invoked in *Gardens*, it is interrupted by white soldiers. The dancers flee but not all are captured. This repeated presentation of the Ghost Dance ceremony, its interruption and the flight of the dancers clearly suggests Silko's vision of white failure to eradicate Indian culture and religion. Departures are always followed by returns. Indian religion, unlike the patriarchal Christianity which dismisses white Hattie's feminist reading, is inclusive. Such adaptability continues the struggle to maintain religious sovereignty.

Sherman Alexie's (Spokane) novel, *Indian Killer* (1996), also employs the Ghost Dance as a central metaphor of resistance against past and present injustice committed against Native Americans. Alexie's tribe did not participate in the Ghost Dance yet he uses it as a powerful pan-tribal assertion of united sovereignty. *Indian Killer* begins in the winter of 1968–1969 with the brutal removal of John Smith from his Native mother and his placement in a white family. This is a reminder of the Indian adoption Project (1958–1967) which systematically removed Native children from their parents to live with white families. The year of 1968 was of course an important one in African-American Civil Rights history when the American Indian Movement also began to agitate for Native American Civil Rights. Alexie's character John, lacking any tribal affiliation, is clearly damaged by his adoption. According to Laura Szanto Furlan: "Loss of tribal identity and knowledge of home are the worst losses that can be imagined. In the world that Alexie imagines one cannot in fact be Indian without them" (105). John is dislocated from his tribal identity but is negatively defined as essentially Indian by the whites among whom he is raised. As Arnold Krupat writes of men like John: "They are Indian because a racist society treats them as Indians" (*Red Matters* 116).

Alexie shows Seattle's white community feverishly indulging in racial hatred, stirred up by radio host, Truck Shultz, when an anonymous killer murders and scalps his victims. Racially prejudiced white society is sure the killer is Indian. Indeed, it is true that John's struggle to come to terms with the loss of his tribal identity does manifest itself in what Krupat calls, "murderous rage" (*Red Matters* 103). Is John so damaged by cultural dislocation that he kills whites? While such an interpretation is possible, Alexie alludes throughout to pan-tribalism as a viable source of identity and resistance for displaced Indians such as John. Lisa Tatonetti has argued that although pan-Indianism is by no means accepted by all Native peoples, the common ground it implies "authorizes Alexie's use of the Ghost Dance"(6). In Alexie's "pan-Indian aesthetic" Spokane character Marie Ploatkin can say: "So maybe this Indian Killer is a product of the Ghost Dance. Maybe ten Indians are Ghost Dancing. Maybe a hundred" (313). Alexie draws on the historical significance of the Ghost Dance to depict the movement as a "potential impetus for Indigenous coalition" (Tatonetti 2). Jack Wilson (ironically named after the prophet Wovoka), a wannabe Indian, and Reggie, a Spokane, discuss the Indian Killer. While white Wilson thinks a "real" Indian would not be capable of the murders, Reggie replies: "Maybe you should be wondering what Indian wouldn't do it" (184). Reggie believes a pan-Indian incentive for retribution is widespread. When Wilson details the massacre at Wounded Knee, Reggie stresses this was the killing of Indians by whites. The massacre was Indian killing on a large scale and offers a clear motive for the revenge-killing of whites. After this interchange at the bar, Alexie writes:

> Within a few hours nearly every Indian in Seattle knew about the scalping. Most Indians believed it was just racist paranoia, but a few felt a strange combination of relief and fear as if an apocalyptic prophecy was just beginning to come true.
>
> (185)

Tatonetti argues that it is not the static image of Wounded Knee that remains after Reggie and Wilson's conversation but the "rebellious echo of the Ghost Dance" (17–18). Alexie's final chapter suggests the revival of the Ghost Dance amongst pan-Indian Native groups: the killer is joined in a ritualistic dance by many Indians with varied tribal affiliations. For Alexie, the Ghost Dance demonstrates the possibility of revolution as a pan-tribal cultural act which, like his own storytelling, reaffirms community by means of Native religious ritual. At the same time Alexie refuses a tidy solution to the mystery killer's identity. Even at the novel's end, the Indian killer remains either a killer of Indians, or an Indian who kills.

The Ghost Dance is likely to continue to provide inspiration for literary works that engage with the issue of religious freedom; such use of the movement will remain within the long history of Indian religious and spiritual resistance in written form. Despite continued governmental failure to protect indigenous religious freedoms, Native Americans have maintained a strong connection to their traditional spiritual practices and ceremonies. This has been achieved in no small part through the strength of their communities and their respective spiritual bonds. Religious sovereignty remains fundamental to the continuing struggle to keep community alive. Although designed to protect Native American freedom of religion, as guaranteed under the First Amendment of the United States Constitution, acts such as the AIRFA in many ways remain obstacles to sovereignty because of federal self-interest. There is a clear history of non-Indian property and economic gain taking precedence over Native American religious concerns. Until Native American religious sovereignty is fully secured – a project which in itself is dependent upon a wider set of restorations of Indian status, resources, land and opportunity – the Ghost Dance and its intertribal legacy will persist as a significant metaphor for tribal resistance and spiritual revival.

Notes

1 For a detailed debate on the sovereign legal status of Native tribes from the 1950s to the 1980s see Wilkinson.
2 Keith Thomas's *Religion and the Decline of Magic* (1971) provides an excellent analysis of a flourishing of magic in seventeenth-century England that was met with fear by Protestants who attempted to remove popular forms of magic from Christianity.

Works cited

Alexie, Sherman. *Indian Killer*. New York: Grove, 1996.
American Indian Religious Freedom Act of 1978, Pub. L. no. 95-341. 92 Stat. 469 (1978).
Apess, William. *Indian Nullification of the Unconstitutional Laws of Massachusetts Relative to the Marshpee Tribe*. Boston: Jonathan Howe, 1835.
——. *Son of the Forest. On Our Own Ground: The Complete Writings of William Apess*. Ed. Barry O'Connell. Amherst: University of Massachusetts Press, 1992. 3–52.
Callahan, S. Alice. *Wynema: A Child of the Forest*. Ed. A. LaVonne Brown Ruoff. Lincoln: University of Nebraska Press, 1997.
Constitution of the United States. 1788. Online. www.archives.gov/exhibits/charters/constitution_transcript.html
Deloria, Vine, Jr. *God is Red*. New York: Grosset & Dunlap, 1973.
Dussias, Allison M. "Ghost Dance and Holy Ghost: The Echoes of Nineteenth-Century Christianization Policy in Twentieth-Century Native American Free Exercise Cases." *Stanford Law Review* 49. 4 (1997): 773–852.
Eastman, Charles Alexander. *From Deep in the Woods to Civilization*. Mineola, NY: Dover Publications, 2003.
——. *The Soul of the Indian*. Boston: Houghton Mifflin, 1911.
Furlan, Laura Szanto. *"Like a Cannibal in Manhattan": Post-Relocation Urban Indian Narratives*. Thesis. University of California, Santa Barbara, 2006.
Harjo, Suzan Shown. "American Indian Religious Freedom Act After Twenty-Five Years: An Introduction." *Wicazo Sa Review* 19. 2 (2004): 129–36.

Krupat, Arnold. *Red Matters: Native American Studies*. Philadelphia: University of Pennsylvania Press, 2002.

Momaday, N. Scott. *House Made of Dawn*. New York: Harper & Row, 1968.

Mooney, James. *The Ghost Dance Religion and the Sioux Outbreak of 1890*. 1896. Rpt. Lincoln: University of Nebraska Press, 1991.

Murray, David. *Forked Tongues: Speech, Writing and Representation in North American Indian Texts*. Bloomington: Indiana University Press, 1991.

———. "Translation and Mediation." *The Cambridge Companion to Native American Literature*. Ed. Joy Porter & Kenneth M. Roemer. Cambridge: Cambridge University Press, 2005. 69–83.

Nelson, Robert M. "Leslie Marmon Silko: Storyteller." *The Cambridge Companion to Native American Literature*. Ed. Joy Porter & Kenneth M. Roemer. Cambridge: Cambridge University Press, 2005. 245–56.

O'Brien, Sharon. "A Legal Analysis of the American Indian Religious Freedom Act." *Handbook of American Indian Religious Freedom*. Ed. Christopher Vecsey. New York: Crossroad, 1991.

Occom, Samson. *A Sermon Preached at the Execution of Moses Paul, an Indian*. New Haven, CT: T & S. Green, 1772.

———. "A Short Narrative of My Life." *The Elders Wrote: An Anthology of Early Prose by North American Indians, 1768–1931*. Ed. Bernd Peyer. Berlin: Dietrich Reimer Verlag, 1982. 12–18.

Ortiz, Simon J. "Towards a National Indian Literature: Cultural Authenticity in Nationalism." *MELUS* 8. 2 (1981): 7–12.

Petoskey, John. "Indians and the First Amendment." *American Indian Policy in the Twentieth Century*. Ed. Vine Deloria Jr. Norman: University of Oklahoma Press, 1985. 221–38.

Peyer, Brend. "Non-Fiction Prose." *The Cambridge Companion to Native American Literature*. Ed. Joy Porter & Kenneth M. Roemer. Cambridge: Cambridge University Press, 2005. 105–24.

Prucha, Francis Paul. *Documents of United States Indian Policy*. 3rd ed. Lincoln: University of Nebraska Press, 2000.

Regier, A.M. "Revolutionary Enunciatory Spaces: Ghost Dancing, Transatlantic Travel, and Modernist Arson in *Gardens in the Dunes*." *MFS Modern Fiction Studies* 51. 1 (2005): 134–57.

Silko, Leslie Marmon. *Ceremony*. New York: Viking Penguin, 1977.

———. *Gardens in the Dunes*. New York: Simon & Schuster, 1999.

Tatonetti, Lisa. "Dancing That Way, Things Began to Change: The Ghost Dance as Pantribal Metaphor in Sherman Alexie's Writing." *Sherman Alexie: A Collection of Critical Essays*. Ed. Jeff Bergland & Jan Roush. Salt Lake City: University of Utah Press, 2010. 1–24.

Thomas, Keith. *Religion and the Decline of Magic*. New York: Scribner, 1971.

Tinker, George E. *American Indian Liberation: A Theology of Sovereignty*. Maryknoll, NY: Orbis, 2008.

———. *Spirit and Resistance: Political Theology and American Indian Liberation*. Minneapolis, MN: Fortress, 2004.

Turner, Frederic Jackson. *The Significance of the Frontier in American History*. 1893. Rpt. Harmondsworth, UK: Penguin, 2008.

Warrior, Robert Allen. "Intellectual Sovereignty and the Struggle for an American Indian Future." *Wicazo Sa Review* 8. 1 (1992): 1–20.

———. *The People and the Word: Reading Native Nonfiction*. Minneapolis: University of Minnesota Press, 2005.

Washburn, Kathleen Grace. "Indigenous Modernity and the Making of Americans, 1890–1935." Thesis. University of California, Los Angeles, 2008.

Weaver, Jace. "Losing My Religion: Native American Religious Traditions and American Indian Religious Freedom." *Other Words: American Indian Literature, Law and Culture*. Norman: University of Oklahoma Press, 2001.

———. *That the People Might Live: Native American Literatures and Native American Communities*. New York: Oxford University Press, 1997.

Weaver, Jace, Craig S. Womack & Robert Warrior, *American Indian Literary Nationalism*. Albuquerque: University of New Mexico Press, 2006.

Wilkinson, Charles F. *American Indians, Time, and the Law: Native Societies in a Modern Constitutional Democracy*. New Haven, CT: Yale University Press, 1987.

Womack, Craig S. *Red on Red: Native American Literary Separatism*. Minneapolis: University of Minnesota Press, 1999.

Wong, Hertha D. Sweet. "Native American Life Writing." *The Cambridge Companion to Native American Literature*. Ed. Joy Porter & Kenneth M. Roemer. Cambridge: Cambridge University Press, 2005. 125–44.

23

Native American Activism and Survival

Political, Legal, Cultural

Bruce E. Johansen

Activism began as soon as Native peoples were forced to re-define their lives according to the dictates of the immigrants. Given that conquest and oppression tend to foster activism to assert rights, this is a history with a very long legal as well as political record. Some changes, such as horses, were accepted, and others resisted, from the Europeans' first landfall. The Marshall Trilogy (1820s, 1830s) that has fundamentally shaped relations with the U.S. government for almost two centuries, was a product largely of Cherokee activism. Over the years, a large number of court cases have been brought as activist vehicles to reclaim resources guaranteed under treaties (the Boldt fishing rights case will be examined below, as an example of political protest provoking a legal proceeding). Add to legal and ground-level protest activism through music: Johnny Cash's *Bitter Tears: Ballads of the American Indian* and Floyd Red Crow Westerman will be examined as two examples among many. Literary and political activism will be exemplified by Vine Deloria Jr.

Protest, recognition, and revival

The modern assertion of Native American civil-rights protest had actually begun with "fish-ins" near Puget Sound during the middle 1960s when most of America woke up to it with the Alcatraz occupation five years later. In 1968, the American Indian movement was barely a blip on the national radar when it organized to protest police brutality in Minneapolis. For the next decade, however, its members convulsed America's conscience with a series of high-profile events that raised issues of treaty rights and economic injustice.

The occupation of Alcatraz has been abundantly covered as history ("Alcatraz and Activism"; "Alcatraz"; Johnson 1999, 2001; Johnson & Nagel; Shreve; Smith & Warrior; Talbot). Largely ignored outside its own region, a similar confrontation at Fort Lawton, in Seattle, produced what the Alcatraz occupation sought but failed to achieve: an enduring community center (KCTS n. pag.). The Fort Lawton site, on park land in the midst of the Seattle urban area, was much more practical than an island in San Francisco Bay. The island site was ideal for isolating people (thus the prison). The Daybreak Star, the center built in what is now Discovery Park, was the opposite: close to the city, and easy to reach (Parham; Reyes).

273

After Alcatraz, a nation-spanning caravan, the Trail of Broken Treaties, traversed the country from three locations in the West (Los Angeles, San Francisco, and Seattle) during the autumn of 1972, arriving in Washington, D.C. days before elections, and barricading the Bureau of Indian Affairs headquarters. Months later, early in 1973, the hamlet of Wounded Knee was occupied on the Pine Ridge reservation. In 1976, another caravan, the Trail of Self Determination, crossed the country. At the same time, the U.S. government undertook a series of legal prosecutions to break AIM apart and increase factional infighting that resulted in the murders of Anna Mae Aquash and others at and near Pine Ridge. At least 66 AIM members and supporters were killed at or near Pine Ridge between 1973 and 1976 with very little attention from federal officials, who are responsible for investigating major crimes on U.S. Indian reservations.

The energy of the movement continued, however, in many legal initiatives to recognize treaty rights, one of the best-known protests that led to the "Boldt Decision" in 1974, upheld by higher courts between 1975 and 1979 (examined below) that recognized fishing rights in Western Washington (American Friends; Bruce Brown; Ralph Johnson; Miller; U.S. Commission; Woods). Many other legal battles have been engaged, notably the Sioux (Lakota) claim to the Black Hills (Lazarus). Activists' energy also has gone into many protests of Indian sports mascots, such as the Washington Redskins, Cleveland Indians, and Atlanta Braves (King).

Many Native peoples also took economic development into their own hands to break out of the poverty cycle, notably by starting various gambling enterprises. On a minority of reservations where such establishments have done well, an economic revival has ensued. This, too, is a measure of activism. The Muckleshoots (southeast of Seattle), for example, were down to their last half-acre of commonly owned land when Alcatraz was occupied. By 2014, they had built their own schools and were providing scholarships and housing, among other things (Johansen & Bill). Notably, in 2013, the Muckleshoots purchased land in parts of their ancient range for more than $300 million.[1]

Political and legal activism: the right to fish

To Pacific Northwest Native American peoples, the salmon was as central to economic life as the buffalo on the plains; 80 to 90 per cent of the protein in the Native peoples' diet was comprised of fish and shellfish. The salmon was more than food; it was the center of a way of life. Among the catch were Chinook, coho, sockeye, chum, pink salmon, and steelhead. These fish were also smoked and dried for storage, and for trade. Fishing methods included nets, weirs, funnel snares, grills, set nets, and spears. Beginning with the first visitors, the immigrants were astonished by the abundance of salmon. Lewis and Clark noted "great quants. [quantities] of salmon" (Bruce Brown 14) when they passed along the Columbia River during 1805. In 1854, George Suckley, who was describing the land for a railroad survey, wrote that salmon were "one of the striking wonders of the region ... These fish ... astonish by number, and confuse with variety" (Suckley n. pag.). The immigrants very quickly came to appreciate the economic value of salmon. A newspaper account in *The Columbia*n (of Olympia), January 15, 1853 mentioned that dried salmon had been shipped to China. The salmon became a marketable commodity across a broad area with construction of the transcontinental railroad in the late nineteenth century (later, refrigeration made the fish even more portable). Vacuum canning became available in 1866, seven years before the railroad linked the Pacific Northwest's fisheries to the rest of the world.

The State of Washington's courts regularly upheld restrictions on Indian fishing; Washington State courts agreed with the state fish and game bureaucracy's assertion that the treaty phrase "in common with" meant "no different from other citizens" (Ziontz 85). An example was *State v. Towessnutte* (February 4, 1916) (89 Wash. 478), in which the State Supreme Court "held that treaty Indians fishing at usual and accustomed places off-reservation were subject to state fishing regulations in the same manner as everyone else" (Lane 97).

> The premise of Indian sovereignty we reject … . The Indian was a child, and a dangerous child, to be both protected and restrained … . Neither Rome nor sagacious Britain ever dealt more liberally with their subject races than we with these savage tribes, whom it is generally tempting and always easy to destroy and whom we have so often permitted to squander vast areas of fertile land before our eyes.
>
> (Wilkinson 53)

As the state pressured Native people to restrict their fishing to reservations, the total number of fish available to everyone was falling as well. In 1914, in Washington State, about 16 million fish were caught annually. By the 1920s annual catches had declined to an annual average of 6 million. In the late 1930s, following construction of several large hydroelectric dams on the Columbia River and its tributaries, the annual catch had fallen to as low as 3 million. By the 1970s, with more aggressive conservation measures in place, including construction of fish ladders at most major dams, the annual catch rose to 4 to 6 million (Physical Yield 89).

Native fishing people resisted state restriction on their fishing rights as early as 1897, when a commercial fishing company interfered with the Lummi's harvest at a favored spot at Point Roberts and Lummi Island, off their reservation. In *United States v. Winans* (1905), the U.S. Supreme Court upheld treaty provisions that allowed Indians to fish at usual and accustomed places (even if the land had come under private ownership) in a case involving a white-owned fish wheel at a location traditionally used by the Yakama. The court put forth "the reserved-rights doctrine" which stated that Indians reserved rights to themselves and granted certain rights to others. This doctrine has become important across the United States in many treaty-rights cases.

By the 1950s and early 1960s, Native peoples who had signed the Medicine Creek and Point Elliott treaties, among others, were having a difficult time harvesting enough fish to survive. As fish runs declined, state efforts to enforce its arbitrary policies became more brutal. By the early 1960s, state fisheries police were conducting wholesale arrests of Indians, confiscating their boats and nets. The increasing intensity of fishing-rights protests during the 1960s was a matter of survival – emphasized when the fishing people banded together in a group that they named the Survival of American Indians Association.

Everywhere, in the fishing controversy, activists found the fingerprints of Hank Adams, "tireless, fiery, chain-smoking, lights-out brilliant, and soul-deep loyal to a sacred undertaking" (Wilkinson 44). He enticed Charles Kuralt, then a famous correspondent for CBS News, to cover the "fish-ins" at Frank's Landing. Adams also played a major role in writing, and raising funds to publish, the American Friends' report *Uncommon Controversy*, which provided a sober, scholarly analysis of treaty fishing rights. The protests came to be called "fish-ins," a conscious reference to the black sit-ins at southern lunch counters during the civil-rights movement. As people fished, by night, they "loaded bright, freshly cleaned Nisqually salmon into a plain white truck bound for sale in San Francisco's Union Square, properly launched into the dark with a Frank's Landing send-off of muffled laughter and *sotto voce* whispers of "go get 'em!" and "You're doing the Great Spirit's work!" (Wilkinson 42).

On 3 March 1964, the National Youth Council summoned Native peoples from across the United States to join fishing people in Western Washington for a rally on the grounds of the State Capitol in Olympia. In *Red Power Rising* (2011), Bradley Shreve wrote that 1,500 to 5,000 people gathered, making the demonstration "the largest intertribal protest ever assembled" (130). Charles Wilkinson, in *Messages from Frank's Landing*, put the figure at 2,000 (44). To defend their fishing rights, Puget Sound Native peoples called upon non-Indian allies, most notably the multi-ethnic collation forming in Seattle around such issues as the Indian occupation of Fort Lawton, the birth of El Centro de la Raza, and minority hiring on federal and state construction sites. Seattle was unusual for its alliances across racial lines; at the same time that defense of fishing rights reached fever pitch, Latinos, Asians, Black, and white allies were asserting economic rights and identity in the urban area. They aided each other.

The fish-ins assumed a familiar pattern:

> The game wardens – a dozen to almost fifty – would descend the banks in a stone-faced scramble toward a few [Indian] men in a canoe or skiff unloading salmon from a gillnet. Usually the [Indians] would give passive resistance – dead weight – and five officers or more would drag the men up the rugged banks toward the waiting vehicles. The dragging often got rough, with much pushing and shoving, many arms twisted way up the back, and numerous cold-cock punches. The billyclubs made their thuds. Sometimes the Indian men struck back. Sometimes Indian people on the banks threw stones and sticks at the intruders. The stench of tear gas hung in the air.
>
> (Wilkinson 38)

The ground-level fishing wars peaked on September 9, 1970 during a fish-in on the Puyallup River near Tacoma, as a multi-ethnic camp of about a hundred fishing-rights supporters standing vigil for an array of treaty Indians on the river was torn apart by about 300 police in riot gear who arrested about sixty people. Four shots were fired at the police, who then dispersed the crowd with a volley of their own fire and a haze of tear gas. This confrontation contributed to the filing of *United States v. Washington*, which produced the Boldt ruling. The growing scale of the conflict over fishing rights prompted federal attorneys to make it a priority.

Judge George H. Boldt's 1974 decision in *U.S. v. Washington*, which allowed Native people access to as much as half the catch, challenged the allocation of legal power in an ambit much broader than fishing alone. The treaties could no longer be dismissed by the state or subject solely to its own definition by police power. Native peoples became equal in the eyes of the law. The ruling also contained several other endorsements of sovereignty that were not specific to fishing, holding that the state could not discriminate against Native peoples, and that the intent of Congress was to enhance Native self-government. The decision was upheld on appeal during the 1970s to the U.S. Supreme Court despite the state's efforts to subvert it.

Activism in the creative arts

American Indian activism has been widespread in musical expression, a sample of which is provided by one Native American performer, Floyd Red Crow Westerman, and a notable non-Indian, Johnny Cash. These are only two examples of a large array of talent, not only in music, but also in drama, visual arts, and film. One will recall that Marlon Brando famously turned down an Oscar for best actor in *The Godfather* during the 1973 occupation of Wounded Knee (Brando).

An influential Native singer and actor, Floyd Red Crow Westerman (1936–2007) was known to large audiences for his role as the wise old sachem Ten Bears in *Dances with Wolves* (1990) and he played a shaman who was consulted by Jim Morrison in Oliver Stone's *The Doors* (1991). Westerman was very popular outside the United States, where he performed at least sixty times. Before (and during) his career as an actor for mass audiences, Westerman was known in Native America as a folksinger and activist. His recordings included: "Custer Died for Your Sins," based on his close friend Vine Deloria Jr.'s book of the same title), "Indian Country," and "The Land is Your Mother."

The American Indian Movement became a major activity for Westerman shortly after its formation in 1968. He also acted as a spokesman for the International Indian Treaty Council, traveling around the world and appearing before the United Nations to advocate improved social and economic conditions for indigenous peoples. In 1982, these themes and environmental issues were the main focus of his third collection of recorded songs, "This Land Is Your Mother."

Westerman passed on to the spirit world 13 December 2007 at Cedars Sinai Hospital in Los Angeles, following complications from leukemia. Mohawk journalist Doug George-Kanentiio described him this way in an e-mail to the author 18 December 2007:

> Floyd ... was not egotistical or full of rage. He went through the emotional and physical traumas of the notorious boarding school system yet whenever I met him he was given to laughter and ready for a good story. He was, in many ways, like his great friend Vine Deloria: aware of the absurdities of life but enjoying his time here. He was a strong presence on and off the stage and played a really hard guitar.
>
> (George-Kanentiio, 2007)

On 1 October 1964, just as the modern Native American civil-rights and cultural revival was beginning, the notable country musician Johnny Cash released *Bitter Tears: Ballads of the American Indian*, a remarkable album of eight songs that heralded the movement with assistance from American Indian song writers and activists. The album is recalled today throughout Native America for its prescient nature. At the time, Cash waged a battle with record-company executives and radio stations to gain airplay. While Columbia Records did not deny Cash release of *Bitter Tears* after his best-selling hit "Ring of Fire," the company did very little to promote it. Radio and print media nearly ignored the album upon its initial release.

Early in his life, Cash thought he had Cherokee and Mohawk ancestry, but he researched his family and found this not to be the case (Cash was English, and Scots-Irish). While researching, he also learned of how unfairly American Indians were being treated, and *Bitter Tears* was a response to Cash's desire to do something about the situation in his own creative realm. Cash was known throughout Indian Country for his support of Native-rights issues. *Bitter Tears*, with its salute to treaty rights in "As Long As the Grass Shall Grow," and the haunting "Ballad of Ira Hayes" was Cash's twentieth album. Five of the eight songs on *Bitter Tears* were written or co-authored by American Indian musician and activist Peter La Farge. The lyrics were at once bitter, ironic, and humorous; its sarcastic needling of George Armstrong Custer echoed through many Native American jokes. Cash had first heard La Farge, who was Narragansett, perform "The Ballad of Ira Hayes" ten years earlier in New York City. He became a friend of La Farge, who was described as "a former rodeo cowboy, playwright, actor and Navy intelligence operative ... was also the son of longtime Native activist and novelist Oliver La Farge, who had won a Pulitzer Prize for his 1930 Navajo love story, *Laughing Boy*" (D'Ambrosio "Bitter Tears" n. pag.).

Columbia Records' executives thought *Bitter Tears* lacked commercial potential. Angry, Cash bought a full-page advertisement in *Billboard*. Some radio stations responded to Cash's characterization of them as "gutless" in that ad by taking all of his music off air for a time. They were forced to relent as the controversy propelled both the "Ballad of Ira Hayes" and *Bitter Tears* up the Country Music charts. In July 1972, President Richard M. Nixon asked Cash to visit him at the White House, and requested that he sing "Okie from Muskogee" and "Welfare Cadillac." Cash ignored Nixon's request and instead sang "The Ballad of Ira Hayes," and two anti-war songs, enduring a stone-cold glare from Nixon. In his eulogy for Cash, who died in 2003, the actor Kris Kristofferson said he was a "holy terror ... a dark and dangerous force of nature that also stood for mercy and justice for his fellow human beings" (qtd. in D'Ambrosio "Bitter Tears" n. pag.). "Johnny wanted more than the hillbilly jangle," Peter La Farge wrote later. "He was hungry for the depth and truth heard only in the folk field (at least until Johnny came along). The secret is simple: Johnny has the heart of a folksinger in the purest sense" (qtd. in D'Ambrosio, "Bitter Tears" n. pag.).

Literary activist: Vine Deloria Jr.

The cardinal example of Native American literary activism is Vine Deloria Jr. (1933–2005), a Standing Rock Sioux, who first became nationally known during the late 1960s, following publication of his book *Custer Died for Your Sins*. His role in the national and international conversation regarding Native American issues rose with the organization of the American Indian Movement and other activist groups during the late 1960s and 1970s. Deloria also rose to national prominence as a spokesman for Native American self-determination movements, becoming a widely respected professor, author, and social critic in several fields, including law, religion, and political science, as well as Native American Studies. He was the best-known founder of Native American studies as a field of scholarly inquiry in the late twentieth century.

By the late 1990s, Deloria was described as:

> [T]he most significant voice in this generation regarding the presentation and analysis of contemporary Indian affairs, their history, present shape, and meaning … . No other voice, Indian or white, has as full a command of the overall data of Indian history or affairs, and no other voice has the moral force, the honesty, to admit mistakes and to redress them, or the edge to bite through the layers of soft tissue, through the stereotypes, myths, and outright lies, to the bone … marrow of Indian affairs.
>
> (Dunsmore 411).

During April 1970, Deloria twice visited Alcatraz during the Indian occupation of the island. He was impressed by the occupiers' boldness and energy, but believed they were inexperienced. Deloria told a press conference that "only ten Indians in the country are qualified to negotiate with the federal government," implying that none of the ten were present at Alcatraz (Smith & Warrior 82). The occupiers' governing council took notice of press reports quoting Deloria on April 3, and sent him a letter, asking for help, citing "our dire need for consultation" (Smith & Warrior 82). Deloria described the seizure of Alcatraz as a "masterstroke of Indian activism," even as he faulted its organizers' inexperience (Johnson et al. 30). About ten years after the occupation of Alcatraz ended, Deloria visited the island and heard a surprisingly mild and pro-Indian explanation of the occupation from a Park Service guide. Deloria's own assessment was more blunt:

> The Indians were well-represented in the media from the Alcatraz occupation through the Wounded Knee trials, but, unfortunately, each event dealt primarily with the symbols of oppression and did not project possible courses of action that might be taken to solve problems.
>
> (Johnson et al. 50)

Deloria saw potential in the younger movements, but also a danger of factionalism between them and older groups. Deloria wrote that "urban Indians have become the cutting edge of the new nationalism … [even as] the tribal leaders were cringing in fear that the activists would totally control Indian affairs" (Smith & Warrior 122). He wrote as the younger activists captivated national attention via the seizure of Alcatraz and other initiatives. As a best-selling author whose work heralded the explosion in Native American civil-rights activity (*Custer Died for Your Sins* was published in 1969, just as AIM was organizing), Deloria was the best-known Native intellectual of his time, perhaps of all time. As the "father" of Native American studies, he had ties to students who formed the backbone of both the National Indian Youth Council (NIYC) and AIM. He also had ties to both reservation and urban peoples, and so formed a unique bridge between rural and urban, older and younger.

Throughout his life, Deloria wrote a number of books and articles that took issue with Eurocentric interpretations of reality. His early books, such as *Custer Died for Your Sins* (1969), *We Talk, You Listen* (1970), and *Of Utmost Good Faith* (1971) continued to spread to new, younger audiences. In all of his works, Deloria has asserted Native American rights of occupancy to the land. Under international law, according to Deloria, Native American nations possess an equitable title of occupancy over lands upon which they live, "and this occupancy was not to be disturbed except by voluntary and lawful sales of lands to the European country claiming the legal title to the area in question" (qtd. in Lyons et al. 283). Deloria's writings also compare the metaphysics of Native American and European points of view, especially in legal and religious matters. In *God is Red* (1973), Deloria argued that American Indian spiritual traditions, far from being out-of-date, are more congruent with the needs of the modern world than Christianity, which he said fosters imperialism and disregard for Earth's ecological future. In *God is Red*, Deloria also contrasts Native American religion's melding of life with a concept of sacred place to the artificiality of Old World doctrines. (On Deloria's life and works, see Deloria; Dunsmore; "In Memoriam"; Wilkins "Native Visionary".)

These profiles of Westerman, Cash, and Deloria are only a sliver of American Indian activism's personal side. Intense social needs compel people of conscience into forms of activism related to their unique skills and talents A few examples include: Rebecca L. Adamson, Cherokee business developer and activist in economic revival; Mohawk John Kim Bell, a Canadian orchestra conductor, also an educational activist; Mohawk Ernest Benedict, educator, political leader, and spiritual leader; Lehman Brightman, Lakota and Creek educator and activist; Elouise Cobell, banker and initiator of the Individual Indian Monies class-action suit; John EchoHawk, Pawnee attorney and Indian-rights advocate; John Kahionhes Fadden and his father Ray, Mohawk artists, educators, and activists; Doug George-Kanentiio, Mohawk writer and activist; Tim Giago, Oglala Lakota (Sioux) journalist, newspaper publisher, and activist; John Herrington, Chickasaw astronaut and educational activist; Winona LaDuke, Anishinaabe (Ojibway) environmental activist, writer, and political figure; Phil Lucas, Choctaw filmmaker and activist; James Luna, Luiseño performance artist who strives to raise consciousness; Oren Lyons, Onondaga political leader, artist, lacrosse player, philosopher, and activist; Barbara Alice Mann, Seneca scholar, author, and activist; Billy Mills, Oglala Lakota distance runner and inspirational speaker; John C. Mohawk, Seneca educator, author, and activist; Buffy Sainte-Marie, Cree folksinger and activist; Joanne Shenandoah (Tekalihwa:khwa) Oneida musician and activist; Jay C. Silverheels, Mohawk actor and labor organizer; Wes Studi, Cherokee actor and activist; John Trudell, Santee Sioux activist, poet, and musician; Sheila Watt-Cloutier, Inuit political activist, political leader, and environmentalist; and W. Richard West, Southern Cheyenne and Arapaho lawyer and founding director of the National Museum of the American Indian.

Conclusion: the outcomes of activism

What does the Native American wave of activism have to show two generations later? Some things have changed, and others have not. Much of Native America is taking part in a revival due to the fact that many demands taken as rabble-rousing several decades ago have become policy. Among outside observers of Indian Country, a popular trope is that the various American Indian movements dissolved into internecine squabbles. That has been a factor, but many commentators fail to observe how deeply the goals of Native American activism in the 1960s and 1970s have become enmeshed in governance today. Forty years ago, the American Indian Movement (AIM) protested beer sales to drunken Oglala Sioux at Whiteclay, Nebraska. Today, the Oglala Lakota tribal council at Pine Ridge has filed suit against the major beer companies that distribute their wares in that tiny border town, seeking $500 million in damages for ruined Native lives. The companies have sought to have the suit dismissed on grounds of discrimination, arguing that they have a right to profit, and Indians have a right to get drunk. Such an abuse of the First Amendment might cause Thomas Jefferson to roll over in his grave. Just as in 1970, Indians are still buying the beer and falling down drunk. As the world changes around it, Whiteclay, the town that beer built, seems immune. But now, in Western Washington, fishing rights sought by members of the Survival of American Indians Association are legally established, and the fishing tribes co-manage the resource with the state that arrested them while ripping their nets and seizing their boats 40 years ago. Across North America, Native American languages are being revived. Elsewhere, parts of the Coalition for Navajo Liberation's program are Navajo Nation policy now. The mining and milling of uranium is illegal in Navajo Country, after two generations of Navajo pain and suffering stemming from the radioactive rock. Native graves and remains are legally protected and human remains are being returned to their owners.

Note

1 For much more detail on AIM activism during its most active period, see: See Banks & Erdoes; Dee Brown; Burnette & Koster; Churchill & Vander Wall; Hendricks; Jaimes; Johansen; Johansen & Maestas; Johnson et al.; Josephy; Matthiessen; Means; Messerschmidt; "Revolutionary Activities"; Shreve; Smith & Warrior; Steiner.

Works cited

Alcatraz and American Indian Activism: A Photographic History of the 1969–1971 Occupation of Alcatraz Island by Indians of All Tribes, Inc. Web. Accessed 4 Aug. 2014. http://www.csulb.edu/~gcampus/libarts/amindian/alcatraz/index.html

"Alcatraz is Not an Island: Timeline of Indian Activism." Public Broadcasting System, 2002. n. pag. Web. Accessed 10 Nov. 2011. http://www.pbs.org/itvs/alcatrazisnotanisland/timeline.html

American Friends Service Committee. *Uncommon Controversy: Fishing Rights of the Muckleshoot, Puyallup, and Nisqually Indians.* Seattle: University of Washington Press, 1970.

American Indian Movement: The home pages for AIM, headquartered in the Twin Cities. n.d., n. pag. Web. Accessed 4 Jan. 2007. http://www.aimovement.org/

Banks, Dennis & Richard Erdoes. *Ojibwa Warrior: Dennis Banks and the Rise of the American Indian Movement.* Norman: University of Oklahoma Press, 2004.

Brando, Marlon. "The Godfather: That Unfinished Oscar Speech." *New York Times* 30 March 1973, n. pag. Web. Accessed 15 Aug. 2014. http://www.nytimes.com/packages/html/movies/bestpictures/godfather-ar3.html

Brown, Bruce. *Mountain in the Clouds: A Search for the Wild Salmon.* New York: Simon & Schuster, 1982.

Brown, Dee. *Bury My Heart at Wounded Knee: An Indian History of the American West.* New York: Bantam Books, 1970.

Burnette, Robert, with John Koster. *The Road to Wounded Knee.* New York: Bantam Books, 1974.

Cash, Johnny. *Bitter Tears: Ballads of the American Indian*. Columbia Records, 1964.

Churchill, Ward & Jim Vander Wall. *Agents of Repression: The FBI's Secret Wars Against the Black Panther Party and the American Indian Movement*. Boston: South End Press, 2002.

The Columbian (of Olympia), 15 January 1853. Bruce E. Johansen with Willard Bill, Sr. *Up from the Ashes: Nation-building at Muckleshoot*. Auburn, WA: The Muckleshoot Indian Tribe, 2014.

D'Ambrosio, Antonino. "The Bitter Tears of Johnny Cash: The Untold Story of Johnny Cash, Protest Singer and Native American Activist, and his Feud with the Music Industry." Salon.com. n. pag. Web. Accessed 8 Nov. 2009. http://www.salon.com/2009/11/09/johnny_cash_2/

Deloria, Vine, Jr. *Custer Died for Your Sins: An Indian Manifesto*. 1969. Norman: University of Oklahoma Press, 1988.

——. *God is Red*. 1973. Golden: Fulcrum, 2003.

——. comp. *Of Utmost Good Faith*. New York: Simon & Schuster, 1971.

——. *We Talk, You Listen: New Tribes, New Turf*. New York: Macmillan, 1970.

Dunsmore, Roger. "Vine Deloria, Jr." *Handbook of Native American Literature*. Ed. Andrew Wiget. New York: Garland Publishing, 1996. 411–15.

George-Kanentiio, Doug. Personal e-mail correspondence. 1 May 2007.

Hendricks, Steve. *The Unquiet Grave: The FBI and the Struggle for the Soul of Indian Country*. New York: Thunder's Mouth Press, 2006.

"In Memoriam: Vine Deloria, Jr." *Indian Country Today* 17 Nov. 2005. n. pag. Web. http://www.indiancountry.com/content.cfm?id=1096411939

Jaimes, M. Annette, ed. *The State of Native America: Genocide, Colonization and Resistance*. Boston: South End Press, 1992.

Johansen, Bruce E. "Peltier and the Posse." *The Nation*, 1 Oct. 1977. 304–07.

Johansen, Bruce E. & Roberto F. Maestas. *Wasi'chu: The Continuing Indian Wars*. New York: Monthly Review Press, 1979.

Johansen, Bruce E. & Willard Bill, Sr. *Up from the Ashes: Nation-building at Muckleshoot*. Auburn, WA: The Muckleshoot Indian Tribe, 2014.

Johnson, Ralph W. "The States Versus Indian Off-reservation Fishing: A United States Supreme Court Error." *Washington Law Review* 47. 2 (1972): 207–36.

Johnson, Troy R. *Alcatraz is Not an Island*. Documentary Film. San Francisco: Diamond Island Productions, 1999.

——. "The Roots of Contemporary Native American Activism." *Major Problems in American Indian History*. Ed. Albert Hurtado & Peter Iverson. Boston: Houghton-Mifflin, 2001. 472–83.

Johnson, Troy R. & Joane Nagel, eds. "Alcatraz Revisited: The 25th Anniversary of The Occupation." Special issue. *American Indian Culture & Research Journal* 18. 4 (1994): 1–253.

Johnson, Troy R., Joane Nagel & Duane Champaign, eds. *American Indian Activism: Alcatraz to the Longest Walk*. Urbana: University of Illinois Press, 1996.

Josephy, Alvin, Jr. *The American Indian Fight for Freedom*. New Haven: Yale University Press, 1978.

——. *Now That the Buffalo's Gone: A Study of Today's American Indians*. New York: Knopf, 1982.

——. *Red Power: The American Indians' Fight for Freedom*. New York: American Heritage Press, 1971.

——. "Wounded Knee and All That: What the Indians Want." *New York Times Sunday Magazine* 18 Mar. 1973, 18–19, 66–83.

Josephy, Alvin, Jr., Joane Nagel & Troy Johnson, eds. *Red Power: The American Indians' Fight for Freedom*. Lincoln: University of Nebraska Press, 1999.

KCTS 9 TV (PBS, Seattle). "Bob Santos, Roberto Maestas, and Larry Gossett Recall Their Activism in Seattle." 13 Nov. 2009. n. pag. Web. Accessed 3 July 2012. https://www.youtube.com/watch?v=eCGeWRxEwxM

King, C. Richard, ed. *The Native American Mascot Controversy: A Handbook*. Lanham, MD: Scarecrow Press, 2010.

Lane, Barbara. "The Muckleshoot Indians and the White River: A Report Prepared for the Muckleshoot Indian Tribe." Sept. 1980. MIT Preservation Program Archive.

Lazarus, Edward. *Black Hills, White Justice: The Sioux Nation v. the United States: 1775 to the Present.* New York: HarperCollins, 1991.

Lyons, Oren, John Mohawk, Vine Deloria Jr., Laurence Hauptman, Howard Berman, Donald A. Grinde Jr., Curtis Berkey & Robert Venables. *Exiled in the Land of the Free: Democracy, Indian Nations, and the Constitution.* Santa Fe, NM: Clear Light Publishers, 1992.

Matthiessen, Peter. *In the Spirit of Crazy Horse.* New York: Viking, 1991.

Means, Russell, with Marvin J. Wolf. *Where White Men Fear to Tread: The Autobiography of Russell Means.* New York: St. Martin's Press, 1995.

Messerschmidt, James W. *The Trial of Leonard Peltier.* Boston: South End Press, 1983.

Miller, Bruce J. "The Press, the Boldt Decision, and Indian–White Relations." *American Indian Culture & Research Journal* 17. 2 (1993): 75–98.

Parham, Vera. "Something Worth Going up That Hill For." *Columbia Magazine* 21. 3 (Fall 2007): 24–32.Web. Accessed 20 Mar. 2010. http://columbia.washingtonhistory.org/magazine/articles/2007/0307/0307-a3.aspx

"Physical Yield of Washington State Salmon Fisheries, 1989–1974." Russel L. Barsh, *The Washington Fishing Rights Controversy: An Economic Critique.* Monograph Series, University of Washington Graduate School of Business Administration, 89, 197.

"Revolutionary Activities within the United States: The American Indian Movement: Report of the Subcommittee to Investigate the Administration of the Internal Security Act and Other Internal Security Laws of the Committee on the Judiciary," United States Senate, Ninety-fourth Congress, second session., September, 1976. OCLC 657741708.

Reyes, Lawney L. *Bernie Whitebear: An Urban Indian's Quest for Justice.* Tucson: University of Arizona Press, 2006.

Shreve, Bradley. *Red Power Rising: The National Indian Youth Council and the Origins of Native Activism.* Norman: University of Oklahoma Press, 2011.

Smith, Paul Chaat & Robert Allen Warrior. *Like a Hurricane: The American Indian Movement from Alcatraz to Wounded Knee.* New York: New Press, 1996.

State v. Towessnutte (February 4, 1916) (89 Wash. 478).

Steiner, Stan. *The New Indians.* New York: Harper & Row, 1968.

Suckley, G. "Report Upon the Fisheries Collected on the Survey: Report Upon the Salmonidae." *Reports of the Explorations … 1854. The Pacific Railroad Report.* Washington, D.C.: Thomas H. Ford, 1860.

Talbot, Steve. "Free Alcatraz: The Culture of Native American Liberation." *Journal of Ethnic Studies* 6. 3 (Fall 1978): 80–89.

United States v. Washington 384 F. Supp. 312 (1974).

United States v. Winans (1905).

U.S. Commission on Civil Rights. "Fishing in Western Washington – a Treaty Right, a Clash of Cultures." *Indian Tribes, a Continuing Quest for Survival: A Report of the United States Commission on Civil Rights.* Washington: U.S. Government Printing Office, 1981. 61–100.

Westerman, Floyd. *Custer Died For Your Sins.* Light in the Attic Records, 1982.

——. *Indian Country.* Perception Records, 1970.

——. *The Land is Your Mother.* Light in the Attic Records, 1982.

Wilkins, David E., ed. *The Hank Adams Reader: An Exemplary Native American Activist and the Unleashing of Indigenous Sovereignty.* Golden: Fulcrum, 2011.

——. "Native Visionary Spoke for All Disadvantaged Americans." *Indian Country Today.* n.d., n. pag. Web. Accessed 1 Dec. 2005. http://www.indiancountry.com/content.cfm?id=1096412026

Wilkinson, Charles. *Messages from Frank's Landing: A Story of Salmon, Treaties, and the American Way.* Seattle: University of Washington Press, 2000.

Woods, Fronda. "Who's in Charge of Fishing?" *Oregon Historical Quarterly* 106. 3 (Fall 2005): 412–41.

Ziontz, Alvin J. *A Lawyer in Indian Country: A Memoir.* Seattle: University of Washington Press, 2009.

24
Identity, Culture, Community, and Nation
Literary Theory as Politics and Praxis

Kirby Brown

Those coming to Native American literary studies today benefit from an ever-growing body of theoretically sophisticated and ethically committed scholarship rooted in theories and methodologies emerging from the challenges, aspirations, and visions of contemporary Native communities. While certainly a state of affairs to celebrate, I think it's important to remember that this was not always case. From the late 1970s through the mid-1990s, Native literary studies concerned itself primarily with questions of identity and authenticity, its relationship to existing literary and formal traditions, and the capacity of Native writing to mediate or challenge Euroamerican claims to epistemological and cultural authority. As such, these approaches often privileged non-Native intellectual questions and theoretical paradigms over the lived experiences and contemporary social and political realities of Native peoples. In an effort to better align intellectual production with those realities, interventions over the last two and a half decades have redirected the field back to the politics of sovereignty, self-determination, and nationhood from which Native Studies emerged out of the political activism of the 1960s and 70s. Recent trends across Native and Indigenous studies, however, have begun to interrogate the theoretical limitations and practical utility of such terms for tribal peoples, positing Indigenous-centered concepts of social and political life which many feel align more productively with tribal values and commitments and are better equipped to advance efforts toward decolonization and Indigenous resurgence.

Central to such projects have been rigorous attempts to theorize the relationships between identity, culture, community, nation, and experience, and to openly contemplate the political, philosophical, and ethical commitments of scholarship and intellectual work for and upon Native peoples and nations. This chapter broadly surveys the contours, organizing ideas, and theoretical interventions that have defined these conversations, focusing specifically on how scholars understand various articulations and experiences of community and nationhood across Indian Country and the theoretical and political questions they attempt to address. I seek here to map my own continually developing understanding of this body of work, and in doing so to strive for breadth and coverage rather than depth and comprehensiveness. To these ends, the first section provides a sketch of the first two decades of scholarship from the 1970s through the mid-1990s, while the next section explores the formative intervention of American Indian Literary Nationalism in the mid-1990s. The

IDENTITY, CULTURE, COMMUNITY, AND NATION

following section explores how questions of modernity, gender and transnational studies encourage us to rethink nationhood and community within the contexts of global and hemispheric relations, followed by a conclusion exploring the emerging field of indigenous resurgence theory grounded in *collective* decolonial resistance to the settler-state motivated by the revitalization of *tribally specific* values, beliefs, practices, and relations exercised at the local level. Though not properly "literary" in method, this exciting body of work models ideas of nationhood and community anchored to inherent rights to autonomy and self-determination more firmly rooted in indigenous understandings of cultural and political life. Its emergence from and ongoing ties to contemporary political and revitalization movements at both local and tribal-international levels – from resistance to Bill C-31 and efforts to incorporate indigenous lands into settler governance structures to the Oka Crisis and Idle No More Movement to Missing and Murdered Awareness and anti-black, red, and brown racial violence – remind us of the very real material and embodied implications of intellectual and activist work. Overall, the story I hope to tell is less one of opposition and rupture than one of a field "gaining knowledge" capable not only of helping us better understand Native *texts*, but also connecting that work to the immediate and ongoing *contexts* that continue to inform Native *life*.

Early literary scholarship: from identity and authenticity to resistance, mediation, and postmodern play

Broadly speaking, the early years of Native literary scholarship concerned itself primarily with questions over who or what "counted" as Indian (politics, history, culture, region, blood/descent); what marked a text as authentically or identifiably Native (authorial identity, identifiable cultural or historical content, formal influences linked to orality or ceremony, spirituality, language); and the relationship of Native literatures to existing ethnic, national, and formal traditions. In the first monograph devoted exclusively to Native literatures, Charles Larson (1978) suggests a combination of tribal affiliation, community recognition, and an emerging political consciousness of resistance and separatism evident in the literature of the 1960s and 70s as markers of both American Indian identity and literary quality, while Kenneth Lincoln (1983) looks to a text's "grounding" in and expression of "tribalism" understood as a widely shared "consciousness" of relationality and kinship most powerfully evident in the content, forms, themes, styles, and structures of oral and ceremonial traditions. Combining Larson's interest in aesthetic quality with Lincoln's emphasis on culture and tradition, Alan Velie (1982) explores the intercultural character of Native literature and how it speaks both *from* and *across* Native and Euroamerican cultural traditions and literary forms. In the first explicitly feminist treatment of Native literature – indeed, the first Native voice in this early period – Paula Gunn Allen (1986) explores what she terms a "gynocratic" respect for female intellectual, political, and maternal labor evident in Laguna and other Native cultures within the crucial contexts of family, history, language, and place that inform Native cultural and political identities.

More heavily informed by Euroamerican critical theory, a series of studies by Arnold Krupat (1989, 1998, 2002), Greg Sarris (1993), Louis Owens (1994, 1998, 2001), James Ruppert (1995), Susan Berry Brill de Ramirez (1999) and Gerald Vizenor (1998, 1999) address questions commonly aligned with the "culture wars" of the late-1980s through

285

the 1990s: identity, discourse, and U.S. cultural politics; canonicity, power, and privilege; relationships between margins, centers, and the "contact zones" resting in between; and possibilities (or not) for cosmopolitanist/cross-cultural mediation and exchange. Across his career, Krupat leverages critical theory as a mechanism to resist the essentializing impulses of ahistorical and strictly formalist approaches to texts, as well as the perpetuation of dominant understandings of canonicity that marginalize Native and other ethnic/postcolonial writing. Suspicious of a politics of difference bent upon uncritical affirmations of one's own theoretical, social, and political commitments, Krupat develops a historically and politically informed "cosmopolitanist" emphasis on what texts share – anti-imperial, anti-racist, anti-colonial critique – across traditions, histories, and cultures. Owens's work shares this anti-colonial critique, recovering mixed-blood identities not as markers of tragedy, degeneration, and inauthenticity, but as hybrid sites where racial, cultural, and political identity; problems of coloniality, (il)legibility, and historical erasure; and complicated relationships between blood, family, history, place, nation, and discourse are most acutely negotiated and contested. Vizenor mobilizes the emancipatory potential of mixed-blood discourse and the politics of postmodern linguistic play to lay waste to the "manifest manners" of colonial binaries and explode the "terminal creeds" of surveillance, containment, nostalgia, tragedy, and death in which Native peoples are often framed. In their place Vizenor posits the now ubiquitous concept of "survivance," both a vision and methodology of tribal life anchored to an appreciation for irony, ambiguity, humor, and play, and a celebration of chance, multiplicity, contingency, and innovation. Studies by Sarris, Ruppert, and Ramirez are also concerned with questions of discourse, specifically the ways in which the process of inter-/cross-cultural communication transforms both writer-speaker and listener-reader by destabilizing the respective epistemological and experiential fields through which they enter the context of exchange. Echoing Krupat, Owens, and Vizenor, they celebrate the potential of "mixed" discursive spaces in which new relationships, identities, and understandings might productively be formed, while also noting circumstances and conditions where communication and translation/exchange break down.

Collectively, this early body of scholarship outlines the questions, concerns, problems, and parameters that in many ways continue to define the field. Larson's privileging of political identity and community recognition over blood quantum and rote self-identification; Lincoln's, Allen's, and Ramirez's emphases on culturally and tribally specific methodologies rooted in dynamic "traditions" as "grounded" frames through which to engage Native writing; and the explicitly "political" approaches to literary studies advocated by Krupat, Owens, and Vizenor anticipate similar positions taken up by literary nationalists and theorists of indigenous resurgence decades later. Similarly, Velie's early attention to intercultural exchange/influence and Krupat's understanding of the anti-colonial potentials of a developing transnational, hemispheric indigenism not only look forward to later explorations of mediation and translation, but also contemporary investments in questions of transnational conflict, exchange, and alliance across difference. Allen's and Sarris's contributions strike me as especially pivotal. Combined with her attention to Laguna oral and cultural traditions, Allen's proto-intersectional framework, attention to the gendered operations of coloniality, and willingness to engage in internal critique, introduced many of the central questions that continue to motivate scholars working across women's, gender, settler-colonial, and indigenous studies today. Similarly, by anchoring his study through his and others' interactions with the Pomo elder Mabel McKay, Sarris situates "community" as *a central* analytic connected to a *living* cultural and political community located in a *specific* place in the *here and now*.

The success and influence of these early studies also intensified some of the methodological and critical tendencies they introduced to the field to which subsequent scholars – many of them Native – would respond. Though this work had done a great deal to *theorize* identity and the contexts of textual, cultural, discursive, and communicative exchange, what had it done to address the *material* and *political* conditions, lived experiences, and social relations through which those identities were negotiated? While its celebration of borders, boundaries, hybridities, and postmodern slippage sought to liberate Native identities from colonialist discourse, how could such moves support the kinds of authoritative claims to identity, territories, resources, and rights upon which Native sovereignty and self-determination depend? How might such approaches speak to questions of sovereignty, treaty relationships, or the ongoing connection not only to discursive communities but also to specific *national* communities? It was out of this shifting milieu that American Indian Literary Nationalism emerged.

American Indian Literary Nationalism: sovereignty, nation, and experience as critical methodology

To paraphrase Paula Gunn Allen, strange things begin to happen when the focus in American Indian literary studies shifts from a Euroamerican to a Native American critical axis. Theoretically, American Indian Literary Nationalism (AILN) holds categories such as nation, community, and the politics of sovereignty and self-determination at the center of its critical practice. Methodologically, it privileges Native cultural and intellectual traditions, experiences, and perspectives as authoritative sources of knowledge and theory; engages the variety of genres and forms – including non-fiction – in which Native peoples have exercised self-representation; recovers previously neglected writers, texts, and traditions; advances both tribally specific and comparative approaches to Native texts; and demands that scholarship explicitly address the political, social, economic, and intellectual challenges facing contemporary Native nations and communities. AILN thus sought to return explicitly political and ethical mandates to the field dedicated to the needs, priorities, and experiences of Native peoples and nations.

One might consider this affirmation of tribal sovereignty within the multiple contexts of Native experience to be one of the central thematics/tensions uniting nationalist scholarship. While some have retrospectively located this impulse in Simon Ortiz's 1982 essay "Towards a National Indian Literature," AILN as we know it today coalesced in a series of essays and monographs published by Native writers from the early 1990s through the mid-2000s. A strong, early, and consistent voice in this redirection was Elizabeth Cook-Lynn. Rooted in a conviction that intellectual and cultural production "contribute to the politics of possession and dispossession" and a commitment to Native Studies' original mission of "defending Indigenous nationhood in America," Cook-Lynn's critical practice begins and ends with tribal nations ("Intellectualism" 126; *Why* 31; "Who" 11; "American Indian Studies" 24). Under this paradigm, identity is not simply a function of culture, consciousness, or discourse, but also of sovereignty, citizenship, territory, and the indigenous politics of recognition. This is not to suggest that other markers of identity are unimportant to

Cook-Lynn, or that nationhood, in a political sense, is the horizon of experience for Native peoples. It is simply to acknowledge that identity claims have political implications for tribal sovereignty and are thus better left to the authority of tribal nations themselves. By framing identity in terms of rights and tying those rights to the political sovereignty of the tribal nations in which they are legally invested, Cook-Lynn's nationalism holds the sovereign right of Indian nations to self-definition intact while also critically engaging "what it means to be Indian in tribal America" ("Intellectualism" 134).

Though different in approach and method, Robert Warrior's *Tribal Secrets: Recovering American Indian Intellectual Traditions* (1995) and *The People and Word: Reading Native Non-Fiction* (2005), Jace Weaver's *That the People Might Live: American Literatures and Native American Community* (1997), and Craig Womack's *Red on Red: Native American Literary Separatism* (1999) offer a variety of visions of what nationalist work which takes Cook-Lynn's critiques seriously might look like. As his titles suggest, Warrior's project shifts the emphasis from questions of literary form, identity, and oppositional politics to the recovery of the history of ideas, traditions, and mediums through which Native writers have understood themselves as Native peoples, a practice Warrior terms "intellectual sovereignty." Grounded in Native cultural, historical, political, and intellectual traditions, intellectual sovereignty is both a critical methodology of privileging Native voices and an ongoing reflective practice of contemplating and envisioning the multiple possibilities for Native life. Weaver's compendious survey of Native intellectual production across a wide array of genres, forms, theoretical traditions, and historical contexts considers nationhood alongside other community formations – "reservation, rural, urban, tribal, pan-Indian, traditional, Christian," and familial – through which Native peoples navigate personal and collective experience in an ongoing context of colonialism (43, 45). Though more expansive in scope than other critics, Weaver understands both identity and community not as free-floating signifiers of self-definition, but rather as experiential categories rooted in *specific relationships* to family, history, and place (38, 43). It is precisely Native literatures' exploration of and "proactive" commitments to such intersections – what Weaver terms "communitism" – that marks both its value and its politics (ix, xiii, 43, 45, 162). Womack examines such intersections in his tribally specific exploration of Mvskogee-Creek history, politics, and literature. Attending to everything from Creek constitutionalism and the oral tradition to historical romances, critical regionalism, and intertribal gender performances – all framed within a brilliant fictional epistolary exchange between Creek traditionalists! – Womack's separatism-as-methodology considers tribal literatures as Native national traditions *in their own right* and *on their own terms* (137–39, 239). In their arguments for tribal sovereignty, the privileging of tribal voices and experiences, and the importance of tribal-national and other communities to Native Studies, AILN scholars don't so much deny intersecting, overlapping, contested, or mediated experiences as they suggest that for such things to have meaning *as Native experiences* they must necessarily be understood from the wide diversity of contexts relevant to *Native life*.

To say that the influence of these studies was seismic would be an understatement, because virtually everyone engaged in post-AILN Native literary studies recognizes both nationhood and sovereignty as foundations upon which crucial political and legal relationships between Native communities and settler-states exist. Because such relations are predicated on the perpetual dispossession, disruption, and elimination of Native land and life, however, both nationhood and sovereignty are extended in AILN and related work

IDENTITY, CULTURE, COMMUNITY, AND NATION

to address such disruptions. As a result, both terms are embedded in a complex matrix of governance, kinship, culture, history, experience, story, and place. In addition to histories of governance, Womack defines nationhood as "a people's idea of themselves, their imaginings of who they are" as well as the "ongoing expression of a tribal voice through imagination, language, and literature" (14). Christopher Teuton (2012) picks up on the power of story, imagination, and language not simply to preserve culture but also to perpetually renew it, and in doing so (re)constitute "the national" via the situated relationships formed in local communities. Focusing on the intersections of kinship, culture, and nation, Daniel Heath Justice (2006) explores nationhood not just as the process of storied political and cultural imaginings, but as the ongoing expression of tribal "peoplehood," an understanding of national community rooted less in legal understandings of citizenship than the familial, historical, cultural, and political relations through which many Native peoples continue to reckon community and belonging. In addition to being "situated" within tribal historical, cultural, and political contexts, most nationalists also understand nationhood as "located" in specific territories and geographies. Place thus emerges as central components of Cook-Lynn's nationalism, Womack's understanding of Creek identity and experience, and Ortiz's emphases on the centrality of land in his "land-language-culture" triad of Native identity. Both Lisa Brooks (2008) and Sean Teuton (2008) advance these commitments in their comparative readings of how Native identities are constituted through linguistic, experiential, and long-standing storied relations between people, place, and landscape.

Taken together, *tribal*-nationhood broadly marks itself in these and other studies in its emphasis on imagination and plurality rather than definition and dogma, on an ethic of peoplehood and community over administrative and bureaucratic affiliations to state authority, and on storied and familial relations to place as crucial contexts for legitimizing legal and political claims rather than through executive orders and legislative fiats. Sovereignty, understood within such contexts, is more than a theory of coercive power invested in states or a norm of political authority tied to nations. Rather, sovereignty also emerges as a methodology and experiential practice of self-determined life and living through which Native peoples continue to imagine and reflect upon who they are and where/what they want to be. In this way, scholars now speak of plural sovereignties ranging from human rights-based understandings of "personal" and "popular" sovereignty to representational, visual, and cultural sovereignties to the emergent field of sovereign erotics advanced by scholars of Indigenous queer and two-spirit writing. Such formulations suggest concepts of sovereignty that are, to paraphrase Justice, as much about ethics and relationships as they are politics and power. In these contexts, scholars now consider both nationhood and sovereignty less as rigid political abstractions than socially symbolic forms of Indigenous anti-colonial resistance, agency, and experience. In theory – if not always in practice – AILN doesn't so much advocate intellectual, political, cultural, or literary separatism as it *locates* the points of exchange, conflict, and convergence within the political, social, cultural, and historical contexts of nationhood and sovereignty through which such relations have meaning and significance *for Native peoples*.

The distinction between theory and practice mentioned above is an important one, for as much as literary nationalism sought to account for a wide range of Native voices and experience from within intersecting tribally specific and wider frameworks, its focus on nationhood, sovereignty, and the cultural politics of recognition often elided other equally important questions facing tribal communities. Not least of these include the problematic relationships between modernity, tradition, and nation, and the intersections between transnationalism, globalization, and gender violence. It is to these interventions that I now turn.

Modernity, transnationalism, and the limits of nation

One project of AILN was to reconcile conventional understandings of tribal authenticity and tradition with contemporary forms of representation and political authority that define discursive and legal relationships with settler-states. Careful neither to romanticize nor universalize tribal cultures and traditions, nationalists consistently frame tradition as a diverse array of cultural practices, beliefs, and relations capable of adaptation, change, *and* maintaining continuity across history. Both Warrior and Justice understand tradition broadly not in terms of identity or authenticity, but as a richly nuanced, complex, and, more importantly, *ongoing* process of survival, adaptation, and self-determination. Speaking of the relationships between traditional and contemporary forms of governance, Brooks similarly aligns tribal constitutionalism in a long history of indigenous self-governance and governmental structures. Pushing further, Womack claims everything from constitutional law and the English language to various modes and forms of writing as "traditional" for Native peoples well over five hundred years into colonization, "no matter how much it deviates from what people did one or two hundred years ago" (42). Though scholars like Krupat acknowledge both the utility and limits of Womack's position – that is, as a point past which retaining Native "values and worldviews" is rendered moot – they have largely left the category of tradition largely intact (*Red Matters* 21–22).

Two recent studies by Scott Lyons (2010) and Joshua Nelson (2014), however, challenge nationalism's attachment to tradition and what comes off at times as its uncritical affirmation of nationhood and sovereignty. Lyons interrogates the tendency of nationalist discourse to rely on undertheorized concepts like culture and tradition as ahistorical markers of authenticity and identity at the expense of exploring how Native peoples have productively engaged modernity within the coercive contexts of settler-colonialism. In what he terms a "realist nationalist" approach to Native Studies and Native politics anchored neither to cultural separatism nor to oppositional politics, Lyons models a contemporary ethic of Native intellectual and political thought upon the x-marks – graphic "signatures" of assent made in treaties and other political agreements – of Indians who engaged modernity not as a *fait accompli* of colonial dominance but as a legitimate, viable, and necessary strategy to ensure the survivance of their communities *in the modern world*. Rather than attempting to force tradition into ideologies of nationalism, Lyons suggests that individual tribal nations decide what kind of citizen they want to produce – traditional or otherwise – and craft their legal and political institutions accordingly. Lyons thus seeks not to reconcile tradition with modernity and nationalism, but to hold them in a perpetually open-ended conversation about the distinctly modern futures of Native nation-peoples. Nelson's text similarly interrogates colonialist binaries that continue to structure even the most thoughtful and rigorous work in Native Studies. Of particular concern are the ways both nationalists and cosmopolitanists, despite their anti-colonial designs, remain problematically committed to centralized state authority – whether tribal or otherwise – as potential sites for resistance and liberation (12–25). Focusing less on identifiable markers of "tradition" or "assimilation" than flexible "dispositions" and "principled practices" rooted in local, distributed authority, consensus decision-making, a respect for dissent, and ethics of hospitality and inclusivity, Nelson offers what he terms "indigenous anarchism," "a pluralist, community-centered political philosophy that looks to practices that preceded and surpass the nation-state," as a corrective for increasingly centralized modes of Native governance (4, 26, 32). With this anarchic frame as its foundation, *Progressive Traditions* seeks not to define or identify what counts as "progress" or "tradition" but to explore the "surprising range of strategies" – some recognizable, some anomalous – through which Cherokees "[combine] old and new ways of doing things as they employ traditional adaptive strategies to resolve cultural and historical problems" (xiii). Though both studies embrace "the new," and thus understandings of Indigenous nationhood as a constant negotiation with difference and modernity, it's important to note that Nelson is much less enthusiastic than Lyons about the potentials for "modernization" and the increasingly centralized, bureaucratic relations toward which it seems to gravitate. Despite this difference, both studies frame modernity not as a problem in need of reconciliation or resolution, but as yet another set of social and cultural circumstances in longer histories of creation, emergence, migration, movement, and becoming through which Native peoples have understood themselves as *both* tribal *and* modern.

If tensions between tradition, modernity, and nationhood represent one challenge for Native scholarship in the twenty-first century, accounting for the global imbrication of Native peoples and nations within larger, transnational economic, political, historical, cultural and methodological contexts constitutes another. A series of theoretically related yet methodologically distinct studies by Shari Huhndorf (2009), Mishuana Goeman (2013), James Cox (2012) and Chad Allen (2012) explore the possibilities of transnational/transindigenous methodologies to address some of nationalism's potential blindspots. Informed by indigenous feminist critiques of settler-colonialism, Huhndorf and Goeman explore the intersections of gender, transnational/settler-colonial discourse, indigenous self-representation, and the centrality of women in decolonization projects. Huhndorf's study situates itself on the political and discursive borders of U.S.–Canadian-indigenous nations and within the disciplinary tension between post-national American studies' interrogation of U.S. imperialism and its elision of ongoing colonial relations, and nationalist-oriented Native studies' commitments to sovereignty and self-determination and its refusal to meaningfully address extra-national questions of patriarchy and gender violence. Exploring both colonialist and indigenous representations of Native peoples and lands across a wide variety of expressive forms, Huhndorf tackles the ways in which the global dissemination of Native texts at times works against the anti-colonialist intentions of their producers, and identifies the emergence of an "indigenous feminist" critique which interrogates colonialist positionings of Native women as "objects of conquest and violence" and counters cultural "return" narratives with explorations of cross-border, urban, and other liminal experiences that define contemporary Native life and art (4, 19). Goeman takes up and advances this critique by (re)situating Native women at the center of both tribal- and settler-national communities, exploring how their gendered mappings of space and nation in poetry, novels, short stories, and performance not only counter patriarchal settler mappings of difference but also imagine alternative understandings of identity, power, community, and place relevant to contemporary Native experience. Combining a fluid and processual conceptualization of tradition with a theoretical understanding of how space maps social relations, Goeman's project is neither one of recovery/return nor "remythologizing" Native national space, but rather a study of how contemporary Native women's writing opens possibilities for embodied spatial, social, and political relations informed but not overdetermined by normative geographies of gender violence and state power.

Where these studies organize themselves around important intersections between gender, sexuality, and settler-colonial violence, Cox and Allen deploy transnational cartographies in an effort to expand Native literary studies into hemispheric political and global cultural contexts. Organized by a historicist methodology of "comparative indigeneities" across U.S., Mexican, and tribal-national histories, Cox challenges understandings of early twentieth-century Native cultural production as disorganized and politically ambivalent, recovering it instead as a revolutionary engagement with the possibilities for hemispheric indigenous politics well ahead of contemporary efforts in indigenous scholarship. The study tracks how twentieth-century writers from Todd Downing, Lynn Riggs, and D'Arcy McNickle to Gerald Vizenor and Leslie Silko variously imagine indigenous Mexico as a "landscape resonant with exciting anti-colonial possibilities that were to them much less visible, or non-existent, in the United States" (3). Whether conceived as a thoroughly indigenous space punctuated by colonialism, a potential site of violent anti-colonial resistance, a hemispheric geography of tribal diplomacy and kinship, or an imagined location of indigenous revolution, what emerges is an oft-elided, decidedly transnational tradition of indigenous self-determination and a hemispheric politics of belonging cutting across "local, tribal national, transnational and continental" contexts (204). Allen also engages projects of recovery and revision, though to slightly different purposes. Acknowledging that the diversity of indigenous cultures in the United States – much less around the world! – still demands rigorous attention to local specificities, Allen argues that methodologies of recovery, interpretation, and "purposeful juxtapositions" *across* indigenous difference are useful tools to complicate understandings of and approaches to presumably well-covered ground in U.S. Native literary studies. Further, a "multiperspectival" approach to authorship, aesthetic form, and the "extra-literary" technologies through which indigenous peoples express themselves and their understandings of the world can supplement current interpretive methodologies, particularly with respect to "texts" that self-consciously combine materials, representations, technologies, and forms from multiple indigenous traditions. Where Cox's study recovers intersecting histories of colonial violence, migration, immigration, and belonging in order to open Native literary studies to the possibility of speaking to both the tribally specific and hemispheric contexts that continue to frame indigenous experiences in the Americas, for Allen the potential for trans-Indigenous studies-as-methodology functions to complicate and expand upon available approaches to indigenous literary and cultural studies in the United States.

In a critical and political moment defined not only by struggles for *tribal sovereignty* but also by global demands for *indigenous rights* to autonomy, mobility, health, safety, reproduction, economic security, and others, methods such as those advocated above constitute necessary interventions not simply to make sense of an increasingly interconnected, globalized world, but also to imagine potentials for more broadly intersectional coalitional politics and intellectual programs. That said, contemporary scholarship must still contend with the variety of alarming threats to political, social, cultural, community, and individual life facing Native communities. Combined with internal struggles over identity, belonging, and disenrollment often structured by colonialist understandings of race, gender, sexuality, and nation, the question becomes how to strike a balance between addressing the broader contexts and relationships in which Native peoples find themselves and the intensely local issues tribal communities face on a day-to-day basis. By way of conclusion, I turn to the emerging field of indigenous resurgence theory as one site where such negotiations are being theorized and practiced.

More than survival: refusing recognition, suspending damage, and cultural revitalization through indigenous resurgence

Though sharing political commitments to indigenous nationhood and inherent rights to cultural, political, and territorial autonomy with literary nationalists, and theoretical commitments to interrogate the intersectional dynamics of state power with settler-colonial and critical transnational studies, what seems to distinguish indigenous resurgence theory from other approaches are its concomitant commitments to *collective* critique of and resistance to settler-state structures of politics, power, and representation, coupled with – if not motivated by – the revitalization of *community-specific* indigenous traditions (Alfred 2005). With this dual-pronged approach, studies range in scope from broad theoretical critiques and discursive analyses of settler-colonial power to local analyses of internal community dynamics and grass-roots cultural revitalization. Eve Tuck and K. Wayne Yang (2012), Dian Million (2013), and Glen Coulthard (2014) each levy strong theoretical critiques against discourses and structures of reconciliation, recognition, and other "settler moves to innocence" as alibis for ongoing neoliberal state violence against Indigenous peoples and lands. Employing tribally specific frameworks anchored in political science, ethnography and history, and literary and cultural studies, respectively, Steve Russell (2010), Audra Simpson (2014), and Joshua Nelson (2014) historicize and critique the discursive, legal, and institutional forces through which the United States and Canada work to reframe and naturalize Cherokee and Mohawk identities according to settler norms, processes which produce efforts to alienate, disenroll, and/or expel bodies that don't neatly align with racialized and gendered markers of identity, status, and recognition. In her ethnographic study of Yakama cultural revitalization and activism, Michelle Jacob (2014) documents the power of grass-roots, family- and community-centered efforts to reinvigorate intergenerational relationships and (re)constitute resurgent communities independent of official structures of state or tribal support, commitments to self-determined community activism also shared by Nishnaabeg writer, scholar, activist, poet, and mother, Leanne Simpson in her intensely personal affirmation of indigenous resurgence and re-emergence (2011).

As such studies suggest, indigenous resurgence theorists understand settler-colonialism not as a historical event of a regrettable colonialist past, but as an ongoing structure of relations predicated upon the perpetual elimination of indigenous life and land. From this critical position, they externally critique any and all attempts at reconciliation, resolution, and healing from within state-mandated parameters that leave the legitimacy of settler nations intact, while internally engaging in efforts to decolonize colonialist understandings of social and political relations that have found their way into tribal communities' social, legal, and political structures. Scholars such as L. Simpson, A. Simpson, Tuck, Jacob, and Million working within explicitly decolonizing feminist frameworks bring much-needed attention to the affective intersections of heteropatriarchal settler power, gender, sexual violence, and indigenous life. This work importantly recovers understandings of individual, cultural, and political life as intensely embodied affectively and emotionally "felt" experiences mapped onto and running through indigenous minds, bodies, and spirits. Exchanging disabling rhetorics of victimization, pathology, and damage for affirmative positions of desire, aspiration, imagination, vitality, and vision (Tuck 2009, L. Simpson, Million), indigenous resurgence scholarship practices a dual politics of refusal/contention and affirmation, "turning away" from the legitimizing gaze of settler authority and toward revitalized tribal values, beliefs, practices, and relationships as resurgent, self-generated, transformative models of self-determination and resilience (Alfred, A. Simpson, Coulthard, Jacob, L. Simpson).

"Revitalization" for scholars of indigenous resurgence is less about a return to pristine, pre-contact indigenous lifeways than a "self-conscious traditionalism" anchored in customary relations of family, place, and politics modeled in traditional knowledge and cultural practices (Alfred *Peace* 16). For Taiaiake Alfred, revitalization is a pragmatic revaluation of "certain common beliefs, values, and principles that form the persistent core of a community's culture" which speak most effectively to contemporary indigenous life, a formulation that recalls Nelson's emphasis on "dispositions" and "principled practices" (*Peace* 52–53). Though affirming the "fluidity" and flexibility of indigenous traditions, Leanne Simpson locates the promise of revitalization less in the "content" of what is recovered than in the reinvigorated contexts and extended family relationships the performance of such practices make possible (42–43). As Glen Coulthard argues, such relations are primarily constituted in place; thus, one of the contexts of relations that must be renewed is with the land itself. Understood not simply as a material resource or marker of political territory, land constitutes for Coulthard "a system of reciprocal relations and obligations" which structures a "grounded," "place-based" ethic of non-exploitative, non-dominating, respectful social practices and relations between human and non-human communities (13, 60). Recovering a revitalized sense of social and political relations grounded not in the absolute sovereignty of a centralized, coercive state, but in extended family relations; practiced and storied relationships with culture and place; political commitments to distributed authority, consensus decision-making, and a respect for dissent; all organized by lived ethics of inclusivity, hospitality, and reciprocity form the decolonizing core of indigenous resurgence theory and the vision of nationhood it advances. As Million writes, indigenous resurgence "speak[s] to, and from, life, an ancient … vital imaginary for a different politic for our times, for our nations, for our worlds (24).

Works cited

Alfred, Taiaiake. *Peace, Power & Righteousness: An Indigenous Manifesto*. Oxford: Oxford University Press, 1993.

——. *Wasáse: Indigenous Pathways to Action and Freedom*. Toronto: University of Toronto Press, 2005.

Allen, Chadwick. *TransIndigenous: Methodologies for Global Indigenous Studies*. Minneapolis: University of Minnesota Press, 2012.

Allen, Paula Gunn. *The Sacred Hoop: Recovering the Feminine in American Indian Traditions*. Boston: Beacon Press, 1986.

Brill de Ramírez, Susan Berry. *Contemporary American Indian Literatures and the Oral Tradition.* Tucson: University of Arizona Press, 1999.

Brooks, Lisa. *The Common Pot: The Recovery of Native Space in the Northeast.* Minneapolis: University of Minnesota Press, 2008.

Cook-Lynn, Elizabeth. "American Indian Intellectualism and the New Indian Story." *Natives and Academics Researching and Writing About American Indians.* Ed. Devon A. Mihesuah. Lincoln: University of Nebraska Press, 1998. 111–38.

——. "American Indian Studies: An Overview. Keynote Address at the Native Studies Conference, Yale University, February 5, 1998." *Wicazo Sa Review* 14. 2 (Autumn 1999): 14–24.

——. "Who Stole Native American Studies?" *Wicazo Sa Review* 12. 1 (Spring 1997): 9–28.

——. *Why I Can't Read Wallace Stegner and Other Essays: A Tribal Voice.* Madison: University of Wisconsin Press, 1996.

Coulthard, Glen Sean. *Red Skin, White Masks: Rejecting the Colonial Politics of Recognition.* Minneapolis: University of Minnesota Press, 2014.

Cox, James H. *The Red Land to the South: American Indian Writers and Indigenous Mexico.* Minneapolis: University of Minnesota Press, 2012.

Goeman, Mishuana. *Mark My Words: Native Women Mapping Our Nations.* Minneapolis: University of Minnesota Press, 2013.

Huhndorf, Shari. *Mapping the Americas: The Transnational Politics of Contemporary Native Culture.* Ithaca, NY: Cornell University Press, 2009.

Jacob, Michelle. *Yakama Rising: Indigenous Cultural Revitalization, Activism, and Healing.* Tucson: University of Arizona Press, 2014.

Justice, Daniel Heath. *Our Fire Survives the Storm: A Cherokee Literary History.* Minneapolis: University of Minnesota Press, 2006.

Krupat, Arnold. *Red Matters: Native American Studies.* Philadelphia: University of Pennsylvania Press, 2002.

——. *The Turn to the Native: Studies in Criticism and Culture.* Lincoln: University of Nebraska Press, 1998.

——. *The Voice in the Margin: Native American Literature and the Canon.* Berkeley: University of California Press, 1989.

Larson, Charles R. *American Indian Fiction.* Albuquerque: University of New Mexico Press, 1978.

Lincoln, Kenneth. *Native American Renaissance.* Berkeley: University of California Press, 1983.

Lyons, Scott Richard. *X-Marks: Native Signatures of Assent.* Minneapolis: University of Minnesota Press, 2010.

Million, Dian. *Therapeutic Nations: Healing in an Age of Indigenous Human Rights.* Tucson: University of Arizona Press, 2013.

Nelson, Joshua D. *Progressive Traditions: Identity in Cherokee Literature and Culture.* Norman: University of Oklahoma Press, 2014.

Ortiz, Simon. "Towards a National Indian Literature: Cultural Authenticity in Nationalism." *MELUS* 8. 2 (Summer 1981): 7–12.

Owens, Louis. *I Hear the Train: Inventions, Reflections, Refractions.* Norman: University of Oklahoma Press, 2001.

——. *Mixedblood Messages: Literature, Film, Family, Place.* Norman: University of Oklahoma Press, 1998.

——. *Other Destinies: Understanding the American Indian Novel.* Norman: University of Oklahoma Press, 1994.

Ruppert, James. *Mediation in Contemporary Native American Fiction.* Norman: University of Oklahoma Press, 1995.

Russell, Steve. *Sequoyah Rising: Problems in Post-Colonial Tribal Governance.* Durham, NC: Carolina Academic Press, 2010.

Sarris, Greg. *Keeping Slug Woman Alive: A Holistic Approach to American Indian Texts*. Berkeley: University of California Press, 1993.

Simpson, Audra. *Mohawk Interruptus: Political Life Across the Borders of Settler States*. Durham, NC: Duke University Press, 2014.

Simpson, Leanne. *Dancing on Our Turtle's Back: Stories of Nishnaabeg Re-Creation, Resurgence, and a New Emergence*. Winnipeg, MB: Arbeiter Ring Publishing, 2011.

Teuton, Christopher B. *Cherokee Stories of the Turtle Island Liars' Club*. Chapel Hill: University of North Carolina Press, 2012.

Teuton, Sean Kicummah. *Red Land, Red Power: Grounding Knowledge in the American Indian Novel*. Durham, NC: Duke University Press, 2008.

Tuck, Eve. "Suspending Damage: A Letter to Communities." *Harvard Education Review* 79. 3 (Fall 2009): 409–27.

Tuck, Eve & K. Wayne Yang. "Decolonization is Not a Metaphor." *Decolonization: Indigeneity, Education & Society* 1. 1 (2012): 1–40.

Velie, Alan R. *Four American Indian Literary Masters: N. Scott Momaday, James Welch, Leslie Silko, and Gerald Vizenor*. Norman: University of Oklahoma Press, 1982.

Vizenor, Gerald. *Fugitive Poses: Native American Scenes of Absence and Presence*. Lincoln: University of Nebraska Press, 1998.

——. *Manifest Manners: Narratives of Postindian Survivance*. Lincoln: University of Nebraska Press, 1999.

Warrior, Robert Allen. *The People and the Word: Reading Native Non-Fiction*. Minneapolis: University of Minnesota Press, 2005.

——. *Tribal Secrets: Recovering American Indian Intellectual Traditions*. Minneapolis: University of Minnesota Press, 1995.

Weaver, Jace. *That the People Might Live: Native American Literatures and Native American Community*. Oxford: Oxford University Press, 1997.

Womack, Craig. *Red on Red: Native American Literary Separatism*. Minneapolis: University of Minnesota Press, 1999.

Part IV
TRADITIONS

25

Indigenous Literacy and Language

Birgit Brander Rasmussen

It is not known when writing first emerged in the Americas. Petroglyphs are found in many parts of the hemisphere, but they are not well understood. While some petroglyphs are ancient, others may have been part of systems of literacy also inscribed on less durable media of inscription common in the Northeast, like wood and birch bark. At least one ancient petroglyph has been linked to the Mi'kmaq script, *komqwe-jwi'kaskl* (Mallery; Greenfield). We know that Native peoples in the Northeast used such hieroglyphic scripts, inscribed on the trunks of trees and on birch bark, long before Europeans arrived. Once colonial settlement began, Native peoples added pen and paper to their repertoire of literacy systems, which also included wampum in the Northeast and quipus in the Andes. Because of colonial violence, our knowledge of indigenous literacies and literatures often remains fragmented and inadequate. For now, a history of writing in the Americas must begin in Olmec country in 900 BC.

The "Cascajal block," an iPad-sized rock slab inscribed with a previously unknown script, was discovered in a pile of debris at a quarry in present-day Veracruz, Mexico, in 1999. It has been linked by dating and stylistic analysis to the Olmec who flourished in the region between 1200 and 400 BC (Del Carmen Rodriquez Martinez). The inscription on the Cascajal block remains undeciphered. Each new discovery is thus also a reminder of how much we have yet to learn.

Scholars have argued that later writing systems in the region derive from Olmec script (Pohl). Maya civilization reached its apex between the fourth and tenth centuries AD; the Zapotec declined a few centuries earlier. The Aztec and the Mixtec were flourishing by the time Europeans arrived in the hemisphere. They all had writing (Marcus). Because they are similar to European forms of literacy, particularly illustrated manuscripts, Aztec scrolls attracted the attention of Spanish scholars immediately – and vice-versa. In 1524, Aztec Tlamatinime met with Spanish friars outside Tenochtitlan, present-day Mexico City, and presented their respective conceptions of literacy, religion, and epistemology. This exchange was recorded by the Franciscan friar Bernardino de Sahagún in Spanish and alphabetized Nahuatl (Klor de Alva).

Sahagún worked with Aztec scribes to produce this and other texts that brought into dialogue Spanish and Aztec language, script, and conceptions of literacy. At sites like Colegio de Santa Cruz at Tlatelolco, European and indigenous scholars taught each other about their respective writing systems and languages. Together they produced culturally hybrid documents uniquely rooted in the colonial context, including work like the *Florentine*

Codex and the books of *Chilam Balam*. As in Europe, literacy was for the elite and their functionaries. Aztec tlacuilo or amatlacuilo were a distinct professional class just like scribes in Europe and for that matter like quipucamayoc in the Andes.

In the Northeast, where literacy seems to have been more universal, missionaries also played a key role in early literacy exchanges with Native peoples. A Franciscan missionary named Christian Le Clerq, who spent time among the Mi'kmaq in the seventeenth century, attempted to learn their writing system from children. He added some signs he invented himself and thus produced a hybrid writing system he intended to use to teach the Mi'kmaq about Christianity. Out of this experiment emerged what eventually became the *Oukateguennes Kignamatinoer*, or Hieroglyphic Prayer, which entered European print culture in 1866 when it was published in Vienna.

While there were other important literary forms and media in the hemisphere, from wampum in the Northeast to quipus in the Andes, the most widespread form of writing in the Americas seem to have been various forms of pictography (see Brander Rasmussen *Queequeg's Coffin*). From the Andes to Panama, throughout Meso-America, across the North American Plains to Alaska, in the Woodlands, along the eastern seaboard, and throughout the Northeast, pictography was used to record and transmit information ranging from the personal to the historical and the sacred.

Elizabeth Hill Boone has argued that pictographic scripts fit multi-lingual environments like the Americas because of their ability to traverse linguistic barriers (16). Pictographic scripts communicate concepts and ideas that can be spoken in a variety of languages, as we see today with pictographic signs on smart phones, in airports, and in "user manuals." That means Mixtec speakers could read an Aztec document so long as they were literate in the script, even if they didn't speak the language.

While Maya writing was syllabic, Hill Boone argues that Aztec writing conveys meaning primarily through the pictorial elements on the page or rock surface, with phonetic glyphs incorporated into the visual narrative (20). This may also have been the case for pictography from the Great Plains where glyphic elements and grammatical markers seem to have been integrated into the pictorial narrative. Or perhaps the pictorial served as a visual elaboration of the glyphic elements as suggested by recent analysis of Kiowa and Cheyenne sketchbooks from Fort Marion in Florida (see Brander Rasmussen "Toward"). Plains pictography remains understudied as a form of writing and its relationship to language is poorly understood.

Some of the best-known examples of North American pictography are tribal histories painted on buffalo hide called *wan'iyetu wo'wapi* by the Dakota. Such winter counts emerged as a common form of historical documentation among plains communities in the early decades of the nineteenth century. Groups like the Lakota and Dakota migrated west out of the Great Lakes area during the eighteenth century. On the plains, buffalo hides replaced birch bark as the surface on which men recorded tribal histories and autobiographical narratives known as coup tales. Coup tales are autobiographical accounts of heroic warrior exploits (Wong). Winter counts, on the other hand, were communally produced. A council of elders would gather to determine what to record as the most significant event of each year. However, many winter counts are identified by the name of an individual author like Lone Dog, American Horse, or Cloud Shield.[1] With the arrival of paper, new versions of the genre emerged, like Amos Bad Heart Bull's *A Pictographic History of Oglala Sioux*.

With new media and tools came new narratives and literary forms. Having once moved from the confines of birch bark paper to the vast expanse of the buffalo hide, pictographic writers now adapted to the limited space of ledgerbook pages and began to exploit the new capacities of the colored pen. One of the most fascinating archives of Plains pictography "sketchbooks" was produced in Fort Marion by Cheyenne and Kiowa captives who experimented with new and fused narrative forms in a way that enables close, comparative analysis of individual-author variations on the same story.

Despite significant differences in pictography from the Northeast, the Woodlands, and the Plains, we can track some continuities across time and space. For example, in one "sketch book" from Fort Marion, Etahdleuh Doanmoe uses a convention from Plains pictography that is similar to conventions from Woodlands pictography centuries earlier: the representation of captives as anonymous figures stripped of individual markers of identification like facial markings or regalia (Earenfight).

Woodlands and Plains pictography seem to combine pictorial elements, grammatical markers like hoofmarks to indicate the progression of time, and also hieroglyphic signs that are related to spoken or sign language. In his epic philological ethnography, entitled *Picture-Writing of the American Indians*, Garrick Mallery notes that pictographic signs sometimes correspond to sign language gestures for the same word. For example, the sign for "sky" in Ojibwe pictography is a particular curve that matches the sign language gesture for the same word (Mallery 694).

While the relationship between North American pictography and language remains understudied, Europeans in the colonial period often commented on the masterful use of metaphoric language in indigenous oratory. Is there a relationship between spoken "figures of speech" and graphic signs like pictographs, and if so, can we map regional and tribal variations? Yet again, we must confront how little most of us know. Doing so, in turn, alerts us to a history of colonial violence that is responsible for the destruction of almost all Mayan codices and most Incan quipus, the erasure of entire literary traditions, along with death and human suffering on a vast scale.

It also confronts us with great methodological challenges – and opportunities. If we can gather disparate fragments and read absences creatively, we might gain new insights. By way of example, analysis of a single pictograph from the Northeast can teach us a lot, because a good deal is known about its relationship to language, even though we have only a visual description of the pictograph and no extant document. Joseph-François Lafitau describes a particular glyph in detail and provides a great deal of linguistic, etymological, cultural, and semiotic context for its analysis (114–15). This glyph was made by "cross-hatches," resembling, perhaps, an elaborate version of the modern-day pictograph known as "hash-tag." It was understood to represent a mattress and signify "war." Lafitau relates that the Iroquois and Huron words for war are *n'ondoutagette* and *gaskenrhagette*, respectively. He then breaks down the words etymologically, explaining that "ondouta" refers to a reed that was used to make portable mattresses while "gagetton" means "to carry." When going on military campaigns, denoted by this glyph in indigenous documents or postings that Lafitau witnessed, warriors would carry their own portable mattresses. "Mattress-carrying" came to mean going to war just like "pen" might represent the activity of writing. The cross-hatch pictograph then represented both the concept "war" and the compound word *n'ondoutagette*.

Such compound words are common in many indigenous American language families, including Nahuatl and Algonquian. These languages are polysynthetic, which means linguistic roots and grammatical modifiers combine to create compound words that can function like sentences with nouns, verbs, and other linguistic elements combined into one word (Mithun qtd. in Gray 3). Polysynthetic languages with a high degree of metaphoric speech may correspond particularly well to pictographic forms of writing.

Perhaps in contrast to more phonetic writing, like Mayan or Sequoyan, scripts that were more pictographic sometimes functioned in conjunction with an oral performance or exegesis. James Lockhart argues that it was this oral performance, rather than indigenous forms of writing, which alphabetic script replaced in central Mexico in the centuries following the arrival of the Spanish (335). On the North American plains, oral performances were also linked to graphic accounts. Joseph White Bull's autobiography, which combines pictographic elements and syllabic script, might represent a North American example comparable to Lockhart's discussion.[2] This would mean that manuscripts like White Bull's can be understood as using syllabic script to replace the now absent oral performance that would normally accompany a pictographic autobiographical account.

But perhaps this distinction between image and text, performance and explication, is entirely too rigid and Eurocentric. Certainly, it is rooted in Western rather than Native American culture. The Aztec did not distinguish between writing and painting. Neither did the Mohegans, who still use the word *wuskuswang* to refer to both activities (Fitzgerald 52). That means such a distinction may be not only Eurocentric, but also misleading and obfuscating. Reminding us that alphabetic script is "comprised entirely of visual symbols; those tiny little works of art we call letters," Dean Rader breaks down the distinction between image and text. He argues that in Native American cultural production, "image-texts" combine the visual, the verbal, and the performative: "what connects oral, written, and visual gestures is that they rely on language and that they intend an audience … blending the lexical and the pictorial is critical for Native people" (300). Rader reminds us that Anishinaabe literary critic and creative writer Gerald Vizenor uses words like "song pictures," "song poems," and "pictomyths" to describe the glyphs on sacred Ojibwe Midewiwin scrolls (301).

N. Scott Momaday, whose landmark book *The Way to Rainy Mountain* is often seen as the start of the "Native American Renaissance" in literature, includes pictographic materials as an integral aspect of the narrative. The pictographic sections in the book are produced by Momaday's father, Alfred Momaday. This means that the pictographic becomes a site in the book where traditional literary forms are transmitted across the generations, coexisting with oral, historical, and anthropological modes of knowing. This is a particularly interesting move because Momaday and his father are descendants of one of the Fort Marion captives, Mamadaty. The period that Momaday describes as the golden age of the Kiowa, when they acquired horses and became Plains peoples, is also the golden age of buffalo-hide based pictography.

Winter counts and coup tales are masculine genres, while basketry and quillwork are feminine genres. Stephanie Fitzgerald reads a Mohegan basket in its linguistic, cultural, narrative, and political context as a retelling of the original Mohegan migration story at a time when Samson Occom lead a move to Brotherton that split the tribe politically and geographically (52–56). Like winter counts, such baskets were gendered and communally produced genres that linked oral and textual narrative. Malea Powell uses the technique and metaphor of basketry to structure "a Native Rhetorics Story," demonstrating how this form remains relevant to contemporary native writing just like pictography informs Momaday's literary debut.

INDIGENOUS LITERACY AND LANGUAGE

In addition to pictography and alphabetic script, two other literary forms require mention in an overview of literacy in the Americas, namely Northeastern wampum and Andean quipus. Iroquois and Algonquin peoples used wampum as a medium of communication and documentation. Although wampum became a form of currency in the colonial era, that function was never primary to native peoples. Wampum served a number of important purposes. This discussion will dwell on some of the ways in which wampum served as a communicative and archival medium, a form of literacy.

Wampum is made from white and dark purple quahog shells strung to form strings or belts. Wampum strings carried and documented shorter messages while belts recorded larger agreements. It is unknown when people first began to use wampum in this way. According to the Iroquois, who call themselves Haudenosaunee, the use of wampum in diplomacy is linked to the emergence of the League sometime between AD 1400 and 1600 (*Handbook of North American Indians* 420). One of the most important wampum belts, called the Hiawatha Belt, documents the founding of the Iroquois League while the Dust Fan Belt records the League's constitution. Tribal members continue to assert the documentary authority of wampum, presenting belts as legally binding documents in international assemblies like the United Nations. In 1988, for example, an Iroquois diplomat appeared in Geneva, Switzerland before the UN Human Rights Commission's Working Group on Indigenous Populations to explicate the Two Row Wampum Belt. On the belt, two dark rows are embedded in three lighter rows which

> symbolize vessels,
> traveling down the same river together.
> One will be for the Original People, their laws, their customs,
> and the other for the European people and their laws and customs.
> We will each travel the river together,
> but each in our own boat.
> And neither of us will try to steer the others' vessel.[3]

The Two-Row records an agreement between ancestors of contemporary Iroquois and European peoples to interact "like brothers" (metaphoric language for distinct, equal, and sovereign polities in a nation-to-nation relationship) rather than "like father and son" (a hierarchical and parochial relationship). Traditionally, wampum belts were not pictographic although settlers like Pennsylvania's founder, William Penn, began to create designs with images symbolizing the agreement in ways that conformed to European visual culture (Druke 89).

Like wampum in the Northeast, quipus in the Andes confront us with a kind of literacy that is radically different from alphabetic script. Made of rope, quipus encode information in strings on which are knots of various size, color, and design, using a decimal principle (Ascher & Ascher). These strings are attached to a central cord and read in a manner that is both tactile (like Braille) and also visual. The Spanish permitted the use of quipus relating to accounting and property in courtrooms and some were transcribed alphabetically. However, just as colonial authorities destroyed most Mayan codices because they were seen as a threat to biblical authority, so they also banned the use of quipus. There are no currently known transcriptions of existing quipus and the code of the quipu remains unknown.

At the time of conquest, quipus were constructed and read by a small class of functionaries called quipucamayoc. Historians, called amautas also used quipus "in place of letters" (Fernando de Montesinos qtd. in Hyland 132–33). In addition, quipus were used to record genealogies, tax information, and also narrative. Along with a more pictographic system called tocapu, quipus were used in the Andes even before the Inca created a centralized state. Under Tupac Yupanqui, the tenth ruler in the line, quipus became central to the administration of the Inca state apparatus (Brokaw 137). For a long time, scholars considered them merely mnemonic devices, but there is now emerging evidence that quipus record verbs and other grammatical structures (Urton). Perhaps we can better appreciate the complex capabilities of a mathematical system of information technology in the computer age than scholars in the nineteenth and twentieth centuries could.

The coexistence of radically different forms of writing, leading to novel experiments testing their commensurability, remains one of the most fascinating, if understudied, stories of American literature from the colonial period. Unfortunately, colonial authorities eventually came to regard indigenous literacies like codices and quipus as competing writing systems and ordered their destruction. In 1652, Diego de Landa issued an Auto de Fé ordering the destruction of most indigenous documents in the Yucatán. In 1583, the Lima Council of Bishops likewise issued an edict to ban all quipus except those relating to taxes and property. This campaign of destruction was so successful that few quipus survive and none have been deciphered.

Pictography in North America did not become a target for wholesale destruction in the same way, even though literacy and books have certainly been important sites of struggle. Throughout the nineteenth century, pictography remained a significant form of literacy among native peoples. New writing systems, like Sequoyah's Cherokee Syllabary, also emerged and offered new ways of recording native languages and producing native literature.

The arrival of Europeans impacted indigenous writing systems in important ways and heralded the introduction of a previously unknown form of writing in the Western hemisphere. Native peoples adapted the European alphabet to their own purposes very quickly. One of the most important, early indigenous alphabetic texts is the *Popul Vuh*, the sacred book of the Maya. Some of the earliest native alphabetic writers include Samson Occom from Mohegan along with Garcilasco de la Vega and Guaman Poma from the Andes. In the centuries that followed, alphabetic literacy spread throughout the continent by force and by choice. By the late twentieth century it appeared as if the alphabet had indeed "conquered" the Americas.

Few scholars of writing, who classified Native American pictography as a "limited, dead-end means of communication," could have anticipated that pictographic expression would once again emerge triumphant in the twenty-first century (DeFrancis 47). During the digital age, pictography has returned to become a global language on smartphones and in other digital media. In the Americas, Native people use Emoji and other contemporary pictography, and participate in digital literacy like everyone else. In fact, Native people on digital media have coined a new term, "NDN," that replaces the Columbian misnomer "Indians" in ways that are simultaneously playful and radically decolonizing. NDN is a pictoglyph made of alphabetic letters.

Such exciting developments mean that we must end our history of writing in the Western hemisphere the way we began, by acknowledging that it is provisional and still unfolding.

INDIGENOUS LITERACY AND LANGUAGE

Only this can be said with certainty: we still have much to learn and understand about literacy and its relationship to language in the Americas. And we have much to gain.

Notes

1 Extant winter counts are rare. The Smithsonian houses those made by Lone Dog, American Horse, The Flame, The Swan, Battiste Good, and Cloud Shield, along with a few others. Examples can now be viewed on the Internet at http://wintercounts.si.edu/html_version/html/thewintercounts.html.
2 The White Bull manuscript resides at the Chester Fritz Library at the University of North Dakota, OGL #183. For an accessible, published version, see James H. Howard, ed. and trans. *Lakota Warrior*.
3 The Two Row Wampum Belt, along with the text it records and some background information, can be viewed online at http://www.ganienkeh.net/2row.html. The original source cited is Huron Miller, trans. *Turtle: Native American Center for the Living Arts Quarterly Edition Newspaper* (Winter, 1980).

Works cited

Ascher, Marcia and Robert Ascher, *Code of the Quipu: A Study in Media and Mathematics*. Ann Arbor: University of Michigan Press, 1981.

Bad Heart Bull, Amos. *A Pictographic History of the Oglala Sioux*. Ed. Helen H. Blish. Lincoln: University of Nebraska Press, 1967.

Brander Rasmussen, Birgit. *Queequeg's Coffin: Indigenous Literacies and Early American Literature*. Durham, NC: Duke University Press, 2012.

——. "Toward a New Literacy History of the West: Etahdleuh Doanmoe's Captivity Narrative." *Contested Spaces of Early America*. Ed. Juliana Barr & Edward Countryman. Philadelphia: University of Philadelphia Press, 2014. 257–75.

Brokaw, Galen. "The Poetics of *Khipu* Historiography: Felipe Guaman Poma de Ayala's *Nueva corónica y buen gobierno*." *Colonial Latin American Review* II. 2 (2002): 111–47.

DeFrancis, John. *Visible Speech: The Diverse Oneness of Writing Systems*. Honolulu: University of Hawaii Press, 1989.

Del Carmen Rodriquez Martinez, Maria, et al. "Oldest Writing in the New World." *Science* 313 (15 Sept. 2006): 1610–14.

Druke, Mary. "Iroquois Treaties: Common Form, Varying Interpretations." *The History and Culture of Iroquois Diplomacy: An Interdisciplinary Guide to the Treaties of the Six Nations and Their League*. Ed. Francis Jennings, William N. Fenton, Mary A. Druke & David R. Miller. Syracuse, NY: Syracuse University Press, 1985. 85–98.

Earenfight, Phili, ed. *A Kiowa's Odyssey: Sketchbook from Fort Marion*, Seattle: University of Washington Press, 2007.

Fitzgerald, Stephanie. "The Cultural Work of a Mogehan Painted Basket." *Early Native Literacies in New England. A Documentary and Critical Anthology*. Ed. Kristina Bross & Hilary E. Wyss. Amherst: University of Massachusetts Press, 2008. 52–56.

Gray, Edward G. "Introduction." *The Language Encounter in the Americas, 1492–1800*. Ed. Edward G. Gray & Norman Fiering. New York: Berghahn, 2000. 1–14.

Greenfield, Bruce. "The Mi'kmaq Hieroglyphic Prayer Book: Writing and Christianity in Maritime Canada, 1675–1921." *The Language Encounter in the Americas, 1492–1800*. Ed. Edward G. Gray & Norman Fiering. New York: Berghahn, 2000. 189–214.

Handbook of North American Indians. Vol 15. Ed. Bruce G. Trigger. Washington: Smithsonian Institution, 1978.

Hill Boone, Elisabeth. "Introduction." *Writing Without Words: Alternative Literacies in Mesoamerica and the Andes*. Ed. Elisabeth Hill Boone & Walter D. Mignolo. Durham, NC: Duke University Press, 1994. 3–26.

Howard, James H., ed. and trans. *Lakota Warrior*. Lincoln: University of Nebraska Press, 1998.

Hyland, Sabine. *The Jesuit and the Incas: The Extraordinary Life of Padre Blas Valera, S.J.* Ann Arbor: University of Michigan Press, 2003.

Klor de Alva, Jorge, trans. "The Aztec–Spanish Dialogues of 1524," trans. Miguel Leon-Portilla. *Alcheringa/Ethnopoetics* 4. 2 (1980): 52–193.

Lafitau, Joseph-François. *Customs of the American Indians Compared with the Customs of Primitive Times*, 2 vols. Ed. and trans. William N. Fenton & Elisabeth L. Moore. Toronto: Champlain Society, 1977.

Lockhart, James. *The Nahuas After the Conquest: A Social and Cultural History of the Indians of Central Mexico, Sixteenth through Eighteenth Centuries*. Stanford, CA: Stanford University Press, 1992.

Mallery, Garrick. *Picture-Writing of the American Indians*, 2 vols. New York: Dover, 1972.

Marcus, Joyce. *Mesoamerican Writing Systems: Propaganda, Myth, and History in Four Ancient Civilizations*. Princeton, NJ: Princeton University Press, 1992.

Momaday, N. Scott. *The Way to Rainy Mountain*. Albuquerque: University of New Mexico Press, 1976.

Pohl, Mary E. D., Kevin O. Pope & Christopher von Nagy. "Olmec Origins of Mesoamerican Writing." *Science* 298 (6 Dec. 2002): 1984–87.

Powell, Malea. "A Basket is a Basket Because … Telling a Native Rhetorics Story." *The Oxford Handbook of Indigenous American Literature*. Ed. James H. Cox & Daniel Heath Justice. Oxford: Oxford University Press, 2014. 471–88.

Rader, Dean. "Reading the Visual, Seeing the Verbal: Text and Image in Recent American Indian Literature and Art." *The Oxford Handbook of Indigenous American Literature*. Ed. James H. Cox & Daniel Heath Justice. Oxford: Oxford University Press, 2014. 299–317.

Urton, Gary. *Signs of the Inca Khipu: Binary Coding in the Andean Knotted-String Records*. Austin: University of Texas Press, 2003.

Wong, Hertha. *Sending My Heart Back Across the Years: Tradition and Innovation in Native American Autobiography*. New York: Oxford University Press, 1992.

26
Native American Voices in Colonial North America

Kathryn N. Gray

The presence of Native American voices in the literatures of settler-colonial America can be difficult to detect and, at times, difficult to decipher. While encounters with Native American people are articulated in the travel narratives, religious tracts, war narratives and promotional pamphlets of the colonial period, Native Americans are rarely given the opportunity to articulate their own response to the new colonial landscape. Indeed, perhaps the most iconic Native American intermediaries from the early Anglo-colonial period, Matoaks or Amonute, more commonly known as Pocahontas, and Tisquantum, more usually called Squanto, are never given the opportunity to articulate their own experiences; for example, it is John Smith's accounts of New England which offer the most fulsome accounts of their experiences. (Smith, *A True Relation* [1608] and *General History of Virginia* [1624]). By way of uncovering the fragmentary evidence of early literary and language encounters of Native interlocutors in the early colonial period, it is useful to turn to the narratives and texts of religious experience. These accounts offer some of the most intriguing, if problematic, articulations of identity by Native American individuals and communities in this early colonial environment. Taking Puritan New England as its focus, since Native conversion to Christianity in this colonial landscape demanded an unusually high level of engagement with the written word, this chapter seeks to examine some of the earliest articulations of Native American self-definition as it developed through the lens of Christian theology in the seventeenth and early eighteenth centuries. While these experiences offer only a partial account of Native experience in colonial North America, as many Native Americans rejected Christianity – most famously, Metacom, or King Philip, who refused to acquiesce to colonial rule – I argue that the collective fragments of praying Indian voices articulate the formation of an early Native American literary identity.

This chapter begins with an assessment of scribal acts, the orthographic work that fashioned written traces of Native languages, as well as the production of largely religious texts in the Massachusett dialect of Algonquian. The effects of this textual reproduction of oral languages are analyzed to map the complexities of Native self-fashioning through expressive engagement with Christianity and through the material form of the text. I argue that the recovery of Christian Indian voices and identities from the colonial records and publications of the New England colonies, Massachusetts Bay and Martha's Vineyard particularly, offers glimpses of Native self-fashioning which precedes the more fulsome and coherent body of manuscripts and published works left by Samson Occom, often considered to be the father of Native American literature (see Brooks).

307

Scribal cultures: marks, signs and the orthographic process

The introduction of handwritten and printed text to largely oral cultures and communities in seventeenth-century New England forced indigenous people to reconsider many, if not all, of their practices and traditions. Native Americans practiced other kinds of literacies, including the recording of trade and negotiation in wampum-belts, carvings and hieroglyphs, for example (see, for example, Thorowgood *Jews in America* 60; Williams *Key* 61; Murray *Forked Tongues*), but the introduction of the Roman alphabet to the spoken word of the Algonquian language sparked significant changes to Native American processes of self-definition. The introduction of this new form of certification, communication and representation, was a varied and haphazard process and early colonial records evidence different levels of literacy among Natives: there are marks and signatures of tribal negotiators, as well as a small number of letters, or references to letters, that indicate a more developed ability to communicate in written forms. For example, an inter-tribal peace treaty between Weetowish, a Narragensett leader, and Uncas, Sachem to the Mohegans is verified in the colonial records with Weetowish's mark, in place of a signature ("September, 1644" *Records of the Plymouth Colony* 30); a letter of "voluntary subjection" to Charles I is, again, marked by Narragansett leaders, Pessicus and Collounicus ("Letter of Pessicus and Collounicus, Naheganset May 24th 1644" Appendix *Records of the Plymouth Colony* 416); a land sale agreement of 1664 is documented by the signatures of four members of the Narragansett (Awashous, Quissoquus, Neneglad and Scuttup, "September 7th, 1664" Appendix *Records of the Plymouth Colony* 449); and Metacom was sent paper and ink to help facilitate the end of hostage negotiations in the conflict of 1675 (*Massachusetts Archive Collection* 68: 193 qtd. in Wyss 39; see also Lepore). As well, letters received in London, written by praying Indians, including those educated at Harvard's Indian College, demonstrate an ability to correspond with colonial and English recipients. Specifically, in March 1683, sixteen praying Indians of Natick signed a letter to John Eliot, asking for more assistance to help sustain the missionary work,[1] and in the archives of the Royal Society in London are two unusual manuscripts written by seventeenth-century Native American scholars Caleb Cheeshateaumauk and Eleazar Judus. Caleb's is dedicate to his "honoured benefactors" in London, and Eleazar dedicates his address to his late teacher, Thomas Thacher, who settled in New England in 1635 (see the transcripts of these original manuscripts and their translations in Hochbruck & Dudensing-Reichel; see also Morison). These addresses are no more than a page long and are written largely in Latin with some sections of Eleazar's text also in Greek. Finally, Matthew Mayhew in his *A Brief Narrative*, alludes to a lost letter written by praying Indians living on the west of Martha's Vineyard at the time of King Philip's War which notes their refusal to surrender their weapons to the English:

> they were unwilling to deliver their Arms, unless the English would propose some mean for their safety and livelihood: with this return they drew a Writing in their own Language, which I have often read, and would have Verbatim inserted, but cannot at present find it; the substance was, that as they had Submitted to the Crown of England, so they resolved to Assist the English on these Islands against their enemies.
>
> (35)

This survey of textual engagement, from simple marks to compositions in Latin and Greek, serves to emphasize the much larger point that the introduction of the written word into the oral cultures of North America had a direct impact on the ways in which certain aspects of society, including aspects of political, economic, military and religious engagement, were recorded and verified.

Facilitating a more sustained engagement with text were the attempts of colonial linguists to transform Algonquian dialects into written forms. In the mid-seventeenth century, William Wood, Roger Williams, John Eliot, and Abraham Pierson endeavored to create orthographies of Algonquian dialects, including Naumkeag, Narragansett and Massachusett, through the use of the Roman alphabet. Wood and Williams in their respective publications, sought to teach English or colonial travelers and traders some useful words and phrases that might help them communicate with indigenous people of New England more effectively. Pierson and Eliot had a different purpose, which was to help the Indians "know the True GOD" according to Pierson (n.p.) or, in Eliot's case, "bring the Indian Language into RULES ... for the furtherance of the Gospel among them" (*Indian Grammar* n. pag.). Eliot became relatively prolific in his publication of Algonquian language texts, publishing a total of twelve texts, including instructional language primers, *Indian Grammar Begun*, *The Logic Primer* and *"Our Indians ABC"*, as well as scriptural texts, principally, the complete Bible.[2] While it is fair to say that it was John Eliot's vision and persistence that led to the publication of the Algonquian Bible and many other religious texts and manuals in this period, it is also important to remember the Native translators and typesetters who, in the most practical and material ways, brought the texts into existence. Cockenoe, John Sassomon, Job Nesutan, Monequasson, and James Printer, were certainly able to read in both English and in Massachusett, and without them, Eliot would not have been able to produce a sizable body of Algonquian-language material. The records are relatively quiet on the contribution of the translators, but there are a few occasions where the translators are given at least some recognition. In the closing statement of *The Indian Grammar*, for example, Eliot refers to:

> a pregnant witted young man, *who had been a Servant in an English house, who pretty well understood our Language, better than he could speak it, and well understood his own Language, and hath a clear pronunciation: Him I made my* Interpreter.
> (n. pag.; see also Tooker; Murray *Forked Tongues*; Cogley; Wyss)

There is, of course, an emerging problem: the transformation of spoken Algonquian dialects into the Roman alphabet, the publication of that language in print, and the mission-colonizer's unapologetic attempts to use text to convert Native Americans to Christianity, presents many difficulties in assessing examples of Native self-fashioning in the written accounts of this period. After all, the very form of the text and its unambiguous religious motivations were intended to erase tribal practices, not find new expression for them. And this is the heart of the dilemma in relation to Native literary studies in colonial North America. George Tinker, Francis Jennings and James P. Ronda to name just a few, have argued that manuscripts and publications that contain early examples of Native American literacy only provide the dominant ideological narrative which the colonial missionary wishes to present (see Tinker; Jennings; Ronda). More recently, however, a growing body of work, broadly predicated on theories of autoethnography and performativity, argues that early examples of Native American literacy should be incorporated into a larger discussion about cultural negotiation and Native eloquence (Wyss; Gustafson; Bross; Bellin; White).

One example might serve to illustrate the interpretative difficulties of these texts and the significance of methodological awareness. In his *Indian Converts* (1727), Experience Mayhew narrates the lives of generations of Wampanoag Christian converts of Martha's Vineyard, from around 1640 until the 1720s. It is a sizable collection in four parts, offering accounts of "Godly Ministers," "Good Men," "Religious Women" and "Pious Children." The collection is prefaced by his intention to show that the "Preaching of the Gospel to the Aboriginal Natives of this Land, has not been in vain; but that there has been some desirable Fruit and Effect thereof" (xx). He goes to some lengths to assure his reader that everything he includes, events and descriptions of individuals that he or others have witnessed, have come from a number of verifiable sources. He also states: "I shall, as occasion offers, translate and insert some such Passages written by them in their own Language, as I think will be subservient to the End herein aimed at" (xxiii). The dominant religious discourse of the colonial missionary is unambiguously asserted and it is impossible to interpret what follows without acknowledging this framework. Within this text and others – most significantly, perhaps, John Eliot's collection of "Indian Tracts" published between 1643 and 1670 – are the transcribed speeches of Native penitents, each of whom are recorded in forms constituted by the colonial missionary, and only a cautious reading can unravel glimpses of Native self-definition.

Reference to one example, the conversion of Hiacoomes on Martha's Vineyard, helps articulate the parameters of this argument. In the first section of his *Indian Converts*, Mayhew reproduces a version of Hiacoomes' religious conversion, noting his eloquence, leadership and his denunciation of the Pawwaws. In this context, Pawwaw is the name given to the shaman or medicine man. Embedded in Hiacoomes' biographical sketch, however, is the story of a former Sachim; the anonymous Sachim is also a powerful leader who chooses to follow Hiacoomes' teachings. The Sachim confesses that in the past he has used the form of the snake to wound or kill an opponent but, since following Hiacoomes' example, he no longer follows that path:

> having seriously considered the said Hiacoomes's Assertion, that none of the Pawwaws could hurt him, since his God whom he now served was the great God to whom theirs was subservient, he resolved to worship the true God. And he further added, That from the time of his doing so, for seven Years, the said Snake gave his great Disturbance; but, that he never after his praying to god in Christ, employed that said Snake in any thing; about which time the said Snake ceased to appear to him.
>
> (7)

As is the case in many, if not all, documented and published forms of Native conversion, this example articulates the colonial fantasy of Native Americans who willingly choose Christian forms of spirituality over tribal forms and, furthermore, are adept proselytizers within their own communities. Indeed, John Eliot went so far as to write and publish *Indian Dialogues*, a semi-fictional text which traces the proselytizing potential of key praying Indians. We can hardly expect a Puritan missionary to publicize an alternative point of view; Native criticism of Christianity, or Native re-interpretations of Christianity, find little room for textual expression in pamphlets and publications emerging from colonial New England. In this climate of censorship and in relation to Eliot's *Dialogues* in particular, David Murray, James P. Rhonda and Henry W. Bowden assert that the Puritan absolutist approach to religious and civil practice left no room for cultural negotiation (see Murray *Forked Tongues*; Eliot, *Indian Dialogues*). From this interpretative point of view it is difficult see beyond the ideological framework within which Native identity is fashioned.

Yet, in this example and others, it is possible to detect glimpses of self-fashioning. It is important to note, for example, that the Sachim chooses *between* belief systems, he suggests that there is a dominant god, but he does not deny the existence, or possibility of different systems of belief. In another example from this early period of religious encounter, Wequash, a Pequot warrior, and one of John Eliot's first converts in Massachusetts Bay, articulated his conversion in a similar vein, with reference to the Christian god's superior status as a warrior:

> This man (Captain Wequash) a few years since, seeing and beholding the mighty power of God in our English Forces, how they fell upon the *Pegans*, where divers hundreds of then were slaine in an houre: The Lord, as a God of glory in great terrour did appear into the Soule and Conscience of this poore Wretch, that very act; and though before that time he had low apprehensions of our God, having conceived hime to be (as he said) but a *Musketto* God, or a God unto a flye; and as meane thoughts of the English that served this God, that they were silly weake men; yet from that time he was convinced and persuaded that our God was a most dreadfull God; and that one *English* man by the help of his God was able to slay and put to flight an hundred *Indians*.
>
> (*New England's First Fruits* 61)

These snippets of speeches and conversations allow us to understand that Massachusett, Pequot, Wampanoag, and other tribal affiliates in the New England colony, self-fashioned individual and collective identities on the basis of pragmatic, survivalist politics. Considered through an autoethnographic lens, whereby descriptions of the self are mediated through representational forms constructed by others,[3] these two examples ask us to look beyond the dominating Puritan agenda and consider that Native converts did not deny the validity of tribal medicines, practices or customs but, rather, they choose a path that might mitigate the many new threats posed by colonization, including loss of life through disease, enforced removal, and conflict.

These performed identities, captured only in glimpses in colonial documents (even those performances shaped by colonial ideology or theology) may reveal something more radical than the colonial translator or editor realized. Moments of colonial ignorance might be exploited, in some instances, to reveal insight into more complex cultural negotiations of Native self-fashioning. One example is an account of a child's burial in colonial Massachusetts:

although the *English* do not usually meet in companies to pray together after such sad occasions, yet it seems God stird up their hearts thus to doe; what the substance of their prayer was I cannot certainly learn ... Tutaswampe did express such zeale in prayer with such variety of gracious expressions, and abundance of teares, both of himself and most of his company, that the woods rang againe with their sighes and prayers ...

(Shepard 137–38)

The community meet together to mourn the child in ways that the colonial onlooker admits he does not fully understand: they say prayers, they weep, and they mourn collectively. We might reasonably suppose that if this is not something that they already practice, it is, at least, a new part of a ritual of burial which they bring to their understanding of Christian burial. It is possible to read this as a hybrid performance, fashioned from two different sets of practices. Further, Craig White draws attention to the fact that the burial site is by a tree, a place which resonates with tribal spiritual belief systems (White 455). The performance of an ostensibly Christian burial can be reconsidered and redefined through the gaps left by colonial ignorance. In this example, and in other praying Indian speeches and practices recorded by Eliot, the Mayhews, and others, the performances of Native self-definition can be more fully understood within a dual perspective, one that accommodates the worldview of the Puritan scribe as well as the worldview of the Native speakers and participants (see Roach; Bellin).

As these examples serve to demonstrate, Native involvement with literacy and literature took many forms: from simple marks, signatures and letters, in the work of Native translators and typesetters, and in the speeches and practices of Native American converts to Christianity. Indeed, through the publication of the Bible and language primers, Native literacy is further evidenced in the marginal, handwritten notes of a community of readers in the surviving copies of John Eliot's Algonquian Bible (Bragdon & Goddard). Collectively, these traces of literacy signal the existence of a Native scribal culture not often recognized in the histories and literatures of seventeenth- and eighteenth-century colonial North America. Through these interactions with the written word, and through the lens of religious conversion, a community of Native Christians in New England participated in a complex and controversial process of cultural self-definition, a process which also found traction in Native responses to the materiality of the book.

Text as object

In Anglo-American colonial studies, one of the most intriguing and most noted representations of early Native engagements with the materiality of the text is Thomas Hariot's depiction of indigenous inhabitants of Virginia receiving the Bible and pressing it to their skin: "yet would many be glad to touch it, to embrace it, to kisse it ... ."[4] While Hariot perceives this to be a naïve response to the power of the written word, when considered in the context of Native articulations of the material qualities of text, this physical response can be interpreted more productively as part of continuous and ongoing processes of cultural understanding and self-definition. Roger Williams' *Key into the Language of America* (1634), a language primer which several commentators

NATIVE AMERICAN VOICES IN COLONIAL NORTH AMERICA

agree (Murray, "Roger Williams' Key"; Scanlan; Schweitzer) offers some insight into the traditions and perceptions of the Narragansett with whom he lived for several years, highlights the growing response to the materiality of text in two distinct ways. First, he offers an appropriation of the word for "letter": "Wussuckwhèke," "A letter which they so call from Wussuckwhómmin, to paint; for, having no letters, their painting comes the nearest" (61), noting the practical adaptation of concept and language to accommodate the new conceptual form of the written word. Second, in his chapter, "Of Religion, the soule, &c.," Williams offers a summary of the polytheistic belief system, whereby certain natural phenomena, the sun, the moon, the sea and fire, are designated a particular deity, and further notes their response to the "*English-mans* God" (123): "... when they talke amongst themselves of the *English* ships, and great buildings, of plowing their Fields, and especially of Bookes and Letters, they will end thus: *Manittôwock* They are Gods: *Cummanittôo* &c" (126). New forms of travel, husbandry and communication, as mentioned here, are incorporated into pre-existing interpretative strategies, demonstrating Native ability to accommodate new phenomena, including the material qualities of the text, into their expanding worldview.

Intriguing and suggestive appreciations of the material qualities of the text find a sure foothold in the articulation of religious negotiation or transformation in this period in two distinct ways. One way is to make distinctions between the "non-literate" Native and the new, "literate" Christian Native: for example, Hiacoomes, an early convert to Christianity on Martha's Vineyard in the 1640s, is said to have carried with him an English language primer (Whitfield 177), after he was able to read, as a material marker of his new cultural self-definition. Another manifestation of the material text requires a more nuanced interpretation. The ostensibly verbatim transcription of a dream from an anonymous "Indian" in Massachusetts Bay, who claims to have had a premonition about the arrival of the English man and his "book," writes the colonial missionary and his Bible into the cultural negotiations of Native self-definition:

> That about two years before the *English* came over into those parts there was a great mortality among the *Indians*, and one night he could not sleep above half the night, after which hee fell into a dream, in which he did think he saw a great many men come to those parts in cloths, just as the *English* are now apparelled, and among them there arose a man all in black, with a thing in his hand which hee now sees was all one *English* mans book ...
>
> (Shepard 119)

This account can, quite clearly, be interpreted from a colonial point of view, accommodating the "black man," or Puritan missionary, within a providential narrative, whereby their arrival is predicated and sanctioned by a higher spiritual authority. Alternatively, if we read this speech from a Native point of view, the speaker uses his dream, or prophecy, as a point of entry into the new colonial environment. By writing his own premonition, or dream, into the fabric of recent history, the speaker comes close to finding a position through which he can, potentially, renegotiate individual and collective Native identity. Far from a naïve response the material text, for Native individuals and communities, the text as object, served as a cultural marker against which they tried to redefine and represent their present circumstances.

Uncovering fragments of Native literacies and self-definition in the colonial records of the seventeenth and eighteenth centuries is a piecemeal pursuit. By contrast, in the latter half of the eighteenth century, Samson Occom produced a large body of letters, diaries, sermons, and an autobiography, offering a more sustained but, still, conflicted account of the effects of text and religion on Native communities in the Anglo-American colonial world. With access to ink, paper and, on occasion, a publisher, Occom had the opportunity to articulate his experiences, good and bad, with more control than his Christian Indian predecessors of the New England colonies. Still, the marks, letters, and transcriptions of Native voices in the colonial records show a keen awareness of the political expediency of the written word among Native communities, dexterous linguistic skill on the part of many translators, named and un-named, as well as the intellectual rigor of converts and scholars who expounded biblical text as part of their religious conversion in the praying towns of New England, or in an academic environment at the Indian College at Harvard. While it is often difficult, at times impossible, to uncover anything beyond the dominant Christian discourse of the period, these documents bear witness to a community of writers, readers, and interlocutors, who engaged with the new literacies of colonization in an attempt to define their presence in an unpredictable, difficult, and dangerous colonial landscape.

Notes

1 The original letter is held in the Guildhall Library in London: "From 16 Indians at Natick." The markers and signatories, all of whom resided in Natick, include: Olt Waban, John Maqoof, Daniel Takawompait, Thomas Tray, Nemiah, Nataniel, John Moquah, Olt Nuomont, Olt Jetro, Olt Nosauwunna, Olt Maquis, Nellem Hahatun, Jams, John Awaquin, Thomas Waban, Simon Betoqkom.
2 William Kellaway uses the term, "Indian Library," in his overview of the financing and printing of Eliot's translations. John Eliot's Algonquian language texts include: *A Christian Covenanting Confession* (1660); trans. *Mamvsse Wunneetupanatamwe Up-Biblum God* (*The Holy Bible containing the Old Testament and the New*, 1663); trans. *Mamvsse Wunneetupanatamwe Up-Biblum God* (*The Holy Bible containing the Old Testament and the New* rev. ed. 1685); *Nehtuhpeh peisses ut mayut, A Primer in the Language of the Algonquian Indians* (1684); *The Indian Grammar Begun* (1666); *The Logic Primer* (1672); trans. *The Psalter* (1658); trans. *Wusku Wuttestamentum Nullordumun Jesus Christ* (New Testament, 1661); *The Book of Genesis* (1655); non-extant texts: Psalms (1658), and Matthew (1655).
3 Wyss uses the term "autoethnography" (75–80) in relation to Mayhew's *Indian Converts*, specifically as it is defined by Mary Louise Pratt, in *Imperial Eyes*, where the "colonized subjects undertake to represent themselves in ways that engage with the colonizer's own terms" (7).
4 Hariot, "A Brief and True Report" (86). In comparison with the Jesuit Mission, James Axtell notes that the Jesuits encourage the objectification of the Bible in a deliberate attempt to perpetuate the myth of the shamanic qualities of the book and those who could read from it (304–05).

Works cited

Axtell, James. "The Power of Print in the Eastern Woodlands." *William and Mary Quarterly* 44. 2 (April 1987): 300–09.
Bellin, Joshua David. "John Eliot's Playing Indian." *Early American Literature* 42. 1 (2007): 1–30.
Bragdon, Kathleen J. & Ives Goddard, *Native Writings in Massachusett*. 2 vols. Philadelphia: American Philosophical Society, 1988.

Brooks, Joanna, ed. *The Collected Writings of Samson Occom, Mohegan: Leadership and Literature in Eighteenth-Century Native America.* New York: Oxford University Press, 2006.

Bross, Kristina. *Dry Bones and Indian Sermons: Praying Indians in Colonial America.* Ithaca, NY: Cornell University Press, 2004.

Cogley, Richard E. *John Eliot's Mission to the Indians Before King Philip's War.* Cambridge, MA: Harvard University Press, 1999.

Eliot, John. *A Christian Covenanting Confession.* Cambridge, Massachusetts. 1660.

——. *Indian Dialogues: A Study in Cultural Interaction.* 1671. Ed. Henry W. Bowden & James P. Ronda. Westport, CT: Greenwood Press, 1980.

——. *The Indian Grammar Begun.* 1666. Rpt. Bedford, MA: Applewood Books, 2001.

——. *The Logic Primer.* 1672. Rpt. Cleveland, OH: The Burrows Brothers Company, 1904.

——. *Our Indians ABC.* Cambridge, 1671.

"From 16 Indians at Natick, Massachusetts, to the Rev John Eliot, 19th March 1683," *New England Company Archives.* Guildhall Library, London, Ms 07957.

Gustafson, Sandra M. *Eloquence is Power: Oratory and Performance in Early America.* Chapel Hill: Omohundro Institute of Early American History and Culture, University of North Carolina Press, 2000.

Hariot, Thomas. "A Brief and True Report of the New found Land of Virginia, 1588." *The English Literature of America 1500–1800.* Ed. Myra Jehlen & Michael Warner. New York: Routledge, 1997. 64–89.

Hochbruck, Wolfgang & Beatrix Dudensing-Reichel. "'Honoratissimi Benefactors': Native American Students and Two Seventeenth Century Texts in the University Tradition." *Early Native American Writing: New Critical Essays.* Ed. Helen Jaskowski. Cambridge: Cambridge University Press, 1996. 1–14.

Jennings, Francis. *The Invasion Within: Indians, Colonisation, and the Cant of Conquest.* 1975. New York: W.W. Norton, 1976.

Kellaway, William. *The New England Company 1649–1776: Missionary Society to the American Indians.* Westport, CT: Greenwood Press, 1975.

Lepore, Jill. "Dead Men Tell No Tales: John Sassamon and the Fatal Consequences of Literacy." *American Quarterly* 46. 4 (1994): 479–512.

Mayhew, Experience. *Indian Converts: Or Some Account of the Lives and Dying Speeches of a Considerable Number of the Christianized Indians of Martha's Vineyard in New England.* 1727. Rpt. Whitefish, MT: Kessinger Publishing, 2005.

Mayhew, Matthew. *A Brief Narrative of the Success which the Gospel hath had, among the Indians of Martha's Vineyard (and Places Adjacent) in New-England.* Boston, 1694.

Morison, Samuel Eliot. *Harvard College in the Seventeenth Century.* 2 vols. Cambridge, MA: Harvard University Press, 1936.

Murray, David. *Forked Tongues: Speech, Writing and Representation in North American Indian Texts.* Bloomington: Indiana University Press, 1991.

——. "Using Roger Williams' Key into America." *Symbiosis, A Journal of Anglo-American Literary Relations* 1. 2 (October 1997): 237–53.

New England's First Fruits (London, 1643). *The Eliot Tracts: With Letters from John Eliot to Thomas Thorowgood and Richard Baxter.* Ed. Michael P. Clark. Westport, CT: Praeger, 2003. 56–78.

Occom, Samson. *The Collected Writings of Samson Occom, Mohegan: Leadership and Literature in Eighteenth-Century Native America.* Ed. Joanna Brooks. New York: Oxford University Press, 2006.

Pierson, Abraham. *Some Helps for the Indians* (1658), appended to *A Further Accompt of the Progresse of the Gospel* (1659). *The Eliot Tracts: With Letters from John Eliot to Thomas Thorowgood and Richard Baxter.* Ed. Michael P. Clark. Westport, CT: Praeger, 2003. 321–53.

Pratt, Mary Louise. *Imperial Eyes: Travel Writing and Transculturation.* London: Routledge, 1992.

Records of the Plymouth Colony, Acts of the Commissioners of the United Colonies in New England, 1643–1651. Ed. David Pulsifer, Vol. 1. New York: AMS Press, 1968.

Roach, Joseph. "Culture and Performance in the Circum-Atlantic World." *Performativity and Performance*. Ed. Andrew Parker & Eve Kosofsky Sedgwick. London: Routledge, 1995. 124–36.

Ronda, James P. "'We are Well as We are': An Indian Critique of Seventeenth-Century Christian Missions." *William and Mary Quarterly* Third Series. 34. 1 (1977): 66–82.

Scanlan, Thomas. *Colonial Writing and the New World 1583–1671: Allegories of Desire*. Cambridge: Cambridge University Press, 1999.

Schweitzer, Ivy. *The Work of Self-Representation: Lyric Poetry in Colonial New England*. Chapel Hill: The University of North Carolina Press, 1991.

Shepard, Thomas. *Clear Sun-Shine of the Gospel. The Eliot Tracts: With Letters from John Eliot to Thomas Thorowgood and Richard Baxter*. Ed. Michael P. Clark. Westport, CT: Praeger, 2003. 101–41.

Smith, John. *General History of Virginia*. 1624. 2 vols. Glasgow: James MacLehose & Sons; New York: Macmillan, 1907. Web. Accessed 23 Dec. 2014. https://archive.org/details/generallhistorie01smit; https://archive.org/details/generalhistorieo02smituoft

——. *A True Relation of Virginia*. 1608. Web. Accessed 23 Dec. 2014. https://archive.org/details/truerelationofvi01smit

Thorowgood, Thomas. *Jews in America* (1650) London, 1669.

Tinker, George E. *Missionary Conquest: The Gospel and Native American Cultural Genocide*. Minneapolis, MN: Fortress Press, 1993.

Tooker, William Wallace. *John Eliot's First Indian Interpreter, Cockenoe-de-Long Island*. New York: Francis P. Harper, 1896.

White, Craig. "The Praying Indians Speeches as Texts of Massachusett Oral Culture." *Early American Literature* 38. 3 (Fall 2003): 437–67.

Whitfield. Henry. *The Light Appearing More and More Towards the Perfect Day* (1651). *The Eliot Tracts: With Letters from John Eliot to Thomas Thorowgood and Richard Baxter*. Ed. Michael P. Clark. Westport, CT: Praeger, 2003. 169–210.

Williams, Roger. *A Key into the Language of America* (1643). Bedford, MA: Applewood Books, 1936.

Wyss, Hilary E. *Writing Indians: Literacy, Christianity, and Native Community in Early America*. Amherst: University of Massachusetts Press, 2000.

27
Early Native American Writing

Drew Lopenzina

The earliest known document by a Native American employing western notions of literacy in North America is a 1663 letter written in Latin by the Wampanoag, Caleb Cheeshateaumauk. When I tell people this they hardly know what to make of it. Native peoples in the seventeenth century are supposed to be sitting down to Thanksgiving dinner with Pilgrims or raiding unsuspecting frontier villages, not corresponding with Puritans in arcane scholarly languages. The phrase itself, "early Native American writing," must strike many as an oxymoron, an inherent contradiction in terms, given that America's indigenous peoples are largely assumed to have been primarily *oral* cultures standing in fast resistance to the forces of western civilization. While such an assumption is not entirely incorrect, it simplifies the dynamics of colonization in ways that are highly beneficial to the colonizer. Cheeshateaumauk's seemingly paradoxical document opens a path into a much richer and possibly revolutionary understanding of America's early colonial and precolonial history – one in which Native people write.

To begin, we should note that the process of colonization, which properly understood is a series of violent usurpations followed by sustained coercive control, benefits greatly from the imposition of rhetorical binaries, imagined opposites, that are often rooted in culturally biased assumptions. For instance, if western colonizers coming to America from Europe in the sixteenth and seventeenth centuries tended to understand themselves as carrying "civilization" along with them, then it must follow that those they colonized were "uncivilized" – a savage and lawless people in need of having western values thrust upon them. If western colonizers tended to see themselves as bearing the one true religion (regardless of their vast disagreements as to what that religion actually was or how it should be practiced), then it follows that the spiritual customs of the colonized must be seen as false religion, heathenistic or, just as likely, non-existent. Religion was something that had to be brought to America's indigenous peoples, almost like a shiny new gift for them to open and admire. By the same token, literacy was understood to be the highest watermark of a civilized people. After all, it was through literacy that the great ideas, laws, customs and artistic expressions of western culture had been preserved. It is the written word, *scripture*, that enshrines the very word of God, insuring its ability to pass, presumably unaltered, across generations tracing divine intentions back to their origins. As European colonists began planting themselves in what they perceived to be a new world, it was arguably writing, more than anything else, that represented for them their cultural superiority, the difference between savagery and civilization. As the Puritan settler Roger Williams observed, when Native people encountered European technologies, and "especially of Books and Letters," they would exclaim "Manittowock, They are Gods" (126).

These types of claims remain historically persuasive because western settler culture deployed them almost without fail. The reams upon reams of first-hand reports from explorers, conquistadors, adventurers, priests, pillagers, and pilgrims viewed the Americas through an extremely biased cultural lens, often motivated by economic considerations, and later histories only served to build on and exponentially reinforce earlier observations. Such claims were further enshrined by the literary romances of writers like James Fenimore Cooper who, in popular novels such as *The Last of the Mohicans*, crafted a brand of Indian ready made for vanishing – noble savages whose nobility was best expressed by their apparent willingness to escort themselves off the stage of the nineteenth century.

These seductive fictions remained unchallenged, for the most part, until the last few decades of the twentieth century when, in response to advances in civil rights gained in the 60s and 70s, Native peoples began to enter the universities in greater numbers, as students, professors and cultural commentators. These Native scholars found deep flaws in the assumptions that had been posted about them over four hundred years of colonial representation. Their response, although hardly surprising, was not well received and remains controversial to this day. It consisted basically of this premise: Native peoples of the Americas were not like "foxes and wild beasts" gallivanting through the forest primeval, as early Puritan settlers had asserted (Cushman 91), nor were they merciless savages looking to advance their warrior credentials through the "undistinguished Destruction of all Ages, Sexes and Conditions" as stated in our Declaration of Independence. They were in fact people with rich and complex communal structures consisting of laws, religion, tradition, art, community, agriculture, and, yes, even writing of their own. Their collective customs, if different from what Europeans practiced, were every bit as worthy of the title "civilization."

One of the great ironies in all this is that the evidence for Native religion, laws, and writing can be found in the very reports of the colonizers who so readily denigrated their existence. For instance, colonists frequently were witness to, and participants in, Native ceremonies involving the exchange of wampum – purple and white beads fashioned from the quahog shell, that when strung together in belts, represented for many Native people of the northeast, a diplomatic agreement that cleared a path for consolation of grief, forgiveness of past trespasses, and reconciliation of differences. Colonists were fascinated by the ritual structure of wampum exchange and it can be seen in practice from the earliest accounts of the French Jesuits, to the literature of the Puritans, to the political negotiations of the United States' fledgling democracy. George Washington, in his early frontier escapades, was a frequent participant in wampum exchange, agreeing in the parlance of the custom to wipe the tears from his eyes, the dust from his ears, and the obstructions from his throat, so that he might deal with honesty and clarity and not be blinded by bloodlust or grief. Arthur Parker, an early nineteenth-century Seneca historian, explained that wampum, from its creation, was designed so that "the strings would become words and lift the darkness with which they are covered. Holding these in my hands, my words would be true" (Parker "Constitution" 52). If the Seneca, and their larger confederacy, the Five Nations of the Iroquois, were a people rooted in oral traditions, wampum played a central role in the preservation of their historical, political, and religious customs – it represented "the rules of good life and laws of good government" (Parker "Origin" 405). Perhaps not surprisingly,

Natives often had the sense that the versions of treaties documented by Europeans had not been faithfully recorded or implemented. The wampum itself was the true heart of a treaty negotiation and is still regarded by Natives, to this day, as more durable and binding than anything western literacy could preserve. Benjamin Franklin, although he understood little of the spiritual significance of wampum, was impressed enough to remark that it provided "the Records of the Council ... they preserve Traditions of the Stipulation of Treaties 100 years back; which when we compare with our Writings, we always find exact" (855).

Native communities coming into contact with colonizers, far from avoiding the tool of European writing, actively sought to acquire it, largely for their own protection. They realized that if they were going to live in proximity with Europeans, whether as neighbors or as adversaries, they would need to avail themselves of this important form of intercultural communication. Contemporary Native scholars, like Abenaki historian Lisa Brooks, are interested in the ways in which, when Native people were introduced to western forms of literacy, they often brought it into conformity with their own traditions, creating new syncretic forms of expression that had their roots in indigenous custom. Brooks notes that "transformations occurred when the European system entered Native space. Birchbark messages became letters and petitions, wampum records became treaties" (13). Native people began actively weaving European traditions of scripture into their own traditions of cultural and historical record keeping.

In South America and Mexico the move to adopting western literacy had been under way since the sixteenth century. The densely populated and hierarchical civilizations that blossomed in these regions had already developed elaborate means of preserving traditions, history and customs in bound books, or codices, and often there was a class of traditional scribes who had been trained in such arts and were able to transition all the more readily to western practices of inscription when the Spaniards became the controlling power in the region. Among these was Don Felipe Guaman Poma de Ayala, the Andean historian whose 1,200-page multi-lingual account of Incan civilization drew primarily from indigenous sources to relate the epic history of his people. Few of the codices of Aztec and Mayan civilization have survived. The Spaniards regarded these records as sacrilegious and did all within their power to wipe them from the face of the earth. Even so, Native scribes steeped in traditions of inscription were in position to preserve their sacred texts like the Mayan *Popul-Vuh* and the *Chilam Balam* from the holocaust of the conquistadors and these written volumes remain a part of that living oral tradition.

Caleb Cheeshateaumauk, mentioned at the start of this chapter, wrote his letter in Latin to demonstrate for English audiences his progress as a student at Harvard College. He was one of at least five Native students to attend Harvard in its earliest enthusiasm for Indian education in the mid-1600s and he lived in the building known as the Indian College which also housed New England's first printing press, maintained by the young Nipmuc Indian, James Printer. In Cheeshateaumauk's letter, he thanked his English benefactors for taking an interest in his education and noted how Orpheus, the musician from Greek mythology, stood as a symbol for the cultivation of western arts and their ability to animate "the forests and rocks" and render "tamer the ferocious beasts" (Hochbruck & Dudensing-Reichel 5). Cheeshateaumauk, who presumably excelled in astronomy, geography, philosophy and rhetoric, and also spoke English, Greek and Hebrew alongside his indigenous Algonquian language, somewhat tactfully neglected to emphasize that Orpheus was, himself, a figure from oral tradition and represented artistic and intellectual achievement outside the realm of European writing. But Cheeshateaumauk's letter provided proof of the successes the Puritans were achieving in their stated goal of "educating the Indians."

The Puritans were interested in teaching local Natives to read and write because it was the first step to being able to read God's word in the bible and to subsequently acquire Christianity. This became a great project for the scripturally centered Puritans and they were able to produce, through the offices of multi-lingual Natives like Cheeshateaumauk, North America's first bible printed in the Algonquian language. If the Puritans hoped the Natives would quickly become compliant Christian servants, however, Native peoples had their own motives for acquiring the tool of literacy. From the very start of colonization they found themselves drawn into land transfers with the settler population, not because they were eager to give up their land, but because they found it a necessity of peaceful coexistence. Natives became fluent in the drawing up of land deeds and used the tool of literacy to try to preserve and protect their holdings. In the hundreds of deeds drawn up by Native writers in the seventeenth and eighteenth centuries, many of them in the Algonquian language, one word that appears over and over is "michime," which translates as "forever," and speaks poignantly to the collective hopes of Native communities to maintain their traditional land base in a time of great hostility and upheaval (Goddard & Bragdon 97).

A telling example of this hope can be seen in the life and career of the Mohegan, Samson Occom. Occom, as a young man, saw the once expansive territory of his people chiseled away by settler encroachment. Weakened by a century of colonial calamity including pandemic disease, warfare and other continuous pressures of colonization, the Mohegans found themselves culturally weakened, without means, and in constant legal contestation with the settler authorities over the title to their traditional lands. Having testified on behalf of his people as a young man and seen how the colonial legal process failed them again and again, Occom went to a local Connecticut minister, Eleazar Wheelock, to acquire an English education and, specifically, to learn Latin, the language of law. The price of such an education, not surprisingly, was Christian conversion, the longstanding demand of the colonial endeavor and the only sphere, short of warfare, in which a Native individual might hope to affect positive change for his people. Occom excelled as a student and within a few years was able to take up the post as missionary to the Montauk Indians of Long Island. As he wrote in his 1768 autobiographical account, he had long felt "if I Could once Learn to Read I Would Instruct the poor Children" and he notes he talked frequently to local Native communities of this goal (54).

Occom's extraordinary advocacy for Native peoples in New England led to his becoming an ordained minister and traveling to England for two and half years to raise money for a proposed Indian College. This college would be the fulfillment of his lifelong goal to educate Native youths so the coming generation might have the tools at their disposal to preserve their heritage and compete in a hostile cultural and economic environment. Occom was a sensation in both England and Scotland. People flocked to see the "Indian Preacher," expecting, perhaps, to partake in some colorful display of savage supplication, but encountering instead the poised and soft spoken Mohegan minister who parlayed his rhetorical talents into an eloquent plea for what were referred to by white audiences of the time as the "poor Indians."

Occom raised some £12,000 for the Indian College, but when he returned to the colonies, he was viewed as having overstepped his bounds, grown too prideful for an Indian, and immediate steps were taken to knock him back down to his proper station. Wheelock

EARLY NATIVE AMERICAN WRITING

accused Occom of public drunkenness to anyone who would listen. Occom's neighbors testified that he had grown "heretical" (Blodgett 116). And the monies Occom raised, instead of being channeled into Indian education, were used instead to found Dartmouth College, an all-white institution headed by Wheelock himself. Occom was well-versed at this point in the fine-tuned treacheries of his colonial neighbors, but as an Indian with few acknowledged rights and no institutional backing, there was little he could do about it. Publicly at least, he maintained his mild outlook, but writing to Wheelock in 1771, Occom offered his jaded impression of Wheelock's college, that instead of becoming "alma Mater, she will be too alba mater" for his tastes (98). In other words, instead of fulfilling the traditional role of alma mater (mother of the soul), the college had become alba mater (mother of the whites) and as such was of little use to the Indians. Occom continued:

> I verily thought once that your Institution was Intended Purely for the poor Indians [and] with this thought I cheerfully Ventur'd my Body & Soul, left my Country, my poor young Family all my friends and Relations, to sail over the Boisterous Seas to England, to help forward your School ... but when we got Home behold all the glory had decay'd and now I am afraid, we shall be Deem'd as Liars and Deceivers in Europe, unless you gather Indians quickly to your College.
>
> (99)

Wheelock's betrayal, far from representing the end of Occom's career, proved a pivotal point for the Mohegan minister. In the next few years he severed his ties with the Christian missionary outfits that had originally sponsored him, published a popular book of hymns, a best-selling sermon, and spearheaded an indigenous revivalist movement that provided not only a spiritual home for many Native people of New England, but became the political impetus for a number of Natives to move themselves westward to pioneer their own settlement on lands gifted them by the Oneida Indians in modern-day upstate New York – as far away as they could get from white settler entanglements. Occom was assisted in this endeavor by a number of literate Natives, including the Montauks, David and Jacob Fowler, and his young son-in-law, Joseph Johnson, a fellow Mohegan who used his literary fluency tirelessly to lobby both Native and white leaders to secure the lands needed for settlement.

Johnson, a talented student who, like Occom, had first studied under Wheelock, was sent at the age of fifteen to assist the white missionary, Samuel Kirkland, who had been stationed amongst the Oneida in the 1760s. Johnson, chaffing under Kirkland's authoritarian expectations, ultimately joined up with his Oneida charges and, as Kirkland observed, "turn'd pagan for about a week – painted, sung – danc'd – drank & whor'd it, [with] some of the savage Indians he cou'd find" (qtd. in Murray 59). Kirkland's comments, when stripped of their racist underpinnings, implied simply that Johnson enjoyed the company of his fellow Natives over that of the missionary. Following his falling out with Kirkland, Johnson, like many young Native men at the time, spent a year and a half seeing the world from the deck of a whaling ship, before returning home and reconnecting with his Mohegan community. In Johnson's private journals one may trace the internal struggles of a passionate young man fighting to find a place amidst a time of great struggle and crisis for New England Natives. He mourns the passing of his father who died fighting alongside the English in the French and Indian Wars, he comments upon his day to day labors, which as

321

an economically marginalized Native were prodigious, and he earnestly reflects on his place in the world and the precarious condition of his soul. He writes:

> Altho I have been whire dangers were and great dangers too the year Past, I have been preserved on the mighty Waters, and have been kept safe from the rage of the Great whales who obey his Voice ... O that his goodness might lead me to true repentance.
>
> (126)

Johnson rallies himself under Samson Occom's example and learns how to deploy Christian rhetoric as a tool for individual and community advancement, receiving his preaching license in 1774 and embarking on a furious campaign to write a new homeland into being for his people. Aware that relations between the colonies and England were fast eroding and that a cry for independence was in the air, Johnson proclaimed, in one of his many letters to colonial officials:

> Liberty is admired by all noble spirits, and Gentleman, let me with humility tell you, that I have exerted myself, used my uttermost endeavours to help my poor Brethren in New England; to bring them out of Bondage, as it were, and to lead them into a land of Liberty, where they and their Children might live in peace.
>
> (225)

Ironically, for Johnson to accomplish this, he had to lead his people away from their homelands and out of the very "land of liberty" for which the colonists were preparing to do battle.

Johnson had proven so skillful at negotiating the intercultural borderlands between the colonies and the Five Nations that, as the revolutionary war broke out, he was enlisted by General Washington to broker a promise of neutrality with the Iroquois. He died of unknown causes somewhere on route to carrying out this delicate diplomatic assignment. The colonial world, particularly in wartime, was a dangerous place for Indians, and if Johnson died in service to the very colonizing powers that had done so much to disenfranchise his people of their lands and rights, this was a fate that had been shared by his father and thousands of other Natives who have served under the flag of the United States government. Nevertheless, Johnson's efforts ultimately resulted in the formation of the Brothertown settlement, which, although he didn't live to see it come to full fruition, stands as a bold, largely forgotten, initiative by Native peoples to forge their own pioneer community on America's famed frontier. Ironically, Brothertown, with its wood frame houses, well-ordered streets, and centralized Christian meetinghouse, was built by Mohegans just a few short miles from Cooperstown, the site where many of James Fenimore Cooper's fictitious Mohicans played out their assigned literary roles as doomed noble savages destined to retreat quietly into the dark forest primeval of cultural oblivion.

The Brothertown movement was one defined by Native American literary practices, a community of indigenous peoples, both men and women, who corresponded with one another, wrote letters and petitions to public officials, published books, sermons, and newspaper articles, all in the service of carving out a peaceful existence for themselves on the far extreme of colonial expansion. From Brothertown emerged other writers and political actors such as the Mohican writer Hendrick Aupaumut who lead a brigade of Native scouts in the Revolutionary War and later wrote of his travels to the "western country" as he tried to secure new lands and alliances for his people. Stockbridge Indians, John Wannuaucon Quinney and Thomas Commuck also contributed to the large body of textual production by Mahican and "Stockbridge" Indians who saw their attempts at establishing safe and stable communities constantly challenged by greedy white settlers. As the United States forced its way further into the Ohio Valley in the early nineteenth century, more Native individuals sought the use of print discourse to lobby for their rights and try to safeguard their lands.

The War of 1812 saw the emergence of Native leaders on the British Canadian side like the Cherokee, Captain John Norton, who was adopted by the Mohawk under Joseph Brant and whose little known journal, written in 1816 but published long after his death in 1970, chronicled his stirring engagements in the major campaigns of that war. Norton's journal, a massive literary accomplishment some 530 printed pages in length, attempts to view Iroquois, or Haudenosaunee, culture through a wide lens, taking in their history, their religious beliefs, their formation as a confederated people, and their story of creation itself. By offering this epic scope, Norton hoped to demonstrate that the Iroquois were, indeed, a civilized people and he specifically worked to establish their long-held cultural commitment to notions of peace, order, and justice. He did this in order to counteract rampant claims, particularly during wartime, that Indians were all savage murderers whose style of warfare merited a policy of "no-mercy" from their more "civilized" opponents. As Norton understood, the insistent historical claim to Indian "savagery" was repeatedly used as justification for whites to murder indiscriminately Indian men, women and children, and divest them of their lands and inheritance. Like many other early Native writers, Norton gained access not only to literacy through his immersion in Christian rhetoric, but moral authority amongst white audiences. Among his other varied accomplishments, he was able to translate the Gospel of John into the Mohawk language. But his association with Christian ideas and spirituality did not prevent him from authoring a Native-centered history of the world and apparently he saw no contradiction in forwarding indigenous views of creation alongside his Christian views.

Another politically engaged community of Native writers could be found amongst the Cherokee, as they spearheaded a resistance to Andrew Jackson's Indian removal policies in the 1820s and 30s. Under extreme pressure from the federal government to uproot their lives and push west of the Mississippi, the Cherokee hunkered down instead and began broadcasting their plight to the world through the offices of the *Cherokee Phoenix*, a newspaper printed by the Cherokee nation under the guidance of Cherokee editor Elias Boudinot. The *Cherokee Phoenix* is a rightly famous institution as it provided tangible proofs of the Cherokee as an "improving" people capable of keeping up with the modern innovations and demands of settler culture. In furtherance of such rhetorical goals, the Cherokee adopted their own constitution largely modeled after the United States' Constitution, created their own centralized seat of government in New Echota (in present day northwest Georgia), and circulated their struggle for cultural autonomy across the country (and into Europe as well) through their nationally distributed newspaper which was printed in both the English and Cherokee languages. Their massive propaganda campaign was reinforced by Cherokee speakers, David Brown, John Ridge, and Boudinot himself, who toured the country lobbying for their cause.

The Cherokee, like many other Native peoples, found themselves in the impossible situation of having to argue their own value as human beings to a dominant culture that had already cast them in the role of sub-human savages. The Removal Act, passed by Congress in 1830, was insidious enough to suggest that the determination forcefully to remove Native peoples from their own lands was actually an act of benevolence, undertaken for the "Red Man's" own good. By removing all eastern Indians to western territories in Oklahoma, the argument went, the United States would afford its "Indian children" time to "catch up," so that when western civilization eventually found its way there, Native peoples might be better prepared for the "gifts" of civilization. Such was the thinking, even though Native peoples had been fully engaged in western life, religion, literacy, and culture for roughly two hundred years. Many of the Cherokee lived in frame houses, had sizable plantations, and some even kept slaves (one of those "gifts" of civilization). But none of this mattered. The United States preferred its fantasy of Native savagery to the claims of those resisting removal and, although in the end even the Supreme Court decided that the Removal Act was unconstitutional, the U.S. army was enlisted to enforce it regardless and the Cherokee were relocated at gunpoint, suffering enormous casualties along the way as a result of the horrendous conditions of their forced march.

If Samson Occom was the first Native American to publish his own works, William Apess, a Pequot, was the first to publish, in 1829, a book-length narrative of his life, entitled *A Son of the Forest*. Apess's life is representative in many ways of the traumas suffered by a colonized people. He grew up in an atmosphere of poverty, neglect, and abuse, was indentured out at a very young age to labor for white families, and when he escaped his persecution under this system, found himself quickly enlisted in the U.S. army and swept off at the age of fifteen to fight for the country of his colonizers in the War of 1812. Despite all of these hardships, Apess used his natural genius to scrape together an education and, when he returned home years later, turned to preaching, writing books, and advocating for Native rights throughout the northeast. An ordained minister in the Protestant Methodist church, Apess authored at least five major works in his short lifetime, all of them searingly critical of the treatment of "people of color" in America. Apess used his rhetorical skills to hold a mirror up to the dominant white culture, reversing the lens by which they had historically scorned and denigrated Native peoples and projected that image back upon themselves. In his masterful, *Eulogy on King Philip* (1836), Apess wrote:

> the Pilgrims landed at Plymouth, and without asking liberty from anyone they possessed themselves of a portion of the country, and built themselves houses, and then made a treaty, and commanded them [Indians] to accede to it. This, if now done, it would be called an insult, and every white man would be called to go out and act the part of patriot, to defend their country's right ... and yet the Indians (though many were dissatisfied), without the shedding of blood or imprisoning anyone, bore it. And yet for their kindness ... they were called savages.
>
> (281)

Not only did Apess use his literary skills to forward progressive notions of racial tolerance and social justice but he was, perhaps, America's first successful practitioner of civil disobedience, deploying peaceful tactics of resistance to help achieve rights for his Native "brethren."

While Apess forged his fiery rhetoric through a reframing of the historical and religious practices of white culture, unveiling its blatant hypocrisies, other Native writers of his time engaged in different types of literary endeavors. David Cusick, a Tuscarora who also served under the United States in the War of 1812, first published his *Sketches of Ancient History of the Six Nations* in 1825, recounting his version of the Iroquois creation story and making a case for the sustained significance of Iroquois culture, religion, and literature. In so doing, Cusick was not only reaffirming the values of his people but he was posting an argument against Indian Removal policies of the time by positing his people not as "moving toward civilization," but as having always already been there. The Ojibwe writer Jane Johnston Schoolcraft was yet another who used her literary talents to relate assorted folktales of her people, preserve traditional songs, and compose poetry. Married to the Indian Agent cum ethnographer Henry Rowe Schoolcraft in 1823, she was more deeply immersed in domi- nant literary forms than many of her Native peers, but she often drew from Ojibwe literary traditions as well. Her Ojibwe name alone, Bamewawagezhikaquay (Woman of the Sound the Stars Make Rushing through the Sky), speaks profoundly to the poetic sensibilities of her people. Her verse ranged in topic from the death of a child, to an honor poem for her grandfather, to tributes to nature and poems of devotion. Johnston's familiarity with domi- nant aesthetic conventions can at times mask her deep Ojibwe moorings to the land and the fact that so many of her poems were written originally in her Native language.

George Copway, like Schoolcraft, was also Ojibwe and in his *The Life, History, and Travels, of Kah-ge-ga-gah-bowh* (1847), he tells of his traditional upbringing in the great north woods of Ontario, Minnesota and Michigan, his eventual conversion to Christianity, and his life and work as a missionary among the Indians. Copway's work, published in 1846, was perhaps the most popular of the Native-authored literary texts up to this moment, as it skillfully synthesized elements of "savage" culture, so thrilling to white audiences, with messages of Christian piety that signaled a new day for the so-called red man of the forest. He told of his first encounter with a bear as a child, the long seasonal journeys by foot and canoe to visit the white trading posts in Canada, and the coming of the Methodists to his woodland home, leading to his conversion in 1830. His marriage to a white English woman was presided over by Peter Jones, another writing Ojibwe missionary. Copway, like many of his literary forbears walked a fine line between preserving and celebrating his indigenous tradition and delineating a path for Native people to safely negotiate under the pressures of colonialism.

Contemporary readers often have a difficult time reconciling early Native literary activism with the prominent presence of Christian rhetoric that pervades these works. The adoption of Christianity continues to appear as a disappointing surrender of traditional culture and identity. But Native people of the time didn't necessarily see it this way. As a colonized people they did not have the luxury of maintaining pristine notions of Indian identity, nor would such a thing have been possible. Often the dominant culture's idea of what constitutes "authentic" Native identity is already one based on romantic fallacies largely perpetuated by white literary practices. Individuals like Caleb Cheeshateaumauk, Samson Occom, Joseph Johnson, William Apess and others lived in times of cultural vio- lence and suffering for their people. It is best to understand them not as figures in flight from a romantic primitive past (they knew of no such world), but rather as individuals grappling with the historical and cultural forces in front of them. If Christianity provided a path for them to function on the colonial stage, it didn't necessarily mean an absolute relinquishing of traditional practices and beliefs. But there was no venue for them to publish such attitudes, no American printer interested in forwarding such spiritualities. Nevertheless, Native writers were almost uniformly critical of Christianity as it was practiced by the whites. As Apess would wryly assert of Christian missionary efforts, "your doctrine is very good, but the whole course of your conduct is decidedly at variance with your profession – we think the whites need fully as much religious instruction as we do" (33). Or, put more succinctly, perhaps, in the private diary of nineteenth-century Mohegan medicine woman Fidelia Fiedling, "Those people who can say much, /Half of what they say is not true as they say it" (575). If one looks and listens carefully, however, a sense of Native spirituality can be apprehended, swift running, like an underground current, through the body of these written texts, and as the Cherokee writer, Thomas King, notes "if you know where to stand, you can hear the two of them talking to each other" (101–02).

When Native Americans engaged in writing in colonial America, it was typically not for leisure or entertainment as was so often the case among white writers. The economic and cultural conditions under which they labored left very little space for such entertainments. And yet they wrote with both Native and white audiences in mind, understanding that their stories might help turn the tide for struggling Native communities, affording a new consideration of their rights and privileges as the people who first occupied this land and, if their predictions prove true, will continue to occupy it "michime" – forever.

Works cited

Apess, William. *On Our Own Ground: The Complete Writings of William Apess, a Pequot.* Ed. Barry O'Connell. Amherst: University of Massachusetts Press, 1992.

Aupaumut, Hendrick. "A Short Narration of My Last Journey to the Western Country." *Early Native Literacies in New England: A Documentary and Critical Anthology.* Ed. Kristina Bross & Hilary E. Wyss. Amherst: University of Massachusetts Press, 2008. 224–37.

Blodgett, Harold. *Samson Occom.* Hanover, NH: Dartmouth College Publications, 1935.

Boudinot, Elias. *Cherokee Editor: The Writings of Elias Boudinot,* Ed. Theda Perdue. Athens: University of Georgia Press, 1983.

Brooks, Lisa. *The Common Pot: The Recovery of Native Space in the Northeast.* Minneapolis: University of Minneapolis Press, 2008.

Cooper, James Fenimore. *The Last of the Mohicans.* 1826. Rpt. New York: Oxford University Press, 1980.

Copway, George. *Life, Letters and Speeches.* Ed. A. Lavonne Brown Ruoff & Donald B. Smith. Lincoln: University of Nebraska Press, 1997.

Cushman, Robert. "Reasons and Considerations Touching the Lawlessness of Removing out of England into the parts of America." 1622. Rpt. *Mourt's Relation: A Journal of the Pilgrims at Plymouth.* Ed. Dwight B. Heath. Bedford, MA: Applewood Books, 1963. 88–96.

Cusick, David. *Sketches of Ancient History of the Six Nations* (1828). Ed. Paul Royster. Lincoln: University of Nebraska Press, Faculty Publications, UNL Libraries. Web. Accessed 28 Dec. 2014. http://digitalcommons.unl.edu/cgi/viewcontent.cgiarticle=1027&context=libraryscience

Fielding, Fidelia. "The Truth of Tomorrow." *Dawnland Voices: An Anthology of Indigenous Writings from New England.* Ed. Siobhan Senier. Lincoln: University of Nebraska Press, 2014. 573–76.

Franklin, Benjamin. "Remarks Concerning the Savages." *The Heath Anthology of American Literature.* Vol. A. 6th ed. Ed. Paul Lauter. Boston: Houghton Mifflin Harcourt, 2009. 854–57.

Goddard, Ives & Kathleen J. Bragdon. *Native Writings in Massachusetts.* Philadelphia: American Philosophical Society, 1988.

Hochbruck, Wolfgang & Beatrix Dudensing-Reichel. "'Honoratissimi Benefactores': Native American Students and Two Seventeenth Century Texts in the University Tradition." *Early Native American Writing: New Critical Essays*. Ed. Helen Jaskoski. Cambridge: Cambridge University Press, 1996. 1–14.

Johnson, Joseph. *To do Good to My Indian Brethren: The Writings of Joseph Johnson, 1751–1776*. Ed. Laura J. Murray. Amherst: University of Massachusetts Press, 1998.

King, Thomas. *The Truth about Stories: A Native Narrative*. Minneapolis: University of Minnesota Press, 2003.

Murray, Laura J. "The Early Letters." *To do Good to My Indian Brethren: The Writings of Joseph Johnson, 1751–1776*. Ed. Laura J. Murray. Amherst: University of Massachusetts Press, 1998. 50.

Norton, John. *The Journal of Major John Norton*. Ed. Carl F. Klinck & James J. Talman. 1816. Rpt. Toronto: The Champlain Society, 1970. Web. Accessed 27 Dec. 2014. http://link.library.utoronto.ca/champlain

Occom, Samson. *The Collected Writings of Samson Occom, Mohegan: Leadership and Literature in Eighteenth-Century Native America*. Ed. Joanna Brooks. New York: Oxford University Press, 2006.

Parker, Arthur C. "The Constitution of the Five Nations." *Parker on the Iroquois*. Ed. William N. Fenton. Syracuse, NY: Syracuse University Press, 1968. 7–118.

——. "The Origin of the Longhouse." *Seneca Myths & Folk Tales*. 1923. Rpt. Lincoln: University of Nebraska Press, 1989. 403–06.

Schoolcraft, Jane Johnston. "To the Pine Tree." *The Sound the Stars Make Rushing Through the Sky: The Writings of Jane Johnston Schoolcraft*. Ed. Robert Dale Parker. Philadelphia: University of Pennsylvania Press, 2007. 89–90.

Williams, Roger. *A Key into the Language of America*. Bedford, MA: Applewood Books, 1936.

28

The Historical and Literary Role of Folklore, Storytelling, and the Oral Tradition in Native American Literatures

Susan Berry Brill de Ramírez

To understand any written literature, attention needs to be paid to its craft, its distinctive language and rhetoric, its style and form, its literariness. This is especially true for Native American literatures which are deeply informed by their respective tribal traditions of storytelling and oratory. And to begin to understand Native American literature, attention must be paid to the language, form, rhetoric, and literariness which are (1) in many cases reflective of present and past oral traditions and (2) integrally tied to tribal literary and linguistic heritage and influence. While the primacy of oral traditions as historically significant is a fact for all literatures, Native American literature stands out due to its ancestrally and culturally genetic positioning between its traditional, tribal oral cultures, languages, and rituals and its place as part of the larger American and Canadian literary canons. The precedence of orality in relation to literacy and textuality is a global fact: in terms of chronology, all written literatures have oral literary traditions as precedent and formative. However, for all of the tribes of North America, the shift to a predominantly written culture has been relatively recent within the global history of writing – for many tribes, largely occurring just within the past two centuries.

Through the government policies of removal, relocation, and termination, tribal cultures and traditions were disrupted as entire tribes were removed from their ancestral land, tribal communities were broken up and divested of their land rights altogether, generations were divided through the removal of children into boarding and residential schools or into foster and adoptive homes, and adults and families were removed to work in urban communities during government relocation efforts. The concomitant, subsequent, and continuing assimilationist efforts, deeply tied to natural resource acquisition moves for lands and mineral rights and later combined with the radical shifts to globalization in the twentieth and early twenty-first centuries, English language dominance, and digital technologies, have all propelled tribes and their cultures quickly forward into predominantly written, textual, and digital cultures.

However, in looking at the craft and literariness of Native American literatures over the course of the last several centuries, it is crucial that orality not be perceived solely in terms of chronology, for Indigenous oral cultures and traditions endure alongside the development of Native written literatures. Predominant delineations between the oral and literate during the greater part of the twentieth century reductively viewed traditional orality as of a piece, negligibly recognizing the extensive diversity and complexity of linguistic forms in oral cultures. The ethnocentric primitivist lens directed towards traditional oral cultures was then extrapolated into simplistically reductive and pat distinctions between the oral and the literate (with, of course, the literate being viewed as the more complex, diverse, and sophisticated). In fact, orality has far greater capabilities in regards to symbolic and metaphoric richness due to the added possibilities inherent in performative, auditory, visual, and intersubjective language (Scheub 276–77; Tedlock *Spoken Word* 3, 55).

The vast majority of the scholarship on language change throughout time has posited the fundamental difference between oral and written communications which, in turn, have been viewed in terms of the divide between the West and nonwestern worlds. By and large, linguistic studies of orality have tended in two general directions: 1) contemporary research into the linguistic, paralinguistic, psychological, and other behavioral aspects of conversation as they relate to the event of conversing, and 2) ethnolinguistic studies of orality that have focused on predominantly oral cultures that have viewed orality within a primitivistic and exoticizing lens, focusing on oral storytelling, folklore and myth, ethnological life histories, and spiritually oriented prayers, chants, stories, and rituals. Many ethnolinguistic studies of modernist primitivism privileged those aspects of orality that involved the creative intricacies of poetic craft in the articulations of storytellers, singers, chanters, and poets. Often, literary language and craft that was oral was, thereby, misread and misinterpreted through foci on the content of what was being said, the information that was being related, the ideas that were being expressed, rather than attention to the "how" of what was being said – the craft behind and within the telling.

In viewing traditional oral cultures through a primitivist lens, the deeply connotative language of skilled storytellers and singers was, thereby, inaccessible to researchers who stayed at the surface levels of denotation. Within this framework, it was written language that was viewed as more complex in its diverse forms, but this was an unfair and erroneous contrast, for the oral language was being misread and misinterpreted as simplistic, when in fact it was far from that. Regardless of culture or time, it is literary and deliberatively symbolic language that is far more complex than straightforward denotative language – and this is the case regardless of whether the language is oral or written. Orality has the potential to be even more complex than writing. For example, the work of highly crafted oral storytellers, bards, and healers is far more complex than written literature due to 1) the heteroglossic multivocality inherent in the oral event (Kroskrity 196; Simard 245), 2) the translations and revisions possible in retellings (Brill de Ramírez 138–47), and 3) the coded, symbolic, and figurative language inherent in metaphorically and metonymically rich tellings (Wilson xiii).

Oral communications and written literature reflect both conversive and discursive modes of interpersonal communication. Conversive communication uses language as a means towards the larger ends of interpersonal and intersubjective relations, as communication (linguistic, paralinguistic, performative) affects personal, interpersonal, and community well-being and growth (Kroeber 8–9; Attinasi & Friedrich 43, 50). Here, language is the tool for relational ends. Interactive orality can also take the form of discourse which draws upon the interpersonal possibilities to convey diverse linguistic and signifying ends. Whereas the conversive mode with the prefix "con-" (with or together) and the Latin root *vertere* (to turn, to change, to translate) has the relational sense of turning with, the term "discourse" conveys positionality, bridging, and movement between positions (running from point to point). Indeed the Latin word *conversatio* has the senses of "intercourse, manner of life": intercourse in contrast to discourse. This distinction is important in approaching the rhetorical diversity and richness that infuses the work of Indigenous writers globally and Native American writers in the United States and Canada, for at the heart of Native American literature is the articulation of community, tribe, nation, and interpersonal connection.

The diversity of rhetoric in Native literatures can be seen in the modal range of writing by three regional writers from the American Southwest. Simon J. Ortiz (Acoma Pueblo), Leslie Marmon Silko (Laguna Pueblo), and Ofelia Zepeda (Tohono O'odham) have all worked to incorporate diverse modes of communication in their print creative work. Ortiz and Zepeda consciously interweave their tribal oral storytelling traditions and their Native languages with and within their creative writing which, in turn, includes both prose and poetic forms. Silko goes further as she interweaves visual art, short prose fiction, life-history narratives, poetry, traditional oral stories, photography, and long prose fiction in various configurations in each of her works. For each of these writers, the intersections of worlds and world views display the inclusivity of their tribal lenses that are rooted with tribe and place while including a broadly open outward lens. The realms of the fictive and the factual, the historical and the mythical, the personal and the tribal and the global, and the human and the nonhuman are interwoven within the authors' linguistic creations. This inclusive inter-relationality is manifested with a storyteller's fluidity of openness and a permeability of grace that invites their readers literally to step into the worlds of the writers' words. Their writing conveys an intimacy of language that "familiarizes" the literary world into the world of the reader (or, if one will, listener-reader). Where Viktor Shklovsky noted the process of "defamiliarisation of the ordinary" within literature, Ortiz, Silko and Zepeda are masters of the process of "familiarization" as they craft the tribal, the historical, the personal, the regional, the previously distant, alien, unknown, forgotten and marginalized into remarkably accessible, deeply engaging, and intimately familiar literary worlds.

In Ofelia Zepeda's poem "Deer Dance Exhibition," she exemplifies a linguistic connectivity as a tribal respondent responds to an outside interlocutor's intrusive questions. Rather than responding in an oppositional manner, the tribal speaker responds conversively, trying to assist the outsider to step forward and participate within the larger scope of the event rather than merely seeking superficial information and objectifying the event as a viewer from without. In the poem, Zepeda demonstrates the linguistic tools by which a traditional storyteller reaches out to listeners as co-creative participants in the unfolding story, but in the crafting of the poem, we see these traditionally oral tools as played out within the written realm of the text. Repeatedly, the outsider asks informational questions that demonstrate an objectifying and distanced perspective upon the unfolding tribal deer dance, inquiring about the sounds of the drum, the dancer's clothing, including the hooves and cocoons that replicate a deer's hooves and the sounds of the deer's steps. In response, the conversive response of the tribal member is not distancing but rather familiarly conversational, offering language as a familiarizing vehicle towards connection. When the tribal member invites the interlocutor to see the dancer as a deer and to "Listen" and hear the dancer's sounds as the footsteps of the deer, these are invitations to enter the imaginary-real

FOLKLORE, STORYTELLING, AND ORAL TRADITION

world of the deer dance ceremony through the sensory means of the visual and auditory imaginations. The questioner seeks the surface level of the *factual real* while what is offered is the ceremonial storytelling and performance of the *magical real*.

Zepeda's poem is therefore quite interesting from a rhetorical perspective. Because the poem presents two speakers who communicate in two very different manners: one who is distanced and objectifying, utilizing language as means towards informational acquisition and the other who responds relationally and intersubjectively, Zepeda's poem opens up the deer dance event as the tribal member's direct address speaks more broadly to both the interlocutor in the poem and, too, the poem's readers as listener-readers. In this way, both poetic questioner and readers are invited to literally step into the world of the poem and the deer dance, to see the deer that is invoked and visualized, to listen to and hear the sounds of the boy's dancing and, thereby, the sounds of the deer. In the only lines of the poem that consist of just one word, Zepeda speaks directly to us in the encouraging and elicitive word: "Listen." The blank space that follows these single word lines is the silent space offered to the listener(s) within the poem and the listener-readers of the poem to silently listen and, perchance, imagine, realize, and hear the presence of the deer. In this way, Zepeda reminds her readers that the role of listeners within stories is as embodied persons participative within the unfolding story. This is expected during the actual ceremony of a traditional ritual deer dance. This is also expected in the oral storytelling responses of the speaker in the poem. Further, Zepeda utilizes the open space of poetry to provide the openings for an orally informed and engaged reader-response in which the reader as listener-reader is called to take an interactively co-creative role in the developing story of the poem.

Simon J. Ortiz utilizes such co-creative cues in his poem "That's the Place Indians Talk About" in which line breaks, empty space through indentation and short one- and two-word lines, along with the textual orality elicited in repeated linguistic cues such as in the words "talk," "talks," "talking," "hear," and "listen" and the vocative "you listen" coalesce as Ortiz invites his readers as listener-readers to join him and the speaking persona of the poem as fellow listeners to an old Paiute man. In this way, Ortiz invites the broad and diverse range of his readers, whether Indigenous or diasporic, literally to enter the world of the storytelling old man as co-participant listeners to his poignant story of enduring colonization and disenfranchisement and, too, a people's efforts to overcome the appropriation of sacred lands by a U.S. government military installation. Ortiz's poetic crafting, spacing, meter, caesura and enjambment, repetition, and chiasmus come together with particular skill to elicit the orality of the old man's storytelling voice and its relationally co-creative effect. The old man explains the natural and sacred power of the Coso Hot Springs in this way:

> When you pray. /U/
> When you talk to the hot springs. /U/ | /U//
> You talk with it when it talks to you. U/U/ | U/ | /U/
> Something from there, /UU/
> from down in there is talking to you. U/U/ | U/U | U/
> You could hear it. /U/U or U/ | /U
> You listen. / | /U
>   Listen. /U
> You can hear it. /U/U

(Woven Stone 31, 33)

SUSAN BERRY BRILL DE RAMÍREZ

Following in the tradition of interactive oral storytelling, Ortiz and the speaker of his poem speak directly to us, inviting us more closely into the events of the story. The voice shifts to a second person voice from the initial first person storytelling and further elicits a participatory response from the reader, inviting us to become actual participants in the unfolding story. The rhythm and meter of the poem create additional openings for reader response. The first five lines quoted above end with accented beats that draw out the lines in connection, while the shorter four ending lines end with unaccented beats that open up the lines to the listener-reader's response.

After the short halting line "You could hear it" (read either more quickly as a ditrochaeus /U/U [double trochee with emphasis on the listener-reader "You"] or with the added pause of an emphatic iamb followed by a single trochee U/ | /U pointing to possibility: here in the listener-reader's potential engagement "You could" with "could" being accented), Ortiz follows this with a line break and spacing that almost fills up the line, spacing that invites his readers to consider the very idea of people who not only go to a sacred place, who not only offer prayers at that place, but who listen deeply and hear the power of that place – a possibility that is textually opened up and reaches beyond the page to the reader as listener. Then Ortiz includes an especially significant line break followed by additional spacing on the subsequent line with two trochees separated by the emphatic opening of an extended silence: "You listen. /Listen." The first of these two lines ("You listen.") explains to his readers the listening practice of those who go on pilgrimage to the Coso Hot Springs. The subsequent line break is followed by an extended blank line that leads to the directive: "Listen" that is aligned at the right side of that line. The blank space between "You listen." and "Listen." is the textual silence for the listener-reader to imagine and possibly hear the sacred power of place in a John Cagean sense of sonorous presence within silence. As Ortiz explains, "A story is not only told but it is also listened to; it becomes whole in its expression and perception" ("Always" 57).

Through the rhetorical connectivity of storytelling and literature, diverse listeners and listener-readers are enabled to make deep, meaningful, and experiential connections that cut across times, places, cultures, and worlds. As Ortiz comments about his writing:

> There is a certain power that is compelling in the oral narrative as spoken by a storyteller simply because the spoken work is so immediate and intimate. I wanted to show that the narrative style and technique could be expressed as written narrative and that it would have the same participatory force and validity as words spoken and listened to.
>
> ("Always" 66)

C. A. Bowers underscores the importance of this very interactive relationship between storylisteners and storytellers regarding stories told by traditional Native elders: "in order for an elder to tell a coherent story the listener must know how to participate in the relationship" (176–77). The interactive rhetoric of storytelling and similarly informed written Native literatures utilizes silence, second person direct address, the inclusive first person plural, embodied sensory referents, elicitive and engaging rhythms and pacing, various empathic and emphatic markers, as well as other conversative strategies that elicit participant involvement in the engaging, connective, and relational communications.

FOLKLORE, STORYTELLING, AND ORAL TRADITION

In her pioneering collection *Storyteller*, Silko explicitly experiments with different forms of literary craft in one coherent volume that articulates the voice of a storyteller in oral, poetic, prose, and even pictorial form. The collection includes photographs, short prose fiction, poetry, traditional myths, her own creative stories that are crafted as traditional myths, and personal family life-history narratives, all of which are interwoven within the larger framework of the book's three thematic Laguna Pueblo lenses of Yellow Woman stories, Gambler stories, and coyote stories. These three broad thematic foci provide examples of how stories are told and retold multiple times and in diverse ways, in some cases, with changes even within one longer and complex creative piece. Since oral storytelling is directly framed within the storytelling event, all who are present are contributory to directions, references, and even characterizations of the unfolding story. Additionally, the narrative structure of traditional oral storytelling is episodic in which different stories overlap, converge and diverge, informing each other with new significance as they are meaningfully interrelated by storyteller and listener alike.

In drawing upon the work of folklorists and ethnographers who experimented with ways to present orally related stories on paper, Silko has accordingly experimented with ways to convey the power, voice, emphasis, tonality and rhythm of interactive orality in her creative writing. Like Ortiz, Silko demonstrates a sophisticated use of spacing on the page for the storyteller's/writer's silence and the listener's/reader's space for co-creative response. She also uses indentation and other spacing along with changes in font to bring additional levels of multivocality into the readings, which in many ways are crafted as textual storytelling events. Acknowledging the limits of textuality, Silko nevertheless demonstrates the remarkable ways by which co-creative orality can be effected via the medium of print.

The relationality of oral storytelling is extended to include the broader relations that cross species and include nonhuman "persons." In oral storytelling traditions around the world, whether as sacred stories, fairy tales, folklore, or myths, interpersonal relations often extend beyond the bounds of human interactions. Through the extended biotic and spirit realms, nonhumans are depicted as intentional and communicative persons. Many Native American and Aboriginal Canadian authors comfortably embrace such inclusively diverse relationality as nonhuman beings have their respective personhood acknowledged, embraced, and presented. In Silko's novels *Ceremony* and *Gardens in the Dunes*, she takes such an environmental turn in depicting conversative relations across species. In *Ceremony*, the lead character Tayo struggles to come into relationship with his fellow humans: whether family members, his tribal community, or others. The ecosystemic holism that is part and parcel of all Native American tribal traditions is presented as key to a person's well-being, and Tayo needs to come into relationship with all of creation.

Silko relates that as a child, he saw no boundaries: communications could even straddle different worlds and times, including mythic and sacred beings. His healing beyond the traumas of an absent mother, an unknown father, an abusive aunt who raised him, the racism experienced in being an Indian in America, and the global violence of World War II that surrounded him and took the life of his beloved cousin when they were in the military, takes the form of his transforming relationship with Ts'eh Montaño, a traditional Indigenous herbalist/spirit person who becomes his lover and who, mysteriously, may actually be the sacred mountain that overlooks his Laguna Pueblo. Tayo's life is also saved by a mountain lion who later reappears as Ts'eh Montaño's Indigenous husband who is introduced in mythic terms as "the Hunter." As Tayo comes into intersubjective relationship with Ts'eh Montaño, he is shown integrating himself into the sacred ancestral landscape of his Laguna Pueblo people, and consequent to this integration is Tayo's healing integration into his tribe and family.

Silko, Ortiz, and Zepeda demonstrate the diverse ways in which Native American literary works interweave the oral and the written within texts that range along the continuum from the conversive where language and story serve the ends of interpersonal connection to the discursive in which interpersonal interactions provide the means towards the ends of language, positionality, and information. While the rhetorical devices of connection combined with the symbolic, coded, and rhythmic languages of poetry and story are part of literatures worldwide (Foley 2002), the specific histories of conquest and colonization in the West have brought Native oral traditions into much closer convergence with creative writing in the work of the various Indigenous writers of North America. Let me delineate a number of the specific elements of Native American and Canadian literatures that evidence their respective tribal, métis, and pan-tribal oral cultures and traditions. An introduction to these oral elements as manifested in conversively informed writing is presented in my earlier volume *Contemporary American Indian Literatures and the Oral Tradition* (221–23).

Narrative and poetic structures

Native American literary works demonstrate many of the structural elements of oral storytelling that are constitutive of meaning, individual development and well-being, and community cohesiveness (Kroeber 19–26; Scheub 47–51). *Episodic structures* include different stories told in conjunction with each other. All of these episodes or stories are meaningfully interrelated, with each offering a pathway into subsequent and prior stories and vignettes. The listener or reader is invited and empowered to make and discern the complexity of meaning in this structuring. These structures are, accordingly, *associational* in that each part is meaningfully associated with each other part. In this sort of interwoven structure, meaning is understood through the unfolding tapestry of stories and vignettes that shed light on each other. To try to understand any one story or vignette in isolation would be to miss important interconnective links. This structure of *interconnectedness* and *interdependency* guides listener-readers in seeing the larger design. The larger story comes into being through each listener-reader's co-creative weaving together of the parts in various meaningful ways (Ruppert 134). Additionally, *framing devices*, often with traditional beginnings and endings interweave diverse stories into a larger coherence (Wiget 12).

While it is true that the storyteller places particular stories in literal proximity and thematic relevance with and to others, it is the listener-reader's interpretive effort that completes the storytelling circle and brings the stories to meaningful fruition. This is further manifested in the *sophisticated interweaving of diverse worlds, persons, places, and times* (including even the mythic and the historic, the real and the imagined, the extraordinary and the everyday). It is important to note that structure is central to a storytelling unfolding. The focus is rarely on a character, a place, or a time; the larger focus is on the interwoven story and its inter-relational meanings. *Open spacing* on the page, whether through poetic line and stanza breaks, open spacing within lines, or blank sections of pages create the open space of *silence* that in oral storytelling gives emphatic significance to what precedes and/or

FOLKLORE, STORYTELLING, AND ORAL TRADITION

succeeds moments of silence. The silence is also a conversive opening for the listener's reflective, interpretive, co-creative, and, at times, actual vocal response (Kroskrity 196).

Participation

The nature of a storytelling circle is such that each participant, whether storyteller or listener, is equally important to the development of the unfolding stories. Much like points on a circle, each person is a co-equal point on the circumference of the circle. The geometric image of a circle also demonstrates that every point on the circle is connected to every other point and that no one point achieves the sort of linear primacy that would be evident, say, in the three defining points of a semiotic triangle. Furthermore, in a circle, every point is crucial to the holism and completion of the circle. The absence of any one point breaks up the circle. As Silko explains in *Storyteller*, the coherence of the storytelling circle event is key because the storyteller's words are directly informed by his or her interactions with the listeners: "You must be very quiet and listen respectfully. Otherwise the storyteller might get upset and pout and not say another word all night" (254). This reflects the conversative nature of storytelling. Far from a monologic presentation, the ideal telling is intersubjectively respectful, holistically engaging, and collaboratively meaningful. Through *relational and experiential engagements* with language, participants gain potentially transformative understandings (Teuton xvi–xvii).

In traditional Indigenous storytelling, the *co-equal importance of every participant* involved is evidenced in the relationality that pervades the event. For example, in the ethnographic "autobiographies" and life-histories of Native people, the storyteller-informants go to great lengths to de-emphasize themselves so there is no primacy given to their persons nor their storytelling voice. Tewa/Hopi elder Albert Yava explains this regarding his stories that were ethnographically published as his life history:

> If I seem to say a lot about myself, it is really my times that I am thinking about. I am merely the person who happened to be there at a particular time. It is hard to put down something with myself as a center of interest – that is, to say I did this or that. It makes me out as important, which isn't the way I see it. We Tewas and Hopis don't think of ourselves that way.
>
> (Yava 4)

This *de-emphasis of the storyteller* also reinforces *the co-creative nature of storytelling*: that the story is not the product of the storyteller alone, but rather the collaborative effort of all involved in the story, including the characters in the story – whether fictional or actual, whether present during the storytelling event or not (Tedlock & Mannheim 9). Each person receives a respective degree of emphasis but primarily in terms of the *intersubjective relationality* and *interdependence* that brings together all persons participant in the story-world (storyteller, listeners, characters in the story), each with subjectivity, intentionality, and importance (Ortiz *Speaking* xiii; Zumthor 9). Each individual is primarily important, not in and of himself or herself but rather within relational terms (Simard 245). As part of the story, characters (human and nonhuman) are framed within tribal and indigenous terms of *relational senses of self* which can be seen linguistically in the Diné or Navajo language in which there is no abstract word for mother; instead there are applied referents that convey a people's relationships to their actual mothers (e.g., shima' for my mother, nihima' for our mother). Additionally the *minimalism* by which characters in the story are sketched further emphasizes their lack of primacy and the co-creative telling that requires completion through the interpretive contributions of listeners and listener-readers who flesh out the skeletal oral/written text into full story (Frey xiv, 153, 172).

Voice and diction

There are many strategies that storytellers use to assist listeners' participation in the story. Two of these are *voice shifts* that work to elicit increased listener connection to and participation in the story. Voice shifts to a *second person direct address* in which the storyteller speaks directly to the listeners provide a familiarizing communication in which the storyteller and the listener come into direct conversation with each other. Here the storyteller speaks directly to the listener "you" in a rhetorical conveyance that brings the listener directly into the story. Additional voice shifts with the equally inclusive *first person plural* "we" provides a rhetorical orientation in which the storyteller speaks for the listeners and the storyteller as a unified body; in this way, listeners are invited to join the storyteller within a common perceptual perspective (Blaeser 29). These and other voice shifts provide significant twists and turns in a developing story to bring listeners more closely into a story and, at other times, may represent a rhetorical distance and protective coding. This is especially common in stories told in multigenerational audiences where adult allusions are protectively coded and geared towards adults and away from children.

Such multigenerational storytelling also utilizes strategic word choices and images to convey stories in diverse ways and with simultaneous levels of meaning so that a story can be enjoyed, understood, and appreciated by all listeners even though aspects of meaning are not accessible to every listener in the same ways. The co-creative nature of storytelling manifests such strategic coding and richness of meaning even where one turn of phrase or included image is provided for select listeners. Diverse word choices are often used to assist in conveying meaning and providing connection. Such connective and *linking words, names, phrases, and even sounds* interrelate persons, situations, places, vignettes and stories in meaningful ways. Also *traditional storytelling words and phrases* ("They say ..." or "A long time ago ...") provide linguistic, tribal, and regional significations and contexts, such as the solemnity of historical tradition or mythic time (Kroskrity 195).

Articulation and indication

There are many rhetorical tools that Indigenous storytellers and writers use to articulate and indicate meaningful directives for their storylistener and listener-reader engagements with/in stories, poems, novels, and other forms of literary genre. William M. Clements's volume *Oratory in Native North America* presents historical records that document elements of rhetorical performance (2002). *Repetition* is commonly used by Native storytellers and writers. In fact, generations of ethnographers misunderstand the importance of this literary device, erroneously assuming that Native storytellers were confused in their retelling

FOLKLORE, STORYTELLING, AND ORAL TRADITION

of stories and vignettes, and then editing out the repetitions in presumptively factual, life-history ethnographies. But literary and oral storytelling is far more complex in its rhetorical directions than is the case for more straightforward texts. The device of repetition provides added emphasis and highlighted attention to whatever is being repeated. Also, the repetition of select terms, phrases, lines, vignettes, and stories provide meaningful opportunities for learning with deepened and different understandings that come from each repetition, especially when the repetition occurs within a different or related context. Analogous to the literary usage of repetition are the connective tools of *parallelism* and *chiasmus*. The *pacing* and *rhythms* of literary language serve the larger purposes of meaning, including the role played by silence and rhythmic openings for listener/reader response (Frey 21–22; Scheub 94–102).

The subtleties of oral and written literature are most commonly recognized in the various tools of figurative language. Native writers draw upon their tribal storytelling traditions as well as the traditions of written literature in their use of *symbolism*, *metaphor*, *metonymy*, *irony*, and *coding* (Blaeser 33; Scheub 23–29, 126–44; Beck & Walters 59–60). While individual storytellers and writers will embed signifying cues for their listeners and readers, distinctive in Native American literatures is the intersubjective recognition of the reader's crucial role in a story's creation. Accordingly, there is greater openness and *ambiguity* in the writing for reader-response (Simard 245). This connective empowerment of the reader utilizes the tool of *familiarization* with phrasing, allusions, and referents that help bring the world of the story or poem into the reader's own world. This contrasts with the Russian formalist concept of defamiliarization which works to make the familiar unfamiliar and, thereby, more literary. In the work of many Native writers, the converse is drawn upon as familiarization brings near and makes understandable the unfamiliar, such as the mythic, the ancient, the imagined, and the distant. Articulative concision and absence in the forms of *understatement*, *omission*, and *minimalism* with places, characters, situations de-emphasized, absented, or sketched rather than fleshed out further permit listeners' and listener-readers' participation in the co-creative aspects of Indigenous storytelling (Blaeser 32).

Community

The interactive and relational impetus central to Native storytelling traditions and their literary influence informs Native American literatures with a clear sense of the importance of the writing to the authors' respective tribal and other affiliative communities (Larson 53–54). Accordingly, many of the oral tools for interpersonal connection are drawn upon by Native writers, as their literary language reaches out to connect with their readers. *Humor* provides a lighthearted, and at times poignantly ironic, way to bring readers and those participant in a storytelling event together in empathic and emotional sharing (Frey 175). *Pauses* and *silence* are emphatically significant, but they are more deliberately used as tools for reader-response and reflective space for deepened understanding. *Situational familiarity* in which the storyteller brings the story into the listeners' and listener-readers' worlds to facilitate their entries into, and participation in, the story, along with specific *interpersonal references* that point to readers' own lives, provide additional connective strategies that bring participants together within the unfolding storyworld. A broadening *ecosystemic holism* where one's sense of community includes all creatures regardless of their

337

species, including the conveyance of interspecies personhood, communicates tribal world views that inclusively embrace diverse life forms within the storytelling world and, concomitantly, within each participant's own perception and life. Even marginal and trickster characters such as coyote or raven are depicted as integral members of the community and with their own value (Owens 29). In this way, *circles of inclusion* welcome all into the storytelling circle, including the efforts necessary to insure that all can follow, understand, and fully participate in the story. Many Native writers include glosses, notes, translations, and prose sections that provide added information to assist their readers' entries into and understandings of their literary work.

The extent to which tribal oral traditions are deliberative or residual in the work of specific Native writers varies from writer to writer. For example, writers who speak their tribal languages infuse the rhythms and elements of those languages more directly into their written work. This being said, virtually all Native writers are participative in Indigenous communities (tribal, reservation, urban, pan-tribal), are familiar with Indigenous rhythms and traditional stories to varying degrees, and draw upon Indigenous elements as relevant to their writing. For example, regarding Gerald Vizenor's creative writing, Kimberly M. Blaeser points to the "multidirectional referential quality of oral tradition, the dialogic nature that forms and sustains community, and the vitality of oral culture" (29). Native American and Canadian First Nations writers demonstrate how literary work can be meaningfully informed by and connected to ancestral traditions and communities (whether genetic, tribal, or otherwise affiliative). This chapter provides an introductory grammar or primer for the range of oral storytelling tools that are drawn upon and utilized by Native writers in their poetry, prose, drama, and other literary work. The colonialist imperatives of Manifest Destiny worldwide sought to impose strict western literary structures and directives upon a world that was becoming increasingly literate. Native writers in the United States and Canada have worked to resist such colonialist strictures and divisions by producing richly complex, intricately inclusive, rhetorically innovative, and radically Indigenous literary work.

Works cited

Attinasi, John & Paul Friedrich. "Dialogic Breakthrough: Catalysis and Synthesis in Life-Changing Dialogue." *The Dialogic Emergence of Culture*. Ed. Dennis Tedlock & Bruce Mannheim. Urbana: University of Illinois Press, 1995. 33–53.

Beck, Peggy V. & Anna Lee Walters. *The Sacred: Ways of Knowledge, Sources of Life*. Tsaile, AZ: Navajo Community Press, 1992.

Blaeser, Kimberly M. *Gerald Vizenor: Writing in the Oral Tradition*. Norman: University of Oklahoma Press, 1996.

Bowers, C. A. *Educating for an Ecologically Sustainable Culture: Rethinking Moral Education, Creativity, Intelligence, and Other Modern Orthodoxies*. Albany: State University of New York Press, 1995.

Brill de Ramírez, Susan Berry. *Contemporary American Indian Literatures and the Oral Tradition*. Tucson: University of Arizona Press, 1999.

Clements, William M. *Oratory in Native North America*. Tucson: University of Arizona Press, 2002.

Foley, John Miles. *How to Read an Oral Poem*. Urbana: University of Illinois Press, 2002.

Frey, Rodney, ed. *Stories that Make the World*. Norman: University of Oklahoma Press, 1995.

Kroeber, Karl. *Retelling/Rereading*. New Brunswick, NJ: Rutgers University Press, 1992.

FOLKLORE, STORYTELLING, AND ORAL TRADITION

Kroskrity, Paul V. "Growing with Stories: Line, Verse, and Genre in an Arizona Tewa Text." *Journal of Anthropological Research* 41. 2 (1985): 183–99.

Larson, Sidner. "Native American Aesthetics: An Attitude of Relationship." *MELUS* 17. 3 (1991–1992): 53–67.

Ortiz, Simon J. "Always the Stories." *Coyote Was Here: Essays on Contemporary Native American Literary and Political Mobilization*. Ed. Bo Schöler. Aarhus, Denmark: SEKLOS, 1984. 57–69.

——, ed. *Speaking for the Generations*. Tucson: University of Arizona Press, 1998.

——. *Woven Stone*. Tucson: University of Arizona Press, 1992.

Owens, Louis. *Other Destinies: Understanding the American Indian Novel*. Norman: University of Oklahoma Press, 1992.

Ruppert, James. *Mediation in Contemporary Native American Fiction*. Norman: University of Oklahoma Press, 1995.

Scheub, Harold. *Story*. Madison: University of Wisconsin Press, 1998.

Shklovsky, Viktor. "Art as Technique." *Russian Formalist Criticism: Four Essays*. Ed. Lee T. Lemon & Marion J. Reiss. Lincoln: University of Nebraska Press, 1965. 3–24.

Silko, Leslie Marmon. *Ceremony*. New York: Penguin, 1977.

——. *Gardens in the Dunes*. New York: Simon & Schuster, 2000.

——. *Storyteller*. New York: Arcade, 1981.

Simard, Rodney. "American Indian Literatures, Authenticity, and the Canon." *World Literature Today* 66. 2 (1992): 243–48.

Tedlock, Dennis. *The Spoken Word and the Work of Interpretation*. Philadelphia: University of Pennsylvania, 1983.

Tedlock, Dennis & Bruce Mannheim, eds. *The Dialogic Emergence of Culture*. Urbana: University of Illinois Press, 1995.

Teuton, Christopher B. *Deep Water: The Textual Continuum in American Indian Literature*. Lincoln: University of Nebraska Press, 2010.

Wiget, Andrew. "Native American Oral Literatures: A Critical Orientation." *Dictionary of Native American Literature*. Ed. Andrew Wiget. New York: Garland, 1994. 3–18.

Wilson, Michael D. *Writing Home: Indigenous Narratives of Resistance*. East Lansing: University of Michigan Press, 2008.

Yava, Albert. *Big Falling Snow: A Tewa-Hopi Indian's Life and Times and the History and Traditions of His People*. Ed. Harold Courlander. 1978. Rpt. Albuquerque: University of New Mexico Press, 1992.

Zepeda, Ofelia. *Ocean Power*. Tucson: University of Arizona Press, 1995.

Zumthor, Paul. *Oral Poetry: An Introduction*. Minneapolis: University of Minnesota Press, 1990.

29

Spinning the Binary

Visual Cultures and Literary Aesthetics

David Stirrup

In his multimedia study of the political aesthetics of Native American visual, cinematic, and literary arts, Dean Rader notes the peculiar absence "in the already-meager discourse about Native public art" of its "first forms" such as "petroglyphs, pictographs, and geoglyphs" (*Engaged Resistance* 204). Acknowledging debates over the "meaning" of such forms, and illuminating, as he does elsewhere, the strikingly diverse generic (and cross-genre) range of visual-verbal art forms in North America, which would also include such "textual" objects and structures as baskets, beaded moccasins and tunics, medallions, hide coverings, mounds, and more (see also "Reading the Visual") he nevertheless avows "that one of the functions of this early symbolic action was to express something specific about a culture and a place" (*Engaged Resistance* 204). Rader's observation is acute as well as intriguing, not least because it belies decades of debate in archaeology, anthropology, (art) history, and, more recently, literary studies, as to exactly what *form* such expression represents. These debates, which are centered most squarely on distinctions between "rock art" and "picture-writing," between, in other words, aesthetic practice ("designs and figures") and the graphic representation of speech acts, can perhaps best be represented in their polarization by two fairly insistent claims. On the one hand, Birgit Brander Rasmussen has recently asserted that "Contrary to common belief, the confrontation between European and indigenous people in the Americas was often a clash between literate cultures" (2–3). For Gordon Brotherston "jejune Western pronouncements on what does and does not constitute script, and the categorical binary that separates oral from written, have proved especially inept when applied to the wealth of literary media in native America" (4).

John DeFrancis, on the other hand, in pursuit of a universal framework (a "diverse oneness") in which to situate the Chinese logogram, condemns too open a definition of what constitutes writing, reiterating the truism that "isolated Indian pictographs communicate only as much as such limited symbolizations as heraldic insignia placed on coats of arms, the male-female figures seen on restroom doors, and 'No Left Turn' or 'Steep Incline' warnings pictured on highway signs" (35). Yet he evaluates only the extensive early nineteenth-century documentation of pictography by Henry Rowe Schoolcraft and Garrick Mallery. There is no sense, in other words, of consultation with Indigenous intellectuals, or rigorous examination of the pictograph's mnemonic, social, or relational function. Drawing conclusions about the limitations of the form in this fashion, then, DeFrancis arguably evokes the colonizing logics against which Daniel Heath Justice warns where he writes: "In discussing diverse Indigenous textualities and writing systems, there is danger in inadvertently locating non- or extra-alphabetic texts in an evolutionary trajectory by which the 'alternative' textualities are those that are illegible to a mainstream audience" (302). DeFrancis's insistence that pictographic writing is not *writing* (35) and that it neither does nor could constitute a full system of writing (47) does not then preclude its status as alternative (or parallel) literacy. Nor does it negate the self-evident fact that the existence of the considerable wealth of texts inscribed on bone, stone, bark, hide, and more, which also give rise to new forms as alternative technologies emerge, exposes a fundamental flaw in conventional histories of the "book" in North America (see Warkentin for an excellent discussion of this question in a Canadian context). This chapter will explore some of the ways in which contemporary Native authors engage and employ those "first forms of indigenous public art," and how those first forms feed a visual aesthetic that develops into a broader engagement with the visual arts.

Within Native literary studies, then, there is a gathering conversation around what Elisabeth Hill Boone and Walter Mignolo call the "alternative literacies" of Native North America (see Rasmussen; Sinclair & Cariou; Kelsey *Tribal Theory*; Low). In much of the conversation to date, connections between visual and literary media have been wrought in order to explore and examine the relationship between text and image in specifically Indigenous Studies (as opposed to conventional art historical) terms (see Cummings). The emphasis of this work has tended so far to fall on the use of text by visual artists, with some small reflection on those literary artists who make use of visual images in their work (see Bernardin "Seeing Memory"; Kelsey *Reading the Wampum*; Rader "Reading the Visual"). Yet a brief survey of literary production in North America reveals a striking prevalence of both literal and metaphoric use of these alternative literacies, both manifest as such and for their contribution to the visual cultures of the continent. That relationship, as Christopher Teuton points out in *Deep Waters: The Textual Continuum in Native American Literature*, is neither arbitrary nor simply aesthetic, but rather bridges the perceived binary, long troubled by Native literary studies, of oral and written (see also Noodin; Stirrup). That so-called divide connotes the ruptures of the colonial moment, deeply embedded as it is in what James Cox and Daniel Heath Justice see as a now outmoded concern with "identity, authenticity, hybridity, and cultural mediation" (1). Furthermore, for Justice, it represents a wider

> cultural investment in the idea of Indigenous peoples being consigned to the realm of the oral, as such a move conveniently, perhaps cynically, locates Indigenous knowledge outside of the sphere of legitimized cultural capital and thus relegates Indigenous intellectual and creative productions to the realm of fanciful prehistory.
>
> ("Indigenous Writing" 293)

In an immediately "productive" sense, for Rader, "One might argue that Native artists combine text and image in order to replicate the immersive experience of oratory and the visual experience of ritual and performance" ("Reading the Visual" 300), and to invoke the often expressive function of visual materials more broadly. The obvious counter to DeFrancis's isolating interpretation of the function of individual pictographs, that immersive experience constitutes what Matt Cohen calls the "broader world of meaning-making," which "usually involved a complex set of symbols and stories that depended upon many kinds of inscription and performance for their meaning" (309). At the levels, then, of both aesthetic experience and ethical concern, the blurring and erasing of conventionally held generic boundaries between the "visual" and "literary" cultures of Native North America both contribute to and draw from the legacy of the long tradition of "the sign system of text-images," as Denise Low-Weso puts it, that "sustain Indigenous sovereignty" (Low 84–85). Beyond the mnemonic function of such sign systems, understanding of the integration of image- and mark-making into dream and visionary traditions, as well as the sign-making, map-making, and historiographic purview of graphic, visual recording systems has remained relatively under-examined. When examined, as Rasmussen notes in this volume, it has tended to be looked at with too rigid a sense of genre and medium.

Among those who in recent years have begun illuminating these lines of connection, Louise Erdrich wrote in her 2004 memoir *Books and Islands in Ojibwe Country* that "these islands, which I long to read, are books in themselves":

> *Mazina'iganan* is the word for "books" in Ojibwemowin or Anishinabemowin, and *mazinapikiniganan* is the word for 'rock paintings'. ... The Ojibwe had been using the word *mazinibaganjigan* for years to describe dental pictographs made on birchbark, perhaps the first books made in North America ... People have probably been writing books in North America since at least 2000 B.C. Or painting islands.
> (5, emphasis in the original)

Writing of the painted rocks at Lake of the Woods, Erdrich's apparently expansive definition of writing – one that explicitly refuses conventional distinctions between the visual and the literary arts (*writing* books, *painting* islands) – is picked up by Lisa Brooks in *The Common Pot*, where she relates Erdrich's explanation that "The Ojibwe people ... synthesized the oral and written tradition by keeping mnemonic scrolls of inscribed birchbark" (*Books and Islands* 10–11) to other traditions and understandings of the graphic arts: "For Abenakis, as well as for Mayans, Mixtecs, and Ojibwes, writing and drawing are both forms of image making" (Brooks, xxi). "Native writers," she continues, "spin the binary between word and image" (xxi).

The logical extension of these connections – for Brooks, for Craig Womack on whom she draws, and for others – is the establishing of a framework of understanding of literacies and visual languages that precede, survive, and transcend the colonial erasure of Indigenous texts, the imposition of alphabetic text, and the intellectual denial of older practices in inherited taxonomies. Several essays in this volume, indeed, invest in these arguments to varying degrees, testifying to its gathering momentum in the field. This chapter will not go so far as to continue the explication of image *as* text, focusing instead on the interaction between images and texts – on the visual cultures of Native literary production – but there are two discursive contexts worth outlining in wrapping up this section. The first, clear in Brooks's analysis, is demonstrated in Niigaanwewidam James Sinclair's introduction to *Manitowapow* where he relates literary form to the land in terms that are intrinsic to the relational praxis of Indigenous knowledges: "Systems of writing have been used in Manitowapow since time immemorial. Often employed alongside oral traditions, these texts record interactions among people and express connections to animals, spirit beings, and other creatures" (7), while the images painted on rocks "represent the complex ecological and spiritual systems embedded in particular places" (8). Beyond any question of Indigenous aesthetics, then, the relationship between visual languages and parallel Indigenous literacies also addresses the ethics of decolonization – of Indigenous presence in, marks on, and reading through particular environments. This is not to infer a static or immobile (in both time and space) notion of indigeneity, but to relate contemporary conceptions and representations of Indigenous sovereignty to those embedded practices. The second discursive context, then, also of decolonizing significance, relates those painted rocks to the politics of writing per se. In "bush/writing" Peter Kulchyski writes of the "teaching rocks" of Peterborough, Ontario that when "assimilate[d]" to "the category of literature" "retain a stronger destabilizing power" (262) relative to what he calls "the writing of the state" to which Indigenous peoples are asked to surrender. Inquiring what it means to call that which has "been compared to visual art" *literature*, in order to call up its power "to disturb the very being of literature," he asks "what kind of literature inscribes itself on rock?" (262).

To think about the visual in relation to the literature of Native North America, then, is to engage with both this rich visual archive and the relational, ethical, and decolonial practices that are intimately connected with it. Active articulations of the relationship between narrative (both spoken and written) and visual art forms in contemporary Native literature go at least as far back as the moment Kenneth Lincoln designated the "Renaissance" in Native American Literature. Writing of an exchange between Kiowa author N. Scott Momaday and Gus Blaisdell at the University of New Mexico Press prior to the publication of *The Way to Rainy Mountain*, Kenneth Lincoln cites Momaday's terse response to the suggestion of a third party reader. The suggestion concerns the syntax governing Momaday's description of the sight of a cricket, perched on a handrail, framed against the moon. The viewer's proximity to the cricket, and the trick of perspective, render the tiny creature proportionate to its lunar ground. In a letter to Blaisdell, Lincoln reports:

> Momaday replied simply: "Leave it alone. You don't seem to realize (as of course X doesn't) that this is one of the great images in our literature. If you lay a hand on it, I will cut your heart out." Momaday explained further, "I give some thought to what I write; I consider the alternatives. In every detail, this image is exactly what I want."
>
> (Lincoln 104)

As many commentators have noted, that same image is then represented visually in Al Momaday's line-drawing on the following page (see Teuton and Bernardin among others). Representative of "landmarks, icons, that indicate the right way … signs on a path" (Rader "Reading the Visual" 302), Momaday's response to Blaisdell also gestures to a number of other aspects. On the one hand, it expresses a kind of literary visual sovereignty, in the author's resistance to alteration of "one of the great images of our literature." Evocative of the relational aspect of traditional storytelling, this makes an obvious claim for an understanding of the oral archive *as* literature. Yet that "our" is deliberately ambiguous in the context of Momaday's emergence on the literary scene as both a self-identifying Native American writer and an arch proponent of high modernist technique. He lays claim here, then, to both *the image itself* and to formal imagism and, in doing so, to both the living oral literary archive and its fundamental centrality to what Craig Womack will later insist on as the inverse understanding of the American canon: "tribal literatures are not some branch waiting to be grafted onto the main trunk. Tribal literatures are the *tree*" (6–7). In this formative exchange, then, we note several of the particular intellectual, ethical, and aesthetic histories to which the visual-verbal relationship attends.

To be sure, Momaday's second book is probably the most high profile of a number of such composites, but it is by no means an isolated phenomenon, nor was it the first. Among Gerald Vizenor's early poetic output, his retranslations of Frances Densmore's transcriptions of Anishinaabe dreamsongs were notable on the one hand for his interspersal of "pictomyths" with his re-expressions and on the other for initiating his career-long articulation of the significance of the visual and material practices of the Anishinaabe to their oral and visionary tradition (and, of course, vice versa). Vizenor's fourth publication, *Summer in the Spring: Anishinaabe Lyric Poems and Stories* (1965), which, as Adam Spry explains was re-edited several times over the final four decades of the twentieth century, includes a range of representations of pictographs first published in Densmore's *Chippewa Music* and W. J. Hoffman's *The Mide'wiwin or 'Grand Medicine Society' of the Ojibway*. Always designated "pictomyths" by Vizenor, "The *anishinaabe* drew pictures of their dream songs, visions, stories, and ideas on birchbark" (*Summer* 11, original emphasis). Lending a sense of material, performative vitality to the literary rendering of oral songs and stories, the interplay between text and images "emphasizes the values of the oral language rather than a total imposition of the philosophies of grammar and translation" (20).

Such visual-verbal experimentation was also occurring north of the colonial border, in a slightly different way. In 1970, the year after Momaday was awarded his Pulitzer Prize, Shoshone-Cree-Salish poet and painter Sock-a-jaw-wu, or Marion Sarain Stump published *There is My People Sleeping*, a product of his "overtly visual poetic depictions" (McKenzie 79). Stump, who moved to Alberta from the United States in the mid-60s, working as a rancher, as an art instructor at the Saskatchewan Indian Cultural Centre, and as an actor, exhibiting his paintings and working on his first book (Armstrong & Grauer 80). Influenced by an earlier generation of artists of the U.S. southwest, as well as contemporaries from Native art schools such as Santa Fe alongside select European artists, and drawing a direct correlation between image and text, Stump described, according to Stephanie McKenzie, "a fully formed pictographic tradition and how this concrete system serves as the basis for his poetic artistry" (79). McKenzie pairs Stump's text with Marty Dunn's *Red on White: The Biography of Duke Redbird*, but she notes "the disproportionate number of works from the [Native Canadian] Renaissance which include images" (79). Stump's endeavor stands out in its milieu precisely because it is a creative production, albeit the text is minimal and highly fragmented. Nevertheless, significant editions of traditional stories preceded it in Canada at this time and also were illustrated. These include works by artist-writers who were also deeply invested in pictographic traditions, such as George Clutesi's *Son of Raven, Son of Deer* (1967), illustrated by Clutesi himself and Norval Morriseau's self-illustrated *Legends of My People: the Great Ojibway* (1965). In Morriseau's case, the relationship between word and image, and the spiritual nature of his material – the revelation of which was objected to by some of his nation – offers perhaps the most explicit correlation between the twentieth-century image text and its older precursors.

The interweaving of visual and verbal, then, describes an aesthetic that, by no means universal, might nevertheless be said to offer common ground in an ethics of seeing and storying experience that embraces polyvalency and resists the absolute primacy of any one form. It persists in fairly direct illustrative terms, such as in the collaborations between Anishinaabe poet Mark Turcotte and his wife Kathleen Presnell (*Songs of Our Ancestors*

[1995], *The Feathered Heart* [1995], and more), or in Peter Blue Cloud's (Aroniawenrate) comical accompaniments to his own *Elderberry Flute Song: Contemporary Coyote Tales* (1982); and in more complex, dialogic expression in, for example, Alexie's *Old Shirts and New Skins* (1993; illustrated by Elizabeth Woody). Or the deft interplay both through word and photograph, of poetry and clay figure in Nora Noranjo-Morse's *Mud Woman: Poems from the Clay* (1992). That these texts are re-emerging in discussions that attend precisely to the interpenetration of movement and meaning between picture and text, is perhaps testament to several factors, but there are three that are relatively self-evident: the first speaks to the extraordinary range (and powerful political implications) of decolonial articulations of Indigenous sovereignty. Although critical challenges to the territorially bound (and therefore colonially implicated) nature of sovereignty as understood in relation to the nation state arguably find their champion in Vine Deloria Jr., it was in the early 1990s, with Robert Warrior's examination of Deloria and Warrior's call to recognize the intellectual sovereignty of Native-centered historiography that those bounded notions began truly to unravel (*Tribal Secrets*). In a similar move, art and film scholars such as Jolene Rickard and Michelle Raheja have turned to questions of *visual* sovereignty within their respective fields, questions that perhaps underlie much of the inquiry into the image text, and certainly offer means of understanding that interaction as more than simply the semiotic encoding of the marketing of "Indianness." The second context is simply the burgeoning of Native owned-and-developed visual media, which would include the ever-increasing exposure of Indigenous film and television media, along with other media such as digital and graphic media.

Thirdly, but by no means finally, the rise to prominence of increasing numbers of exciting visual artists working variously and to different ends with narrative, text, Indigenous sign systems and decorative motifs, popular cultural narratives and symbols, and decolonizing methodologies related to "colonial" documents such as maps, treaties, ID cards, street signs, and so on, and the embrace by literary scholars of the intersections between visual and textual forms promises to continue in its significance. Thus, artists such as Nadia Myre, Andrea Carlson, Christi Belcourtt, Jeffrey Veregge, America Meredith, Hulleah Tsinhnahjinnie, and Rickard herself, join other internationally renowned artists such as Hock E Aye Vi Edgar Heap of Birds, Jaune Quick-To-See-Smith, George Longfish and others in the critical purview of literary scholars as well as scholars of the visual arts (see Rader; McGlennan). In a similar vein, the heightened visibility of Indigenous texts that relate not only to cultural identification but, explicitly, to political and diplomatic understandings, texts such as those represented by Haudenosaunee wampum belts, provides a meeting point between text (in all its possibilities) and image in the work of many Haudenosaunee visual artists, including Alan Michelson, Shelley Niro, Greg Hill, G. Peter Jemison, Joey David, and, of course, most pertinently in this context, the "innovative mash-ups" (Rader "Reading the Visual" 308) of Eric Gansworth.

Gansworth's interplay of image and text – sometimes an organizing metaphor, such as in *Nickel Eclipse* (2001) – is often more theoretically searching, such that, as Bernardin argues, "Gansworth's aesthetic collaboration of text and image reaffirms foundational Haudenosaunee ways of knowing aimed at ensuring survival" ("Seeing" 178). Gansworth's work is also worth pausing on briefly for its insight into visual culture of another kind. In her introduction to *Visualities: Perspectives on Contemporary American Indian Film and Art*, Denise K. Cummings notes that "visuality concerns the field of vision as a site of power and social control" (xiv). While, for Mirzoeff – the image, and control of the image – paradoxically, becomes the means by which people as objects are "blinded" in the hierarchy of Imperial visuality, it also becomes a significant means of resistance and the reappropriation of autonomy. Central to this dynamic, the question of who controls the images and what those images are can be seen to be central to the dialogue between text and image. We need think only of such iconic images as the various portraits of Pocahontas/Matoake/Amunate/Rebecca Rolfe, Benjamin West's *The Death of General Wolfe*, or John Vanderlyn's *The Death of Jane McRea* to glimpse the legacy of the visual rhetorics of empire; that it is precisely through such images, the highly visual literary portrayals of *"indians"* by authors such as James Fenimore Cooper, and, of course, the visuality of the Wild West Show and the cinematic Western, that popular perceptions of who (and what) Native peoples are illuminates the dominance of images over the realities of lived experience. Writers such as Gansworth, along with many other contemporary writers, artists, and filmmakers, though by no means bound in a one-dimensional tussle with the colonial legacy, construct a form of countervisuality that entirely disrupts and displaces the singular identities placed on Native people through popular (mis)representation. This functions in a figurative sense in Gansworth's work, through his "densely cross-pollinated iconography of Haudenosaunee stories and referents drawn from popular culture and music," (Bernardin "Seeing" 178), as well as European art conventions and artists. It also functions in a more literal sense, in a novel such as *Mending Skins* (2005), featuring the Seventh Annual Conference of the Society for Protection and Reclamation of Indian Images, kitsch-Indian obsessed art historian Annie Boans (daughter of the intimidating Tuscarora woman, Shirley Mounter), and a comical-yet-nuanced examination of the internalization of and internal conflict over popular cultural stereotypes of Indianness.

In a somewhat different, but no less powerful production, Heid Erdrich's video poem "Pre-Occupied" similarly employs a range of popular and iconic imagery, including Langston Hughes' rivers (from "The Negro Speaks of Rivers"), maps, the Occupy Movement, PopArt, a superman cartoon, stereotypes of Native Americans, environmental devastation, and much more, along with Indigenous iconography in the form of the spiral. The extended video ends with a version of John Lennon's famous song "Imagine" ("G'pkwenmaag Noongwa"), translated into Anishinaabemowin by Howard Kimewon and Margaret Noodin (credited as Noori), and sung by Noodin. This video captures and recalibrates the Occupy movement in relation to historical acts of occupation and oppression. In doing so, it examines questions of land occupancy and ownership, rights versus responsibility, popular vernaculars of heroism, and the competing countervisualities of Occupy and Indigenous sovereignty movements. Insofar as the countervisual is about the attempt to change the perceived "real" in which it takes place, the video poem becomes a means of re-presenting Occupy as an inheritor of the logic of imperial visuality, revealing the disparity between an Indigenous "real" and the biopolitical spaces and capitalist rhetorics within which Settler Colonialism operates.

While "Pre-Occupied" captures the vitality of contemporary Indigenous protest through the adaptation of old forms to new technologies, it returns us to a very different, but no less "resistant" form at the end of the nineteenth century. Ledger art as it developed in the nineteenth century (particularly after the imprisonment of warriors at Fort Marion, Florida) has a well-charted connection back to Plains graphic traditions (see Keyser), maintaining and in some ways developing the narrative forms of pictorial art associated with inscription on bark and painting on stone and hide. That latter pictographic tradition – frequently designated a "supplement" (whether "dangerous" or not remains unspecified) to the oral tradition (Hail xv) – found its expression among incarcerated warriors using colored pencils and used ledger books. Denise Low-Weso ascribes the winter count – often spiraling pictographic accounts of historic events – to this same tradition, insisting that "As my students and I have encountered these sign-texts, European categories collapse. The images assert a legitimate alternative literacy" (Low 85). The sense of resistance to imposition is multiple in that notion. The ledger drawings themselves sustained individual agency and Indigenous sovereignty through that final period of containment; they defiantly combined traditional techniques with contemporary materials such that practitioners created the palimpsestic ground of a "space of foreign calculations, thereby transforming the nature of their own drawing and the ledger book itself, creating a middle place, an in-between place, in a place of writing" (Blume 40); and we might, then, re-introduce Kulchyski's question here, and ask what kind of literature – and therefore what kind of destabilizing power – such creations represent in direct relation to the structural (state) forms of literacy the ledger books and the fort-prisons invoke.

Ledger art, of course, persists in a variety of forms from the relatively straight contemporary iterations of the historic form represented by Dolores Purdy Corcoran, Terence Guardipee or Linda Haukaas, to the often more playful work of Dwayne Wilcox and especially Dallin Maybee. Beyond those representative practices, though, Low-Weso points out that ledger art texts "inform contemporary writers' history and methods. They are vehicles of continuity, following historic and personal narratives into the present time" (Low 84). In particular, she picks out James Welch's *Fool's Crow* for its recounting of "events that are in the Newberry ledger book" (84–85), but other examples spring to mind. Lance Henson's poetry collection *A Cheyenne Sketchbook* (1985) evokes the form in its title alone, while Diane Glancy's *Lone Dog's Winter Count* (1991) more explicitly claims continuity to "this idea of commemoration[, w]ith contemporary pictographs in the form of poems" (jacket blurb).

The literalness of that latter claim does a disservice to the rich complexity of Glancy's poetry here – not because pictography itself cannot be complex, but because the blurb infers a kind of ekphrastic representation of the visual form that the poems do not simply (or simplistically) serve up. Instead, they evoke the full relational and processual nature of the multiform tradition in which the winter count performs. "The tribe waits for the voice of Lone Dog to pierce the silence," one triplet in "Lone Dog's Winter Count" begins; "to father thought/like children running into their heads" (13). The relationship between the act of recording and the document as utterance; the generalized audience and the select voice reading-remembering; and the temporal flow forwards and backwards across generations that the poems invoke, speak to survivance, even as individual poems contrast the desire to draw with the violence of writing as instructed in residential schools ("The First Reader: Santee Training School, 1873"), or navigate the psychic and even epistemological ground, shifting in the sudden changes of the late nineteenth-century Plains ("Portrait of Lone Dog"). The appropriative gesture of Glancy's subject – she is of Cherokee descent, while Lone Dog's Winter Count is a Yanktonais Nakota text – is not isolated with regard to the Plains tradition. Indeed, over many years, ledger art in particular has engrossed and at times aesthetically motivated the aforementioned Gerald Vizenor.

While for a writer like Leslie Marmon Silko, whose well-known evocations of Sand Painting in *Ceremony*, entwine that nation- and geographically specific form into a polyphonic narrative of healing, in which *all* immediately available cultural material is potentially the stuff of ceremony, Vizenor reaches next door, as it were, to the vital *motion* of the Plains pictographic tradition to complement his already extensive engagement with the practices of the Anishinaabeg.

> The warriors and their horses are pictured in motion, the artistic transmotion of native sovereignty. The scenes and motion were of memories and consciousness … The transmotion of ledger art is a creative connection to the motion of horses depicted in winter counts and heraldic hide paintings … . Native transmotion is seen in the raised hooves of horses, the voice lines, traces of arrows, the curve of feathers, footprints, and the trail of buffalo blood in a hunt.
>
> *(Fugitive Poses* 179)

The active, dynamic, and visionary presence of the visual motif here – not only a *picture* but lines, traces, curves, prints, trails, *marks* of narrative and markers of sovereignty – echoes, Low-Weso suggests, the obviative (fourth person) presence Vizenor identifies in oral testimony. As such, she writes, "The 'presence' is the body of tradition that, in the ledger texts, interacts with image-texts" (Low 85). The transcendent (and transient) qualities implicit in this (trans)motion are present elsewhere in Vizenor's work, such as in his haiku, as in the haiku of fellow Anishinaabeg poets Gordon Henry Jr. and Kimberly Blaeser, all three of them evoking the dreamsong in forms at once visionary and imagistic. Henry, too, creates artists like his "Prisoner of Haiku" Elijah Cold Crow (*The Light People*, 1994), for whom the evocation of cultural motifs and foundational stories in the smoke of his arson attacks against federal buildings similarly (though perhaps more provocatively!) combines signifiers of visual (artistic) practices and ceremonial forms with literary resistance.

The aesthetic gestures of Vizenor's investment in ledger art circulate more widely still, of course, through the figure of the blue horse. "Howling Wolf," he writes, "created blue, red, and green horses, the transmotion of memories as a political prisoner. He painted his bright horses several years before the birth of the artist Franz Marc" (*Fugitive Poses* 179). And yet the German expressionist, like his "native expressionist" forebear, "painted many animals in several colors; his most notable creations are sensuous horses in rich chromatic hues of blue, the spiritual tease of blue horses" (*Fugitive Poses* 179). Vizenor artfully explores these connections with Marc and other members of the early modernist collective Der Blaue Reiter in novels like *Shrouds of White Earth* (2010) and in poems such as "Blue Horses." The poem begins:

> painted horses
> prison riders
> by morning
> blue in the canyons
> green and brown
> western posts
> forever mounted
> in ledger art
>
> *(Almost Ashore* 25)

Simultaneously pointing to the creative liberation encapsulated by the horses, the transcendent blue that shimmers medicinally on the edge of possibility throughout Vizenor's work, and the image of restraint and containment (the posts, the double meaning of "mounted") from which they tirelessly move, the poem comments on the ironic juxtaposition of prison art with the commercialization of the form that was to follow, as the "prison riders" are "crowned by museums" and "old world curators" who "envy the race/primitive art/and native liberty." In that process, however, Vizenor reveals another liberation as the "ledger mounts" – literally mounted and framed, no longer vital and medicinal in the battlefield books of their creators – "ride again/with franz marc/chagall/kandinsky/and quick to see." Leaving the riders outriding the processes of nomenclature and classification that seek – and Vizenor provocatively identifies envy as the cause – to fix the images and their creators in a static museum moment, indeed to write the Native subject out all together, the final stanza stresses the transformational aspect of transmotion, understanding the process as reciprocal, seeing the motifs in ledger art and its traditional precursors as transcending ethnic or cultural boundaries, and as possessing their own life. That life brings Howling Wolf and the contemporary Salish-Kootenai artist Jaune Quick-to-See Smith into contact with non-Native artists – clearly connecting the animal leitmotifs in the primitivist and spiritual enthusiasms of Der Blaue Reiter artists and the folk-art influence and heavy symbolism of Chagall's work, to a dynamic, possibly dialectical, and indigenous-centered (rather than European-framed) continuum. Indeed, in his discussion of "Native Cosmototemic Art," which ranges from the caves at Lascaux to European modernism to contemporary Native painters, Vizenor writes "There are no direct traditions or evolution of art, of course, but the scenes of natural motion and the elements of artistic perception and dimension were obvious connections between some ancient rock art and innovative painters" (46).

The direct engagement of artists is by no means unique to Vizenor. Chagall makes an appearance among other Native and non-Native luminaries in Gansworth's *Nickel Eclipse*, while Louise Erdrich treats the murals of Mexican artist Clemente Orozco in poetic form ("Orozco's Christ," for instance, appears in her second book of poetry, *Baptism of Desire*; his *The Epic of American Civilization* is displayed in the Baker Memorial Library at her alma mater, Dartmouth College) and the "*indian*" painter George Catlin himself in prose (*Shadow Tag*). Erdrich, in fact, features artists – and art forms – in several of her books: painting in *Shadow Tag*, sculpture in *The Painted Drum*, beading in *The Antelope Wife* and *Four Souls*, the dreamt design for the skin of a drum in *The Painted Drum*, and more. A mixture of Native and non-Native, and performing signifying or theoretical functions in terms of cultural reclamation, spiritual awakening, political resistance, and more, the visual contributes significantly and regularly to Erdrich's literary aesthetic. Cherokee author Thomas King also deploys an artist – Monroe Swimmer – in his 1999 novel, *Truth and Bright Water*. There, Swimmer engages in various strategies designed, quite literally, to paint out the impositions of the colonial world. Beginning by painting Natives back in to (restoring) museum-held landscapes, Swimmer takes his work to an even more literal level in his pursuit of reversing the colonial erasure of Indigenous peoples and spaces by painting out a church that sits like the heaving prow of a ship overlooking the Canada–U.S. border in the Canadian Prairies.

If King's character works on the land painting out the markers of colonial imposition, Vizenor's latest novel, *Blue Ravens*, sets about storying Indigenous presence in the Twin

Cities and Paris, France and throughout the French theatre of World War I. While one brother, Basile Hudson Beaulieu, writes and narrates their travels, Aloysius Beaulieu, inscribes his totemic blue ravens on the surfaces of the urban landscapes they move through. Throughout his work, Vizenor stresses the visual in the verbal, using such coinages as "word cinemas" to describe the visual-oral-performative (if not-quite anti-writing) bent of his poetics, generating a clear sense of both his imagistic allegiances *and* his aesthetic rooting in the ethical affiliations of the pictographic tradition. There is an echo of this in the work of another octogenarian author of great renown. Writing of Mohawk poet Maurice Kenny's 1992 *Tekonwatonti/Molly Brant 1735–1795: Poems of War*, for instance, Lisa Brooks writes:

> In Kenny's work [the] craft of creating "word-pictures" in place is rooted both in modernist imagism and Indigenous pictographic writing. Kenny, like his heroine Aliquippa, seeks neither "honor nor loot" but "only to write/on the rock, paint color for the grandchildren."
>
> ("Painting" 112)

Writing on the rock, writing on the page, forming what Brooks calls a "glyphic representation" in words that conjure images to displace and re-place: image and text, verbal and visual; and integrated whole rather than a category divide, that unsettles the heavy burden of text in favor of a relational aesthetic that simultaneously evokes ways of seeing alongside ways of reading, and a relational ethic that foregrounds the power and the pressure of making marks on surfaces, whether they be letters, images, or both.

Works cited

Alexie, Sherman. *Old Shirts & New Skins*. Los Angeles: American Indian Studies Center, University of California, Los Angeles, 1993.

Armstrong, Jeanette C. & Lally Grauer, eds. *Native Poetry in Canada: A Contemporary Anthology*. Peterborough, ON: Broadview Press, 2001.

Bernardin, Susan. "Seeing Memory, Storying Memory: Printup Hope, Rickard, Gansworth." *Visualities: Perspectives on Contemporary American Literature*. Oxford: Oxford University Press, 2014. 161–88.

Blue Cloud, Peter. *Elderberry Flute Song: Contemporary Coyote Tales*. Trumansburg, NY: The Crossing Press, 1982.

Blume, Anna. "In a Place of Writing." *Plains Indian Drawings 1865–1935: Pages from a Visual History*. Ed. Janet Catherine Berlo. New York: Harry N. Abrams, 1996. 40–44.

Boone, Elisabeth Hill & Walter D. Mignolo eds. *Writing Without Words: Alternative Literacies in Mesoamerica and the Andes*. Durham, NC: Duke University Press, 1994.

Brooks, Lisa. *The Common Pot: The Recovery of Native Space in the Northeast*. Minneapolis: University of Minnesota Press, 2008.

——."Painting 'Word-Pictures' in Place: Maurice Kenny's Empathetic Imagination of *Tekonwatonti/ Molly Brant*." *Maurice Kenny: Celebrations of a Mohawk Writer*. Ed. Penelope Myrtle Kelsey. Albany: State University of New York Press, 2011. 97–118.

Brotherston, Gordon. *Book of the Fourth World: Reading the Native Americas Through Their Literature*. Cambridge: Cambridge University Press, 1992.

Clutesi, George. *Son of Raven, Son of Deer: Fables of the Tse-Shaht People*. Sidney, BC: Gray's Publishing, 1967.

Cohen, Matt. "A History of Books in Native North America." *The World of Indigenous North America.* Ed. Robert Warrior. New York: Routledge, 2015. 308–29.

Cox, James A. & Daniel Heath Justice, eds. *The Oxford Handbook of Indigenous American Literature.* Oxford: Oxford University Press, 2014.

Cummings, Denise K., ed. *Visualities: Perspectives on Contemporary American Indian Film and Art.* East Lansing: Michigan State University Press, 2011.

DeFrancis, John. *Visible Speech: The Diverse Oneness of Writing Systems.* Honolulu: University of Hawaii Press, 1989.

Dunn, Martin F. *Red on White: The Biography of Duke Redbird.* Toronto: New Press, 1971.

Erdrich, Heid. "Pre-Occupied." Co-Directed by R. Vincent Moniz Jr.; Art Director and Animator, Jonathan Thunder. 2013. Web. Accessed 1 Feb. 2015. http://heiderdrich.com/video/pre-occupied/

Erdrich, Louise. *The Antelope Wife.* New York: HarperCollins, 1998.

——. *Baptism of Desire: Poems.* New York: Harper Perennial, 1989.

——. *Books and Islands in Ojibwe Country.* Washington, DC: National Geographic Books, 2003.

——. *Four Souls.* New York: HarperCollins, 2004.

——. *The Painted Drum.* New York: HarperCollins, 2005.

——.*Shadow Tag.* New York: Harper, 2010.

Gansworth, Eric. *Mending Skins.* Lincoln: University of Nebraska Press, 2005.

——. *Nickel Eclipse: Iroquois Moon.* East Lansing: Michigan State University Press, 2001.

Glancy, Diane. *Lone Dog's Winter Count.* Albuquerque: West End Press, 1991.

Hail, Barbara. "Foreword." Richard Pearce. *Women and Ledger Art: Four Contemporary Native American Artists.* Tucson: University of Arizona Press, 2013.

Henry, Gordon, Jr. *The Light People.* East Lansing: Michigan State University Press, 2003.

Henson, Lance. *A Cheyenne Sketchbook: Selected Poems 1970–1991.* Greenfield Center NY: Greenfield Review Press, 1985.

Justice, Daniel Heath. "Indigenous Writing." *The World of Indigenous North America.* Ed. Robert Warrior. New York: Routledge, 2015. 291–307.

Kelsey, Penelope Myrtle. *Reading the Wampum: Essays on Hodinöhsö:ni' Visual Code and Epistemological Recovery.* Syracuse, NY: Syracuse University Press, 2014.

——. *Tribal Theory in Native American Literature: Dakota and Haudenosaunee Writing and Indigenous Worldviews.* Lincoln: University of Nebraska Press, 2008.

Keyser, James D. *The Five Crows Ledger: Biographic Warrior Art of the Flathead.* Salt Lake City: University of Utah Press, 2000.

King, Thomas. *Truth and Bright Water.* Toronto: HarperCollins Canada, 2009.

Kulchyski, Peter. "bush/writing: embodied deconstruction, traces of community, and writing against the state in indigenous acts of inscription." *Shifting the Ground of Canadian Literary Studies.* Ed. Smaro Kamboureli & Robert Zacharias. Waterloo, ON: Wilfrid Laurier University Press, 2012. 249–68.

Lincoln, Kenneth. "Tai-Me to Rainy Mountain: The Makings of American Indian Literature." *American Indian Quarterly* 10. 2 (1986): 101–17.

Low, Denise. "Composite Indigenous Genre: Cheyenne Ledger Art as Literature." *Studies in American Indian Literatures* 18. 2 (2006): 83–104.

McGlennan, Molly. "Horizon Lines, Medicine Painting, and Moose Calling: The Visual/Performative Storytelling of Three Anishinaabeg Artists." *Centering Anishinaabeg Studies: Understanding the World Through Stories.* Ed. Jill Doerfler, Niigaanwewidam James Sinclair & Heidi Kiiwetinepinesiik Stark. East Lansing: Michigan State University Press, 2013. 341–62.

McKenzie, Stephanie. *Before the Country: Native Renaissance, Canadian Mythology.* Toronto: University of Toronto Press, 2007.

Mirzoeff, Nicholas. "On Visuality." *Journal of Visual Culture* 5. 1 (2006): 53–79.

——. *The Right to Look: A Counterhistory of Visuality.* Durham, NC and London: Duke University Press, 2011.

Morriseau, Norval. *Legends of My People: The Great Ojibway.* Whitby, ON: McGraw-Hill Ryerson, 1977.

Noodin, Margaret. *Bawaajimo: A Dialect of Dreams in Anishinaabe Language and Literature.* East Lansing: Michigan State University Press, 2014.

Noranjo-Morse, Nora. *Mud Woman: Poems from the Clay.* Tempe: University of Arizona Press, 1992.

Rader, Dean. *Engaged Resistance: American Indian Art, Literature, and Film from Alcatraz to the NMAI.* Austin: University of Texas Press, 2011.

——. "Reading the Visual, Seeing the Verbal: Text and Image in Recent American Indian Literature and Art." *The Oxford Handbook of Indigenous American Literature.* Oxford: Oxford University Press, 2014. 299–317.

Rasmussen, Birgit Brander. *Queequeg's Coffin: Indigenous Literacies and Early American Literature.* Durham, NC: Duke University Press, 2012.

Silko, Leslie Marmon. *Ceremony.* New York: Viking Penguin, 1977.

Sinclair, Niigaanwewidam James & Warren Cariou, eds. *Manitowapow: Aboriginal Writings from the Land of Water.* Winnipeg: Highwater Press, 2011.

Spry, Adam. "'It May be Revolutionary in Character': The *Progress*, a New Tribal Hermeneutics, and the Literary Re-Expression of the Anishinaabe Oral Tradition in *Summer in the Spring.*" *The Poetry and Poetics of Gerald Vizenor.* Ed. Deborah Madsen. Albuquerque: University of New Mexico Press, 2012. 23–43.

Stirrup, David. "'To the Indian Names are Subjoined a Mark and Seal': Tracing the Terrain of Ojibwe Literature." *Literature Compass* 7. 6 (2010): 370–86.

Stump, Sarain. *There is My People Sleeping.* Sidney, BC: Gray's Publishing, 1970.

Teuton, Christopher B. *Deep Waters: The Textual Continuum in American Indian Literature.* Lincoln: University of Nebraska Press, 2010.

Turcotte, Mark & Kathleen Presnell. *The Feathered Heart.* Chicago: MARCH/Abrazo Press, 1995.

——. *Songs of Our Ancestors: Poems About Native Americans.* Chicago: Childrens Press, 1995.

Vizenor, Gerald. *Almost Ashore.* Cambridge: Salt, 2006.

——. *Blue Ravens.* Middletown, CT: Wesleyan University Press, 2014.

——. *Fugitive Poses: Native American Indian Scenes of Presence and Absence.* Lincoln: University of Nebraska Press, 1998.

——. "Native Cosmototemic Art." *Sakahan: International Indigenous Art.* Ed. Greg A. Hill, Candice Hopkins & Christine Lalonde. Ottawa: National Gallery of Canada, 2013. 41–52.

——. *Shrouds of White Earth.* Albany: State University of New York Press, 2010.

——. *Summer in the Spring: Anishinaabe Lyric Poems and Stories* (new edition). Norman: University of Oklahoma Press, 1993.

Warkentin, Germaine. "In Search of 'The Word of the Other': Aboriginal Sign Systems and the History of the Book in Canada." *Book History* 2.1 (1999): 1–27.

Warrior, Robert Allen. *Tribal Secrets: Recovering American Indian Intellectual Traditions.* Minneapolis: University of Minnesota Press, 1995.

Welch, James. *Fool's Crow.* New York: Viking, 1986.

Womack, Craig S. *Red on Red: Native American Literary Separatism.* Minneapolis: University of Minnesota Press, 1999.

30

Indigenous Hermeneutics through Ceremony
Song, Language, and Dance

Diveena S. Marcus

The foundational knowledge systems of Indigenous people of North America are based upon oral tradition: as spoken word, through songs and performance. The effective expression of Indigenous peoples' cultural knowledge is through their languages. Indigenous languages are derived from and live within each significant territorial "homeland" region. Indigenous cultures have been analyzed by anthropologists and archeologists. Their creation myths and prophesies have been translated by ethnographers. But what is the hermeneutics vis-à-vis these original cultures that is essentially within Aboriginal knowledge? What hermeneutical significance is placed within cultural values for Indigenous people? These questions support an inclusive understanding of Indigenous peoples and their epistemologies. To facilitate this investigation through an Indigenous perspective, I offer personal insights from my diverse Indigenous and Native American Tamalko culture of Native California and of Indigenous knowledge keepers respected in their communities with whom I have established relationships. This chapter is presented with regard to and in appreciation of Indigenous hermeneutics attributed to Native American ceremony and its components of language, song and performance.

An ethnohistorical survey

My positionality in this chapter embraces and honors my matriarchal ancestry of the Tamalko Coast Miwok and Southern Pomo original peoples from the Sonoma and Marin Counties of North Central Indigenous California. Tamalko descendants thrive today within a community renamed during the federal status process as the Federated Indians of Graton Rancheria.[1]

Unlike the majority of Indigenous groups in North America, most California tribal communities have remained upon their ancestral homelands and claim their beginnings from time immemorial. In addition, many California Indigenous peoples' survival depended upon the miscegenation of newcomer minorities and non-Indigenous settlers (see Heizer). For the majority of California Indigenous peoples, we had and continue to have affiliations with a diverse background of Indigenous heritages. Within my community of Tamalko relatives, there are mixed heritages from the Mexican, Italian and South Pacific communities. From my patriarchal lineage I have cultural affiliations with the Filipino Bicolano Community from Luzon, Philippines. Though I have distant Aztec, Portuguese and "White" blood as well, I identify with my Tamalko heritage.

Keith Basso points out that:

> investigations have shown that indigenous populations may adapt with exquisite intricacy to the physical conditions of their existence (including, of course, the presence of other human populations), and the modifications in these conditions may have a range of dynamic effects on the structure and the organization of social institutions, ... And it is individuals, not social institutions, who make and act on cultural meanings.
>
> (67)

Though I practice traditional spirituality and life ways, it is not the Tamalko way to talk about what we do or what we believe unless we are asked or are confronted. Religion and spirituality are private and personal affairs for my *inniiko* (relatives). Nevertheless, today California Indigenous people are coming out into society to make their presence known in the world. I resonate to this quotation in *Kaandossiwin: How We Come to Know*:

> Coming out as Indigenous, you know, coming out as not only Indigenous, but coming out as embracing Indigenous worldviews and ways of being and ways of knowing, and ways of doing things because these things all have operated in my life, all my life.
>
> (Absolon 74)

The knowledge I have acquired from my Tamalko *inniiko* continues to assist me along my life journey. My ancestors and my homeland environment have endured waves of Diasporas, genocide and extermination brought on by foreign invader contact for more than five hundred years. Many of my ancestors chose not to survive the inundating attacks. For those that did, I am a product of their legacy. Without their determination to live I would not be here. I choose to take responsibility out of my deep respect for them to continue to reciprocate their lives through efforts such as this discourse as a means of restoring their values in our world today.

Lynn Fox was long-time curator of the *Jessie Parker* Indian Museum at the Santa Rosa Junior College and a devoted advocate for the regional Indigenous peoples. She took me to my early California Native ceremonies at Kuleloklo in Point Reyes Sea Shore National Park. Those ceremonies were facilitated by Coast Miwok/Pomo Elder and knowledge keeper Lanny Pinola. It was through the *towis wuṣki* (good hearts) of both Lynn and Lanny that my heart and mind opened to my mother's relatives and our ancient ancestors through ceremony. From that first encounter, I could not separate myself from the music and the desire to be in ceremony. I eventually apprenticed with Dennis Borilla (who had worked with Lanny in ceremony). I supported Dennis as an accompanying traditional ceremonial singer for his doctoring and family ceremonies. Since those earlier days I have acquired life and research experience in the Hawaiian Islands, Montana with the Absarooke (Crow), Piegan BlackFeet in South Dakota (Yankton/Dakota community), and in Ontario Canadian Territories of the Haudenosaunee (Six Nations) and Anishinaabe (where I apprenticed with Midewiwin Fourth Degree Elder Edna Manitowabi). The focus of my personal life and my academic interests has continued to be concentrated within the spiritual and philosophical aspects of consciousness.

An Indigenous perspective is an ideology based upon lived and living experiences. There is no one supreme scholar or entity that can be labeled the source or bearer of the Indigenous knowledge system. There are no ancient tablets, texts, or artifacts that hold the secrets. Indigenous knowledge exists through the unbroken sequences of living practices that draw their wisdom back to its source, Spirit. In the 2001 documentary film, *In the Light of Reverence*, Lakota scholar Vine Deloria Jr. states that ceremony comes out of an experience rather than a philosophical reason to explain things. The Indigenous spiritual journey is an experience of consistent relationship with the spiritual dimensions of life. Once this is accomplished as a life way, there is an outlook on life as sacred. The sacred connection can offer emotional and psychological relief regarding a situation of concern as a healing or a process of transformation: for example, Richard Erdoes' documentation of Lakota Lame Deer's coming-of-age vision quest or John Neihardt's accounts of Black Elk's visions. It can offer spiritual gifts like songs for healing and blessing, which are typically found within California Indigenous cultures (Hinton 42–43; Margolin & Montijo 83–85). Documented through oral narrative by Garter Snake Woman in *The Seven Visions of Bull Lodge*, the Pipe and the medicine initiations were the gifts given to the last Gros Ventre pipe carrier Bull Lodge. Winnemem Wintu Chief Caleen Sisk gives examples of the gifts that emerge within her community:

> Well it brings people together. Getting ourselves ready to show up to represent those things that we heard and feel as our sacred tradition. I think it comes about within the heart in ceremony that a lot of people realize what they can do.
>
> (Sisk)

In *In the Light of Reverence* Deloria discloses, about Indigenous religious practices, "[they] don't understand the whole thing, they just know that it works … if you don't understand it leave it to the mysterious". It works because the experience creates a bond of people and purpose as well as to an environmental place of belonging. I fasted with four other women when I began to work with Elder Edna Manitowabi. All of us participating came into the fasting camp with different intentions and from different Indigenous communities. In spite of that, when it was over there was a transformational spiritual link that I do not believe will ever be broken between us. I also believe that the spiritual experience deepens our identity and personal power with Spirit which incites a rededication or responsibility to the community and to Mother Earth, especially when you realize that what you are intending manifests.

The last ceremony in which I participated with the Winnemem Wintu was their annual *Coonrod* ceremony. It was a ceremony to honor and pray for the renewal of the people and the earth, in particular the Winnemem environmental homelands. The Fire and Water ceremony, which had not been done for hundreds of years, was enacted during *Coonrod*. Throughout the entire year of 2014 California was experiencing a draught of epic proportions with approximately 631,434 acres destroyed by fire. Many of us living in the northern high country were evacuated from our homes. One month after that ceremony took place rains came down upon Northern California and sacred *Bulyum Puyuik* (Mount

Shasta) regained her beautiful glaciers. As a member of the traditional community, you are required to be committed to the process. Your involvement is needed, whether it is cooking, setting up the space, gathering foods, keeping the fire, assisting elders, or taking care of the children. Wintu Ricardo Torres, Chair of Sacramento Native American Health Center, revealed:

> I'd be at work at the University and I'd get a call, "we need you tonight". I'd drive after work there. Sing all night. Leave there maybe four in the morning and come back. Go to my house and shower and come back to work. That was the kind of stuff we were doing.
>
> (Torres)

For traditional Indigenous communities, ceremony is a way of life.

During my early spiritual experiences, tribal ceremony was not protected. Even though the American Indian Religious Freedom Act (Public Law No. 95-341, 92 Stat. 469) was passed in 1978, it did not provide religious freedom without restrictions. Cherokee MD Lewis Mehl-Madrona explains in *Coyote Medicine* the conditions of the times: "Although school children learn that the Constitution protects freedom of religion, Native Americans were long denied the right to practice theirs. We were forbidden from congregating. We were not allowed to keep sacred objects, including pipes and eagle feathers" (Mehl-Madrona 36). In the early times, the ceremonies I attended were "underground" events. Unfortunately it has been and continues to be through many trials and tribulations that Native people who try to live their traditional culture endure. An excellent historical example of Native American tenacity and adherence to their spiritual traditions is the *Lyng vs. Northwest Cemetery* legal case. In 1987 northern California tribes Karuk, Yurok, and Tolowa under the Northwest Cemetery Association fought the U.S. Supreme Court for the use and for the protection of their traditional sacred Chimney Rock site in the Siskiyou Wilderness area. It was not until 1998 that the U.S. Federal Government passed an amendment to the bill H.R. 4155 "in order to provide for the management of federal lands in a way that doesn't frustrate the traditional religions and religious purposes of Native Americans" (see Bowers & Carpenter).

However, even though a bill is passed it does not guarantee or provide enforcement of the law or protection for those Indigenous communities and people who are trying to practice their religion. Unfortunately many non-Indigenous people are not sufficiently familiar with the relationship between federal governments and their Indigenous peoples to know what is accepted within society as a legislative reality and do not have the capacity to respect Indigenous ideologies and practices (see Berta on unrecognized tribes and their sacred sites on public lands). Hence dominant society's ignorance regarding Indigenous cultural and spiritual misappropriation is understandable. David Peat addresses this quite clearly:

> Cultural appropriation is not simply the act of taking something away from a people, it is also using something in a way that is inappropriate, disrespectful and distorted. How easy it is for a well meaning outsider to interpret what he has seen and experienced and in the process has misrepresented the knowledge and worldview of Indigenous people. How easy it is to study a ceremony, story, or area of knowledge out of its context, employing Western critical paradigms and

values ... In this way, after five hundred years of misunderstanding, the First People continue to suffer the denigration of their most sacred practices and the disruption of their ways of life.

(17)

The reality underlying this attitude is a long history of violence. But despite our long traumatic history tied to foreign invaders upon our homelands we continue to work to re-cultivate our beautiful culture. As Haudenosaunee John Mohawk has stated: "It is the Creator's way that mountains rise and fall, rivers change their course, islands appear, disappear, and reappear in new form – but always there is maintained a spiritual consistency throughout the universe" (Barreiro 5). It is this spiritual consistency that is translated through the Indigenous voice and its perspective.

Ceremony: Ma yayyu hine 'ununni 'unu (Our Call to our Great Mother)

One of the most perplexing concepts to comprehend from the perspective of a colonized ideology is the value of Indigenous peoples' oral histories or what is referred to as their myths. Paradoxically, the dominant culture has based its legal, moral and philosophical authenticity on the Christian myth. Empirical studies cannot offer solid scientific evidence or historical fact based upon this myth, but nonetheless it is the foundation of the culture. Likewise, oral histories within Indigenous myths are filled with intriguing hermeneutic elements similar to myths from the Bible (Marcus 6). However, from an Indigenous perspective there are no hermeneutical elements comparable with Western interpretations of the sacred.

The word hermeneutics originates in a European context as a tool to decipher/translate sacred texts, or rather to write/edit the Christian Bible, which was the documentation of ancient oral recollections for hermeneutical study. The present Bible has over 40 authors and was written over a period of 1,500 years that commenced 400 years after the death of its central prophet Jesus Christ. And the hermeneutical interpretative process has been changing and evolving since the Council of Nicaea in AD 325. The Aristotelian style of hermeneutical analysis (of words and symbols) through the ages and in conjunction with contemporary media technology has expanded interpretation of the non-physical sacred into a theoretical methodology used in research within various disciplines of the humanities and social sciences. For the Indigenous traditionalist focused on the spiritual journey, one must adapt with the earth despite colonial domination that promotes theories that justify and rationalize an ideology of power and control. It is affirming the conscious inner lifeline attached to the mysterious power of Spirit that guides Indigenous people through chaos and confusion. John Mohawk confirms, "That way is not theory – it is living and all the universe of life" (Barreiro 5). Furthermore, Mohawk scholar and Indigenous environmentalist Dan Longboat claims, "Ceremony, and storytelling are agents that inspired inner consciousness within our human lives and world, rather than its contemporary value placed upon it from the dominant society for the primary use of entertainment and/or propaganda" (Longboat).

Frank LaPena, Wintu elder and artist, in his article "Wintu Sacred Geography" describes how the Olelbis, (the entire invisible energy and power of the earth and universe) is everywhere constantly in motion and never stagnant. Aleut elder and knowledge keeper Larry Merculieff refers to this energy and power as the Sacred Feminine (see Earth and Spirit Council). Merculieff relates this essence of knowledge and power from his recollections of Aleut practices during traditional hunting and ceremonies. Tewa scholar Greg Cajete defines further, "This very participation in procreation brings with it certain responsibilities and understandings that must be maintained, the kinds of understandings that today we call an 'ecological compact' or spiritual ecology" (38). Western man has defined this creative living force as God. Indigenous hermeneutics are the emerging visions based upon oral participative experiences in contemporary life which include the spiritual. Like the Saints of the Middles Ages, Indigenous people interpret their spiritual experiences and through these oral practices laws and codes of ethics and principles have been established as protocols within living traditions for thousands of years.

Within traditional Indigenous knowledge systems such as the Haudenosaunee Great Law and Anishinaabe Seven Grandfather Teachings, there is a prominent spiritual order that embraces concepts of peace, cooperation, harmony, balance, kinship, health, and respect (see Benton-Banai; Thomas). These aspects of Indigenous traditions are impossible to learn from within an institutional context because Indigenous traditional spiritual knowledge originates from the natural environment and is inherent within the cosmological indigenous culture (see Basso; Cajete; Colorado; Cordova; Dumont; Ermine). Many components and details of this sacred cultural knowledge cannot be exposed outside of traditional relations of transfer because of the fact that everything about a particular Indigenous knowledge is directed toward personal experience and is entrusted intimately within ceremony and/ or ritual.

> Words are rare and therefore dear. They are jealously preserved in the ear and in the mind. Words are spoken with great care, and they are heard. They matter, and they must not be taken for granted: they must be taken seriously and they must be remembered.
>
> (Momaday 15)

Momaday's statement is a teaching shared by Anishinaabe Elder Shirley Williams in a poem about her father, "When I Was Small": prayers, rituals and ceremonies are not to be documented, for they are enacted as spiritual covenants and as consecrations of events as well as for transformation. Even though the sacred is found alive everywhere in everything and in every moment, it is not realized unless it is sought out. The ceremonial context is the forum where human beings make the effort to relate to the sacred. Chief Caleen Sisk defines this calling:

> It would be like if you're in trouble or something happens to you and you start calling out for your mom even though she's nowhere around to hear you. Sometimes women can actually hear the child. For Wintu that is our mother, and if you want help you call for those helpers.
>
> (*In the Light of Reverence*)

In Indigenous California cosmology there are three worlds (see Bean). The upper and lower worlds are inhabited by powerful beings and the middle world where humans and all of life and the life spirit exist. I refer to this creative force as *'ununni 'unu*, which translates from *Tamal Machchawko* (Coast Miwok) as the Great Mother. All Indigenous peoples have origin stories that educate them about how and why they belong to the earth. They were either made from the earth as Indigenous California peoples (see Merriam), were given life and sustenance from the planet as the Eastern peoples (see Benton-Banai) and the Hawaiians (see Meyer *Ho'oulu* 98), or actually emerged from the earth like the Dine (see Berlo & Philips 37) and the Kiowa (see Momaday). It is the middle world where all forces can come together. For Indigenous California people, music and songs in particular, form the medium that traverses the worlds and enables us to find our way to *'ununni unu* as a blessing and prayer. In the California Miwok origin story "The Birth of Wek and the Creation of Man," Wek, a pre-human creator was awaiting the advent of the first humans. Wek loves the music of the singing Elderberry tree and plants it all over the land so that humans will have music in their experience (Merriam 67–73). This story tells me that my ancestors were loved and provided for. The Creators prepared our homelands for our ancient grandparents to live a cultured existence within a multidimensional world. Bruno Nettle, ethnographer and author of *Blackfoot Musical Thought* says, "Music for the Blackfoot is the language that is used by Spirit to speak to humans" (129). For Indigenous California traditionalists, songs are real entities and have specific powers and intentions just as all living beings do: "It is as if the song were a being, and it came to a person, almost like an animal might come to a person. The song was thought of as a living thing that would allow itself to be sung" (Margolin & Montijo 83). Traditional song is a gift from our spiritual elders. When experienced and practiced ceremonially, it empowers cultural intelligence and pays respect to all our relations.

Four guiding Indigenous principles

There are four guiding principles – Relationship, Respect, Responsibility and Reciprocity – that are intrinsically hermeneutically aligned and understood through Indigenous ceremony and the spiritual way of life (see Battiste; Brant-Castellano; Cajete; Couture; Fixico; Meyer *Ho'oulu*; Simpson; Smith).

> Spiritual and intellectual integrity is achieved on Turtle Island by the interplay of human and more-than-human consciousness. The experience of imagination is minding all things. Minding all things performs the spiritual conservation of all things. All things comprise the Indigenous mind and Indigenous minds are composed of all things.
>
> (Sheridan & Longboat 365)

Sheridan and Longboat are referring to relationship-building and the sustaining consciousness that ceremony does for our awareness within our existing planetary relationships and the potentiality of building relationships within the worlds and dimensions of the universe.

Ceremony is what builds Indigenous spiritual and intellectual integrity by adhering to respectful protocols. Participating in ceremony is paying due respect to all our relationships. By being mindful of the gifts of our lives within our own talents and abilities, we become more attuned to our place within our community and the environment. Our prayers are for guidance as to how we can best offer ourselves as we learn to play our part in respect to cultural sustainability. Hawaiian scholar Manulani Meyer explains pule, a traditional chant/prayer protocol: "It is the invoking of other powers and it is true recognition of the diversity that cultural people represent. Pule is not dogmatic and not exclusive. Saying pule is like knocking on a door before one enters" (Meyer 38). Pule is respectful action towards all relationships; respectful action towards our relationships by preparing space through song is basic ceremonial protocol.

When we receive a tangible gift from Spirit such as a song, we have a responsibility to use it for the benefit of everyone. An understanding of this principle of responsibility can best be illustrated regarding Winnemem language and culture. "In the beginning all the creatures came out of the spring on Mount Shasta. Human had no voice. So Salmon gave her voice to Human. In return Human promised to speak for Salmon" (*Dancing Salmon Home*). Responsibility is a promise that our ancestors made with the rest of creation to support each other. There are no arguments within the biological sciences that our planet evolved perfectly for human habitation. Traditional Indigenous people believe we have benefitted from this beautiful world and we are part of its evolution. Much like the spiritual and transformational bond I have with my fasting sisters, we humans have become bonded to each other and to the rest of the non-human peoples in our earthly environment through our living relational experiences. Our Indigenous languages are powerful mediums given to us by very distinctive and ancient ancestral entities from times and worlds that are hard to grasp in the conceptual terms of Eurowestern thought. Regardless, many of our traditional human ancestors did not forget their responsibilities. California endangered language activist Ohlone Vince Medina speaks proudly of his Chochenyo legacy:

Oh, glorious fighters, ancestors, people of defiance, people of wisdom, gravity breakers. Today, as a result of your refusal to surrender language, we as modern *Ohlone* can speak words once again. Because of the scribbles on parchment paper, the land hears *Chochenyo* a second time. It has been inside us all along. The words caress us like a grandmother, comfort us like a song, and bring us dignity and connect us to the East Bay, the place we love. My elders, my heroes, you saved it from ever being forgotten. We will not relinquish *Chochenyo*, for it thrives in the footsteps of giants.

(Linsteadt & Margolin 75)

Reciprocating wisdom and gifts given through this world and others is the right action of doing for others as well as protecting what is left for those who will be next upon the evolutionary journey. The process of reciprocal action is considered prayer. Within the ceremonial context the power of prayer in action is the dance. For most California tribes their warriors are ceremonial warriors. Ethnographer Theodora Kroeber described how Indigenous California peoples "did not believe in war. When it came it disrupted the medi-tated tenors of life in which they believed" (29). However, our dancing intent is similar to the Plains Sun Dancers. Dancers go through a purification ritual, fast, drink no water and dance during the entire four days of the ceremony. Their dancing prayer battle is to preserve their sacred sites and to balance the injustices committed against their culture and people. The dancer offers his spirit and life force, all of himself to the cause; David Martinez proclaimed: "If they raise that dam (Shasta Dam) if it happens in my life time and I'm still capable, as a warrior I will go down and I will dance until water covers me until I drown" (qtd. in "David Martinez" n. pag.; see also Berta).

Tamalko traditionalist and spiritual practitioner David Carrio says of Ceremony:

> It [ceremony] means everything. Like Christian "holy". And ceremony is where ever you are. Like how you live your life. How you wash your cloths. That's ceremony. Everything you do. How you prepare your food. How you treat your food. I try to respect the food … to show that respect … . I'm trying to show respect for Mother Earth and what she's given me to survive. Ceremony means everything.
>
> (Carrio)

Indigenous hermeneutics is the living voices and actions of ancient principles best understood through ceremony. As ceremonial consciousness, Indigenous hermeneutics maintain a relationship of spiritual consistency within traditional Indigenous communities and life ways.

Note

1 Many California tribes were federally terminated in the 1950s. Half of California's original peoples are still seeking reinstatement (Federal Recognition). The Federated Indians of Graton Rancheria regained federal status in 2000.

Works cited

Absolon, Kathleen E. *Kaandossiwin: How We Come To Know*. Black Point, NS: Fernwood Publishing, 2011.

Barreiro, Jose. *Thinking in Indian: A John Mohawk Reader*. Golden, CO: Fulcrum, 2010.

Basso, Keith H. *Wisdom Sits in Places: Landscape and Language among the Western Apache*. Albuquerque: University of New Mexico Press, 1996.

Battiste, Marie. "Enabling the Autumn Seed: Toward a Decolonized Approach to Aboriginal Knowledge, Language, and Education." *Canadian Journal of Native Education* 22. 1 (1988): 16–27.

Bean, Lowell, J. *California Indian Shamanism*. Menlo Park, CA: Malki-Ballena Press, 1992.

Benton-Banai, Edward. *The Mishomis Book: The Voice of the Ojibway*. Hayward, WI: Red School House, 1988.

Berlo, Janet C. & Ruth B. Phillips. *Native North American Art*. Oxford: Oxford University Press, 1998.

Berta, Charlotte. "'Don't Drown Our Culture' – New Short Doc Demands Senators Boxer and Feinstein Address Winnemem Justice Issues Relating to the Shasta Dam Raise." *Winnemem Wintu*. Winnemem Wintu Tribe, 21 July 2014. Web. Accessed 18 Sept. 2014. http://www.winnememwintu.us/tag/coming-of-age-ceremony/

Bowers, Amy & Kristen A. Carpenter. "Challenging the Narrative of Conquest: The Story of Lyng vs. Northwest Indian Cemetery Protection Association." *Indian Law Stories*. Ed. Carole Goldberg, Kevin K. Washburn & Phillip R. Frickey. New York: Thomson Reuters Foundation Press, 2011.

Brant-Castellano, M. "Updating Aboriginal Traditions of Knowledge." *Indigenous Knowledges in Global Contexts: Multiple Readings of our World*. Ed. G. Sefa Dei, B. Hall & D. Rosenburg. Toronto: University of Toronto Press, 2000. 21–36.

Cajete, Gregory. *Native Science: Natural Laws of Interdependence*. Santa Fe, NM: Clear Light, 2000.

Carrio, David. Personal Interview. Santa Rosa, California. 25 Sept. 2014.

Colorado, Pam. "Bridging Native and Western Science." *Convergence* 21. 2/3 (1988): 49–68.

Cordova, Viola F. *How It is: The Native American Philosophy of V.F. Cordova*. Ed. Kathleen Dean Moore, Kurt Peters, Ted Jojola & Amber Lacy. Tucson: University of Arizona Press, 2007.

Couture, J. "Explorations in Native Knowing." *The Cultural Maze: Complex Questions on Native Destiny in Western Canada*. Ed. J. W. Friesen. Calgary, AB: Detselig Enterprises, 1991. 53–76.

——. "Native and Non-native Encounter: A Personal Experience." *Challenging the Conventional – Essays in Honor of Ed Newberry*. Ed. W. Cragg. Burlington, ON: Trinity Press, 1989. 123–54.

——. "Traditional Native Thinking, Feeling, and Learning: Some Thoughts on the Relationship between Native Values and the Practice of Native Education." *Contemporary Educational Issues: The Canadian Mosaic*. Ed. S. McCann & L. Stewlin. Toronto: Copp Clark Pitman, 1987.

Dancing Salmon Home. Dir. Will Doolittle. Moving Image Productions. 2012.

"David Martinez Brave Faces Portrait Gallery." *Stand Against Stigma*. Health and Human Services Agency. Web. Accessed 18 Sept. 2014. http://www.co.shasta.ca.us/index/hhsa_index/mental_wellness/stand_against_stigma/brave-faces-portrait-gallery/david_martinez.aspx

Dumont, James. "Journey to Daylight-Land: Through Objiwa Eyes." *Laurentian University Review* 8. 2 (1976): 31–43.

Earth and Spirit Council. "Larry Merculieff: Indigenous Voices." Online Video Clip. YouTube. 14 July 2011.

Erdoes, Richard & John Lame Deer. *Lame Deer, Seeker of Visions*. New York: Washington Square Press, 1994.

Ermine, Willie. "Aboriginal Epistemology." *First Nations Education in Canada: The Circle Unfolds*. Ed. Marie Battiste & Jean Barman. Vancouver: University of British Columbia Press, 1995. 101–12.

Fixico, D. *The American Indian Mind in a Linear World: American Indian Studies and Traditional Knowledge*. New York: Routledge, 2003.

Garter Snake Woman, Fred P. Gone & George P. Horse Capture, eds. *The Seven Visions of Bull Lodge*. Lincoln: University of Nebraska Press, 1992.

Heizer, Robert F. *The Destruction of California Indians*. Lincoln: University of Nebraska Press, 1993.

——. *The Other Californians: Prejudice and Discrimination under Spain, Mexico, and the United States to 1920*. Berkeley: University of California Press, 1977.

Hinton, Leanne. *Flutes of Fire*. Berkeley, CA: Heyday Books, 1994.

In the Light of Reverence. Dir. Christopher McLeod. Sacred Land Film Project. 2003.

Kroeber, Theodora & R.F. Heizer. *Almost Ancestors: The First Californians*. San Francisco: Sierra Book Club, 1968.

LaPena, Frank. "Wintu Spiritual Geography." *California Indian Shamanism*. Ed. Lowell John Bean. Menlo Park, CA: Malki-Ballena Press, 1992. 211–25.

Linsteadt, Sylvia & Malcolm Margolin. *Wonderments of the East Bay*. Berkeley, CA: Heyday Books, 2014.

Longboat, Dan. "Introduction to Indigenous Food Systems". Trent University, Ontario, Canada. 12 Feb. 2013. Lecture.

Marcus, Diveena. "Sounds from the Heart: Native American Language and Song". M.A. Thesis. Montana State University, 2011.

Margolin, Malcolm & Yolanda Montijo. *Native Ways*. Berkeley, CA: Heyday Books, 1995.

Mehl-Madrona, Lewis. *Coyote Medicine*. New York: Scribner, 1997.

Merriam, Hart C., ed. *The Dawn of the Word: Myths and Tales of the Miwok Indians of California*. Lincoln: University of Nebraska Press, 1993.

Meyer, Manulani. A. *Ho'oulu: Our Time of Becoming*. Honolulu: 'Ai Pohaku Press, 2003.

Momaday, Scott N. *The Way to Rainy Mountain*. Albuquerque: University of New Mexico Press, 1976.

Neihardt, John G. *Black Elk Speaks*: Lincoln: University of Nebraska Press, 1968.

Nettle, Bruno. *Blackfoot Musical Thought: Comparative Perspectives*. Kent, OH: Kent State University Press, 1989.

Peat, David F. *Blackfoot Physics*. Boston: Weiser Books, 2002.

Sheridan, Joe & Dan Longboat. "The Haudenosaunee Imagination and the Ecology of the Sacred." *Space and Culture* 9. 4 (2006): 365–81.

Simpson, L. "Stories, Dreams and Ceremonies: Anishinaabe Ways of Learning." *Tribal College Journal of American Indian Higher Education*, 11. A (2000): 26–29.

Sisk, Caleen. Personal Interview. Siskiyou County, California. 18 Sept. 2014.

Smith, L. T. *Decolonizing Methodologies, Research and Indigenous Peoples*. London: Zed Books, 1999.

Thomas, Jake. "Gayanashagowa: The Great Binding Law." 2009. Web. Accessed 18 Sept. 2013. http://www.utulsa.edu/law/classes/rice/constitutional/Six_Nations_Const.htm

Torres, Ricardo. Personal Interview. Sacramento, California. 30 Sept. 2014.

Williams, Shirley Ida. "When I Was Small." *First Voices*. Ed. Patricia A. Monture & Patricia D. McGuire. Toronto: Inanna Publications & Education, 2009. 437–40.

31

Native American Intellectuals
Moundbuilders of Yesterday, Today, and Tomorrow

Cari M. Carpenter

In three spare lines of a poem in her collection *Blood Run*, mixed-blood poet Allison Adelle Hedge Coke manages to capture both the vibrancy and the vulnerability of the earthen mound in what is now known as Blood Run National Historic Landmark Site. Writing from the perspective of the mound itself, which is associated with active words like "releasing," "remembering," and "gathering," she describes the mound's attempts to protect its holdings and, in the process, to determine present political conditions:

Somehow, perhaps remembering
from my tilled base, barely protecting gatherings

a finger reaches out to test the temperature.

(ll. 15–17)

In the final line, the mound is equated to a single finger that literally embodies the human remains – and human memories – within.

We can extend this voice to the Newark mounds in present-day Ohio, which have also been subject to the depredations of "civilization": a golf course now exists near this National Heritage Site that has been nominated as an Eighth Wonder of the World. While archaeologists date the Newark mounds at two thousand years old, it is only recently that non-Natives have acknowledged them for the wonders they are. In 1982, Ray Hively, an astronomer, and Robert Horn, a philosopher, published their findings in the essay "Geometry and Astronomy in Prehistoric Ohio." Hively and Horn detail how the Octagon Mound was built to trace the 18-year cycle of the moon. Despite the complexity of the cycle, Hively and Horn note that the Indigenous Hopewell builders were able to construct the mound so that it would track all eight alignments during the lunar cycle.

On particular dates, those standing on the Observatory Mound could see the moon rising above the walls. The mounds' location in modern-day Ohio was the center of a vast Indigenous landscape, and as such, they might be viewed as an earthen embodiment of Native intellectualism. Today, Marti L. Chaatsmith (Comanche) notes, 16,000 conical mounds still exist in the United States, representing the footprints of an extensive earthen design that once stretched throughout the entire Ohio Valley:

Figure 31.1 Three-dimensional reconstruction of a moonrise over the Newark Earthworks. http://indiancountrytodaymedianetwork.com/2013/06/07/newark-american-indian-mounds-eighth-wonder-world-you-decide-149763. Copyright CERHAS/University of Cincinnati, www.ancientohiotrail.org. Reprinted with permission of John E. Hancock.

The form of the Octagon Earthworks is a pictograph of two different shapes joined together. The small perfect circle outside the walls of the octagon calls for ceremony. The open entryways of the octagon invite people to enter the site. Following the walkway, people enter the circle. Observatory Mound offers a view of the rising moon at its peak in standstill moments. The circle, ubiquitous among Indigenous cultures as a symbol of life's cycles, could represent the physical world, while the rising moon above the octagon brings the spiritual world closer, signaling that it is time for community events to begin – or end.

(196–97)

The mounds thus enact a connection between mind and spirit, material and immaterial, that symbolizes Indigenous intellectualism at its core. In turn, Native intellectualism helps individuals orient themselves to the landscape; like the walls of the octagon, these guiding thoughts use natural materials to offer a new way of seeing the world.

Reading and writing, we are taught in the western tradition, is essential to higher thought, and as such are key markers of "civilization." But what about human life before the written word? When we learn of the moundbuilders of present-day Ohio, it seems preposterous to limit intellectualism to such a narrow span of human existence. Although the examples of Indigenous intellectualism are as diverse as Indigenous peoples themselves – who today belong to over 560 federally recognized tribes and hundreds more state and unrecognized tribes in the United States – they share a core challenge to western conceptions of ingenuity, creativity, and the production of knowledge. Appropriately, the first meeting of the Society of American Indians, a nineteenth-century association of Indigenous intellectuals, chose to gather at the Newark mounds. If we define "intellectualism" too narrowly, we end up missing evidence of tremendous human insight like the earthen mounds.

While a deservedly thorough account would require an exhaustive (and exhausting) consideration of Native peoples across this landscape and over centuries, for the sake of efficiency I have chosen to focus this chapter on four instances of Indigenous intellectualism: early material culture; the activism of the Pequod minister William Apess; the rhetorical strategies of Northern Paiute Sarah Winnemucca Hopkins; and finally, intellectuals today who not only offer insights into previous examples of Native ingenuity, but produce new forms altogether. Admittedly, this list is shaped by my specialty in literature and feminist studies; any other scholar of Native American Studies would likely produce a somewhat different list. So rather than suggesting that the sum total of Native intellectualism is represented in these few pages, I offer them simply as samples of a much larger group that, together, constitutes the vibrant Indigenous intellectualism of yesterday, today, and tomorrow.

When we broaden our conception of intellectualism, it emerges in multiple forms, as scholars like mixed-blood scholars Malea Powell and Angela M. Haas have shown in their study of material culture like wampum and basketry. The Two-Row wampum of the Haudenosaunee (Iroquois Confederacy), for example, was used as a representation of the desired relationship between the Confederacy and the United States, in which the two would exist in parallel positions, neither interfering with the other. As a symbol of the union of multiple, even conflicting entities, wampum is symbolically equivalent to the Constitution of the United States; indeed the Iroquois Confederacy was an inspiration for the organization of the U.S. government. Angela M. Haas has shown how wampum embodies memory and, as such, is a powerful form of rhetoric that she likens to current-day hypertext. The original conception of hypertext was imagined as "an associative system for indexing, storing, retrieving, and delivering of memories," a description that resonates with wampum's material form (82). Malea Powell likens rhetorics to basket making: "A basket is a basket because of how it's made, how it means, how it holds" (471). Like wampum, baskets are means of holding – of preserving – a culture's stories and memories. In this sense it is another kind of text, another means of communication. In many cases, Powell argues, Native forms are the basis upon which other texts have been created: she refers, for example, to a song known as the "Sioux National Anthem" that has found its way into more recent Native fiction, like Kiowa author N. Scott Momaday's novel *House Made of Dawn*, as well as Native poetry. So there is no firm distinction between material and literary texts; like a basket, their individual strands are woven together over time. We might extend this understanding of baskets as entities that "hold" the core materials of human existence to the mounds themselves – not only as holders of human remains, but various forms of cultural knowledge.

Both of the nineteenth-century figures I examine, William Apess and Sarah Winnemucca Hopkins, managed to convey their messages in terms sanctioned by western culture: they were both talented writers and speakers who argued for Native rights. Both also offer subtle critiques of the assumptions of that culture even while ostensibly embracing it – and it is in those moments of critique that they are most successful. They managed, in other words, to use the master's tools to dismantle his house – all while appearing to conform to his expectations. This was particularly strategic in the nineteenth century, when Native rights were under a wide-scale assault. In this sense, they may seem to have succeeded because they were able to imitate non-Native intellectualism. Indeed. But they did not stop there; rather, I argue, these tactics are only the first steps in an elaborate campaign that, like the mounds themselves, combined material knowledge with abstract spiritualism. In other words, like the ancient moundbuilders, Apess and Winnemucca both build concrete forms of resistance in ways that challenge and even transcend western knowledge.

William Apess

A mixed-blood Pequot born in Massachusetts in 1798, William Apess became a Methodist minister in 1829. In 1833, as an "itinerant revivalist" (*The Experiences* 102), he visited a Mashpee settlement and was troubled by the patronizing attitude of Reverend Fish, a white man, and the infringement on Mashpees' rights. He then undertook a campaign for self-government and, specifically, the protection of timber on Mashpee land, drafting a Mashpee Declaration of Independence that was influenced by John Calhoun's Nullification Doctrine (Hutchins 104). As Lisa Brooks has documented, the protection of timber was particularly important in an era marked by over-logging. That June, Apess and two Mashpees prevented a white man from carrying a load of wood from the parsonage, thus signaling the Mashpees' claim to self-government. Although Apess was sentenced to prison for thirty days for seizing the wood, a year later, a higher court passed an act "restoring Mashpee to the status of an unincorporated district" that could control its own affairs (Hutchins 108). This victory was thanks in part to the persuasiveness of white lawyer Benjamin Hallett, who compared their claiming of the stolen wood to the American colonists' tea party. The victory in the Mashpee case was one of the few successes in a century marked by Native dispossession. As Theresa Strouth Gaul has argued, Apess's *Indian Nullification* (1835) integrates Hallett's legal discourse with Mashpee accounts, so that "white legal precedents are this time mobilized on behalf of Mashpee claims against white interests" (286).

A number of scholars have described Apess as a profound intellectual; Robert Warrior (Osage), for example, contends that Apess is the nineteenth-century Native American intellectual who best speaks to present Native American concerns. While Warrior claims Apess's "Eulogy on King Philip" as "the pinnacle of Apess's intellectual career" (1), I focus on Apess's sermon "An Indian's Looking-Glass for the White Man" from his collection *The Experiences of Five Christian Indians of the Pequod Tribe* (1833). I have found that students who pick up Apess's essay expect something akin to the image of a defeated Indian man perched on the edge of a cliff, with suicide far preferable to Native existence in the nineteenth century. What they get instead is a remarkably confident voice that seems like an artful prelude to Martin Luther King, with Apess's words "Perhaps some unholy, unprincipled men would cry out, the skin was not good enough; but stop friends – I am not talking about the skin, but about principles" (Apess 156). My students often comment on the Christian discourse that he uses so effectively, so that an ostensible justification of mistreatment is instead a vibrant defense of equality. In one of the most effective passages, he writes:

But, reader, I acknowledge that this is a confused world, and I am not seeking for office; but merely placing before you the black inconsistency that you place before me – which is ten times blacker than any skin that you will find in the Universe.

(157)

Here the racially loaded language of "darkness" instead becomes a marker of ignorance, so that Apess detaches "darkness" from skin color – and all the inequality associated with it – and makes it instead a quality that *anyone* (in this case, the whites who mistakenly claim superiority) can possess. Using precise logic he masterfully dislodges all of the assumptions that support a "natural" connection between Christianity, whiteness, and superiority, most impressively through the use of rhetorical questions that appear to invite rather than lecture the reader. Consider the following:

Did you ever hear or read of Christ teaching his disciples that they ought to despise one because his skin was different from theirs? Jesus Christ being a Jew, and those of his Apostles certainly were not whites – and did not he who completed the plan of salvation complete it for the whites as well as for the Jews, and others? And were not the whites the most degraded people on the earth at that time? And none were more so, for they sacrificed their children to dumb idols!

And did not St. Paul labor more abundantly for building up a christian nation amongst you than any of the Apostles. And you know as well as I that you are not indebted to a principle beneath a white skin for your religious services, but to a colored one.

(O'Connell 158)

The white Christian reader is thus in a quandary: a minister has effectively redefined the religion to disrupt the white privilege it previously enabled. George Ashwell notes that Apess's authority derives from "his ability to exploit white cultural forms" (qtd. in Gaul 276). Further, Robert Warrior argues that instead of seeing Christianity as a betrayal of his Pequot identity, Apess found in republican Methodism a means of critiquing the oppression of American Indians as "unchristian." In Warrior's words, "In holding up a looking-glass to his white readers, Apess turns an intellectual corner in terms of his willingness to confront his public directly" (*The People and the Word* 32). In Lisa Brooks's words:

When Apess and the Mashpees put their resolutions in writing, they bound themselves together in a promise to enact them. The tribe used writing to pledge commitments and actions, to persuade political bodies, to communicate with neighboring communities, to record communal decisions, and to clearly delineate Native space. Thus, well into the nineteenth century, writing was operating in forms similar to wampum and *awikhiganak*.

(260)

Like the Newark mounds themselves, these words expose our limited understanding of the extent of Native intellectualism.

Sarah Winnemucca Hopkins

Like William Apess, Sarah Winnemucca excelled at knowing when to use western forms to convey her message and when to challenge those very forms. Although Warrior contrasts Apess and Winnemucca, noting the latter's willingness to indulge her audience by "playing Indian," I argue that Winnemucca offered a similar kind of intellectual prowess. While most scholarship of Winnemucca has focused on her book *Life Among the Piutes* (1883), I would like to consider how an unpublished transcript of her 1884 testimony to the House of Representative's Indian Affairs Committee indicates her acumen.[1] Likely the only woman in the room – and most assuredly the only American Indian – Winnemucca argued forcibly for a restoration of Malheur Reservation to the Northern Paiutes.

Her astute approach is evident from her first few words, when she answers a question about how the dispossession of the reservation came about by beginning earlier, in a time when the Northern Paiutes were treated decently by Agent Samuel Parrish. By starting here, Winnemucca is able to construct the Northern Paiutes as hardworking people who quickly acceded to Parrish's agrarian plan for the reservation. Here she recalls her father's response to Parrish: "It is now nearly fifteen years that we have waited on the reservation and no one has tried to teach us, and here we are, poor, and we are glad you have come, and we are willing to work" (2). By starting here, and then taking up eight pages of the transcript, she asserts her control over the direction of the proceedings and is able to illustrate the sharp contrast between Parrish and William Rinehart, the agent who instigates Paiute removal. In other words, instead of beginning with the dismal – and stereotypical – portrait of a defeated people, she describes them in accordance with an American model of self-reliance and agrarian usefulness. While Native Americans were frequently accused of "wasting" land in the nineteenth century by not farming it, Winnemucca recalls gathering a harvest of watermelons and potatoes and building schoolhouses, the epitome of Anglo-American education. This work is set in an idyllic space, complete with music song "in the Indian language also," an appealing vision that both solidifies Northern Paiute adoption of "American" customs and reminds the listener of her distinct racial identity. This is not, then, a whole-cloth adoption of Anglo-American ideology; instead, she integrates it with aspects of Northern Paiute culture to mold a powerful argument.

The transcript indicates the calculated nature of Winnemucca's comments. She continues, for example, with a story of how a Judge Curry of Oregon had petitioned for a part of the reservation – a detail not included in *Life Among the Piutes*. She next recounts the Northern Paiute response:

> The people said "does our father want to play with us as if we were little children? Why did he give it to us in the first place: why didn't he keep it?" So we told Sam to tell our big father, our good father, that we did not want to sell. We said our white brothers have got all they want: leave us this one.
>
> (4)

This protest is notable for its polite decline: it both acknowledges U.S. power and asserts the Paiutes' own. The transcript indicates that it was the brother-in-law of Curry, William Rinehart, who replaced Samuel Parrish in an instance of President Grant's "Peace Policy," in which secular agents were replaced with Christians. This was a policy that the Paiutes found baffling, in that it removed a good agent and installed a dictatorial and duplicitous one. But even before we hear details about Rinehart's mismanagement, we associate him with a man who greedily sought part of the Malheur Reservation. Her tone changes markedly at this point: "So many little children, so many women, so many old men, so many young men – were turned over to him just the same as you would turn your stock over to a person who bought them" (5). In Rinehart's words, the reservation is the U.S. President's land instead of their own; they are simply its laborers. Again, Winnemucca describes the Northern Paiute's willingness to work, but in much more guarded language: "Now of course we could not disobey as we lived there, and we worked for the money. The boys and women went to work and worked six days faithfully" (7). She then details his underhanded insistence that they use their pay to buy clothes and food, which Parrish had freely provided. Rinehart has thus violated both Northern Paiute and Anglo-American concepts of fairness and responsibility.

Throughout, Winnemucca's language offers a pointed critique of Rinehart and other whites who seek to dispossess the Paiutes. As she does in *Life Among the Piutes*, Winnemucca uses the phrase "of course" to underline the common sense and integrity of the Northern Paiutes in the face of Rinehart's duplicity: "Of course we could not disobey" (7) and "we had a row of course right away" (8). Winnemucca is not above using stereotypical language, but she does so with quotation marks so as to differentiate between the whites' words and her own. For instance, she describes another tribe who "as you call it 'went on the war path'" (8). At the same time, then, she uses language her audience would recognize as its own *and* asserts it as distinct from hers. She goes on to refer to their "medicine man – as you would call it," calling attention to the distinction between white conceptions of the world and her own. She goes on to voice their protest: "We said that we did not want to be played with like children" (8). In repeating this protest, she makes it more difficult for the legislators before her to treat her like a child. Winnemucca concludes this section with a description, familiar to readers of *Life Among the Piutes*, of her valiant rescue of her people from the Paiutes. Her extensive answer to the first question thus underscores her people's integrity and her own bravery – a sharp contrast from the tale of defeat that we might expect.

Although the remainder of the testimony is of a more predictable question-and-answer format, Winnemucca continues to hold her own: when the chairman asks who this agent was, she responds, "I think you must all be acquainted with [the name], Mr. Rinehart." Although we don't know the precise tone in which this was spoken, the words suggest a certain impatience on Winnemucca's part: a sense that she won't allow them to pretend innocence of the "Indian Ring" that, along with Rinehart, cast aspersions upon her character. A later response echoes this: when Mr. George asks her who was the person she accused of selling "firewater," she says, "Why ... our agent" (18). Her description of the Paiutes' forced removal to the Yakima Reservation employs the sentimentality with which her readers would be familiar, a language designed to win the hearts of the audience. Showing her dexterity as a rhetorician, she emphasizes the vulnerability and innocence of her people in order to make the removal all the more tragic:

> The women were crying because they were carrying their little frozen children in their arms, and of course the soldiers never could stop, and they would dig into the snow as deep as over your head, to try to dig a grave, and even if they wanted to dig

a grave they could not, and the only way the mother could do [this] was to stop off to one side and dig out a little hole and stick her little frozen child under the snow.

(10)

In her words the bodies of dead children are literally "strung along the side of the road frozen to death for nothing" (10). One of Winnemucca's skills as a rhetorician, then, is to use words to mold the earthen landscape her audience envisions.

As if uncomfortable lingering too long in sentimentality, however, Winnemucca changes tactics. The Paiute's "pleas" for Malheur quickly turn from the President's action to her own: "He asked them to give it back to us, which they did, and I will show how I got it" (11). This is followed by her confident proclamation, "I got the reservation. I got 100 acres for each head of a family to work on and live on, and I got it all back" (11). This apparent victory occurs despite the fact that the government did not, in fact, follow through with their promise, leaving the Paiutes to feel "trifled with" (11). She then returns to the language of "pleading and begging," perhaps believing this the best strategy at that point. Describing Rinehart and Curry as a "lion [who] was lying there with his mouth open ready to shut their teeth down upon them" (12), she again uses her words to paint a particularly effective picture of her enemies.

The remainder of the transcript is a back-and-forth exchange in which Winnemucca continues to shift her rhetoric, standing her own throughout. She reminds the committee that this was her people's original land, and notes that she has spoken not only to the Commissioner of Indian Affairs but to the Secretary of the Interior and even the President of the United States, claiming "their eyes are not open yet" (13). Her initial strategy of focusing on the Northern Paiutes' agrarian labor proves useful as the legislators return to this topic, asking about their part in the construction of an irrigation ditch – suggesting it is this kind of work that gives them a right to the land. Winnemucca enthusiastically goes along, noting their construction not only of the ditch but their clearing of land, cutting of fence railings, and road work. Winnemucca's husband Hopkins makes a rare comment at this point, describing Rinehart's appointment of a storekeeper to care for government buildings on the reservation. The fact that he says so little during the testimony is further evidence that Sarah Winnemucca did not allow her position as a woman to impede her authority; she did not rely, in other words, on her white husband (who would likely occupy a much more privileged position in this environment) to craft her argument. This fight, another kind of earthen mound, is hers alone.

Moundbuilding today

William Apess and Sarah Winnemucca Hopkins lived in times when there were very few public models of Native intellectualism. Thus they were required to fashion resistance with a limited cache of materials. Today, thanks to the development of Native American studies programs in colleges and universities throughout the country, American Indians have much more support for the production and circulation of their ideas. Native American literature was taken more seriously after 1969, when N. Scott Momaday won the Pulitzer Prize for *House Made of Dawn*, and formative novels like mixed-blood author James Welch's *Winter in the Blood* (1974) and Laguna Pueblo author Leslie Marmon Silko's *Ceremony*

(1974) appeared. And like any academic field, Native American studies has evolved since the first NAS programs were established in the early 1970s; concern has moved from recovery (though such projects still, necessarily, exist) to critical theory. Early theorists in this tradition were Vine Deloria Jr. (Standing Rock Sioux), whose book *Custer Died for Your Sins* (1969) was a tremendously influential study, as was an early exploration of stereotypes of American Indian women by Rayna Green (Cherokee). Intellectuals like Paula Gunn Allen inaugurated Native feminist theory, emphasizing the early gynocentrism of tribes – an emphasis that some would later criticize as essentialist, but that offered a groundbreaking introduction to the importance of studying Native women and Native women's literature. The early essay "Towards a National Indian Literature: Cultural Authenticity in Nationalism" by Simon Ortiz (Acoma Pueblo) would become important to the later American Indian nationalist movement, while Gerald Vizenor (White Earth Anishinaabe) embraced the poststructuralist theory that was so critical to other forms of literary study. The perseverance of Vizenor's theory is evident in the production of the new journal *Transmotion*, which is dedicated to scholarship his works have inspired.

Another important early work in Native American Studies was Robert Warrior's *The People and the Word*, which considers American Indian intellectual history with a focus on Vine Deloria and John Joseph Mathews (Osage), pursues a literary analysis of Mathews's novel *Sundown*, and finally makes an argument for what he calls "intellectual sovereignty" as a means of moving beyond essentialism and dealing with political sovereignty and other concerns of Native people. David Martinez (Gila River Pima) also offers important histories of Native intellectuals, such as Charles Eastman (Santee Sioux) and Vine Deloria Jr., as do scholars like Fred Hoxie, Maureen Konkle, and Cherokee scholar Jace Weaver.

In 2006, a branch of thought called "American Indian Literary Nationalism" (AILN) emerged, following in Warrior's, Weaver's, and, originally, Simon Ortiz's footsteps as a call for Indian nationhood. AILN was most forcefully articulated in Craig Womack's *Red on Red*, *American Indian Literary Nationalism* by Jace Weaver, Warrior, and Womack, and the collection *Reasoning Together* with Lisa Brooks (Abenaki). AILN developed partly in response to Elvia Pulitano's book *Toward a Native American Critical Theory*, which Weaver, Warrior, and Womack argued mischaracterized their theory as essentialist. This initial acrimony became in 2011, at the Emory University panel "Cosmopolitanism and Nationalism in Native American Literature," a healthy debate about the role of sovereignty in Native American Studies.[2]

Since that time the conversation has continued to evolve, with most scholars emphasizing the importance of tribal (rather than a Pan-Indian) knowledge: studies have come to focus more specifically on, for example, the literature and history of scholars' own tribes: Cherokee (Daniel Heath Justice), Haudenosaunee (Penelope Kelsey) Diné (Jennifer Denetdale), Muscogee Creek (Craig Womack), and Native Hawaii (Noenoe Silva). At the same time, the field has expanded in certain ways, with an increased consideration of globalization and transnationalism (Huhndorf) or, in Chadwick Allen's terms, "trans-Indigeneity." Much scholarship has challenged stereotypical, limiting concepts of Native identity, such as *Playing Indian* and *Indians in Unexpected Places* by Phil Deloria, *Native Hubs* by Reyna Ramirez (Winnebago), and *Indian Blues: American Indians and the Politics of Music, 1879–1934* by John Troutman. Others, such as Brenda Child (Red Lake Ojibwe), K. Tsianina Lomawaima (Mvskoke/Creek Nation), and Amelia Katanski have contributed to, and revised, accounts of Native American history by examining boarding schools. Recent work by Mark Rifkin, Daniel Heath Justice, Deborah Miranda (Ohlone-Costanoan Esselen Nation of California), and Lisa Tatonetti have made important inroads into the intersections of queer theory and Native American studies. Increased awareness of the importance of preserving Native languages has manifested in a host of language programs, activism, and research by Anishinaabe scholars Margaret Noodin and David Treuer. Sovereignty remains a major topic, from the work of Kahnawake scholars Taiaiake Alfred and Audra Simpson, Kevin Bruyneel's *Third Space of Sovereignty*, and *X-Marks* by Scott Richard Lyons (Ojibwe/Dakota), which examines the complex ways American Indians have navigated sovereignty within and on the edges of the U.S. nation.

Transit of Empire by Jodi Byrd (Chickasaw) represents yet another turn in the field: the recentering of Native American studies at the center of theory rather than a voice from its margins. Byrd argues that it is "Indianness" that the United States largely relies upon in order to enact imperialism. The importance of her book was evident at the 2014 Native American Indigenous Studies Conference, where two panels were dedicated to it. Byrd's work marks a crucial turn from Native intellectualism on the edges of society, as it was constructed in Apess's and Winnemucca's time, to a central locus for critical thought.

But to return to one of Robert Warrior's central questions, what responsibility do Native intellectuals have for Native Americans beyond the academy? Andrea Smith models the kind of engaged intellectualism that Warrior envisions in Apess; she combines extensive scholarship on violence against Native women with grassroots community organizing such as INCITE! Winona LaDuke (White Earth Ojibwe) offers a similar model, as a writer, activist, and director of the environmental organization Honor the Earth. As she argues, the production and preservation of wild rice is key to the cultural sovereignty and survival of the Anishinaabe. Likewise, Suzan Harjo (Cheyenne and Hodulgee Muscogee), director of the Morning Star Institute and author of a number of poems and essays, has been at the forefront of legal battles such as NAGPRA and the racist name of an NFL team. And as mixed-blood historian Donald Fixico reminds us in his book *The American Indian Mind in a Linear World*, we should not limit the term "Native American intellectual" to the academy; many American Indian people, particularly elders, hold a wisdom that, like the mounds themselves, is minimized only to our collective detriment.

Allison Adelle Hedge Coke's brilliant poetry collection *Blood Run*, which speaks the voices of various constituents of a present-day, 700-year-old moundbuilding site, is built in a fashion nearly as complex as the mounds themselves: an elaborate indigenous mathematical matrix explicated by Chadwick Allen's award-winning essay "Serpentine Figures, Sinuous Relations: Thematic Geography in Allison Hedge Coke's *Blood Run*." While participating in a panel at the Native American Literary Symposium in 2010, Hedge Coke responded to Allen's presentation with the admission that she never thought anyone would decipher the pattern of the poems. These poems' creation – and their interpretation – require an intellectualism not always included in the western imaginary, and they represent exactly the kind of thought that I would argue is key to Indigenous intellectualism: a careful observation of natural forms and an ability to replicate or interpret those forms in a creative way. Allison Adelle Hedge Coke captures this sentiment in one of "The Mounds" poems of *Blood Run*:

Latin precise in accordance; constellation rise; cyclic phenomena; lunar cycle; solar event; in the matter of being positioned relevant to all that was – will be. Measured by line, multidimensional, geometrical design, envisioned, embraced, made form from rope lines calculating paths, fiery loved ones guiding us here in this world from far beyond.

(ll. 11–14)

Here the language of past and present converge, signaling an intellectualism that draws us together.

Notes

1 Unpublished ms; Sally Zanjani private papers, University of Nevada.
2 This panel exemplifies the kind of collaboration between Native and non-Native scholars of American Indian Studies that is ideal. In keeping with the Indigenous-centered scope of this collection, I emphasize scholarship done by Native Americans (in part by indicating their tribal affiliation in parentheses after their names). I believe, though, that I would be remiss in leaving out non-Native scholars who have also contributed to the field. Perhaps Craig Womack says it best in his defense of his use of "sovereignty" in *American Indian Literary Nationalism*: "There is no claim in *Red on Red* that nationhood is pure, purely Indian or purely anything, or authentic. The book, instead, concerns itself with how sovereignty might be relevant to modern Indian life. Once again, it is philosophically untenable to assume sovereignty constitutes an inherent demand for purity, isolation, and authenticity. Since sovereignty, by definition, has to do with government-to-government relations, it has everything to do with intersections and exchanges between inside and outside worlds" (111)

Works cited

Alfred, Taiaiake, "Sovereignty." 1999. Rpt in *Sovereignty Matters: Locations of Contestation and Struggle in Indigenous Struggles for Self-Determination.* Ed. Joanne Barker. Lincoln: University of Nebraska Press, 2006. 33–50.
Allen, Chadwick. "Serpentine Figures, Sinuous Relations: Thematic Geography in Allison Hedge Coke's *Blood Run.*" *American Literature* 82. 4 (2010): 807–34.
——. *Trans-Indigenous: Methodologies for Global Native Literary Studies.* Minneapolis: University of Minnesota Press, 2012.
Allen, Paula Gunn. *The Sacred Hoop: Recovering the Feminine in American Indian Traditions.* Boston: Beacon, 1986.
Apess, William. *The Experiences of Five Christian Indians of the Pequod Tribe.* 1833. Rpt in *On Our Own Ground: The Complete Writing of William Apess.* Ed. Barry O'Connell. Amherst: University of Massachusetts Press, 1992. 59–101.
——. *Indian Nullification.* Boston: Press of Jonathan Howe, 1835. Project Gutenberg. 24 Dec. 2014.
Brooks, Lisa. *The Common Pot: The Recovery of Native Space in the Northeast.* Minneapolis: University of Minnesota Press, 2008.
Brooks, Lisa et al. "Cosmopolitanism and Nationalism in Native American Literature: A Panel Discussion." *Southern Spaces.* Emory University. Web. Accessed 21 June 2011. http://southernspaces. org/2011/cosmopolitanism-and-nationalism-native-american-literature-panel-discussion
Bruyneel, Kevin. *The Third Space of Sovereignty: The Postcolonial Politics of U.S.–Indigenous Relations.* Minneapolis: University of Minnesota Press, 2007.

NATIVE AMERICAN INTELLECTUALS

Byrd, Jodi. *The Transit of Empire: Indigenous Critiques of Colonialism*. Minneapolis: University of Minnesota Press, 2011.

Chaatsmith, Marti. "Singing at a Center of the Indian World: The SAI and Ohio Earthworks." *American Indian Quarterly* 37.3 (Summer 2013): 181–98.

Child, Brenda J. *Boarding School Seasons: American Indian Families, 1900–1940*. Lincoln: University of Nebraska Press, 1998.

Deloria, Philip J. *Indians in Unexpected Places*. Lawrence: University Press of Kansas, 2004.

——. *Playing Indian*. New Haven, CT: Yale University Press, 1998.

Deloria, Vine, Jr. *Custer Died for Your Sins: An Indian Manifesto*. 1969. Norman: University of Oklahoma Press, 2008.

Denetdale, Jennifer. *Reclaiming Diné History: The Legacies of Chief Manuelito and Juanita*. Tucson: University of Arizona Press, 2007.

Driskill, Qwo-Li, Daniel Heath Justice, Deborah Miranda & Lisa Tatonetti, eds. *Sovereign Erotics: A Collection of Two-Spirit Literature*. Tucson: University of Arizona Press, 2011.

Eastman, Charles. *From the Deep Woods to Civilization: Chapters in the Autobiography of an Indian*. Boston: Little, Brown, 1916.

Fixico, Donald. *The American Indian Mind in a Linear World*. 2003. New York: Routledge, 2013.

Gaul, Therese Strouth. "Genre and Public Discourse in William Apess's *Indian Nullification*." *ATQ: 19th Century American Literature and Culture* 15. 3 (2001): 276–92.

Green, Rayna. "The Tribe Called Wannabee: Playing Indian in America and Europe." *Folklore* 99. 1 (1988): 30–55.

Haas, Angela. "Wampum as Hypertext: An American Indian Intellectual Tradition of Multimedia Theory and Practice." *Studies in American Indian Literature* 19.4 (2007): 77–100.

Hallett, Benjamin. "Rights of the Marshpee Indians." 1834. Rpt. in *Indian Nullification of the Unconstitutional Laws of Massachusetts, Relative to the Marshpee Tribe: or, the Pretended Riot Explained*. William Apes [sic]. Boston: Jonathan Howe, Printer, 1835. 7–8. Web. Accessed 25 Nov. 2014. https://archive.org/details/indiannullificat00apes

Hedge Coke, Allison. *Blood Run*. London: Salt, 2006.

Hively, Ray & Robert Horn. "Geometry and Astronomy in Prehistoric Ohio." *Archaeoastronomy* 4 (1982): 1–20.

Hopkins, Sarah Winnemucca. *Life Among the Piutes: Their Wrongs and Claims*. 1883. Vintage West Series. Reno: University of Nevada Press, 1994.

Hoxie, Frederick E. *This Indian Country: American Indian Activists and the Place They Made*. New York: Penguin, 2013.

Huhndorf, Shari M. *Mapping the Americas: The Transnational Politics of Contemporary Native Culture*. Ithaca, NY: Cornell University Press, 2009.

Hutchins, Francis G. *Mashpee, The Story of Cape Cod's Indian Town*. West Franklin, NH: Amarta, 1979.

Justice, Daniel Heath. *Our Fire Survives the Storm: A Cherokee Literary History*. Minneapolis: University of Minnesota Press, 2006.

Katanski, Amelia. *Learning to Write 'Indian': The Boarding School Experience and American Indian Literature*. Norman: University of Oklahoma Press, 2005.

Kelsey, Penelope Myrtle. *Tribal Theory in American Indian Literature: Dakota and Haudenosaunee Writing and Indigenous Worldviews*. Lincoln: University of Nebraska Press, 2008.

Konkle, Maureen. *Writing Indian Nations: Native Intellectuals and the Politics of Historiography, 1827–1863*. Chapel Hill: University of North Carolina Press, 2004.

Lomawaima, Tsianina K. *They Called It Prairie Light: The Story of Chilocco Indian School*. Lincoln: University of Nebraska Press, 1994.

Lyons, Scott Richard. *X-Marks: Native Signatures of Assent*. Minneapolis: University of Minnesota Press, 2010.

375

Martinez, David. *Dakota Philosopher: Charles Eastman and American Indian Thought*. Minneapolis: Minnesota Historical Society Press, 2009.

Mathews, John Joseph. *Sundown*. 1934. Norman: University of Oklahoma Press, 1988.

Momaday, N. Scott. *House Made of Dawn*. 1968. New York: HarperCollins, 2010.

Noodin, Margaret. *Bawaajimo: A Dialect of Dreams in Anishinaabe Language and Literature*. East Lansing: Michigan State University Press, 2014.

O'Connell, Barry, ed. *On Our Own Ground: The Complete Writing of William Apess*. Amherst: University of Massachusetts Press, 1992.

Ortiz, Simon. "Towards a National Indian Literature: Cultural Authenticity in Nationalism." 1981. *American Indian Literary Nationalism*. Ed. Jace Weaver, Craig S. Womack & Robert Warrior. Albuquerque: University of New Mexico Press, 2006. 253–60.

Powell, Malea. "Rhetorics of Survivance: How American Indians Use Writing." *College Composition and Communication* 53. 3 (2002): 396–434.

Pulitano, Elvira. *Toward a Native American Critical Theory*. Lincoln: University of Nebraska Press, 2003.

Ramirez, Rayna. *Native Hubs: Culture, Community, and Belonging in Silicon Valley and Beyond*. Durham, NC: Duke University Press, 2007.

Rifkin, Mark. *When Did Indians Become Straight? Kinship, the History of Sexuality, and Native Sovereignty*. Oxford: Oxford University Press, 2010.

Silko, Leslie Marmon. *Ceremony*. 1977. New York: Penguin, 2006.

Silva, Noenoe K. *Aloha Betrayed: Native Hawaiian Resistance to American Colonialism*. Durham: Duke University Press, 2004.

Simpson, Audra. *Mohawk Interruptus: Political Life Across the Borders of Settler States*. Durham, NC: Duke University Press, 2014.

Simpson, Audra & Andrea Smith, eds. *Theorizing Native Studies*. Durham, NC: Duke University Press, 2014.

Smith, Andrea. *Conquest: Sexual Violence and American Indian Genocide*. Cambridge, MA: South End Press, 2005.

Treuer, David. *Native American Fiction: A User's Manual*. Minneapolis, MN: Graywolf Press, 2006.

Troutman, John. *Indian Blues: American Indians and the Politics of Music, 1879–1934*. Norman: University of Oklahoma Press, 2009.

United States. Cong. House. Committee on Indian Affairs. 48th Cong. 1st sess. Washington, D.C.: GPO, 22 April 1884.

Vizenor, Gerald. *Fugitive Poses: Native American Indian Scenes of Absence and Presence*. Lincoln: University of Nebraska Press, 2000.

Warrior, Robert. *The People and the Word: Reading Native Nonfiction*. Minneapolis: University of Minnesota Press, 2005.

Weaver, Jace. *That the People Might Live: Native American Literatures and Native American Community*. New York: Oxford University Press, 1997.

Weaver, Jace, Craig S. Womack & Robert Warrior. *American Indian Literary Nationalism*. Albuquerque: University of New Mexico Press, 2006.

Welch, James. *Winter in the Blood*. 1974. New York: Penguin, 2008.

Womack, Craig S. *Red on Red: Native American Literary Separatism*. Minneapolis: University of Minnesota Press, 1999.

Womack, Craig S., Daniel Heath Justice & Christopher B. Teuton. *Reasoning Together: The Native Critics Collective*. Norman: University of Oklahoma Press, 2008.

Part V
LITERARY FORMS

32

Crossing the Bering Strait
Transpacific Turns and Native Literatures

Iping Liang

In *The Trickster of Liberty: Native Heirs to a Wild Baronage* (1988), Anishinaabe American writer and critic Gerald Vizenor turns his eye to the watery crossroads between North America and Asia. In this episodic narrative, Vizenor creates a fictional tribal township by the name of Patronia, which is owned by the trickster patriarch Luster Browne. In his self-fashioned oral tradition, Vizenor recounts the family saga of three generations of the Brownes in the wild baronage. To celebrate the birth of his first grandchild, Luster Browne or "Lusterbow claimed that he heard the echo of her name (China Browne) when he shouted into a panic hole, down to the other side of the earth, to the other world" (*Trickster* 15). Hence, the first grandchild is named "China Browne."

If the connotation of China as "the other world" seems to suggest the exotic and outlandish customs of China, or Asia, at large, it's a misconception in disguise. Native Americans have had close interactions with Asia.[1] Gerald Vizenor, among others, not only writes about his experiences in China and Japan, but also incorporates Asian literary traditions into his trickster discourses. A well-known author of haiku, Vizenor combines the tradition of Anishinaabe trickster with that of Monkey King from the Chinese classic, *The Journey to the West*. If "crossreading" – "the way in which all of us engage texts across some kind of cultural boundary or conceptual horizon" is a "precondition" (Owens 5), Native American writers' adoption of Asian literary forms is, I argue, a form of "crosswriting" (see Owens 3–11; Pulitano 2003, 101–43). In the spirit of "crosswriting," this chapter investigates literary border-crossings between Native America and Asia. First, I focus on the transpacific turn in Native American literature by looking at the career of Gerald Vizenor as a point of reference. Then, I examine the influence of Asian literary forms and philosophical contexts in Native American writing by centering on the works of Gerald Vizenor, Mary TallMountain, Nora Marks Dauenhauer, and William Oandasan. Points of impact between Native American and indigenous Asian writers are then highlighted in my discussion of Ainu writer Shigeru Kayano in Japan and Atayal writer Walis Norgan in Taiwan.

The transpacific turn

As anthropologists have researched, there are numerous historical records of geographical border-crossing between Native America and Asia. Linda Lizut Helstern points out, "the best-known story about Indians, after all, is the story of their migration to the Americas from their original Asian homelands" (136). In *The Trickster of Liberty*, China Browne's brother, Ginseng Browne, is involved in the ginseng trade with the Chinese, and he tells a white postman:

> "The Chinese, you see, are one of the long lost tribes, our brothers," said the trickster with a smile. "You must have heard about the Bering Strait? Well, we migrated from here to there, and now they are coming back. So you see, this is their real homeland"
>
> (136)

By revoking the anthropological myth, Vizenor re-routes the trajectory and "reimagines" how the Chinese would cross the Bering Strait to "come home" to North America. That is to say, the Chinese are virtually Native: they are one of the "lost tribes" of Native America.

Despite the controversy regarding the Bering Strait hypothesis, there have been close relationships between Native America and Asia. For example, the ginseng trade portrayed in *The Trickster of Liberty* had been thriving between North America and China.[2] As early as 1784, when the Empress of China set sail from New York harbor to Canton, there were 30 tons of American ginseng aboard, all of native species. In 1854 Commodore Matthew Perry opened Japan not only to western trade and culture, but also to the influence of American Indian policy, which affected Japanese colonial domination over the Ainu (see Medak-Saltzman 2008). In more recent times, Native Americans have been brought to Asia by war. In Leslie Marmon Silko's *Ceremony*, Tayo's uncle joins the war and sees his Native brothers in the Philippine jungles. In Linda Hogan's *People of the Whale*, Thomas joins the war and meets his second wife in Vietnam. Vizenor's enlistment in the Korean War and chance arrival in Japan introduces him to haiku, which was getting popular as a result of the American occupation of Japan (1945–1972). In addition, the use of the Navajo Code in the Battle of Okinawa has been recognized as an instance of "global indigenous encounter" (see Medak-Saltzman 2010).

Critics such as Danika Medak-Saltzman, Elvira Pulitano, and Brigitte Georgi-Findlay have argued that there has been a transnational turn in Native American literature. In her introduction to *Transatlantic Voices: Interpretations of Native North American Literatures,* Pulitano states that European scholars "take the Atlantic as a site of cross-cultural exchange and circulation of ideas, a bridge linking in the Old and New Worlds" (xiii). Drawing on Paul Gilroy's *The Black Atlantic*, Pulitano observes that European scholars "interested in transnational and intercultural perspectives have found in the Atlantic a fruitful, creative space around which to articulate ideas on ethnicity, race, gender, class, sovereignty, nationalism, migration, and language in an increasingly globalized world" (xiii). She draws on recent developments in the fields of postcolonialism and globalization to argue that Native North American literary studies could benefit from dialogues with these critical discourses.

Likewise, Brigitte Georgi-Findley in "Transatlantic Crossings: New Developments in the Contemporary North American Novel" argues that there has been a "cosmopolitan" trend in recent novels by Native American authors. She contends that "many recent novels explore transcultural connections and point to the instability of ethnic and national identities by tracing affinities between people beyond culture, ethnicity, and nationality" (89). By examining the characteristics of Native American authors – from the "blood memory" of N. Scott Momaday, the "mixedblood frontier" of Louis Owens, the modernist influences from Hemingway, Eliot, and Faulkner, and the postindian "trickster discourse" of Gerald Vizenor – Georgi-Findley regards the "Native encounter with Europe" as a new theme of recent Native American novels. Citing *Gardens in the Dunes* and *Heartsong of Charging Elk* as examples, she argues that both Leslie Marmon Silko and James Welch "explore the boundaries of culture by pointing to transcultural connections and the instability of ethnic and national identities" (105). Moreover, Georgi-Findley argues:

> [if] Silko uses Europe as a positive, contrastive foil in order to explore the failures of white America, Welch explores the way Europeans use Indians to express their criticism of or ambivalence toward America, masking the realities of racial exclusion in their own societies.
>
> (105)

While I find the critiques of Pulitano and Georgi-Findlay to be inspiring, they fail to address transpacific dialogues between Native America and Asia. If we take Vizenor as a case study, his military service in Japan in the 50s and his subsequent volumes of haiku poetry signify Vizenor's transpacific turn. In 1987 Vizenor published *Griever: An American Monkey King in China*, focusing on trickster travels in China. A year later, *The Trickster of Liberty* reverses the trafficking by having the Chinese cross the Bering Strait and return to Native America. While Japan and China have served as important "sites and transits" (see Shirley Lim), I maintain that there have been two-way crossings between Native America and Asia. In the following discussion, I examine Native American writers' adoption of Asian literary forms, as well as the reception and influence of Native American literature among Asian indigenous writers.

Haiku poetics

In terms of Asian literary form, haiku is undoubtedly the most dominant style of "cross-writing" that has been adopted by American writers. Charles Trumbull explains in "The American Haiku Movement" that haiku poems had been written by American writers as early as the 1930s and that haiku poetry and Asian philosophies resurged as a result of the occupation of Japan. Kenneth Yasuda published *The Japanese Haiku* in 1957, which opened the door to the haiku renaissance in America. Harold G. Henderson published *An Introduction to Haiku* in 1958; R. H. Blyth, who served in Japan during the Occupation years, published *A History of Haiku* in 1963. In addition, the Beat generation poets, such as Kenneth Rexroth, Gary Snyder, Jack Kerouac, and Allen Ginsberg helped to promote the popularity of haiku. The result has been remarkable. As Karen Jackson Ford claims, "haiku was 'no longer synonymous with Japan'" (333).

In the context of American poetry, haiku has, however, become "synonymous with Native America" (Ford 336). As Ford observes in her excellent contextualization of the affinities between Native America and Japan: "US haiku writers have persistently employed haiku as a form for poems about Native peoples" (336). Gerald Vizenor is clearly the most well-established Native American haiku poet. To date, Vizenor has published thirteen books of haiku. Kimberly Blaeser notes, "Vizenor's army tour included a stint in Japan ... [and] the Japanese experience brought Vizenor into intimate contact with the haiku tradition" (258).

381

In *The Poetry and Poetics of Gerald Vizenor*, the most comprehensive single-volume of criticism concerning Vizenor's poetry to date, Deborah Madsen states: "Vizenor has explained his discovery of haiku and its proximity to Anishinaabe dream songs as a key to his poetics of survivance" (x). Madsen and her contributors further the scholarship of Vizenor's poetry and poetics in three ways. First, as Madsen notes, "the repetition of tropes has become Vizenor's signature phraseology" (xiv). Critics comment on Vizenor's repeated "reimaginings, revisions, and returns" to the same tropes and themes; notably, the violent death of his father, the killing of the squirrel, and the rewrites of *Summer in the Spring*. Second, they pay attention to the extensive influence of haiku upon Vizenor's prose (Madsen xi). This is particularly important because haiku has become not only the form, but also the aesthetics of his *corpus*. As Madsen observes, "the language that Vizenor uses to describe his aesthetic clearly derives from his writing of poetry and particularly the discipline of composing haiku poems" (*Understanding* 21). Third, David Moore's notion of "haiku hermeneutics" registers the ambiguity, indeterminacy and openness that distinguishes Vizenor's texts (Madsen xxi), a notion that Madsen describes as "haiku-inspired poetics" – "the promise of experiences as an imagined dreamscape, grounded in, but transforming, the natural world" (xxi).

Moore's notion of "haiku hermeneutics" characterizes Vizenor's hybrid poetics. Comparing Frances Densmore's translation of Anishinaabe dream songs and Vizenor's haiku poems, Adam Spry argues that "if Densmore's Japanese style is incidental, Vizenor's is decidedly purposeful" (35). By comparing different versions of "Song of the Crows," Spry notes how Vizenor removes the punctuation marks and the first-person pronoun to endow the original poem with a "greater indeterminancy ... [and thus] transform the Densmore transcription into an 'open text,'" as Blaeser has argued (qtd. in Spry 35). Traces of this indeterminancy can also be observed in Vizenor's prose work. In *Bearheart: The Heirship Chronicles*, Proude Cedarfair is introduced in "Morning Prelude" presiding over the cedar nation. When he is taking a bath in the *misisibi*, "the clown crows wait in the trees" (6). As the crows are waiting, the silence and stillness seems to suggest an implied event or action, thus creating a moment of "potent pause," which is a feature of Vizenor's haiku poetics. Another trait is Vizenor's tendency to craft concise, haiku-like headings, like the twelve chapter titles in *Chair of Tears*, which are "almost exclusively" rendered in two-word four-syllable phrases – "Captain Eighty," "Chair of Tears," "Removal Treaty," "Full House Casino," "Panic Hole Chancery," "Irony Dogs," "Skin Dunk," "Last Lecture," "Postindian Holograms," "Denivance Press," "Stray Visions," and "Earthdiver Auction" – and this has been a feature of Vizenor's chapter headings. Most importantly, unlike the elegiac sorrow associated with the Vanishing Indian ideology, Vizenor conveys in haiku the very presence of the Anishinaabe people. In the 1993 edition of *Summer in the Spring*, Vizenor writes, "all around/the sky/with my sound/i come to you" (28). While critics have commented on the effacement and impersonality of haiku, I argue that the use of the first person pronoun in the lower case signifies, however, the non-authentic and non-mythological definition of the "varionative" – a notion that Vizenor discusses in *Fugitive Poses* and is also a point well-argued by Ford (343). It is also possible to interpret the figure of the "i" as the personification of the crane. The first-person, lower-cased "i" therefore speaks the everlasting re-sounding of the crane clan. Haiku is, in essence, "[Vizenor's] aesthetic survivance" (*Postindian* 65).

Mary TallMountain (1918–1994), Nora Marks Dauenhauer (1927–), and William Oandasan (1947–1992) are other notable Native American haiku poets. TallMountain was born in Nulato, Alaska, located one hundred miles south of the Arctic Circle. Her

CROSSING THE BERING STRAIT

troubled life evidences the historical turmoil Native Athabaskan People had lived through. When TallMountain was born in 1918, it was only fifty years after the Alaska Purchase. The Native Athabaskan people experienced the change of federal government from Russia to the United States. Her Koyukon/Athabaskan/Russian mother met her Scottish/Irish/American father and gave birth to her and her younger brother. The cultural clash, the political disruption, the loss of her mother, and her adoption by a Caucasian couple at the age of six all left indelible marks of trauma and became the primary motivation for writing. The poem, "Indian Blood," concerns the humiliation she experienced in what she calls the "Outside," the term coined by TallMountain to indicate the "outside" of her Native village in Nulato. TallMountain recalls a performance in which she participated at school. When she stumbled over the "slivered board" ("Indian Blood" l. 3) on stage, she was ridiculed by the audience who shouted at her, "Do you live in an igloo?" Feeling deeply ashamed, she describes the traumatized experience: how the protagonist bit her finger at night until it was punctured with dark-colored moon-like drops of "Indian blood."

The image of "moons of dark/Indian blood" suggests a haiku-like opposition between dark and paleness, Indian-ness and whiteness; her wearisome life had been worsened by radical cancer and serious bouts of alcoholism. Paula Gunn Allen recalled how often TallMountain had been hospitalized, and discharged, and how the cycle had continued. In addition, her twenty-year residence in the San Francisco Tenderloin district, associating with the street people, the immigrants, and the homeless, had deepened her understanding of underclass misery. TallMountain began to write poems in the 60s and continued to publish until the 90s. In a career spanning over thirty years, she had overcome many barriers and shone through with a "quiet confidence among a people" (Breinig 71). Allen regarded TallMountain as a Coyote, "that quintessential old survivor" (2–3). TallMountain published seven collections of poetry and is positive about her Native Athabaskan heritage. Caroline Heller recounts the lively gathering among women writers in the Tenderloin, in which TallMountain took part, by combining drama and TallMountain's "talk story" of a poem "Soogha Brother,"[3] dedicated to her brother whom she "never knew."[4]

As Gabrielle Welford argues, TallMountain's "writing is that of a healer, a re-membering of self and others" (141). She writes to "go home" and the haiku poetics comes to her by way of a spirit animal. In her most anthologized poem, "The Last Wolf," TallMountain gives a voice to years of dislocation, disruption, and disinheritance in the figure of a "last wolf." In the beginning, the last wolf is rushing toward the narrator through the damaged city. The narrator describes the wolf's passage through the urban wasteland to the room where she sits. The narrator watches the wolf scurry across the floor and lay his muzzle on the white sheet of the bed. She notices that his eyes are glowing yellow and his eyebrows are trembling. At this moment, the wolf stops and the narrator comes to a sudden realization – she knows what they have done to the wolf. Clearly, "what they have done" is the total destruction of nature. The poem ends with a haiku moment of epiphany: while the wolf and the narrator stand together in witness of the "ruined city," they also give testimony to the survivance of Native Athabaska.

If haiku produces as a sudden realization for TallMountain, it functions differently in the hands of Nora Marks Dauenhauer. Born in 1927, Dauenhauer is from the Tlingit Nation, located on the Pacific Northwest Coast of North America. The Tlingit People are the "people of the tide," surrounded by the Pacific Ocean on the west coast. Widely known for her collections and translations of Tlingit oral tradition, Dauenhauer has published two books of poetry and is recognized for her "haiku-like poems [that] are reminiscent of traditional Tlingit songs" (Russell 30). Like TallMountain, Dauenhauer expresses a strong haiku aesthetics. In "The Droning Shaman," she describes the Bering Sea as a "droning shaman" whose mouth is creased with the spray and misty foam that wash up the St. Paul Island. The poem captures an imagistic glimpse of the Bering Sea. While "spraying" and "cleaning" suggest the sea in motion, the misty figure of the "droning shaman," however, implies a timeless mystery. As Andrea Lerner observes, the poem is highly place-centered, rendered with a heightened awareness of the Tlingit Nation (37).

While TallMountain writes to heal the childhood trauma of dislocation and disinheritance, Dauenhauer does so to preserve and revive the Native Tlingit language. Under the pressure of the dominant society, Dauenhauer plays the role of a linguistic physician to maintain the oral tradition. While she aims to preserve the tradition, she also understands the necessity of adaptation. The juxtaposition of both tradition and adaptation characterizes the conversational, playful, and inviting tone of the narrative in "How To Make Good Baked Salmon." While the poem is literally a Tlingit cook book about "making good baked salmon," the Tlingit sacred fish, it is also a survival kit for sustainability. For example, the opening stanza shows how flexible a modern Tlingit would "make good baked salmon." Instead of traditional bar-b-q sticks of alder wood, he/she would make do with the oven. Instead of the river salmon which would cost $4.99 a pound in the supermarket, the modern Tlingit would make do with the salmon poached from the river. While the oven has replaced alder sticks, the humor and irony implied in the poached salmon signifies a radical change in the traditional way life. Most importantly, the repetition of "in this case" suggests on the one hand the fast pace of modern life, and on the other the continuity of the oral tradition. The price sign of "$4.99 a pound," moreover, renders a highly visual haiku-like image of modern life in the supermarket.

Caskey Russell argues that the "How To" poem is a "tool of self-definition," functioning as a "powerful expression of Tlingit culture and sense of place" (29). Likewise, in "My Grandfather, Blind and Nearly Deaf," Dauenhauer writes about the family experience of a boat ride in a storm. While her father and brothers are trying to brave the storm, she stays inside the cabin and informs her grandfather about what is happening. She describes how she would look at her grandfather's long eyebrows and get very close, for both of them like to see by getting close. In a conversational and carefree idiom, the narrator communicates an important message: in the storm of modernity, the Tlingit tradition will be preserved if one can get "really close to see." Pausing the poem with the action "of seeing," Dauenhauer also suggests a haiku moment of epiphany.

While both TallMountain and Dauenhauer are Native from Alaska, William Oandasan was born on the Round Valley Reservation in northern California. A pioneer of Native American literature in the 70s, Oandasan was of mixed Yuki and Filipino heritage. He published three volumes of haiku poems and *Round Valley Songs* won the American Book Award from the Before Columbus Foundation in 1985. Like Dauenhauer, Oandasan writes place-based haiku poetry of the Ukomno'm, the Valley People. In "Grandmother's Land," Oandasan paints a landscape intertwined with ancestry and redwood trees, as the flesh and blood of the family become entangled with the grandmother's womb of redwood for five generations. As the flesh and blood of the family grow like the branches, leaves and sprouts of the redwood tree, the "grandmother's land" is now the womb-land of the Valley People. In his interview with Joseph Bruchac, Oandasan explained he was first attracted to the "little nature poems" of haiku, which is an imagistic registry of the natural environment in Round Valley (3). He disciplined himself in the practice of haiku, which liberated the poem from any "'interference from the writer'" (qtd. in Ford 351). A haiku poem from the collection, *Earth and Sky* (1976), depicts an eagle. While the "cloudy sky" draws the horizontal plane, "the plummeting hawk" flashes a vertical line of flight. Together, they secure the fugitive imagery of a flying eagle against the horizon, a scene common in northern California. The haiku, "Marking Time," is also remarkable as it "marks time" by rendering the marks of seventeen "X's." While the seventeen "X's" are related to the seventeen syllables in haiku, the pictographic nature of the mark "X" reminds us of Native American drawings on caves and rocks. As it suggests the timelessness of Native Peoples, it also mocks the senselessness of any marking of time by the calendar. Ford further argues that "haiku 'marks' time by measuring it in syllables, by noting the specific details of life, and by abiding in the imaginative spaces emptied by displacement and loss" (350–51). That is to say, while "'marking time' is the opposite of vanishing" (Ford 351), haiku aesthetics marks the everlasting presence of Native Americans.

As the poetic form of haiku originated from Japan, it is interesting to observe how Oandasan expresses his concern with Japan. When the poem was written in 1984, it was already forty years after World War II. The shadows of the atomic bombing in Hiroshima still "hang" "over the valley and earth" like a holocaust. As alarming as Native American writers' reaction to atomic bombing is, I explore how Asian indigenous writers respond to the holocaust of Native Americans in the following section.

The transpacific intimacies

My framework of "transpacific intimacies" among Native Peoples in America, Japan, and Taiwan draws upon the work of Danika Medak-Saltzman (see "Staging Empire"). As Medak-Saltzman contends, the Japanese colonial domination of the Ainu was heavily influenced by U.S. federal Indian policy. The repercussions of this impact were threefold. First, the colonial policy caused the annexation of the Ainu Moshir (the Ainu land), which became the territory of Japan in 1869 and was subsequently renamed as modern-day Hokkaido. Second, if we compare the Ainu in Japan with the Athabaskan in Alaska, we realize that what the Ainu had experienced was actually similar to that of the Athabaskan after the signing of the Alaska Purchase in 1867. That is to say, the imposition of American Indian policy had actually caused the destruction of Native life ways across the Bering Strait – encompassing the Ainu, the Athabaska, and the Tlingit. Third, when Japan colonized Taiwan (the island of Formosa) in 1895, it continued the same policy of colonial domination and caused the Jomonization of Taiwan indigenous peoples. While the Ainu and Taiwan Indigenous Peoples had been subject to colonial domination in Japan, it was really a mimicry of American Indian policy. Hence, what I call "transpacific intimacies" signifies the close interconnectedness among Native Peoples across the Bering Strait, which is also evidenced in Native American and Indigenous Asian literatures.[5]

The most famous Ainu writer is Shigeru Kayano (1926–2006), who shared many similarities with his Alaskan Tlingit neighbor Nora Dauenhauer. Like her, Kayano had experienced the disintegration of the Native way of life after Japanese colonial settlement. As a native speaker of the Ainu language, Kayano became concerned with the loss of his native tongue and, like Dauenhauer, he tried hard to preserve the oral tradition and compiled the first Japanese–Ainu dictionary. In *Our Land Was a Forest: An Ainu Memoir*, which was first published in Japanese in 1980 and translated into English in 1994, Kayano recounts the three-generation family saga. He begins with his grandfather who was a "slave" to the *shamo*, the Japanese government, then moves to his father who was once arrested for "poaching" salmon (Siddle "On Being"): an incident of the kind about which Dauenhauer also writes. Finally, he turns to himself and his difficult attempts to assert his Ainu identity against the onslaught of dominant Japanese culture. More politically radical than Dauenhauer, Kayano campaigned for and helped to pass the Ainu Cultural Promotion Law in 1997, which "recognizes the Ainu as a separate ethnic nation (*minzoku*) within Japan" (Siddle "On Being"). As Benjamin Carson notes, "the history of the struggle between the Ainu and the Japanese mirrors in significant ways the ongoing conflict between American Indian nations within the United States" (443). I would argue that Shigeru Kayano is the Ainu counterpart of writers like Nora Dauenhauer and Gerald Vizenor: simple and uncluttered in language, but forceful and oppositional in politics.

Taiwan indigenous peoples have gone through colonization in two phases. First, they suffered from Jomonization between 1895 and 1945 during the Japanese occupation. Second, they have been under the domination of Chinese culture ever since the Kuomingtang came to Taiwan in 1949. Born in 1961, Walis Norgan is from the Atayal, the largest tribe in Taiwan. To date, he has published more than twenty books in Chinese, including prose, poetry, and short stories. Like Kayano, Walis is opposed to the colonial regime. In his award-winning essay, "Reading in Seven Days," he juxtaposes the history of the Atayal with that of American Indians. Divided into seven days, the narrative recounts a reading of Dee Brown's *Bury My Heart at Wounded Knee* across a period of seven days by reflecting on numerous American Indian incidents, such as Columbus and his "discovery" of the "Indios"; Little Crow, who criticized the "white man's devil water"; the defeat of the Southern Cheyennes in 1867; the death of Crazy Horse in 1877; the flight of Chief Joseph of the Nez Perces in 1877; and the final laments of Black Elk – "A people's dream died there. It was a beautiful dream … the nation's hoop is broken and scattered. There is no center any longer and the sacred tree is dead" (Walis "Reading" n. pag.). Memories of Atayal's history are interlaced with this Native American history – the loss of traditional hunting grounds, the 1921 earthquake, the flooding of the sacred river, and the bankruptcy of the Atayal tradition. While the reading continues, it ends abruptly on the seventh day with the assertion: "God ought to repose, for all deities have woven great misfortunes" (Walis "Reading" n. pag.). Reminiscent of the pause in TallMountain's "Last Wolf," the "repose" in "Reading in Seven Days" bespeaks the similar "great misfortunes" that have befallen both Native America and Indigenous Asia.

Conclusion

In her discussion of Arnold Krupat's notion of "cosmopolitan comparativism," Deborah Madsen argues for a "kind of intercultural translation" (*Native* 15), which could be compared to a literary "third space akin to Homi Bhabha's concept of a cosmopolitan space" that is situated outside of the fixed logocentric binarism, that is, "a space of transculturality or what Helmbrecht Breinig calls 'transdifference'" (14–15). Madsen's notion of "intercultural translation" and Breinig's conception of "transdifference" complement my discussions of the intercultural transdifferences between Native America and Asian indigenous writers. While Vizenor, TallMountain, Dauenhauer, and Oandasan transform the Japanese haiku and make it a particular Native American aesthetics, Kayano and Walis join forces with Native American resistance. Their literatures witness an ongoing tradition of "stories of survivance" that cross the Bering Strait.

Notes

1 The scope of this chapter is however limited to East Asia, mainly China, Japan, Taiwan, and to some extent Korea, Russia, Vietnam and the Philippines.
2 American ginseng is a herbaceous perennial plant native to deciduous forests from southern Quebec and Minnesota, south to Louisiana and Georgia. Commercial harvesting of American ginseng roots began in the early eighteenth century, when European colonists recognized its similarity to the Asian species highly valued in traditional medicine (see Schorger).
3 "Soogha" is the Athabaskan word for brother.
4 TallMountain was adopted by the Outside at age six and never saw her mother and brother. Her mother passed away two years later and her brother, whom she "never knew," died at the age of seventeen.
5 For anthropological research in this regard, please see Noboru Adachi et al, who argue that "Moreover, the fact that Hokkaido Jomons shared haplogroup D1 with Native Americans validates the hypothesized genetic affinity of the Jomon people to Native Americans, providing direct evidence for the genetic relationships between these populations." In addition, there's been cultural exchange between the Ainu and Native Peoples in the Northwest. Between 2009 and 2010, the Burke Museum at the University of Washington and the Ainu Association of Hokkaido in Japan co-sponsored Tribal Canoe Journeys, celebrating the canoe paddling tradition along the Native Pacific Northwest Coast. Ainu representatives spoke with Northwestern tribal groups (through a translator) about the common struggles they have experienced relating to colonization. Dr. Deana Dartt-Newton, Curator of Native American Ethnography at the Burke Museum said, "We had no idea, really, the extent to which these indigenous peoples have experienced the same histories of discrimination and oppression" (Dartt-Newton).

Works cited

Adachi, Noboru, et al. "Mitochondrial DNA Analysis of Jomon Skeletons from the Funadomari Site, Hokkaido, and Its Implication for the Origins of Native American." *American Journal of Physical Anthropology*. n. pag., n.d. Web. Accessed 28 Jan. 2015. http://onlinelibrary.wiley.com/doi/10.1002/ajpa.20923/abstract

Allen, Paula Gunn. Foreword. *The Light on the Tent Wall: A Bridging*. Los Angeles: UCLA American Indian Studies Center, 1990. 1–4.

Blaeser, Kimberly. "Gerald Vizenor: Postindian Liberation." *The Cambridge Companion to Native American Literature*. Ed. Joy Porter & Kenneth M. Roemer. Cambridge: Cambridge University Press, 2005. 257–69.

Blyth, R.H. *A History of Haiku*. 2 vols. Tokyo: Hokuseido Press, 1963.

Breinig, Jeane Coburn. "Review: *The Light on the Tent Wall: A Bridging*." *Studies in American Indian Literatures* 3. 4 (1991): 70–72.

Brown, Dee. *Bury My Heart at Wounded Knee: An Indian History of the American West*. New York: Holt, Rinehart & Winston, 1971.

Bruchac, Joseph. "The Poet is a Voice: An Interview with William Oandasan, 2/12/85." *Wicazo Sa Review* 2. 1 (Spring 1986): 2–9.

Carson, Benjamin. "Ainu and Anishinaabe Stories of Survivance: Shigeru Kayano, Katsuichi Honda, and Gerald Vizenor." *Tokyo Cross-Cultural Studies* 2 (2009): 443–49. Web. Accessed 30 Jan. 2015. http://kuir.jm.kansai-u.ac.jp/dspace/handle/10112/3251

Dartt-Newton, Deana. n.d., n. pag. Web. Accessed 28 Jan. 2015. http://www.artsci.washington.edu/newsletter/Sept10/Ainu.asp

Dauenhauer, Nora. *The Droning Shaman: Poems.* Hains, AK: Black Current, 1988.

——. *Life Woven with Song.* Tucson: University of Arizona Press, 2000.

Ford, Karen Jackson. "Marking Time in Native America: Haiku, Elegy, Survival." *American Literature* 81. 2 (June 2009): 333–59.

Georgi-Findley, Brigitte. "Transatlantic Crossings: New Developments in the Contemporary North American Novel." *Transatlantic Voices: Interpretations of Native North American Literatures.* Ed. Elvira Pulitano. Lincoln: University of Nebraska Press, 2007. 89–107.

Gilroy, Paul. *The Black Atlantic: Modernity and Double-Consciousness.* Cambridge, MA: Harvard University Press, 1993.

Heller, Caroline, ed. *Until We are Strong Together: Women Writers in the Tenderloin.* New York: Teachers College Press, 1997.

Helstern, Linda Lizut. "*Griever: An American Monkey King in China*: A Cross-cultural Re-membering." *Loosening the Seams: Interpretations of Gerald Vizenor.* Ed. A. Robert Lee. Bowling Green, OH: Bowling Green State University Press, 2000. 136–54.

Henderson, Harold G. *An Introduction to Haiku.* New York: Doubleday, 1958.

Hogan, Linda. *People of the Whale.* New York: W.W.Norton, 2009.

Kayano, Shigeru. *Our Land was a Forest: An Ainu Memoir.* Boulder, CO: Westview Press, 1994.

Lerner, Andrea. "Review: The Droning Shaman." *Studies in American Indian Literatures* 2. 4 (1990): 36–38.

Lim, Shirley Geok-lin, ed. *Transnational Asian American Literature: Sites and Transits.* Philadelphia: Temple University Press, 2006.

Madsen, Deborah L. Introduction. *Native Authenticity: Transnational Perspectives on Native American Literary Studies.* Albany: State University of New York Press, 2010. 1–18.

——. *The Poetry and Poetics of Gerald Vizenor.* Albuquerque: University of New Mexico Press, 2012.

——. *Understanding Gerald Vizenor.* Columbia: University of South Carolina, 2009.

Medak-Saltzman, Danika. "Staging Empire: The Display and Erasure of Indigenous Peoples in Japanese and American Nation Building Projects, 1860–1904." Ph.D. diss. University of California, Berkeley, 2008.

——. "Transnational Indigenous Exchange: Rethinking Global Interactions of Indigenous Peoples at the 1904 St. Louis Exposition." *American Quarterly* 62. 3 (2010): 591–615.

Oandasan, William. *Earth & Sky: A Sequence of Contraries in Haiku Form.* Laguna, NM: A Press, 1976.

——. "Grandmothers Land." Poetry Foundation, n.d. Web. Accessed 28 Jan. 2015. http://www.poetryfoundation.org/poem/238544

——. *Round Valley Songs.* Minneapolis: West End Press, 1984.

Owens, Louis. *Mixedblood Messages: Literature, Film, Family, Place.* Norman: University of Oklahoma, 2001.

Pulitano, Elvira. *Toward a Native American Critical Theory.* Lincoln: University of Nebraska Press, 2003.

——, ed. *Transatlantic Voices: Interpretations of Native North American Literatures.* Lincoln: University of Nebraska Press, 2007.

Russell, Caskey. "Tools of Self Definition: Nora Marks Dauenhauer's 'How to Make Good Baked Salmon.'" *Studies in American Indian Literatures* 2nd ser. 16. 3 (Fall 2004): 29–46.

Schorger, A. W. "Ginseng: A Pioneer Resource." *Transactions of the Wisconsin Academy of Sciences, Arts and Letters* 57 (1969): 65–74.

Siddle, Richard. "On Being and Becoming Ainu." Review of *Our Land Was a Forest: An Ainu Memoir* by Shigeru Kayano. Boulder, CO: Westview Press, 1994. Web. Accessed 28 Jan. 2015. http://www.h-net.org/reviews/showrev.php?id=1198

Silko, Leslie Marmon. *Ceremony*. New York: Viking Penguin, 1977.

——. *Gardens in the Dunes*. New York: Simon & Schuster, 2000.

Spry, Adam. "'It May be Revolutionary in Character': The *Progress*, a New Tribal Hermeneutics, and the Literary Re-expression of the Anishinaabe Oral Tradition in *Summer in the Spring*." *The Poetry and Poetics of Gerald Vizenor*. Ed. Deborah Madsen. Albuquerque: University of New Mexico Press, 2012. 23–42.

TallMountain, Mary. "Indian Blood." n.d., n. pag. Web. Accessed 28 Jan. 2015. https://sites.google.com/site/ mtallmountain/indian-blood

——. "The Last Wolf." Poetry 180. n.d., n. pag. Web. Accessed 28 Jan. 2015. http://www.loc.gov/poetry/180/167.html

Trumbull, Charles. "The American Haiku Movement: Part I: Haiku in English." *Modern Haiku* 36. 3 (Autumn 2005): 1–24.

Vizenor, Gerald. *Bearheart: The Heirship Chronicles*. Minneapolis: University of Minnesota Press, 1979.

——. *Chair of Tears*. Lincoln: University of Nebraska Press, 2012.

——. *Fugitive Poses: Native American Indian Scenes of Absence and Presence*. Lincoln: University of Nebraska Press, 1998.

——. *Summer in the Spring: Anishinaabe Lyric Poems and Stories*, New Edition. Norman: University of Oklahoma Press, 1993.

——. *The Trickster of Liberty: Native Heirs to a Wild Baronage*. Norman: University of Oklahoma Press, 2005.

Vizenor, Gerald & A. Robert Lee. *Postindian Conversations*. Lincoln: University of Nebraska Press, 1999.

Walis Norgan. "Reading in Seven Days." n.d., n. pag. Web. Accessed 28 Jan. 2015. http://www.wlsh.tyc. edu.tw/blog/files/6-4747-5025.php

Welch, James. *The Heartsong of Charging Elk*. New York: Anchor Books, 2001.

Welford, Gabrielle. "Mary TallMountain's Writing: Healing the Heart – Going Home." *ARIEL: A Review of International English Literature*. 25. 1 (January 1994): 136–54.

Yasuda, Kenneth. *The Japanese Haiku: Its Essential Nature and History*. 1957. Rpt. Boston: Tuttle Publishing, 2001.

33

Reverse Assimilation

Native Appropriations of Euro-American Conventions

Kenneth M. Roemer

The Cinderella paradigm

Frank Hamilton Cushing (1857–1900), the respected collector of Zuni oral narratives, pioneered a form of immersion anthropology that encouraged cross-cultural sharing, including story sharing. Hence, it is not surprising that when he encountered stories that seemed to incorporate non-Zuni plots, characters, and morals, he did not consider them inauthentic or corrupted but as examples of the dynamic evolution of cultures. One of the most striking examples of this dynamism is the version of "The Poor Turkey Girl," published in his *Zuni Folk Tales* (54–64) that, after Cushing's death, received wide circulation retitled as "Cinderella," in the "Tales Borrowed from Europeans" section of Stith Thompson's *Tales of North American Indians* (225–31) and even wider circulation today in a children's book (Pollock). There is some debate about the degree the story should be categorized as "borrowed" (Austin xxv–xxvi), since there is a long-established sub-genre of Zuni *telapenaawe* (fictional stories [Tedlock xvi]) that features the poor turkey girl. The exact degree of borrowing would be almost impossible to determine. Nevertheless, "Poor Turkey Girl"/"Cinderella" can still serve as a provocative model of the transformative powers of Native oral and written literatures.

Much of the plot is the same: a poor young woman longs to attend festivities for the upper classes; she is transformed by magical powers; she attends but fails to return at the stated hour and is once again reduced to her lowly position. If this were all there were to the Zuni narrative, then the exchange would be a passive appropriation. Instead, the Zuni storytellers (mediated through Cushing's English translation) reinvented the Cinderella story for a Zuni audience and for Zuni purposes. In the Anglo-European version, Cinderella's duties are domestic. In the Zuni version, there is no mention of her family. Instead, she has significant community responsibilities – caring for flocks of turkey. In an endnote to a modern translation, Dennis Tedlock indicates that turkeys were significant to the Zuni; they were domesticated for feathers and meat (73). Instead of a non-human Fairy Godmother, the primary agent of change is the biggest "Gobbler" in the young girl's flock, and his powers are communal; all the turkeys participate in the singing and the wing brushing that bring about the transformations.

Possibly the most significant acts of reinvention are narrative truncation and a strict adherence to community responsibility. The turkeys conclude that the young woman has forgotten them and that, under these circumstances, their "irksome captivity" is intolerable (Cushing 61). They run off toward a canyon. Their tracks are visible to this day in rock formations, and their heritage obvious in the abundance of wild turkeys in the area (Cushing 63). Thus the story is reinvented to explain local geographical and habitat phenomenon. As for the young woman, "she was the same poor Turkey girl that she was before" but without her flock. There is no explanation as to how she will survive. The story just stops: "Thus shortens my story" (Cushing 64). Zuni storytellers not only repositioned the narrative in a familiar geography inhabited by important non-human animals, they also radically shifted the emphasis from miraculous but human-like agency (Fairy Godmother) to non-human communal animal agency (the Gobbler and his community of turkeys) and re-imagined an individualistic tale of transformation from cruelty and poverty to love and elevated stature to a story about life-sustaining community responsibility. As Joseph Peynetas, one of Dennis Tedlock's twentieth-century Zuni storytellers observes, "Our lives depend on ... thoughtfulness .... Just because there's a dance doesn't relieve you from any responsibilities" (qtd. in Tedlock 73).

"Reinventing the enemy's language"

I have dwelled on the Zuni reinvention of the Cinderella story because it is an appropriate paradigm for a dynamic process that Joy Harjo and Gloria Bird announce in the title of their anthology *Reinventing the Enemy's Language* (1997). Even before the English language crossed the Atlantic, extensive trade routes throughout North and South America involved exchanges of goods and stories. Reinventions among indigenous cultures were an obvious precursor to the reinventions of English language conventions. Since the publication of literature in English by Native authors, this process has continued in a multitude of forms. The roll-call of eighteenth- through twenty-first-century reinventions could fill many pages. Here is a brief sampling: Samson Occom (1723–1792) – execution sermon; Jane Johnston Schoolcraft (1800–1841) – Anglo-American metrics and poetic genres; William Apess (1798–1839) – the Christian conversion narrative; John Rollin Ridge (1827–1867) – sensationalistic journalism and adventure narrative; E. Pauline Johnson (1861–1913) and S. Alice Callahan (1868–1894) – sentimental domestic fiction; Alexander Posey (1873–1908) – satiric dialect newspaper columns; John Joseph Mathews (1894–1979) – philosophical memoir à la *Walden*; Ella C. Deloria (1889–1971) – ethnographic discourse; N. Scott Momaday (1934–), Leslie Marmon Silko (1948–), Louise Erdrich (1954–) various Modernist experiments; and LeAnne Howe (1951–) murder mystery and sports literature. The reinventions haven't been limited to Euro-American incorporations: witness the poetry of James Welch (1940–2003) inspired by Peruvian surrealism and Gerald Vizenor's (1934–) excellent haiku poems.

For decades, but especially since the publication of articles similar to Jack Forbes's "Colonialism and Native American Literature" in 1987 and Elizabeth Cook-Lynn's "The American Indian Fiction Writer" in 1993, the incorporation of non-indigenous styles and conventions has inspired debates about authenticity, sovereignty, and responsibility. If we adhered strictly to what Henry Louis Gates refers to as the "ethnic descent of authors" (293), then there is no controversy as long as publishers, editors, readers, and Indian communities can agree on the definition of a "Native American author," (which is, of course, a controversial topic in itself). Gates posits an extreme descent position: if Shakespeare had one African ancestor, he would "head the list" of African authors (293). Acceptance of this position should eliminate criticism of texts that depend almost entirely on Euro-American conventions and do not include "Indian" topics. Hence the best-seller *Gorky Park* (1981) by the Senecu del Sur/ Yaqui, Martin Cruz Smith (1941–), would deserve entry into the canon of American Indian literature, despite its murder mystery conventions and Soviet characters and setting. I doubt that Forbes or Cook-Lynn would criticize Cruz, since neither he nor his publisher promote *Gorky Park* as an "Indian novel." Cook-Lynn's primary targets are "cosmopolitan" texts that are promoted as Indian or Native literature but seek approval from mainstream publishers by depending primarily on Euro-American criteria for "good literature," defined say, by New Critical or Poststructuralist standards. This critical viewpoint in its more strident forms certainly limits artistic freedom, constricts the Native literary canon, and robs it of its ability to evolve. But this criticism does raise a fundamental question: How much incorporation of non-indigenous conventions does it take before the "Native" in an "Indian" text becomes silenced?

In one relatively brief chapter, I can't pretend to answer this question. Instead, what I can offer are a few case studies that represent historical breadth and genre diversity: Howe's novel *Shell Shaker* (2001), a Schoolcraft poem, Mathews' life narrative *Talking to the Moon* (1945), and Momaday's mixed-genre *The Way to Rainy Mountain* (1969). In all these cases, the authors appropriated Euro- or Anglo-American conventions. But the indigenous was definitely not silenced. Instead, as in the case of the Zuni Cinderella story, these authors reinvented the conventions for their tribal or Pan-Indian purposes.

Who done it maybe didn't

At the dramatic center of Howe's *Shell Shaker* is a murder mystery: who killed the corrupt tribal chief of the Choctaw? Borrowing from murder mystery conventions is not unique to Howe. There is even at least one other contemporary Choctaw murder mystery, Louis Owens' *The Sharpest Sight* (1992). *Shell Shaker* is especially interesting because of the ways Howe embeds the mystery conventions in historical–mythical contexts and in tragic episodes of mass murders and how she invites readers to question their epistemological assumptions and rational processes: how they gain and process evidence and use it to understand, to "solve" an event.

Shell Shaker is a parallel Choctaw history of powerful women, corrupt male leaders, love, and murder. The primary contemporary murder mystery – did Auda Billy kill her corrupt lover Redford McAlester? – is framed and surrounded by histories of killings. Important episodes spoken by the eighteenth-century voice of Shakbatina, a woman born into the peacemaker tradition of the first Shell Shaker, frame the novel (1–16, 222). Dramatized mythic times immemorial, the sixteenth century (Desoto's impact), and the nineteenth century (Trail of Tears) intermingle with the primary historical juxtaposed periods: the eighteenth century during the French and Indian Wars (especially 1738–1747, primarily in what is now Louisiana and Mississippi) and in Durant, Oklahoma, during late September, 1991. The historical juxtapositions invite readers to perceive individual killing in the contexts of mass killings and invite them to see obvious parallels, especially between the eighteenth century and late twentieth century: in both eras, the lovers (Anoleta and Auda) of corrupt leaders (Red Shoes and McAlester) are accused of murder (victims: Red Shoes' other wife and McAlester), and the accused women's mothers (Shakbatina and Susan Billy) volunteer to sacrifice their lives for their daughters. Thus, the specific instance of McAlester's murder becomes a reincarnation of violence that, to quote Shakbatina, represent times when "past and present collide into a single moment" (222).

The parallel/colliding juxtapositions of *Shell Shaker* go beyond inviting readers to question their notions of separate times and blur the meanings of mass and individualized murders. Monika Barbara Siebert's article "Repugnant Aboriginality" does not focus on Howe's use of murder mystery conventions, but her discussion of the conclusion of the Auda–McAlester mystery (103–05) suggests how Howe reinvents murder mystery conventions and asks readers to question their assumptions about justice, agency, and perception from Choctaw viewpoints.

A mystery is supposed to "solve" "who done it." At first, it appears this happens in *Shell Shaker*. Before the conclusion, most readers have probably concluded that McAlester's lover Auda is innocent and that another unscrupulous character is the murderer. In a dramatic courtroom scene an elder produces hard evidence (taped phone conversations) that exonerate Auda; a warrant is issued for the murderer. Case closed. But on the last page of the novel, the voice of the eighteenth-century woman who opened the novel re-enters with an alternate "solution." Shakbatina reveals that she was in the room with Auda when she pointed the gun at McAlester; she "slipped [her] hands in front of [Auda's] hands, and together "the day was [theirs]" (222). Auda couldn't remember what happened; she had blanked out, the murder weapon nearby. The courtroom "solution" presents her as a victim of framing. Shakbatina's version gives Auda and Shakbatina agency and connection with a long line of clan mothers/peacekeepers whose duty was to eliminate corrupt leaders (Seibert 104). Auda's family line connects her to these clan mothers (Hollrah 77). Now she is connected by deed as well as lineage. One "solution" is valid in a "rational" courtroom sense, the other in a traditional Choctaw matriarchal cosmology. Instead of finding a pat solution that ends the mystery, Howe reinvents the expected "solution," undermines any smugness readers might have about knowing "who done it," and invites them to ponder Choctaw worldview truths that exist outside the domain of courtrooms.

Invoking reinvention

For his excellent work of literary recovery, *The Sound the Stars Make Rushing Through the Sky: The Writings of Jane Johnston Schoolcraft* (2007), Robert Dale Parker asked Dennis Jones, Heidi Stark, and James Vukelich to create a new translation of a poem written originally in Ojibwe by Schoolcraft (49). The new translation is remarkably accessible and relevant for twenty-first-century readers. Parker compares it to Imagist and haiku poetry, and the topic – a parent's lament over her children's departure for boarding school – seems significantly ahead of its time for a poem composed in the 1830s. Here is the stanza at the heart of the lament:

> My little daughter
> My little son
> I leave them behind
> Far away land.

(ll.6–9)[1]

The two versions created in the 1830s would not be very accessible to most modern readers. One is in Ojibwe: "Ne dau nis ainse e/Ne gwis is ainse e/Ishe nau gun ug wau/Waus saw a kom eg "(ll.6–9). Schoolcraft's husband Henry, the respected ethnographer and geologist, created the other version. Jane Schoolcraft's eighteen brief lines became six stanzas of six-lined rhymed couplets in iambic tetrameter (141–42). It's not until the end of the poem that we find lines equivalent to Jane Schoolcraft's lament: "For there I must leave the dear jewels I love, /The dearest of gifts from my Master above" (ll.35–36).

The rigid meter and rhyme scheme and the stereotypes ("sported the plume" l.15) of Henry Schoolcraft's version would seem outdated and offensive to many modern readers. But, as Parker rightly reminds us, this is the way readers "preferred poems ... in the style of their time" (49). It's inappropriate to criticize Schoolcraft for allowing her Ojibwe poems to be transformed in English or to fault her for presenting her own English language poems "in the style of their times." Her Ojibwe poems would be incomprehensible to most readers, and poems not in familiar forms might not be recognized as poems. But it is appropriate to ask, did she simply pour Ojibwe wine into "their times" poetic forms, or do some of her poems represent reinventions of the non-Native conventions?

One poem that does reinvent is "Invocation To my Maternal Grand-father on hearing his descent from Chippewa ancestors misrepresented" (99–100). "Invocation" does reinforce the Noble Savage stereotype and much of the diction will seem outdated to modern readers (e.g., "Thou saw'st the fell foes of thy nation expire?" [l.24]). But, in at least three ways, Schoolcraft is reinventing the genre and poetics for Ojibwe purposes. In Euro-American contexts, invocations typically invoke or summon the assistance of Christian or Hebrew deities or deified civic leaders like Washington or Lincoln. In this case, Schoolcraft's persona speaks to her maternal grandfather, Waubojeeg, and, in the opening, identifies him, not with Christian or Anglo-American associations, but with "the mark of the noble deer" (l.1). He was a member of the reindeer clan (Parker 100). The poetics are also innovative; in terms of metrics, Parker considers the poem Schoolcraft's "most intricate" (100). He features the version that was published in the *Southern Literary Messenger* (1860) because it had undergone less "meddling" by other hands (100). The other versions Parker includes use a conventional heroic couplet form. The *Messenger* version uses an equally noble but more complex form. Here is the opening stanza:

> Rise bravest chief! of the mark of the noble deer.
>> With eagle glance,
>> Resume thy lance,
> And wield again thy warlike spear!
>> The foes of thy line,
>> With coward design,
> Have dared with black envy to garble the truth.
> And stain with falsehood thy valorous youth.

(ll.1–8)

Parker offers an astute reading of the complex metrics of the first three lines (46), but a reader doesn't have to be versed in poetics to see how Schoolcraft has abandoned the regular iambic pentameter and pairs of rhymed couplets for a more complex rhyme scheme (abbaccdd) and varied the line lengths and positioning to draw attention to the significant celebratory words of short centered lines ("thy name," "proclaim" [ll.34–35]) and calls for remembrance ("Or those e're forget, /Who are mortal men yet," [ll.18–19]). Parker emphasizes the poetic characteristics of the poem, but he does not stress the redirection of the genre. Instead of asking for assistance from the honorable ancestor, the speaker is offering assistance to him by asserting his Ojibwe heritage and thus countering the false representation of him as "Sioux." Parker explains that Waubojeeg "had two Sioux half-brothers" (100), but he was Ojibwe. Thus, Schoolcraft bestows positive agency on an Anglo-American genre typically associated with drawing agency from elsewhere (deities or founding fathers/mothers) and uses this agency for her family and Ojibwe purposes.

More than a change from pond to prairie

In the first line of the Foreword to the 1981 edition of *Talking to the Moon* (1945), Elizabeth Mathews announces the primary literary model for her husband's book: "This is John Joseph Mathews' *Walden*" (ix). The parallels are obvious. Mathews left "civilization" to live in solitude in a small cabin (sandstone rather than Thoreau's wood) for an extended period (ten years rather than Thoreau's two). Both authors narrate their sojourns in the form of a one-year seasonal cycle (Thoreau ends in spring; Mathews ends with the "Light-of-Day-Returns-Moon" when hints of spring appear); and neither spends much time discussing events beyond their surroundings (Mathews does make mention of World War II in parts of his last chapters). Their reasons for their sojourns represent the most significant parallels. Mathews' explanations often echo Thoreau's proclamations in "Where I Lived and What I Lived for": "I came to the blackjacks [oaks] as a man who had pulled himself out of the roaring river of civilization to rest for a while … ." (3). Mathews wanted to "become part of the flowing so far as I was able; to learn something of the moods of [this] little corner of the earth. … my perceptive powers had been dulled by the artificialities and the crowding and the elbowing of men in Europe and America … ." (2). And when those perceptions were refreshed (Thoreau would say awakened), he, like Thoreau, offered engaging descriptions of his daily life and of the plants and animals that shared his "little corner of the earth." Again like Thoreau, these descriptions were often touchstones for the philosophical ruminations that convinced Robert Warrior, in *Tribal Secrets* (1995), to include Mathews in his pantheon of the American Indian intellectual tradition.

If we only take the above-mentioned similarities into account, we might conclude that Mathews' borrowings were basically attempts to appeal to a wide, non-Indian reading audience. But there is much more to take into account. Both authors take great sensual and intellectual pleasure in their surroundings, but Mathews punctuates his expert enumerations of plants and animals and attempts to grasp their meanings with an acute awareness of the smallness of his (and by implication the human) place in the scheme of nature and a delight in freedom from the need to generate meaning. The best expression of these attitudes occurs in Chapter XI:

> I am not smug as I sit here. I am small and overpowered by the primitive forces, but there is no fear. Instead there is only the true freedom that man can feel; the serenity that comes with the absence of emotion and the complete absence of man's pitiful urge to express himself; … .

My thoughts come like the breezes that move through the pines and in their passing leave nothing to disturb ... .

(177)

When Mathews does succumb to the "pitiful urge" to make meaning from what he sees and experiences, his cataloguing of plant and animal species and his use of animals as touchstones for speculations do suggest a privileging of the human point of view, despite his feelings of smallness. But, unlike some of Thoreau's engaging descriptions of what he calls his "brute neighbors," Mathews' description of many bird species, of the strange dance of a rabbit seen from his window (220), or a chance encounter with the mysterious play of a cougar (219–20), suggest an interdependent biological community rather than a transcendental correspondence. Robert Warrior offers extended analyses of Mathews' theory about animal-human behavior ranging from survival behavior, to play that involves practice for survival, to the ornamental that seems to have little to do with survival or practice for survival and can lead to beautiful creations or destructive ideologies when they are divorced from the laws of nature (e.g., Warrior 61–63; Mathews 213–26, 232–33). Mathews' theories of life seem much closer to Loren Eiseley's *Immense Journey* (1957) evolutionary flow of life or Osage concepts of inter-species communities of interdependence than to transcendental correspondences.

Mathews' representations of time and place also suggest reinventions of *Walden*. Mathews divides each of the seasons into three sub-seasons that are named by Osage moons; for example, "Planting Moon," "Buffalo-Pawing-Earth Moon," "Buffalo-Breeding Moon," "Deer-Breeding Moon," "Coon-Breeding Moon," "Baby-Bear Moon." These labels do more than make time sound Osage. They emphasize the seasonal interdependencies between the people and their environment.

And that environment is perceived differently from Thoreau's perceptions of his "little corner." This is not only because, as Elizabeth Mathews mentions, *Talking to the Moon* "is a *Walden* of plains and prairies" (ix). Thoreau's place is a marvelous matter of convenience and chance: it is not far from Concord, and his mentor, Ralph Waldo Emerson, happened to own a piece of land near Walden Pond and allowed Thoreau to build his cabin there. Mathews' place has little to do with convenience or chance. His three ridges of blackjacks that "push their prows south into the sea of prairie" are far removed from any cities in Oklahoma (1). But, unlike Thoreau's escape from home, this retreat is home. It is a family place: "My father had built the first house in the blackjacks by the spring at the head of the canyon" (1). This was Mathews' family and tribal land. His responsibility to the land goes beyond his efforts to minimize any disruptions to the natural "flow" of blackjack-prairie country. He shares a few Osage stories, including why an Osage clan chose as its symbol the spider who gained their respect by proclaiming: "wherever I go I build my house and wherever I build my house all come in" (142). "For Posterity," he helps facilitate the portrait painting of several elders during a stifling hot summer (126–36). Most importantly, he sees himself as an urgently needed voice for the land and the people. Eagle-That-Gets-What-He-Wants "often asks his wife to send for me ... ." As this elder tells Mathews, "'Seems like now these things will not be remembered by the people who will follow, if you do not write them down in a book'" (86). True, Thoreau does mention a few human visitors. But, for Mathews, people – his father and his Osage – are integral parts of his place no matter how far he is from "civilization." Mathews reinvents Thoreau's escape as a re-entry into an

Osage community homeland teeming with fellow creatures slithering, crawling, standing, and flying and all a part of grand biological evolutions and urges: his "little corner of the earth which had given me being … ." (2).

Modernism Kiowaized

Many of N. Scott Momaday's works feature reinventions of Euro-American conventions; certainly his Pulitzer Prize winning novel *House Made of Dawn* (1968) offers complex borrowings from Faulkner and Hemingway. But the most interesting example seems an unlikely choice. *The Way to Rainy Mountain* (1969), which has become Momaday's most frequently read book, appears to be his most "Indian" – specifically Kiowa – book. His father's black and white line drawings echo traditional plains art and the styles of the Kiowa Five/Six (Wunder 81, 86–88). The stories recreated on the left-hand side of the page are Kiowa tribal or family stories; the historical accounts and descriptions of objects on the right-hand side reflect Kiowa history and culture; the personal memories and reflections on the right, with the exception of one childhood memory of riding a "red roan" in New Mexico (67), are all about Kiowa landscapes and figures. But the arrangement[2] and genres of the book and the ironies and complexities of the final poem demonstrate Momaday's ability to reinvent Modernist forms and philosophy to serve Kiowa as well as Pan-Indian viewpoints.

Section XVII, which focuses on Kiowa women, demonstrates Momaday's Kiowazation of Modernism. Modernists were known for literary experimentation, including using structures that emphasized fragmentation, juxtaposition, and genre mixing. As with all the other twenty-four sections that make up the body of *The Way to Rainy Mountain*, Momaday divides section XVII into three paragraph-length texts in different font styles separated by significant amounts of white space. (Unfortunately, in some of the recent editions the text is double-spaced and the white space shrinks.) In a poem such as T. S. Eliot's "Love Song of Alfred J. Prufrock," one implied effect of the fragmentation is the suggestion of the disjointed nature of modern reality. In this section, the white space instead invites readers to savor each "voice" more than if all three were merged together in a typical book-reading experience. Possibly even more important is that very early in the book – first with a brief phrase in the Prologue ("What remains is fragmentary … ." [4]) and then in the Introduction description of the military defeat of the Kiowa, the imprisonment of the Kiowa at Fort Sill, and the suppression of the Sun Dance – Momaday implies that presenting Kiowa history and culture as a nicely unified narrative that fills pages with text would represent an inaccurate and unethical portrayal. Fragments and large gaps are much more accurate visual and textual representations of the assault on Kiowa culture, especially during the nineteenth century.

The initial version of *The Way to Rainy Mountain* was a one-genre book. *The Journey of the Tai-me* (1967) was a hand-printed collection of 33 Kiowa and family stories (Lincoln 101–17). Momaday's mentor, Yvor Winters, encouraged Momaday to add other genres – the historical/factual accounts and personal memories, which Momaday initially called commentaries ("The Man Made of Words" 106). The story and two commentaries – the three voices – of section XVII undermine Euro-American concepts of genre barriers and stereotypes of indigenous women. The opening miraculous, though possible, narrative tells of a rash man's sudden blindness in a "whirlwind," his family's exile, his ability, with the help of his wife's eyesight, to hunt a buffalo, his wife's desertion with the meat, his desperate survival tactics and return to camp, and his wife's exile because she deserted him and lied. She said "enemy warriors" killed him (58). The second voice offers two greatly condensed versions of tragic events documented in the Kiowa's *Calendar History of The Kiowa Indians* (Mooney 233, 280–01): one woman is stabbed (1843), the other forced to wait in the snow until her feet froze (1851–1852). Neither had committed any wrongdoing. The third voice is a vignette profile of Momaday's great-great-grandmother. Although she was a captive and a slave (the only two categories "held in lower status" than women) and of mixed heritage ("blue eyes"), she became a "figure in the tribe," owning a "great herd of cattle" and riding horseback "as well as any man" (59).

Although Momaday has been criticized for lack of complexity and a patriarchal viewpoint in his portrayal of women characters in *House Made of Dawn* and *The Ancient Child* (1989) (Donovan 74–98), the three voices in XVII obviously critique one-dimensional views of women and Kiowa patriarchal views. The oral narrative suggests a justified punishment, though this judgment should be qualified, since the first woman in the storytelling section was trying to preserve the life of her child. The second historical voice offers a harsh documented view of mid-nineteenth-century patriarchal treatment of Kiowa women. The third family/personal remembrance reveals a Kiowa's woman's ability to gain respect and rise above the patriarchal oppression. This section complicates one-dimensional concepts of traditional Kiowa women and their treatment.

Juxtaposing these three voices also undercuts conventional Euro-American genre distinctions by blurring the boundaries between the three genres and thus suggesting that the representation of Kiowa history demands a reinvention of genre concepts. Early in *The Way to Rainy Mountain*, the three genres are quite distinct. But by the time readers encounter section XVII, genre lines are blurring. The story derived from oral traditions is miraculous, but the two astounding events are not impossible: the strong winds and dust on the plains can damage eyes, and an exceptional hunter, if told when the animal is "directly in front of me," could bring the buffalo down (58). The events of cruelty documented in the Kiowa calendar seem almost too cruel to believe, and the family/personal voice is documented with the reproduction of the words on Kau-au-ointy's gravestone. Of course, long before section XVII and certainly in XVII, it is clear that Kiowa history cannot and should not be represented with just one genre: written history. Kiowa history and by implication all indigenous histories must include oral histories and personal reflections and writing that blurs genre lines and reminds us that indigenous genres often differ significantly from Euro-American genres.

British-American conventions mediated through his mentor Yvor Winters (Morgan 43) undoubtedly influenced Momaday's last words to his personal history of the Kiowa. "Rainy Mountain Cemetery" consists of two quintains (five lines) with a regular ababc rhyme scheme and lines that are quite consistently iambic pentameter (89). Momaday's first biographer, Matthias Schubnell, implies Winter's influence by comparing the poem to Winters' "To the Holy Spirit – From a Deserted Graveyard in the Salinas Valley" (206).

But, as the conclusion to *The Way to Rainy Mountain*, the poem takes on an inventive, almost subversive, function. By the time non-Native readers finish the Epilogue, they may feel confident in their understanding of Kiowa history. They have been introduced to significant ethnographic information and historical events, to many of the most important Kiowa oral narratives, and to the impact of the history and narratives on an important Kiowa family, including an important author. And the Epilogue figure Ko-sahn and her memory of an old woman who helped prepare the earth for Sun Dancers seemingly bridge the gap between past and present with the old woman's sung words, "As old as I am, I still have the feeling of play" (88). The controlled form of the poem that follows would further emphasize this coming to certainty if it were not for the disturbing and complex nature of the words within the form.

There are layers upon layers of irony and ambiguity in these lines (89). The poem begins with the words "Most is your name … ." (l.1), and yet the speaker never mentions his grandmother's or any other name. This nameless name is "Deranged in death "and yet the "mind to be inheres" (l.2); the mix of verb tenses and word connotations suggest both absolute dejection and a vital desire for meaning. In the next two lines the word combinations "nominal unknown" and "wake of nothing audible" raise fundamental questions: if the meaning can be named ("nominal"), can it also be "unknown"? A "wake" reverberates, but our senses can't grasp the vibrations. They are "inaudible" (4–5)? The first lines of the second stanza shift to the clarity of "The early sun, as red as a hunter's moon, /Runs in the plain. The mountain burns and shines" (ll.6–7). But the "silence" of "the long approaching noon" and the "shadow" that the nameless "name" defines" (ll.8–9) seem to snuff out the clarity and vitality and lead to the final line filled with hard sounds and dark imagery: "And death this cold, black density of stone" (l.10).

The terminal harshness of the ending contrasts drastically with the rejuvenating song of "As old as I am, I still have the feeling of play," and the ambiguities of the poem undercut readers' ability to assume they can comprehend the disastrous endings and wondrous continuities of Kiowa history. Thus, a controlled Anglo-American form in which the first four lines of abab often lead to a conclusion is reinvented as a means of undermining our ability to name, control, and understand the fragmented, tragic, and vital history of the Kiowa.

Celebrating creative transformations

In his well-known essay "Towards a National Indian Literature: Cultural Authenticity in Nationalism" (2001), Simon Ortiz recalls Catholic fiesta days at Acoma Pueblo that "within the Acqumeh community" became "authentic Acqumeh ceremonies":

> This is so because this celebration speaks of the creative ability of Indian people to gather many forms of the socio-political colonizing force which beset them and to make these forms meaningful in their own terms.

> (120)

He further proclaims that this "creative" and "nationalistic" impulse is alive and well: "Today's writing by Indian authors is a continuation of that elemental impulse" (121). My Cinderella paradigm, the brief enumeration of authors from Occom to Howe, and the four examples of fiction, poetry, life narrative, and mixed genre demonstrate that the gathering and transforming of "many [foreign] forms" has gone on for a long time and continues into the twenty-first century. It ensures that the best storytelling and writing by Native Americans will continue to counter static concepts of Indian authenticity and purity with dynamic reinventions of the enemy's words.

Notes

1 I depended on the historical and biographical facts provided by Parker relating to Schoolcraft's poems. I take responsibility for any flaws in the interpretations.
2 The primary designer for the page layouts was Bruce Gentry. Momaday was delighted with the design (*Way to Rainy Mountain* 90; Roemer 3).

Works cited

Austin, Mary, "Introduction." Frank Hamilton Cushing. *Zuni Folk Tales*, 1901. New York: Knopf, 1931. xix–xxix.

Cook-Lynn. "The American Indian Fiction Writer: Cosmopolitanism, Nationalism, The Third World, and First Nation Sovereignty." *Wicazo Sa Review* 9. 2 (1993): 26–36.

Cushing, Frank Hamilton. *Zuni Folk Tales*, 1901. New York: Knopf, 1931.

Donovan, Kathleen M. *Feminist Readings of Native American Literature*. Tucson: University of Arizona Press, 1998.

Eiseley, Loren. *The Immense Journey*. New York: Random House, 1957.

Forbes, Jack. "Colonialism and Native American Literature: Analysis." *Wicazo Sa Review* 3. 2 (1987): 17–23.

Gates, Henry Louis, Jr. "Ethnic and Minority' Studies." *Introduction to Scholarship in Modern Languages and Literature*, 2nd ed. Ed. Joseph Gibaldi. New York: MLA, 1992. 288–302.

Harjo, Joy & Gloria Bird, eds. *Reinventing the Enemy's Language*. New York: Norton, 1997.

Hollrah, Patrice. "Decolonizing the Choctaw: LeAnne Howe's *Shell Shaker*." *American Indian Quarterly* 28. 1/2 (2004): 73–85.

Howe, LeAnne. *Shell Shaker*. San Francisco: Aunt Lute Books, 2001.

Lincoln, Kenneth, "Tai-me to Rainy Mountain: The Makings of American Indian Literature." *American Indian Quarterly* 10 (1986): 101–17.

Mathews, John Joseph. *Talking to the Moon*, 1945. Norman: University of Oklahoma Press, 1981.

Momaday, N. Scott. *The Ancient Child*. New York: Doubleday, 1989.

——. *House Made of Dawn*. New York: Harper, 1968.

——. *The Journey of the Tai-me*. Santa Barbara: Privately printed, 1967.

——. "The Man Made of Words." *Nothing but the Truth*. Ed. John L. Purdy & James Ruppert. Upper Saddle River, NJ: Prentice Hall, 2001. 82–93.

——. *The Way to Rainy Mountain*. Albuquerque: University of New Mexico Press, 1969.

Mooney, James. *Calendar History of the Kiowa Indians*, 1898. Washington: Smithsonian, 1979.

Morgan, Phyllis. *N. Scott Momaday: Remembering Ancestors, Earth, and Traditions, an Annotated Bio-Bibliography*. Norman: University of Oklahoma Press, 2010.

Ortiz, Simon, "Towards a National Literature: Cultural Authenticity in Nationalism." *Nothing but the Truth*. Ed. John L. Purdy & James Ruppert. Upper Saddle River, NJ: Prentice Hall, 2001. 120–25.

Owens, Louis. *The Sharpest Sight*. Norman: University of Oklahoma Press, 1992.

Parker, Robert Dale, ed. *The Sound the Stars Make Rushing Through the Sky: The Writings of Jane Johnston Schoolcraft*. Philadelphia: University of Pennsylvania Press, 2007.

Pollock, Penny. *The Turkey Girl: A Zuni Cinderella Story*. New York: Little, Brown, 1996.

Roemer, Kenneth, ed. *Approaches to Teaching Momaday's* The Way to Rainy Mountain. New York: MLA, 1988.

Schubnell, Matthias. *N. Scott Momaday*. Norman: University of Oklahoma Press, 1985.

Siebert, Monika Barbara. "Repugnant Aboriginality: LeAnne Howe's *Shell Shaker* and Indigenous Representation in the Age of Multiculturalism." *American Literature* 83 (2011): 93–119.

Smith, Martin Cruz. *Gorky Park*. New York: Random, 1981.

Tedlock, Dennis, ed. and trans. *Finding the Center: Narrative Poetry of the Zuni Indians*. New York: Dial, 1972.

Thompson, Stith, ed. *Tales of North American Indians, Selected and Annotated by Stith Thompson, 1929*. Bloomington: Indiana University Press, 1972.

Warrior, Robert Allen. *Tribal Secrets: Recovering American Indian Intellectual Traditions*. Minneapolis: University of Minnesota Press, 1995.

Wunder, John R. *The Kiowa*. New York: Chelsea, 1989.

34
From As-Told-To Stories to Indigenous Communal Narratives

Stephanie A. Sellers

Formerly the standard in texts by Indigenous informants, the As-Told-To stories of the past were written by EuroAmerican ethnographers and have become a somewhat dated genre of texts that have given way to a new genre of writing by primarily, but not exclusively, Native American writer-scholars and their communities. These new texts I define as Indigenous Communal Narratives, and they are powerful antidotes to the cultural and historic misrepresentations still prevalent in mainstream American culture and educational systems. The Indigenous Communal Narratives of today often spring from previously published monographs and are reprinted with comprehensive additions to the text that include nation-specific historiographies, language definitions, tribal voices from the era of the text and of today, and provide a counter-narrative to the ethnocentric texts the As-Told-To publications presented. Often criticized and delegitimized by mainstream historians as "revisionist history," the Indigenous Communal Narratives are literary products that counter blatant misinformation about Indigenous nations and peoples and place the responsibility and privilege of speaking about one's own history and culture into the appropriate hands. Some examples of recent Indigenous Communal Narratives are *Mourning Dove: A Salishan Autobiography*, edited by Jay Miller (1994) about the first Native American woman author, Christine Quintasket, of the Colville Federated Tribes of East Washington State, and *The Life and Traditions of the Red Man: A Rediscovered Treasure of Native American Literature* edited by Annette Kolodny, which I will use as a case study in forthcoming analysis of the Indigenous Communal Narrative genre.

As-Told-To stories

The American As-Told-To narratives of the past were primarily written from late in the nineteenth century to early in the twentieth century, and were the products of university anthropologists and individuals curious about "Indians" who were attempting to save Indigenous cultures from perceived annihilation. This literary genre reinforced the "white savior" trope and still is enacted today by EuroAmerican media, academics, and missionaries who perceive Indigenous nations as helpless and lacking the agency to address concerns in their own communities. Some examples of these As-Told-To texts include the famous work

Black Elk Speaks by John G. Neihardt (1932), *Pretty-Shield: Medicine Woman of the Crows* by Frank B. Linderman (1932), and *Crashing Thunder: The Autobiography of an American Indian* by Paul Radin (1926). The practice of what was later termed "Salvage Ethnography" arose in this era from the Anthropology discipline. This era occurred after outright military engagement between the United States and Indigenous armies primarily ended and other tools to destroy Native peoples took a more prominent role (like the Boarding School era). Salvage Ethnography created not only a body of writings called the As-Told-To genre, but also a body of photography, paintings, and films by EuroAmericans like Edward Curtis (photography), George Catlin (paintings), and Robert Flaherty (film).

Works from this era continue to shape American and international conceptualizations of Indigenous peoples of North America. They are still widely consumed in museums, libraries, and college classrooms as authentic representations of the images, words, and worldviews of Indigenous peoples when quite often what is presented by the EuroAmericans who created them could not be further from their cultural truths. Corrective historical and cultural materials by Indigenous peoples are often omitted when these materials are presented, thus creating by default the perception that the settlers' materials are factual testaments about Indigenous histories and cultures. Unless directly schooled in scholarly methodologies that interrogate the Eurocentric worldview, not even graduate students will recognize what questions to ask of these texts. Hence, the poisoning of the historic record continues as the inaccurate body of scholarship born from this genre grows.

Importantly, Salvage Ethnography fixes Indigenous peoples as artifacts in an often romanticized, but nearly always, long-dead past and utterly dismisses the living peoples and nations of today. These literary and visual works reinforce a cultural trope that there was once a "pure cultural state" of Indigenous peoples that is not only gone, but that renders currently living Native peoples as culturally inauthentic and inferior to their ancestors. This widespread belief allows colonial systems of oppression to ignore current needs and legal claims made by Native nations. The EuroAmerican colonial perspective revives with each new generation the belief that the settlers define Native cultural identity, and the As-Told-To genre strongly facilitates this phenomenon. Literary Salvage Ethnography used as a stand-alone legitimate Indigenous voice, without critical literary analysis by Indigenous scholars and tribal councils' input on language, customs, and history, has significant political backlash in matters such as repatriation of Indigenous property and Native land claims, among others.

In addition to the concerns created by the Salvage Ethnography model, the literary conceptualizations of Indigenous cultures in the As-Told-To stories convey a monolithic, authoritative, singular voice speaking for the whole nation in the form of autobiography. Such ethnographic narratives run counter to the cultural value of communal ethics at the foundation of most all First Nations. A value of communal ethics means all members of the community, including the earth, animals, plants, and luminaries, are sentient participants in the human experience and thus must be considered and included in human matters. The stories created about Native individuals by EuroAmerican ethnographers at the turn of the last century did not come from a communal perspective but, instead, their publications were a single-voiced narrative, often with their own ethnocentric interpretations alongside the Indigenous stories. Centralizing the experiences of one individual, especially seeing an individual human being as existing separately from her/his community and the larger biosphere, is utterly foreign to Indigenous peoples. Whereas the literary tradition in

English follows a central heroic figure (solely a male until recently) struggling against either internal or external forces and working to resolve this conflict within the framework of the literary product, the Indigenous literary tradition does not follow this strategy.

Indigenous writing traditionally was used for recording events of national concern (like minutes of meetings, land use, astrological events, good hunting, and so on) and as timekeeping calendars. Some mediums for this writing included dyed and carved clam shells sewn into belts called wampum (which are still made today), birch bark books, engraved stone tablets, painted animal hides, and carved wooden staffs, among others. These forms of writing were not understood as singular-narratives by an individual author about the deeds of notable individuals, but were understood primarily as the property and reflections of the nation kept by individuals specifically chosen and assigned with the responsibility to care for these national records. Therefore, when EuroAmerican ethnographers were meeting with Indigenous informants for their cultural story, an ancient form of Indigenous storytelling and record keeping was broken and departed from, creating an entirely new literary genre in North America. The poetry, song-poems, and storytelling were (and still are) primarily kept in the oral tradition, since these literary forms are valued as best transmitted by the living community rather than fixed in place and time by some form of writing. Hence the poems and stories are kept alive by the specially trained and ritually appointed storykeepers of the day.

Importantly, Native Americans who learned to read and write in English did author autobiographical works as early as the mid-1700s, while conveying much about their particular nation's culture. Two of the earliest examples are the works of Samson Occom (Mohegan), *A Short Autobiography of My Life*, written in 1768 and William Apess (Pequot), *A Son of the Forest: The Experience of William Apes, a Native of the Forest, Written by Himself*, written in 1829. The scholar Lisa Brooks (Abenaki) writes authoritatively about early Indigenous writings in her book *The Common Pot: The Recovery of Native Space in the Northeast* (2008), which discusses the writings of Occom and Apess as well as the first American protest writing from the 1700s by Indigenous authors.

In addition to concerns about how the As-Told-To genre distorts images of Indigenous cultures and histories up until present times and its secondary assertion that Indigenous peoples did (and could) not write and needed European settlers to do it for them, there are also issues with this genre concerning gender. A little known practice of many Indigenous nations of North America is gendered protocols for the transmission of culture, dreams, and visions. This means that men transmitted men's culture to other men, and women transmitted their knowledge to other women. In the nations northeast of the Mississippi, this practice was demonstrated through the appointment of speakers on gendered councils. The Seneca scholar Barbara Alice Mann discusses this Haudenosaunee (Iroquois) practice at length in her work *Iroquoian Women: The Gantowisas* (2006). The protocol stems from a worldview that conceptualizes a gendered biosphere and thus structures human governing and social systems from that belief. Therefore, the protocols were (and often still are) closely adhered to in order to keep the biosphere in balance.

Though there is great cultural variance among the nations in relation to gendered practices, Indigenous gendered protocols certainly impacted the As-Told-To genre in significant ways. First, nearly all the ethnographers traveling to gain information from Indigenous peoples were male. This means primarily Indigenous men are going to be willing to speak to the male ethnographer in order to follow gendered speaking protocols.

There are few As-Told-To stories written from an Indigenous woman informant. The genre is comprised of almost entirely male informants, which reinforces the European cultural practice of patriarchy and falsely applies it to Indigenous nations where it very often did not exist. In other words, readers of this genre unaware of the gendered protocols assume by default that Indigenous nations centralized and more highly valued the experiences of men over those of women, as accounts of European and non-Indigenous American history do. What non-Indigenous readers of this genre do not know is that the male Indigenous informant is transmitting the cultural voice and practices of the men along with his personal experiences, and that the cultural voice and practices of the women are quite often as highly valued in that particular nation. In some Indigenous nations, the women's voices are culturally more central and important than the men's. Nevertheless, some evidence of cross-gender disclosure of cultural practices and beliefs are at times contained in the As-Told-To genre as Indigenous informants felt the need to have certain events recorded for future generations and thus did not strictly adhere to the gendered protocols of their cultures.

Black Elk Speaks and the As-Told-To genre

Despite significant challenges in the As-Told-To genre that simply reinforce stereotypes of Native North Americans, some of the works contribute valuable cultural and historic information about Indigenous nations, particularly now that nation-specific cultural and literary criticism have amended the original editions. Some As-Told-To works are outstanding examples of poetic-literature and spiritual inspiration. For example, the famous work *Black Elk Speaks* by the ethnographer John G. Neihardt, published in 1932, has been translated into more than twenty languages and in the year 2000 was chosen as one of the Top Ten Spiritual books of the century (Deloria xxxviii). Neihardt was funded in May 1931 by a New York publisher, William Morrow, to gather the stories of Lakota medicine man Black Elk and produce a monograph (243).

Though the strengths of this classic in American literature are well known, there remain lasting concerns that are the direct result of the As-Told-To genre. From the keen analysis of literary scholars and critics (some of whom are Lakota), we know that Neihardt changed many key passages, or made assumptions, from Black Elk's oral transmissions that cast what was stated as solely Black Elk's perspective into a decidedly Eurocentric point-of-view that was actually Neihardt's. Indeed, only after a major expansion of the original edition in 2014, which brought together decades of critical discourse concerning the book, can the depth of Neihardt's intrusions on Black Elk's meanings be truly recognized. For example, the infamous last paragraphs of the book that are presented as the despairing words of a weeping Black Elk expressing an image of brokenness and hopelessness for his people and their worldview, are actually the constructs of Neihardt the ethnographer.

As the Lakota scholar Raymond J. DeMallie observes in the amplification notes of the book, the original transcript of Black Elk's words demonstrates an altogether different position of hopeless despair. DeMallie writes, "The phrase 'lean to hear my feeble voice' is Neihardt's (330). The transcript has 'thus I will send up a voice'" (330). Neihardt writes the words "despair" and "pitiful old man" in these last lines of the book as being uttered by Black Elk when, according to the actual original transcript, Black Elk either did not use those words or the words he did choose do not have the same meaning in Lakota as they do in English (330). Though these points may seem irrelevant, the omissions and additions reinforce the Vanishing Indian trope so popular in Neihardt's time and, unfortunately, still prevalent today. The hopeless despair of this section is shaped by Neihardt – a despair made famous by its repetition across academic disciplines, by environmental organizations, and in literary works – and attributed to the experience of all Indigenous peoples, thus continuing the colonizer's narrative. DeMallie writes that the experience Black Elk had at the site of his original medicine vision "offered hope for reviving the tree that never bloomed" (330), but this sentiment did not make its way into Neihardt's book. I must add that many literary scholars directly challenge the supposition that the tree never bloomed and that the sacred hoop to which Black Elk refers is broken, since these are Eurocentric concepts of Time and generalized EuroAmerican beliefs about Native Americans.

In the final passage of the book, when he is praying at the site of his original medicine vision, Black Elk finishes his prayer by referring to Neihardt and his daughters with the line, "I offer this pipe that we may see many happy days" (330). Neihardt omits this line that conveys an image of a positive future and the binding together of not just Black Elk and Neihardt as family, but, as DeMallie states, "represented continuity with generations yet to come, [for] both Lakotas and whites" (330). This omission from the book is certainly a missed opportunity for a more holistic view of Indigenous and settler relations, but such a view does not mesh with the popular Vanished Indian that, on some level, Neihardt must have believed.

The 2014 Bison Books edition of *Black Elk Speaks* from the University of Nebraska Press includes critical scholarly discourse, an appendix of definitions of Lakota vocabulary, maps, and cultural information from Lakota scholars. This newest edition, edited by Philip J. Deloria, includes prefaces from the 1932, 1961, and 1972 editions, along with important essays and images from Neihardt's family members and Lakota people. Fortunately, in its current incarnation, *Black Elk Speaks* is beginning very much to resemble an Indigenous Communal Narrative.

Indigenous Communal Narrative: an emerging literary genre

Centralizing the Indigenous communal perspective to maintain cultural authenticity is best conveyed in the new literary genre I refer to as Indigenous Communal Narrative (ICN). This genre may centralize one Indigenous person, as do the As-Told-To genres, but it also takes into account full consideration of that individual's nation via consultation and collaboration with the nation's Tribal Council, nation-specific historians and scholars, and his/her living descendants. In this genre, the culture and history of the Indigenous nation is made apparent through the experiences of the individual because the author's voice is not merely centralizing her/his own experiences as an Informant with a EuroAmerican transcriber, but instead uses the singular-plural or communal voice of his/her nation. Also, in the Indigenous Communal Narrative, the end product is to reveal the nation's larger history rather than turn the Informant into a singular, "special," or heroic individual separate from the community.

Case study: *The Life and Traditions of the Red Man: A Rediscovered Treasure of Native American Literature*

A recent work that exemplifies the Indigenous Communal Narrative genre is *The Life and Traditions of the Red Man: A Rediscovered Treasure of Native American Literature* by Annette Kolodny (2007). This work serves as an excellent case study for this discussion about not only the criteria, but the merits, of an ICN. Joseph Nicolar was a Penobscot elder who lived in the 1800s and wrote an original book about his people. Annette Kolodny, a EuroAmerican academic, edited and annotated the book, and included a history of the Penobscots; Charles Norman Shay, the grandson of Joseph Nicolar, wrote the Preface. The Penobscot Tribal Council also contributed to the work.

In 1893 *The Life and Traditions of the Red Man* was self-published by Joseph Nicolar (Penobscot) in Bangor, Maine by the C.H. Glass & Co. Printers (Kolodny 35). Nicolar had served six terms as the Penobscot representative to the Maine State Legislature in Augusta and was astutely aware of the alarming political policies unfolding in the United States during this time (36). Nicolar's original publication uses a storytelling style to share the traditional stories of his people. Some chapter topics include: the Creation story of Klos-kur-beh and his adventures, the First Mother who changed into corn and tobacco, the first white man's track, the fish famine, war between the Penobscots and the May-Quays (Mohawks), and history of when the grand council of northeastern nations was established.

Nicolar's book is not autobiographical, but is about the Penobscot nation. He recounts traditional Penobscot material culture, practices, and worldview in his stories. He does so while presenting the challenges of colonization and an altered Penobscot world that simultaneously includes and refashions Christian beliefs around their original culture. He finishes the body of his work with the ominous line "The red man was now ready to be converted and resigned himself to wait for the future fate that may come" (194), and then adds six pages of pre-contact Penobscot practices and vocabulary to conclude the book. The last six pages are little more than a compilation of important traditional information, as if added in haste to preserve every detail he could remember. The book ends with a reference to Casco Bay in Maine with the final line "this great medicine water was called 'K'chit-ka-bi'" (200), an observation that suggests religious conversion may have been at hand, but nevertheless Penobscot language and traditions must be preserved.

Kolodny's edition, which includes Nicolar's entire publication in its original form, opens with a drawing of a traditional Penobscot design, then a Preface by Charles Norman Shay. Shay's three-page statement includes a photograph of Shay next to a painted portrait of his grandfather (x) and his belief that Nicolar's book is "a preservation of what he knew, what he'd heard and learned directly ... so that those who came later might learn and understand" (xi). Shay recalls his first impression of reading his grandfather's book after he returned from serving in World War II by saying "I remember being impressed by the accomplishment of writing and publishing a text so full of detailed information ... my grandfather managed to do it in an era when Indians were looked down upon" (ix). Kolodny's important inclusion of Shay's experiences adds a contemporary voice to the work that demonstrates the continuation not only of Nicolar's lineage, but of the Penobscot people. This counters the Vanishing Indian myth and firmly places the Penobscot people in the now.

After the Preface, Kolodny discloses in the Acknowledgements section that her methods are grounded in communal ethics and the cultural value of the collective narrative. She demonstrates her methods by noting that she

> repeatedly received both encouragement and good advice from James Sappier, Chief of the Penobscot Nation, and from Arnie Neptune, a revered Penobscot elder and spiritual leader ... and that she was welcomed by the Director of the Penobscot Nation's Department of Culture and Historic Preservation.
>
> (xiii)

Along with these recognized Penobscot leaders, Kolodny also notes her relationship with the living descendants of Nicolar, as well as time she spent with experts on Penobscot language and lore. A number of non-Penobscot experts were also consulted to complete the work. In the space of three pages, Kolodny presents a dense listing of recognized experts that makes her work a collective narrative and demonstrates attributes that are the hallmark of a work in the ICN genre.

Next in the book's offerings is a 34-page section titled "A Summary History of the Penobscot Nation" written by Kolodny that opens with a statement from James Sappier, Penobscot Elder, at a meeting of the New England Law Review in 2002. In this section, she opens with an etymology of the word Penobscot that immediately reveals both meaning and cultural values of the People. She then plunges into a discussion of the Eastern Algonquian dialect noting how a cultural value of communal ethics is supported linguistically; human habitation in Maine from eleven thousand years ago; migrations and trade routes; climatic changes including ice ages, periods of warming, and glacial movements; and lifestyles of early Indigenous peoples from this region. Kolodny uses the terms "indwelling sanctity of the world" and "intimate reciprocal relationships" (5) in her analysis of Penobscot cultural values gained from her experience with primary sources that demonstrates her depth of understanding of the Penobscot worldview.

In addition to these observations, the Summary History section also includes a brief history of the earliest experiences of Indigenous and European settler contact, noting that diseases and warfare "killed off as much as 90 percent of New England's [I]ndigenous populations within the first one hundred years of contact" (8). She recounts the near impossibility of eastern Indigenous nations remaining neutral between the French and English struggles at the time of early colonization and of the destruction of the Penobscot way of life by early settlers. For example, settlers' hogs uprooted Indigenous clam and oyster beds, settlers leveled forests, and trapped the beaver to near extinction (10). In addition to these cultural disruptions involving availability of the land's bounty, Kolodny astutely includes a discussion of the role the Christians played in disturbing Penobscot traditions, along with a seemingly unending list of wars that either directly involved or deeply affected the nation. This section also includes the chilling reminder of when the colonial government declared "the Penobscot tribe of Indians to be enemies ... and [colonists were to] embrace all opportunities of pursuing, captivating, killing and destroying all and every of the aforesaid Indians" (12). Next, Kolodny includes a lengthy summary of Penobscot actions to protect their sovereignty and land rights. Throughout the History section, she notes population numbers over the centuries, as well.

Finally, the Summary History includes photographs of sites key to the Penobscot, a recounting of contemporary struggles the people face, like chemical pollutants affecting their health and the fish in their rivers, hydroelectric dams, unemployment, and prejudice against Natives. The current structures of their government are noted as well. The section finishes with Kolodny's statement that "Above all, they are warriors still, a proud Nation fighting to protect its sovereignty, its heritage, and its riverine ecosystem" (32).

Following the Summary History section is Kolodny's 53-page Introduction that presents a highly researched and informed presentation of American history from this time period as it relates more broadly to Native peoples, and to the Penobscot specifically. Included in the Introduction is a keenly insightful analysis of Nicolar's original text. Kolodny discusses many prevailing cultural values from nations of the Eastern Woodlands that are present in Nicolar's work about the Penobscots. Some of these cultural values are the primacy of land in determining Indigenous origins; the importance and practice of kinship ties among individuals, clans and nations; the presence of multiple creators (rather than a monotheistic origination); the centrality of women deities and women in the nations; the important role of Uncle in childrearing; and how cultural traditions are born from the land who is understood to be a living being.

In the Introduction, Kolodny goes to great lengths to outline key political events, noting the Indian Appropriation Act of 1871, the General Allotment or Dawes Act of 1887, and the 1893 World's Columbian Exposition at the national celebration of the quadricentennial of Columbus's "discovery" of America (36–37), among other anti-Indigenous policies. Concerning the Exposition in Chicago, Kolodny recounts the opening parade at the dedicatory ceremonies that featured uniform-clad Indigenous children from the Carlisle Indian School that reinforced (especially to Nicolar) "that the Indian was either a relic of some earlier stage of human development, bound for extinction, or a people who would have to become thoroughly assimilated ... in order to survive" (38). Placing the Indigenous writer's work in historical context, as is relevant to his experience and not history as it is derived from images of the master narrative, is important. Kolodny accomplishes that task well in the Introduction and soundly reinforces the centrality of the Indigenous voice as a speaker with agency and vision.

In the final section of the Introduction, Kolodny looks more broadly at the impact Nicolar's work has made upon academics. She notes that "anthropologists, ethnologists, ethnohistorians, and folklore specialists have been content to mine Nicolar's book" and that these researchers differ greatly from most historians specializing in the American colonial period who ignore Nicolar's work because they are "frustrated by the difficulty of aligning his narrative with any corresponding EuroAmerican chronology of battles, significant occurrences, or identifiable priestly arrivals" (75). Though this observation is insightful, what primarily matters for this discussion about the ICN genre is that, as a chronicler, Kolodny has the experience and wisdom to recognize this academic phenomenon that is about centralizing the Indigenous voice, not creating yet another ethnocentric narrative about Indians. The early As-Told-To literary genre reinforces that ethnocentric narrative. Though it may appear to be a dispassionate, academic observation on her part, her statement is quite radical and speaks to fundamental issues concerning a nation and its higher educational system that continues to struggle with the disgraceful events that surround their inceptions. This avoidance is played out in the way Indigenous histories are taught to American grade school and university students, in both content and methodology, and is thus one reason why the stereotypes and misinformation about Native cultures are so pervasive and pernicious. A stronger argument for the value and necessity of the creation and inclusion of works in the ICN genre cannot be found.

Kolodny's final statements in the Introduction, which come just before her lengthy amplification Notes section, educate readers about oral transmission and then remark that Nicolar's text focuses on "a single sustained narrative that told an *Indian* story from an *Indian* point of view ... the result is a written text that still retains some of the elements of its oral sources" [italics in the original] (77). She finishes with explicit statements about Nicolar's intentions for writing *The Life and Traditions of the Red Man*. Kolodny notes "first, it was meant to attract a white readership ... second [it] reinforced the viability of Indigenous self-representation" (78). Importantly, Kolodny's assessment that Nicolar's work is about a heritage "that will ensure the Penobscots' survival, even under the unhappy present circumstances forced upon them by the white man" (79) is a fundamental perspective for a chronicler of an Indigenous narrative. The writer or editor of an Indigenous Communal Narrative must unwaveringly adhere to a position of Indigenous continuance, as that is simply the state of the nations today.

After the Introduction by Kolodny, she offers a few pages of comments on the history of Nicolar's original text. She recounts dates of reprintings, errors and typos that have been corrected, explanations about inconsistencies in the spelling of Penobscot names and terms, and so forth. There is an explanation about the "double curve design elements" throughout the book, which she notes are Penobscot traditional designs from beadwork, baskets, and other weavings from Nicolar's era (92). Last, Kolodny asserts that Nicolar's work is a "major literary achievement" that brings together storytellers across the ages and proves that "Native ancestors still speak" (92). This short section also contains a studio photographic portrait of Joseph Nicolar from the 1893 edition.

The next section of the book is Nicolar's original work, which is 105 pages in length. He recounts traditional stories that lay the foundation of the Penobscot's cultural worldview that includes the sanctity of the earth, gendering protocols, and cycles of the earth from which the people shape daily life. Origins of important plants, like corn and tobacco, are told, as are stories about human relationship with animals. Complex cultural philosophies are interwoven with stories that seem to be straightforward retellings. For example, the number seven is central to most all the ceremonial stories, and this number is fundamental in Penobscot cosmology and the ordering of the universe.

Kolodny has added footnotes to explain geography, Penobscot terms, and added historic information to assist readers. Next, she adds a twelve-page section of Notes expanding on his text. The final voice of this edition is an Afterword by Bonnie D. Newsom, Director of Cultural and Historic Preservation of the Penobscot Nation. In the Afterword, Newsom directly states "the Penobscot Nation's endorsement of this republication" and "we want to thank Professor Kolodny for her extensive research, her cooperation with us" (214). Closing the book is a six-page listing of Works Consulted and Recommendations for Further Reading section.

Conclusion

Joseph Nicolar states clearly in the book's original Preface that only a red man can "give the public the full account of all the pure traditions which have been handed down from the beginning of the red man's world" (35). As Kolodny skillfully assesses in her analysis of Nicolar's original literary text, the book's purpose was to fix the Penobscot people unmistakably in their homeland; to teach the worldview and traditions of his people using an important deity from Wabanaki culture (Klos-ker-beh); and to affirm the continuance of the Penobscot.

The literary genre of Indigenous Communal Narrative is fundamentally about Indigenous self-representation and offers a form that does so through a multi-voiced, Native-centered narrative. This can be accomplished by using previously published Salvage Ethnography-type books (As-Told-To stories) and histories that may have been narrowly presented and that most likely reflected colonized tropes, like the Vanishing Indian, Princess-Squaw or Savage-Warrior stereotypes.

Kolodny's publication expounding on the previously published literary work of Penobscot elder Joseph Nicolar could not be a better example of the Indigenous Communal Narrative genre. From the breadth of collective voices to the depth of Kolodny's wisdom in Native American Studies, the book is a model of de-colonizing methodology that first and foremost centralizes the Indigenous writer's voice and his nation's cultural and historical experiences.

Works cited

Apess, William. *A Son of the Forest*. 1829. Rpt. *On Our Own Ground: The Complete Writings of William Apess, a Pequot*. Ed. Barry O'Connell. Amherst: University of Massachusetts Press, 1992. 1–56.

Brooks, Joanna, ed. *The Collected Writings of Samson Occom, Mohegan: Literature and Leadership in Eighteenth-Century Native America*. New York: Oxford University Press, 2006.

Brooks, Lisa. *The Common Pot: The Recovery of Native Space in the Northeast*. Minneapolis: University Minnesota Press, 2008.

Deloria, Philip J., ed. *Black Elks Speaks: The Complete Edition*. Lincoln: University Nebraska Press, 2014.

DeMallie, Raymond, ed. *The Sixth Grandfather: Black Elk's Teachings Given to John G. Neihardt*. University Nebraska Press, 1985.

Kolodny, Annette, ed. *The Life and Traditions of the Red Man: A Rediscovered Treasure of Native American Literature*. Durham, NC: Duke University Press, 2007.

Linderman, Frank B. *Pretty-Shield: Medicine Woman of the Crows*. 1932. Rpt. Lincoln: University of Nebraska Press, 1972.

Mann, Barbara Alice. *Iroquoian Women: The Gantowisas*. New York: Peter Lang, 2006.

Miller, Jay, ed. *Mourning Dove: A Salishan Autobiography*. Lincoln: University of Nebraska Press, 1994.

Neihardt, John G. *Black Elk Speaks*. 1932. Rpt. Lincoln: University of Nebraska Press, 1961.

Occom, Samson. *A Short Narrative of My Life* in Bernd Peyer, *The Elders Wrote: An Anthology of Early Prose by North American Indians, 1768–1931*. Berlin: Dietrich Reimer Verlag, 1982. 12–18.

O'Connell, Barry, ed. *On Our Own Ground: The Complete Writings of William Apess, a Pequot*. Amherst: University of Massachusetts Press, 1992.

Radin, Paul, ed. *Crashing Thunder: The Autobiography of an American Indian*. 1926, 1954. Rpt. Ann Arbor: University of Michigan Press, 1999.

35
Native Short Story
Authorships, Styles

A. Robert Lee

Legacy

Story, storytelling, as in all indigenous tradition, lies at the very core of Native American culture. From the outset and across the wider geography of the Americas, Bering Strait to Tierra del Fuego, the Caribbean to Hawai'i, this has meant the spoken word, a vast, enactive thesaurus of legend, storying and song in a plurality of historic languages. They each bear nothing if not memory, the one or another prism into habitations of time and land. Whether Kiowa creation myth, Navajo coyote and other trickster fable, Hopi tales of clan and adventure, Anishinaabe-Chippewa woodland narrative, Sioux accounts of horse and buffalo, Pueblo and Cherokee fables of childhood and witchery, or Cree versions of cosmology, their fashioning has always allowed for improvisation, spontaneity in styles of delivery. That holds, equally, for each other tribal-oral portrait of community, love, war, craft, medicine, latterly even city life, and always comic mishap and tease. It is a legacy, of which a compendious and hugely indicative collection would be *American Indian Myths and Legends* (1985), that provides the necessary hinterland to native *written* authorship, "story" in general and specifically short stories whether reservation or increasingly beyond-reservation based.

To speak of Native short story publication as a force in its own right is also to situate it within the spectrum of the Native novel and poetry, along with Native autobiography, drama, and the plethora of evidentiary and discursive writing. Since Scott Momaday's *House Made of Dawn* (1968), his virtuoso homing novel of Abel as Jemez Pueblo mixed-blood caught between the colliding worlds of the World War II Asian Pacific and Indian Country, California and Laguna New Mexico, it may well be that longer narrative fiction has tended to win the limelight. But that in no way diminishes short story achievement, be it as early tier, one-off, author collection, cycle, or edited anthology.

Antecedents

If the novel looks to John Rollins Ridge's *The Life and Times of Joaquín Murieta* (1854) as inaugural text, albeit by a Cherokee-descended writer with Mexican banditry as subject, so the short story has its working first benchmarks. Zitkala-Sa, Yankton Sioux activist, Carlisle Indian School teacher, violinist, opera writer, contributor to *Atlantic Monthly* and *Harper's*, and also known under her English-language name of Gertrude Simmons Bonnin, gives one kind of pointer. Her political writings may well have had the stronger impact but both *Old Indian Legends* (1901), pitched mainly for children, and *American Indian Stories* (1921), with their mix of autobiography, essay and fiction and focus on the intricacies of Sioux legacy and the costs of assimilation, show a ready enough virtuosity. Charles Eastman, the Santee Sioux physician who attended at Wounded Knee in 1890 and whose *Indian Boyhood* (1902) won a considerable readership, gives pointers of another kind. Following his interpretations of tribal culture and his animal and war stories, first published in *Harper's* and other leading magazines, he successively collected stories in *Red Hunters and Animal People* (1904), *Old Indian Days* (1907) and *Smoky Days Wigwam Evenings: Indian Tales Retold* (1910).

Alexander Posey's *Fus Fixico Letters*, the work of an Oklahoma Muscogee Creek satirist with a shrewd eye to federal and tribal politics, and published in his Eufaula newspaper *Indian Journal* in the 1900s, offers a case in point. Behind the ostensible epistolary form lies a fund of canny story-creation and character. E. Pauline Johnson's *Legends of Vancouver* (1911), *The Shagganappi* (1913) and *The Moccasin Maker* (1913), as the posthumously collected stories of a celebrity Six Nations Canadian Mohawk poet and touring actress, take on a mix of Native terrains. Whatever the occasional dips of style they encompass an ambitiously bicoastal span of Iroquois to Squamish history.

Mourning Dove's *Coyote Stories* (1933), by the Okanogan author (also known as Christal Quintasket) of *Cogewea, the Half-Breed* (1927) with its Montana ranch setting and inter-cultural relationships, transcribes grandmother-told tribal legend into on-the-page story. John Milton Oskison, the Cherokee autobiographical novelist of *Brothers Three* (1935), begins his career with the religious-themed and titled story "Only the Master Shall Praise." D'Arcy McNickle (Cree-Métis, enrolled Salish), best known for *The Surrounded* (1936) as the frontier territorial clash of Flathead, Spanish and white-American writ, bequeaths the western-frontier and international stories posthumously collected in *The Hawk is Hungry* (1992). John Joseph Mathews' *The Osages: Children of the Middle Waters* (1961) offers a trove of documentary tribal custom and timeline, but is most notable for how it resorts to material deftly sourced from the talk-stories of his own Osage origins.

Each of the earlier names differs as much in their story-styling as in cultural ancestry. They also, several times over, confirm that Native authors fall under no absolute obligation to write only Native-themed work. Undoubtedly the roster of written Native short story has moved into fuller come-uppance under the pen of moderns and contemporaries in the wake of Momaday. But these first strata were, and remain, necessary pathways.

Author gallery

To alight upon any one selection of stories might well risk looking arbitrary, especially given the formidable variety at hand in range of theme and operative design. Oral voice, be it the storytelling of tribal elder, gamester, different womanhoods, or even children, readily presses from behind the written form. Settings run from the legendary and tribal-historical to the present-day, from rez to city, land to road, HUD housing to casino. Family and community are told in hues variously fond and otherwise. Retellings of coyote as up-setter, a breaker of rules, are to be found alongside modern tales of love fever or dispossession. Postmodern narration makes a bow. Who, too, could doubt the ironic turn, at one reach stories given over to tragedy large or small, and at another, to comic pratfall or dark laughter? Native short storytelling has yielded nothing if not the full menu.

Perhaps appropriately one can open with Scott Momaday's "She is Beautiful in Her Whole Being" (Lesley *Talking Leaves*), from *The Ancient Child* (1989), a composition engagingly seamed in bear, pollen and star myth. This love story of Set and Grey conjures a far older story from behind its apparent contemporaneity, the damaged Kiowa man who finds redemption in his Navajo lover recently returned from an America outside the world of her mother's Arizona-Lukachukai *Diné* people. Grey's life-ancestry of Navajo custom and language, as much as her beauty, and its renewal of Set's spirit as much as body in the shared life of their hogan and their subsequent vision ceremony of joining, bespeaks the continuity of what the story designates "tradition out of time" (207). Legend so elides into life, spirit into body – as it does again in short fiction like "Bone Girl" (Trafzer *Earth Song, Sky Spirit*) by Joseph Bruchac (Abenaki) with its respect for "Indian ghost" meaning, and "This is a Story" (King *All My Relations*) by Jeannette C. Armstrong (Okanagan) with its Coyote/Kyoti folklore narrative of Canadian ancestral salmon-run as against the latter-day river of dam and oil slick.

A yet more specific sense of place presses in "Fear and Recourse" (*Earth Song, Sky Spirit*), a meticulous fictionalization by the veteran Mohawk poet and fiction writer Maurice Kenny of the events leading to the 1868 bluecoat cavalry attack on Black Kettle and his southern Cheyenne at Washita, Oklahoma. Beginning from the perspective of Black Kettle's daughter, Monahsetah, the story offers a line of remembrance into Comanche near-evisceration. The effect is one of story documentary that includes tribal divisions over whether to attack or make peace with settler whites, the memory of the Sand Creek Massacre of the Cheyenne in 1864, actual citings from military figures like Generals Sherman and Sheridan, and the invocation of the Washita River encampment before the murderous attack under the command of George Custer. It interlaces Black Kettle's peace overtures with extracts from white soldier war letters and diaries. The Plains are invoked as one-time buffalo plenty but now turned famine and bitter winter privation by destructive white hunting. Kenny keeps the connecting layers of his story tight, above all their implication of place as tribal memory.

Other locales enter the story spectrum in a variety of ways. In "From Aboard the Night Train" (*Earth Song, Sky Spirit*) Kimberly Blaeser (Anishinaabe) has her Native-born narrator rail-travel back to her reservation township first home. The rail journey, Wisconsin to Minnesota, yields memories of seeing a Fourth of July celebration, a summer stay in France's Haute-Savoie, and nightmares of being at risk in some violent major city. Both on arrival, and on her return trip home, an Our Town reservation panorama of twenty years previous comes into view: main street and store, eatery and hotel, even a funeral parlor. But the presiding change is the casino, "Las Vegas-style gambling" in its gains-and-losses significance for the Native community. That leads on to thoughts of other transformations, noise over quiet, satellite TV where once there was the parlor and veranda. A closing metaphor summons the TV report of a returning Russian cosmonaut, his balance uncertain, after a sixteen-month stay in space. This Native home, one among many, has likewise become shifting ground, for good or not, subject to the folds of change like any other America.

In "Snatched Away" (*Talking Leaves*) Mary TallMountain (Koyukon Athabascan), much acclaimed for her poem "There is No Word for Goodbye," develops an intricate memory-fiction set upon the sub-Arctic Yukon River and close to the bankside towns of

Nulato and Kaltag. The Yukon, variously calm and in "fierce, frowning mood," at once Native and non-Native habitation, and a place of death and yet sustaining salmon run, mirrors the community life evolved on and about its presence. The figure of the fisherman Clem Stone, his loss of his Athabaskan wife Mary Joe to tuberculosis, of their children by adoption, and of her brother Andy to a river drowning, fuses into a literal as much as metaphoric time and tide story. Past memory of all he has learned from the community plays alongside present life to make for highly accomplished, not to say contemplative fabling as Clem steers his way one more time along the river ("Indian. Indianness. The words floated through his thoughts." 266).

Native family, and within it childhood, necessarily finds an array of voice of which Ruby Slipperjack (Ontario Fort Hope Anishinaabe) gives a rich vignette in "Coal Oil, Crayons and Schoolbooks" (*All My Relations*). Its unnamed narrator tells a working-day: bacon and coffee breakfast in a reserve cabin home, cold weather, outhouse, morning trout-catch, sibling play and scurry, schoolroom, clothesline, forgotten key, and the presence of a kindly elder called Medicine Man. The account exudes warmest intimacy, a First Nations round of everyday communal life. For Greg Sarris (Miwok-Pomo) in "Slaughterhouse" (*Earth Song, Sky Spirit*) the focus is more one of disconnection, that of an ethnically mixed California boy-adolescent set within seedy, run-down "in-town-reservation-living." Frankie's peer status in his Santa Rosa Avenue gang, his disjunctive home of drink-addled father, disheveled Aunt Julia and other relatives, the would-be sexual pursuit of Caroline, and his adventuring into a local barn made over into a brothel, all ply into dark portraiture. The image of family here is one of uncertain Native circuit, lives close to broken wheel.

If humor, wry subversive wit, beckons, then Gerald Vizenor (Anishinaabe-Chippewa) has long established his claim. A story like "Almost Browne" (*Landfill Meditation*), in common with other trickster-themed work of a kind with the novels *Bearheart* (1978) and *Griever: An American Monkey King in China* (1986), does duty, full of play, contrariety, yet serious enough within its lattices of irony. Born in a hatchback at the border of the White Earth reservation with white Minnesota, neither quite one hue nor another, Almost in his role as entrepreneur of Blank Books wins every satiric laurel. In his own genealogical mix, and his travels from the Midwest to Berkeley, Vizenor teases the very notion of any one fixed "Indian" identity, some pan-tribal aggregate based on Columbus's mistaken map. Native culture, past and ongoing, tribe-specific, languaged on its own terms, remains unwritten as it were. The blank books, accordingly, and among other aims, represent Vizenor's witty if uncompromising aim at the vacuity of the cliché Red Indian, each endlessly seductive (not to say financially profitable) Hollywood romance or comic-strip version.

For Rayna Green (Cherokee) in "High Cotton" (*That's What She Said*) the target is a whiskey-drinker husband, Will, bamboozled in his DTs into thinking his church-woman wife in her flannel gown is the down-from-heaven figure of Jesus calling him to sobriety. Told as though feisty kitchen-talk by a Tahlequah, Oklahoma Cherokee grandmother to her young kinswoman Ramona, it runs full of cryptic aside, off the cuff comedy. Infinitely to the point the narrator, long seasoned in married ways, terms the happenings (and by implication the storytelling) "snakebite medicine." Linda Hogan (Chickasaw) offers another kind of woman-centered story in "Aunt Moon's Young Man" (*Talking Leaves*), that which circles around Bess Evening, Chickasaw spinster medicine-woman whose affair with Isaac, a younger full-blood native man, puts her wartime Pickens, Oklahoma small town neighborhood into a frenzy of church and street gossip. The girl-narrator, Sis, her own family "mixed like Heinz 57," gives the story just the right measure: Bess's role as *curandera*, mentor, lover of Isaac who beats the menfolk at poker, and the woman who sends her on her way to college life with herbs and feather and the image of a "small beautiful woman in my eye."

An equally agile irony plays into "Moccasins Don't Have High Heels" (Velie *American Indian Literature*) by the Choctaw fiction writer and playwright LeAnne Howe. Told as breezy vernacular, swearing included, it gives a brief first-person diary of a Native woman who, in the wake of market greed and crash, disgustedly bows out of her office bond-trading job ("I was getting rid of my high heels and putting on my moccasins"). The itinerary that follows involves acerbic swipes at more "Indian" stereotypes, and at Reagan-era predations on the environment, Wild West hoopla, and archeology's digging up native bones. No more "Indians" as margin, periphery, shadow, runs the story's staccato ending.

Tom King's "The One About Coyote Going West" (*All My Relations*) uses the archetypal trickster figure to fashion a savvy, colloquial story "all about who found us Indians" (68). European discovery history, be it by Norsemen, Columbus or Jacques Cartier, attracts different parodic hits. Coyote's own "discovery" story leads into a duck-clan rite of passage, curious fowl having grown impatient with his trickster's digressions and mistakes who turn themselves into Indians. The upshot is genial creation-myth, edged in fun, about-turn, quirk, even excremental smell, but nothing if not a lien on self-owned tribal culture.

Story cycles

The modern story cycle vaunts well enough known landmarks, whether James Joyce's *Dubliners* with its vernacular city-world of Ireland or Sherwood Anderson's *Winesburg, Ohio* with its portrait of American small-town claustrophobia. But it has also been a favored genre in Native authorship, not least, perhaps, for how it un-privileges the one presiding storyline or storyteller. Rarely has that worked to shrewder advantage than in Louise Erdrich's *Love Medicine* (1984), fourteen pieces to which four more were added in the 1993 edition and which was further revised in 2009, and with which she made her considerable public bow as a writer. As the narration shifts from one voice of disclosure to the next over a span of six decades the complex Anishinaabe-Chippewa and mixed dynasties of North Dakota's Turtle Mountain Reservation come increasingly into view. The result is a kind of reservation story consortium, a cross-plied and greatly affecting map of inter-layered tribal and white family, memory, loves, fissures, place, and above all, voice.

"The World's Greatest Fishermen," in four parts, sets the cycle in motion with its account of June Kashpaw who walks to death in night-time snows and Chinook wind outside of Williston, North Dakota ("oil boomtown") after bar-drinking and a casual sexual encounter with a "mud engineer." Her demise, that of a woman lost to her own best promise, and its aftermath for her divorced husband Gordie, her niece Albertine Johnson and mother Zelda, her Grandmother Kashpaw and Great-uncle Eli, her cousin Nector, and the family adoptee Lipsha Morrissey, supplies a kind of warning shadow for the lives still to be unfolded. This is reservation culture toughly told as damage, missed chance, love which can turn bitter. Other Kashpaws and Lamartines enter, together with the Lazarres, Pillagers, Morrisseys, Nanapushes and Adares, each severally bound into a linking but broken hoop. Yet for each crack or fissure there is connection, life-histories whose very divergence and dark, at times comic, ironies themselves make a revolving circle.

The stories, in turn, deal with the tensions between a French-exported Catholicism and Chippewa belief ("Saint Marie" and "Flesh and Blood"); the unexpected, comic turns of tribal conjure as against Catholic observance in affairs of the heart ("Love Medicine"); the role of drink and alcoholism in Chippewa history ("Crown of Thorns"); sexual permutations within an extended family regime ("Lulu's Boys"); Vietnam and the return of the damaged Henry Lamartine ("The Red Convertible"); and actual tribal reality in an era of mythified or cartoon Indians ("The Plunge of the Brave"). As serious in implication as these themes evidently are, Erdrich keeps them free of solemnity or sentimentalism. Narrators, accordingly, can settle old scores, adjust the record as fits, complain or justify, only to have correctives supplied by others in the wheel. Erdrich's deftness, throughout, is to make a one idiom of story precisely imply the circle of all the others.

For Diane Glancy (Cherokee) in *Firesticks* (1993) a different cycle-strategy holds. The six-part "Firesticks" acts as a spine, a coordinating story line. Its portrait of Turle, fortyish, seen-it-all or seen-most-of-it diner waitress in Guthrie, Oklahoma, her taking up with the truck-driving and migrant worker Navorn, their trip to Frederick to see her ailing father (his death to follow), and their eventual uncertain resolve for a road life together, is told as a gapped sequence within and between the collection's other stories. Each "Firesticks" episode works to a timescale in which later can precede earlier events. Taken together they also throw a light on the accompanying shorter narratives, writing she teasingly designates in *The Voice That Was in Travel* (1999) "connectives and *disconnectives*" (vii).

These stories can be spaced elliptically like the "The First Indian Pilot" with its boyhood avian fantasy, or take the form of a girl's cryptic diary like "A Family to Which Nothing Happened" in which accidents, death, tornado and sexual harassment of her friend Linda Elson, all bypass the township banality which is her own life. "Stamp Dance," the styling close to imagism, offers the mixed-blood boy Mack's absorption in philately as a figurative route into buffalo, war-bonnet and avian escape from his round of food-stamp minimums and a father lost-in-action in Vietnam. "A Phenomenon of Light" links the spiritual elation of the narrator's seeing the beauteous reflection of Mount St. Helens in Spirit Lake with the flatness, and craters, in her own life. A vignette like "Proverb, American" playfully teases the genesis and then the need to organize words each "running loose" as if they were lexical free spirits (134). It makes for an oblique but elucidatory comment on how *Firesticks* seeks to arc its own various word-stories into the one overall cycle.

Author collections

Any given selection, once again, can look arbitrary, but key volumes make for a serious plenty. Collections by names already mentioned necessarily feature, whether Louise Erdrich's omnibus *The Red Convertible: Selected and New Stories, 1978–2008* (2009); Tom King's coyote tease of targets from anthropology to the RCMP in *One Good Story, That One* (1993), and his both native and multicultural span in the equivocally named *A Short History of Indians in Canada* (2005); or the different gamester pieces like "Ice Tricksters," with its tricky liberation fable, and "The Psychotaxidermist," with its mock trial format and reflexive take on native storytelling, that accompany "Almost Browne" in Gerald Vizenor's *Landfill Meditation: Crossblood Stories* (1988).

Equally, established authorship has not gone missing. Simon Ortiz (Acoma Pueblo) brings the seasoned poet's ear of *Woven Stone* (1992) and *Out There Somewhere* (2002) to his *Men on the Moon: Collected Short Stories* (1999). This easefully told mix of life-stories range through the title-story's ironic contemplation of an age of astronauts for reservation culture ("Men on the Moon"), Pueblo upbringing and family life ("What Indians Do"), Idaho migrant labor ("Woman Singing"), Vietnam and a lost son ("To Change Life in a Good Way"), and West Coast hippie-wannabes ("The San Francisco Indians"). Elizabeth Cook-Lynn (Crow Creek Sioux), the tenacious founder-editor of *Wicazo Sa Review* and novelist of *Aurelia: A Crow Creek Trilogy* (1999), writes *The Power of Horses and Other Stories* (1990) with their portraiture of Upper Plains reservation life whether family dysfunction ("Last Days of a Squaw Man"), sad-comic missionary blunder ("A Visit from Reverend Tileston"), or grand-maternal love of dynasty and earth ("Mahpiyato").

Maurice Kenny, veteran poet, gives greatly assured expression to his Haudenosaunee Mohawk legacy as well as other tribal history in *Tortured Skins and Other Short Fiction* (2000). His stories display a nuanced exploration of white ethnocidal policy (in the case of the southern Cheyenne "Black Kettle: Fear and Rescue" and "Forked Tongues"), the complexities of bear signification and shape-shifter myth ("Bacon" and "Blue Jacket"), and the eco-imperative of human to wildlife kinship ("One More"). His forte is to situate tribal realms of past inside the present, Haudenosaunee/Iroquois practice and craft as it throws illumination upon a contrary modernity. Joseph Bruchac, long-time all-rounder as poet, musician, anthologist, founder of the Greenfield Review Press and Center, and storyteller of both adult and children's fiction, also mines a range of U.S.–Canadian lore, in his case Abenaki, rarely with livelier returns than in *Turtle Meat and Other Stories* (1992). Whether a laconic piece like the title-story with its clash of generations in which Homer and Amalia, themselves old-turtle-like, persist in ancestral ways as against their would-be contemporary daughter, or "The Fox Den" with its portrait of the Abenaki as tribal fox-people both hunters and hunted, the collection displays a shrewd insider touch for tribal ways of continuance and knowing.

Ralph Salisbury (Cherokee-Shawnee), whose autobiography *So Far, So Good* (2013) traces his mixed-blood poet's life, a "medicine path" as he calls it, from impoverished Depression-era farm Iowa to World War II, Korea, and Pacific Northwest academia, has long shown his hand as a short story talent with issues of masculinity, rite of passage, and war as keystone themes. His likely best-known volume, *The Indian Who Bombed Berlin and Other Stories* (2009), offers the poetically fine-threaded drama of a Native boy's coming of age ("Bathsheba's Bath, Bull Durham, and a Bottle of Old Grandad"), Native sexual stereotype and actuality set in a world of European diplomacy ("The New World Invades the Old"), and the epiphanic war encounter at the heart of the title-story ("The Indian Who Bombed Berlin").

Anna Lee Walters (Pawnee and Otoe-Missouria) creates a delicate octet of stories in *The Sun Is Not Merciful* (1985), not least her clear-eyed story of alcoholic damage in "The Warriors," careful parsing of a reservation girl's molestation and relationship to her mother in "The Apparitions," and updated telling of a celebrated native rebirth myth in "The Resurrection of John Stink." Michael Dorris (Modoc) writes with great exactness if a certain airlessness in the fourteen stories of *Working Men* (1993), whether the burial of a drowned child by a pond-designer obsessed with precise measurement and his wife in "The Benchmark" or the re-plaiting of an Alaskan tribal folktale of marital betrayal, spirit-wife and all too unwitting anthropologist in "Shining Agate." In Adrian C. Louis (Paiute), and his collection *Wild Indians and Other Creatures* (1996), Native short fiction has a battler, coyote and raven stories given sardonic hard edge both for themselves and as they play into and upset seeming actual lives, be they Sioux marriage, veteran but also gay Gulf War soldiery, affectingly, a Downs child, or even white enquirers after the supposed truth of the film, *A Man Called Horse*.

Contemporaries? None can be said to have achieved greater sway than Sherman Alexie (Spokane-Coeur d'Alene). His storytelling invention, often wickedly funny, serious, as seamed in modern reservation habits and ways, whether centered in Coeur d'Alene Pacific Northwest tribal history and myth or not, has put him at the forefront of Native authorship. His prolific shorter work, nine or so collections, in common with novels like *Reservation Blues* (1995) with Thomas Builds-The-Fire as griot, lowers an irreverent, ironic but always engaging eye upon Americas both tribal and otherwise, not to say their longstanding cultural interface.

The Lone Ranger and Tonto Fist Fight in Heaven (1993) yields a story like "Indian Education" unfolded as the First to Twelfth Grade paradigmatic diary of a reservation boy's life full of creativity yet lived within a circuit of HUD, welfare, basketball, and posed classroom photographs. *The Toughest Indian in the World* (2000) has Alexie showing his ironic paces in "Dear John Wayne," a story told as though a futurist (and trickster) interview with the Coeur d'Alene centenarian woman Etta Joseph in which she recalls her love-affair with Wayne, Marion Morrison as she knew him under his original name, and which took place ironically even as he was playing the whitest of homesteaders: Ethan Edwards in John Ford's *The Searchers*. Both stories bespeak rare wit, pointers to a present-day mastery of Native American revels.

Alexie can look to generational, and equally prolific, company. *Bleed Into Me: A Book of Stories* (2005), by Stephen Graham Jones (Blackfeet), one book in an output of more than thirty, catches at out-of-kilter families each of mixed-blood heritage, notably in the dead-son portrait of the title-story and of flawed parentage of the "Halloween." In "Discovering America," in the voice of a playwright writing the one-acter *The Time That Indian Started Killing Everybody*, Jones takes a laconic shy at the modern cultural footfalls of Columbus, the ways in which Native America has been taken out of history by mainstream "Indian" kitsch and paraphernalia. Anita Endrezze (Yaqui), much recognized for her poetry and artwork, turns to a range of world folk-myth in *Butterfly Moon* (2012), the spectrum ranging from sixteen-century Yaqui evisceration ("White Butterflies") through to contemporary shape-shifters ("The Vampire and the Moth Woman").

Canadian First Nations author collections, and not to sidestep the story contributions of Ruby Slipperjack along with those of Peter Blue Cloud (Mohawk), Jeannette Armstrong (Okanagan) and Joan Crate (Cree) and of which Thomas King's *All My Relations* (1990) gives an important selection, has been its own imaginative force. Basil Johnston (Ontario Anishinaabe), voluminous author and an Anishinaabe as well as English speaker, offers Runyonesque drollery in *Ojibway Tales: Moose Meat and Wild Rice* (1978), whether "Yellow Cloud's Battle with the Sprits" in which the trickster-demon Windigo gets conflated with a local white preacher's car headlights, or a lake-fishing pastiche at the expense of the Department of Indian Affairs like "A Sign of the Times."

Beth Brant (Mohawk), First Nations sovereignty and gender activist, gives voice to a range of woman-focused Native experience in *Food and Spirits: Stories* (1991), variously

"This is History" with its gynocentric turtle-creation mythology and "Wild Turkeys" as the story-memoir of a long-ago abusive relationship. E. Donald Two-Rivers (Anishinaabe), Ontario-born but long resident in Chicago and an established playwright, creates a tough gallery of Native city-lives in *Survivor's Medicine* (1998), typically crime and its aftermath as in "Joe Walks-Bear Comes Home" or broken minds as in "Smoking Gun Syndrome." Joseph Boyden (Métis), novelist of the *Three Day Road* (2005) with its account of the wounds and then healing of two Canadian-Cree soldiers in World War I, covers a wide range in his debut collection *Born with a Tooth* (2001). Centered in a northern Ontario reserve and given over to accounts of youth damage ("Gasoline"), intoxicants ("Painted Tongue"), even a punk band ("You Don't Want to Know What Jenny Two Bears Did"), it closes with a subtly orchestrated and reflexive story-quartet in which contesting viewpoints seek to understand the suicide of the tribal student Linda Cheechoo.

Anthologies

These, a sampling of which is given in the "Works Cited" list below, have played an altogether necessary part in making known the Native/First Nations authorship on offer. General anthologies from Erdoes and Ortiz (1985) to Velie (1979, 1991) give situating tribal-cultural and literary context. Story compilations, King (1990), Lesley (1991), Trafzer (1992), Blaisdell (2014), all serve to emphasize the sense of literary variety and heft. In Green (1984), Allen (1989), Harjo and Bird (1997), (1984) and Wong (2008) Native womanist voice has its deserved representation. Other gatherings of relevant story work would not be difficult to locate, any more than still emerging authorship. But given in survey or otherwise there can be no doubt of wide efficacy, hugely distinctive galleries of short story born of Native legacy within the United States and Canada and increasingly also worlds yet beyond.

Works cited

Allen, Paula Gunn, ed. *Spider Woman's Granddaughters: Traditional Tales and Contemporary Writing by Native American Women*. Boston: Beacon Press, 1989.
Alexie, Sherman. *Blasphemy: New and Selected Stories*. New York: 2012.
——. *The Business of Fancydancing: Stories and Poems*. Brooklyn, NY: Hanging Loose Press, 1992.
——. *Face*. Brooklyn, NY: Hanging Loose Press, 2009.
——. *First Indian on the Moon*. Brooklyn, NY: Hanging Loose Press, 1993.
——. *The Lone Ranger and Tonto Fist Fight in Heaven*. New York: Atlantic Monthly Press, 1993.
——. *Reservation Blues*. New York: Atlantic Monthly, 1995.
——. *Tattoo Tears*. Spokane, WA: Sherman Alexie, 1992.
——. *Ten Little Indians: Stories*. New York: Grove Press, 2003.
——. *The Toughest Indian in the World*. New York: Atlantic Monthly, 2000.
——. *War Dances*. New York: Grove Press, 2009.
Blaisdell, Bob, ed. *Great Short Stories by Contemporary Native American Writers*. Mineola, NY: Dover Publications, 2014.
Boyden, Joseph. *Born with a Tooth*. Toronto: Cormorant Books, 2001.
——. *Three Day Road*. Toronto: Penguin, 2005.

Brant, Beth. *Food and Spirits: Stories*. Ithaca, NY: Firebrand, 1991.

Bruchac, Joseph. *Turtle Meat and Other Stories*. Duluth, MN: Holy Cow! Press, 1992.

Cook-Lynn, Elizabeth. *Aurelia: A Crow Creek Trilogy*. Niwot: University Press of Colorado, 1999.

——. *The Power of Horses and Other Stories*. New York: Arcade, 1990.

Dorris, Michael. *Working Men: Stories*. New York: Henry Holt, 1993.

Dove, Mourning (Hum-Ishu-Ma, Christal Quintasket). *Cogewea, the Half-Blood: Given Through Sho-Powtan: A Depiction of the Great Montana Cattle Range*. Boston: Four Seas, 1927. Rpt. Lincoln: University of Nebraska Press, 1990.

——. *Coyote Stories*. Caldwell, ID: Caxton Press, 1933. Rpt. Lincoln: University of Nebraska Press, 1990.

Eastman, Charles. *Indian Boyhood*. New York: McClure, 1902.

——. *Old Indian Days*. New York: McClure, 1907.

——. *Red Hunters and Animal People*. New York: Harper & Brothers, 1904.

——. *Smoky Day's Wigwam Evenings: Indian Tales Retold*. Boston: Little, Brown and Company, 1910.

Endrezze, Anita. *Butterfly Moon: Short Stories*. Tucson: University of Arizona Press, 2012.

Erdoes, Richard & Alfonso Ortiz, eds. *American Indian Myths and Legends*. New York: Pantheon, 1985.

Erdrich, Louise. *Love Medicine*. New York: Henry Holt, 1986; expanded version, 1993; newly revised edition (P.S.). New York: HarperCollins, 2009.

——. *The Red Convertible: Selected and New Stories 1978–2009*. New York: HarperCollins, 2009.

Fisher, Dexter, ed. *American Indian Stories*. Lincoln: University of Nebraska Press, 1985.

Glancy, Diane. *Firesticks*. Norman: University of Oklahoma Press, 1993.

——. *The Voice That Was in Travel: Stories*. Norman: University of Oklahoma Press, 1999.

Green, Rayna, ed. *That's What She Said: Contemporary Poetry and Fiction by Native American Women*. Bloomington: Indiana University Press, 1984.

Harjo, Joy & Gloria Bird, eds. *Reinventing the Enemy's Language: Contemporary Native Women's Writing of North America*. New York: W.W. Norton, 1997.

Johnson, E. Pauline. *Legends of Vancouver*. Vancouver: G.S. Forsyth, 1911.

——. *The Moccasin Maker*. 1913. Rpt. Tucson: The University of Arizona Press, 1987.

——. *The Shagganappi*. Toronto: Briggs, 1913.

Johnston, Basil. *Ojibway Tales: Moose Meat and Wild Rice*. Toronto: McClelland & Stewart, 1978.

Jones, Stephen Graham. *Bleed Into Me: A Book of Stories*. Lincoln: University of Nebraska Press, 2005.

Kenny, Maurice. *Tortured Skins and Other Short Fiction*. East Lansing: Michigan State University Press, 2000.

King, Thomas. *All My Relations: An Anthology of Contemporary Native Fiction*. Toronto: McClelland & Stewart, 1990.

——. *One Good Story, That One: Stories*. Toronto: HarperPerennial, 1993.

——. *A Short History of Indians in Canada*. New York: HarperCollins, 2005.

——. *The Truth About Stories: A Native Narrative*. Minneapolis: University of Minnesota Press, 2003.

Lesley, Craig, ed. *Talking Leaves: Contemporary Native American Short Stories*. New York: Dell-Laurel, 1991.

Louis, Adrian C. *Wild Indians and Other Creatures*. Reno: University of Nevada Press, 1996.

Mathews, John Joseph. *The Osages: Children of the Middle Waters*. Norman: University of Oklahoma Press, 1961.

McNickle, D'Arcy. *The Hawk is Hungry*. Ed. Birgit Hans. Tucson: University of Arizona Press, 1992.

——. *The Surrounded*. New York: Dodd, Mead, 1936.

Momaday, N. Scott. *The Ancient Child*. New York: Doubleday, 1989.

——. *House Made of Dawn*. New York: Harper & Row, 1968.

Ortiz, Simon. *Men on the Moon: Collected Stories*. Tucson: University of Arizona Press, 1999.

———. *Out There Somewhere*. Tucson: University of Arizona Press, 2002.

———. *Woven Stone*. Tucson: University of Arizona Press, 1992.

Oskison, John. *Brothers Three*. New York: Macmillan, 1935.

Posey, Alexander. *The Fus Fixico Letters*. Ed. Daniel F. Littlefield. Lincoln: University of Nebraska Press, 1993.

Ridge, John Rollin (Yellow Bird). *The Life and Adventures of Joaquín Murieta, the Celebrated California Bandit*. 1854. Rpt. Norman: University of Oklahoma Press, 1977.

Salisbury, Ralph. *The Indian Who Bombed Berlin and Other Stories*. East Lansing: Michigan State University Press, 2009.

———. *So Far, So Good*. Lincoln: University of Nebraska Press, 2013.

Silko, Leslie Marmon. *Ceremony*. New York: Viking Press, 1972.

Trafzer, Clifford E., ed. *Earth Song, Sky Spirit: Short Stories of the Contemporary Native American Experience*. New York: Doubleday-Anchor, 1992.

Two-Rivers, E. Donald. *Survivor's Medicine: Short Stories*. Norman: University of Oklahoma Press, 1998.

Velie, Alan R., ed. *American Indian Literature: An Anthology*. 1979. Rev. ed. Norman: University of Oklahoma, 1991.

Vizenor, Gerald. *Darkness in Saint Louis Bearheart*. Minneapolis, MN: Truck Press, 1978. Rev. and rpt. as *Bearheart: The Heirship Chronicles*. Minneapolis: University of Minnesota Press, 1990.

———. *Griever: An American Monkey King in China*. Normal: Illinois State University/Fiction Collective. 1986. Rpt. Minneapolis: University of Minnesota Press, 1990.

———. *Landfill Meditation: Crossblood Stories*. Hanover, NH: Wesleyan University Press/University Press of New England, 1991.

Walters, Anna Lee. *The Sun is Not Merciful*. Ithaca, NY: Firebrand Books, 1985.

Wong, Hertha D. Sweet, Lauren Stewart Muller & Janet Sequoya Magdaleno, eds. *Reckonings: Contemporary Short Fiction by Native American Women*. New York: Oxford University Press, 2008.

Zitkala-sa/Zitkala-sha/Red Bird (Gertrude Simmons Bonnin). *American Indian Stories*. Washington, D.C.: Hayworth. 1921. Rpt. Lincoln: University of Nebraska Press, 1985.

———. *Old Indian Legends*. Boston: Ginn. 1901. Rpt. Lincoln: University of Nebraska Press, 2001.

36

"A New Legacy for Future Generations"

Native North American Performance and Drama

Birgit Däwes

Of the many genres in the North American literary landscape, Indigenous performance and drama are both the oldest and most innovative, the most misrepresented and resistant. Long displaced into the fields of anthropology and religious studies, the richly diverse performance traditions of Native North America have been subject to colonial oppression, prohibition, cultural genocide, and other forms of exploitative power, continuously appropriated and overwritten by colonial discourse. For centuries, practices of "playing Indian" (Deloria) in plays about, not by, Native Americans and First Nations people have dominated North American stages. With exponentially growing numbers of published and produced plays, audiences, readers, and critics have at last begun to leave both the gravitational pull of these "dubious simulations of native scenes" (Vizenor "Transmotion") and the disciplinary grip of primitivist and exoticist desires for a stereotypical Other. Increasingly visible and internationally successful, contemporary Indigenous North American drama radically resists processes of cultural appropriation, replaces hegemonic forms of representation with original voices, and redefines the American stage from the vantage points of its oldest origins.

As Ojibway playwright Drew Hayden Taylor aptly puts it, Native theater is "as old as this country, as old as the people who have been here for thousands of years, as old as the stories that are still told today. It is merely the presentation that has changed" (52). Ranging from Kwakiutl mystery plays to Hopi clown dances, from the ceremonial cycles associated with mound-building (see Howe "Story") to contemporary comedies, performative traditions have been primary modes of cultural expression across the continent for millennia. In the late nineteenth and twentieth centuries, some of these traditions were transformed into pan-tribal and more secular art forms, such as powwows, pageants, or scripted plays, which also incorporated European-American and Asian theatrical styles – but were clearly directed against the frozen, "ethnostalgic" (Owens 139) images that had governed the scene at least since John Augustus Stone's *Metamora, or, The Last of the Wampanoags* (FP 1829).

In the twentieth century, when Lynn Riggs (albeit largely without reference to his Cherokee heritage) achieved recognition with theatrical milestones such as *The Cherokee Night* (FP 1932), *Green Grow the Lilacs* (1931, adapted into the musical *Oklahoma!* in 1943),

423

and *Out of Dust* (1949), the development of modern Native drama gained momentum. Significant advances toward a theater movement included the establishment of the first contemporary Native American theater group, the American Indian Drama Company in New York in 1956, the foundation of the performance section at the Institute of American Indian Arts (IAIA) in Santa Fe in 1966, and the formation of theater companies in the 1970s, such as Hanay Geiogamah's American Indian Theater Ensemble (1972) and Spiderwoman Theater (1975) in New York, Red Earth Performing Arts in Seattle (1974), and James Buller's Native Theater School (1975) in Toronto. Other companies followed suit: from Native Earth Performing Arts (1982) in Toronto and De-Ba-Jeh-Mu-Jig Theater Company on Manitoulin Island, Ontario (1984), all the way to the establishment of Native Voices at the Autry National Center of the American West, "America's leading Native American theatre company," according to its website ("Native Voices"), in 1994.

In the emergence of Indigenous North American drama as a genre, different performative styles have diversified conventional terminologies and forms. Kermit Hunter's *Unto These Hills*, for instance, which was first staged in 1950 and is thus one of the oldest outdoor historical dramas in the United States, exemplifies the dynamic continuity of a historical pageant in Cherokee, North Carolina: while authored by a non-Native writer, it has recently been rewritten into a new, historically more accurate version by Linda W. Squirrel, with choreography by Sicangu Lakota playwright Larissa FastHorse, and it currently features a dominantly Cherokee cast. In 2014, the Oklahoma City Theater Company celebrated its fifth annual Native American New Play Festival, the Native Voices at the Autry's annual festival of New Plays went into its sixteenth round in Los Angeles, and Weesageechak Begins to Dance – Native Earth Performing Arts' annual festival of theater, dance, music, poetry, and multidisciplinary works by Indigenous artists – celebrated its twenty-seventh successful staging. With a vibrant contemporary scene and recent productions such as Robert Owens Greygrass's "Ghostlands of an Urban NDN" (2012), Yvette Nolan's "The Unplugging" (2014), or Ty Defoe's musical "Clouds are Pillows for the Moon" (2014), the creative force of the genre seems far from nearing exhaustion.

Native North American drama and the canon

There has been much debate about what constitutes Native theater, and since colonial practices of cultural appropriation, simulation, and misrepresentation have overshadowed its development for a long time, one of its key questions is that of authorship. "Native theater," according to Choctaw playwright LeAnne Howe, "is theater that is written by natives, and performed by native, tribal, indigenous, American Indian, Native American actors. It comes from a native voice and perspective" ("Native" 63). In its contemporary context, therefore, Native North American drama can be defined as performance events (including the scripts which provide the blueprints for those events) produced for an audience for multiple, overlapping purposes (of education, entertainment, memory, cultural and spiritual celebration and enrichment, individual and collective identity construction and the stabilization of communities), authorized, regardless of their themes, by a Native American or First Nations individual or group (persons consciously affiliated with one or several of the sovereign indigenous tribal groups of the United States or Canada), usually in English and/or indigenous languages (see Däwes, *Native Theater* 88).

Quite problematically, critics still occasionally succumb to the temptation to measure Native theater against European-American forms, which are implicitly taken to be superior: Alexander Pettit, for instance, writes even in a 2014 survey article that "aesthetically and intellectually, the best Native drama is as good as anything now being written, anywhere" (267). In spite of such arguments of "quality," or of "great writing" (Pettit 280), which perpetuate the tacit Eurocentric ideology of the genre's marginal status, the visibility of Native drama has been much increased by the publication of nine anthologies of three or more plays by different Native American or First Nations dramatists between 1999 and 2009, edited, respectively, by D'Aponte (1999), Geiogamah and Darby (1999), Kane, Daniels, and Clements (2001), Hodgson (2002), Mojica and Knowles (2003), Darby and Fitzgerald (2003), Huston-Findley and Howard (2008), Mojica and Knowles (2009), and Armstrong et al. (2009).[1] Hundreds of plays by Native American and First Nations playwrights and theater groups have been produced and published since the early 1970s, and access to this abundance of material is increasingly improving: the Native American Women Playwrights' Archive at Miami University in Oxford, Ohio, houses an ever-expanding collection of both published and unpublished plays (see Howard; Huston-Findley), and Alexander Street Press's *North American Indian Drama*, a digital full-text collection of more than 250 Indigenous plays, is searchable by semantic parameters. Despite the abundance of primary sources, scholarship in the field is only just beginning to evolve. With a few notable earlier exceptions – such as Jeffrey Huntsman's investigation of traditional ritual drama and contemporary forms in *Ethnic Theatre in the United States* (1983), Christopher Bigsby's chapter on "American Indian Theatre" in *A Critical Introduction to Twentieth-Century American Drama* (1985), or Sally Ann Heath's unpublished dissertation on "The Development of Native American Theater Companies in the Continental United States" (1995) – it took until the early 2000s for an academic discourse to develop, and yet, besides a few survey articles in handbooks and literary companions (by Haugo, Huhndorf, Pettit and Valentino), only a handful of English-language, book-length publications exclusively dedicated to mapping Native North American drama have been published to date (Geiogamah & Darby; Wilmer; Stanlake; Däwes). As Shari Huhndorf puts it, "drama remains the most overlooked genre in Native American literatures" (313).

Native North American drama is a "multi-faceted movement" (Haugo 202), marked by remarkable diversity in both form and content. From early productions in the 1970s, such as *The Dress* by Nora Benedict (Mohawk) in 1970, Kiowa playwright Hanay Geiogamah's *Body Indian* in 1972, and George Kenny's *October Stranger* in 1977 to Dew Hayden Taylor's comedies – like his famous "Blues quartet," including *The Bootlegger Blues* (1990), *The Baby Blues* (1995), *The Buz'Gem Blues* (2001), and *The Berlin Blues* (2007), as well as the more recent "Cerulean Blue" (2009) – and from the first historical pageants performed at the Six Nations Reserve's Forest Theatre in Ontario, Canada, in the 1940s to twenty-first century drama by important female playwrights such as Marie Clements – like *Burning Vision* (2003), *The Edward Curtis Project* (2010) or *Tombs of the Vanishing Indian* (2012); Diane Glancy – like *The Woman Who Was a Red Deer Dressed for the Deer Dance* (2005), *Salvage* (2008), "The Reason for Crows" (2011) or "The Bird House" (2011); or Larissa FastHorse – like *Average Family* (2007), *Teaching Disco Square Dancing to Our Elders: A Class Presentation* (2011), "Hunka" (2012), *Cherokee Family Reunion* (2012), or "Landless" (2015) – forms and styles include social drama, agit-prop, tragedy, musicals, history and memory plays, vaudeville, outdoor historical drama, and comedy, mixing or alternating realist and expressionist, mimetic, carnivalesque, and burlesque styles, kitchen-sink frameworks and universal symbolism.

Spiderwoman Theater – a theater group of Kuna and Rappahannock descent and "the oldest continually running women's theater company in North America" (Abbott 165) – works with a creative process called "storyweaving," in which autobiographical experiences of the group members are fashioned into performative tapestries of both individual and collective memory. In *Persistence of Memory* (FP 2007), for instance, core members Lisa Mayo, Gloria Miguel, and Muriel Miguel mix videos and staged excerpts from some of their previous plays – including "Women in Violence" (1976), "Lysistrata Numbah" (1977), *Sun, Moon, and Feather* (1981), *Winnetou's Snake Oil Show from Wigwam City* (1988), *Power Pipes* (1993), *Rever-ber-ber-rations* (1990), Murielle Borst's "More than Feathers and Beads" (1996), and Monique Mojica's *Princess Pocahontas and the Blue Spots* (1991) – into a pluralistic, multi-media, and meta-representational show of healing, a "gathering of energies and memories" (Spiderwoman Theater 42) that celebrates the female experience, continuity, and survivance.

Tomson Highway has contributed substantial impulses of magic realism with his fictitious community of Wasaychigan Hill Reserve in Ontario. *The Rez Sisters* (1986), for instance, revolves around seven women who dream of attending the "biggest bingo in the world" (27). Along the way, each woman's story is unfolded, revealing struggles with domestic violence, rape, jealousy, and loss of love, but the play concludes, after further tragedy, on a note of empowerment and hope, with Nanabush, the Ojibway trickster, dancing "triumphantly" on a community roof. The gender-shifting trickster figure, Cree and Ojibway language elements, music and dance, a life-affirming sense of humor, and an emphasis on healing have also become trademarks of Highway's other plays, including *Dry Lips Oughta Move to Kapuskasing* (FP 1987), *Rose* (FP 1999), *Ernestine Shuswap Gets Her Trout* (FP 2005), and *The (Post) Mistress* (FP 2011). In its manifestations across the continent and with effective outreach around the globe, the genre thus constitutes one of the most manifold and dynamic practices of what Gerald Vizenor terms "survivance": "an active sense of presence over absence, deracination, and oblivion; survivance is the continuance of stories" (*Native Liberty* 85).

Coordinates of Native American drama

Because of its sheer diversity among 566 federally recognized Native American nations in the United States and 634 First Nations in Canada, the compartmentalization of Native North American theater and drama into fixed categories is an impossible venture. There are, however, a number of recurrent characteristics that help to describe the genre, regardless of the variety of its themes. Christy Stanlake, for instance, sees the concepts of "platiality" (39), "storying and tribalography" (118), and "uncontainable identities" (164) as central categories for the analysis of Native drama. In addition to (and interwoven with) these, a few more coordinates can be identified that facilitate the mapping of the genre:

1   the use of fluid, multiple, shifting, and non-essentialist identities that may also transcend boundaries between human, animal and spirit; this also includes the presence of literal or symbolic trickster figures on stage;
2   a strong emphasis on community in both a national and a transnational sense, in which the principle of inclusion, connection, and intercultural exchange is favored over separatism or individual interests;

3 a deeply political engagement of individual memory and North American history at large, and/or the inclusion of mythical, spiritual and metaphysical elements into contemporary plots;
4 non-linear, cyclical, and ritualistic time patterns and radically inclusive understandings of space, which often merge geographical settings with spiritual, non-material, or "mythic" spaces (Darby x);
5 multilingual and heteroglossic outlines of dialogue as well as a merging of English and Indigenous languages;
6 formats that rely strongly on the performative power of storytelling, music, rhythm, and dance;
7 a pluralistic use of diverse media that challenges conventional concepts of representation; and importantly,
8 an empowering sense of humor that can range from kitchen-sink comedy to historical sarcasm.

This list is far from authoritative or exhaustive, and not all of these elements are necessarily used, but they provide practical starting points for studying the genre and indicate the abundant contribution of Indigenous North American drama to the global literary landscape. In the following discussion, two exemplary analyses – of both a "classic" and a recent play, both set in Anadarko, Oklahoma – may illustrate how these elements overlap, recur, and work together in contemporary contexts.

Personal is political: Hanay Geiogamah's Body Indian

When Hanay Geiogamah's *Body Indian* was first performed in October 1972 at the LaMaMa Experimental Theater Club in downtown New York City, theater critic McCandlish Phillips enthusiastically pronounced it the beginning of a new era:

> [w]hen the history of the American Indian theater is written in, say, the year 2054, it will probably record that it all began back in 1972 in a narrow loft at 74A East Fourth Street on New York's Lower East Side.
>
> (56)

Body Indian presents eleven characters – alternately drinking and passing out – in a run-down condominium near the railroad tracks in Anadarko, Oklahoma. The plot begins with the arrival of Bobby Lee, "a crippled alcoholic in his mid-thirties" (6), who once lost a leg while he was passed out on railway tracks (15). He wants to join an Alcoholics Anonymous program, but needs "a relative to sign [his] papers" (19), so he goes to his Uncle Howard's apartment. Welcomed by Thompson, another friend or relative, he accepts the invitation to attend a party: "Well, I'lll beee! B–obbye Leee! Come in, hites [friend], come in! Long time no see!" (11). In changing constellations but repeating plot patterns, the group drinks excessively, accompanied by the sound of "drums and rattles" (13); and at the end of each of the five scenes, after Bobby Lee passes out, he is thoroughly searched for money by his friends and relatives. Significantly, these recurrent rituals are accompanied by the sound of a rushing train and its blasting whistle, as well as "color slide projections of railroad tracks, taken at sharp angles and flashing in rapid sequence" (17) on the back wall. The cruelty of the action is disrupted by the fact that each new scene opens with "no indication that anything wicked has taken place" (17), substituting an apparent linearity of plot with a cyclical or spiral-like structure. The repeated rituals culminate in the final scene, when Howard and Thompson "brutally" (35) remove his artificial leg to pawn it at the "white man bootleggers" (35) for more alcohol. When Bobby realizes that his leg has been taken for a second time, there is "a sardonic smile fixed on his face" and he closes the cyclical structure of the play by repeating the initial greeting, this time to himself: "Well, h–ell–o, Bobby Lee. How are you, hites? Lo–ng time no ... seee" (36). The play ends in an expressionist crescendo of train sounds, track visuals, and the flashing of train lights, during which Bobby Lee relives the "horror" of being run over and losing his leg (36).

At first glance, the picture looks simple, bleak, and easily summarized: the victimized body of Bobby Lee seems to symbolize the situation of contemporary Native Americans in the United States, marked by injury, immobility, exploitation, poverty, and addiction. In terms of corporeal semiotics, the "Indian body" in this play has been maimed, diseased, impoverished, and dismantled, offering an expressive visual signifier of ethnic oppression. This oppression includes the introduction of alcohol by Europeans, but it is most graphically symbolized through the train that cut off Bobby Lee's leg. As Leo Marx famously puts it, the locomotive was the "leading symbol of the new industrial power," which, as a prototypical "machine," entered the pastoral "garden" of nature (27), effectively eliminating the traditional ways of life of many Indigenous American tribes. In this sense, the reappearance of the railway tracks in their frightening and flashing form of "sharp angles" (*Body Indian* 17), together with the all-encompassing sound of the train whistle, also imply the recurrent colonial trauma of an entire population.

Instead of drawing a dichotomous line between Indigenous victimhood and European-American colonization, however, the play refrains from easy solutions and quite explicitly points to the responsibility within the Native community, as well. What *Body Indian* clearly illuminates is that if any hope is imaginable for a better future, for an escape from the traps of historical conditions, alcoholism, and financial disaster, this hope requires pan-tribal solidarity – especially at a time when the Indigenous community continues to be torn apart by power struggles (such as in the American Indian Movement), conflicts over territory, as between the Navajo and the Hopi (Pinazzi 182), or by the ongoing "culture wars" (Lincoln 4) over authenticity, nationalism, and representation.

Furthermore, in its statement against any kind of biological or national essentialism, *Body Indian* also openly involves the audience: from the very beginning of the play, when a train's "loud, rushing sound" signals "to the audience that the play is beginning" (9), viewers are explicitly included in the events on stage. During the first act of victimization, the stage direction stipulates that "[t]he cast freezes. The drum and rattles grow intense. Expressions of fear slowly cross over the cast's faces as they look directly toward the audience" (16). The viewers' acts of voyeurism and silent witnessing are disturbed by this contact between stage and auditorium, and in scene three, the cast even reaches physically "toward the audience" (24), as if to summon intervention. Finally, on the point of climax, when Bobby's leg is removed, "[t]he others begin, one by one, to rise and stand around the bed to watch, hiding the operation from the audience" (35). Geiogamah works with increasing levels of uneasiness to involve the viewers, exposing their silent complicity, and thus collapsing the protective borderline between stage and auditorium that protects what Alan Filewod has termed the "colonial gaze" (21).

This strategy holds audiences accountable for their role in representational processes, and especially for the political implications of their gaze. Through the repeated shifts between interior and exterior systems of communication, viewers are ultimately included in the "body Indian," which is effectively merged into a general human entity, regardless of gender, race, class, age, or other lines of difference. With this humanity comes responsibility – for empathy and social justice as much as for historical contextualization and a commitment to the future. Hence, despite the foregrounding of helplessness, alcoholism, poverty, injustice, hypocrisy, and intracultural exploitation, *Body Indian*'s ultimate force is its combination of subversiveness and optimism.

Past is present is future: Mary Kathryn Nagle's "Manahatta" (2013)

Over the past three years, a number of young voices have emerged on the theatrical scene. Together with Larissa FastHorse (Sicangu Lakota), Vickie Ramirez (Tuscarora), Emily Johnson (Yup'ik), and Tara Beagan (Ntlakapamux), Mary Kathryn Nagle, a Cherokee lawyer and playwright based in New York City, is among the most prolific of these voices. After early plays (such as "To the 7th Degree," "Miss Lead," or "Waaxe's Law"), her award-winning play on Hurricane Katrina, *Welcome to Chalmette,* was published in 2011.

"Manahatta," first presented as a reading in March 2013 at the Public Theater, New York, received a full production in Oklahoma City in May 2014. The play tells the story of Jane Snake, a young Lenape woman from Oklahoma, who returns to her ancestral homelands on Manhattan to pursue a career in investment banking. Besides conflicts with her father Robert, and her sister Debra, who disapprove of her immersion in American capitalism, she weathers the storms of the 2008 financial crisis during which her employer, the historical investment bank Lehman Brothers, has to file for bankruptcy. From her geographical distance, she has to deal with numerous family issues: her mother dies while she is absent for a job interview, her sister's application for a grant to establish a Lenape language program is rejected, and their father finds himself unable to pay the rates on his mortgage to pay his medical bills, risking eviction and the selling of his home.

The experience of Jane's family is closely intertwined with the historical purchase of Manhattan by the Dutch in 1626, and its devastating consequences for the Lenape. Scenes alternate between Anadarko, Oklahoma (also the setting of *Body Indian*) and Manhattan; and within the latter, the plot shifts back and forth between the seventeenth and twenty-first centuries. As Jane is learning her trade of selling investment packages on Wall Street, for instance, a parallel scene shows Peter Minuit, the historical governor of the Dutch West India Company, trading beaver pelts and guns with Lenape leaders Tamanend and Se-ket-tu-may-qua. Following a revisionist historical agenda that many Native North American plays share, this scene shows that the "selling" of Manahatta was based on a mere misunderstanding of the concept of ownership, and on the Europeans' lack of intercultural respect:

TAMANEND (*to Peter Minuit*): Because we now consider you our brother, we invite you
to call Manahatta your home. But anyone who calls Manahatta home must know this:
the Creator gave us Manahatta. Here in the *helape chen kwaelas*, Manahatta is sacred.
PETER MINUIT (*to Assistant*): What did he say?
ASSISTANT: I have no idea.
Peter Minuit hands Assistant one of the glasses and offers a toast.
PETER MINUIT: To Manahatta!

(35)

The Lenape language phrase echoes down through the centuries; it is also used by Robert
(6, 19), and its translation is not given until the last line of the play, when Jane has an
office facing the East River where she can see the *helape chen kwaelas*, "the place where the
sun is born" (139).

Language, communication, and misunderstandings constitute a central pillar of the play,
and the two time levels also illustrate that these are tied closely to two different economies
clashing on the island of Manhattan. Whereas Europeans – from Peter Minuit and Peter
Stuyvesant to the contemporary CEOs of Wall Street – believe in maximum monetary gain
("there's no such thing as enough in the New World" [42]), the Lenape have a different,
less profit-oriented understanding of trade. As Se-ket-tu-may-qua puts it: "We both want
what's best for each other. You know we aren't looking to just walk away with something
for ourselves" (46). The conflict resulting from these different economic systems soon esca-
lates: more and more Lenape are shot or massacred (98), and eventually forced away. The
very name of Wall Street still bears this colonial legacy, as explained by Peter Stuyvesant:
"we need to build a wall. You know, to keep the Indians out" (105). In a clear gesture of
survivance, however, Jane not only returns to Wall Street, she also makes it to the top of
the European-American hierarchy. Her success eventually bridges both systems, as symbolized by the traditional wampum necklace that she wears in New York: Robert tells her:

When your grandma, your great-great-great-however many greats grandma made
this necklace, wampum meant something very special to our people. To the
Dutch, it seemed as though it was a form of currency. But it was more than that. ...
Wampum was sacred, and it was a sign of respect.

(134)

While the clash between Indigenous and European-American economies still impacts
Jane's family – from the legacy of broken treaties (19) and the nineteenth-century forced
removal of the Lenape to Oklahoma (109) to her mother's violent boarding school experience (81) – the lines of conflict are not laid out exclusively between Native and non-Native
Americans in the play. Instead, as in *Body Indian*, the notion of cultural difference is diversified by aspects of lifestyle and choice: whereas Jane, for instance, is interested in a healthy,
low-calorie diet, her sister and father insist on eating frybread as a symbol of tradition and
resilience, regardless of the cardiovascular harm it causes. Similarly, while Jane wants to
use her prosperity to pay her family's debt, Debra charges her with materialism and lack of
respect: "you went off to school, you learned how to be white, and you're good at it" (132).
In the end, however, Jane manages to save her home and is reconciled with both her father
and her sister, who finally endorse her career choice. This conciliatory stance effectively

denounces ethnic dichotomies, yet without erasing cultural difference or glossing over historical injustice.

The most important element in the play – illustrating both the dynamic concept of identity and the permeability of temporal boundaries – is its temporal continuum, underlined, on the level of characters, by the double or triple casting: all actors play roles in both the seventeenth and the twenty-first centuries. The actress who plays Jane in the present also impersonates Tamanend's daughter Le-le-wa'-you, and both Peter Minuit and Peter Stuyvesant recur in Dick Fuld, Jane's boss at Lehman Brothers. The transitions between past and present do not merely rely on stage directions, but they are smoothly enhanced by semantic, symbolic, and material elements, including conversational topics such as ownership (32, 84, 86), literal or metaphorical guns (116), or an envelope held both by Minuit and Jane (89). The continuity between time levels not only signifies the close ties between contemporary characters and their ancestors, but it also indicates that history repeats itself, in this play even literally: four hundred years after Peter Minuit brings brandy to the Lenape ("This bottle is a fine, or rather, a *great*, indeed I think the greatest, spirit ever made" [31]), Dick Fuld repeats these exact same words while celebrating a business success with brandy – to which Jane responds, just like her ancestor Tamanend: "It's different" (117). Such repetitions with variations also underline the cyclical structure of the play: not only does Debra send Jane back to Wall Street with their mother's last words, in another repetition of "Machi. Machi Manahatta. [Go home! Go home to Manhattan!]" (22, 134), but the epilogue, in which Jane – now in a top position at JP Morgan – interviews a Delaware war veteran returning from Afghanistan for a job, is almost an exact re-enactment of the play's opening: like her previous supervisor Joe, she slightly mocks the candidate, until he tells her that she had been a role model for him: "The first Indian to run a major investment bank. ... I read about you. And I was like, I'm going to get into Stanford. I'm going to do what she did, because I know I can" (137).

In spite of the first impression that it is primarily an indictment of colonial injustice, the play ends on an optimistic note, celebrating Jane's top career in investment banking and honoring her Lenape heritage. The play features humor and a dynamic concept of time, and – like *Body Indian* – it also calls for a responsibility of reception. As Jane puts it when she talks about her love for mathematics: "Math is just a bunch of patterns, and once you've spotted the pattern, you never have to guess what'll happen next because it's already happened" (118). Like a motto for the entire play, this statement calls on the audience to contextualize the patterns, to notice historical injustice, and to rewrite contemporary analogies into new constellations.

As these two examples demonstrate, Native theater is an ideal laboratory for sociopolitical criticism, ethical intervention, and cultural work on a transnational scale; it allows for the negotiation of Native images and Native identities, of cultural difference, memory, and tradition, as well as of issues of sovereignty, agency, and community. Although colonial and missionary history, social inequality, violence, and racism are among the more widely recurrent themes on Native stages, the overall tone is far from pessimistic or bleak. There is just as much emphasis on humor and healing, and works by writers as diverse as William Yellow Robe Jr. (Assiniboine), Daniel David Moses (Delaware), Gerald Vizenor (Anishinaabe), Floyd Favel (Cree), Joseph Dandurand (Salish), Terry Gomez (Comanche), Arigon Starr (Kickapoo/Creek), Bruce King (Oneida), Laura Shamas (Chickasaw), and Rebecca

Belmore (Anishinaabe) all share a deep commitment to resistance, recovery, and futurity. As Spiderwoman Theater note in the preface to *Persistence of Memory*:

> We have told our stories over kitchen tables, on our front steps, in our communities, on the stages of New York, Berlin, Auckland, and Beijing. It is important to be home again and connect our stories of the past to our future. Our future is the generations who will take their stories out into the world of the new millennium and who will create a new legacy for their future generations.
>
> (42)

This quotation not only summarizes their lifetime achievement in both a national and a transnational framework, but it aptly describes the current outlook of Indigenous drama in Canada and the United States.

Note

1 In addition to these, Native North American drama has been published in at least twenty-eight more general anthologies, and there are numerous collections of three or more plays by individual playwrights, such as Hanay Geiogamah, Diane Glancy, Bruce King, N. Scott Momaday, Yvette Nolan, Lynn Riggs, E. Donald Two-Rivers, and William S. Yellow Robe Jr. These do not yet include the large number of plays published individually or in journals.

Works cited

Abbott, Larry. "Spiderwoman Theater and the Tapestry of Story." *The Canadian Journal of Native Studies* XIV. 1 (1996): 165–80.

Armstrong, Ann Elizabeth, Kelli Lyon Johnson & William A. Wortman, eds. *Performing Worlds into Being: Native American Women's Theater*. Oxford, OH: Miami University Press, 2009.

Bigsby, Christopher W. E. "American Indian Theatre." *A Critical Introduction to Twentieth-Century American Drama*. Vol. 3: *Beyond Broadway*. Cambridge: Cambridge University Press, 1985. 365–74.

D'Aponte, Mimi Gisolfi. "Introduction." *Seventh Generation: An Anthology of Native American Plays*. Ed. Mimi Gisolfi D'Aponte. New York: Theatre Communications Group, 1999. ix–xxiii.

Darby, Jaye T. "Introduction: A Talking Circle on Native Theater." *American Indian Theater in Performance: A Reader*. Ed. Hanay Geiogamah & Jaye T. Darby. Los Angeles: UCLA American Indian Studies Center, 2000. iii–xv.

Darby, Jaye T. & Stephanie Fitzgerald, eds. *Keepers of the Morning Star: An Anthology of Native Women's Theater*. Los Angeles: UCLA American Indian Studies Center, 2003.

Däwes, Birgit, ed. *Indigenous North American Drama: A Multivocal History*. Albany: State University of New York Press, 2013.

——. *Native North American Theater in a Global Age: Sites of Identity Construction and Transdifference*. Heidelberg: Winter, 2007.

Deloria, Philip J. *Playing Indian*. New Haven, CT: Yale University Press, 1998.

Filewod, Alan. "Averting the Colonizing Gaze: Notes on Watching Native Theatre." *Aboriginal Voices: Amerindian, Inuit, and Sami Theatre*. Ed. Per Brask & William Morgan. Baltimore, MD: Johns Hopkins University Press, 1992. 17–28.

Geiogamah, Hanay. "Body Indian." *Seventh Generation: An Anthology of Native American Plays*. Ed. Mimi Gisolfi D'Aponte. New York: Theatre Communications Group, 1999. 1–38.

Geiogamah, Hanay & Jaye T. Darby, eds. *American Indian Theater in Performance: A Reader*. Los Angeles: UCLA American Indian Studies Center, 2000.

——, eds. *Stories of Our Way: An Anthology of American Indian Plays*. Los Angeles: UCLA American Indian Studies Center, 1999.

Haugo, Ann. "American Indian Theatre." *The Cambridge Companion to Native American Literature*. Ed. Joy Porter & Kenneth M. Roemer. Cambridge: Cambridge University Press, 2005. 189–204.

Heath, Sally Ann. "The Development of Native American Theater Companies in the Continental United States." Diss. University of Colorado at Boulder, 1995. Unpublished Manuscript.

Highway, Tomson. *The Rez Sisters*. Saskatoon, SK: Fifth House Publishers, 1988.

Hodgson, Heather, ed. *The Great Gift of Tears: Four Aboriginal Plays*. Regina, SK: Coteau Books, 2002.

Howard, Rebecca. "The Native American Women Playwrights Archive: Adding Voices." *Journal of Dramatic Theory and Criticism* 14. 1 (1999): 109–16.

Howe, LeAnne. "Native Theater: Who Will Create the 'Native Cue'?" *Native Playwrights' Newsletter* 7 (Spring 1995): 62–63.

——. "The Story of Movement: Natives and Performance Culture." *The Oxford Handbook of Indigenous American Literature*. Ed. James Cox & Daniel Heath Justice. New York: Oxford University Press, 2014. 250–65.

Huhndorf, Shari. "American Indian Drama and the Politics of Performance." *The Columbia Guide to American Indian Literatures of the United States Since 1945*. Ed. Eric Cheyfitz. New York: Columbia University Press, 2006. 288–318.

Huntsman, Jeffrey. "Native American Theater." *Ethnic Theater in the United States*. Ed. Maxine Schwartz Seller. Westport, CT: Greenwood, 1983. 355–85.

Huston-Findley, Shirley A. & Rebecca Howard, eds. *Footpaths and Bridges: Voices from the Native American Women Playwrights Archive*. Ann Arbor: University of Michigan Press, 2008.

Kane, Margo, Greg Daniels & Marie Clements. *DraMétis: Three Métis Plays*. Penticton, BC: Theytus Books, 2001.

Lincoln, Kenneth. *Speak Like Singing: Classics of Native American Literature*. Albuquerque: University of New Mexico Press, 2007.

Marx, Leo. *The Machine in the Garden: Technology and the Pastoral Ideal in America*. 1964. Rpt. Oxford: Oxford University Press, 2000.

Mojica, Monique & Ric Knowles, eds. *Staging Coyote's Dream: An Anthology of First Nations Drama in English*. Toronto: Playwrights Union of Canada Press, 2003.

——, eds. *Staging Coyote's Dream* vol. II. Toronto: Playwrights of Canada Press, 2009.

Nagle, Mary Kathryn. "Manahatta." Unpublished playscript, 2012.

"Native Voices at the Autry." *Autry National Center of the American West*. Autry.org. 2014. Web. Accessed 3 Jan. 2015. http://theautry.org/theater-native-voices

Owens, Louis. "Courting the Stone Age: Native Authenticity in Gerald Vizenor's *Ishi and the Wood Ducks*." *Multilingua: Journal of Cross-Cultural and Interlanguage Communication* 18. 2–3 (1999): 135–47.

Pettit, Alexander. "Published Native American Drama, 1970–2011." *The Oxford Handbook of Indigenous American Literature*. Ed. James Cox & Daniel Heath Justice. New York: Oxford University Press, 2014. 266–83.

Phillips, McCandlish. "Indian Theater Group: Strong Beginning." *The New York Times* 9 November 1972: 56.

Pinazzi, Annamaria. "The Theater of Hanay Geiogamah." *American Indian Theater in Performance: A Reader*. Ed. Hanay Geiogamah & Jaye T. Darby. Los Angeles: UCLA American Indian Studies Center, 2000. 175–94.

Riggs, Lynn. *The Cherokee Night and Other Plays*. Norman: University of Oklahoma Press, 2003.

Spiderwoman Theater. "Persistence of Memory." *Performing Worlds into Being: Native American Women's Theater*. Oxford, OH: Miami University Press, 2009. 42–56.

Stanlake, Christy. *Native American Drama: A Critical Perspective*. Cambridge: Cambridge University Press, 2009.

Taylor, Drew Hayden. "The Re-Appearance of the Trickster: Native Theatre in Canada." *On-Stage and Off-Stage: English Canadian Drama in Discourse*. Ed. Albert-Reiner Glaap & Rolf Althof. St. John's, NF: Breakwater, 1996. 51–59.

Valentino, Gina. "Theater Renaissance: Resituating the Place of Drama in the Native American Renaissance." *The Native American Renaissance: Literary Imagination and Achievement*. Ed. Alan R. Velie & A. Robert Lee. Norman: University of Oklahoma Press, 2013. 295–306.

Vizenor, Gerald. "Literary Transmotion: Survivance and Totemic Motion in Native American Indian Art and Literature." *Twenty-First Century Perspectives on Indigenous Studies: Native North America in (Trans)Motion*. Ed. Birgit Däwes, Karsten Fitz & Sabine Meyer. New York: Routledge, 2015. 17–30.

———. *Native Liberty: Natural Reason and Cultural Survivance*. Lincoln: University of Nebraska Press, 2009.

Wilmer, Steven E., ed. *Native American Performance and Representation*. Tucson: University of Arizona Press, 2009.

37

Native American Poetry
Loosening the Bonds of Representation

David L. Moore and Kathryn W. Shanley

Native American poetic expression, in both the oral and the written traditions, can deepen readers' appreciation for the nature of language itself, as Indigenous poetics reflect myriad ways humans and the more-than-human world speak to each other. Modern and ancient Indigenous expression reflects how the nature of language and the language of nature intersect. Even within human language usage, such academic categories and genre divisions as poetry and prose may not apply to Indigenous traditions of storytelling, orality, and poetic voice.[1] Rooted in song, story, prayer, chant, curse, oath, or joke, oral traditions embed themselves within the written. They are not prior epistemologies but vibrant threads of a living, aesthetic weave. Like the reversibility of a Navajo rug, Indigenous literatures inextricably blend written and oral forms. The power of a song to change the rain or to affect the harvest becomes a modern poem to change minds, laws, history, or human perception. As Kiowa poet and novelist N. Scott Momaday writes:

> By means of words one can bring about physical change in the universe. By means of words one can quiet the raging weather, bring forth the harvest, ward off evil, rid the body of sickness and pain, subdue an enemy, capture the heart of a lover, live in the proper way, and venture beyond death.
>
> (Momaday 15–16)

The spoken word equals extraordinary power in what Vine Deloria Jr. terms "the world we used to live in," and carries forward into the twenty-first century in old and new ways, in ceremony and in contemporary social discourse.

With attention to this intersection of language and nature, care must be taken, however, in the study of Native American poetry, neither to allow a stereotypical view of Indigenous people as "one with nature" nor to lose the vibrancy and challenge of contemporary realities. Offering nuanced and incisive visions of human experience within various settler-colonial spaces and their own homelands (there are over 560 federally recognized tribes in the United States), Native poets are difficult to categorize. Yet their relatedness does come across in the shared political imperative to self-identify, in sustaining themes relevant to Indigenous people, and in belief in the importance of remaining Native.

Native poetic power carries a burden to overcome (mis)understandings – stereotypes and ignorance of historical difference – when textual focus in figurative language and lyrical impulse must balance contextual explanation and other cross-cultural aesthetic imperatives.

Transmitting appropriate cultural heritage becomes a defining feature, indeed, an imperative of Native American poetry, however slippery or opaque the links may be to various readers. Thus, Klallam poet and editor Duane Niatum describes how Native poetry can simultaneously embody tradition and the modern, a communal and an individual voice in "the poetry of a new generation and the spirit of an age-old people. ... That spirit has not died. On the contrary, it has grown and is growing" (ix).

Similarly, Anishinaabe poet and scholar Kimberly Blaeser explains of Native poets, "For the poems ... give voice not only to the experiences of the contemporary authors themselves, but extend themselves in subject, imagery, and form to forge connections with the literary and cultural history of tribal communities everywhere" (412). Indeed, Blaeser attempts a workable definition of Indigenous poetry:

> the possibilities of a Native poetics infused with echoes of the song poems and ceremonial literatures of the tribes, born out of the indigenous revolution, filled with the dialogues of intertextuality, sometimes linked to the cadences and constructions of "an-other" language, frequently self-conscious, and often resistant to genre distinctions and formal structures.
>
> (412)

Tradition and revolution, dialogue and resistance, reciprocity and sovereignty here weave together.

Balancing such factors is key in reading Native voices. In one poem we may study tribal specificity, individual style, and broad Indigenous values, as Niatum lists them, "common concerns: kinship, Nature, art as a part of tribal religion, and cultural survival and rebirth" (x). Indeed, we are dealing here with a realm of expression where EuroAmerican categories of "group" and "individual," "universal" and "particular," even "spirit" and "matter" may break down. Yet Niatum, like many critics, identifies one further, crucial aspect of Indigenous poetry: "It is precisely this sense of coming from the land and not to it that gives the Native American voice its clarity and range" (xi). Far from the often romantic, "imperialist nostalgia" in nature writing by EuroAmerican settler colonialists – who may continue to be shaped by the tired ideology of "manifest destiny" – Native American expression arises out of a "living heritage of place and tradition ... giving them power to encounter and grapple with both contemporary issues ... and age-old questions of meaning and existence" (xi). A poetry of place affirms the land and its voices. We may see in such poets as Lois Red Elk (Dakota, b. 1940), Linda Hogan (Chickasaw, b. 1947), Luci Tapahonso (Navajo, b. 1953), James Welch (Blackfeet/Gros Ventre, 1940–2003), Ray A. Young Bear (Meskwaki, b. 1950), Leslie Marmon Silko (Laguna, b. 1947), Louise Erdrich (Chippewa, b. 1954), Ofelia Zepeda (Tohono O'odham, b. 1952), Elizabeth Woody (Navajo/Warm Springs/Wasco/Yakama, b. 1959), Laura Tohe (Navajo, b. 1952), Sherwin Bitsui (Navajo, b. 1975) and many others how their unique individual voices, while addressing contemporary issues, are grounded in ancient lands.

Thus this literary history of Native American poetry focuses more on place than on period. Rather than trace a chronology, we keep in mind the voice of the land as we listen to voices of the people across time.[2] Until the late twentieth century, Native American writers were usually working in isolation, without a collective or a "movement" that we now might identify in retrospect as a "period." It was not until after N. Scott Momaday's 1969 Pulitzer Prize for fiction with his novel *House Made of Dawn* that a critical mass of

Native American writers blossomed in many directions. Then as before, Native poets and prose writers were connected in using English, the master's language, to dismantle the master's house; that is to deconstruct stereotypes and to rewrite the narratives of "the vanishing Indian" and "manifest destiny." As U.S. imperialist policies were systematically affecting and changing cultures, Indigenous literary creations remained rooted in places. Thus we may read a poetry of connection around political statements of survivance. This aesthetic and politic of interconnection is a substratum of the ground we trace in the poetry.

On that ground, we trace the links of ongoing oral traditions to literary ones in major writers and publications from the nineteenth through the twenty-first century, while attending to five thematic dynamics of the songs, prayers, and poems across the years. These five themes reflect Blaeser's and Niatum's definitions above, and they emerge often in a historical context of oppression by gender, class, and race: ritual healing, political sovereignty, cultural affirmation, individual humanity, and, underneath all of these, an indigenous sense of the musical power of language itself.

Ritual healing on the land

Choosing place-based poetics as an organizing principle for this chapter runs the risk of evoking a nostalgia for past realities and imaginaries, but Indian Country *is* fundamentally defined by Indigenous homelands – complicated by tribal tenure and sovereignty in any given place. "Medicine Song," by Dan Hanna (Havasupai) and translated by Leanne Hinton expresses the healing connections to place. It begins with the lines, "The land we were given. ... It is right here." The word "given" takes on a spiritual meaning tied to belonging. Most lines in the fifteen-page song are repeated, as the singer lays "claim" to the canyon through naming, singing the geographical features. In the manner of one who wants another to be aware of his presence, he repeatedly says, "This is what I'm thinking." Then he identifies his purpose for being there:

> Here we arrive
> Here we arrive
>
> An illness
> An illness
>
> I sit down
> I sit down
>
> I sing myself a song
> I sing myself a song
>
> This is what I'm thinking
> This is what I'm thinking
>
> A medicine spirit
> A medicine spirit. ...

(30)

DAVID L. MOORE AND KATHRYN W. SHANLEY

Larry Evers and Ofelia Zepeda, the editors, explain: "The word *bay gjama*, which is translated as 'an illness'... refers to a straying from the rightful road, the development of a disharmony with nature ..." (19). They introduce the song to us as having a "rich description of Havasu Canyon. At the end, the song refers to some boulders which lie in a certain place, which, when one lies down on them, absorb illness" (19). The song illustrates what N. Scott Momaday (Kiowa) means in:

> None of us lives apart from the land entirely; such an isolation is unimaginable. We have sooner or later to come to terms with the world around us. ... to imagine who and what we are with respect to the earth and sky. I am talking about an act of imagination. ...
>
> ("Words" 53)

We place ourselves through ritual and imagination where we can be known and can thereby be healed, according to Hanna and Momaday.

Carter Revard (Osage/Ponca, b. 1931), poet and literary scholar, captures the significance of being from someplace real, in his poem "In Oklahoma":

> When you leave a Real City, as Gertrude Stein did, and go to Oakland, as she did, there is no there, there. When you are a Hartford insurance executive, as Wallace Stevens was, and you have never been to Oklahoma, as he had not, you can invent people to dance there, and you can call them Bonnie and Josie. But a THERE depends on how, in the beginning, the wind breathes upon the surface.
>
> (*Eagle Nation* 3)

The orality in Revard's rhythmic repetitions and parallel structure serve to highlight the dimensions of tradition at play in his philosophy and aesthetic of belonging to a place. Like Hanna, Revard speaks the details into his imagination of Oklahoma. He writes: "White clouds sail slowly across the pure blue pond. Turtles poke their heads up, watch the Indian man casting, reeling, casting, reeling ... . See friends, it's not a flyover here. Come down from your planes and you'll understand. Here" (*Eagle Nation* 3). Revard beckons the passer-by to stop in and observe the interconnectedness of being in a place, asks him even to partake by sharing the fried fish family meal; it illustrates what Susan Berry Brill de Ramirez calls the "conversive," an interaction rather than a discursive act (Brill de Ramírez 1999).

Political sovereignty on the land under siege

Revard's insistence on the ground and Hanna's healing ritual among the rocks both sing of this fundamental value in the land. But it has not always been possible for Native poets to make those affirmations. For example, in the late nineteenth and early twentieth century, Western-educated Indian poets and other intellectuals were caught in a dilemma. The twin federal policies for assimilation, by "civilizing" Indians in boarding schools and by remaking them into farmers through land allotment, had dominated their communities. Assimilation had reined in a deeper ideology of annihilation only officially. Boarding schools and their oppressions undercut the cultures, the families, and indeed the psyches of American Indian populations. Similarly, allotment and its corruptions undercut the tribal land base and eliminated prospects for economic development. The repressive policies of the federal executive and its Bureau of Indian Affairs, of the anti-Indian judicial system, of a Congress interested only in its own "plenary power" over reviled tribes, and of a military dedicated to violent control, were added to the greed of demagogues in local territories and states with their own militias ready and willing to commit war crimes. At the turn of the century, barely a quarter-million Native Americans had survived centuries of disease and warfare.

In such an historic nadir, which path were educated American Indians to offer their people against this onslaught that would blithely destroy the Indigenous populations? Very often this turn-of-the-century generation had to choose assimilation – because in reality there was no choice when annihilation was the only alternative. It wasn't until another generation in the 1930s, and then further another generation in the 1970s, that the politics of tribal self-governance, self-determination, and sovereignty reconsolidated to provide real alternatives for Indian communities.

Among turn-of-the-twentieth-century Native writers such as Charles Eastman/Ohiyesa (Dakota, 1858–1939) and Gertrude Simmons Bonnin/Zitkala-Sa (Dakota, 1876–1938), poets such as Carlos Montezuma/Wassaja (Apache, 1866–1923) and E. Pauline Johnson (Mohawk, 1861–1913) published works that reflected those pressured times of cultural and economic stress as well as the potency of poetry itself to affirm human expression and survivance. Montezuma's and Johnson's quite different voices reflect opposite approaches to formal English structures, to nostalgic reference to a lost past, and to a conflicted sense of historical fatalism, while both affirm the strength of their cultural values in contrast to those of the settler colonials.

For example, Montezuma, who was an educator and activist as well as a writer, published the following manifesto poem, "Changing is not Vanishing," in 1916. It bears striking resemblance to some of the expansive thinking of much later southwestern Indigenous writers at the other end of the century, such as Simon Ortiz (Acoma) in his book-length poem *from Sand Creek* (1981) or Leslie Marmon Silko (Laguna) in her novel *Almanac of the Dead* (1991), as well as legions of Indigenous writers who resist erasure by proclaiming "we are still here."

> Who says the Indian race is vanishing?
> The Indians will not vanish.
> The feathers, paint and moccasins will vanish, but the Indians, — never!
> Just as long as there is a drop of human blood in America, the Indians will not vanish.
> His spirit is everywhere; the American Indian will not vanish.
> He has changed externally but he has not vanished.
> He is an industrial and commercial man, competing with the world;
> he has not vanished.
> Wherever you see an Indian upholding the standard of his race,
> there you see the Indian man; he has not vanished.
> The man part of the Indian is here, there, and everywhere.
> The Indian race vanishing? No, never! The race will live on and prosper forever.
>
> (Montezuma)

Celebrating ordinary language and extraordinary, radical affirmations, Montezuma negates the words vanish, vanished, and vanishing nine times in a poem of ten sentences and twelve lines. He subverts a major American narrative of "the vanishing Indian," a story of erasure on which the nation is built, justifying dispossession of Indian land. Against the stereotype of "feathers, paint and moccasins," Montezuma affirms that Indian people and communities will "prosper forever." It is worth emphasizing how deeply engrained those stereotypes were when Montezuma tried to deflate them. "Feathers, paint and moccasins" had been institutionalized in his day by decades of dime novels, which only re-enacted similar stereotypes in James Fenimore Cooper and his early nineteenth-century "literary" contemporaries. In addition, these images were already enshrined in the growing Hollywood industry of his time. The poem's subtle equation of the "Indian race" with "human blood" offers a vision of kinship, identity, community, and authenticity that confounds America's racial categories in its complexity. Now, a century later, his poem remains relevant to current controversies about stereotypical sports mascots in their "feathers, paint and moccasins."

A very different, representative poem is from E. Pauline Johnson, who "was one of the most widely read Indian authors in the United States," as well as in Canada and England (Ruoff 66). Her prolific and popular turn-of-the-twentieth-century output includes a narrative, "The Pilot of the Plains," which does some of the same work as Montezuma's piece, but from an opposite strategy. Where he straightforwardly asserts Indigenous difference and adaptability, Johnson melodramatically affirms connection and universality as a road to survival. Her poem recounts the legend of a Native "maiden," Yakonwita, awaiting the return of her "Pale-face" lover. Her kinsmen expect the worst of him, "Thus they taunted her, declaring, 'He remembers naught of thee:/Likely some white maid he wooeth, far beyond the inland sea.'" Yet unlike parallel contemporary narratives of colonial relations such as John Luther Long's "Madame Butterfly" (1898) or even Mourning Dove's *Co-ge-wea* (1927), where a colonialist lover proves untrue, this "white" lover, caught tragically in a winter storm while trying to return to her, can declare, "I am Pale, but I am true!" It is not necessary to speculate how such a story fulfilled the personal or political dreams of Johnson, a mixed-blood herself, whose Mohawk name, *Tekahionwake*, translates as "double-life." Yet the poem certainly envisions racial reconciliation – though any "happy ending" is deferred romantically to a reunion only in the afterlife. Eternally searching for her lost lover, the "maiden, misty as the autumn rains, /[is] Guiding with her lamp of moonlight/Hunters lost upon the plains" (Johnson).

In a few representative lines from the long narrative poem we may see the stylistic formality and the romantic turn of colonial divisions building toward the tragic conclusion, resonant with a dream of love:

"Yakonwita, Yakonwita," O the dreariness that strains
Through the voice that calling, quivers, till a whisper but remains!
"Yakonwita, Yakonwita,
    I am lost upon the plains!"
But the Silent Spirit hushed him, lulled him as he cried anew,
"Save me, save me, O belovèd, I am Pale, but I am true!
Yakonwita, Yakonwita,
    I am dying, love, for you!"

NATIVE AMERICAN POETRY

Leagues afar, across the prairie, she had risen from her bed,
Roused her kinsmen from their slumber: "He has come tonight," she said.
"I can hear him calling, calling,
    But his voice is as the dead."

(Johnson)

After her kinsmen also hear "a spirit-voice [calling] faintly, 'I am dying, love, for you,'" they wail in sympathy, "'O Yakonwita, /He was Pale, but he was true!'" She disappears into the storm to search for him, "And they never saw her more" – except for lost Indian hunters, "Late at night ... when the starlight clouds or wanes," and she guides them home. The inviolable romance is completed for both "white" and "Indian" desire, with clear overtones of Pocahontas or Sacajawea – yet in perfect contrast to the historic nadir of Indian/white relations in the early twentieth century when assimilation policies masked the near annihilation of Indians.

Cultural affirmation on the land

The near edge of such annihilation energizes much of Indigenous poetry, even into the later twentieth century. Indeed it forms the framing structure of one of the most significant works of Indigenous poetry, which we will discuss further below, *from Sand Creek*, by Simon Ortiz. Among the major poets of the latter twentieth and early twenty-first centuries, Ortiz (b. 1941) offers a unique voice from his Acoma "Sky City" Pueblo perspective. Rooted in traditional culture and language as well as being widely traveled, Ortiz pours politics and history, tradition and revolt, song and sharp analysis into his poetry, fiction, and essays. In approximately two dozen books, he is able to speak on behalf of the American land, and especially the red rocks of his homeland, as in this excerpt from the poem "Culture and the Universe":

> ... *Lean into me.*
> The universe
> sings in quiet meditation.
>
> We are wordless:
>   I am in you.
>
> Without knowing why
> culture needs our knowledge
> we are one self in the canyon.
>
>   And the stone wall
> I lean upon spins me
> wordless and silent
> to the reach of stars
> and to the heavens within. ...

(*Out There Somewhere* 104–05)

Simultaneous with these ancient interconnections, Ortiz may critique postcolonial identities, as in a prose poem, "What Indians?" from the same collection, excerpted here:

> ... Like other colonized Indigenous peoples, cultures, and communities throughout the world, Native Americans have experienced and endured identities imposed upon them by colonial powers, most of which originated in Europe. This imposition has resulted to a great extent – more than we admit and realize – in the loss of a sense of a centered human self and the weakening and loss of Indigenous cultural identity.
>
> (45)

Ortiz both invokes that "centered human self" and laments its loss in American history.

Establishing that fundamental critique, Ortiz' book-length poem *from Sand Creek: Rising In This Heart Which Is Our America* (1981) is one of the most important long poems of the twentieth century, for its lyric revaluations of history and identity in both Native America and America at large. Struggling to contemplate the Sand Creek Massacre of 1864 in Colorado, one of the lowest points in American history, Ortiz is able to articulate beyond history:

> This America
> has been a burden
> of steel and mad
> death,
> but, look now,
> there are flowers
> and new grass
> and a spring wind
> rising
> from Sand Creek.
>
> (9)

The poem's short sections navigate psychological compassion across the American spectrum, recognizing militia men lonely for their own brutalized humanity, and their victims on the open prairie, and the descendants of these tragic figures buried in the post-traumatic psyche of the American frontier. Through the worst of America's ongoing "Indian Wars," Ortiz is able to envision a real American dream beyond inequality and injustice:

> That dream
> shall have a name
> after all,
> and it will not be vengeful
> but wealthy with love
> and compassion
> and knowledge.
> And it will rise
> in this heart
> which is our America.
>
> (95)

NATIVE AMERICAN POETRY

The thematic achievements of *from Sand Creek* owe an aesthetic debt to N. Scott Momaday's classic *The Way to Rainy Mountain* (1969), for its deployment of multiple discourses in each double-page unit of the book-length poem. Where Momaday (Kiowa, b. 1934) employs three voices, the historical, mythical, and the personal, which eventually blend, Ortiz sets up a dialectic between the journalistic and the poetic discourses on facing pages. The effect is a compelling mix of rational analysis and passionate sensation, leading to "this heart/ which is our America" – as he reclaims the land.

Individual humanity on the land

Along with Ortiz, Joy Harjo (Mvskoke/Creek, b. 1951) shares the stage as a pre-eminent Native American poet since the latter twentieth century. Her poems frequently connect to the land through the long history of horses in Native America. A jazz musician as well as a poet, Harjo employs the image of horses as an intense and pounding trope for human passions, especially when those emotions clash or connect with nature, with other humans, and with history. In "She Had Some Horses," the title poem of her 1983 collection, the narrator begins in the natural world where horses stand for "bodies of sand," "maps drawn of blood," "skins of ocean water," and "blue air of sky" (63). Repetition of the words "She had some horses" or "She had horses who ..." recall to the ear the uniform sound of galloping hooves offering a complicated sense of near and far, comfort and threat, power and powerlessness. Next the poet steadily complicates Indigenous existence, suggesting how suffering emerges, and how humans themselves evolve out of earth. The poem moves through imagery of bodies to more violent word choices, words like "splintered" and "spit," and finally to an outright statement of self-loathing and fear. Harjo's horses take on human complication. "She had some horses who were fur and teeth ... clay and would break ... were splintered red cliff." Gradually, the imagery reveals how life under colonial circumstances brings devastation and despair: "horses" cry "in their beer," "spit at male queens who made them/afraid of themselves" (63). Those who do not lie, who tell the truth "were stripped/ bare of their tongues" (63). Reconciliation in the end consists of an embrace of seeming opposites, love and hate.

In another poem in the collection, "Two Horses," the narrator speaks of herself as driven purely in a burst of love, "... I am a horse running towards/a cracked sky where there are countless dawns/breaking simultaneously" (65). According to Norma Wilson,

> Harjo is convinced that, as in ceremonies, stories, and oratory, the use of repetition in poems can transform a statement into a "litany," giving the participant or reader "a way to enter in to what is being said and a way to emerge whole but changed."
>
> (Wilson 113)

Horses stand for dynamic and dramatic healing, a ritual rebuilding of hope through grounding in place and natural energy. Harjo invokes horses in a way that suggests an exhaustion of grief through passionate engagement with life.

Janice Gould (Koyangk'auwi Maidu, b. 1949) pulls together a similar theme of reconciliation through the images of winter: "I liked the way the city slowed/to accommodate

Nature ... /the rounded hills and orchards/all lay in a deep frosty dream. ... horses in pastures, breath steaming icicles/hanging from their shaggy coats" ("Snow" 63). The poem ends with a strong belief in healing and a connection between human contentment and being in the natural world, as the poet brings her past into line with her present. The steaming breath of the horse links to the steaming atmosphere of sex and love.

> ... the laughter
> that resounds in frozen air,
> the first shove through January snowfall.
> After years I grew up,
> married a woman who isn't crazy.
> I like to imagine how I've come back to kiss her,
> time after time on snowy mornings,
> her lips warm,
> the room steaming,
> the smell of sex still in our bed
> delicious as sweet rolls and tangerines.
>
> (67)

Like so many poets, Gould evokes the pure erotic to forge the poem's link to natural power and the seasonal cycles.

A poignantly ironic example of place-centeredness comes to life in Joy Harjo's "The Woman Hanging from the Thirteenth Floor Window." As a despairing single mother dangles from a window "on the east side of Chicago," "on the Indian side of town," the narrator imagines what she sees, hears, thinks, and remembers (35–36). On the one hand, she is not alone; indeed, she sees "other women/hanging from many-floored windows." Surrounded by others' voices, she knows the terror of menacing "gigantic men" and of people calling to her to jump. Some voices are comforting like the voice of her grandmother. The places that call to her are her home "up north" with its "waterfalls and pines" and "Chicago streets" (37). The woman's dilemma twists with her in the wind as the poem ends by turning backward on itself and the two possibilities. "She thinks she remembers listening to her own life/break loose, as she falls from the 13th floor/window on the east side of Chicago, or she/climbs back up to claim herself again" (37). The woman hangs suspended paradoxically outside of time and space, yet she inhabits a center of both lost and found purpose. Her dilemma rivets us as observers to her fate.

By contrast in tone but similar in unflinching observation, Adrian C. Louis (Lovelock Paiute, b. 1946), in "Manifest Destination," finds himself in a small border-town in Nebraska, just off the Pine Ridge Oglala Lakota Reservation. The poem title's pun on a fundamental American motto carries all the weight of history and irony. Known for his harsh depictions of American Indian lives and homelands, Louis offers a scathing critique of the town's weather and inhabitants. Like Harjo's "woman" who lives in intense and perpetual pain, Louis's first-person narrator expresses a troubled, sour grief for his situation:

> Every other day I grieve for the me
> that was and every man or woman
> I see fills me with contempt.

Nine out of ten Skins in town are
hang-around-the-fort welfare addicts. ...

(157)

He goes on to claim that the sad state Indians find themselves in does not embarrass him, because "the white people are even worse" (157). He concludes that "Every single thing about this/town is sadly second-rate," and he dubs it "Cowturdville" and "Panhandle town." Yet in the end, the land offers reprieve for the pitiful: "Thunderheads are forming/and the sweet-ass rain/of forgiveness is in the air" (158).

Power of language on the land

Sherman Alexie (Spokane, b. 1966) launched himself as a bold voice in a flood of half a dozen books of poems in the 1990s, while he was also producing short story collections, novels, and films, plus displaying his talents as a stand-up comic and as reigning "world heavyweight poetry bout champion." Twenty years later he has more than twenty major publications, winning major awards. Often referring to his Spokane Reservation in Washington State, Alexie's poetry and prose ranges, like his own career and like more than half of the Native population of the United States, into America's urban centers as well. Ironic dynamics of leaving and returning play out in his poems. His poetic structures are informal with a tone of convincing authority and poignant insight, again usually turning on irony. "You have to understand that white people invented/irony," says the narrative voice in his poem titled "The American Artificial Limb Company" (*One Stick Song* 33). Alexie's narrations mirror the ironic American practice of treaty-writing and treaty-breaking; such irony may indeed permeate much of the literary expression of Native American writers across the centuries, caught as they too often are in the distresses of history, in the ironic reversals of desire and despair, but Alexie is a case apart. Through his commanding wit and ironic attitude, he takes on the world for its hypocrisy and ignorance. He takes Native literature in new dimensions of self-reflection, as he reaffirms Native lives and Native nationhood.

Perhaps Alexie's formulation – that poetry equates to anger multiplied by imagination – which reoccurs as a leitmotiv in several of his books (e.g., *Old Shirts, New Skins* xi), provides a key into the interwoven aesthetics and politics of his and other Native Americans' art. Where Poetry stands for agency, for an affirmation of personal and communal power as a Native American artist, Anger, to Alexie, is a positive, freeing force of recognition and resistance to an entire history of injustice, while Imagination here directs that freedom toward visions of liberation. Alexie's formula is a manifesto for artistic survivance, to use Gerald Vizenor's crucial term of resistance and survival in a strength beyond despair.

Another specific aesthetic formulation, this by Vizenor (Anishinaabe, b. 1934), helps us to understand Indigenous poetics and practices more broadly. A prolific poet, novelist, filmmaker, and trickster theorist, Vizenor, who discovered Japanese haiku as a young soldier, reflects on "haiku hermeneutics" in Indigenous writing ("Envoy" 30, 32). Language both hides and represents. Haiku hermeneutics recognizes and manipulates the semiotic structure of representation itself, affirming beyond the slippery signifier a natural reality that always stands like a shadow outside of cultural, especially literary, expression. "Shadows tease and loosen the bonds of representation" (*Manifest Manners* 72). Although words are powerful, language cannot contain or control reality, just as the standard American stereotypes about Indians cannot contain or control Indigenous tribal realities, neither cultural practices nor legal sovereignties. Yet, knowing these linguistic limitations, every poet strives paradoxically to push the poem beyond words, to touch a natural reality. Thus Vizenor's haiku hermeneutics play with language to trick us out of such stereotypes or "terminal creeds" about so-called vanishing Indians. By challenging and tricking those stereotypes, Indigenous writers "loosen the bonds of representation" between the dominant signifier and the sign of Indigeneity, so that into that gap they may present images more natural and historical. This technique simultaneously recognizes a natural, Indigenous presence on the land while denying imperial erasures. His theory indeed applies to the work of many Indigenous poets who push language beyond its limits to represent Indigenous experience.

Politics matter in Native American poetics. In fact, a haiku hermeneutics quickly illuminates that dynamic of aesthetics and ethics. As Qwo-Li Driskill states, "The idea that poetry should abstain from politics does nothing for struggles toward liberation" (223). She writes of Gregory Scofield's poetry as embodying "the complexities of identities" arising "from political and cultural histories often denied by a racist/colonial culture" (223). This representative sampling of Native American poetry does not pretend to encompass such a vibrant and changing field of expression, but perhaps it can serve to tease out the resistance to erasure and the persistence of interconnectedness in the field.

Notes

1 Thanks to Professor P. Jane Hafen (Taos) at the University of Nevada, Las Vegas for articulating this distinction.
2 For a thorough chronology, see both Ruoff pp. 62–115 and Blaeser.

Works cited

Alexie, Sherman. *Old Shirts, New Skins*. Los Angeles: UCLA American Indian Studies, 1993.
——. *One Stick Song*. Brooklyn, NY: Hanging Loose Press, 2000.
Blaeser, Kimberly. "The Possibilities of a Native Poetics." *Nothing But the Truth: An Anthology of Native American Literature*. Ed. John L. Purdy & James Ruppert. Upper Saddle River, NJ: Prentice Hall, 2001. 412–15.
Brill de Ramirez, Susan Berry. *Contemporary American Indian Literature and the Oral Tradition*. Tucson: University of Arizona Press, 1999.
Driskill, Qwo-Li. "Call Me Brother: Two-Spiritedness, the Erotic, and Mixedblood Memory as Sites of Sovereignty and Resistance in Gregory Scofield's Poetry." *Speak to Me Words: Essays on Contemporary American Indian Poetry*. Ed. Dean Rader & Janice Gould. Tucson: University of Arizona Press, 2003. 222–34.
Gould, Janice. "Snow." *Earthquake Weather: Poems*. Tucson: University of Arizona Press, 1996. 63–67.
Hanna, Dan. "Medicine Song." *Home Places: Contemporary Native American Writing from Sun Tracks*. Ed. Larry Evers & Ofelia Zepeda. Tucson: University of Arizona Press, 1995. 19–34.
Harjo, Joy. *She Had Some Horses: Poems*. New York: Thunder's Mouth Press, 1983.
——. "The Woman Hanging From the Thirteenth Floor Window." *How We Became Human: New and Selected Poems: 1975–2002*. New York: W.W. Norton, 2002. 35–37.

Johnson, E. Pauline. "The Pilot of the Plains." Web. Accessed 2 March 2015. http://digital.library.upenn.edu/women/garvin/poets/johnson.html

Louis, Adrian C. "Manifest Destinations." *Fire*. No. 9 (September 1999): 157–58.

Momaday, N. Scott. "Man Made of Words." *Indian Voices: The First Convocation of American Indian Scholars*. San Francisco: The Indian Historian Press, 1970. 49–62.

———. *Way to Rainy Mountain*. 1969. Rpt. Albuquerque: University of New Mexico Press, 2010.

Montezuma, Carlos. "Changing is not Vanishing." Web. Accessed 2 March 2015. http://www.graphicclassics.com/pgs/Montezuma_Changing%20is%20not%20Vanishing.pdf

Mourning Dove (Humishuma). *Cogewea, the Half Blood: A Depiction of the Great Montana Cattle Range*. 1927. Rpt. Lincoln: University of Nebraska Press, 1981.

Niatum, Duane. "Preface." *Harper's Anthology of 20th Century Native American Poetry*. Ed. Duane Niatum. San Francisco: Harper San Francisco, 1988. ix–xii.

Ortiz, Simon J. *from Sand Creek*. Tucson: University of Arizona Press, 2000.

———. *Out There Somewhere*. Tucson: University of Arizona Press, 2002.

Revard, Carter. "In Oklahoma." *An Eagle Nation*. Tucson: University of Arizona Press, 1993. 3.

Ruoff, A. LaVonne Brown. *American Indian Literatures: An Introduction, Bibliographic Review, and Selected Bibliography*. New York: Modern Literature Association, 1990.

Silko, Leslie Marmon. *Almanac of the Dead*. New York: Viking Penguin, 1991.

Vizenor, Gerald. (1993) "An Envoy to Haiku." *Shadow Distance: A Gerald Vizenor Reader*. Ed. A. Robert Lee. Hanover, NH: University Press of New England, 1994. 25–32.

———. (1993) *Manifest Manners: Postindian Warriors of Survivance*. Lincoln: University of Nebraska Press, 1999.

Wilson, Norma C. *The Nature of Native American Poetry*. Albuquerque: University of New Mexico Press, 2001.

38

Native American Novels
The Renaissance, the Homing Plot, and Beyond

John Gamber

The argument could be made that the Native American Renaissance, the period labeled by Kenneth Lincoln in his 1983 text of the same name and marking the increase in positive critical responses to and popularity of Native American literature, began with a novel. I refer specifically to Kiowa author N. Scott Momaday's *House Made of Dawn*, which was awarded the Pulitzer Prize in 1969. Lincoln's text describes the increased output of critical work engaging with Native American literature during the late 1970s. Certainly, Momaday's receipt of the Pulitzer put not only him, but also other Native authors on critics' radar.[1] In any event, Native American literature's rise has certainly rested on the back of its novels to a large extent. Indeed, while prominent authors including Native literature's most prominent presence, Sherman Alexie (Spokane/Coeur d'Alene), might think of themselves as writers broadly or poets primarily, their prose, and especially their novels, are especially visible. None of this is meant to take away from other genres of Native literary production or Native art generally, of course. It simply signals the realities of literary consumption right now.

This chapter addresses Native American-authored novels especially since this increase in their popularity. However, we would be remiss if we did not discuss the fact that Native people have not only been writing, but publishing novels for over a century and a half. Cherokee author John Rollin Ridge's *The Life and Adventures of Joaquín Murrieta, the Celebrated California Bandit*, published in 1854, stands as the first. This novel fictionalizes Murrieta's exploits, painting him as a force of vengeance against the cruelties of U.S. citizens (Murrieta was born in Mexico) against people of color, women, and the poor. This novel is also regarded as the first written in the (then five-year-old) state of California.

Creek author Alice Callahan is credited as being the first Native woman to have published a novel, *Wynema: A Child of the Forest* in 1891. While Ridge's text makes use of Western dime novels' episodic formula to address (and in certain instances to replicate or reinforce) racialized injustices in the United States and by its citizens, Callahan wields sentimental interiority to demonstrate the possibility and necessity for change in U.S. policy toward Native people (including, but certainly not limited to, allotment), as well as to the misunderstandings between white and Native people and to Anglo racial and cultural supremacism. It is worth noting as well that Mourning Dove's *Cogewea the Half-Blood: A Depiction of the Great Montana Cattle Range* (1927) was thought to be the first novel published by a Native woman, until the rediscovery of Callahan's in the 1990s.

Published not far on *Cogewea*'s heels came D'Arcy McNickle's (Salish Kootenai) *The Surrounded* (1936). This novel lies first chronologically on the list of novels that William Bevis famously labeled Native American "homing plots," narratives about Native protagonists leaving their tribal homelands but returning home to re-engage with their communities and families. Notably, in these novels, he asserts, the mostly young male protagonists find failure and destruction in their journeys and must come home to heal. Bevis differentiates these narratives from classic European *bildungsroman* in which a character sets off into the world in order to come home more fully formed. There is more to Bevis's reading, however, and this should perhaps be re-examined, as the homing plot is often explained in these overly simplistic terms. *The Surrounded*'s protagonist, Archilde, returns to the Salish/Kootenai reservation from Portland, Oregon, where he has found some success as a fiddler. He does not return home damaged, though there may be some concern that his career has placed him in proximity with undesirable folks. After returning to his family, which includes a tense relationship with his Spanish father, Archilde suffers a series of indignities, including harassment by law enforcement. As Bevis explains, McNickle's "novel does not present Archilde as simply sucked into a depressing situation, although he certainly is; the novel applauds his return to Indian roots" (583). *The Surrounded* demonstrates a kind of ambivalence about Archilde's return home: it may show him dragged down as an individual, but it also lauds him for recognizing a communal importance greater than himself. Moreover, it demonstrates his growth as a member of his community, becoming more familiar with its people and cultural practices.

The ambivalence of this novel may reflect the era in which it was written. While the later texts that Bevis discusses come from the late-1960s or later (the era of Native American legal self-determination), *The Surrounded* grows out of the 1930s, fresh on the heels of the Indian Reorganization Act of 1934 (aka the Indian New Deal) that followed the much more overtly assimilationist and profoundly destructive allotment era. *The Surrounded* represents a text that arises out of the aftermath of allotment, the period of massive land loss for Native people. Crafting a protagonist who is materially and professionally successful away from the Native community, who returns, nonetheless to that community, marks Archilde as the successful product of some of the assimilative processes that drove allotment. That said, McNickle's attempts to find a publisher for this novel, and their demands for revision, certainly shaped some of the text's ambivalence on this front. McNickle had attempted to publish this novel under the title *The Hungry Generations*, only to have it rejected by *The Surrounded*'s eventual publisher, Harcourt Brace (Owens 239). Whereas *The Surrounded* concludes with Archilde being arrested for a murder he did not commit, in *The Hungry Generations* the charges are dismissed and Archilde returns to his family's land that he has inherited following his father's death. Moreover, *The Hungry Generations* includes a lengthy section that discusses Archilde's journey to Paris, completely absent in *The Surrounded*, and his encounter with a French woman whom he will wed at the novel's end. Archilde, as a character, becomes more an emblem of assimilation in the earlier draft, and a more tragic, even doomed one in the later one. This distinction carries important political implications. If the assimilationist narrative wins the day, Native people who refuse to yield become responsible for their own marginalization. If the Naturalist narrative endures, Native people become far more sympathetic (albeit a sympathy that likely takes the form of pity).

Prior to Louise Erdrich's (Chippewa) successes, which I will discuss later, the two most critically successful Native authored novels were Momaday's *House Made of Dawn* (1969), and Leslie Marmon Silko's (Laguna) *Ceremony* (1977). These texts, moreover, occupy central positions within the mode of the homing plot. *House Made of Dawn* follows its protagonist, Abel, beginning with his return to Jemez Pueblo following World War II. In perhaps one of the most oft-quoted lines in the Native American canon, Abel arrives home by bus and "stepped heavily to the ground and reeled. He was drunk, and he fell against his grandfather and did not know him" (9). Abel's lack of recognition of his grandfather emblematizes his cultural confusion, which is exacerbated by the fact that he is tribally mixed; his father was not from Jemez. Reeling and lost at home, Abel murders a man following a feast day competition, is convicted of murder, and incarcerated. Upon his release, he relocates to Los Angeles where, despite finding some community among fellow relocated Indians, his life continues to shamble. He drinks to excess and eventually quits his job. A police officer badly beats Abel, whose friends subsequently buy him a train ticket to return home where he re-engages with Jemez culture and begins to heal both physically and psychically.

Ceremony's narrative bears many similarities to that of *House Made of Dawn*, though key differences exist. Both central characters have parents from communities outside of their Pueblo communities, both are brought away from their homes, Abel by his incarceration, *Ceremony*'s Tayo by the Second World War. Tayo returns from his service in the Pacific theater having been subjected to the Bataan Death March and suffering from symptoms akin to PTSD. Tayo eventually begins to mend under the guidance of Betonie, a Navajo healer, who emphasizes the dangers of denying the possibilities of change within Native cultures, of accepting an ethnographic fallacy that true Native communities do not adapt. To that end, Betonie reminds both Tayo and the reader, "things that don't shift and grow are dead things" (126). Too often, Native people are cast as subjects only of the past, but, like so many texts of the Native canon, *Ceremony* refuses the settler-colonial nation its vanished indigenous populations.

Read alongside one another, *House Made of Dawn* and *Ceremony* demonstrate temporally specific elements of their homing plots, specifically those of the American Indian Relocation policies of the Termination Era, smack dab in the middle of which each of this novels is set. This program contributed to the massive demographic shift within Indian Country since its inception. Indeed, while today nearly 70 percent of Native people live in cities, at the dawn of World War II, only 8 percent did (compared to just over half of U.S. citizens generally). While these shifts reflect the demographic changes of the United States as a whole, they are significantly disproportionate for Native Americans. While many political movements grew from the critical mass of Native people from various nations in specific urban settings, and while they in many ways launched Native issues into mainstream American consciousness, they also grew out of the failures of the Relocation Program to fulfill its promises. Specifically, we note a number of narratives of cultural dislocation, of poverty arising from the lack of (promised) training and preparation, new encounters of racialized marginalization, as well as increases in drug abuse and violence that follow in the wake of urban relocation. These elements are conspicuous in the novels that appear in this historical moment.[2]

While these novels reinforce tropes of relocated Native people as *dislocated*, not all novels do, nor do all post-renaissance texts portray homing plots. Plenty of texts focus on characters set within their communities exclusively; others show successful Native characters in urban environments. In short, the Native American canon is rich and diverse. As such, we turn now to texts that offer alternatives to the homing plot traditions in various ways and to varying degrees. Some, like the works of Gerald Vizenor (Anishinaabe), examine the positive roles of Native mobility, while those of Sherman Alexie demonstrate the potentials for healthy Native communities in cities or away from one's reservation. Moreover, we note a number of complications to simplistic notions of what Native American literature can or should be in the narrative devices wielded by Louise Erdrich. That said, the definitions and limits of Native identity continues as a major trope in the work of all of these authors.

Until recently, when Sherman Alexie claimed the mantle, Louise Erdrich stood as the single most popular and successful contemporary Native author. Erdrich has published fourteen novels, beginning with her 1984 *Love Medicine*, and has received countless accolades, including the National Book Award for *The Round House* (2012). Erdrich's work is especially renowned for her recurring characters (Lipsha and Nanapush stand as ready examples) and settings across multiple novels, eliciting comparisons to William Faulkner's imaginative Yoknapatawpha County and its denizens. Similarly, her novels frequently employ multiple narrators (including, at times, other-than-human ones, such as dogs), a convention often read to represent the tribal aspects of her writing, an insistence that the entire community must join in the storytelling for it to be true or accurate. Such a reading, though, as David Treuer (Ojibwe) notes, might place an overdetermined reading of Native context within a Native author's work despite the fact that this device, like the novel itself, has grown from a number of non-Native sources (4). Along these lines, the reader must bear in mind that in much of her writing, Erdrich includes white as well as Native narrators. Indeed, her second novel, *The Beet Queen*, centers on the white characters in Argus, North Dakota, with Native characters occupying positions in the periphery. Moreover, Erdrich often focuses attention on mixed-race characters and communities, an element that comes to the fore in a great deal of Native American literature of the 1980s and 1990s.

In a particularly interesting move, Erdrich radically revised her 1998 novel *The Antelope Wife* in 2012 (as she did *Love Medicine* [1984] in 1993 and again in 2009) so that while the two versions begin similarly, they depart wildly from one another after that. Erdrich writes out much of the tragedy of the text, including the death of some major characters who now survive through the novel's end. Erdrich refers to these changes as corrections, asserting that she has made *The Antelope Wife* into the novel that it was always supposed to be. The original text includes an author's note, "This novel was written before the death of my husband. He is remembered with love by all of his family" (n. pag.). The need for such a note stems from the fact that the novel's primary antagonist, Richard Whiteheart Beads, ultimately commits suicide, a conjunction of events with some similarities to the suicide of Erdrich's husband, Michael Dorris. The dedication to the revised version reads simply, "To Aza," Erdrich's daughter, a powerful inversion that privileges life over death, and future generations over an arguably tragic past.

Such changes, though, do more than shed light on some of the motivations for Erdrich's changes to her own novel. Indeed, they beg critical questions about the novel itself. If two radically different versions of this text exist, which one is *The Antelope Wife*? Is either one? Must we read both to say we have read the text? While Erdrich insists her changes were simply needed because she had failed to create the novel she intended, we can also read its revision as a continuation of her multiple narrator approach to writing. If her other texts require multiple voices in order to communicate a proper story, the same could be said about novels themselves. A single version of a story might be bounded, might seem whole, but a story told from multiple perspectives shows that the singular version never was, and never could be, complete. Perhaps our attachment to novels as bounded stories, fixed and final, represents an attachment to incomplete stories. Perhaps Erdrich has found a new method of "writing in the oral tradition," to paraphrase Kimberly Blaeser's (Anishinaabe) work on Gerald Vizenor.

While Vizenor's work is not nearly as popularly read as Erdrich's, it is certainly no less influential in the realm of Native American novels, nor is he less prolific, with over a dozen novels under his belt as well as collections of poetry, short stories, and collected Ojibwe songs. Moreover, Vizenor is the author of some of the most influential critical and theoretical works in the field of Native American Studies, including *Manifest Manners: Narratives of Postindian Survivance* (1999) and *Fugitive Poses: Native American Scenes of Absence and Presence* (1998). All of this is to say nothing of his contributions to the White Earth Nation's revision of its constitution (to a White Earth specific, rather than collective Minnesota Chippewa, governmental structure).

Vizenor has explained, time and time again, that his writing attempts to participate in tribal traditions of storytelling, particularly by eschewing the static, the tragic, or the facile, in favor of the fluid, the comic, the tricky, and the complex (see *Postindian Conversations*). His novels tend to utilize a metaliterary technique that insists that they be understood as stories, not reality, but stories that can nonetheless *shape* reality. Part and parcel of that fluidity is Vizenor's use of revision in his written texts. Certainly, these revisions are most noticeable in his multiple editions of *Summer in the Spring: Anishinaabe Lyric Poems and Stories*, originally published in 1965, but revised in 1970, again in 1981, and yet again in 1993 (see Spry). However, we also see this compulsion to revise in the changes Vizenor applied to his 1978 *Darkness in Saint Louis Bearheart* in order to craft 1990's *Bearheart: The Heirship Chronicles* in 1990, the latter recast with a different framing device.[3]

Vizenor's novels stand out among Native American texts particularly for their settings in nations outside the United States. His most recent *Blue Ravens* (2014) follows two young men from White Earth who serve in World War I, return to Minnesota, but ultimately relocate back to Paris. However, this examination of Native people abroad is hardly new in Vizenor's work. *Griever: An American Monkey King in China* (1986) draws on comparative trickster traditions to set an Anishinaabe teacher in Tianjin, China, while *Hiroshima Bugi: Atomu 57* (2003), which pitches itself an a Native kabuki novel, portrays a protagonist who is of Anishinaabe and Japanese descent, a product of a soldier's stationing in Japan as an interpreter for General MacArthur. Such narratives of travel push against the homing plot in important ways, as Native experiences away from tribal nations serve as sources of not only personal, but also communal growth. Not all their experiences are negative and communities become expanded to include people from all over the world.

While Vizenor may be unique for his recurring attention to Native protagonists abroad, his novels are not alone in that move. Indeed, renowned authors such as James Welch (Blackfeet) and Silko have crafted narratives of Native protagonists who venture to Europe. Welch's *The Heartsong of Charging Elk* (2001) follows the Lakota eponymous central character from the Stronghold in what would soon thereafter become South Dakota (the novel begins in 1898) as he travels to Europe with Buffalo Bill's Wild West Show. It is worth noting that this temporal setting allows Charging Elk, who witnessed the Battle of the Little Big Horn as a child, to not be present for the Wounded Knee Massacre. Charging Elk, however, falls ill and becomes hospitalized while the troupe travels on. Due to a series of bureaucratic snafus, Charging Elk is unable to leave France. His attempts to return to the United States are hampered by the fact that Native people had not achieved universal citizenship at this point in history.[4] However, this quirk of citizenship eventually benefits him. He is incarcerated for murder, but freed because his sentence erroneously came under the auspices of French/United States treaties regarding the treatment of their citizens within one another's judicial systems. Once this oversight is realized by French officials, Charging Elk is freed. He, like the protagonists in Vizenor's *Blue Ravens*, opts to remain in France, becoming naturalized through his marriage to a French woman. In each of these French-set texts, and in contrast to Vizenor's East Asian-set novels, the authors play with the colonial/ metropole binary, demonstrating the movements to the latter from the former. Ironically, these characters often come to feel they have avenues toward a decreased marginalization within the European seats of the racialized colonialism that they face in their indigenous homelands in the United States.

Silko's addition to this collection of texts set in Europe comes in the form of *Gardens in the Dunes* (1999), which follows Indigo, a young Native girl, during the same time period as *The Heartsong of Charging Elk*, the 1890s through the early 1900s. This being a period of aggressive attempts by the United States to assimilate Native people, Indigo is taken from her family and brought to the Sherman Indian Institute in Riverside, California. Indigo is eventually adopted by a white couple who bring her across the United States to New York, and across the Atlantic to Europe. While Indigo ultimately returns home to the novel's titular gardens, she also comes to recognize similarities between indigenous American and European relationships to space and place, connections that often take the form of gardens maintained by women. Silko's novel, as such, fits within an ecofeminist canon as well. Finally, the temporal settings of these novels also allow their authors to adopt the tone of nineteenth-century literature, a device that might otherwise seem out of place in the work of contemporary Native American authors, as each demonstrates an affinity for the sentimental narratives of the Victorian era.

While Sherman Alexie stands at the center of the Native American literary world, much of his work falls into the genres of short story and poetry. Indeed, he often notes that he thinks of himself as a poet first and foremost.[5] He has written three novels, *Reservation Blues* (1995), *Indian Killer* (1996), and *Flight* (2007) – the last of which might more rightly be categorized as a novella. The mainstays of Alexie's novels, however, are similar to those of his other prose: a mixture of dark, painful moments that drift into hilarious, unanticipated punch lines. Another common thread that runs throughout these novels (as well as the mixed-genre young adult novel, 2007's *The Absolutely True Diary of a Part Time Indian*) is the presence of a young Native male protagonist who is some form of misfit in his own community. In *Reservation Blues*, that misfit comes in the form of Thomas Build-the-Fire, one of Alexie's recurring names whose personality shifts a bit from text to text (many will recognize him as the misfit of *Smoke Signals*, the critically acclaimed film for which Alexie wrote the screenplay). In *Indian Killer*, it is John Smith, a Native young man adopted by a white suburban family, who knows nothing about his Native community, or even from what community his birth parents came. In *Flight*, it is Zits, another orphaned character

453

who bounces around foster families until he begins to bounce around in time and space, *Slaughterhouse Five* style.

Alexie owes some of his success to his approach that allows popular and non-Native readers to understand contemporary Native people stripped of any stereotyping exoticism. Absent are the elements of magic realism that exist in texts like *Ceremony*, Erdrich's *Tracks*, or more contemporary works like Craig Womack's (Creek) *Drowning in Fire*, which I will discuss below. *Reservation Blues*'s Thomas is a contemporary young person who, along with friends and romantic interests starts a rock and blues band. *Indian Killer*'s John is a construction worker with dissociative issues; his narrative overlaps with those of a number of Native college students. *Flight*'s Zits goes to school, has relatively minor run-ins with the police, and makes references to pop culture icons from Kanye West to Stephen King.

A number of more recent novels from authors who are not as widely discussed as the likes of Erdrich, Alexie, Silko, Vizenor, and Welch demonstrate some of the innovations authors are making within Native American literature broadly and novels more specifically. Craig Womack's *Drowning in Fire* (2001) deserves attention for a number of reasons. First, Womack is a key figure in Native American Literary Nationalism, a movement that aims to increase the tribal specificity in Native literature as well as to foster critical approaches that are politically committed to improving conditions and strengthening sovereignty for Native people and nations. *Drowning in Fire*, in keeping with these moves, focuses on the Mvskoke (Creek) Nation, with a young protagonist who begins to move across time to the era of the Crazy Snake Rebellion of 1909 (which responded to Oklahoma Statehood in 1907). That is, its focus is specific to a particular, politically defined community, an example of the literary work that Womack calls for in his critical monograph *Red on Red: Native American Literary Separatism* (1999). Moreover, this novel follows a gay protagonist as he comes of age in extremely conservative and bitterly homophobic 1970s Oklahoma. Novel-length texts with detailed examinations of Native LGBTQ communities and individuals remain rare, and Womack's deft text works to change that.

Another critic cum novelist making waves in Native literature is David Treuer, who pairs his most recent novel *The Translation of Dr. Apelles* (2008) with his critical *Native American Fiction: A User's Manual* (2006). This latter text argues for an approach to reading Native literature that moves away from identitarian issues toward an appreciation of texts' formal qualities. Too often, Treuer contends, readers assume some kind of cultural insight or authenticity in these narratives, an ethnographic voyeurism, rather than understanding them as carefully crafted stories. To that end, Treuer offers *The Translation of Dr. Apelles* as a counter to those reader expectations. His novel pairs the story of the eponymous Doctor, a translator of Native languages, and his romantic interest, Campaspe, with the story he appears to be translating from a Native American language. In truth, though, the story is the second-century Greek pastoral of Daphnis and Chloe being translated into an Ojibwe context, while the romantic plot is merely a story that Apelles is inventing. This novel, then, works against much of the canon of Native American novels, denying expectations of stereotypical old-timey Indians in particular.

I conclude with a brief discussion of the work of the bafflingly prolific Stephen Graham Jones (Blackfeet), whose work demonstrates novelistic innovation on two fronts. First, he has written three novels – *The Fast Red Road: A Plainsong* (2000), *The Bird is Gone: A Manifesto* (2003), and *Ledfeather* (2008) – that clearly fit within the Native American canon, populated almost entirely by Native characters, but which push it in fascinating directions. In *The Bird is Gone*, for example, Jones imagines a near-future world in which the Great Plains (through a legal accident) are returned to Native ownership. This text represents the growing field of Native Futurism, speculative fiction from a Native perspective. Jones's move allows him to imagine a truly postcolonial Native nation, a thought experiment that is far more difficult to conduct in a text set in the present. Nonetheless, *The Bird is Gone* does not offer an idealized or utopian state, but a sketchy, dangerous one, full of violence and drug abuse. At the same time, Jones is a "genre" writer who is especially known for his horror and zombie narratives in over ten novels apart from the aforementioned three. His *Demon Theory* (2006), for example, is a book that imagines a series of murders that were made into horror movies which the book in turn narrativises, riffing off of and parodying horror films as a genre but with a fanboy-like encyclopedic knowledge thereof. Meanwhile, *Zombie Bake Off* (2012) describes a bake off in Lubbock, Texas that is crashed by a group of profession wrestlers, in all their over-the-top glory. Tensions rise, but culminate when a batch of infected baked goods start turning characters into zombies.

Such work begs the question, what is Native American literature? Is it work that carries overt themes easily recognized as unique to Native people? Is it literature with clearly Native characters? If so, then much of Jones's work does not fit the bill. But, why should Native literature be relegated to only those definitions? Why should Native authors not be allowed to pursue their narrative passions, whether they examine the white citizens of a North Dakota town as in Erdrich's *The Beet Queen* or the zombies and monsters that populate Jones's work? The simple and obvious answer, of course, is that they shouldn't. Native literature and Native writers are profoundly and increasingly diverse in their work, and Native novels continue to express that diversity.

Notes

1 The rise of multiculturalism during this era is certainly closely related to all of these events.
2 We should note as well that the increase in Native writing and publishing in this era mirrors those of other marginalized communities (in Chicano literature, for example) in which veterans, taking advantage of the GI Bill, often became the first people in their families to attend and graduate from colleges and universities.
3 Bearheart begins with a chapter titled "Letter to the Reader" a strangely Victorian invocation, allusion and device. In some ways, Vizenor's move from poetry to the novel is akin to the shift in generic emphasis between the Romantic and Victorian eras. Of course, this convention predates these eras, tracing back to the dawn of the novel in *Don Quixote* and continuing through perhaps its most famous U.S. iteration in *Uncle Tom's Cabin*. However, this epistolary frame exists only in this chapter, which Teuton asserts moves this later version of the novel from "political statement" to one that "highlights aesthetic issues" (105).
4 All Native Americans acquired citizenship in 1924, though some Native people were granted citizenship in exchange for accepting allotment.
5 Alexie asserted between the publication of his novels, for example, "I think I'm a poet with short story inclinations" (Poetry Society).

Works cited

Alexie, Sherman. *The Absolutely True Diary of a Part-Time Indian*. New York: Little, Brown, 2007.
———. *Flight*. New York: Grove, 2007.
———. *Indian Killer*. New York: Warner, 1996.
———. *Reservation Blues*. New York: Warner, 1996.

Bevis, William. "Native American Novels: Homing In." *Recovering the Word: Essays on Native American Literature*. Ed. Brian Swann & Arnold Krupat. Berkeley: University of California Press, 1987. 580–620.

Blaeser, Kimberly M. *Gerald Vizenor: Writing in the Oral Tradition*. Norman: University of Oklahoma Press, 1996.

Callahan, S. Alice. *Wynema: A Child of the Forest*. Ed. A. LaVonne Brown Ruoff. Lincoln: University of Nebraska Press, 1997.

Erdrich, Louise. *The Antelope Wife*. New York: Harper, 1998.

——. *The Beet Queen*. New York: Bantam, 1986.

——. *Love Medicine*. New York: Harper, 1984.

——. *The Round House*. New York: Harper, 2012.

——. *Tracks*. New York: Holt, 1988.

Jones, Stephen Graham. *The Bird is Gone*. Tallahassee, FL: FC2, 2003.

——. *Demon Theory*. San Francisco: MacAdams/Cage, 2006.

——. *The Fast Red Road: A Plainsong*. Tallahassee, FL: FC2, 2002.

——. *Ledfeather*. Tuscaloosa, FL: FC2, 2008.

——. *Zombie Bake Off*. Portland, OR: Lazy Fascist Press, 2012.

Lincoln, Kenneth. *The Native American Renaissance*. Berkeley: University of California Press, 1983.

McNickle, D'Arcy. *The Hungry Generations*. Ed. Birgit Hans. Albuquerque: University of New Mexico Press, 2007.

——. *The Surrounded*. Albuquerque: University of New Mexico Press, 1964.

Momaday, N. Scott. *House Made of Dawn*. New York: Harper, 1968.

Mourning Dove. *Cogewea the Half Blood: A Depiction of the Great Montana Cattle Range*. Lincoln: University of Nebraska Press, 1981.

Owens, Louis. "The Red Road to Nowhere: D'Arcy McNickle's *The Surrounded* and *The Hungry Generations*." *American Indian Quarterly* 13.3 (1989): 239–48.

Poetry Society of America. "A Conversation: Sherman Alexie and Diane Thiel." Web. Accessed 14 Dec. 2014. https://www.poetrysociety.org/psa/poetry/crossroads/interviews/2009-09-04/

Ridge, John Rollin. *The Life and Adventures of Joaquín Murrieta, the Celebrated California Bandit*. Norman: University of Oklahoma Press, 1955.

Silko, Leslie Marmon. *Ceremony*. New York: Penguin, 1977.

——. *Gardens in the Dunes*. New York: Scribner, 1999.

Smoke Signals. Chris Eyre, dir. Miramax, 1998.

Spry, Adam. "'It May be Revolutionary in Character:' *The Progress*, a New Tribal Hermeneutics, and the Literary Re-expression of the Anishinaabe Oral Tradition in *Summer in the Spring*." *The Poetry and Poetics of Gerald Vizenor*. Ed. Deborah L. Madsen. Albuquerque: University of New Mexico Press, 2012. 23–42.

Teuton, Christopher B. *Deep Waters: The Textual Continuum in American Indian Literature*. Lincoln: University of Nebraska Press, 2010.

Treuer, David. *Native American Fiction: A User's Manual*. Saint Paul, MN: Graywolf Press, 2006.

——. *The Translation of Dr. Apelles*. New York: Vintage, 2008.

Vizenor, Gerald. *Bearheart: The Heirship Chronicles*. Minneapolis: University of Minnesota Press, 1990.

——. *Blue Ravens*. Middletown, CT: Wesleyan University Press, 2014.

——. *Darkness in Saint Louis Bearheart*. St. Paul, MN: Truck Press, 1978.

——. *Fugitive Poses: Native American Scenes of Absence and Presence*. Lincoln: University of Nebraska Press, 2000.

——. *Griever: An American Monkey King in China*. Minneapolis: University of Minnesota Press, 1987.

——. *Hiroshima Bugi: Atomu 57*. Lincoln: University of Nebraska Press, 2003.

NATIVE AMERICAN NOVELS

——. *Manifest Manners: Narratives on Postindian Survivance*. Lincoln: University of Nebraska Press, 1999.

——. *Summer in the Spring: Anishinaabe Lyric Poems and Stories*. Norman: University of Oklahoma Press, 1993.

Vizenor, Gerald & A. Robert Lee. *Postindian Conversations*. Lincoln: University of Nebraska Press, 1999.

Vonnegut, Kurt. *Slaughterhouse Five*. New York: Delacorte, 1969.

Welch, James. *The Heartsong of Charging Elk*. New York: Anchor, 2001.

Womack, Craig. *Drowning in Fire*. Tucson: University of Arizona Press, 2001.

——. *Red on Red: Native American Literary Separatism*. Minneapolis: University of Minnesota Press, 1999.

39

Film in the Blood, Something in the Eye
Voice and Vision in Native American Cinema

Theodore C. Van Alst Jr.

Ask, "What is Native American cinema?" of just about anyone, and you'll likely get a very different answer from every person you question. Responses (with exceptions, certainly) will range from "Is there really such a thing as Native American cinema" (one of my long-ago advisors)? to "I've never heard of that before" (students, with fair regularity), or even, "I loved *Dances with Wolves*" (still). These reactions of course reflect the influence of Hollywood, American ideology, and cold hard cash. It follows then that much Native (including here American Indian/Native American, First Nations, Aboriginal, Indigenous, and other terms that reflect indigenous peoples in the language) film comprises resistance. There is an impulse to tell everyone that we are still here, that Manifest Destiny (both in the United States and globally) was not a successful project, that with the advent of digital cinema we can tell our stories, and that often we must expand and rethink not just modes of production, but also modes of distribution. Many Native productions evince a decidedly activist streak: they often focus on issues of indigenous language loss and reclamation, and the land itself takes on the role of a cinematic character in ways not seen in non-Native films. Indigenous cinema frequently offers a certain, not necessarily *poly*vocality, but rather an *equi*vocality to its characters that makes the viewer pay close attention to who is speaking as well as what they are saying. This is often crucial in the context of the social and cultural relationships being portrayed. Narration matters.

A long cinematic history of Hollywood speaking on "behalf" of Native people and characters necessitates a reworking of and attention to narrative structure in Native film. A sample filmography of works ostensibly *about* rather than *by* Native people would include films ranging from Thomas Edison's *Sioux Ghost Dance* (1894) and D.W. Griffith's *The Battle at Elderbush Gulch* (1913) to the much-beloved *Last of the Mohicans* (adapted, made, and remade at least 18 times with a new production rumored to be currently in the works), the 2013 remake of *The Lone Ranger,* and yet another version of *Peter Pan* (2015). In contrast, what we might term "Native Cinema" – that is, films made *by* Native artists – would include works that range from James Young Deer and Lillian St. Cyr's body of work that dates from 1910, right up through the work of Alanis Obamsawin including *Incident at Restigouche* (1984) and *Kanehsatake: 270 Years of Resistance* (1993); Chris Eyre's *Smoke Signals* (1998), *Skins* (2002), *Law and Order* (2008), and *Friday Night Lights* (2008–2011); Sterlin Harjo's *Four Sheets to the Wind* (2007), *Barking Water* (2009), *This May Be the Last*

458

Time (2014) and *Meeko* (2015); and many more young Indigenous filmmakers who seem to expand the form almost daily. As Sium and Ritskes note:

> Indigenous stories are a reclamation of Indigenous voice, Indigenous land, and Indigenous sovereignty. They are vital to decolonization. Indigenous storytelling works to both deconstruct colonial ways of coming to know, as well as construct alternatives – recognizing that these two processes do not happen in a linear trajectory; if we are waiting for the dismantling of colonial structures before we focus on rebuilding Indigenous and decolonial alternatives, we will always be too late.
>
> (viii)

I posit that echoes of Louis Riel's 1885 words, "My people will sleep for one hundred years, but when they awake it will be the artists who give them back their spirit" (Cariou & Sinclair 6), now arc and shine in the digital world; when Native people use digital and social media we often imbue them with both latent and realized artistic tendencies and indigenous aesthetics. We know how to transmit our message in recognizable and resonant ways, and have adopted social and digital media in exciting and effective fashion. We consider that the Native Literary Renaissance told our stories after 500 years of contact in inventive and poignant, lyrical and gritty, incisive and shattering ways. As we begin to imagine ourselves after a millennium or more of interaction with settlers, it has become obvious that we must engage in long-term planning and stewardship as well as a reclamation of Indigenous spaces and places to ensure the survival of everyone. We recognize that the past centuries have not been good for the land, water, air, and animals under the suzerainty of settler administration. While it may not be practical to imagine these realms without the settlers, we can certainly conceive of these lands without their (guiding) hands. Filmic artists show us and tell us what these worlds can be; activists work digitally to translate "moccasins on the ground" to make them realities. From the Idle No More movement to the Cowboy and Indian Alliance against the KXL pipeline, Indigenous people turn cyberdreams into concrete change for all. Vital intersections between Native artistry and activism are more than compelling Indigenous subjects for study; they are essential components in everyone's understanding of this new millennium.

This, then, is no small part of the larger aim of Native cinema. To tell Native stories. Stories that resist colonial structures, stories that reclaim histories and rewrite understanding. But ultimately Native cinema tells stories that transcend, that imagine futures free of shackling tropes and expectations, futures devoid of both othering gazes and unreal expectations. Stories, then, that are in the end, merely human. Human stories. Those are the stories of Native cinema. As we move deeper into this Indigenous millennium, these are the stories that will point the way forward.

James Welch's novel *Winter in the Blood* is a startling and plaintive work about love, loss, redemption, and life lived hard, but it's also an experimental and humorous look at the America of its time, an invaluable snapshot in the understanding of our shared experience. Its particular Hi-Line setting is finite enough to launch into universals, and its author- and readership is at times uniquely Indian. Can hometown-boys-made-good Alex and Andrew Smith direct this micro-epic work in a way that captures all of those locavore desires and nostalgic cravings, while producing a work macro- enough to engage the rest of us, Native and non-Native, Montanan and non-Montanan alike? Their cinematic adaptation of

Winter in the Blood signals a new page in Native/non-Native artistic collaboration, and this chapter will examine in part a cinematic adaptation of a pillar of the Native American Literary Renaissance, and also consider a key difference between Native and non-Native filmic adaptations.

Of course we have to ask: does the novel *Winter in the Blood* actually call out for a cinematic adaption? Writer Ken White seemed to think so (Person, n. pag.), the Smith brothers readily agreed, and Sherman Alexie said: "There are no two white boys in the world I would trust more with this book." (Kramer n. pag.). My answer is: with (or better, because of) its unnamed (and excitingly, potentially unreliable) narrator, it just might. I will also add that the novel itself – full of experimental moments, shifting chronologies, smash and jump cuts, and skewed eyeline matches – seems preternaturally disposed to cinematic translation. Before proceeding, though, we would do well to consider the *how* of what such an adaption might look like, since, as we know, for classic Hollywood productions, the camera ideally serves as an anonymous, reliable, single-thread narrator. However, the filmic adaptation of *Winter in the Blood* immediately indicates that we may be moving towards an encounter with something else entirely, because in the Smiths' particular vision the narrator is named, rather than leaving him in the form of Welch's still-undeveloped, free-floating signifier. Starting from this point of view then, I will investigate the ways in which this particular cinematic adaptation achieves but one of many possible translations.

Of particular interest is the reliability of this newly named narrator. In the novel, after the scene where he and Dougie roll the white man in the bar, we end with him outside Minough's; this is followed by a smash cut to a new chapter that finds him sitting and drinking with the as-yet-unidentified Airplane Man (this of course, is The Man Who Tore Up His Plane Ticket – a name which I've always seen as a teasing "Indian-style" name – but who will, for the purposes of discussion and ease of use, be known by his movie moniker, "Airplane Man"), squirming under the awkwardness of possibly chatting up the man he just helped his "wife's" brother rob in a tavern bathroom. It is not entirely clear that he did not roll the Airplane Man in the bathroom (just as it is never entirely clear whether the narrator and Agnes are actually married), and the ambiguity in the transition from the Airplane Man's address to the narrator, "we're trying to solve *your* problems" results in our narrator's internal dialogue reading thusly: "The only problem I had now was trying to stay out of the way of the man I had helped Dougie roll. That was the only problem that was still clear to me. The others had gone away" (45).

In the film version, he has just helped Dougie roll not a white man but Raymond Long Knife, whose drunken rodeoesque kicking in the imaginary chute of the stall floor either kills the now much louder and seemingly non-diegetic jukebox that has been rocking along during the scene or – since we cannot know the layout of the bar – the jukebox is simply close enough to the wall to which it backs up to make the needle jump off the record. The confusion of those of us who are working with both the film and the novel is compounded by the fact that actor David Morse (who plays the Airplane Man) has dyed his hair red for the film, as we recall the description in the novel of the drunk: "Beside him a large white man dozed, his head resting on his freckled forearms. His hat was pushed back almost to his shoulders. A cigarette smoldered in the ashtray next to his curly red hair" (42). At this moment in the film, and those that follow? Well, for now we'll just say: the film is starker and colder than the novel. These tones and tales seem readily apparent in Chaske

FILM IN THE BLOOD, SOMETHING IN THE EYE

Spencer's complex and inspired portrayal of Virgil First Raise. Recalling that the narrator has no name in the novel, Andrew Smith told Peter Orner in a *Cut Bank* interview:

> You know, Jim [Welch] doesn't name the narrator/hero in the novel, because he says he hadn't earned a name until the last pages of the story. We've called our hero "Virgil," but you'll never hear another character in the film call him by his name: he hasn't earned it yet.
>
> (Orner n. pag.)

Some thoughts of my own on the naming of the narrator in the cinematic version follow. First of all, I'm going to suggest the principle of "poetic" license. Publius Vergilius Maro, or *Virgil*, as most of us know him, penned a couple of pieces that are likely germane to our writers' vision of just who the younger First Raise is, what he might mean in a broader American context, and what he might mean to this story. Consider Virgil's *The Aeneid*, the Homerian epic that works to describe Aeneas's founding of a nation that would become an empire. Reading/viewing for mood and tone, and searching for redemption as we frequently do here in America, we recall the presence of the fictionalized Virgil himself as Dante Alighieri's tour guide through the *Inferno* and *Purgatorio* of *La Divina Commedia*. I've discarded Robbie Robertson's Virgil Caine from *The Night They Drove Old Dixie Down*, and pretty quickly ruled out James Gandolfini's Virgil in *True Romance*, but, as in all works of fiction, you're welcome to read as you will. The undetermined source of the narrator's name sets the tone for our inquiry into the unreliability of just about every character in the novel and the film (mentioning of course that other kind of "unreliability" that we see in so many stories, that of Virgil's tragic father, the elder First Raise).

Inside the Pomp Room we are introduced to the invisible cigarettes of the ever-smoke-ring-blowing Barmaid; Virgil describing how:

> Standing a few feet away from me, a barmaid leaned on her tray. She poked the ice cubes in her Coke with her finger and glared at herself in the mirror. Although I couldn't see a cigarette near her, she was blowing smoke rings.
>
> (47)

She implies a wink through the fourth wall when she tiredly responds, "I wouldn't know – I'm new here," to the narrator, who has been complaining, "I don't understand the people around here." That wink comes alive when he says, "She blew more smoke rings. There was still no cigarette near her" (48). And at the Airplane Man's own introduction he "winked at the bartender, who had been listening, then ordered another boilermaker for me and a double scotch for himself" (46). Since we are on the subject of winking and its possible signification regarding unreliability, among other things, I will add here the figure of the narrator as well, who says, "I winked at myself in the mirror and the barmaid, who had returned, glared back" (48). What then to make of this bawdy and misogynistic passage from Lame Bull delivered with what other than:

> "All right then ..." He leaned forward and winked at me. "Boy, you're going to catch her this time, I feel it in my bone – I mean bones – catchum, holdum, shrinkum – you got to treat these women rough once in a while or else they forget."
>
> (71)

Well now. The "winking" motif keeps going. The Airplane Man: "'But there are no fish in the river.' He grimaced. Then winked ..." (87). The bartender at Gable's: "... He jerked his thumb at me and winked at another customer. Randolph Scott" (117). All this winking somehow ... dates this novel, even more explicitly than the Randolph Scott reference. Do people wink anymore? Is that still a thing? An unironic wink? Who winks? Now that we are on edge and more than a little uncomfortable, we note that the mood continues. Consider the odd sequence where the Barmaid insists she caught "seven goldeyes in the river just that morning" and then is rushed by the Airplane Man who "suddenly ... jerked upright and roared" before "swerving out the door and into the night at the last minute ..." (51). This slides directly into the bizarre opening dream sequence of Chapter 16 (52), complete with a girl "gutted like a fat rainbow" and "wanted men with ape faces, cuffed sleeves, and blue hands," whereupon Teresa gives birth to Amos the orange-legged duck. As our narrator slouches toward alertness, we are left as always, deeply (but mostly happily) unsure of his reliability; he reassures us that our perception should in fact be reeling by telling us, "I don't know whether I was asleep or awake during this last scene, but the boy changed quickly into a pale ceiling" (53). And the narrator himself certainly does not help his own case for reliability: here he says about the Airplane Man and the Barmaid:

> He was from the east, and she from the west, they couldn't have known each other. Or it had been a joke, they had played a trick on me – but for what purpose, I was nothing to anybody. Or – that's it. I had imagined the whole thing in my drunken state. Neither of them existed ...
>
> (57)

In the film version of this sequence, not to be outdone, the Airplane Man pitches in with his own brand of unreliability, first setting up the narrator with a sharp truth: "I saw you on the ankle express this morning." The narrator dutifully flashes back via a lovely montage of the hood ornament of a driverless '55 or '56 Mercury Monterey (Figure 39.1); a bloody, muddy leg and boot (Figure 39.2); and a deep-focus Hi-Line twilight with a fuzzy, unnamed figure in the foreground (Figure 39.3), – all accompanied by the trailing blast of a car horn. The Airplane Man's pitch to get First Raise on board as his driver into Canada lurches down a bit of a drunken alley though, when he follows that up by saying, "Seeking visions, or whatever it is you people do." The significance of this line is particularly ambiguous. The sequence began with the Airplane Man ordering another round of drinks by saying, "Barmaid. Circle the wagon," and he follows this allusion to generic Westerns by alluding loosely to the vision-quest. We – and our heavy-lidded narrator, who narrows his eyes and says, "Hey. You don't know me" – are quickly thrown back into the arena of unreliability, when the Airplane Man replies: "Oh, sure I do, brother. Helped you out of that fracas the other night." "Fracas?" Here, the Airplane Man gets his own green-tinted absinthian dream-like close-up, and busts out some old-timey boxing moves as he recounts the barroom brawl (Figure 39.4).

"Breaks my little glass heart, you don't remember ... well, we were all Dick Van Dyke drunk. It gets a little foggy." Viewers are probably feeling a bit foggy, too – perfectly, woozily so – as one of the director/writers, Alex Smith clarifies:

Figure 39.1 The Mercury Monterey. *Winter in the Blood*, Copyright Ranchwater Films, 2013. 98 minutes, released by Kino Lorber Films. Alex and Andrew Smith, Dirs. Reprinted with the permission of Alex and Andrew Smith.

Figure 39.2 The Boot. *Winter in the Blood*, Copyright Ranchwater Films, 2013. 98 minutes, released by Kino Lorber Films. Alex and Andrew Smith, Dirs. Reprinted with the permission of Alex and Andrew Smith.

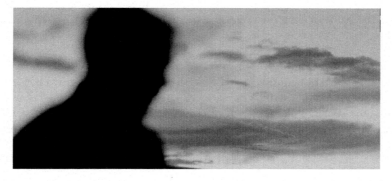

Figure 39.3 Hi-Line Sunset. *Winter in the Blood*, Copyright Ranchwater Films, 2013. 98 minutes, released by Kino Lorber Films. Alex and Andrew Smith, Dirs. Reprinted with the permission of Alex and Andrew Smith.

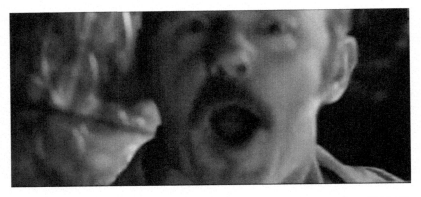

Figure 39.4 The Airplane Man. *Winter in the Blood*, Copyright Ranchwater Films, 2013. 98 minutes, released by Kino Lorber Films. Alex and Andrew Smith, Dirs. Reprinted with the permission of Alex and Andrew Smith.

"Escape and father and danger." "He's really kind of basically trying to get Virgil to a place of uncertainty"…"Jagged shards poking through the veneer of happy drunkenness. There's danger here … this is not a savior … ." "But this hints that there might be a vision quest." "Things aren't as they seem … it's sort of a noir Castaneda/Hunter Thompson disorientation …" "Noir elements … with First Raise as a dupe, a mule …" "White father white hunter all jumbled together in his cracked skull" "It's a warning to Virgil."

(Alex Smith interview)

All of this unreliability in the narration allows for the floating (and fuzzily drunken) feeling that gives us the sense of being unmoored through most of the film, as if we can't quite believe or grasp what's happening to our narrator, and to us by extension. Late in the film only a particularly brutal slap, a vicious moment of the Real, is able to break us out of what's been happening. This portion of the scene between Virgil and Marlene plays in the film just as it does in the novel, with one significant change. Proceeding from Virgil's attack on Marlene the scene in both the novel and the film play this way, with the passage in the novel ending with Marlene's words:

"What did you do that for?" she cried. "Jesus Christ!" The muscles in her neck stood out as she strained to keep her head up. Her arms were pinned beneath my knees. "What kind of a sonofabitch are you, anyway?"… In one tremendous effort she tried to roll me off, but I sat, grave as a stone, on her belly. "If only I could get loose, you dirty bastard, if only …" – her voice strained and muffled against her teeth …"If only I could get loose."

(123)

In the film, "You and me both" replies the narrator. This scene, then, is that irruptive moment of violence hurtling us in crashing fashion to the realization of the pain we inflict, and the pain we've been in, the pain we are often born to, but also the pain we can leave behind. This voice, perhaps more than anything in the film, is what we would do well to take away: the voice of the ultimately reliable narrator we hear in the end.

And here near the end of the film, after the slap, the moment of breath that should linger for a beat or two longer than imaginably might be considered normal—the beat, the echo, that come-back, then, is the void filled in hopeful fashion by Native filmmakers in contrast to one of the things that is happening in the filmed version of *Winter in the Blood*. In review, *Winter* has one memorable instance of Native language use, and that particular moment is very interesting. When addressing his grandmother at one point in the film, Virgil uses the term *unci*, which is a Lakota word rather than Blackfeet (in Pikuni, he'd say "*naahs*"), one that shows actor Chaske Spencer's roots, and brings me to my second point of discussion.

Native language use in non-Native made film signifies many other issues – resistance to language loss, U.S. boarding school language termination programs and other official policies to destroy Native languages, current tribal programs to revitalize and even reconstitute Native languages – which fall largely outside the scope of this chapter, but I can at least begin that conversation here. Director Neil Diamond provides a wonderful point of departure for this discussion of filmic language in his 2008 release *Reel Injun*. There, he shows Diné (Navajo) resistance on screen as he describes how Diné actors would go "off-script in some scenes, joking around, in their language," and no one ever bothered to translate this Native dialogue. A memorable scene between an officer played by Troy Donahue and an uncredited "Chief" from Raoul Walsh's last offering, *A Distant Trumpet* (1964) plays thus:

2ND LT. MATTHEW "MATT" HAZARD. If I do not return, General Quait will find you.
WAR EAGLE – CHIEF OF THE CHIRICAHUA APACHE ARMIES. (In Diné) Just like a snake, you'll be crawling in your own shit.
2ND LT. MATTHEW "MATT" HAZARD. No. He is not a fool. You are.
WAR EAGLE – CHIEF OF THE CHIRICAHUA APACHE ARMIES. Obviously you can't do anything to me. You're a snake crawling in your own shit.

The actor playing "War Eagle" gives us far more interesting retorts than what was subtitled in English on screen, phrases like "I hear you speak. I do not hear it in my heart." Interestingly (and perhaps presciently), in his *New York Times* review of *A Distant Trumpet*, in the spring of the film's release, Bosley Crowther observes that:

The only bright thing in the picture comes when "Shavetail" Lieutenant Donahue, attached to isolated Fort Dependence in Arizona in 1883, finally gets through to Chief War Eagle to ask him to surrender peacefully, and the chief's conversation in his native language is translated with English subtitles at the bottom of the frame. But the humor of this is missed by those who made the film. They play it as straight as the expression – the only one – on Mr. Donohue's face.

(Crowther n. pag.)

Time Out London's review, "A Distant Trumpet," goes one better, referring to the "brilliant" photography, while mentioning that it tends to have its cake and eat it by indulging in a spectacular massacre before introducing the liberal message, but still goes further than most in according respect to the Indian by letting him speak his own language (with subtitles).

(*Time Out* n. pag.)

As you can see, the use of Native language by non-Native directors can be problematic at the least. However, the use of Native language by Native filmmakers is another issue entirely. As I mentioned earlier, language loss and recovery are frequently subjects of exploration as well as thematic elements in Native cinema. In the interests of space, I will focus briefly on the work of just one director here.

Jeff Barnaby's short (11 minutes) film *From Cherry English* (2005) immediately strikes the viewer as one of those works from an artist we are lucky to run into maybe a handful of times in our lives. His subsequent offerings have reinforced that belief in spectacular ways. Barnaby has tackled huge subjects: language and culture loss in *From Cherry English* (which uses a section of Rita Joe's beautiful work "I Lost My Talk") and 2010's *File Under Miscellaneous* (also inspired by a poem, in this case, Neruda's "Walking Around"); drugs and addiction in *The Colony* (2007); and in his latest film, *Rhymes for Young Ghouls* (2013), perhaps the biggest issue of them all: residential schools. Throughout his work, Barnaby bares the fangs of a Native language activist. By turns subtle and savage, he shows us tongues that have been lost, and then found, but were never gone. Whereas non-Native writers and directors use language to place Native characters in the past or otherwise fix them in time, Native writers and directors use Indian languages to project their people into the future.

As David Treuer writes in his discussion of Welch's *Fools Crow* in his book *Native American Fiction*:

it is excruciatingly difficulty to create fully realized Indian characters who exist in their language ... Every other Native American novel, in order to overcome the difficult task of creating Indians in English, has characters who are distant from their cultures and themselves, and the novels describe a process of reaching back.

(107)

Barnaby and others – such as Cedar Sherbert and his 2006 work *Gesture Down (I Don't Sing)*, which is also derived from a poem, this time James Welch's "Gesture Down to Guatemala") – work against the creation of this "distance" for their characters, this divide of language that places Natives in an ideologically constructed past. Rather, these Native filmmakers use language in a way that instantly propels their characters (we might say even projects them) into the future via their tribal languages.

This deeper engagement with communities is a hallmark of many Native directors. In Alex Rogalski's 2007 interview at the Toronto International Film Festival with then first-time attendee Jeff Barnaby, Rogalski reminds the young director: "In an interview about your film *From Cherry English*, I read a quote that said, 'I wrote this piece because I was so pissed off at my own generation.'" To be sure, in that line Barnaby was expressing disappointment at the state of certain issues, but we should by no means construe any cynicism on the director's part. In that same interview, he goes on to say:

Cherry was a funny movie, because it didn't really reflect my artistic ideology so much so much as my aesthetic. The poem it was based on encompassed more of how I thought at the time. I kind of looked at it as a commissioned piece and an opportunity to do a calling card on somebody else's dime. Plus it was for television so my normal heathen approach to filmmaking had to be curbed in lieu of no nudity, minimal violence, and a lead that wasn't a total fucking train wreck, which was fine since I knew what I was getting myself into. ... So when I did *Cherry* I wanted to do something that wasn't so heavy on characterizations and told more of the story through allegory: the allegory revolving around the loss of language and culture to an ever-growing non-native presence.

(Rogalski n. pag.)

Barnaby shows us that resistance via Mi'gMaq language is threaded throughout the narrative, rather than spotlighted or put on focused display. The form is used to describe the function in his films, and the language appears and disappears in aesthetic rather than didactic ways. His passion for his culture and his love for his people infuse his work with an elevated sense of purpose but also a core of incandescence that transcends his often-bleak settings. He provides more insights:

Well first off lemme just say I love my culture, I love being Mi'gMaq, if I were beside God while he was slapping me together, and he was going through his rolodex of races I would stop him at Indian and point out Mi'gMaqs, that very reserve, those very people, this very time. Right Now. Contemporary. And it's really that love affair, that fascination that drives a lot of my characterizations.

(Rogalski n. pag.)

Therein lies the drive that pushes his films (which he writes, directs, edits, and scores) into realms not often approached by other directors. The industry has taken note; Barnaby's films have received multiple awards and accolades. With the feature-length *Rhymes for Young Ghouls* gaining regular distribution (Monterey Media), iTunes and Netflix releases, and DVD sales on Amazon, Native film excitedly looks forward to more from Barnaby. Even as he redefines the language of cinema in the twenty-first century for broader audiences, he continuously advocates for Native language and culture on behalf of us all.

When we return then to Native language use in the Smiths' *Winter in the Blood*, we see that the film does not even straddle a middle ground in this regard. It does not project its users into either the past or the future. Significantly, though, it reflects the collaborative nature of the film and a change in the air. Where in the "old days" Spencer's use of Indian language would have been cut, dubbed, or otherwise edited, the Smiths shrug, and continue the scene. Their cinematic adaptation of *Winter in the Blood* thus gives us reason to reconsider Treuer's sentiments about "almost-happy endings" (184). The Smiths' end scene gives us a seemingly redeemed narrator; a younger version of himself and his brother heading into a sunny field of bright future while an uplifting score rises in the background. Despite the fact that we of course know from our reading of the novel that it will end otherwise, it nevertheless provides a happy visual finale. As we reflect on the ending of both the novel and the film, and the desires of wide-audience readers (and here, "viewers"), we learn a bit more from Treuer: "What readers seem to want and the Native American context can provide is the ultimate evolution of American literature, a kind of literature satisfying to everyone: tragedies with happy endings" (185). And while the necessary and much-needed adaptation of James Welch's novel satisfies quite a few constituencies and achieves much in the field of collaborative filmmaking, we would do well to consider the efforts of Native filmmakers like Jeff Barnaby. His growing body of work has yet to produce anything remotely resembling a happy ending, but the demands of his vision and voice and the stories he tells grow with each new work at the start of this Indigenous millennium.

Works cited

Barnaby, Jeff. Dir. *The Colony*. Perf. Glen Gould, Kaniehtiio Horn. Prospector Films, 2007. DVD.
——. Dir. *File Under Miscellaneous*. Perf. Glen Gould. Prospector Films, 2010. DVD
——. Dir. *From Cherry English*. Perf. Nathaniel Arcand. 2005. DVD.
——. Dir. *Rhymes for Young Ghouls*. Perf. Kawennáhere Devery Jacobs, Glen Gould. Prospector Films, 2013. Film, DVD.
Cariou, Warren & Nigaanwewidam Sinclair. *Manitowapow: Aboriginal Writings from the Land of Water*. Winnipeg, MB: HighWater, 2011.
Crowther, Bosley. "*Muscle Beach Party* (1964) Donahue and Suzanne Pleshette in Western Movies." *New York Times* 28 May 1964. Web. Accessed 9 Dec. 2014. http://www.nytimes.com/movie/revie w?res=9D01E2DB1F3AE13ABC4051DFB366838F679EDE
Diamond, Neil. Dir. *Reel Injun*. Rezolution Pictures, 2009. DVD.
Joe, Rita. "I Lost My Talk." *Synthesis/Regeneration* 5 (Winter 1993). Web. Accessed 17 Dec. 2014. http://www.greens.org/s-r/05/05-32.html
Kramer, Gary M. "Sherman Alexie: 'It's funny that Hollywood would hire an Indian to make white people more likable.'" www.salon.com 31 Oct. 2014. Web. Accessed 1 Nov. 2014. http://www. salon.com/2014/10/31/sherman_alexie_it's_funny_that_hollywood_would_hire_an_indian_to_ make_white_people_more_likable/
Orner, Peter. "Translating James Welch." *CutBank Literary Magazine*. Web. Accessed 9 Sept. 2014. http://www.cutbankonline.org/2013/10/translating-james-welch/
Person, Daniel. "Winter in the Blood." Tvfilm. 9 Sept. 2014. Web. Accessed 1 Nov. 2014. http:// www.cowboysindians.com/Cowboys-Indians/July-2013/Winter-In-The-Blood/
Rogalski, Alex. "Jeff Barnaby and 'The Colony' Directors." www.tiff07.ca Toronto International Film Festival 2007. Web. Accessed 21 Aug. 2007.
Sherbert, Cedar. Dir. *Gesture Down/I Don't Sing*. US: 2006.
Sium, Aman & Eric Ritskes. "Speaking Truth to Power: Indigenous Storytelling as an Act of Living Resistance." *Decolonization: Indigeneity, Education & Society* 2. 1 (2013): i–x. Web. Accessed 1 Feb. 2015. www.decolonization.org
Smith, Alex & Andrew Smith. Dirs. *Winter in the Blood*. Ranchwater, 2013. Film, DVD.
Time Out London. "A Distant Trumpet." n.d., n. pag. Web. Accessed 9 Dec. 2014. http://www.timeout. com/london/film/a-distant-trumpet
Treuer, David. *Native American Fiction: A User's Manual*. Minneapolis, MN. Graywolf Books, 2006.
Walsh, Raoul. Dir. *A Distant Trumpet*. Perf. Troy Donahue, Suzanne Pleshette, Claude Akins. Warner Bros, 1964. Warner VOD. 28 Sept. 2013. Accessed 9 Dec. 2014.
Welch, James. "Gesture Down to Guatemala." *Riding the Earthboy 40*. 1971. Rpt. New York: Penguin, 2004. 12.
——. *Winter in the Blood*. New York: Penguin Books, 1986.

40

Indigenous Uncanniness
Windigo Revisited and Popular Culture

Sarah Henzi

The field of Indigenous literatures of North America focuses largely on the novel, drama and poetry. Certain genres have not been given sufficient, if any, critical reception within the field: science fiction, fantasy, the graphic novel, and the (revisited) gothic novel. These alternative works seek to bring the supernatural and the mythical up-to-date and into dialogue with the modern world: *Windigo, Wendigo, Whitiko*, Feaster, Boiled Face, Hair Eater or Skin Walker, vampire or zombie, the mysterious world of shape-shifters and evil creatures has peopled Indigenous mythology since its beginnings, and these creatures are finding their way into contemporary texts. The works I explore in this chapter – Drew Hayden Taylor's *The Night Wanderer: A Native Gothic Novel* (2007) and its graphic novel adaptation *The Night Wanderer: A Graphic Novel* (2013), the comic book *Darkness Calls*, written and illustrated by Steven Keewatin Sanderson (2011), Armand Garnet Ruffo's feature film *A Windigo Tale* (2009) and Kris Happyjack-McKenzie's short film *Windigo* (2009) – all make reference to vampire-like creatures, who more often than not share characteristics of the *Windigo*. More importantly, their reputation instills fear in the other protagonists, leading them to make choices that are at times more deadly than anticipated. "The oldest and strongest emotion of mankind is fear," wrote H. P. Lovecraft, "and the oldest and strongest kind of fear is fear of the unknown" (3); nevertheless, there is an unquenchable fascination with the uncanny amongst readers and viewers of horror and science fiction. The different depictions and uses of the *Windigo* figure in these modern texts and films go a long way to show how works that make up the field of Indigenous literary studies, despite similarities in terms of the questioning of history, intergenerational gaps, colonial violence, and horizontal patterns of abuse, in no way foster the illusion of being a homogenous whole. In addition, it is interesting to consider how an analysis of literary productions now informs that of film production as well, for societal preoccupations have become so complex and opaque that it is impossible to address them via a totalizing practice of critical reading. In this way, the intersections of text and image convey the complexity of the process of textualizing or otherwise materializing storytelling traditions.

Often coined a "Native Canadian Gothic novel," Eden Robinson's *Monkey Beach* (2000) has been thoroughly analyzed by scholars such as Jennifer Andrews, Grace Dillon and Cynthia Sugars. While *Monkey Beach* not only successfully resists and withstands the categorization of its author as "Native" – despite its predominantly Haisla content – it does so in terms of genre categorization as well: by experimenting with a variety of genres – Canadian Gothic, resistance novel, feminist novel, coming-of-age novel, and revenge novel – Robinson circumvents the expectations of her readership by interrupting the narrative with universal issues such as human suffering and family relationships, as well as more contextualized legacies, such as residential schools, loss of culture, and the destruction of traditional land. By mixing "traditional protocols and modern storytelling" – to borrow the subtitle of Robinson's *Sasquatch at Home* – Robinson's work is best explained as a meta-experimentation of different genres. However, some of these genre-specific interpretations are very useful for an analysis of, for instance, Drew Hayden Taylor's self-dubbed "Native Gothic Novel," *The Night Wanderer* (previously a 1992 play entitled "A Contemporary Gothic Indian Vampire Story"), while keeping in mind the technique of mixing traditional protocols and modern storytelling.

In his own words, Drew Hayden Taylor sought to "culturally appropriate a European legend and Indigenize it" (Words Aloud 6 n. pag.). Through Pierre L'Errant, Taylor characterizes the traditional beastly creature of the *Windigo* within a contemporary setting as a vampire; vampirism, with which Pierre is infected, is represented as the European version of "savagery." This, of course, can be seen as a tongue-in-cheek reproach towards Europeans who brought illness over to their colonies, and purposely spread the deadly infections to Indigenous populations. Like Eden Robinson, as suggested by Cynthia Sugars, "the often-invoked negative imagery conventionally associated with Native peoples (hunting, cannibalism, savagery, primitivism, windigo/sasquatch)" (78) is used strategically: Taylor is "appropriating and reformulating the discourse of savagery" (79). As a result, the violent and the barbaric do not only affect the savage/Native, it is at the heart of white society as well: "The savagery associated with aboriginal identity," Sugars continues, "becomes transfigured as a result of the contagion of the non-Native world and metamorphoses into a kind of psychosis – specifically, an all-consuming hunger for physical and psychological violence" (80). However, although Pierre "engages in a ritualized performance of savagery" (81) and thus engages with the image of the savage as soulless "Other," he resists. In the prologue to *The Night Wanderer*, a grandfather tells his grandchildren about a fight that is going on inside him, "a terrible fight between two wolves" (v) – one is evil and one is good. He tells them that the wolf that will win the fight is the one that will be fed the most. The restraint that Pierre shows throughout the novel by neither feeding the evil wolf nor himself enables him to break free from the cycle of violence he has been enduring for over 300 years; his return to Otter Lake is in fact his redemptive journey home, during which he must fast in order to purify himself before dying. Again, by modernizing the creature, Taylor is able to recreate the mythology of a creature that preys on the weak and isolated, to one that helps the weak and isolated, suggesting that even a being as horrible as a vampire can gain redemption, and reclaim a sense of humanity.

Pierre, however, is not a clear-cut vampire/Wendigo; rather, his elusive nature and his lapses in will-power reveal him to be, on the one hand, untrustworthy and potentially dangerous – he tricks the family into taking him in and, until the end of the novel, the reader is led to believe that he has murdered the two bullies Dale and Chucky – but kind and generous on the other – Pierre comfortingly whispers in Anishinaabe to Granny Ruth in her sleep and patiently teaches Tiffany about the area in which she lives and the history of the people that used to live there. "There is no Elder older than me," he shares (215), leading the reader to believe that he also embodies an Elder who is responsible for generational teachings. Ultimately, whether vampire, *Windigo* or *Weesageechak* – or a combination of all three – Pierre certainly puts into question any given assumptions about what divides physical, spiritual, historical, and imaginative worlds.

INDIGENOUS UNCANNINESS AND POPULAR CULTURE

Reading the gothic novel and the graphic novel side by side sheds some light on these gray zones of Pierre's in/humanity and his inner struggle. On two occasions, Tiffany hurts herself while in close proximity to Pierre; visually, the splashes of red against the ominous gray/black background emphasize the shock and power of the vampire's reaction to blood. Towards the end of the novel, although she is at his mercy, Pierre – who is at his hungriest and weakest – spares the suicidal Tiffany; Pierre sees Tiffany's blood, but he also sees her sorrow. There is an interesting difference at this point in the timeline between the novel and the graphic novel: in the latter, as Tiffany admits that death does not seem to be such a bad idea, Pierre retorts "Very well. I can arrange that" (91). Grabbing her by the throat and pinning her against a tree, it seems Tiffany's death is mere moments away. However, in the next panel, Pierre's eyes go from a deep red back to normal: seeing her fear, he releases her. "I'm sorry," he says, "I just – I wanted to shock you into seeing your life more clearly." (92) He then proceeds to make a fire and to tell her the story of the "Native vampire," after which she decides to go home. In the novel, this scene takes place after he has told her the story; having released her, he disappears into the forest, and she makes a run for home – but falls and hits her head. Pierre returns, "[rips] some moss from a nearby rock and lightly [wipes] the blood from her forehead" (211), and carries her home. He whispers one last thing in Anishinaabe to Granny Ruth in her sleep, and leaves. In fact, both Pierre and Tiffany feel and live with a great sense of isolation and loss; Tiffany is at odds with her family, friends and former boyfriend, and was – in a way – abandoned by her mother, while Pierre, due to his "condition," mourns the loss of his family but also the loss of his humanity. Their nightly conversations in the woods and by the lake – places that are themselves reflective of an uneasy in-betweenness – reveal each character's feelings of nostalgia and displacement, and this despite Tiffany's petulant indifference that unnerves Pierre:

> "You know nothing. You are a young, self-obsessed girl who does not care about those around her. There are a hundred million more terrible and horrible things happening in this world than are happening to you. Circumstances and creatures out there that make your problems so insignificant, it's not worth the calories to speak of them"... At this very minute he wanted to leap to his feet, angry and hungry, and pursue the girl until he found her and took what he wanted ... Earlier, when he'd first arrived, he had come dangerously close to harming her. His heightened sense of smell drank in her aroma ... He could see her veins pulsing with blood. Tiffany did not know and would never know how close she came to joining the countless others that had crossed Pierre's path and not left so quickly or easily.
>
> (184–86)

Although Tiffany has been described as "a female protagonist who does not remain passive or become a victim of the Europeanized vampire who has returned home to reclaim his roots" (James 173), her obliviousness towards fear and danger make way for the novel's severe critique of contemporary youth and their detachment from reality:

> Native mythology was full of dangerous and mysterious creatures – wendigos who were cannibal spirits that ate anything and everyone, spirits that took over a body and made people do crazy things, demon women with sharp elbows and teeth in parts the female body that weren't supposed to have teeth. Tiffany occasionally

471

thought of them when she and her friends played video games. The monsters she battled on Darla's Xbox paled in comparison to some of the stories she'd half heard. Luckily, the beasts she fought on screen were far more real to her than whatever might be out there in the woods.

(16)

Thus, while Sugars suggests that "the story of the windigo was originally intended as an ethical warning against giving in to libidinous impulses, it has also been widely used as a metaphor for the violence of imperialism and the sickness at the heart of the modern capitalist world" (79).[1] *The Night Wanderer* – if we consider it as the Annick Press intended it to be, a young adult novel – appeals to a demographic of potential young "lost souls" in need of guidance, albeit disguised as entertainment. The novel addresses a wide range of issues with which teenagers find themselves confronted, like relationships (whether with friends, family or the opposite sex), divorce, school, popularity, isolation/alienation, and mental health issues, most importantly suicide.

Interestingly, in *The Night Wanderer*, although Pierre is able to coax Tiffany away from "contemplating such an action" (193), he himself commits suicide at the end of the novel. Once again, the graphic novel offers more room for interpretation: the final two-page spread shows Pierre being burnt by the rising sun, and his ashes seemingly take on the shape of a bird, possibly a phoenix. The question begs itself: what makes his suicide acceptable and not Tiffany's? Is his suicide to be read rather as a sacrifice, an end to the monster in him? In an interview with Melissa Montovani, when asked why it was "important to [him] for Pierre, the one who knows most about death, to counsel Tiffany rather than Granny Ruth or one of the other elders in the community," Taylor replied:

I wanted to, somewhere, have in the book, a discussion of death from somebody who was "dead" and somebody who was envying it. I think it's in the book some-where where Pierre warns Tiffany about being wanting [sic] death more than life cause "Death lasts longer." They always say the best drug and alcohol counsellors are people who have been addicts themselves. Why can't the same principle apply to this!?

(n. pag.)

Taylor thus exploits the uncanniness of Pierre's character to reach certain pedagogical goals. For instance, Tiffany's resistance to what "she is taught with white people's text-books" is circumvented by "Pierre's tales [which] give her a Native context for the reality of her ancestors" (Montovani n. pag.). However, Taylor is quick to draw a certain distinction:

Keep in mind, me no go university. Me storyteller. But if I am to try to read the subtext of the question and presume the inference to socio-political perception, humanize it. In journalism, we are taught that a thousand people killed in a land-slide is not a story, it's a statistic. People do not relate to statistics. One person, with a face, a name, and a family, killed by that landslide, is a story. People connect to people. Same with history. The overall view is always important, the personal factor is what grabs and keeps people's attention.

(Montovani n. pag.)

"I've heard these stories all my life but –" admits Tiffany. "[But] you thought they were just stories. You must remember, all stories start somewhere," (201) reminds Pierre. Pierre literally embodies the "link [between] two disparate narrative locations" (McLeod 33) and, in the "cocoon of light and heat" (*Night Wanderer* 202) – despite "the potential for tragedy that always hovered above them" (*Night Wanderer* 203) – creates "a place, a place of speaking and narrating" (McLeod 33) the lineage between his/their ancestors and Tiffany. Thus, by emphasizing the importance and continuance of storytelling, *The Night Wanderer* seeks to offer an interpretation of "what being Anishinabe means" (201), a sense of belonging that Tiffany has lacked, and which has contributed to her overwhelming sense of isolation.

While the novel has long been the genre of choice for young adult fiction, other forms – like the graphic novel – are being used since they bring a graphic texture to the story that offers further entry points into understanding the stakes of the narrative, via facial expressions, landscapes, sound effects, captions, dialogue, points of view, sequences, body language and relationships. For instance, Steven Keewatin Sanderson's comic book *Darkness Calls* and Kris Happyjack-McKenzie's short film *Windigo* both portray young boys who – like Tiffany –are at odds with their surroundings, family, and sense of self; and, like *The Night Wanderer*, both stories deal with teen suicide. In the comic book, "the central character [Kyle] is terrorized for his obesity, but it is other Indigenous kids who torment him because of his physical appearance, not because he is Native" (Sheyahshe 151); in Taylor's novel, Tiffany has to deal with the added pressure of being Anishinaabe – one of the main reasons her relationship with Tony (a non-Native) comes to an end – and living on a reserve – thus adding a physical sense of isolation to her already psychological one. In Happyjack-McKenzie's film, the unnamed protagonist is also bullied for his physical appearance – New Wave hairstyle, piercings, black nail polish – and his brooding demeanor; like Kyle, he enjoys drawing monsters and strange creatures. Both stories also speak of the *Windigo*, a creature that preys on the vulnerable; as with Pierre – whether these beings feed on flesh and blood or not – the ominousness of death and danger, an all-consuming hunger for physical and psychological violence, is always present. "Whitiko," warns Kyle's grandfather, "He's a demon spirit who lives in the woods. If you go into his woods he'll draw you in. He'll use your confusion. He'll use your sadness. And he'll use your fears against you, and he'll eat your spirit" (Sanderson 23).

Rather than modernizing the creature itself into a handsome-looking, well-mannered Native vampire like Drew Hayden Taylor, the Windigo in *Darkness Calls* is projected into a contemporary setting but still takes on the features of a "real" monster, physically and psychologically. Weesageechak, on the other hand, is given "modern accoutrements – armored boots, a souped-up motorcycle, and even a samurai sword"; and although "the feathers and breastplate [may] seem to be a step backwards," Sanderson's purpose was

> to present a character that an Aboriginal youth might mentally conjure when hearing a traditional story ... the youth imagines the hero with feathers. Perhaps because of the influence of stereotypic imagery in popular media, even Indigenous kids (who may, at times, have more direct interaction with Native culture) might have their imagination tainted with the notion of obligatory feathers.
>
> (Sheyahshe 151)

Resonant of Sherman Alexie's time-traveling protagonist in *Flight*, Kyle finds himself in the midst of the battle between Whitiko and Weesageechak; this "body-jumping tactic helps widen the social and cultural framework" (Coulombe 130), as well as the gaps between generations. Notwithstanding, it is the intersection between the visual art and the text of the comic book that permits a continuance between the stories – the way in which the grandfather tells it, and the way Kyle perceives it (Figures 40.1 and 40.2).

The grandfather's story of the battle between Whitiko and Weesageechak, told through the medium of the comic book, serves both as a teaching tool, but also as a tribute to the healing practices that are occurring; practices that mix traditional and modern protocols.

> While there is some play on the noble versus savage dichotomy with the use of the uber-good hero and ultra-evil bad guy, this is an expected element in many traditional Native stories … this contrast serves more to support teaching young people ideas of good and bad behaviour than it does ideas of Indigenous people themselves being inherently either good or bad.
>
> (Sheyahshe 152)

Similar to the two wolves in *The Night Wanderer*, the end of *Darkness Calls* "is all about choice between these two opposing forces … it illustrates the humanity of Native people complete with good and bad idiosyncrasies" (152). In the short film, this choice is represented by the protagonist confronting the *Windigo* at the edge of the woods and calling upon his spiritual guide for support; united, their forces send the *Windigo* away, "in search for others who believe in nothing, weak minds … that initiate evil" – namely, the bullies.

Figure 40.1 Steven Keewatin Sanderson, *Darkness Calls* (2005), 24–25. Copyright Steven Keewatin Sanderson. Reprinted with permission.

Figure 40.2 Steven Keewatin Sanderson, *Darkness Calls* (2005), 40–41. Copyright Steven Keewatin Sanderson. Reprinted with permission.

Taken together, the comic book and the film, although distinctly different stylistic approaches to conveying a similar message, are mutually reinforcing, "each in a certain sense completing the other to produce something more nearly resembling a whole, far stronger together than either could hope to be on its own" (Churchill qtd. in Hill 7). Through the use of images – whether in the graphic novel, the comic book or the film – the effect that words alone convey is reinforced, rendering the story of the past as vivid and quasi-immediate as that of the present. This modernization of the story enables the boys' "victory" over the *Windigo*, or rather, their victory over unhappiness, anxiety, suppressed fear and, ultimately, death (Figure 40.3).

Both the comic book and the film work towards suicide prevention amongst teens: it is at that moment that these youth are most vulnerable and on the verge of becoming the lost souls that *Windigo* seeks to feast on. Metaphorically speaking, the more the *Windigo* "eats" the more he searches for food, or calls for "lost souls"; thus the greater the cycle of violence gets. In this way, both works emphasize the dangers of horizontal violence; specifically, that bullying is a form of rhetorical violence that can exacerbate the conditions that lead an individual to feeling isolated. More importantly, they raise important questions as to each individual's involvement in wrongs, enacted or suffered, and how fictional genres are effective tools in the discussion of ethical concerns. In this way, the issues that are explored in *The Night Wanderer*, *Darkness Calls* and *Windigo*, coupled with the combination of graphic and written narratives, do not only speak to a young adult audience: the intersections of genre lend the material "an equally extraordinary accessibility, thereby making 'the Big Picture' available ... to anyone willing and physically able to look at it" (Churchill qtd. in Hill 20). None of these works condemn the community that surrounds their troubled,

Figure 40.3 Steven Keewatin Sanderson, *Darkness Calls* (2005), 44–45. Copyright Steven Keewatin Sanderson. Reprinted with permission.

damaged protagonists. Rather, their personal recovery, resilience, and growth participate in a far wider healing project that involves and nurtures both families and communities as well.

This leads me to Armand Ruffo's film *A Windigo Tale*. *A Windigo Tale* uses the figure of the Windigo to explore the intergenerational effects of residential schools and horizontal violence through the story of Doris and her strained relationship with her daughter, Lilly. Doris is a survivor of the residential school system; during her time there, not only was she abused, she was impregnated and gave birth to Lilly. She was then married off, as a teenager, to a white Christian man, who continued to abuse her, as well as Lilly. Rather than face her husband, Doris sent Lilly away to the city in an attempt to protect her from her stepfather. Although the viewer only gets glimpses of how horrific was the abuse both women suffered, the camera handling gets very shaky at certain times, expressing the anxiety and uncertainty felt by Doris. And the scenes in which Lilly relives the trauma of sexual abuse are all nearly pitch black, pigmenting the narrative with allusions and elliptical gaps. Did it really happen? To whom, by whom, when, and how?

After Doris's husband's death, the Windigo returns, still "hungry," and focused on the consumption and destruction of its former family; he comes to possess Lilly's boyfriend's body, Dave. As he is about to rape Lilly, Doris breaks the cycle of abuse by defending her daughter from the Windigo, in a way that she never defended her from her abusive stepfather. Thus, by forcing Doris and Lilly to confront their trauma, the two women – together – are able to exorcise the Windigo from Dave's body and reverse the powerful hold it has had on their family.

According to Steven Loft, Ruffo's objective was

> to make an engaging movie while simultaneously being respectful to the people who attended the schools – many of whom did not survive – and their experiences. To do so, [he] chose to return to the mythic roots of narrative itself, and [he] therefore drew inspiration from specific Anishinaabe storytelling traditions ... this creature embodies the violence, the pain, the abuse that so many Aboriginal people in this country have, and continue to feel.
>
> (n. pag.)

However, with the *mise en abîme* created by the parallel storyline – a road trip featuring Harold and his grandson Curtis, during which Harold tells the troubled youth this version of the Windigo story – Ruffo also

> re-imagines a conceptual [safe] space for a reattachment to land, culture and philosophy that many argue has been denied to Aboriginal youth. He teaches his grandson, not by cajoling or "disciplining," but by teaching, by storytelling and by re-acculturating the young man.
>
> (Loft n. pag.)

And, much like *The Night Wanderer* and *Darkness Calls*, "Ruffo presents the realization of *choice* as the final solution: here, the issue isn't about defeating spirits like the Wiindigo, but how Wiindigos present us [with] possibilities for dealing with the problems they bring [or represent]" (Sinclair n. pag.; emphasis mine).

Ruffo certainly achieves a distinct complexity by bridging indigenous mythology and commentary on the contemporary ills of Indigenous communities. The *Windigo* in Ruffo's film is not meant to be a supernatural monster that lurks in the shadows of the forest; rather it is representative of the trauma that lurks in the homes and in the minds of survivors and their children, of post-traumatic distress, of the cycles of abuse that are reproduced, and of the breakdown of families. Furthermore, by having the *Windigo* inhabit twice a white, Christian body, Ruffo – much like Drew Hayden Taylor – suggests that this type of "disease" or "contamination" is not only a "Native" issue; it is a *human* issue. Violence both begets and harms indiscriminately.

However, in many ways, we have to allow it to be both: the *Windigo* has to be that unbelievable, monster figure that continues to lurk inside homes as a result of the residential schools, for to restrict the *Windigo* to being one or the other would be to impose a Western interpretation on a story in which mythology is fictional by default – one of the key arguments that counter the interpretation of Eden Robinson's novel *Monkey Beach* as a "gothic" novel; that is, if we accept "gothic" to be an interpretive model that perpetuates colonialism by inserting mythical creatures or ghosts into a framework that mainstream readers assume is *not* real. The reader/viewer thus has to be satisfied with the gaps, the unconventional story structure and, most importantly, the gray areas between what is "real" and what is story.

In her introduction to *Dead North: Canadian Zombie Fiction*, Silvia Moreno-Garcia suggests,

The undead are the blank slate upon which we project our anxieties. Whether these are fears of technology (medical experiments turning people into monsters), an economic collapse (the zombie apocalypse scenario), a runaway consumerist society (zombie consumption generates more consumption) or simply our fear of death and the corruption of our bodies, the zombie serves as a vessel for our collective dread.

(xii)

Whether zombies or *Windigo*, the premise remains: popular culture is of significant value in its ability to speak beyond linguistic, cultural and intergenerational gaps, and enables a new space in which the mythical and the supernatural are brought into dialogue with the contemporary world. What better way to confront the dread of living than by portraying the hardships of the non-living? But what makes Indigenous popular culture creations different from other productions that exploit the uncanny? First, conventional theories of cultural studies or popular culture have not – so far – accounted for the historical and political specificities of Indigenous productions; quite the opposite, since Indigenous peoples continue to be stereotyped, generalized, and misrepresented in popular culture and mainstream media. The works discussed here seek to rectify the falsity of colonial imagery, and to restore and reaffirm a sense of collective memory and belonging – in particular for the benefit of their young protagonists. And second, as suggested by Dean Rader, "Indian invention tropes are neither scientific nor fictional"; rather, they "play with creation stories, shapeshifters, coyotes, and all that is atemporal, creating a *new genre* that takes indigenous aesthetics to new planes" (86; emphasis mine). Popular fiction enables us to explore alternatives to the violence and inequality that surround us and, perhaps most importantly, it reinstates a space in which conversing and living with the supernatural is regarded as potential rather than trial; a space in which "Native vampires" are "cool" (Taylor *Night Wanderer* 206).

Note

1 See, for instance, Richard Van Camp's short story "On the Wings of This Prayer," where global warming and the Alberta Tar Sands cause a woman to turn into a zombie and become the queen of "The Boiled Faces": "The Tar Sands are ecocide. They will bring Her back ... it is the Tar Sands to blame. This is how the *Wheetago* will return" (168). This concept has also led to the disputed modern medical term "Wendigo psychosis."

Works cited

Alexie, Sherman. *Flight*. New York: Grove/Atlantic, 2007.
Andrews, Jennifer. "Native Canadian Gothic Refigured: Reading Eden Robinson's *Monkey Beach*." *Essays on Canadian Writing* 73 (Spring 2001): 1–24.
Coulombe, Joseph L. "The Efficacy of Humor in Sherman Alexie's *Flight*: Violence, Vulnerability, and the Post-9/11 World." *MELUS* 39. 1 (Spring 2014): 130–48.
Dillon, Grace L. "Miindiwag and Indigenous Diaspora: Eden Robinson's and Celu Amberstone's Forays into 'Postcolonial' Science Fiction and Fantasy." *Extrapolation* 48. 2 (Summer 2007): 219–43.

Happyjack-McKenzie, Kris. *Windigo*. Film. Wapikoni Mobile, 2009.

Hill, Gord. *The 500 Years of Resistance Comic Book*. Vancouver: Arsenal Pulp Press, 2010.

James, Suzanne. "Into the Wild, Again." *Canadian Literature* 198 (Autumn 2008): 172–73.

Loft, Steven. "Curatorial essay accompanying the Cinema Lounge: Steven Loft on Adam [sic] Garnet Ruffo's *A Windigo Tale*." 1 Aug. 2012, n. pag. Web. Accessed 31 Dec. 2014. https://www.winnipegfilmgroup.com/wp-content/uploads/A-Windigo-Tale.docx-bySteven-Loft.docx-4.pdf

Lovecraft, H. P. *Supernatural Horror in Literature*. 1945. Rpt. Mineola, NY: Dover Publications, 1973.

McLeod, Neal. "Coming Home Through Stories." *(Ad)dressing Our Words: Aboriginal Perspectives on Aboriginal Literatures*. Ed. Armand Garnet Ruffo. Penticton, BC: Theytus Books, 2001. 17–36.

Montovani, Melissa. "Interview with Drew Hayden Taylor, Author of *The Night Wanderer*." YA Book Shelf. 26 Oct. 2010, n. pag. Web. Accessed 30 Dec. 2014. http://www.yabookshelf.com/2010/10/interview-with-drew-hayden-taylor-author-ofthe-night-wanderer/

Moreno-Garcia, Silvia, ed. *Dead North: Canadian Zombie Fiction*. Toronto: Exile Editions, 2013.

Rader, Dean. *Engaged Resistance: American Indian Art, Literature, and Film from Alcatraz to the NMAI*. Austin: University of Texas Press, 2011.

Robinson, Eden. *Monkey Beach*. Toronto: Knopf Canada, 2000.

——. *The Sasquatch at Home: Traditional Protocols & Modern Storytelling*. Edmonton: University of Alberta Press, 2011.

Ruffo, Armand Garnet. *A Windigo Tale*. Film. Windigo Productions Inc., 2009.

Sanderson, Steven Keewatin. *Darkness Calls*. Courtenay, BC: Healthy Aboriginal Network, 2011.

Sheyahshe, Michael A. *Native Americans in Comic Books: A Critical Study*. Jefferson, NC: McFarland, 2008.

Sinclair, Niigaanwewidam James. "'Windigo,' 'A Flesh Offering' & 'A Windigo Tale' at imagineNATIVE 2010". *mediaindigena.com*. 21 Oct. 2010, n. pag. Web. Accessed 31 Dec. 2014. http://www.mediaindigena.com/niigonwedom-sinclair/arts-andculture/night-of-the-living-wiindigo-or-the-ab-original-zombie

Sugars, Cynthia. "Strategic Abjection: Windigo Psychosis and the Postindian Subject in Eden Robinson's 'Dogs in Winter'." *Canadian Literature* 181 (Summer 2004): 78–91.

Taylor, Drew Hayden. "*The Night Wanderer*." Words Aloud 6 Spoken Word Festival, Durham, Ontario, Canada. Nov. 2009, n. pag. Web. Accessed 26 Dec. 2014. https://www.youtube.com/watch?v=xpSo1H81c04

——. *The Night Wanderer: A Native Gothic Novel*. Toronto: Annick Press, 2007.

Taylor, Drew Hayden & Anita Kooistra. *The Night Wanderer: A Graphic Novel*. Ill. Michael Wyatt. Toronto: Annick Press, 2013.

Van Camp, Richard. "On the Wings of This Prayer." *Dead North*. Ed. Silvia Moreno-Garcia. Toronto: Exile Editions, 164–73.

41

Future Pasts

Comics, Graphic Novels, and Digital Media

Susan Bernardin

How can we "re-imagine the way we see each other? Can we re-learn to see as human beings?" These are the opening questions posed by Tulalip/Swinomish photographer Matika Wilbur in her Tedx Talk, entitled, "Surviving Disappearance, Re-imagining and Humanizing Native Peoples." Seeking to reframe a tenacious legacy of images of vanished and vanquished Natives and the continued absence of diverse, contemporary Native Americans in mass media, Wilbur launched what she calls "Project 562": a photographic and digital portrait of members from each currently federally recognized Native nation in the United States. In so doing, Wilbur joins a diverse range of Indigenous artists working to visualize, narrate, and imagine the lives, stories, and, most notably, the futures of Native peoples. This final chapter samples the increasing prominence of comics, graphic novels, and digital media in contemporary Native arts and literatures. Whether creating web comics, digital comedic shorts or comic books and graphic novels, Native artists and writers exemplify what Michael Nicoll Yahgulanaas calls a "tradition of innovation" (22 Nov. 2014). In refusing rigid boundaries between literary and visual arts, they also re-animate relationships with visual and sequential storytelling practices that stretch back millennia. Just as these innovative forms affirm dynamic relationships between indigenous pasts and futures, so too do they highlight the primacy of collaboration between genres, media, and artists.

In their introduction to *Comics: A Global History*, authors Dan Mazur and Alexander Danner state that

> the human inclination to tell stories with pictures, to combine image and text, seems universal: Trajan's column, Asian scrolls, medieval tapestries and altarpieces, eighteenth-century broadsheets and Japanese woodblock prints may all be reasonably situated in the "prehistory" of comics.
>
> (8)

To their list one can add codices, petroglyphs and totem poles, just some examples of indigenous visual languages that serve as foundational "texts" for many contemporary Native writers. In *Books and Islands in Ojibwe Country*, Louise Erdrich notes that the root word in the Ojibwe language for rock painting – *mazina* – is the same for "text" or "made image" (11). Referencing birchbark scrolls and petroglyphs as longstanding texts, she claims that for Ojibwe, "books are nothing all that new" (11). In doing so, Erdrich disrupts deeply held assumptions about the divisions between written versus oral language; "modern" versus "traditional"; the present versus the past. Erdrich's statement also gestures to what Craig Womack has called the "vast, and vastly understudied written tradition in America" (2): from Mayan codices to wampum belts, petroglyphs to beading, and winter counts to weaving, Indigenous peoples have used non-alphabetic and visual languages to engage each other and their worlds. As layered forms communication – wampum belts, for example, can be read, touched, seen, recited, and heard – they both embody and compel collaborative efforts of making meaning.

Erdrich shares that the interrelationship of text and image – the hallmark of comic and graphic mediums – is for her "nothing new." Practicing what Dean Rader calls "indigenous interdisciplinarity" (2), many contemporary Native literary works engage in collaborative interplay between literary genres or between text and image. For example, Eric Gansworth (Onondaga) pairs poems and paintings in *Nickel Eclipse: Iroquois Moon* and *A Half-Life of Cardio-Pulmonary Function*; sculptor Nora Naranjo-Morse (Santa Clara Pueblo) pairs poems with photographs of her sculptures in *Mud Woman: Poems from the Clay*. N. Scott Momaday's paintings and illustrations feature prominently in his books; Leslie Silko's mixed-genre memoir, *Storyteller*, includes her father Lee Marmon's photographs. Meanwhile, the extraordinary cross-over success of Sherman Alexie's bestselling young adult novel *The Absolutely True Diary of a Part-Time Indian*, which features cartoons by non-Native graphic artist Ellen Forney, points to other kinds of productive collaborations. Recent collaborations between Native and non-Native writers and artists include two collections: *Native American Classics* and *Trickster: Native American Tales*. The former re-imagines stories by foundational writer-intellectuals working in the late nineteenth and early twentieth century – Gertrude Bonnin, Pauline Johnson, Alex Posey, and Charles Eastman – as well as "as-told-to" narratives adapted by contemporary First Nation writers such as Richard van Camp and Niigaanwewidam James Sinclair. The collaborating Indigenous visual artists, comics artists and cartoonists include Murv Jacobs, Roy Boney Jr., Joseph Erb, Arigon Starr, Jon Proudstar, and Jay Odjick. In the latter, Native educators, storytellers, and writers teamed up with non-Native visual artists to present diverse tribal trickster stories. About the collaboration, editor Matt Dembicki notes that the writers chose the artists out of a pool and "approved the storyboards" (225). Such recent collaborations also suggest that forms of contemporary indigenous visual storytelling function within a network of complex cross-cultural relationships and aesthetic influences.

In an era marked by a renewed vogue for comic superheroes from the DC and Marvel universes and blockbuster movie franchises – *Captain America, Thor, The Avengers, The X-Men, Iron Man* – the exhibit "Comic Art Indigène" opened in Spring 2008. The message of this traveling exhibit is encapsulated by its pairing of two images: a petrograph of a red, white and blue, shield-bearing man from about 1290 and a more recognizable red, white and blue shield-bearing hero, Captain America. This pairing invokes a seemingly surprising convergence of U.S. comics and Indigenous visual storytelling traditions. At the same time, it instigates questions about the different origin stories we can tell about the comics medium. Amy Peltz observes that, "while serialized word-picture combinations go back to ancient Egypt at least, the American strain of the sequential, narrative, printed graphic form we call 'comics' arose about a century ago as a feature of the new Sunday newspaper supplements." The launch of the storied *Superman* comic in 1938 inaugurated what Hillary Chute calls the "so-called Golden Age of comics" (13) whose mass appeal cut across age, class, ethnicity, and region. Its appeal to young readers, coupled with "its assembly-line" production model of "writers, pencillers, inkers and colorists" (Peltz), ensured its diminished status as either literary or visual art form. Antonio Chavarria, curator of "Comic Art Indigène," says that

> comic strips were the first accessible form of mass media made available on reservations, and there was this immediate connection between native people and that type of work. There was no language barrier, and the whimsical stories were a very familiar tradition.
>
> (qtd. in Bradner)

The exhibit draws attention to the still little-known work of artist and educator Eva Mirabal (Taos Pueblo) who enlisted in the Women's Army Corps, or WAC, in World War II, and was asked to create a comic strip for WAC publications. Mirabal's creation, G.I. Gertie, found the comedic in military life. The exhibit also shows how Native cartoonists have wielded the single-panel cartoon, that mainstay of newspaper editorial pages. Marty Two Bulls (Lakota), for *Indian Country Today*, and the late Vincent Craig (Navajo), for *Fort Apache Scout* (White Mountain Apache tribal newspaper) and the *Navajo Times*, use humor to tackle local tribal issues and broader concerns across Indian Country. If the power of the comics medium resides in the complex interplay of text and image, R.C. Harvey argues, then "the single panel cartoon is the haiku of cartooning, its balance of visual and verbal elements essential to its function" (7). A compressed form that relies on the viewer's recognition of the comedic interaction of text and image, the single-panel drawing has also been adopted by Ricardo Cate (Kewa/Santa Domingo Pueblo), who has published a daily cartoon in the *Santa Fe New Mexican* since 2006. Tongva/Ajachmem artist L. Frank is well known throughout indigenous California for the single-panel cartoon "Acorn Soup" which appeared between 1992 and 2006 in *News from Native California*, a quarterly magazine, and was published in book form in 1999. The cartoon's starring contrarian character, Coyote, along with its striking use of reverse-captions (or mirror-writing) that requires readers to actively decode their meaning, signal L. Frank's stratagems of trickster humor designed to both address and redress California Indian histories.

That humor is sorely needed, given the continued hypervisible circulation of cartoonish images and caricatures of Native peoples. Unsurprisingly, there has been little comic relief from the world of comic books. In his 2008 study, *Native Americans in Comic Books*, Michael Sheyashe (Caddo) documents an ongoing representational history rife with formulaic sidekicks, mystical warriors, and shape-shifting animals. As of 2008, there were few Native comic books to disrupt this visual onslaught, save for Jay Odjick's *The Raven* (2004; now a TV series in Canada) and before that Jon Proudstar and Ryan Huna Smith's collaborative but short-lived *Tribal Force* (1996). The prefatorial page of Arigon Starr's 2012 comic book *Super Indian* gleefully teases this history by featuring a bare-chested, bear-fighting, loin-clothed warrior (Figure 41.1) who holds "the mystical knowledge and secrets of the ancient shamans" (Vol. 1).

In the last panel, this figure winks at the reader as the caption wryly adds: "Unfortunately, that warrior and his story are told in another comic book." Starr's playful but emphatic rejection – and redirection – of this representational legacy heralds the comic interventions of her work and that of a growing cohort of Native comics artists.

Figure 41.1 "Shamanic Warrior," from "Super Indian Volume 1." Copyright 2012 Arigon Starr, Wacky Productions Unlimited. Used with permission.

That intervention is embodied by her actual superhero, Super Indian, whose giant "S" emblazoned on his chest and skintight blue suit reference Super Man but whose long black hair and prominent NDN belt buckle announce some vital script changes. Through his efforts to protect his fictional Leaning Oak reservation community, Super Indian also makes visible the transformative potential of Native comic superheroes. In a pivotal scene from the 1998 film *Smoke Signals*, young Victor, having witnessed the effects of alcoholism within his family, delivers a devastating response to his drunk father, Arnold, when asked, "who's your favorite Indian?": "nobody, nobody, nobody." The failure of male family role models and the fraught desire to identify with past indigenous resistance leaders such as Crazy Horse animate Alexie's early writing. Not surprisingly, Alexie reveals in his essay, "Superman and Me": "I learned to read with a Superman comic book."

Meanwhile, artist Larry McNeil recognizes affinities between Superhero comics and cosmological Tlingit narratives: "American Comic book characters have traditionally been about a yearning for heroes to come to the rescue that never did in real life" ("Vanishing Race, 101"). In McNeil's blog about "Comic Art Indigène," he describes intersecting origin stories for what he terms his "comic book aesthetic":

> You could make the argument that comic book heroes are really an extension of the yearning for mythical characters to come to life … Our mythical character is *Raven*, whose main trait is to be simultaneously scrappy and funny. Instead of fighting corrupt politicians like Superman did, he brazenly took on a mendacious, greedy Chief who has lost his way from being the type of forthright and visionary leader that the people desperately needed. The corrupt Chief was the ultimate villain in that he was so greedy that he actually stole light from the world …. Our hero, who was kind of a scoundrel himself, came to the rescue and stole the sun, replacing it back in the sky where it belonged. Raven was white before this, and his act turned him black as he is today, so he paid a price for his audacity, another almost sublime part of the mythology. Raven was a transformer, changing shape at will. Superman was a transformer too.
>
> ("101")

For "Comic Art Indigène," McNeil envisions Tonto punching out Edward Curtis, whose famed photographs froze Indians in the past tense of U.S. life. Tonto punches with words too: "Your 'Vanishing Indian' paradigm just doesn't fit our Native epistemology. Here's to deconstructionist theories." The caption reads: "Tonto gives Edward Curtis a lesson in Native values." McNeil slyly

> transformed Tonto from something of a dimwitted sidekick to the proverbial main hero character. He transforms right before our eyes and starts kicking butt in the post-colonial world, setting disgusting and repugnant people like Edward Curtis straight, with one mighty punch. In this sense, the comic book aesthetic is perfect for what I want to do with my art, especially as Raven acts as a literal foundation for the art.
>
> ("101")

By recasting the popular cultural and literary history of indigenous sidekicks such as Tonto, McNeil gestures toward the transformative potential of re-imagining culture heroes.

In related visual media, Native artists have found rich imaginative terrain in harnessing the enduring popular appeal and cultural power of comic superheroes and indigenizing them. For example, in her stunning experimental digital poem-film, "Pre-Occupied," Heid Erdrich and her collaborators embed a 1942 Superman cartoon, "Electric Earthquake," about an indigenous scientist scheming to wrest back control of Manhattan, as well as an audio clip of "Superman's Song" by the Crash Test Dummies. For Erdrich, these two popular cultural referent points resonate with challenges Native peoples face in trying to be "super people" fighting evils on so many fronts: whether environmental, legal, political, or social. This indigenous comic aesthetic also underlines the aesthetic interventions of artists Diego Romero (Cochiti) and Steven Paul Judd (Kiowa/Choctaw): the former creates pottery with comic designs of under-noted Pueblo histories of resistance; the latter creates temporal juxtapositions and ironic interrelationships through his paired acrylic paintings of "Siouxperwoman" and "Siouxperman." Finally, Jeffrey Veregge (Port Gamble S'Klallam Tribe) re-imagines comic superheroes and sci-fi figures through Coast Salish formline design, a stylized visual language. His striking cover designs for issues of GI Joe and Judge Dredd indigenize comic icons while visualizing Arigon Starr's claim that "Geek culture is alive and well in Indian Country!" (RJM "Beyond the Panel").

For Starr (enrolled Kickapoo; Creek, Cherokee, Seneca), the transformation at the core of superhero comic narratives opens up a space for the transformational possibilities in reframing the world through Indigenous imaginations, experiences, and histories. For Starr, "The thing I love about superhero stories is someone normal transforming into the extraordinary. How would Wolverine or Wonder Woman be different if they came from an Indian nation?" ("Beyond the Panel"). Starr would devour the comic books that her grandfather bought for her during annual family trips to Oklahoma. Many years later, she came up with the idea of Super Indian, recalling, "I've always thought our Native community didn't have enough comic book heroes and most of the ones that were already out there weren't created or drawn by Native artists or writers" ("About Us"). Super Indian is the alter-ego of mild-mannered, dateless Hubert Logan, a janitor at the Leaning Oak Bingo Hall. As a boy, Hubert attended the birthday party of reservation bully, Derek Thunder, where both inadvertently consumed large quantities of commodity cheese tainted with "Rezium" that gave them both superpowers. His origin story, like many of the storylines in the comic, pointedly but humorously reframes multi-generational experiences with legacies of colonization in reservation communities. His origins echo those of Vincent Craig's quintessentially Navajo and incisively political comic hero, "Mutton Man," whose powers derive from eating mutton contaminated by an actual uranium mining accident on the Navajo Reservation in 1979.

Super Indian's enemies are not just unhealthy commodity foods: the "circle of evil" encompasses Wampum Baggs, former reservation history teacher who possesses a wampum belt with mystical powers; Bick Bucks, "the non-Native love flute sensation" who is a "big hit" during "PBS Pledge Break"; Carl Van Erik, "the most famous Native American actor in Hollywood" with "a dubious indigenous pedigree"; and anthropologist and "souvenir hunter" Karl Von Kelheim (Vol. 1).

In "Here Comes the Anthro," Starr invokes a foe familiar to Native communities: Von Kelheim's murderous search for "ancient artifacts" recalls a long history of non-Native academics and collectors eager to extract indigenous knowledge and material items. Super Indian fights non-Natives bent on cultural appropriation and economic exploitation but internal predators as well: corrupt tribal leaders and power-hungry bullies. Luckily, Super Indian has help: his trusty sidekicks include his best friend General Bear (whose alter-ego is Mega Bear) and Diogi, a smart, speaking canine who, having also consumed the cheese, is now a library-card carrying string-theory enthusiast (Figure 41.2).

Moreover, unlike the prototypical superhero, Hubert is embedded in a supportive family who know his secret. He is neither lone wolf, nor sullen outsider. Starr explains:

> I wanted to break the stereotype of the stoic, loner Indian that is persistent in mainstream Native stories. My hero would be a guy who had both parents (unlike Superman or Batman), lived in his community and had friends within that community. Some folks would say that's not "dramatic" enough, but it's pretty easy to find drama in a Native community!
>
> (3 Oct. 2013)

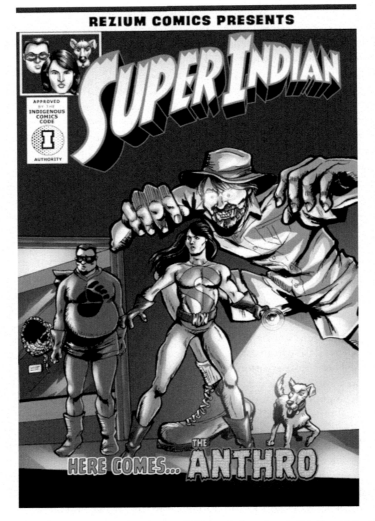

Figure 41.2 Cover of "Here Comes the Anthro," "Super Indian Issue #2." Copyright 2011 Arigon Starr, Wacky Productions Unlimited. Used with permission.

Starr also reframes the still prevalent gender confines of U.S. comics traditions by creating, in close consultation with Laguna Pueblo members, a Native woman superhero: Ka-waika (Laguna) Woman, who was launched as the alter-ego of urban professional Phoebe Francis in *The Curse of Blud Kwan'tum*. On the cover of Issue 6, Ka-waika Woman is carrying a limp Super Indian in a bold visual reversal of conventional scenes of female rescue (Figure 41.3).

By re-imagining a recognizable scene from superhero comics, Starr wrests new narrative possibility out of old stories. Through a dense network of thematic references, Starr's comics also create a network of possible portals for her readers. For example, *Blud Kwan'tum* incorporates indigenous history lessons, Star Trek fan jokes ("We're all in expendable red.

Figure 41.3 Cover of "The Curse of Blud Kwan'Tum, Part II," "Super Indian Issue #6." Copyright 2014 Arigon Starr, Wacky Productions Unlimited. Used with permission.

You know what happens to red shirts"), and a sustained scrutiny of internalized colonization, from blood quantum debates to cinematic inventions. For example, while General Bear and soon-to-be superhero, Phoebe Francis, eagerly consume *Never at Dusk*, Starr's hilarious revamp of the *Twilight* series, vampire *Blud Kwan'tum* sucks the [full] blood out of tribal members with the help of a blood mobile and his "Indian-o-Meter." In so doing, Starr demonstrates the destructive power of popular cultural imaginings about Native peoples, while defusing that power through punning, parody and inversions.

Starr not only engages readers through a network of layered references, but through networking itself: by moving and adapting *Super Indian* from radio and stage performance to a serial web comic and then published volumes, Starr has developed multiple media platforms for disseminating her Native superhero. After the success of an initial radio series, Starr launched *Super Indian* as a weekly web comic in 2011, with half-page installments appearing every Monday. Unlike many comics creators, Starr writes, draws, colors, and inks her stories. In both form and format, this serial digital comic invites interaction from its reader-viewers. First, the comics medium not only relies on the dynamic, shifting interplay of image and narration, but on the constitutive role of readers in forging connections of causality, time, and space across the white spaces, or "gutters" separating individual panels. Put more simply, graphic novelist and comic artist David Mack says, "For me, comics are a collaboration between the reader and the creator" (88). Collaboration extends from the artist's distinctive visual syntax – the formal elements of perspective, panel placement, shape, and size; word or thought balloons – to cross-cultural references peopling *Super Indian*.

Yet the process of devising and sustaining a serial comic is not just about building anticipation for future installments of *Super Indian*: it builds layered relationships with the past. Comics scholar Hillary Chute notes that "the medium of comics compels because it is so capacious, offering layers of words and images – as well as multiple layers of possible temporalities – on each page. Comics conveys several productive tensions in its basic structure" (5). For knowledgeable comics readers, *Super Indian* evokes the "classic" 1980s *X-Men* aesthetic: its saturated colors, square panels, line art, and perspective revisit what Starr simply calls "old school." Her efforts to make *Super Indian* look "dated" are part of a broader imaginative recuperative strategy. Describing *Super Indian* as a "found comic," Starr asks, "*what if* I went into a comic shop and found *Super Indian*"? (18 Oct. 2014). Starr imagines a hidden alternative history of Indigenous comics, one with a Native superhero antecedent. At the same time, her purposeful use of bold, saturated colors refutes the visual script that forever freezes Native peoples in the past tense. Starr knows that "people think of Indians in sepia tones" (18 Oct. 2014). Like Tonto busting Edward Curtis's face, Starr's boldly colorful characters bust the frames of representational confinement.

With the publication of *Volume 1* in 2012, Starr widened the reach and range of her audience. While the weekly web comic privileges readers familiar with reservation communities, tribal politics, and intertribal Indian humor, *Volume 1* includes a glossary of "rez speak" and full-page glossy color tributes to "REAL" Super Indians: iconic athlete Jim Thorpe and prima ballerina Maria Tallchief. These tributes educate "outside" readers but more purposely inform young Native readers who may be unfamiliar with the achievements of earlier generations. Akin to her speculative genealogy of Indigenous comics history, this tactic generates intellectual engagement with indigenous histories. Starr's commitment to youth outreach, coupled with her commitment to generate new and alternative histories of Native graphic stories, extends to INC: the Indigenous Narratives Collective, a comics creation, publication, and distribution venture which she co-founded in 2011 with Lee Francis IV (Laguna Pueblo) and a network of other Native comics artists, including Theo "Teddy" Tso (Paiute), Michael Sheyashe, Jonathan Nelson, and Roy Boney Jr. (Cherokee). INC's aim is to rebuild the comics world through diverse Native lenses, such as the regionally and tribally rooted *Wool of Jonesy*, Jonathan Nelson's purposeful comic about a sheep on the Navajo reservation. Sheep are a centerpiece of Navajo culture, Nelson notes, "a way to survive," but sheep also "are seen as meat, easily influenced, followers ... [so] I've given them this voice where they are able to go beyond the boundaries" (qtd. in Silversmith).

INC's mission statement asks: "What would an alternative Native universe look like? What if Batman or Superman were Native? Who would Native America call on to save their world when threatened by hostile aliens?" Thanks to INC, they might call on Pueblo Jones, in the forthcoming *Raiders of the Lost Art*, co-created by writer Lee Francis IV and artist Kristina Cuthand (Lakota), or call on Captain Paiute, Theo Tso's creation. As Francis states, "Native kids are searching for heroes who look like them ... And here comes Captain Paiute, who screws up anyone who comes trying to hurt the rez – that's his job" (qtd. in Walker). Starr and Francis first hatched the premise of INC through their comic creation of the seal located in the upper-left corner of INC-affiliated publications: "Approved by the Indigenous Comics Code Authority." Comics readers will recognize this cheeky reframing of the "Comics Code Authority," formed in 1954 to regulate comics content, and in existence until 2011. Francis notes, "We know the Comics Code Authority is a censoring body but we wanted to flip the script on that. If you see this Indigenous Comics Code Seal then you know it's Indian approved" (23 Sept. 2014). On its website, INC describes the icon as:

> a symbol of our work as a collective, a way of demonstrating our connection to the past, the culture of comics, and our shared future to promote the art and stories of Indigenous People in a progressive and authentic manner. So rest assured, if you see the Indigenous Comics Code seal of approval, you know you are buying an INC book and helping to support all those Native and Indigenous writers, artists, inkers, colorists, and storytellers who wish to add their work to the comics canon.

At comic cons, at tribal schools, at sequential art and visual storytelling workshops, INC artists share their work and mentor emerging Native comics artists. Its ethos of collaboration extends from writers and artists co-creating Indigenous graphic narratives in diverse genres such as science fiction and fantasy, to its collaborative creation of comic books, beginning with INC's first major comics publication, *Tales of the Mighty Code Talkers* (2014). Much like Starr's tribute to "real Super Indians," *Tales* was instigated by Starr's learning just a few years ago about Choctaw Code Talkers in World War I. An advance digital installment is Roy Boney Jr.'s "We Speak in Secret," whose title, in Cherokee and English, suggests the broader irony framing *Tales*: Native soldiers using their languages at the same time that those languages were banned, forcing children in boarding schools to "speak in secret." This recuperative narrative honors the unsung contributions of Cherokee Code Talkers in World War I – contributions that remained a government secret for many decades – while placing them within an ongoing story of Cherokee resistance and leadership. The final scene names the public law (of 2008) affirming that Code Talkers "deserve immediate recognition for their dedication and valor." The caption below repeats the key word, "recognition": "it is recognition long overdue." These final words are reinforced by the page's visual recognition of Cherokee warriors collaborating across time and space to defend their country. Both Native and U.S. history lesson, Boney's Cherokee comic reflects the broader goals of the volume to create a collaborative space for sharing stories across tribal communities and to honor collaboration as both a creative and intellectual practice of survival.

These goals were first communicated on the cover page of INC's inaugural 2012 publication, *INC Universe*, which features a young girl looking with her grandfather at Starr's installment of *Tales of the Mighty Code Talkers* as he reads the story to her (Figure 41.4).

Figure 41.4 Cover of "INC's Universe #0." Copyright 2012 Arigon Starr, Wacky Productions Unlimited. Used with permission.

This powerful scene of intergenerational and interactive engagement epitomizes INC's collaborative efforts to reframe Native histories while animating Native futures.

INC's growing digital media presence attests to the changing shape of Indigenous visual storytelling for both creators and audiences. Successful Kickstarter campaigns, for example, launched Wilbur's Project 562 and also the forthcoming indigenous comics collection, *Moonshot*, to be published by Alternative History Comics. At the same time, ever-shifting forms of digital and social media direct us to the power and potential of Indigenous artists building relationships with multiple audiences, from local to international, from Indigenous to non-Indigenous. For example, the 1491s, a sketch comedy troupe (Sterlin Harjo, Dallas Goldtooth, Migizi Pensoneau, Bobby Wilson, and Ryan Red Corn), whose members were featured in a volatile "Redskins" segment on Jon Stewart's *The Daily Show*, got their start with "New Moon Wolf Pack Audition" (2009), a YouTube parody of the *Twilight* series. Its website features satirical videos such as "Slapping Medicine Man" but also those from its "Represent" campaign: Native American college students re-presenting the dynamic relationship between contemporaneity and indigeneity. In Tahlequah, Oklahoma, Joseph Erb and Roy Boney Jr. develop language technologies to move the Cherokee language into the future. Erb's animated origin and sci-fi stories revitalize the Cherokee language for current and future speakers: "Hero," for example, champions "superhero Cherokees fighting for their rights in the future" (*blackgummountain*).

Such traditions of innovation extend to the cross-cultural collaboration between the Cook Inlet Tribal Council (CITC) and the game studio, E-Line Media, which it sought out to help create "'Upper One Games,' the first indigenous-owned video game company in the United States" (Boney "Inupiaq"). Told in Inupiaq, its new video game "Kisima Innitchunja"/"Never Alone" was developed around a version of the story of Kunuuksaayuka, or Blizzard Man, by Robert Nasruk Cleveland. His daughter, Minnie Aliitchak Gray, who gave permission for the developers to use this version, was part of a network of collaborators in the game's creation that included Alaska Native elders, youth, and hunters. Gloria O'Neill, CEO of CITC, observes:

> Our people are evolving, and our stories evolve. They continue to evolve, and that's why we love the power of video games. I think they are an amazing medium to evolve the stories with us, as we tell those stories to new generations at home, and to the world. ... A lot of people feel video games and digital media are disconnecting youth and young adults from their culture, their elders and their language. But why not use it to reconnect? That's what we hope to do.
>
> (qtd. in Freeman)

With its collaborative re-imagination of old stories for new contexts, "Never Alone" demonstrates the imaginative possibilities set into motion by the shifting forms and changing lives of Indigenous visual narration. As a closing example that refuses closure, consider the many lives of Michael Nicoll Yahgulanaas's 2009 graphic novel, *Red: A Haida Manga*. Yahgulanaas takes what he calls his cultural birthright – "the complex, ancient iconic art form which is totem poles" (21 Nov. 2014) – and translates it into a new visual language he calls "Haida manga," arising at the intersection of multiple lineages of visual storytelling: U.S. comics, manga, and Haida formline. Conceived as a "bridge to settler society" through its visual narration (CBC), *Red* also shows its kinship with manga, the ubiquitous Japanese comics style that means "images without limit" (CBC). Recalling that earlier generations of Haida fishermen were made welcome in Japanese communities in an era of virulent racism in Canada, Yahgulanaas honors the affinity he sees between peoples and visual storytelling traditions by claiming Haida Manga as part of a Northern Pacific tradition.

A retelling of a pre-contact family and community story from Haida Gwaii (islands off the coast of British Columbia), *Red* offers its readers diverse portals through which to access its lessons about trauma, loss, and reconciliation. It does so by the multiple forms the story takes: *Red* is composed of 108 individual watercolor panels that also form a sequential narrative *and* a large nonlinear formline mural that – as the author's note encourages – can be reconstructed from the pages of the book. The interactive engagement required by these multiple platforms extends to the book's visual and narrative design. Most strikingly, Yahgulanaas dispenses with "gutters": those white spaces that separate panels, or frames, in comics and which indicate shifts in time or space. He likens this distinctive convention of the comics medium to the mindset of settler colonialism: "Someone came and said the land is empty. Therefore ... I get to describe it myself. And I get to control it, I get to cut it up, and I get to own it and sell it" (14 Oct. 2010). In their place, we see instead the signature element of Haida visual language, the formline: a moving black line whose changing dimensions and shapes actually direct the shape of the story. However, Yahgulanaas ultimately finds a term more befitting his arts practice: "frameline." Claiming that "formline" sounds too static, he explains:

a frame is a device that opens a window to limitless opportunities ... And so the frame suggests that there are any number of things hidden within it. So, it's a call for us to go deeper into the work. As opposed to thinking, it's fully presented to me; I'll move on to the next piece.

(22 Nov. 2014)

That call to "go deeper" has deep roots in his life. A vital participant in the decades-long fight to block logging corporations in his home territory of Haida Gwaii, Yahgulanaas later turned his activist aesthetic toward creating public art and graphic narratives that compel audience responsibility and engagement. He extends this vital relationship between aesthetics and activism in a startling invitation to readers at the end of his book: "I welcome you to destroy this book. I welcome you to rip the pages out of their binds ... you can reconstruct this work of art" (109). Like the visual punning characteristic of Haida art, *Red* layers meanings within its form while refusing a single framework for accessing, reading, or seeing its story. By inciting our responsibility to ask questions, find points of contact, and reframe assumptions and perspectives, Yahgulanaas forges interactive pathways between his art and audience. Those pathways do not have an end point: current public programming initiatives with major museums will sustain the life of *Red* well past the pages of his book. In doing so, Yahgulanaas's Haida Manga makes a powerful case for the moving practice of Indigenous literary arts. With ongoing innovations in Indigenous comic, graphic, and digital forms, framelines of possibility abound for envisioning Native futures.

Works cited

1491s. Web. Accessed 14 Jan. 2015.

Alexie, Sherman. "Superman and Me." *Los Angeles Times*. 19 Apr. 1998. Web. Accessed 14 Jan. 2015.

Boney, Roy, Jr. "Inupiaq Culture Comes to the Fore in 'Never Alone.'" *Native Peoples*. Jan./Feb. 2015. Web Accessed 14 Jan. 2015.

——. "We Speak in Secret." *Tales of the Mighty Code Talkers: Volume 1*. INC Comics. Indigenous Narratives Collective. Nov. 2014. Digital release.

Bradner, Liesl. "A Tribal Take on Comic Art." *Los Angeles Times*. 11 May 2008. Web. Accessed 14 Jan. 2015.

Chute, Hillary L. *Graphic Women: Life Narrative and Contemporary Comics*. New York: Columbia University Press, 2010.

Dembicki, Matt, ed. *Trickster, Native American Tales: A Graphic Collection*. Golden, CO: Fulcrum Publishing, 2010.

Erb, Joseph. Blackgummountain. Web. Accessed 14 Jan. 2015.

Erdrich, Heid. "Pre-Occupied." Co-Dirs. Erdrich; R. Vincent Moniz Jr.; Art Dir. and Animator, Jonathan Thunder. Heid E. Erdrich. 2013. Web. Accessed 14 Jan. 2015.

Erdrich, Louise. *Books and Islands in Ojibwe Country*. Washington, D.C.: National Geographic, 2003.

Francis IV, Lee. Personal Interview. 23 Sept. 2014.

Frank, L. *Acorn Soup*. Berkeley, CA: Heyday Books, 1999.

Freeman, Will. "The Story Behind the First Indigenous-Owned Developer, Upper One Games." *Develop.* 18 Nov. 2014. Web. Accessed 14 Jan. 2015.

Harvey, R.C. "Wednesday 'Look Day' and the Freelance Magazine Cartooner." *The Education of a Comics Artist: Visual Narrative in Cartoons, Graphic Novels, and Beyond.* Ed. Michael Dooley & Steven Heller. New York: Allworth Press, 2005. 4–7.

INC Comics. Indigenous Narratives Collective. Web. Accessed 14 Jan. 2015.

Mack, David. "The Whole-Brained Approach: Interview." *The Education of a Comics Artist: Visual Narrative in Cartoons, Graphic Novels, and Beyond.* Ed. Michael Dooley & Steven Heller. New York: Allworth Press, 2005. 86–90.

McNeil, Larry. "Comic Art Indigène: Vanishing Race, 101." 16 Apr. 2008. Web. Accessed 14 Jan. 2015.

Mazur, Dan & Alexander Danner. *Comics: A Global History, 1968 to the Present.* New York: Thames & Hudson, 2014.

Peltz, Amy. "A Visual Turn: Comics and Art after the Graphic Novel." *Art in Print.* 2.6. Web. Accessed 14 Jan. 2015.

Pomplun, Tom, ed., John E. Smelcer & Joe Bruchac, assoc. eds. *Native American Classics. Graphic Classics Vol. 24.* Mount Horeb, WI: Eureka Productions, 2013.

Rader, Dean. *Engaged Resistance: American Indian Art, Literature, and Film from Alcatraz to the NMAI.* Austin: University of Texas Press, 2011.

RJM [Rachel McCarthy James]. "Beyond the Panel: An Interview with Arigon Starr of *Super Indian*: Part 1." *Bitch Media.* 23 Feb. 2012. Web. Accessed 14 Jan. 2015.

Sheyashe, Michael A. *Native Americans in Comic Books: A Critical Study.* Jefferson, NC: McFarland and Company, 2008.

Silversmith, Shondin. "Jonesy Leaves Readers Jonesing for More." *Navajo Times.* 26 Sept. 2013. Web. Accessed 14 Jan. 2015.

Smoke Signals. Dir. Chris Eyre. Miramax. 1998.

Starr, Arigon. "About Us." *Super Indian Comics.* Web. 2012. Accessed 14 Jan. 2015.

——. "The Curse of Blud Kwan'tum: Part 1." *Super Indian Comics.* 11 Nov. 2013. Web. Accessed 14 Jan. 2015.

——. Email to author. 3 Oct. 2013.

——. Personal Interview. 18 Oct. 2014.

——. *Super Indian: Volume 1.* West Hollywood, CA: Wacky Productions, 2012.

——. *Tales of the Mighty Code Talkers #1. INC Comics.* Web. Accessed 11 June 2015. http://www.inccomics.com/products/tales-of-the-mighty-code-talkers-1

Walker, Taté. "New Indigenous Superheroes Save the Day." *Native Peoples.* Nov.–Dec. 2014. Web. Accessed 14 Jan. 2015.

Wilbur, Matika, "Surviving Disappearance, Humanizing and Re-Imagining Native Peoples." Tedx Talk. Seattle, Washington. 23 June 2013. YouTube. Web. Accessed 19 July 2013.

Womack, Craig. *Red on Red: Native American Literary Separatism.* Minneapolis: University of Minnesota Press, 1999.

Yahgulanaas, Michael Nicoll. Artist Talk. American Museum of Natural History. 22 Nov. 2014.

——. Artist Talk. University of British Columbia. 14 Oct. 2010. YouTube. Web. Accessed 14 Jan. 2015.

——. Interview: "Daybreak with Russell Bowers." CBC Radio One. 28 June 2005. Web. Accessed 14 Jan. 2015.

——. Q and A: Reddit AMA. 21–22 Nov. 2014. Web. Accessed 14 Jan. 2015.

——. *Red: A Haida Manga.* Vancouver: Douglas & McIntyre, 2009.

FURTHER READING

Abrams, Herbert L. "Medical Problems of Survivors of Nuclear War: Infection and the Spread of Communicable Disease." *New England Journal of Medicine* 305. 20 (Nov. 1981): 1226–32.

Alfred, Taiaike. "Sovereignty." *A Companion to American Indian History*. Ed. Philip Deloria & Neal Salisbury. New York: Blackwell, 2004. 460–74.

Allen, Chadwick. "Postcolonial Theory and the Discourse of Treaties." *American Quarterly* 52. 1 (March 2000): 59–89.

Allen, Paula Gunn, ed. *Studies in American Indian Literature: Critical Essays and Course Designs*. New York: Modern Language Association, 1983.

Anaya, James. *Indigenous Peoples in International Law*. 2nd ed. Oxford: Oxford University Press, 2004.

Anderson, Wanni W. "Alaskan Haida Stories of Language Growth and Regeneration." *American Indian Quarterly* 30. 1–2 (Winter–Spring 2006): 110–18.

———. *The Dall Sheep Dinner Guest: Inupiaq Narratives of Northwest Alaska*. Fairbanks: University of Alaska Press, 2005.

Antell, Judith A. "Momaday, Welch, and Silko: Expressing the Feminine Principle through Male Alienation." *American Indian Quarterly* 12. 3 (1988): 213–20.

Anzaldúa, Gloria. *Borderlands: The New Mestiza/La Frontera*. San Francisco: Aunt Lute Books, 1987.

Armstrong, Ann Elizabeth, Kelli Lyon Johnson & William A. Wortman, eds. *Performing Worlds into Being: Native American Women's Theater*. Oxford, OH: Miami University Press, 2009.

Armstrong, Jeannette. "Invocation: The Real Power of Aboriginal Women." *Women of the First Nations: Power, Wisdom, and Strength*. Ed. Christine Miller & Patricia Chuchryk. Winnipeg: University of Manitoba Press, 1996. ix–xii.

Baca, Damián & Victor Villaneuva, eds. *Rhetorics of the Americas: 3114 BCE to 2012 CE*. New York: Palgrave Macmillan, 2010.

Bacher, John. "Sharing Ancestral Knowledge: An Interview with Chief Jake Thomas." *Peace Magazine* Mar.–Apr. 1991, p. 17. Web. Accessed June 2013. http://peacemagazine.org/archive/v07n2p17.htm

Balaz, Joe. *After the Drought*. Honolulu: Topgallant Press, 1985.

———. *Electric Laulau*. Honolulu: Hawai'i Dub Music, 1998.

———, ed. *Ho'omānoa: An Anthology of Contemporary Hawaiian Literature*. Honolulu: Ku Pa'a Press, 1989.

———. *OLA*. Honolulu: Tinfish Press, 1996.

Banks, Dennis & Richard Erdoes. *Ojibwa Warrior: Dennis Banks and the Rise of the American Indian Movement*. Norman: University of Oklahoma Press, 2004.

Barnaby, Jeff. Dir. *Red Right Hand*. Nutaaq Media, 2004. DVD.

Barrera-Osorio, Antonio. *Experiencing Nature: The Spanish American Empire and the Early Scientific Revolution*. Austin: University of Texas Press, 2006.

Bataille, Gretchen M., ed. *Native American Representations: First Encounters, Distorted Images, and Literary Appropriations*. Lincoln: Nebraska University Press, 2001.

FURTHER READING

——, ed. *Native American Women: A Biographical Dictionary*. New York: Garland, 1993.

Bataille, Gretchen M. & Kathleen Mullen Sands. *American Indian Women: Telling Their Lives*. 1984. Rpt. Lincoln: University of Nebraska Press, 1987.

Bauman, Richard. "Verbal Art as Performance." *American Anthropologist* 77. 2 (1975): 290–311.

Beidler, Peter G. "Animals and Human Development in the Contemporary American Indian Novel." *Western American Literature* 14. 2 (August 1979): 133–48.

Bevacqua, Michael Lujan, Victoria Leon-Guerrero & Craig Santos Perez, eds. *Chamorro Childhood*. Berkeley: Achiote Press, 2011.

Bighorse, Tiana & Noel Bennett. *Bighorse the Warrior*. Tucson: University of Arizona Press, 1994.

Blackbird, Andrew J. *History of the Ottawa and Chippewa Indians of Michigan*. Ypsilanti: Ypsilantian, 1887.

Blaeser, Kimberly M. "Native Literature: Seeking a Critical Center." *Looking at the Words of Our People: First Nations Analysis of Literature*. Ed. Jeannette Armstrong. Penticton, British Columbia: Theytus, 1993. 51–62.

Bleichmar, Daniela, Paula De Vos, Kristin Huffine & Kevin Sheehan, eds. *Science in the Spanish and Portuguese Empires, 1500–1800*. Stanford, CA: Stanford University Press, 2009.

ᏍᏈ ᎠᎯᏍ ᎠᏲᎨᎢ: ᎫᏣᎪᎠᏫᎧᏞᏲᏍᏲᏴ Roy Boney Jr., Artist. Web. Accessed 4 Dec. 2014.

Brant, Beth. *Mohawk Trail*. Ithaca, NY: Firebrand Books, 1985.

Breinig, Helmbrecht. *Imaginary (Re-)Locations: Tradition, Modernity, and the Market in Contemporary Native American Literature and Culture*. Tübingen: Stauffenburg, 2003.

Brill de Ramírez, Susan Berry. "Literary Explorations into the Poetic Sonority of Contemporary Diné (Navajo) Poetry." *ANQ: A Quarterly Journal of Short Articles, Notes, and Reviews* 24. 3 (2011): 181–92.

——. "Writing the Intertwined Global Histories of Indigeneity and Diasporization: An Ecocritical Articulation of Place, Relationality, and Storytelling in the Poetry of Simon J. Ortiz." *Stories Through Theory/Theory Through Stories: Native American Storytelling and Critique*. Ed. Gordon Henry, Silvia Martinez-Falquina & Nieves Pascual Soler. Lansing: Michigan State University Press, 2009. 159–90.

Brown, Dee. *Bury My Heart at Wounded Knee: An Indian History of the American West*. 1970. Rpt. New York: Henry Holt, 2007.

Bruchac, Joseph, ed. *Survival This Way: Interviews with American Indian Poets*. Tucson: University of Arizona Press, 1987.

Brumble, H. David, III. *American Indian Autobiography*. Lincoln: University of Nebraska Press, 1988.

——. *An Annotated Bibliography of American Indian and Eskimo Autobiographies*. Lincoln: University of Nebraska Press, 1981.

Buscombe, Edward. *'Injuns!': Native Americans in the Movies*. London: Reaktion Books, 2006.

Calabrese, Joseph D. *A Different Medicine: Postcolonial Healing in the Native American Church*. New York: Oxford University Press, 2013.

Carlson, David J. *Sovereign Selves: American Indian Autobiography and the Law*. Urbana: University of Illinois Press, 2006.

Carpenter, Cari M. *Seeing Red: Anger, Sentimentality, and American Indians*. Columbus: Ohio State University Press, 2008.

——. "Tiresias Speaks: Sarah Winnemucca's Hybrid Selves and Genres." *Legacy* 19. 1 (2002): 71–80.

Carr, Helen. *Inventing the American Primitive: Politics, Gender and the Representation of Native American Literary Traditions, 1789–1936*. New York: New York University Press, 1996.

Carroll, Jeffrey, Brandy Nālani McDougall & Georganne Nordstrom, eds. *Huihui: Navigating Art and Literature of the Pacific*. Honolulu: University of Hawai'i Press, 2014.

Carson, Benjamin D. *Sovereignty, Separatism, and Survivance: Ideological Encounters in the Literatures of Native North America*. Cambridge: Cambridge Scholars Publishing, 2009.

Carson, David. *Crossing into Medicine Country: A Journey in Native American Healing*. New York: Arcade Publishing, 2005.

FURTHER READING

Carstarphen, Meta G. & John P. Sanchez, eds. *American Indians and the Mass Media*. Norman: University of Oklahoma Press, 2012.

Cate, Ricardo. *Without Reservations: The Cartoons of Ricardo Cate*. Layton, UT: Gibbs Smith, 2012.

Chaplin, Joyce. *Subject Matter: Technology, the Body, and Science on the Anglo-American Frontier, 1500–1676*. Cambridge, MA: Harvard University Press, 2001.

Chapman, Abraham, ed. *Literature of the American Indians: Views and Interpretations*. New York: New American Library, 1975.

Chari, Sangita & Jaime L. M. Lavallee, eds. *Accomplishing NAGPRA: Perspectives on the Intent, Impact, and Future of the Native American Graves Protection and Repatriation Act*. Corvallis: Oregon State University Press, 2013.

Cheyfitz, Eric, ed. *The Columbia Guide to American Indian Literatures of the United States since 1945*. New York: Columbia University Press, 2006.

Chief Eagle, Dallas. *Winter Count*. Lincoln: University of Nebraska Press, 2003.

Child, Brenda J. *Boarding School Seasons: American Indian Families, 1900–1940*. Lincoln: University of Nebraska Press, 1998.

Churchill, Ward & Jim Vander Wall. *The COINTELPRO Papers: Documents from the FBI's Secret Wars against Dissent in the United States*. 1990. Rpt. Cambridge, MA: South End Press, 2002.

Clements, William M. *Native American Verbal Art: Texts and Contexts*. Tucson: University of Arizona Press, 1996.

Clifford, James & George E. Marcus, eds. *Writing Cultures: The Poetics and Politics of Ethnography*. Berkeley: University of California Press, 1986.

Cobb, Amanda J. "Understanding Tribal Sovereignty: Definitions, Conceptualizations, and Interpretations." *American Studies* 46. 3–4 (2005): 115–32.

Cobb, Daniel. *Native Activism in Cold War America: The Struggle for Sovereignty*. Lawrence: University of Kansas Press, 2010.

Cohen, Felix S. *Handbook of Federal Indian Law*. Washington, D.C.: United States Government Printing Office, 1941.

Colonnese, Tom & Louis Owens, comps. *American Indian Novelists: An Annotated Critical Bibliography*. New York: Garland, 1985.

Coltelli, Laura, ed. *Winged Words: American Indian Writers Speak*. Lincoln: University of Nebraska Press, 1990.

Conley, Robert J. *The Cherokee Dragon: A Novel of the Real People*. New York: St. Martin's Press, 2000.

——. *Cherokee Medicine Man: The Life and Work of a Modern-Day Healer*. Norman: University of Oklahoma Press, 2014.

Cook-Lynn, Elizabeth. *Anti-Indianism in Modern America: A Voice from Tatekeya's Earth*. Urbana: University of Illinois Press, 2001.

——. *New Indians, Old Wars*. Urbana: University of Illinois Press, 2007.

——. *A Separate Country: Postcoloniality and American Indian Nations*. Lubbock: Texas Tech University Press, 2011.

Cox, James H. *Muting White Noise: Native American and European American Novel Traditions*. Norman: University of Oklahoma Press, 2006.

Cox, James H. & Daniel Heath Justice, eds. *The Oxford Handbook of Indigenous American Literature*. New York: Oxford University Press, 2014.

Crosby, Alfred W. *The Columbian Exchange: Biological and Cultural Consequences of 1492*. Westport, CT: Greenwood, 1972.

D'Ambrosio, Antonino. *A Heartbeat and a Guitar: Johnny Cash and the Making of Bitter Tears*. New York: Nation Books, 2009.

D'Aponte, Mimi Gisolfi, ed. *Seventh Generation: An Anthology of Native American Plays*. New York: Theatre Communications Group, 1999.

Dauenhauer, Nora. *Life Woven with Song: Poems*. Tucson: University of Arizona Press, 2000.

FURTHER READING

Davies Wade & Richmond L. Clow. *American Indian Sovereignty and Law: An Annotated Bibliography*. Lanham, MD: Scarecrow Press, 2009.

Däwes, Birgit, ed. *Indigenous North American Drama: A Multivocal History*. Albany: State University of New York Press, 2013

———. *Native North American Theater in a Global Age: Sites of Identity Construction and Transdifference*. Heidelberg: Winter, 2007.

Delbourgo, James, and Nicholas Dew, eds. *Science and Empire in the Atlantic World*. New York: Routledge, 2008.

Deloria, Philip J. *Playing Indian*. New Haven, CT: Yale, 1998.

Deloria, Vine, Jr. *Behind the Trail of Broken Treaties*. New York: Delacorte Press, 1974; Austin: University of Texas Press, 1985.

———. *God is Red: A Native View of Religion*. Golden, CO: Fulcrum Publishing, 2003.

———. "Intellectual Self-Determination and Sovereignty: Looking at the Windmills in Our Minds." *Wicazo Sa Review* 13. 1 (1998): 25–31.

Deloria, Vine, Jr. & Raymond DeMallie. *Documents of American Indian Diplomacy: Treaties, Agreements, and Conventions, 1775–1979*. 2 Vols. Norman: University of Oklahoma Press, 1999.

Deloria, Vine, Jr. & Clifford M. Lytle. *The Nations Within: The Past and Future of American Indian Sovereignty*. New York: Pantheon Books, 1984; 2nd ed. Austin: University of Texas Press, 1998.

Deloria, Vine, Jr. & David Wilkins. *Tribes, Treaties, and Constitutional Tribulations*. Austin: University of Texas Press, 2000.

Demby, Gene. "Updating Centuries-Old Folklore with Puzzles and Power-ups." *Code Switch: Frontiers of Race, Culture, and Ethnicity*. Web. Accessed 30 Nov. 2014.

Denson, Andrew. *Demanding the Cherokee Nation: Indian Autonomy and American Culture, 1830–1900*. Lincoln: University of Nebraska Press, 2004.

Derrida, Jacques. *The Animal That Therefore I Am*. Bronx, NY: Fordham University Press, 2008.

———. *The Beast and the Sovereign*. 2 Vols. Chicago: University of Chicago Press, 2011.

Diamond, Jared. *Guns, Germs, and Steel: The Fates of Human Societies*. New York: Norton, 1997.

Driskill, Qwo-Li. *Walking With Ghosts: Poems*. Cromer, Norfolk: Salt Publishing, 2005.

Driskill, Qwo-Li, Chris Finley, Brian Joseph Gilley & Scott Laura Morgensen, eds. *Queer Indigenous Studies: Critical Interventions in Theory, Politics, and Literature*. Tucson: University of Arizona Press, 2011.

Dudoit, Māhealani & ku'ualoha ho'omanawanui, eds. *'Ōiwi: a native hawaiian journal* 1–4. Honolulu: Kuleana 'Ōiwi Press, 1998, 2002, 2005, 2010.

Dussias, Allison M. "Ghost Dance and Holy Ghost: The Echoes of Nineteenth-Century Christianization Policy in Twentieth-Century Native American Free Exercise Cases." *Stanford Law Review* 49. 4 (1997): 773–852.

Eastman, Charles A. "The North American Indian." *Papers on Inter-Racial Problems, Communicated to the First Universal Races Congress Held at The University of London, July 26–29*. London: P.S. King & Son, 1911.

———. "The Story of Little Big Horn." *The Chautauquan*. (July 1900): 353–59.

Echo Hawk, Walter. *In the Courts of the Conqueror: The Ten Worst Indian Law Cases Ever Decided*. Golden, CO: Fulcrum, 2012.

Epple, Carolyn. "Coming to Terms with Navajo *Nádleehí*: A Critique of *Berdache*, 'Gay,' 'Alternate Gender,' and 'Two-Spirit.'" *American Ethnologist* 25. 2 (1998): 267–90.

Erdrich, Heid. www.heiderdrich.com. Web. Accessed 4 Dec. 2014.

Erdrich, Louise. *The Painted Drum*. New York: HarperCollins, 2005.

———. *The Round House*. New York: HarperCollins, 2012.

Ermine, Willie. "Aboriginal Epistemology." *First Nations Education in Canada: The Circle Unfolds*. Ed. Marie Battiste & Jean Barman. Vancouver: UBC Press, 1995. 101–12.

Ewalt, Margaret R. *Peripheral Wonders: Nature, Knowledge, and Enlightenment in the Eighteenth-Century Orinoco*. Lewisburg, PA: Bucknell University Press, 2009.

FURTHER READING

Fawcett, Melissa Jayne. *The Lasting of the Mohegans*. Uncasville, CT: The Mohegan Tribe, 1995.

——. *Medicine Trail: The Life and Lessons of Gladys Tantaquidgeon*. Tucson: University of Arizona Press, 2000.

Fienup-Riordan, Ann & Lawrence D. Kaplan, eds. *Words of the Real People: Alaska Native Literature in Translation*. Fairbanks: University of Alaska Press, 2007.

Fine-Dare, Kathleen. *The American Indian Repatriation Movement and NAGPRA*. Lincoln: University of Nebraska Press, 2002.

Finnegan, Ruth. *Literacy and Orality*. Oxford: Blackwell, 1988.

Fitz, Karsten, Sabine Meyer & Birgit Däwes, eds. *Twenty-First Century Perspectives on Indigenous Studies: Native North America in (Trans)Motion*. New York: Routledge, 2015.

Fitzgerald, Stephanie & Hilary E. Wyss, "Land and Literacy: The Textualities of Native Studies." *Early American Literature* 45. 2 (2010): 241–50.

Fleck, Richard F., ed. *Critical Perspectives on Native American Fiction*. Washington, D.C.: Three Continents Press, 1993.

Forbes, Jack. "Colonialism and Native American Literature: Analysis." *Wicazo Sa Review* 3. 2 (1987): 17–23.

——. "Intellectual Self-Determination and Sovereignty: Implications for Native Studies and for Native Intellectuals." *Wicazo Sa Review* 13. 1 (1998): 11–23.

Fortunate Eagle, Adam. *Heart of the Rock: The Indian Invasion of Alcatraz*. Norman: University of Oklahoma Press, 2002.

Garrison, Tim Alan. *The Legal Ideology of Removal: The Southern Judiciary and the Sovereignty of Native American Nations*. Athens: University of Georgia Press, 2002.

Geiogamah, Hanay & Jaye T. Darby, eds. *American Indian Theater in Performance: A Reader*. Los Angeles: UCLA American Indian Studies Center, 2000.

Gilley, Brian Joseph. *Becoming Two-Spirit: Gay Identity and Social Acceptance in Indian Country*. Lincoln: University of Nebraska Press, 2006.

Glancy, Diane. *Pushing the Bear: After the Trail of Tears*. Norman: University of Oklahoma Press, 2009.

Gomez, Reid. "The Storyteller's Escape: Sovereignty and Worldview." *Reading Native American Women: Critical/Creative Representations*. Ed. Inés Hernández-Avila. Lanham, MD: Altamira Press, 2005. 145–69.

Gonzalez, Mario & Elizabeth Cook-Lynn. *The Politics of Hallowed Ground: Wounded Knee and the Struggle for Indian Sovereignty*. Urbana: University of Illinois Press, 1998.

Gould, Janice. *Beneath My Heart: Poetry*. Ithaca, NY: Firebrand Books, 1990.

Graveline, Frye Jean. *Circle Works: Transforming Eurocentric Consciousness*. Black Point, Nova Scotia: Fernwood, 1998.

Green, Joyce, ed. *Making Space for Indigenous Feminism*. New York: Zed Books, 2007.

Guerra, Francisco. "Medical Colonization of the New World." *Medical History* 7. 2 (1963): 147–54.

Hall, Dana Naone, ed. *Mālama: Hawaiian Land and Water*. Honolulu: Bamboo Ridge Press, 1985.

Handley, William K. & N. Lewis. *True West: Authenticity and the American West*. Lincoln: Nebraska University Press, 2004.

Hanley, Anne & Carolyn Kremer, eds. *The Alaska Reader: Voices from the North*. Golden, CO: Fulcrum Publishing, 2005.

Hanson, Elizabeth I. *Forever There: Race and Gender in Contemporary Native American Fiction*. New York: Peter Lang, 1989.

Haraway, Donna J. *When Species Meet*. Minneapolis: University of Minnesota Press, 2008.

Harjo, Suzan Shown, ed. *Nation to Nation: Treaties between the United States and American Indian Nations*. Washington, D.C.: Smithsonian Books, 2014.

Harring, Sidney L. *Crow Dog's Case: American Indian Sovereignty, Tribal Law, and United States Law in the Nineteenth Century*. New York: Cambridge University Press, 1994.

FURTHER READING

Healy, Margaret. *Fictions of Disease in Early Modern England: Bodies, Plagues and Politics*. London: Palgrave, 2001.

Hearth, Amy Hill. *Strong Medicine Speaks: A Native American Elder Has Her Say*. New York: Simon & Schuster, 2008.

Hendricks, Steve. *The Unquiet Grave: The FBI and the Struggle for the Soul of Indian Country*. New York: Thunder's Mouth Press, 2006.

Henry, Gordon. *The Light People*. (1994). East Lansing: Michigan State University Press, 2003.

Hernández-Avila, Inés. *Reading Native American Women: Critical/Creative Representations*. Lanham, MD: AltaMira Press, 2005.

Hertzberg, Hazel W. *The Search for an American Indian Identity: Modern Pan-Indian Movements*. Syracuse, NY: Syracuse University Press, 1971.

Highway, Tomson. *Kiss of the Fur Queen: A Novel*. Norton: University of Oklahoma Press, 2006.

Hirsch, Bernard A. "'The Telling Which Continues': Oral Tradition and the Written Word in Leslie Marmon Silko's *Storyteller*." *American Indian Quarterly* 12 (1988): 1–26.

Hirschfelder, Arlene B., comp. *American Indian and Eskimo Authors*. New York: Association on American Indian Affairs, 1973.

Hoffmann, Robert Davis. *Village Boy: Poems of Cultural Identity*. N/A: CreateSpace Independent Publishing Platform, 2014.

Hogan, Linda. *The Book of Medicines: Poems*. Minneapolis, MN: Coffee House, 1993.

——. *People of the Whale*. New York: W.W. Norton, 2009.

Holt, John Dominis. *Hānai: A Poem for Queen Liliʻuokalani*. Honolulu: Topgallant Press, 1986.

hoʻomanawanui, kuʻualoha. *Voices of Fire: Reweaving the Literary Lei of Pele and Hiʻiaka*. Minneapolis: University of Minnesota Press, 2012.

Hopkins, Sarah Winnemucca. *Life among the Piutes: Their Wrongs and Claims*. Reno: University of Nevada, 1994.

Howe, LeAnne, Harvey Markowitz & Denise K. Cummings, eds. *Seeing Red: Hollywood's Pixeled Skins: American Indians and Film*. East Lansing: Michigan State University Press, 2013.

Hoxie, Frederick E. *A Final Promise: The Campaign to Assimilate the Indians, 1880–1920*. Lincoln: University of Nebraska Press, 2001.

Hudson, Brian K. & Dustin Gray, eds. *Animal Studies*. Special issue of *Studies in American Indian Literatures* 25. 4 (2013).

Hughte, Phil. *A Zuni Artist Looks at Frank Hamilton Cushing*. Zuni, NM: Pueblo of Zuni Arts & Crafts/A: Shiwi A-Wan Museum and Heritage Center, 1994.

Hymes, Dell. *"In vain I tried to tell you": Essays in Native American Ethnopoetics*. Philadelphia: University of Pennsylvania, 1981.

Indian Nations. Washington, D.C.: Smithsonian Books, 2014.

Indigenous Foundations. "Land Rights." Online. Accessed June 2013. http://indigenousfoundations. arts.ubc.ca/home/land-rights.html

Irwin, Lee. "Freedom, Law, and Prophecy: A Brief History of Native American Religious Resistance." *American Indian Quarterly* 21. 1 (1997): 35–55.

Iverson, Peter. *Carlos Montezuma and the Changing World of American Indians*. Albuquerque: University of New Mexico Press, 1982.

Jacobs, Sue-Ellen, Wesley Thomas & Sabine Lang, eds. *Two-Spirit People: Native American Gender Identity, Sexuality, and Spirituality*. Urbana: University of Illinois Press, 1997.

Jacobson, Angeline. *Contemporary Native American Literature: A Selected & Partially Annotated Bibliography*. Metuchen, NY: Scarecrow Press, 1977.

Jaimes, M. Annette, ed. *The State of Native America: Genocide, Colonization, and Resistance*. Boston: South End Press, 1992.

Jaimes-Guerrero, M. A. "'Patriarchal Colonialism' and Indigenism: Implications for Native Feminist Spirituality and Native Womanism." *Hypatia* 18. 2 (Spring 2003): 58–69.

FURTHER READING

Jarvis, Brad D. E. *The Brothertown Nation of Indians: Land, Ownership and Nationalism in Early America, 1740–1840*. Lincoln: University of Nebraska Press, 2010.

Jaskoski, Helen. "'A Terrible Sickness among Them': Smallpox and Stories of the Frontier." *Early Native American Writing: New Critical Essays*. Ed. Helen Jaskoski. New York: Cambridge University Press, 1996. 136–57.

Johansen, Bruce. *Encyclopedia of the American Indian Movement*. Westport, CT: Greenwood, 2013.

Johansen, Bruce & Roberto Maestas. *Wasi'chu: The Continuing Indian Wars*. New York: Monthly Review Press, 1979.

Johnson, Troy. *The Indian Occupation of Alcatraz Island and the Rise of Indian Activism*. Urbana: University of Illinois Press, 1996.

Justice, Daniel Heath. *The Way of Thorn and Thunder*. Fantasy Trilogy. Albuquerque: University of New Mexico Press, 2005, 2006, 2007.

Kahakauwila, Kristiana. *This is Paradise*. New York: Hogarth, 2013.

Kalahele, Imaikalani. *Kalahele*. Honolulu: Kalamaku Press, 2002.

Kalter, Susan. *Benjamin Franklin, Pennsylvania, and the First Nations: The Treaties of 1732–62*. Urbana: University of Illinois Press, 2006.

Kane, Joan Naviyuk. *The Cormorant Hunter's Wife*. Fairbanks: University of Alaska Press, 2012.

——. *Hyperboreal*. Pittsburg, PA: University of Pittsburg Press, 2013.

Kaopio, Matthew. *Written in the Sky*. Honolulu: Mutual Publishing, 2002.

Kilcup, Karen L. *Native American Women's Writing: An Anthology c. 1800–1924*. New York: Blackwell, 2000.

Kilpatrick, Jacqueline. *Celluloid Indians: Native Americans and Film*. Lincoln: University of Nebraska Press, 1999.

King, Thomas. *The Inconvenient Indian: A Curious Account of Native People in North America*. Minneapolis: University of Minnesota Press, 2013.

——. *The Truth about Stories: A Native Narrative*. Minneapolis: University of Minnesota Press, 2003.

Konkle, Maureen. *Writing Indian Nations: Native Intellectuals and the Politics of Historiography, 1827–1863*. Chapel Hill: University of North Carolina Press, 2004.

Krueger, Victoria, Bobette Perrone & H. Henrietta Stockel. *Medicine Women, Curanderas, and Women Doctors*. Norman: University of Oklahoma Press, 2012.

Krupat, Arnold. *Ethnocriticism: Ethnography, History, Literature*. Berkeley: University of California Press, 1992.

——. *For Those Who Come After: A Study of Native American Autobiography*. Berkeley: University of California Press, 1985.

——. *Native American Autobiography: An Anthology*. Madison: University of Wisconsin Press, 1994.

——, ed. *New Voices in Native American Literary Criticism*. Washington, D.C.: Smithsonian Institution Press, 1993.

Kymlicka, Will & Sue Donaldson. *Zoopolis: A Political Theory of Animal Rights*. Oxford: Oxford University Press, 2013.

Lacan, Jacques. *The Seminar of Jacques Lacan: Book II: The Ego in Freud's Theory and in the Technique of Psychoanalysis 1954–1955*. New York: W.W. Norton & Company, 1991.

LaDuke, Winona. *Last Woman Standing*. St. Paul, MN: Voyageur Press, 1997.

LaFavor, Carole. *Along the Journey River: A Mystery*. Ithaca, NY: Firebrand Books, 1996.

LaPensée, Elizabeth. "Aboriginal Territories in Cyberspace: Interview with Michael Sheyahshe" Abtec.org. 6 Apr. 2009, n. pag. Web. Accessed 31 Dec. 2014. http://www.abtec.org/blog/?p=118

Lepore, Jill. *The Name of War: King Philip's War and the Origins of American Identity*. New York: Vintage Books, 1998.

Liberty, Margot, ed. *American Indian Intellectuals*. St. Paul, MN: West, 1978.

Littlefield, Daniel F., Jr. & James W. Parins, comps. *American Indian and Alaskan Native Newspapers and Periodicals, 1826–1924*. Westport, CT: Greenwood, 1984.

FURTHER READING

Lomawaima, Tsianina. *They Called It Prairie Light: The Story of Chilocco Indian School*. Lincoln: University of Nebraska Press, 1994.

Lopenzina, Drew. *Red Ink: Native Americans Picking up the Pen in the Colonial Period*. Albany: SUNY Press, 2012.

Love, William Deloss. *Samson Occom and the Christian Indians of New England*. Syracuse, NY: Syracuse University Press, 2000.

Maddox, Lucy. *Citizen Indians: Native American Intellectuals, Race and Reform*. Ithaca, NY: Cornell University Press, 2005.

——. *Removals: Nineteenth-Century American Indian Literature and the Politics of Indian Affairs*. Oxford: Oxford University Press, 1991.

Madsen, Deborah, ed. *The Poetry and Poetics of Gerald Vizenor*. Albuquerque: University of New Mexico Press, 2012.

——. "The Tribal Trajectory of Vizenor's Poetic Career." *The Poetry and Poetics of Gerald Vizenor*. Ed. Deborah Madsen. Albuquerque: University of New Mexico Press, 2012. ix–xxiii.

——. *Understanding Gerald Vizenor*. Columbia: University of South Carolina Press, 2009.

Mālama: Hawaiian Land and Water. Ed. Dana Naone Hall. Honolulu: Bamboo Ridge Press, 1985.

Mander, Jerry & Victoria Tauli-Corpuz, eds. *Paradigm Wars: Indigenous Peoples' Resistance to Globalization*. San Francisco: Sierra Club, 2006.

Martin, Joel W. and Nichols, Mark A., eds. *Native Americans, Christianity, and the Reshaping of the American Religious Landscape*. Chapel Hill: University of North Carolina Press, 2010.

Marubbio, M. Elise & Eric L. Buffalohead, eds. *Native Americans on Film: Conversations, Teaching, and Theory*. Lexington: University Press of Kentucky, 2013.

Mathews, John Joseph. *Wah'Ko-Tah: The Osage and the White Man's Road*. Norman: University of Oklahoma Press, 1932.

McDougall, Brandy Nālani. *The Salt-Wind, Ka Makani Pa'akai*. Honolulu: Kuleana 'Ōiwi Press, 2008.

McDougall, Brandy Nālani & Craig Santos Perez. *Undercurrent*. Honolulu: Hawai'i Dub Machine, 2010.

McLeod, Neal. *Cree Narrative Memory: From Treaties to Contemporary Times*. Saskatoon, Saskatchewan: Purich, 2007.

McPherson, Michael. *All Those Summers*. Honolulu: Watermark Publishing, 2004.

——. *Singing with the Owls*. Honolulu: Petronium Press, 1982.

Mehl-Madrona, Lewis. *Coyote Medicine: Lessons from Native American Healing*. New York: Simon & Schuster, 2011.

Mergler, Wayne, ed. *The Last New Land: Stories of Alaska Past and Present*. Anchorage: Alaska Northwest Books, 1996.

Meyer, Manulani. A. "Hawaiian Hermeneutics and the Triangulation of Meaning: Gross, Subtle, Causal." *Canadian Journal of Native Education*, 27. 2 (2003): 249–55.

Mielke, Laura L. *Moving Encounters: Sympathy and the Indian Question in Antebellum Literature*. Amherst: University of Massachusetts Press, 2008.

Mignolo, Walter D. & Elizabeth Hill Boone, eds. *Writing Without Words: Alternative Literacies in Mesoamerica and the Andes*. Durham, NC: Duke University Press, 1994.

Mihesuah, Devon. *Indigenous American Women: Decolonization, Empowerment, Activism*. Lincoln: University of Nebraska Press, 2003.

Miller, Robert. *Native America, Discovered and Conquered: Thomas Jefferson, Lewis and Clark, and Manifest Destiny*. Lincoln, NE: Bison Books, 2008.

Miranda, Deborah. *Indian Cartography*. Greenfield Center, NY: Greenfield Review Press, 1999.

——. *The Zen of La Llorona*. Cromer, Norfolk: Salt Publishing, 2005.

Momaday, N. Scott. *The Man Made of Words*. New York, St. Martin's Griffin, 1998.

——. "Personal Reflections." *The American Indian and the Problem of History*. Ed. Calvin Martin. New York: Oxford University Press, 1987.

FURTHER READING

Mooney, James. *The Ghost Dance Religion and the Sioux Outbreak of 1890*. Ed. Anthony F.C. Wallace. Chicago: University of Chicago Press, 1965.

Moore, David L. "Decolonializing Criticism: Reading Dialectics and Dialogics in Native American Literatures." *Studies in American Indian Literatures* 6. 4 (1994): 7–35.

——. *That Dream Shall Have a Name: Native Americans Rewriting America*. Lincoln: University of Nebraska Press, 2013.

Moraga, Cherríe & Gloria Anzaldúa, eds. *This Bridge Called My Back: Writings by Radical Women of Color*. Watertown, MA: Persephone Press, 1981.

Murphy, James E. & Sharon M. Murphy. *Let My People Know: American Indian Journalism, 1828–1978*. Norman: University of Oklahoma Press, 1991.

Murray, David. *Forked Tongues: Speech, Writing, and Representation in North American Indian Texts*. Bloomington: Indiana University Press, 1991.

Naranjo, Tito & Rina Swentzell. "Healing Spaces in the Tewa Pueblo World." *American Indian Culture and Research Journal* 13. 3 & 4 (1989): 257–65.

Niezen, Ronald. *Spirit Wars: Native North American Religions in the Age of Nation Building*. Berkeley: University of California Press, 2000.

Noori, Margaret. "Native American Narratives from Early Art to Graphic Novels." *Multicultural Comics: From* Zap *to* Blue Beetle. Austin: University of Texas Press, 2010, 55–72.

Norgren, Jill. *The Cherokee Cases: The Confrontation of Law and Politics*. New York: McGraw Hill, 1996.

Northrup, Jim. *The Rez Road Follies: Canoes, Casinos, Computers, and Birch Bark Baskets*. Minneapolis: University of Minnesota Press, 1999.

Numbers, Ronald L., ed. *Medicine in the New World: New Spain, New France, and New England*. Knoxville: University of Tennessee Press, 1987.

O'Brien, Jean & Amy Den Ouden, eds. *Recognition, Sovereignty Struggles and Indigenous Rights in the United States: A Sourcebook*. Chapel Hill: University of North Carolina Press, 2013.

Odjick, Jay. www.kagagi.squarespace.com. Web. Accessed 4 Dec. 2014.

Ong, Walter J. *Orality and Literacy: The Technologizing of the Word*. New York: Routledge, 1982.

Ortiz, Simon J. *Song, Poetry and Language – Expression and Perception*. Tsaile, AZ: Navajo Community College Press, n.d.

Parrish, Susan Scott. *American Curiosity: Cultures of Natural History in the Colonial British Atlantic World*. Chapel Hill: University of North Carolina Press, 2006.

Penner, Andrea M. "'The Original in Ourselves': Native American Women Writers and the Construction of Indian Women's Identity." Diss. University of New Mexico, 2001.

Perdue, Theda. *Nations Remembered: An Oral History of the Five Civilized Tribes, 1865–1907*. Westport, CT: Greenwood, 1980.

——. "Writing the Ethnohistory of Native Women." *Rethinking American Indian History*. Ed. Donald L. Fixico. Albuquerque: University of New Mexico Press, 1997. 73–87.

Perdue, Theda & Michael D. Green, eds. *The Cherokee Removal: A Brief History with Documents*. Boston: Bedford/St. Martin's, 1995.

Perez-Wendt. *Māhealani*. *Uluhaimalama*. Honolulu: Kuleana ʻŌiwi Press, 2008.

Pevar, Stephen L. *The Rights of Indians and Tribes*. 4th ed. New York: Oxford University Press, 2012.

Pewewardy, Cornel. "From Subhuman to Superhuman: The Evolution of American Indian Images in Comic Books." *American Indian Stereotypes in the World of Children: A Reader and Bibliography*. 2nd ed. Ed. Arlene Hirschfelder, Paulette Fairbanks Molin & Yvonne Wakim. Lanham, MD: Scarecrow Press, 1999. 193–98.

——. "From Subhuman to Superhuman: Images of First Nation Peoples in Comic Books." *Studies in Media and Information Literacy Education* 2. 2 (2002): 1–9.

Peyer, Bernd C. *The Tutor'd Mind: Indian Missionary Writers in Antebellum America*. Amherst: University of Massachusetts Press, 1997.

FURTHER READING

Pinson, Elizabeth. *Alaska's Daughter: An Eskimo Memoir of the Twentieth Century*. Logan: Utah State University Press, 2005.

Pommersheim, Frank. *Braid of Feathers: American Indian Law and Contemporary Tribal Life*. Berkeley: University of California Press, 1997.

Porter, Joy & Kenneth M. Roemer, eds. *The Cambridge Companion to Native American Literature*. New York: Cambridge University Press, 2005.

Powell, Malea. "Sarah Winnemucca Hopkins: Her Wrongs and Claims." *American Indian Rhetorics of Survivance: Word Magic, Word Medicine*. Ed. Ernest Stromberg. Pittsburgh: University of Pittsburgh Press, 2006. 89–127.

Prucha, Francis Paul. *American Indian Treaties: The History of a Political Anomaly*. Berkeley: University of California Press, 1994.

——, ed. *Documents of United State Indian Policy*. 3rd ed. Lincoln: University of Nebraska Press, 2000.

——. *The Great Father: The United States Government and American Indians*. Lincoln: University of Nebraska Press, 1986.

Purdy, John & James Ruppert, eds. *Nothing But the Truth: An Anthology of Native American Literature*. Upper Saddle River, NJ: Prentice Hall, 2001.

Raheja, Michelle H. *Reservation Reelism: Redfacing, Visual Sovereignty, and Representations of Native Americans in Film*. Lincoln: University of Nebraska Press, 2011.

Rainwater, Catherine, ed. *Dreams of Fiery Stars: The Transformations of Native American Fiction*. Philadelphia: University of Pennsylvania Press, 2011.

Rannow, Robin K. "Religion: The First Amendment and the American Indian Religious Freedom Act." *American Indian Law Review* 10. 1 (1982): 151–66.

Revard, Carter. *From the Extinct Volcano, a Bird of Paradise*. Norman, OK: Mongrel Empire Press, 2014.

Richter, Daniel. *The Ordeal of the Longhouse: The Peoples of the Iroquois League in the Era of European Colonization*. Chapel Hill: University of North Carolina Press, 1992.

Rifkin, Mark. *The Erotics of Sovereignty: Queer Native Writing in the Era of Self-Determination*. Minneapolis: University of Minnesota Press, 2012.

——. *When Did Indians Become Straight? Kinship, the History of Sexuality, and Native Sovereignty*. Oxford: Oxford University Press, 2011.

Robertson, Lindsay G. *Conquest by Law: How the Discovery of America Dispossessed the Indigenous Peoples of Their Lands*. Oxford: Oxford University Press, 2005.

Roemer, Kenneth M., ed. *Native American Writers of the United States*. DLB 175. Detroit: Gale Research, 1997.

Rollins, Peter C. & John E. O'Connor, eds. *Hollywood's Indian: The Portrayal of the Native American in Film*. Lexington: University Press of Kentucky, 2003.

Ronda, Jeanne & James P. Ronda. "'As They Were Faithful': Chief Hendrick Aupaumut and the Struggle for Stockbridge Survival, 1757–1830." *American Indian Culture and Research Journal* 3 (1979): 43–55.

Roscoe, Will. *Changing Ones: Third and Fourth Genders in Native North America*. 1998. Rpt. London: Palgrave Macmillan, 2000.

——. *The Zuni Man-Woman*. Albuquerque: University of New Mexico Press, 1992.

Rosenblatt, Louise M. "The Poet as Event." *College English* 26. 2 (1964): 123–28.

Rosenthal, Caroline. *Narrative Deconstructions of Gender in Works by Audrey Thomas, Daphne Marlatt, and Louise Erdrich*. Rochester, NY: Camden House, 2003.

Ross, Gyasi & Michael O. Finley. "Circle of Violence: An Open Letter to People Regarding the Rape and Sexual Assault of Indian Women." *Indian Country Today*. Indian Country Today Media Network, 4 Aug. 2011. n. pag. Web. Accessed 4 Aug. 2014. http://indiancountrytodaymedianetwork. com/2011/08/04/circle-violence-open-letter-people-regarding-rape-and-sexual-assault-indian-women

FURTHER READING

Ross, Luana. "From the 'F' Word to Indigenous/Feminisms." *Wicazo Sa Review* (Fall 2009): 39–52.

Ruoff, A. LaVonne Brown. *American Indian Literatures: An Introduction, Bibliographic Review, and Selected Bibliography.* New York: Modern Language Association, 1990.

———. "The Survival of Tradition: American Indian Oral and Written Narratives." *The Massachusetts Review* 27. 2 (1986): 274–93.

Ruppert, James. "Paula Gunn Allen and Joy Harjo: Closing the Distance between Personal and Mythic Space." *American Indian Quarterly* 7. 1 (1983): 27–40.

Rusco, Elmer R. *A Fateful Time: The Background and Legislative History of the Indian Reorganization Act.* Reno: University of Nevada Press, 2000.

Sanders, William. "At Ten Wolf Lake." *East of the Sun and West of Fort Smith.* Highgate Center, VT: Norilana, 2008. 410–30.

Sarris, Greg. *Grand Avenue: A Novel in Stories.* New York: Penguin, 1995.

———. "On the Road to Lolsel: Conversations with Mabel McKay." *News from Native California* 25. 4 (Summer 1988): 3–6.

Scheckel, Susan. *The Insistence of the Indian: Race and Nationalism in Nineteenth-Century American Culture.* Princeton, NJ: Princeton University Press, 1998.

Scheiding, Oliver, ed. *Native American Studies across Time and Space: Essays on the Indigenous Americas.* Heidelberg: Winter, 2010.

Schmidt, David L. & Murdena Marshall, eds. *Mi'kmaq Hieroglyphic Prayers: Reading in North America's First Indigenous Script.* Halifax, Nova Scotia: Nimbus Publications, 1995.

Schneider, Bethany. "Boudinot's Change: Boudinot, Emerson, and Ross on Cherokee Removal." *English Literary History* 75. 1 (2008): 151–77.

Schoolcraft, Henry Rowe. *Indian Legends.* Ed. Mentor L. Williams. East Lansing: Michigan State University Press, 1991.

Schweninger, Lee. *Imagic Moments: Indigenous North American Film.* Athens: University of Georgia Press, 2013.

———. "'Only an Indian Woman': Sarah Winnemucca and the Heroic Protagonist." *Native American Women in Literature and Culture.* Porto, Portugal: Fernando Pessoa University Press, 1997. 157–61.

Scofield, Gregory. *Love Medicine and One Song.* Vancouver: Raincoast Books, 2000.

———. "You Can Always Count on an Anthropologist (To Set You Straight, Crooked or Somewhere In-between." *Me Sexy: An Exploration of Native Sex and Sexuality.* Ed. Drew Hayden Taylor. Vancouver: Douglas and McIntyre, 2008.

Sears, Vickie. *Simple Songs.* Ithaca, NY: Firebrand Books, 1990.

Senier, Siobhan. *Voices of American Indian Assimilation and Resistance: Helen Hunt Jackson, Sarah Winnemucca, and Victoria Howard.* Norman: University of Oklahoma Press, 2001.

Shanley, Kathryn W. "'Born from the Need to Say': Boundaries and Sovereignties in Native American Literary and Cultural Studies." *Paradoxa* 15 (2001): 3–16.

———. "The Indians America Loves to Love and Read: American Indian Identity and Cultural Appropriation." *Native American Representations: First Encounters, Distorted Images, and Literary Appropriations.* Ed. Gretchen M. Bataille. Lincoln: University of Nebraska Press, 2001. 25–49.

Sherzer, Joel & Anthony C. Woodbury, eds. *Native American Discourse: Poetic and Rhetoric.* Cambridge: Cambridge University Press, 1987.

Silko, Leslie Marmon. "Language and Literature from a Pueblo Indian Perspective." *English Literature: Opening Up the Canon.* Ed. Leslie A. Fiedler & Houston A. Baker Jr. Baltimore, MD: Johns Hopkins University Press, 1981. 54–72.

———. *Yellow Woman and a Beauty of the Spirit.* New York: Simon & Schuster, 1997.

Silva, Cristobal. *Miraculous Plagues: An Epidemiology of Early New England Narrative.* Oxford: Oxford University Press, 2011.

Silverman David J. *Red Brethren: The Brothertown and Stockbridge Indians and the Problem of Race in Early America.* Ithaca, NY: Cornell University Press, 2010.

FURTHER READING

Simpson, Leanne. "Anticolonial Strategies for the Recovery and Maintenance of Indigenous Knowledge." *American Indian Quarterly* 28. 3&4 (2004): 373–84.

Singer, Beverly R. *Wiping the War Paint off the Lens: Native American Film and Video.* Minneapolis: University of Minnesota Press, 2001.

Smith, Andrea. "Queer Theory and Native Studies: The Heteronormativity of Settler Colonialism." *GLQ: A Journal of Lesbian and Gay Studies* 16. 1–2 (2010): 41–68.

Smith, Huston. *A Seat at the Table: In Conversation with Native Americans on Religious Freedoms.* Berkeley: University of California Press, 2006.

Smith, Paul Chaat & Robert Warrior. *Like a Hurricane: The Indian Movement from Alcatraz to Wounded Knee.* New York: The New Press, 1997.

Smith, Rogers M. *Civic Ideals: Conflicting Visions of Citizenship in U.S. History.* New Haven, CT: Yale University Press, 1997.

Sockbeson, Henry. "Repatriation Act Protects Native American Burials and Artifacts." *NARF Legal Review* 16. 1 (Winter 1990/91): 1–4.

Sowell, David. *The Tale of Healer Miguel Perdomo Neira: Medicine, Ideologies, and Power in the Nineteenth-century Andes.* Wilmington, DE: Scholarly Resources, 2001.

Spacks, Ruth. *America's Second Tongue: American Indian Education and the Ownership of English, 1860–1900.* Lincoln: University of Nebraska, 2002.

Spiers, Miriam Brown. "Creating a Haida Manga: The Formline of Social Responsibility in *Red*." *Studies in American Indian Literatures* 26. 3 (Fall 2014): 41–61.

St. Germain, Jill. *Indian Treaty-Making Policies in the United States and Canada, 1867–1877.* Lincoln: University of Nebraska Press. 2001.

Standing Bear, Luther. *Stories of the Sioux* 1934. Rpt. Lincoln: University of Nebraska Press, 2006.

Stanlake, Christy, ed. *Nations Speaking: Indigenous Performances across the Americas.* Special Issue of *Baylor Journal of Theatre and Performance* 4. 1 (Spring 2007).

——. *Native American Drama: A Critical Perspective.* Cambridge: Cambridge University Press, 2009.

State [of Washington] *v. Tulee* 7 Wash. 2d 124, 109 P.2d 280 (1941).

Stearns, Raymond Phineas. *Science in the British Colonies of America.* Urbana: University of Illinois Press, 1970.

Stromberg, Ernest, ed. *American Indian Rhetorics of Survivance: Word Medicine, Word Magic.* Pittsburgh, PA: University of Pittsburgh Press, 2006.

Swann, Brian & Arnold Krupat, eds. *Recovering the Word: Essays on Native American Literature.* Berkeley: University of California Press, 1987.

Takehiro, *Sage U'ilani. Honua.* Honolulu: Kahuaomānoa Press, 2006.

Taylor, Drew Hayden, ed. *Me Sexy: An Exploration of Native Sex and Sexuality.* Vancouver: Douglas & McIntyre, 2008.

Tedlock, Dennis, trans. *Popul Vuh: The Definitive Edition of the Mayan Book of the Dawn of Life and the Glories of Gods and Kings.* New York: Simon & Schuster, 1985.

Tedlock, Dennis & Barbara Tedlock, eds. *Teachings from the American Earth: Indian Religion and Philosophy.* Toronto: Vail Ballou Press, 1975.

Teuton, Sean. "A Question of Relationship: Internationalism and Assimilation in Recent American Indian Studies." *American Literary History* 18 (2006): 152–74.

Thomas, David Hurst. *Skull Wars: Kennewick Man, Archaeology, and the Battle for Native American Identity.* New York: Basic Books, 2000.

Tisinger, Danielle. "Textual Performance and the Western Frontier: Sarah Winnemucca's *Life Among the Piutes.*" *Western American Literature* 37. 2 (2002): 171–94.

Toelken, J. Barre. "The 'Pretty Language' of Yellowman: Genre, Mode, and Texture in Navaho Coyote Narratives." *Genre* 2. 3 (1969): 211–35.

Tohe, Laura. "There is No Word for Feminism in My Language." *Wicazo Sa Review* 15. 2 (2003): 103–10.

FURTHER READING

Trafzer, Clifford E. & Diane E. Weine. *Medicine Ways: Disease, Health, and Survival among Native Americans.* Walnut Creek, CA: AltaMira Press, 2001.

Treuer, David. *Native American Fiction: A User's Manual.* Minneapolis, MN: Graywolf, 2006.

"Tribal Equity Toolkit: Tribal Resolutions and Codes to Support Two Spirit and LGBT Justice in Indian Country." *Lewis and Clark Graduate School of Education and Counseling.* Web. Accessed 21 June 2013. https://graduate.lclark.edu/programs/indigenous_ways_of_knowing/tribal_equity_toolkit/

Udel, Lisa J. "Revision and Resistance: The Politics of Native Women's Motherwork." *Frontiers* XXII. 2 (2001): 43–62.

Vecsey, Christopher, ed. *Handbook of American Indian Religious Freedoms.* New York: The Crossroad Publishing Company, 1991.

Velie, Alan R., ed. *Native American Perspectives on Literature and History.* Norman: University of Oklahoma Press, 1995.

Velie, Alan R. & A. Robert Lee, eds. *The Native American Renaissance: Literary Imagination and Achievement.* Norman: University of Oklahoma Press, 2013.

Venegas, Yolanda. "The Erotics of Racialization: Gender and Sexuality in the Making of California." *Frontiers* 25. 3 (2004): 63–89.

Veregge, Jeffery. Art/Design/Mischief. www.jeffreyveregge.com. Web. Accessed 4 Dec. 2014.

Vizenor, Gerald. "Authored Animals: Creature Tropes in Native American Fiction." *Social Research* 62. 3 (Fall 1995): 661–83.

——. *Chancers.* Norman: University of Oklahoma Press, 2000.

——. *Interior Landscapes: Autobiographical Myths and Metaphors.* 2nd ed. Albany: State University of New York Press. 2009.

——. "Ishi and the Wood Ducks." *Native American Literature: A Brief Introduction and Anthology.* Ed. Gerald Vizenor. New York: HarperCollins, 1995. 299–336.

——. *Native Liberty: Natural Reason and Cultural Survivance.* Lincoln: University of Nebraska Press, 2009.

Voyageur, Cora, David Newhouse & Dan Beavon, eds. *Hidden in Plain Sight: Contributions of Aboriginal Peoples to Canadian Identity and Culture,* Vol. 1. 2nd rev. ed. Toronto: University of Toronto Press, Scholarly Publishing Division, 2005.

Wald, Priscilla. *Contagious: Cultures, Carriers, and the Outbreak Narrative.* Durham, NC: Duke University Press, 2008.

Walker, Cheryl. *Indian Nation: Native American Literature and Nineteenth-Century Nationalisms.* Durham, NC: Duke University Press, 1997.

Wallace, Paul A. W. *White Roots of Peace: The Iroquois Book of Life.* Sante Fe, NM: Clear Light Publishers, 1994.

Wallis, Velma. *Raising Ourselves: A Gwich'in Coming of Age Story from the Yukon River.* Kenmore, WA: Epicenter Press, 2002.

Warrior, Robert, ed. *The World of Indigenous North America.* New York: Routledge, 2014.

Washington Passenger Fishing Vessel 443 U.S. 658 (1979).

Waters, A., ed. *American Indian Thought: Philosophical Essays.* Malden, MA: Blackwell Publishers, 2004.

Weatherford, Jack. *Savages and Civilization: Who Will Survive?* New York: Fawcett Columbine, 1994.

Wendt, Albert, Reina Whaitiri & Robert Sullivan, eds. *Mauri Ola.* Honolulu: University of Hawai'i Press, 2010.

——, eds. *Whetu Moana.* Honolulu: University of Hawai'i Press, 2003.

Westlake, Wayne. *Westlake: Poems by Wayne Kaumualii Westlake (1947–1984).* Ed. Mei-Li Siy & Richard Hamasaki. Honolulu: University of Hawai'i Press, 2009.

Wheeler, Rachel. *To Live Upon Hope: Mohicans and Missionaries in the Eighteenth-Century Northeast.* Ithaca, NY: Cornell University Press, 2008.

FURTHER READING

White, Richard. *The Middle Ground: Indians, Empires and Republics in the Great Lakes Region, 1650–1815*. New York: Cambridge University Press, 1991.

Wiget, Andrew O., ed. *Critical Essays on Native American Literature*. Boston: G. K. Hall, 1985.

———, ed. *Handbook of Native American Literature*. New York: Garland, 1996.

———. *Native American Literature*. Boston: Twayne, 1985.

Wilkins, David. *American Indian Sovereignty and the U.S. Supreme Court: The Masking of Justice*. Austin: University of Texas Press, 1997.

Wilkins, David E. & Heidi Kiiwetinepinesiik Stark. *American Indian Politics and the American Indian Political System*. 3rd ed. New York: Rowman & Littlefield, 2011.

Wilkins, David E. & K. Tsianina Lomawaima. *Uneven Ground: American Indian Sovereignty and Federal Law*. Norman: University of Oklahoma Press, 2001.

Williams, Robert A., Jr. *The American Indian in Western Legal Thought: The Discourse of Conquest*. Oxford: Oxford University Press, 1992.

———. *Like a Loaded Weapon: The Rehnquist Court, Indian Rights, and the Legal History of Racism in the United States*. Minneapolis: University of Minnesota Press, 2005.

Williams, Walter L. *Spirit and the Flesh: Sexual Diversity in American Indian Culture*. Boston: Beacon Press, 1986.

Wilson, Shawn. *Research is Ceremony: Indigenous Research Methods*. Black Point, Nova Scotia: Fernwood Publishing, 2008.

Witalec, Janet, ed. *Native North American Literature*. Detroit: Gale Research, 1994.

Wong, Hertha. *Sending My Heart Back Across the Years: Tradition and Innovation in Native American Autobiography*. New York: Oxford University Press, 1992.

Wyss, Hilary. *Writing Indians: Literacy, Christianity, and Native Community in Early America*. Amherst: University of Massachusetts Press, 2000.

Yahgulanaas, Michael Nicoll. www.mny.ca. Web. Accessed 4 Dec. 2014.

Zolbrod, Paul G. *Reading the Voice: Native American Oral Poetry on the Page*. Salt Lake City: University of Utah Press, 1995.

INDEX

1491s 490

Acosta, Alberto 199
activism: American Indian Movement
(AIM) 7, 66, 111, 118, 183, 261, 273,
277, 281; Coalition for Navajo Liberation
281; Cowboy and Indian Alliance against
the KXL pipeline 246, 259; Fort Lawton
occupation (1970) 273, 276; Idle No
More Movement 105, 285, 459; Missing
and Murdered Awareness 285; Occupation
of Alcatraz Island 141, 273; Occupation of
Kanehsatà:ke & Kahnawà:ke (1990 Oka Crisis)
285; Occupy Movement 346; Puyallup fish-in
(1970) 276; Red Power 7, 66, 178, 276;
Survival of American Indians Association
275, 281; Trail of Self Determination (1976)
274; Wounded Knee occupation (1973) 118,
136, 141, 143, 274, 277
Adams, Hank 36, 275–6
Adamson, Joni 240, 243, 255
Adamson, Rebecca L. 280
Akins, Adrienne 220
Alaska 28–37, 199, 201n4, 382–4, 385, 491:
Alaska Purchase (1867) 383, 385
Alcantara-Camacho, Dåko'ta 47
Alencar, José de 20, 21
Alexie, Sherman 80, 137, 184, 251, 266,
345, 419, 445, 448, 451, 453–4, 460,
474, 483: *The Absolutely True Diary of a
Part Time Indian* 453, 481; "Blankets" 257;
Flight 453, 474; "I Would Steal Horses" 251;
Indian Killer 165, 268–9, 453; *Reservation
Blues* 454
Alfred, Taiaiake 198, 293, 294
Alighieri, Dante 461
Allen, Chadwick 5, 54, 67, 111, 372, 373
Allen, Paula Gunn 84, 100, 101–2, 255, 256,
285, 287, 372, 383

allotment 3, 6, 74, 76–7, 80, 81, 102, 112,
146–54, 157, 163, 168–9, 171–4, 201n4,
241–2, 245, 409, 438–9, 448, 449
American Horse (Wašíčuŋ Tȟašúŋke) 300
American Indian Defense Association 172
Amerika Samoa 39, 41, 43–7
Anderson, Kim 100
Anderson, Sherwood 416
Andes 300, 303–4
Andrei, Mary Anne 246–7
Andrews, Jennifer 469
animals 8, 22, 75, 132, 199, 201n6, 229–36,
239, 240–2, 250, 342, 348, 391, 395–6, 403,
451, 459, 482
Aotearoa/New Zealand 43, 44
Apess, William 112, 114–15, 136, 196–8,
263–4, 324–6, 366–9, 371, 391, 404:
"Eulogy on King Philip" 115, 196, 198, 324,
367; *Indian Nullification* 114, 264, 367; "An
Indian's Looking-Glass for the White Man"
167–8; *Son of the Forest* 112, 114, 264,
324, 404
Apu Ollantay 25n6
Aquash, Anna Mae 274
archaeology 7, 182–3, 340, 364
Arguedas, José María 21–2
Armstrong, Jeannette 414, 419
Ashwell, George 368
Asia 11, 15, 379–87, 423, 480
assimilation 5–7, 58, 76, 77, 85, 112, 154,
157–65, 168, 170, 172, 174–5, 178–9, 184,
219, 220, 266–8, 291, 328, 438–9, 441, 449
Astaire, Fred 142
Atwood, Margaret 65
Aupaumut, Hendrick 205–15, 323
authenticity 3, 20, 64–72, 263, 284, 285–6,
290, 341, 357, 374n2, 391, 399, 406, 428,
440, 454: hobbyism 67; "playing Indian" 64,
423; "whiteshamanism" 67

INDEX

autobiography 10, 29, 30–7, 41, 44, 59–60, 89, 114, 119, 159, 161–2, 163, 263, 302, 342, 386, 402–11, 418: As-Told-To narrative 10, 161–2, 402–6, 409, 411, 481; "autoethnography" 310, 314n3; Indigenous communal narrative 10, 402, 406–11

Awaquin, John 314n1

Awashous 308

Axtell, James 314n4

Bad Heart Bull, Amos 300

Balaz, Joe Puna 43

Banks, Dennis 118

Banner, Stuart 115, 127

Barnaby, Jeff 466–7, 468

Barraclough, Frances Horning 22

Barreiro, Jose 357

Basso, Keith H. 354

Beagan, Tara 429

Beardslee, Lois 103

Beaulieu, David L. 169

Belaney, Archie 66

Belau 49

Belcourtt, Christi 345

Bell, Betty 97

Bell, John Kim 280

Belmore, Rebecca 431–2

Benedict, Ernest 280

Benedict, Nora 425

Beresford, Bruce 23

Berger, Thomas 65, 67–9, 71

Berglund, Jeff 238

Bering Strait 15, 380, 381, 384, 385

Berkhofer, Robert F, Jr. 64, 66

Bernardin, Susan 11, 65, 345

Bernet, John W. 29

Betoqkom, Simon 314n1

Bevacqua, Michael Lujan 47

Bevis, William 75, 78, 449

Bhabha, Homi 70, 386

Bieder, Robert 182–3

Big Cat (Mkhequeh Posees) 214

Big Foot (Spotted Elk, Uŋpȟáŋ Gleška) 265–6

Bigsby, Christopher W. E. 425

Bird, Gloria 391

Bitsui, Sherwin 436

Black Coyote 266

Black Elk (Heȟáka Sápa) 75, 355, 386, 403, 405–6

Black Hawk (Ma-Ka-Tai-Me-She-Kia-Kiak) 146, 149–50, 154

Black Kettle (Mo'ohtavetoo'o) 414, 418

Blaeser, Kimberly 60, 61n5, 338, 348, 381, 382, 414, 436, 437, 452

Blaisdell, Gus 343, 420

blood quantum 3, 6, 58, 64, 67, 169, 175, 240, 286, 487

Blow, Peter 254–5

Blue Cloud, Peter (Aroniawenrate) 345, 419

Blyth, R. H. 381

boarding schools 21, 33, 34, 36, 80–1, 88, 96, 157–65, 189, 206, 238, 240, 261, 277, 328, 347, 393, 430, 438–9, 465, 466, 470, 476–7, 489: Carlisle Indian Industrial School 6, 157, 158, 159, 164, 409, 412; Chemawa Indian School 164; Keams Canyon Boarding School 161; Santee Normal School 159, 347; Sherman Institute 161, 164, 453; Tucson Indian School 56; Wealaka Methodist boarding school 163; Wesleyan Female Institute 163; White's Manual Labor School 158

Boccaccio 249

Boney, Roy, Jr. 481, 488, 489, 490

Bonnin, Ray 159

borders 56–7, 97, 231, 239, 249, 287, 291, 379–81

Borilla, Dennis 354

Borja-Kicho'cho', Kisha 47

Borrows, John J. 129

Borst, Murielle 426

Boudinot, Elias 146, 147–9, 150, 154, 323

Bowden, Henry W. 311

Bowers, C. A. 332

Boyden, Joseph 420

Bradford, William 113

Brando, Marlon 277

Brant, Beth 85, 86, 88, 90, 91, 100, 419

Brant, Joseph (Thayendanegea) 211–14, 323

Brazil 4, 15, 20–1, 24–5

Breinig, Helmbrecht 386, 387

Breinig, Jeane C. 29

Brightman, Lehman 280

Brill de Ramirez, Susan Berry 10, 285, 438

Brinton, Daniel 16

Brooks, Lisa 9, 113, 289, 290, 319, 342, 350, 367, 368, 372, 404

Brother, Farmers (Ho-na-ya-wus) 210

Brotherston, Gordon 340

Brown, Bruce 274

Brown, David 323

Brown, Dee 386

Bruchac, Joseph 30, 384, 414, 418

Bruyneel, Kevin 117, 373

Buffalo Bill's Wild West Show 75, 346, 453

Burns, Randy 85–6

Butcher, Lennie 246

Byrd, Jodi 373

INDEX

Cajete, Gregory 201n6, 218, 358
Calhoun, John 367
Callahan, S. Alice 11, 102, 146, 151–2, 154, 162–3, 266–7, 268, 391, 448
Calloway, Colin G. 113, 115, 116
Camacho-Dungca, Bernadita 47
Camus, Albert 249
Canada 15, 20, 21, 22–3, 88, 238, 246, 249, 293, 325, 344, 349, 417, 426, 491
Cannassatego 114
Caribbean, the 15, 22, 213
Carlson, Andrea 345
Carlson, David J. 5
Carlson, Vada F. 161–2
Carpenter, Cari M. 9, 183
Carpenter, Kristen A. 128
Carrio, David 361
Carruth, Allison 31
Carson, Benjamin 386
Cash, Johnny 273, 277–8, 280
Cate, Ricardo 482
Catlin, George 349, 403
ceremony 101, 262, 330–1, 353–61
Chaatsmith, Marti 364
Chagall, Marc 349
Chavarria, Antonio 482
Cheeshateaumauk, Caleb 10, 308, 317, 319–20, 325
Cheyfitz, Eric 8, 127
Chief Joseph (Hin-mah-too-yah-lat-kekt) 386
Chilam Balam 9, 300, 319
Child, Brenda J. 372
Chile 25
China 274, 379–81, 452
Chrystos 91–3
Church, Benjamin 137
Churchill, Ward 66, 67, 157–8, 475
Chute, Hillary L. 481, 488
cinema 35, 66–7n3, 346, 458–78; *see also* film
citizenship 5–7, 54, 151–4, 157–8, 159, 160, 167–71, 175, 178, 205, 231, 275, 287, 289–90, 448, 453
Clements, William M. 336
Cleveland, Robert Nasruk 491
Clifton, James A. 66
Clinton, Hillary 50
Cloud Shield 300
Clutesi, George 344
Cobell, Elouise 280
Cockenoe 309
Coffey, Wallace 129
Cohen, Felix S. 168, 172
Cohen, John 18
Cohen, Matt 341
Colleps, Donovan Kūhiō 43

Collier, John, Sr. 7, 172–5, 191n3, 261
Collounicus 308
colonialism 1–2, 8, 32, 35, 39–40, 45, 47–8, 115, 123, 139, 192–9, 219, 238, 251, 290–3, 304, 307, 320, 342, 380, 385, 403, 442, 459, 491
colonization 2, 5, 9, 47, 64, 84–5, 89, 96–9, 103, 112, 117, 143, 192, 200, 217, 219, 234, 238–9, 240–1, 243–6, 264, 266, 311, 317, 320, 386, 407–8, 487
Colorado, Pamela 218
Columbus, Christopher 15–16, 136, 197, 198, 386, 409, 415, 416
comics 480–92: "Comic Art Indigène" 481–2, 484; INC Comics 488–90; *Super Indian* 482–3, 485–9; *Wool of Jonesy* 488
Commonwealth of the Northern Mariana Islands (CNMI) 4, 47
Commuck, Thomas 323
community 3, 10, 33, 76, 87, 89, 92, 127, 140, 169, 178, 205, 240, 245, 264–5, 270, 284–94, 329–30, 337–8, 356, 359–60, 403, 404, 406, 428, 449, 475–6
Conley, Robert 236n1
Constitutions: Cherokee Nation (1827) 130, 148, 323; United States 7, 112, 116, 120, 125, 126–7, 130, 147, 167, 168, 173, 194, 195, 260, 270, 323, 324, 356, 366 356, 366; White Earth Nation 129, 132, 452
constitutions, tribal 174–5, 290, 303
Cook, Katsi 244
Cook-Lynn, Elizabeth 112, 119–20, 287–8, 289, 391–2, 418
Cooke, Alistair 16
Coolidge, President Calvin 171
Coolidge, Sherman 171
Cooper, James Fenimore 21, 70, 117, 206, 318, 322, 346, 440
Cooper, Tova 6
Copway George (Kah-Ge-Ga-Gah-Bowh) 10, 20, 325
Corcoran, Dolores Purdy 347
Cortés, Hernán 18, 25n10
cosmopolitanism 4, 52–60, 286, 290, 372, 380, 386–7, 392
Costner, Kevin 60–1n3
Cotera, Maria Eugenia 176–7, 178–9
Coulombe, Joseph L. 474
Coulthard, Glen Sean 293, 294
Cover, Robert. M. 190n1
Cox, James H. 176, 291, 292, 341
Craig, Vincent 482
Crazy Horse (Tashunka Witco) 141, 386, 483
Cronon, William 224
Crosby, Alfred W. 252
Crowther, Bosley 465

INDEX

Cummings, Denise K. 345–6
Curtis, Edward 403, 425, 484, 488
Cushing, Frank Hamilton 390–1
Cushman, Robert 318
Cusick, David 325
Custer, General George Armstrong 135, 278, 414
Cuthand, Kristina 489
Czech Republic 67

D'Ambrosio, Antonino 278
D'Aponte, Mimi Gisolfi 425
Dandurand, Joseph 431
Daniels, Greg 425
Danner, Alexander 480
Darby, Jaye T. 425, 427
Dartt-Newton, Deana 387n5
Daschuk, James 238, 245
Dauenhauer, Nora Marks 29, 32, 199, 379, 382, 383–4, 385–6, 387
Dauenhauer, Richard 29
David, Joey 345
Davidson, Cathy 160
Davis [Hoffmann], Robert 29, 34
Däwes, Birgit 10
decolonization 39, 43, 47, 87–9, 91, 96–9, 102, 103, 118, 131, 190, 195, 245, 285, 293–4, 343, 459
De St. Aubin, Ed 65
Debo, Angie 163
Deer, Sarah 178
Defoe, Daniel 117, 249
Defoe, Ty 424
DeFrancis, John 304, 340–1
Del Carmen Rodriquez Martinez, Maria 299
Deloria, Ella Cara 76, 79, 176–8, 391
Deloria, Philip J. 64, 66, 67, 405, 406, 423
Deloria, Vine, Jr. 1, 118, 120, 131, 135, 168, 170, 172–3, 174, 178, 229–30, 232, 235, 262–3, 265, 273, 277, 278–80, 345, 355, 372, 435
DeMallie, Raymond J. 167, 168, 176, 405, 406
Dembicki, Matt 481
Denetdale, Jennifer Nez 96, 100, 372
Denmark 67
Densmore, Frances 344, 382
Diamond, Jared 234
Diamond, Neil 465
Dias, Gonçalves 20
diaspora 39, 40, 44, 45, 46, 47, 48, 49, 74–6, 354
Díaz, Bernal 17, 18, 19
digital media 11, 304, 328, 345, 425, 458, 459, 480–92
Dillon, Grace L. 469
diplomacy, 113–15, 119, 205–13, 292, 303;
    see also treaties

Direnc, Dilek 220
disease 157, 231–6, 240, 244, 245, 249–58, 408, 428, 439, 477
Doanmoe, Etahdleuh 301
Doctrine of Discovery 112, 120, 123–4, 129–30
Doerfler, Jill 169
Donahue, Troy 465
Donaldson, Laura 138
Donohue, Betty Booth 113
Donovan, Kathleen M. 398
Doolittle, Will 360
Dorris, Michael 418, 451
Dove, Mourning (Hum-Ishu-Ma, Christal Quintasket) 76–7, 82, 402, 413, 440, 448–9
Downing, Todd 292
drama 5, 10, 25n6, 42, 136, 141–3, 423–32:
    American Indian Drama Company 424;
    American Indian Theater Ensemble 424;
    De-Ba-Jeh-Mu-Jig Theater Company 424;
    Institute of American Indian Arts 424;
    LaMaMa Experimental Theater Club 427;
    Naakaahidi Theater 33; Native American
    New Play Festival 424; Native Earth
    Performing Arts 424; Native Theater School
    424; Native Voices, Autry National Center
    of the American West 424; Red Earth
    Performing Arts 424; Six Nations Reserve's
    Forest Theatre 425; Spiderwoman Theater
    424, 432; Weesageechak Begins to Dance 424
Driskill, Qwo-Li 84, 87–8, 89, 91, 446
Druke, Mary 303
Dunavan, Claire Panosian 234
Dunbar-Ortiz, Roxanne 136, 139
Dunn, Martin F. 344
Dunsmore, Roger 279
Dussias, Allison M. 261
Duthu, N. Bruce 184

Earenfight, Phili 301
earthworks (mounds, mound-builders) 1, 9, 182, 190, 301, 340, 365–7, 368, 371, 373–4, 423
Eastman, Charles (Ohiyesa) 136, 158, 159–60, 171, 260, 266, 267–8, 372, 413, 439, 481
Echo-Hawk, Walter R. 182
EchoHawk, John 280
Eco, Umberto 260n3
Edmunds, R. David 169
education 7, 32, 36, 44, 95–6, 157–65, 170–2, 174, 220, 261, 319–21
Edwards, Jonathan 55
Eiseley, Loren 396
Eliot, Rev. John 137, 308, 309, 310–11, 312
Eliot, T. S. 381, 397
Elliot, Captain Matthew 213, 214
Elliott, Michael A. 135

INDEX

Endrezze, Anita 419
environment 36, 48, 50, 54, 82, 217–27, 235–6, 242, 244, 255, 373, 396: dam-building 226, 275, 409; ecocide 224, 478n1; mining 139–40, 199, 220–1, 222–3, 226–7, 239, 243, 254, 281, 485; resource extraction 34, 35, 219, 243; toxic waste 221, 223–5, 226, 235, 243–4, 246, 253–4
epistemology, 8, 33, 56, 102, 105n1, 299, 484
Erb, Joseph 481, 490
Erdoes, Richard 355, 420
Erdrich, Heid 346, 484
Erdrich, Louise 11, 103–4, 112, 136, 137, 184, 238, 239, 240, 251–2, 342, 349, 391, 416–17, 436, 450, 451–2, 480–1: *The Antelope Wife* 238, 349, 451–2; *The Beet Queen* 451, 455; *Books and Islands in Ojibwe Country* 342, 480–1; *Love Medicine* 103–4, 416–17, 451; *The Round House* 104, 451; *Tracks* 103, 112, 239, 240–2, 245, 251–2, 256, 454
essentialism 98, 135, 372, 428
ethnography 89, 159, 293, 301, 403, 411
Ethridge, Robbie Franklyn 139
Everett, Edward 137
Evers, Larry 438
Eyre, Chris 453, 458, 483

Fadden, John Kahionhes 280
FastHorse, Larissa 424, 425, 429
Fatheuer, Thomas 199–200
Faulkner, William 55, 381, 397, 451
Favel, Floyd 431
Federated States of Micronesia 49
feminism 3–4, 84–92, 95–105, 268, 285, 291, 293–4, 372, 453: Ohoyo Indian Women's Conference on Leadership (1983) 100
Fergus, Jim 65, 68, 69, 70
Fienup-Riordan, Ann 37
Figiel, Sia 47
Filewod, Alan 429
film 11, 23, 46, 52, 55, 58, 60–1n3, 345–6, 355, 453, 455, 458–68, 473, 474–7, 483, 484: *Barking Water* 458; *The Battle at Elderbush Gulch* 458; *Clearcut* 52–3, 58; *The Colony* 466; *Dances with Wolves* 61n3, 277, 458; *File Under Miscellaneous* 466; *Four Sheets to the Wind* 458; *Friday Night Lights* 458; *From Cherry English* 466–7; *Gesture Down (I Don't Sing)* 466; *Incident at Restigouche* 458; *Kanehsatake: 270 Years of Resistance* 458; *Last of the Mohicans* 458; *Law and Order* 458; *The Lone Ranger* 458; *Meeko* 459; *Peter Pan* 458; *Rhymes for Young Ghouls* 466, 467; *Sioux Ghost Dance* 458; *Smoke Signals* 453, 458, 483; *This May Be the Last Time* 458–9;

Windigo 469, 473; *A Windigo Tale* 469, 476–7; *Winter in the Blood* 459–65, 467–8; *see also* cinema
Finley, Chris 88
Fitzgerald, Stephanie 302, 425
Fixico, Donald L. 255, 373
Flaherty, Robert 403
Fletcher, Matthew L. M. 123, 124, 125, 127
Florentine Codex 9
Flores, Evelyn 47
Florit, Eugenio 17
Foley, John Miles 334
food 31–2, 159, 214, 238–47, 250, 274–7, 361, 370, 475, 485
Fool's Crow, Frank 178
Forbes, Jack 391–2
Ford, John 61n3, 419
Ford, Karen Jackson 381, 382, 385
Forney, Ellen 481
Fort Marion (Florida) 300, 301, 302, 346
Forte, Maximilian 54
Foucault, Michel 249
Fowler, David 321
Fowler, Jacob 321
Fox, Lynn 354
Francis, Daniel 66, 68
Francis IV, Lee 488, 489
Frank, L. 482
Franklin, Benjamin 113–14, 319
Frazier, Charles 65, 68, 71–2
Frey, Rodney 336, 337
Friedrich, Paul 329
Furlan, Laura Szanto 269

Gamber, John 11, 80
Gandolfini, James 461
Gansworth, Eric 345–6, 349, 481
Gardner, Susan 176
Garibay K., Ángel Maria 19
Garner, Van H. 116
Garrison, Tim Alan 130
Garter Snake Woman 355
Gates, Henry Louis, Jr. 391–2
Gaul, Therese Strouth 367
Geiogamah, Hanay 136, 141–3, 424, 425, 427–9: *Body Indian* 425, 427–9, 430, 431; *Foghorn* 136, 141–3
gender 3–4, 22, 46, 84–92, 95–105, 119, 162, 176–7, 240, 286, 291–3, 294, 302, 404–5, 419–20, 486–7
gendercide 89, 93n5
genocide 96–7, 100–1, 157, 196, 233–6, 251, 408
Gentry, Bruce 400n2
George-Kanentiio, Doug 277, 280

INDEX

Georgi-Findley, Brigitte 380–1
Germany 43, 141
Ghost Dance 152, 165, 257, 260–70
Giago, Tim 280
Gilbert, Willard Sakiestewa 219
Gillan, Jennifer 225
Gilroy, Paul 56, 380
Ginsberg, Allen 381
Glancy, Diane 112, 347, 417, 425
Glover, Jeffrey 135
Goddard, Ives 312, 320
Goeman, Mishuana R. 96, 97, 100, 103, 104, 291–2
Goldie, Terry 64, 66
Goldtooth, Dallas 490
Gomez, Terry 431
Good, Battiste 305n1
Gordon, David M. 218
Gordon, R. 249
Gould, Janice 443–4
Grande, Sandy 96, 100
graphic novel 469, 471, 472–3, 475–6, 480–92: *Darkness Calls* 473–5; *The Night Wanderer* 269, 470, 471, 472; *Red: A Haida Manga* 491–2
Grauer, Lally 344
Gray, Kathryn 10
Gray, Minnie Aliitchak 491
Green, Paul 29
Green, Rayna 100, 372, 415, 420
Green, Samuel 137
Greenblatt, Stephen 137
Greene, Graham 52
Greenfield, Bruce 299
Greygrass, Robert Owens 424
Grinde, Donald A. 224
Grover, Linda LeGarde 80–2, 83
Guåhan (Guam) 4, 39, 47–9
Guardipee, Terence 347
Guatemala 17, 18, 25n2, 139
Gustafson, Sandra M. 310

Haas, Angela 366
Hafen, P. Jane 168, 171
Hahatun, Nellem 314n1
Hail, Barbara 347
Hall, Lisa Kahaleole 98, 100
Hallett, Benjamin 367
Hanna, Dan 437–8
Hanson, William 160
Happyjack-McKenzie, Kris 469, 473
Hariot, Thomas 312
Harjo, Joy 30, 104, 136, 391, 420, 443, 444: *She Had Some Horses* 443; *The Woman Who Fell From the Sky* 136

Harjo, Sterlin 458–9, 490
Harjo, Suzan Shown 262, 373
Harvey, R. C. 482
Hau'ofa, Epeli 50
Haugo, Ann 425
Haukaas, Linda 347
Hauptman, Laurence M. 174–5, 178
Hawai'i 39–43, 44, 45–6, 50, 195, 198, 201n4, 261–2, 359, 360, 372: Kanaka 41, 43; Kanaka Maoli 50n1; Kanaka 'ōiwi 40
Hawaiian Kingdom 40, 41, 42: Queen Lili'uokalani 40, 42
Haycox, Stephen 28
Hayes, Ernestine 28, 29, 30–4, 37
health 171, 199, 221, 244, 247n10, 249–58, 262–3, 408–9, 430
Heap of Birds, Edgar (Hock E Aye Vi) 345
Heath, Sally Ann 425
Hedge Coke, Allison Adele 183, 184, 190, 364, 373–4
Hele, Karl S. 239
Heller, Caroline 383
Helstern, Linda Lizut 379–80
Henderson, Harold G. 381
Henry, Gordon Jr. 184, 348
Hensley, William L. Iġġiaġruk 29, 30, 34–7
Henson, Lance 347
Herrington, John 280
Herzog, Kristin 102
Hewitt, J. N. B. 171
Hiacoomes 310, 313
Highway, Tomson 426
Hill, Errol 22
Hill, Greg 345
Hill Boone, Elisabeth 300, 341
Hinton, Leanne 355, 437
Hively, Ray 364
Hobakon 214
Hobson, Geary 30
Hochbruck, Wolfgang 319
Hodgson, Heather 425
Hoffman, W. J. 344
Hogan, Linda 4, 53, 55, 59–60, 136, 199, 220, 225–6, 230, 231, 233, 380, 415, 436: *Mean Spirit* 226; *People of the Whale* 380; *Power* 53, 217, 220; *Sightings* 225–6; *Solar Storms* 53, 226; *Talking Leaves* 415; *The Woman Who Watches Over the World* 59–60
Hogan, Michael 52
Holland 2, 17, 18, 429, 430
Hollrah, Patrice 393
Holm, Sharon 222
Holt, John Dominis 40–1
ho'omanawanui, ku'ualoha 43

INDEX

Hopkins, Sarah Winnemucca 98, 146, 152–4, 163–4, 366, 369–71
Hoppe-Cruz, Anghet 47
Horinek, Mekasi 246
Horn, Robert 364
Howard, James H. 425
Howe, LeAnne 11, 105n1, 391, 392–3, 416, 424
Hoxie, Frederick E. 372
Hughes, Langston 346
Huhndorf, Roy M. 201n4
Huhndorf, Shari M. 35, 64, 97, 201n4, 241, 245, 291, 372, 425
Hungary 67
Hunter, Kermit 424
hunting 31, 157, 159, 225–6, 239–41, 243–4, 358, 414
Huntsman, Jeffrey 425
Huston-Findley, Shirley A. 425
Hutchins, Francis G. 367
hybridity 4, 9–10, 16, 44, 57–9, 68, 70–2, 143, 255, 263, 268, 286–7, 299–300, 312, 341, 382

identity 1, 2–6, 8, 10, 20, 22, 37, 44–6, 49–50, 52–60, 64–72, 74, 84–92, 96–101, 129, 143, 148–9, 158, 165, 170, 199, 205–6, 222, 269, 284–94, 307, 311, 325, 346, 372, 403, 415, 426, 431, 440, 442, 446, 451, 470
Imbert Enrique Anderson, 17
imperialism 39–50, 96, 112, 123, 127–8, 131–2, 135, 238, 240, 243, 245, 280, 291, 373, 437, 472
Indian policy, US federal 6–8, 76–7, 85, 115, 123, 128, 146–54, 157–8, 168–78, 186, 196–7, 261–2, 323, 369–70, 380, 385
indigeneity 8, 47, 64–72, 198, 343, 446, 490: trans-indigeneity 372
intellectualism 113, 159–60, 217–18, 262, 265, 279, 284, 288, 340–2, 364–74, 395
inter-species relations 30, 199, 229–36, 333, 337–8, 396, 418
Inuit Circumpolar Council 37

Jackson, President Andrew 196, 323
Jackson, Tom 52
Jacob, Michelle 293, 294
Jacobs, Murv 481
Jaimes, Annette M. 99
Japan 47, 48, 379, 380, 381–2, 385–6, 387, 452, 480, 491
Jefferson, President Thomas 147, 149, 182
Jemison, G. Peter 345
Jemison, Mary 69–70
Jennings, Francis 309
Jesuits 20, 23, 164, 314n4, 318

Jetnil-Kijiner, Kathy 49, 50
Jetro, Olt 314n1
Joe, Rita 466
Johansen, Bruce E. 5, 7, 221, 224, 274
Johnson, E. Pauline (Tekahionwake) 136, 391, 413, 439, 440–1, 481
Johnson, Emily 429
Johnson, Joseph 10, 321–2, 325
Johnson, Troy R. 273, 279
Johnson, Sir William 67, 70–2
Johnston, Basil 419
Jones, Dennis 393
Jones, Peter 325
Jones, Stephen Graham 419, 454–5: *The Bird is Gone* 454–5; *Bleed Into Me* 419; *Demon Theory* 455; *Zombie Bake Off* 455
Joyce, James 416
Judd, Steven Paul 484
Judus, Eleazar 308
jurisgenesis 114, 181–90
Justice, Daniel Heath 88, 89, 176, 289, 340–1, 372, 373

Kahakauwila, Kristiana 43
Kalahele, Imaikalani 43
Kamps, Kevin 224
Kanae, Lisa 43
Kane, Joan Naviyuk 29
Kane, Margo 425
Kaopio, Matthew 43
Kassam, Karim-Aly S. 250
Katanski, Amelia 7, 128, 372–3
Kawash, Samira 64
Kayano, Shigeru 379, 385–6, 387
Keali'i, David 43
Kealoha 43
Kellaway, William 314n2
Kelly, Gene 142
Kelm, Mary-Ellen 244, 245
Kelsey, Penelope Myrtle 183, 372
Kemp, Lysander 19
Kenny, George 425
Kenny, Maurice 425
Keokuk 150, 154
Kerouac, Jack 381
Kihleng, Emelihter 49
Kimewon, Howard 346
King, Bruce 431
King, Martin Luther 367
King, Thomas 80, 82–3, 117, 226, 326, 349, 419: *The Back of the Turtle* 82–3; *Green Grass, Running Water* 82, 117, 226; *Medicine River* 82; *Truth and Bright Water* 82, 226, 349
kinship 76, 81, 89, 99, 114, 119, 152, 169, 176–9, 197, 285, 289, 292, 409, 440

INDEX

Kirkland, Samuel 321
Klein, Naomi 219, 225
Klor de Alva, Jorge 299
Kneubuhl, John 44–5, 47
Kneubuhl, Lemanatele Mark 47
Kneubuhl, Victoria Nālani 41–2, 47
Knobloch, Frieda 240
Knowles, Ric 425
Knox, Henry 211, 212, 213
Kollin, Susan 4
Kolodny, Annette 402, 407–11
Konkle, Maureen 372
Kramer, Gary M. 460
Krech III., Shepard 218
Kreiner, Philip 68
Kristofferson, Kris 278
Kroeber, Karl 329, 334
Kroeber, Theodora 360
Kroetsch, Robert 68
Kroskrity, Paul V. 329, 335, 336
Krupat, Arnold 53–4, 56, 59, 61n5, 269, 285, 286, 290, 386
Kulchyski, Peter 343, 347
Kuralt, Charles 275

LaDuke, Winona 184, 221, 239–40, 243–6, 252, 255, 280, 373
La Farge, Oliver 278
La Farge, Peter 278
La Via Campesina 242
Lafitau, Joseph-François 301
Lalemant, Jérôme 20
LaLonde, Chris 4
LaPena, Frank 357
Lamming, George 22
LaRocque, Emma 97–8, 100
Lame Deer John 355
land 6–8, 28, 30, 34, 36–7, 40, 43, 60, 76, 104, 115–16, 120, 123–4, 129–30, 132, 139–42, 146–54, 157, 160, 168–70, 172–4, 192–5, 198–9, 215, 217–27, 238–47, 254, 274–5, 280, 289, 308, 320–6, 328, 342, 346, 353, 369, 371, 385, 396–7, 436–46, 449, 458–9
Landa, Diego de 304
language 9, 15, 28, 39, 40, 53, 84–5, 93n1, 99, 102, 104, 114, 133, 152, 185, 197, 199, 211, 215, 239, 263, 299–305, 307, 312–13, 328–30, 334, 337, 353–61, 370, 373, 382, 424, 435–6, 437, 445–6, 454, 465–7, 489: eradication 40, 158, 159; preservation 243, 246, 281, 360, 373, 386, 407, 458; rights 7, 9, 197, 243
languages, indigenous: Acqumeh 140; Ainu 385–6; Algonquian 206, 301, 307–10, 312–13, 319–20, 408; Anishinaabemowin

53, 93n1, 247n2, 325, 342, 346, 480–1; Aztec 9, 26n11, 299–300, 302, 319; Blackfeet 465; Cahuilla 116; Cherokee 304, 323, 490–1; Cherokee Syllabary 304; Chochenyo 360; Choctaw 57; Chumash 90; Diné (Navajo) 336–7; Guaraní 25n2; Lakota 465; Lenape 430; Maya 17, 299–300, 301, 302, 303, 304, 319, 342, 481; Mi'kMaq (Mi'gMaq) 300, 467; Mixtec 299, 300, 342; Mohawk 323, 440; Nahautl 18, 301; Olmec 299; Quechua 22, 25n2, 199; Sequoyan 302; Tlingit 384; Tupi 25; Winnemem 360; Zapotec 25n2
Larsen, Deborah 65, 68, 69–70
Larson, Charles 285, 286
Larson, Sidner 337
Lauderdale, Pat 219
law 5, 28, 37, 95, 100, 111–21, 123–33, 147, 150–1, 157, 163, 167–76, 181–90, 192–201, 214–15, 220, 224, 226, 235, 260–2, 280, 303, 356, 358: jurisdiction 7, 104, 123, 124–5, 126, 130, 147, 149, 197, 225, 231
laws: Ainu Cultural Promotion Law (1997, 1999) 386; Alaska Native Claims Settlement Act (1971) 28, 37, 201n4; American Indian Religious Freedom Act (1978) 7, 102, 261–2, 356; Animal Welfare Act (1966) 236; Antiquities Act (1906) 182; Archaeological Resources Protection Act (1979) 7, 182; "Boldt Decision" (*U.S. v. Washington*, 1974) 274, 276–7; Burke Act (1906) 168–9; *Cherokee Nation v. Georgia* (1831) 6, 111, 123, 124–5, 126, 129, 167, 194; Clapp Rider (1906, 1907) 169; Curtis Act (1898) 151, 162; *Employment Division v. Smith* (1983) 262; Five Civilized Tribes Act (1906) 162; General Allotment Act (Dawes Act, 1887) 3, 6–7, 76, 150, 152, 157, 158, 159, 162, 163, 168–9, 240, 409; Homestead Act (1862) 240; Humane Slaughter Act (1978) 236; Indian Appropriations Act (1851) 6; Indian Appropriations Act (1871) 5, 6, 111; Indian Child Welfare Act (1978) 7; Indian Citizenship Act (1924) 5, 168–70, 455n4; Indian Civil Rights Act (1968) 7; Indian Civilization Fund Act (1819) 157; Indian Removal Act of 1830 5, 146, 147, 154n3, 324; Indian Reorganization Act (Wheeler-Howard Act, "Indian New Deal," 1934) 7, 77, 154n5, 167–79, 178–9, 449; Indian Self-Determination and Education Assistance Act (1975) 7; Individual Indian Monies suit (*Cobell v. Salazar*, 2009) 280; *Johnson & Graham's Lessee v. McIntosh* (1823) 112, 123–4, 133n1; *Lyng v. Northwest Indian*

515

INDEX

Cemetery Protective Association (1988) 262, 356; Marshall Decisions 5, 8, 111–12, 123–33, 167, 194, 197, 273; National Museum of the American Indian Act (1989) 183, 186, 190; Native American Graves Protection and Repatriation Act (NAGPRA, 1990) 5, 7, 181–90, 373; Nationality Act (1940) 5; Native American Languages Act (1990) 7, 9; Newlands Resolution (1898) 40; *State v. Towessnutte* (1916) 275; "Termination" (1953) 7, 77, 117, 328, 450; Tribal Law and Order Act (2010) 95, 104; *United States v. Nice* (1916) 169–70; *United States v. Sandoval* (1913) 169–70; *United States v. Winans* (1905) 275; Violence Against Women Act (2013) 104; White Earth Land Settlement Act (1985) 245; *Wilson v. Block* (1983) 262; *Worcester v. Georgia* (1832) 123, 126–7, 129, 197

Lazarus, Edward 274
LeClaire, Antoine 149
Le Clerq, Christian 9, 300
Le Jeune, Paul 20
Lea, Ron 52
Lennon, John 346
León-Portilla, Miguel 19
Lerner, Andrea 384
Lesley, Craig 420
Liang, Iping 11
Lincoln, Kenneth 285, 286, 343, 397, 428, 448
Lincoln, President Abraham 394
Linderman, Frank B. 403
Lindstrom, Naomi 21
Lischke, Ute 239
literacies 9–10, 40, 135, 137–8, 150, 299–305, 308–14, 317–26, 328, 341–3, 347, 480–1: basketry 302, 340, 366, 410; beadwork 340, 349, 410, 481; birchbark scrolls 9–10, 11, 319, 342, 344, 480; "Cascajal block" 200; codices 11, 301, 303, 304, 319, 480, 481; comics 480–92; coup tales 300, 302; geoglyphs 9, 340; glyphs 26n11, 300, 302; graphic novel 469, 471–2, 473–5, 480–92; hieroglyphic scripts 9, 17, 299, 301, 308; ledgerbooks 301, 346–9; petroglyphs 9, 11, 299, 340, 480–1; pictographs 9, 304, 348; quillwork 24, 302; quipus 9, 299, 300, 301, 303–4; tocapu 304; totem poles 480, 491; wampum 9, 10, 11, 114, 209–11, 215, 299, 300, 303, 308, 318–19, 341, 345, 366, 368, 404, 430; winter counts (wan'iyetu wo'wapi) 300, 302, 347–8
Little Crow (Thaóyate Dúta) 386
Lobo, Susan 74

Lockhart, James 302
Loft, Steven 477
Lomawaima, K. Tsianina 170, 231, 372
Lone Dog 300, 347
Lone Ranger 117, 458
Long, John Luther 440
Long Lance, Sylvester 67, 71
Longboat, Dan 357, 359
Longfish, George 345
Lopenzina, Drew 9, 10, 11
Lorillard, Christine Metteer 128
Louis, Adrian C. 419, 444–5
Louisiana Purchase 149
Lovecraft, H. P. 469
Low-Weso, Denise 342, 347
Lucas, Phil 280
Luna, James 280
Lyons, Oren 231, 280
Lyons, Scott Richard 176, 290, 373
Lytle, Clifford M. 131, 170, 173–4, 178

MacArthur, General Douglas 452
Mack, David 488
MacLeish, Archibald 25n9
Madrigal, Anthony 219
Madsen, Deborah 53, 65, 382, 386–7
Magalhães, Gonçalves de 20
Mallery, Garrick 299, 301, 340
Malo, Juan 48
Mamadaty 302
manifest destiny 39, 56–7, 71, 103, 186, 253, 338, 436–7, 444, 458
Manitowabi, Edna 355
Mankiller, Principal Chief Wilma 78
Mann, Barbara Alice 280, 404
Mann, Mary 153
Mann, Thomas 249
Maqoof, John 314n1
Maquis, Olt 314n1
Marcus, Diveena 10
Margold, Nathan R. 170, 172
Margolin, Malcolm 355, 359
Marshall, Chief Justice John, 5–6, 8, 111, 123–7, 130–1, 167, 194, 197
Marshall Islands 4, 49
Martínez, David 372
Martinez, David 360–1
Marx, Leo 428
mascots 91, 274, 440
massacres 136, 143, 152, 251, 261, 266, 268, 269, 414, 430, 442, 453: Sand Creek (1864), 414, 439, 441, 442–3; Wounded Knee (1890), 136, 143, 152, 261, 265–6, 266–7, 268, 269, 413
Mather, Cotton 137

516

INDEX

material communicative forms *see* literacies
Mather, Increase 137, 196
Mathews, Elizabeth 395, 396
Mathews, John Joseph 11, 265, 372, 391, 392, 395–7, 413: *The Osages* 413; *Sundown* 372; *Talking to the Moon* 395–7
May, Karl 70
Maybee, Dallin 347
Mayhew, Experience 310, 312, 314n3
Mayhew, Matthew 308, 312
Mayo, Lisa 426
Mazur, Dan 480
McDougall, Brandy Nālani 1, 4
McGregor, Deborah 217–18, 219
McKay, Mabel 286
McKenzie, Stephanie 344
McLeod, Albert 87
McLeod, Neal 473
McMullin, Dan Taulapapa 46–7
McNeil, Larry 484
McNickle, D'Arcy 55, 164, 184–6, 190, 191n3, 226, 292, 413, 449–50: *The Hawk is Hungry* 413; *The Hungry Generations* 449; *The Surrounded* 55, 164, 413, 449–50; *Wind from an Enemy Sky* 184–6, 226, 266
Means, Russell 118, 119
Medak-Saltzman, Danika 380, 385
Medina, Vince 360
Mehl-Madrona, Lewis 356
Melville, Herman 117
Mendiola, Clarissa 47
Merculieff, Larry 358
Meredith, America 345
Meriam, Lewis 7, 171–2: Meriam Report 7, 171–2
Merrell, James H. 113–14
Metacomet (Metacom, "King Philip") 114–15, 136–7, 196, 264, 307
Mexico 18–19, 116, 139, 152, 292, 299, 302, 319, 448
Meyer, Manulani A. 360
Meyer, Sabine N. 5–6
Michelson, Alan 345
Midewiwin (Ojibwe) 302, 355
Midnight Sun 86
Mignolo, Walter 56, 61n7, 341
Miguel, Gloria 426
Miguel, Muriel 426
Mihesuah, Devon 162, 245
military 6, 18, 19–20, 39, 40, 43–4, 47, 48, 49–50, 76, 115, 136, 149, 150–1, 152, 158, 178, 182, 215, 246, 251, 301, 324, 397, 403, 414, 439, 482; *see also* war
Miller, Carol 3, 7, 176
Miller, Jay 402

Million, Dian 293, 294
Mills, Billy 280
Milton, John 82
Mirabal, Eva 482
Miranda, Deborah 4, 84, 85, 87–8, 89–91, 93n5, 373
Mirzoeff, Nicholas 346
Mithun, Marianne 301–2
mixed-race 2, 3–4, 52–60, 64, 77, 139, 162, 163, 440, 451
Moctezuma, Emperor 18
modernism 11, 329, 343, 348, 348, 350, 380–1, 391, 397–9
modernity 3, 31, 32, 37, 56, 77, 117, 143, 151, 249, 264, 280, 285, 290–3, 301, 323, 374n2, 384, 418, 436, 469, 470, 472, 473
Moertl, Heidrun 24
Mohawk, John 230–1, 280, 357
Mojica, Monique 425, 426
Momaday, Alfred 302
Momaday, N. Scott 11, 20, 67, 78–9, 82, 136, 302, 343–4, 358, 271, 380, 391, 397–9, 414, 435, 438, 448, 481: *The Ancient Child* 398, 414; *House Made of Dawn* 78–9, 264, 366, 371, 397, 398, 412, 413, 436, 450; *The Journey of the Tai-me* 397; *The Way to Rainy Mountain* 302, 343, 392, 397–9, 443, 448
Monahsetah 414
Monegal, Emir Rodríguez 16, 25n3
Monequasson 309
Montesinos, Fernando de 304
Montezuma, Carlos (Wassaja) 439–40
Montijo, Yolanda 355, 359
Montovani, Melissa 472
Mooney, James 232, 266
Moore, Brian 23
Moore, David L. 382
Moquah, John 314n1
Morales, President Evo 195
Moreno-Garcia, Silvia 477–8
Morgan, Phyllis 398
Morgensen, Scott 89
Morriseau, Norval 344
Morse, David 460
Morton, Dr. Samuel 182
Mosby, Ian 238
Moses, Daniel David 431
Murra, John 22
Murray, David 209, 210, 263, 264, 311, 312–13
museums 7, 46, 181–9, 261, 280, 349, 354, 387n5, 403, 492: American Museum of Natural History in New York 182; Army Medical Museum 182; Field Museum in Chicago 182; Harvard's Museum of Comparative Zoology 182; Smithsonian Institution 182, 183, 186–9

INDEX

Myre, Nadia 345
myth 3, 11, 20, 21, 24, 53, 66, 91, 101, 112, 117, 140, 158, 160, 232, 319, 329, 333, 336, 337, 353, 357, 392, 412, 414, 418, 419, 420, 443, 469, 470, 471, 477–8, 484: Skin Walker 469; vampire 419, 469–73, 478, 487; Windigo (Wendigo, Whitiko) 238, 241, 247n2, 419, 469–78

Nagle, Mary Kathryn 429–31
Naranjo-Morse, Nora 481
Nataniel 314n1
nation 3, 4, 5–8, 20, 21, 57, 66, 77, 87, 97–8, 112, 119, 124–7, 146–8, 150–1, 153–4, 167–72, 193–200, 205, 207–9, 211, 213–15, 223, 226, 231, 284–94, 402–10, 440
nationalism 20–1, 40, 53, 97–8, 279, 290–1, 399: American Indian literary 54–5, 57, 87, 263, 284, 287–90, 372, 374n2, 454
National Congress of American Indians 95
Native American Rights Fund 183
Native communities: Abenaki 342, 418; Agua Caliente (Cahuilla) 116–17; Ainu 379, 380, 385–6; Aleut (Unangan) 4, 28, 29, 261–2, 358; Anishinaabe (Ojibwe, Chippewa) 53, 80, 129, 214, 238, 239, 242, 246, 247n4, 252, 301, 302, 325, 342, 344, 358, 373, 393–5, 417, 452, 473, 477, 480; Apache 6, 139, 224, 465; Arapaho 6, 265; Atayal 379, 386; Athabaskan 4, 382–3, 385; Attawapiskat 105; Aztec 9, 17–19, 299–300, 302, 319; Bannock 153–4; Carib 15; Cheroenhaka (Nottoway) 3; Cherokee 36, 55, 57, 71–2, 89, 99, 112, 124–7, 129–31, 147–8, 150, 152, 154, 162, 194, 231–6, 273, 278, 291, 293, 304, 323–4, 412, 489, 490–1; Cheyenne 6, 68–9, 265, 300, 301, 386, 414, 418; Chickahominy 3; Chickasaw 59–60, 162; Choctaw 55, 57, 162, 392–3, 489; Coeur d'Alene 419; Columbia River Indians 153; Comanche 6, 414; Creek (Muscogee) 104, 151–2, 154, 162–3, 267, 288, 289; Dakotah 76, 119–20, 176–8, 300; Delaware (Wenaumie) 206, 208–9, 210, 213–14, 216n6, 251; Diné (Navajo) 6, 139, 140, 161, 186, 187–8, 221, 254, 262, 281, 335–6, 380, 412, 428, 435, 450, 465, 485, 488; Eastern Chickahominy 3; Eyak 4; Federated Indians of Graton Rancheria 353, 361n1; Fox 149; Goshute, Skull Valley 224; Haida 4, 28, 491–2; Haisla 469; Haudenosaunee (Iroquois Confederacy) 20, 23, 52, 70, 82, 113–14, 207, 210, 211–12, 214, 216n6, 247n3, 301, 303, 318, 322, 323, 325, 345, 346, 358, 366, 404, 413, 418; Hokkaido Jomon 387n5; Hopi 161, 262, 335, 412,

423, 428; Housatonic 206; Huron 23, 301; Inca 18, 301, 304, 319; Inuit 22–3, 36–7; Iñupiat 28, 29, 35, 36, 491, 492; Karok 262; Kickapoo 149; Kiowa 6, 265, 300, 301, 302, 359, 397–9, 412; Lenape 429–30, 431; Lummi 275; Mahican 206, 323; Mairun 25; Makah 225–6; Massachusett 307, 309, 311; Mattaponi 3; Maya 17, 18, 299, 300, 301, 302, 303, 304, 319, 342, 481; Mi'kMaq (Mi'gMaq) 9, 299, 300, 467; Miami 208; Mingo 251; Miwok 359; Mixtec 299, 300, 342; Modoc 6; Mohawk (Mauquas) 46, 70, 211–12, 244, 247n3, 293, 323; Mohegan 206, 302, 308, 320–1, 322; Mohican (Muhheakunuk) 206–8, 211–13, 215, 216n6, 322; Monacan Indian Nation 3; Monthee 208, 210; Muckleshoot 274; Nansemond 3; Nez Percé 6, 386; Nottoway Indian Tribe 3; Oneida 321; Osage 221, 226, 396–7, 413; Ottawa 208, 214; Paiute 152–4, 257, 265, 369–71; Pamunkey 3, 11n1; Patawomeck 3; Penobscot 407–11; Pequot 264, 311, 368; Pitiguara (Potiguára) 21; Potawatomi 149; Powhatan 3; Pueblos (Acoma, Laguna, Cochiti) 78, 79, 140, 164, 221–2, 254, 255, 333–4, 399, 412, 441, 450, 484, 486; Rappahannock 3, 426; Rarámuri 242; Sahtu Dene 255; Sauk 149–50, 152, 154; Seminole 6, 162; Shawnee 69, 207, 213, 251; Shoshone 265; Sioux (Nadouissiooux) 6, 104–5, 115, 142, 143, 158, 159, 160, 261, 265–7, 281, 366, 412; Spokane 445; Tabajara 21; Taino 15; Tamalko Coast Miwok 353, 354; Tlingit 4, 28, 29, 30, 32, 33, 199, 383–4, 385, 484; Tolowa 262, 356; Tsimshian 4, 28; Upper Mattaponi 3; Ute 6, 159; Wampanoag 113, 114, 115, 137, 196, 310, 311; Wappinger 206; Wyandot 214; Yakama 275, 293; Yupik 4; Yurok 262, 356; Zuni 140, 390–1
Neihardt, John G. 355, 403, 405–6
Nelson, Jonathan 488
Nelson, Joshua B. 239, 290–1, 293, 294
Nelson, Robert 30, 268
Nemiah 314n1
Neneglad 308
Neptune, Arnie 408
Neruda, Pablo 466
Nesutan, Job 309
Nettle, Bruno 359
New Zealand/Aotearoa 43, 44
Newcomb, Steven 192, 200n1
Newsom, Bonnie D. 410
Newsome, Geoffrey 187
newspapers 36, 135, 147, 162, 267, 274, 280, 323, 391, 413, 481, 482: A Wreath of Cherokee Rose Buds 162; American Indian

INDEX

Magazine 159; *Cherokee Phoenix* 147, 323; *Fort Apache Scout* 482; *Indian Country Today* 482; *Navajo Times* 482; *News from Native California* 482; *Santa Fe New Mexican* 482; *Tundra Times* 36

Niatum, Duane 436, 437

Nicolar, Joseph 407–8, 409–11

Niro, Shelley 345

Nixon, President Richard 77, 118, 278

Nolan, Yvette 424

Noodin, Margaret 346, 373

Noranjo-Morse, Nora 345

Norgan, Walis 379, 386

Norgren, Jill 125, 126, 127

Norris, Ada 160

Norton, Captain John 323

Nosauwunna, Olt 314n1

Nuomont, Olt 314n1

O'Brian, Sharon 262

O'Neill, Gloria 491

Oandasan, William 379, 382, 384–5, 387

Obamsawin, Alanis 458

Occom, Samson 10, 136, 263–4, 302, 304, 307, 314, 320–1, 322, 324, 325, 391, 399, 404

oceans, 28, 32, 39, 40, 43, 45, 50, 59, 195, 197, 225–6, 383, 384

Odjick, Jay 481, 482

orality 10, 20, 29, 44, 79, 89, 113, 116, 183, 196, 229, 236, 285, 302, 307, 317, 318, 328–38, 340, 341, 342, 343, 344, 353, 357, 358, 384, 397–8, 404, 410, 435, 438, 452

oratory 20, 29, 99, 114, 301, 328, 341, 443

Orozco, Clemente 349

Osorio, Jamaica 43

Ontario Native Women's Association 95

Ontario Federation of Indian Friendship Centres 95

Orner, Peter 461

Ortiz, Simon J. 136, 199, 263, 287, 289, 330, 331–2, 334, 335, 372, 399, 418, 420, 439, 441–3: *Fight Back* 139–41; *from Sand Creek* 439, 441–3; *Men on the Moon* 418; *Woven Stone* 331–2

Oskison, John 413

O'Toole, Fintan 65, 68, 70–2

Oukateguennes Kignamatinoer (Hieroglyphic Prayer) 300

Owens, Louis 55, 56–8, 61n3, 226, 251, 285, 286, 338, 379, 380–1, 423, 449: *Bone Game* 55; *Mixedblood Messages* 56–8, 61n3; *Nightland* 55; *The Sharpest Sight* 55, 392; *Wolfsong* 226

Owlfeather, M. 85, 87

Palau 4

pan-Indianism 2, 66, 136, 159–60, 266, 268, 269, 288, 334, 338, 372, 392, 397, 415, 423, 428

Parham, Vera 273

Parker, Arthur C. 171, 318

Parker, Robert Dale 393–5

Parrish, Samuel 153, 369, 370

Pascua, Jay Baza 47

Passion, Christy 43

Pat-Borja, Melvin Won 47

Patencio, Chief Francisco 116–17

patriarchy 4, 84, 89, 93n4, 100, 103, 268, 291, 293–4, 398, 405

Patterson, John B. 149

Pawwaw 310

Paz, Octavio 19

Peabody, Elizabeth 153, 163–4

Pearson, Maria 183

Peat, David F. 356

Peltz, Amy 481–2

Penn, William 303

Pensoneau, Migizi 490

Perez, Cecilia "Lee" 47

Perez, Craig Santos 47–8

Perez-Hattori, Anne 47

Perez-Wendt, Māhealani 43

Perkins, Leialoha 43

Perry, Commodore Matthew 380

Peru 18, 21–2, 139, 250, 391

Pessicus 308

Peters, Jesse 220

Peters, Kurt 74

Peters, Richard 113

Peterson, Brenda 225–6

Peterson, Nancy J. 252

Petoskey, John 262

Petrone, Penny 20

Pettit, Alexander 425

Pevar, Stephen L. 174, 175

Peyer, Bernd C. 137, 171, 264

Peynetas, Joseph 391

Phillips, McCandlish 427

Piatote, Beth H. 128

Pickering, Timothy 207–8, 212, 213

Pierson, Abraham 309

Pinazzi, Annamaria 428

Pinola, Lanny 354

Pinson, Elizabeth 29

Piper, Karen 223

Pocahontas (Matoaks, Amonute, Rebecca Rolfe) 3, 307, 346, 441

poetry 29, 42, 43, 45, 48, 49, 50, 91–2, 136, 190, 331, 334, 381–2, 393, 404, 435–46: haiku 11, 348, 379, 380, 381–5, 387, 391, 393, 445–6, 482

Pohl, Mary E. D. 299

Poland 67

Pollock, Penny 390

Poma de Ayala, Don Felipe Guaman 319

INDEX

Popol Vuh 17, 24
popular culture 61n3, 318, 345–6, 454, 469–78, 480–92
Porter, Robert B. 170
Portugal 17, 18, 21, 24, 139
Posey, Alexander 11, 391, 413, 481
postcolonialism 64–5, 68, 97, 198, 286, 380, 442, 455
postmodernism 66, 68, 117, 197, 285–7, 413
Potts, Annie 235–6
Powell, Malea 302, 366
Power, Susan 184
Pratt, Mary Louise 139, 314n3
Pratt, Richard Henry 158
Presnell, Kathleen 344
Price, Hiram 261
Printer, James 136–8, 309, 319
Proudstar, Jon 481, 482
Prucha, Francis Paul 111–12, 113, 261
Puleloa, Michael 43
Pulitano, Elvira 4, 372, 380, 381
Puritans, New England 137, 264, 317, 318, 320

Qoyawayma, Polingaysse 161–2
Quinney, John Wannuaucon 323
Quintasket, Christine *see* Dove, Mourning
Quissoquus 308

Rabelais 249
Rabinal Achi 16–17
race 64, 69, 97–9, 182, 192, 233, 265, 268, 275, 439–40
racism 69, 70, 85, 88, 103, 158, 164, 182, 186, 224, 239, 243, 264, 333, 491
Rader, Dean 302, 340, 478, 481
Radin, Paul 403
Raheja, Michelle 345
Ramirez, Reyna 97, 100, 372
Ramirez, Vickie 429
Rasmussen, Birgit Brander 4, 9, 340, 342
Red Corn, Ryan 490
Red Elk, Lois 436
Red Jacket (Sa-go-ye-wa-tha) 211
Regier, A.M. 268
Reid, Joshua 225
religion 17, 102, 157, 158–9, 162, 183, 206, 260–70, 280, 307–14, 317–26, 354–61, 368, 407: Ghost Dance 152, 165, 257, 260–70; "Praying Indians" 137–8, 308–11, 314; Sun Dance 160, 360–1, 397
Relocation Program, 7, 77–8, 450
removal 5–6, 59, 112, 115, 127, 130–1, 146–54, 163, 181, 182, 196, 323–5, 328, 369–70, 430
Renaissance, Native American 302, 343, 448–54, 459, 460
repatriation 7, 181–90, 403

reservations 5, 6, 67, 76, 78, 80–1, 112, 117, 119, 131–2, 136, 150, 153–4, 157–9, 160, 163–5, 168, 169, 171–3, 178, 201n4, 221, 223–5, 238–9, 244, 247n4, 274–5, 369–71: Akwesasne (St. Regis) Reservation (Mohawk) 244, 246; Flathead Indian Reservation (Confederated Salish and Kootenai Tribes) 164; Laguna Pueblo reservation (Western Keres) 254; Lummi Indian Reservation (Lhaq'temish) 275; Malheur Indian Reservation (Northern Paiute) 153, 369–70, 371; Navajo (Diné) reservation (Navajo Nation) 485, 488; Paiute (Northern) reservations (Pyramid Lake, Walker Lake, Malheur) 153; Pine Ridge Indian Reservation (Oglala Lakota) 136, 266, 267, 274, 444; Round Valley Indian Reservation (Round Valley Indian Tribes) 384; Spokane Indian Reservation (Spokane) 445; Standing Rock Reservation (Dakota, Lakota Sioux) 265; Tongue Ridge Indian Reservation (Northern Cheyenne) 69; Turtle Mountain Indian Reservation (Ojibwe) 416; Uintah and Ouray Reservation (Ute) 159; White Earth (Gaa-waabaabiganikaag) Indian Reservation (Ojibwe) 132, 239, 246, 415; Yakima (Yakama) Indian Reservation (Northern Paiute) 153, 370; Yankton Indian Reservation (Yankton Sioux) 119
Resnik, Judith 175
Revard, Carter 53, 438
Revilla, No'ukahau'oli 43
Rexroth, Kenneth 381
Reyes, Lawney L. 273
Ribeiro, Darcy 24
Richland, Justin B. 178
Rickard, Jolene 345
Ridge, John (Skah-tle-loh-skee) 323
Ridge, John Rollin (Chee-squa-ta-law-ny) 11, 391, 412, 448
Riding In, James 190
Riegelhaupt, Joyce F. 24
Riel, Louis 459
Rifkin, Mark 4, 6, 89, 95, 127–8, 373
Riggs, Lynn 292, 423
Rinehart, William 369–70
Ritskes, Eric 459
RJM (Rachel McCarthy James) 485
Robertson, Lindsay G. 127
Robertson, Robbie 461
Robinson, Eden 269–70, 471
Rock, Harold 36
Roe Cloud, Henry 171
Roemer, Kenneth 11
Rogalski, Alex 466–7

INDEX

Romero, Diego 484
Ronda, James P. 309
Rondon, General Mariano 26n12
Roosevelt, President Franklin D. 172
Roscoe, Will 86
Rose, Wendy 30, 56, 67
Rosenwald, George C. 65
Ross, Chief John 129–30, 148, 149
Rowlandson, Mary 137–8
Ruffo, Armand Garnet 66, 67, 68, 469, 476–7
Ruoff, A. Lavonne Brown 102, 163, 440
Ruppert, James 19, 30, 33, 285, 286, 334
Rusco, Elmer R. 174–5
Russell, Caskey 384
Russell, Steve 293
Russia 28, 34, 383

Safier, Neil 258
Sahagún, Bernardino de 9, 299–300
Sainte-Marie, Buffy 280
Salisbury, Neal 138
Salisbury, Ralph 418
Salmón, Enrique 242, 245
Samoa 4, 39, 41–2, 43–7
Sanchez, Georgianna 59
Sanderson, Steven Keewatin 469, 473–6
Sappier, James 408
Sarris, Greg 285, 286–7, 415
Sassomon, John 309
Scanlan, Thomas 313
Scheiding, Oliver 6
Scheub, Harold 329, 334, 337
Schiller, Friedrich von 249
Schmeckebier, Laurence F. 171
Schneider, Bethany 89
Schoolcraft, Henry Rowe 325, 340
Schoolcraft, Jane Johnston (Bamewawagezhikaquay) 325, 391, 392, 393–5
Schubnell, Matthias 398
Schweitzer, Ivy 313
Scott, Randolph 462
Scuttup 308
Seals, David 226–7
Sehgal, A. Cassidy 224, 225
Sekaquaptewa, Helen 161
self-determination 4, 7–8, 86, 96–8, 131–2, 158, 186, 194, 196, 197, 200, 217, 224, 242–3, 245–6, 261, 289, 292, 294
Sellers, Stephanie 10
Sequoyah 304
Sergeant, John 124–5
Sergeant, Rev. John 206
sexuality 3–4, 21, 23, 46, 84–93, 95–7, 98, 102, 152–3, 292: berdache 84–7, 93n4; heteronormativity 4, 88, 93n1, 294;

homophobia 85–6, 88, 90, 93n5; LGBTQ 86–7, 89, 93n1, 454 (Gay American Indians 85–6); sexual violence 88, 93, 95–7, 104, 120, 152–3, 476; Two Spirit/Queer identities 3–4, 46, 84–93, 289, 373
Shade, Hastings 234–5
Shakespeare, William 25n3, 249, 392
Shamas, Laura 431
Shanley, Kathryn 100
Shay, Charles Norman 407
Shenandoah, Joanne (Tekalihwa:khwa) 280
Shepard, Thomas 313
Sherbert, Cedar 466
Sheridan, General Philip 414
Sheridan, Joe 359
Sherman, General William Tecumseh 414
Sheyahshe, Michael A. 473, 474
Shklovsky, Viktor 330
Shreve, Bradley 276
Shuck-Hall, Sheri M. 139
Siddle, Richard 386
Siebert, Monika Barbara 393
Silko, Leslie Marmon 11, 19, 20, 23–4, 30, 53, 79, 128, 136, 164, 217, 243, 266, 292, 330, 334, 347–8, 391, 436, 452, 454: Almanac of the Dead 24, 79, 103, 135, 250, 253, 254, 439; Ceremony 23, 55, 79, 82, 100, 101–2, 220–3, 225, 254, 264–5, 333–4, 347, 371–2, 380, 450; Gardens in the Dunes 164–5, 255–6, 268, 381, 453; Sacred Water 253–4; Storyteller 164, 333, 335, 481
Silva, Noenoe K. 372
Silver, Peter 135
Silverheels, Jay C. 280
Simard, Rodney 329, 335, 337
Simpson, Audra 293, 294, 373
Simpson, Leanne R. 218, 219, 225, 294
Sinavaiana Gabbard, Caroline 44, 45–6, 47
Sinclair, Niigaanwewidam James 342, 459, 477, 481
Sisk, Chief Caleen 355, 358
Sitting Bull (Tȟatȟáŋka Íyotake) 141, 265–6
Sium, Aman 459
slavery 15, 18, 19–20, 61n7, 115, 151, 162, 213, 324, 398
Sloan, Thomas 171
Smith, Alex 459–60, 462–4
Smith, Andrea 4, 84, 89, 96, 100, 373
Smith, Andrew 459–60, 461, 462
Smith, Captain John 307
Smith, Chad 234–5
Smith, Jaune Quick-To-See 345, 349
Smith, Linda Tuhiwai 96, 100
Smith, Martin Cruz 392
Smith, Paul Chaat 279
Smith, Ryan Huna 482

INDEX

Sneider, Leah 4, 98
Snyder, Gary 381
Society of American Indians (SAI) 159–60, 171, 366
Sollors, Werner 65
Sommer, Doris 21
sovereignty 4, 5–9, 41, 43, 86–9, 92, 96–100, 104–5, 111–20, 123–33, 139–40, 146–54, 162, 165, 190, 193–200, 205–15, 217–27, 231–5, 238–47, 249–58, 260–70, 275–6, 287–9, 342–3, 345, 347–8, 372–3, 408–9, 437, 438–41, 459
Spence, Chief Theresa 105
Spencer, Chaske 460–1, 465, 467
Spruhan, Paul 169
Spry, Adam 344, 382
Squirrel, Linda W. 424
St. Cyr, Lillian 458
Standing Bear, Luther (Ota K'te) 158, 159
Stanlake, Christy 425, 426
Stannard, David E. 251
Stark, Heidi Kiiwetinepinesiik 174, 393
Starr, Arigon 431, 481, 482–3, 485–90
Stein, Gertrude 438
stereotypes 1, 3, 10, 53, 55–8, 65, 68–9, 87, 103, 124, 126, 141, 142–3, 264, 346, 370, 372–3, 394, 397, 405, 409, 423, 435, 440, 446, 473, 485: "noble savage" 53, 55, 64, 66, 70, 137, 141, 318, 322, 394, 474; "Vanishing Indian" 3, 6, 64, 66, 74, 77, 137, 186, 257, 266–7, 318, 382, 385, 406, 407, 411, 437, 439–40, 446, 484
Stevens, James Thomas 46
Stevens, Wallace 438
Stirrup, David 10
Stockton, Sen. John P. 167
Stone, John Augustus 423
Stone, Oliver 277
storytelling 11, 46, 58, 75–6, 82, 90, 114, 116, 128–9, 133, 136, 141, 243, 245, 328–38, 343, 357, 407, 413, 427, 451, 452, 459, 469, 470, 473, 477, 480, 481, 491
Stowe, Harriet Beecher 455n3
Studi, Wes 280
Stump, Marion Sarain (Sock-a-jaw-wu) 344
Suckley, George 274
Sugars, Cynthia 469, 470, 472
Survival of American Indians Association 275
survivance 59, 74–5, 80, 83, 129, 136, 286, 290, 347, 382, 383, 426, 430, 437, 445
Suzack, Cheryl 99, 100
Sweet, Timothy 130

Taimanglo, Tanya Chargualaf 47
Taitano, Lehua 47, 48–9
Taiwan 82, 379, 385–6
Takawompait, Daniel 314n1

Takehiro, Sage U'ilani 43
Talbot, Steve 273
Tallbear, Kim 67
Tallchief, Maria 488
TallMountain, Mary 29, 379, 382–4, 386, 387
Tanner, Helen Hornbeck 213
Tapahonso, Luci 436
Tarter, James 222
Tatonetti, Lisa 88, 269, 373
Tautpuhgtheet 210–11
Taylor, Alan 206, 215
Taylor, Drew Hayden 423, 425, 469, 470–3, 477, 478
Tecumseh 141
Tedlock, Dennis 17, 329, 335, 390, 391
Teller, Edward 36
Teller, Henry M. 261
Teuton, Christopher B. 289, 335, 341
Teuton, Sean Kicummah 176, 289
Thacher, Thomas 308
Thériault, Yves 22–3
Thomas, Keith 270n2
Thompson, Lucy 245
Thompson, Stith 390
Thoreau, Henry David 395–7
Thorpe, Jim 488
Tinker, George E. 138, 260, 262, 309
Tisquantum (Squanto) 307
Tohe, Laura 436
Tompson, Benjamin 137
Torgovnick, Marianna 64
Torres, Ricardo 356
tourism 33, 40, 48, 66, 201
Trafzer, Clifford E. 219, 414, 420
Tragedia del fin del Atahualpa (*The Tragedy of Atahualpa's Final Days*) 25n6
translation 10, 17–18, 19, 22, 46, 48, 85, 93n1, 113, 119, 137–8, 149–50, 160, 185, 197–8, 199, 286, 309, 310, 311, 312, 314, 320, 323, 329, 338, 344, 346, 353, 357, 359, 382, 383–4, 386–7, 390–1, 393, 430, 437, 438, 440, 454, 465, 491
transnationalism 31, 35–6, 37, 54–5, 97, 286, 290–3, 372, 380, 426, 431
Trask, Haunani-Kay 42–3, 198–9, 201n4
trauma 6, 45, 59, 70, 78, 88, 102, 120, 201n4, 277, 324, 333, 357, 383, 384, 428, 442, 476, 477, 491
Tray, Thomas 314n1
treaties 5–6, 9–10, 37, 40, 105, 111–21, 125, 126–7, 130, 131, 141–2, 146–51, 167–8, 194, 197–8, 199, 214, 220, 225–6, 230–1, 233, 236, 238, 241, 245–6, 273–4, 275–6, 308, 319, 324, 445, 453: Creek removal treaties (Treaty of Cusseta, 1832; International Indian Treaty Council 183, 277; reserved-rights doctrine

(1905) 275; Trail of Broken Treaties (1972) 118, 274; Treaty of Fort Laramie (1868) 115, 119, 120, 142; Treaty of Fort Pitt (1778) 111; Treaty of Fort Stanwix (1768, 1784) 115; Treaty of Hopewell (1785, 1786) 126; Treaty of Lancaster (1844) 113–14, 115; Treaty of Medicine Creek (1854) 275; Treaty of Neah Bay (1855) 225–6; Treaty of New Echota (1836) 147–8; Treaty of Point Elliott (1855) 275; Treaty of St. Louis (1804) 149–50; Treaty of Washington ("Treaty with the Yankton Sioux," 1858) 119; Treaty of Washington, 1866) 151
Trennert, Robert A., Jr. 251
Treuer, David 66, 373, 451, 454, 466, 467–8
"tribalism" 100, 164, 285
tribalography 105n1, 426
tribes *see* Native communities
tribes, federal recognition 2–3, 7, 104, 117, 147, 150, 194, 223, 224
trickster, 58, 90, 129, 197, 268, 338, 379–80, 381, 412, 416, 419, 426, 452, 481, 482
Troutman, John 372
Trudell, John 280
Trumbull, Charles 381
Tsinhnahjinnie, Hulleah 345
Tso, Theo "Teddy" 488, 489
Tsosie, Rebecca 127, 129
Tuck, Eve 293, 294
Tupac Yupanqui 304
Turcotte, Mark 344–5
Turner, Dale 127
Turner, Fredrick Jackson 112, 266
Tutaswampe 312
Twain, Mark 55
Two Bulls, Marty 482
Two Rivers, E. Donald 420

Udall, Louise 161
Uncas 308
United Nations 47, 120–1, 192–200, 231, 277, 303: Convention on Indigenous and Tribal Populations Convention (1957) 200n1; Global Indigenous Preparatory Conference 194–6, 197; International Labor Organization: Indigenous and Tribal Peoples Convention (1989) 200n1; United Nations Declaration on the Rights of Indigenous Peoples 2, 5, 8, 120–1, 192–200, 250; United Nations Human Rights Commission's Working Group on Indigenous Populations 303; United Nations Permanent Forum on Indigenous Issues 200n2; World Conference on Indigenous Peoples (2013) 194; World Food Summit (1996) 242; World Health Organization 249

United States, 2, 4, 5, 6, 9, 15, 19–20, 21, 28, 37, 39, 40, 43, 44–5, 49–50, 58, 85, 88, 112, 116, 118, 119–20, 123, 124–7, 130, 132, 139, 142, 147, 148, 149–50, 151, 152, 167–9, 175, 195, 196, 207–15, 221, 226, 234, 240, 249, 260, 261–2, 270, 275, 293, 318, 322, 323–4, 366, 373, 383, 403, 407, 426, 435, 450, 453: Bureau of Indian Affairs 2, 3, 7, 36, 158, 159, 162, 175, 195, 261, 274, 439; Congress 6, 7, 8, 37, 77, 115, 117, 127, 146, 150, 153, 157, 167, 170, 171, 173, 174–5, 181, 183, 186, 195, 196, 225, 260, 261, 276, 324, 439; Declaration of Independence 116, 195, 318; Department of the Interior 6, 43, 153, 171, 174, 175, 195; statehood 4, 28, 36, 40, 454; Supreme Court 2, 123–32, 151, 194, 196, 225, 275, 277, 324, 356
urban Native communities 3, 7, 67, 74–83, 85, 119, 165, 246, 264, 276, 279, 288, 291, 328, 445, 450–1
Urbas, Jeannette 23
Urton, Gary 304

Valentino, Gina 425
Van Camp, Richard 478n1, 481
Vanderlyn, John 346
Vargas Llosa, Mario 22
Vega, Garcilasco de la 304
Velie, Alan R. 285, 286, 420
Veregge, Jeffrey 345, 485
video games 491
Virgil (Publius Vergilius Maro) 461
visuality 10, 11, 245, 300, 302, 303, 340–50, 471, 480–92
Vizenor, Gerald 3, 52–3, 56, 58–9, 64, 67, 75, 86, 111, 129, 131–3, 136, 184, 197, 198, 217, 223–5, 253, 254, 285, 286, 292, 302, 338, 344, 347–50, 372, 379, 380, 381–2, 386, 387, 391, 415, 417, 423, 426, 431, 445–6, 451, 452, 453, 454, 455n3: *Bear Island* 136; *Bearheart* 382, 415, 452, 455n3; *Blue Ravens* 349–50, 452, 453; *Chair of Tears* 131–3, 382; Constitution of the White Earth Nation 129, 132, 452; "Crows Written on the Poplars" 58; *Darkness in Saint Louis Bearheart* 452; *Everlasting Sky* 53; *Fugitive Poses* 3, 53, 58, 67, 348, 382, 452; *Griever* 381, 415, 452; *Hiroshima Bugi* 254, 452; *Hotline Healers* 253; *Landfill Meditation* 223–5, 415, 417; *Manifest Manners* 64, 445–6, 452; *The People Named the Chippewa* 53; *Postindian Conversations* 382; *Summer in the Spring* 344, 382, 452; *Trickster of Liberty* 379, 380, 381
Vogel, Virgil J. 250
Von Hagen, Victor Wolfgang 17–18
Vonnegut, Kurt 454
Vukelich, James 393

INDEX

Waban, Olt 314n1
Waban, Thomas 314n1
Wall, Drucilla Mims 66
Wallis, Velma 29
Walsh, Raoul 465
Walters, Anna Lee 184, 186–9, 190, 337, 418
war 23, 76, 78, 79, 102, 115, 124, 125, 126,
   135–44, 147, 150, 151, 152–3, 177–8, 222,
   233–4, 251, 252, 301, 322–3, 360–1, 380,
   392, 407, 408, 418, 450, 489: American
   Revolutionary War (1775–83) 115, 126,
   205–15, 322–3; Bannock War (1878)
   152–3; Battle of Fallen Timbers (1794) 215;
   Battle of Okinawa (1945) 380; Battle of
   the Little Bighorn (1876) 135, 453; Battle
   of Wishita River (1868) 414, 418; Black
   Hawk War (1832) 149, 150; Crazy Snake
   Rebellion (1909) 454; French and Indian
   Wars (1754–63) 69–70, 135, 321, 392;
   Metacom's War (1675–1676) 115, 136–8,
   196, 308; Mexican-American War (1846–48)
   152; Pueblo Revolt (1680–92) 136, 139–41,
   198–9; Red Cloud's War (1866–68) 115;
   War of 1812 (1812–15) 323, 324, 325
Ward, Nancy 99
Warrior, Robert 54, 57, 113, 176, 182, 263,
   265, 288, 345, 367, 368, 372, 373, 395, 396
Washburn, Kathleen Grace 266, 267
Washington, President George 394
Watson, Blake A. 126
Watt-Cloutier, Sheila 280
Waubojeeg 394–5
Wayne, John 61n3, 419
Weatherford, Jack 250
Weaver, Jace 8, 54, 55, 57, 61n7, 135, 176,
   260, 261, 262, 263, 264, 265, 288, 372
Weetowish 308
Welch, James 55, 136, 391, 436, 454: *Death
   of Jim Loney* 55; *Fools Crow* 112, 253, 347;
   Heartsong of Charging Elk 381, 452; *Winter in
   the Blood* 371, 459–61, 466, 468
Welford, Gabrielle 383
Wendt, Albert 39
Wequash 311
Wernitznig, Dagmar 64, 67
West, Benjamin 346
West, W. Richard 280
Westerman, Floyd Red Crow 52, 273, 277, 280
Westlake, Wayne 43
Wheeler, Rachel 208
Wheeler, Sen. Burton 175
Wheelock, Eleazar 320–1
White, Craig 312
White, Ken 460
White Bull, Joseph 302

Whitfield, Henry 313
Whyte, Kyle Powys 242, 247n4
Wilbur, Matika 480
Wilcox, Dwayne 347
Wilkins, David E. 174, 205, 231
Wilkinson, Charles F. 112, 117, 123, 275–6
Williams, Maria Shaa Tlaá 28–9
Williams, Robert A. Jr. 112–13, 114, 190n1
Williams, Roger 309, 312–13, 317–18
Williams, Shirley Ida 358
Wilson, Bobby 490
Wilson, Michael D. 329
Wilson, Norma C. 443
Wilson, Waziyatawin Angela 218
Winnemucca *see* Hopkins, Sarah
   Winnemucca
Winslow, Edward 182
Winter, Kari J. 241
Winters, Yvor 397, 398
Wirt, William 124, 126
Wisecup, Kelly 253, 258
Wolfe, Nathan D. 234
Womack, Craig 1, 54, 57, 84, 87, 89, 92, 176,
   263, 267, 288, 289, 290, 342, 343, 372,
   374n2, 454, 481
Wong, Hertha Sweet 267
Wood, William 309
Woody, Elizabeth 345, 436
Worcester, Samuel A. 126
Work, Hubert 171
World's Columbian Exposition (1893) 409
Wovoka (Jack Wilson) 265, 267, 269
Wroth, Lawrence 121n2
Wunder, John R. 397
Wyss, Hilary E. 310, 314n3

Ximémez, Francisco, Fr. 17

Yahgulanaas, Michael Nicoll 480, 491–2
Yang, K. Wayne 293
Yasuda, Kenneth 381
Yava, Albert 335
Yellow Robe, William S. 431
Young Bear, Ray A. 436
Young Deer, James 458

Zamir, Shamoon 221
Zanjani, Sally 163
Zepeda, Ofelia 330–1, 334, 436, 438
Zimmerman, Larry J. 183
Ziontz, Alvin J. 275
Zitkala-sa/Zitkala-sha/Red Bird (Gertrude
   Simmons Bonnin) 158–60, 171, 412–3,
   439, 481
Zumthor, Paul 335